JOSS WHEDON

Christopher **Golden** • David **Fury** • Eric **Powell** • Christian **Zanier** • Ryan **Sook**

ANGEL ™

LEGACY EDITION BOOK ONE

Collection Designers
Marie Krupina and **Scott Newman**

Additional Art by
Eric Powell, **Christian Zanier**, **Guy Major**

Original Series Editors
Adam J. Kreutz Gallardo, **Scott Allie**

Legacy Edition Assistant Editor
Gavin Gronenthal

Legacy Edition Associate Editor
Jonathan Manning

Legacy Edition Editor
Jeanine Schaefer

Special Thanks to
Nicole Spiegel and **Carol Roeder**
at **Twentieth Century Fox**,
Sierra Hahn, **Becca J. Sadowsky**.

Originally published by
Dark Horse Comics

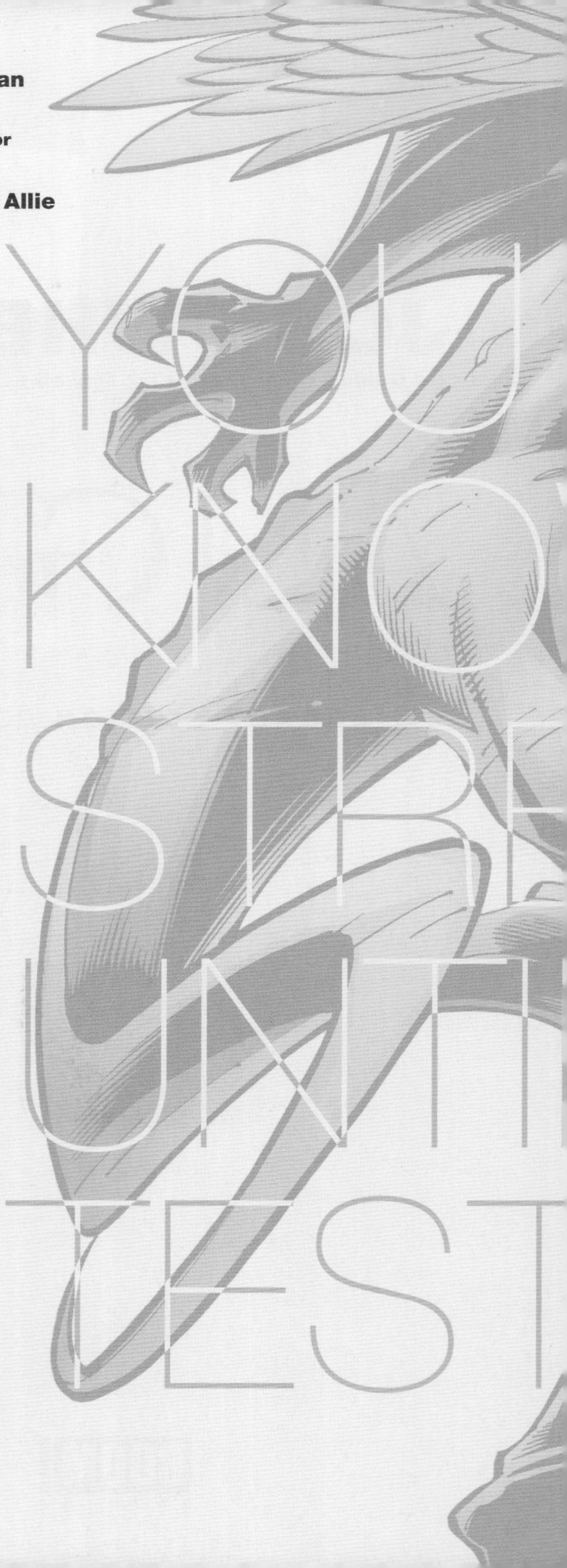

BOOM! Studios, 5670 Wilshire Boulevard, Suite 400,
Los Angeles, CA 90036-5679. Printed in China. First Printing.

ISBN: 978-1-68415-469-2, eISBN: 978-1-64144-586-3

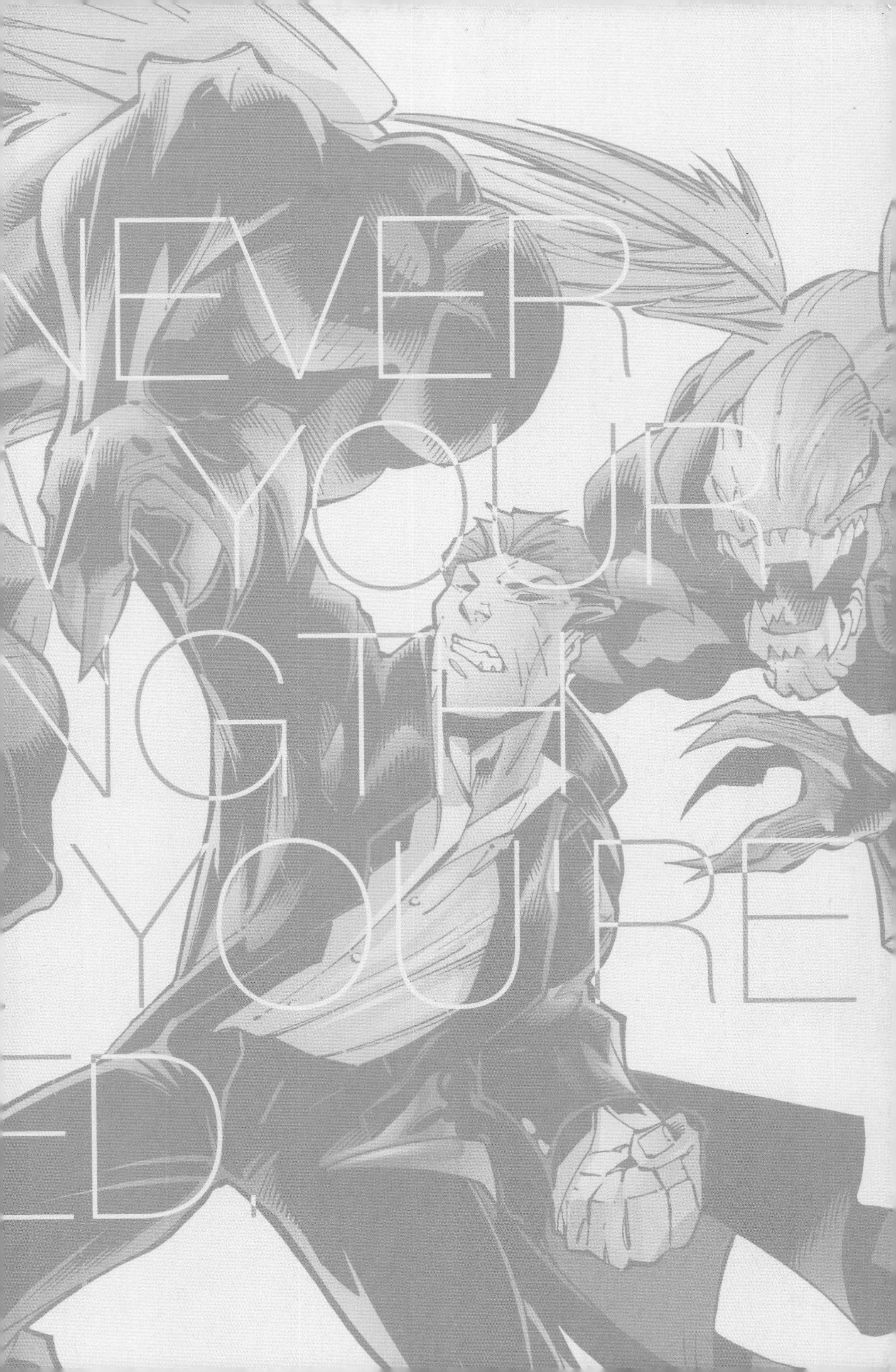
NEVER
YOUR
NGTH
YOU'RE
ED

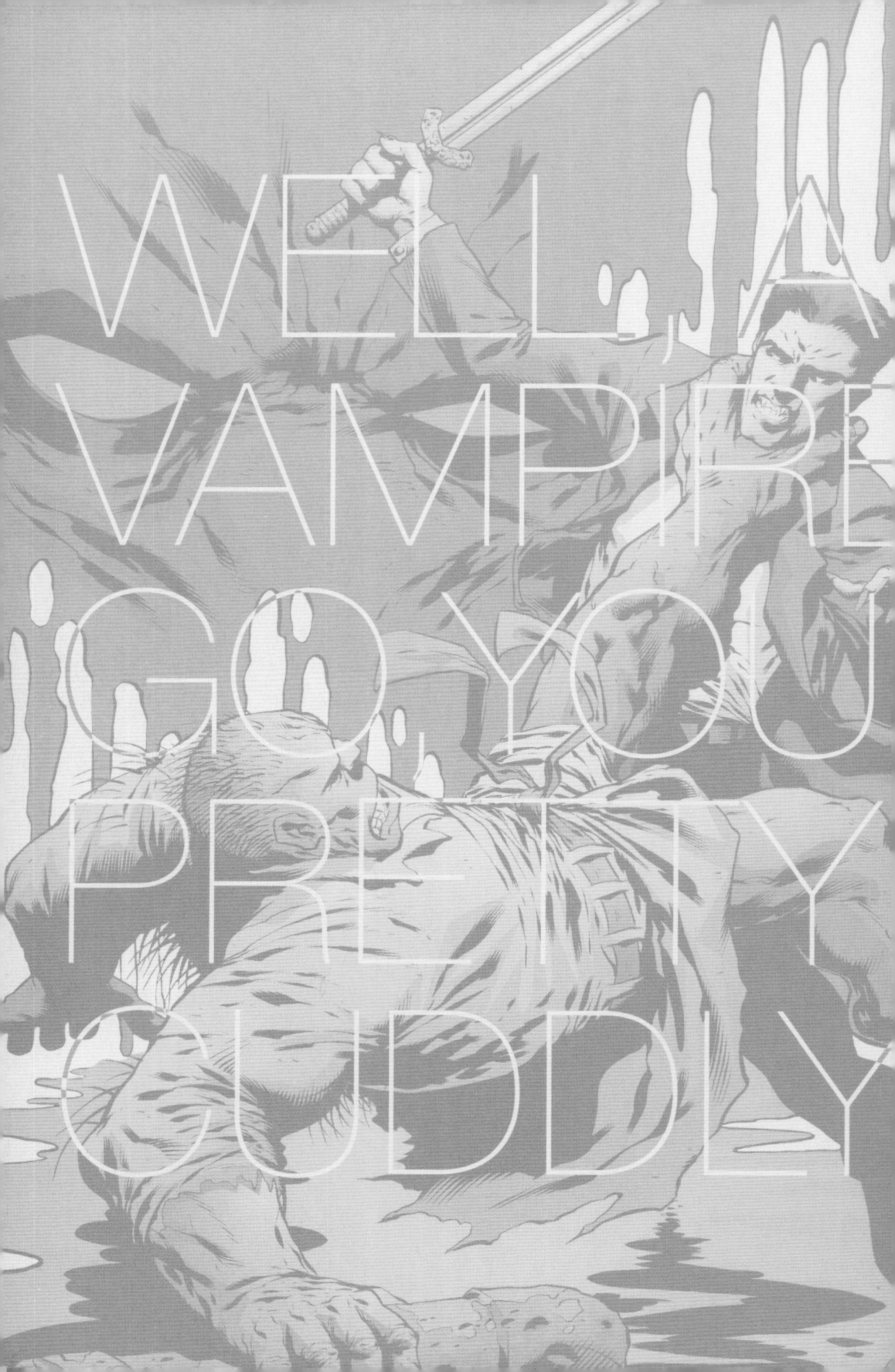
WELL, A
VAMPIRE
GO, YOU
PRETTY
CUDDLY

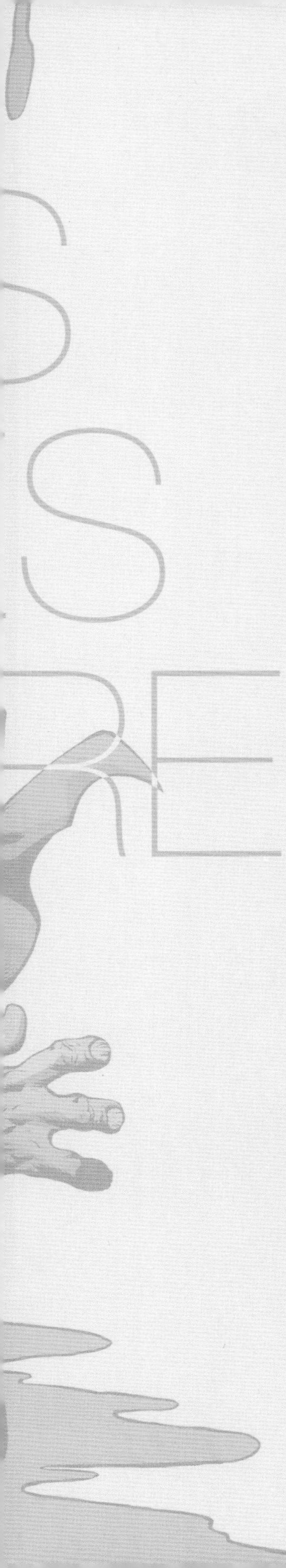

Created By
Joss Whedon
& David Greenwalt

THE HOLLOWER

Script by
Christopher Golden

Pencils by
Héctor C. Gómez

Inks by
Sandu Florea

Colored by
Guy Major

Lettered by
Ken Bruzenak

SURROGATES

Script by
Christopher Golden

Pencils by
Christian Zanier

Background Assists by
Marvin Mariano
& **Draxhall Jump** (Chapter 3)

Inks by
Andy Owens,
with **Jason Minor**
& **Curtis P. Arnold** (Chapter 3)

Colored by
Digital Broome

Lettered by
Clem Robins

THE CHANGELING WIFE

Script by
Christopher Golden

Illustrated by
Eric Powell

Colored by
Guy Major

Lettered by
Pat Brousseau

EARTHLY POSSESSIONS

Script by
Christopher Golden
& **Thomas E. Sniegoski**

Pencils by
Christian Zanier

Background Assists by
Marvin Mariano

Inks by
Andy Owens

Colored by
Digital Broome

Lettered by
Clem Robins

BENEATH THE SURFACE

Script by
Christopher Golden
& **Thomas E. Sniegoski**

Illustrated by
Eric Powell

Colored by
Lee Loughridge

Lettered by
Pat Brousseau

POINT OF ORDER

Script by
David Fury

Illustrated by
Ryan Sook

Colored by
Dave Stewart

Lettered by
Amador Cisneros Jr.

LOVELY, DARK, AND DEEP

Script by
Christopher Golden
& **Thomas E. Sniegoski**

Pencils by
Brian Horton

Inks by
Paul Lee

Colored by
Matt Hollingsworth

Lettered by
Clem Robins

Cover by
Nimit Malavia

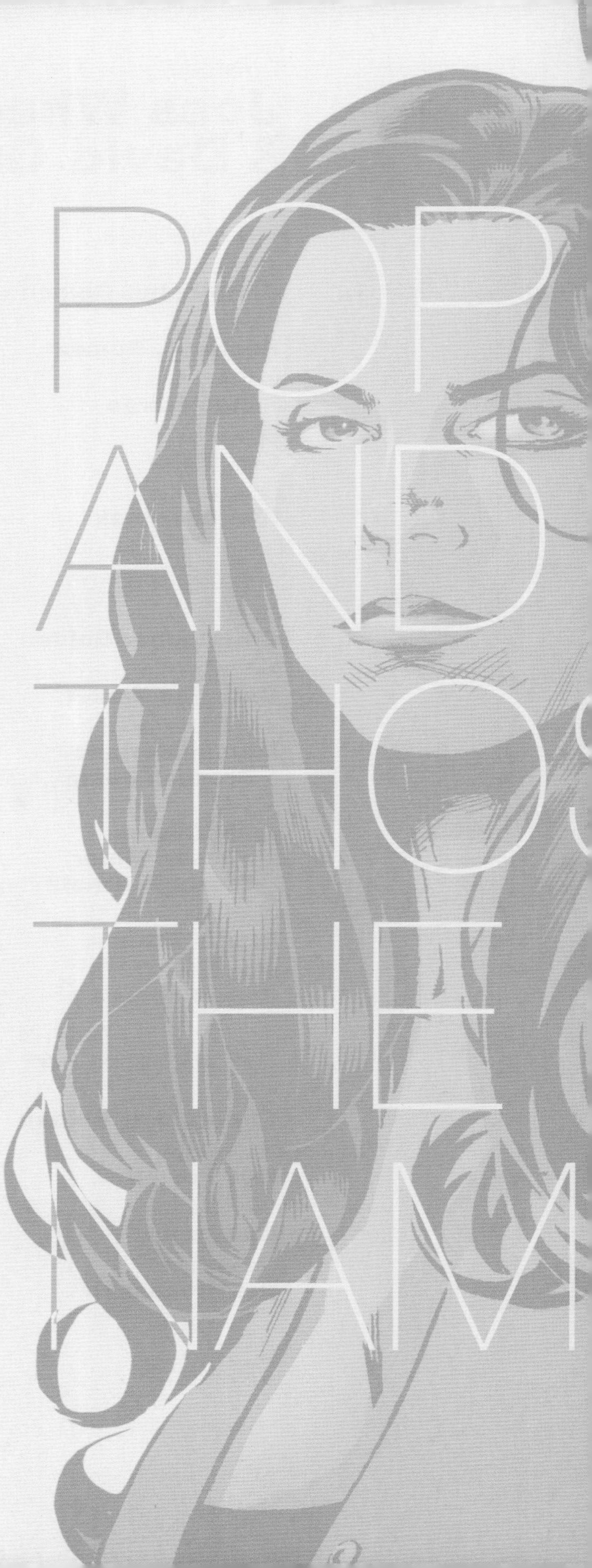
POP
AND
THOS
THE
NAM

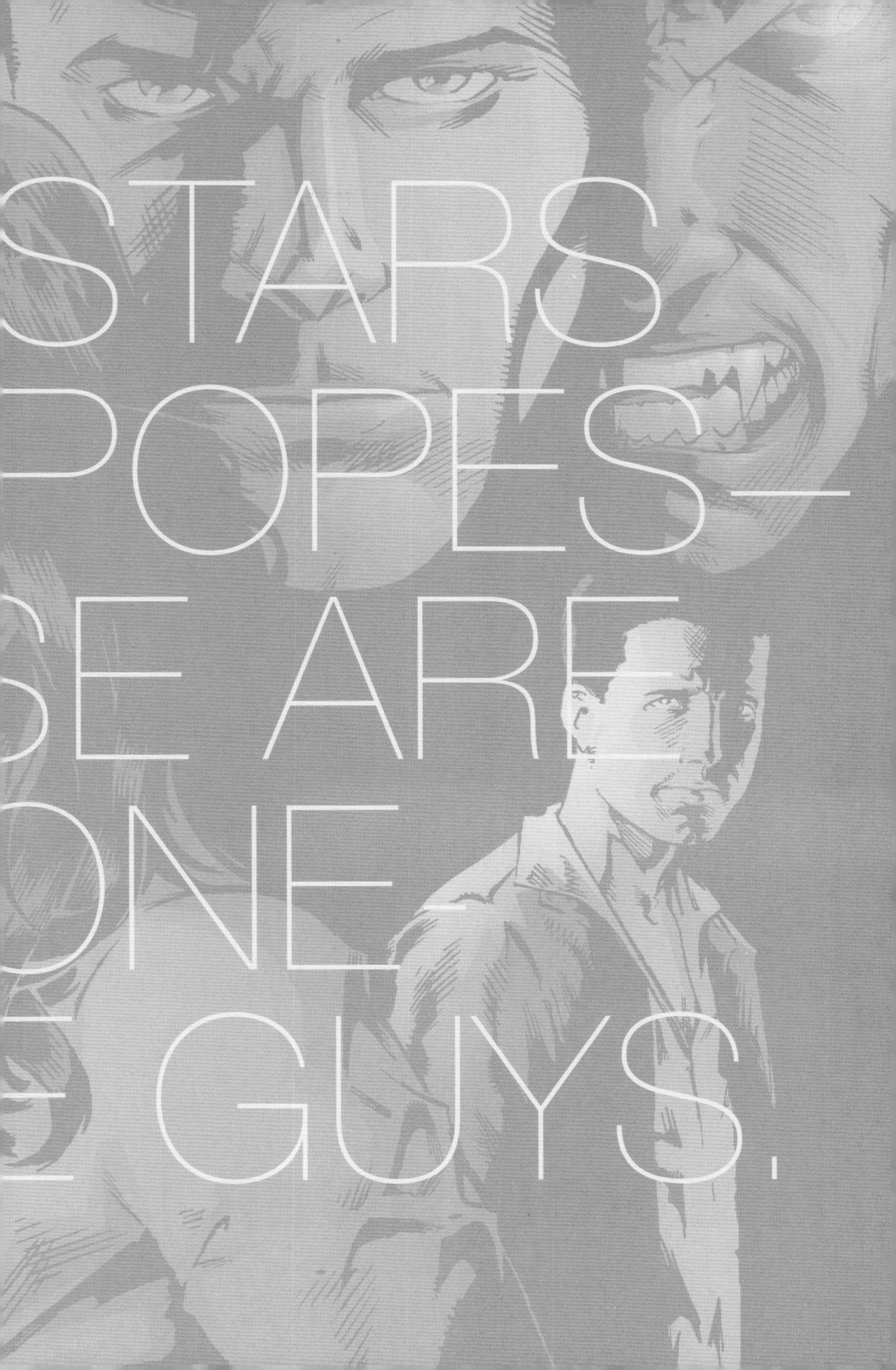

STARS
POPES—
SE ARE
ONE—
GUYS.

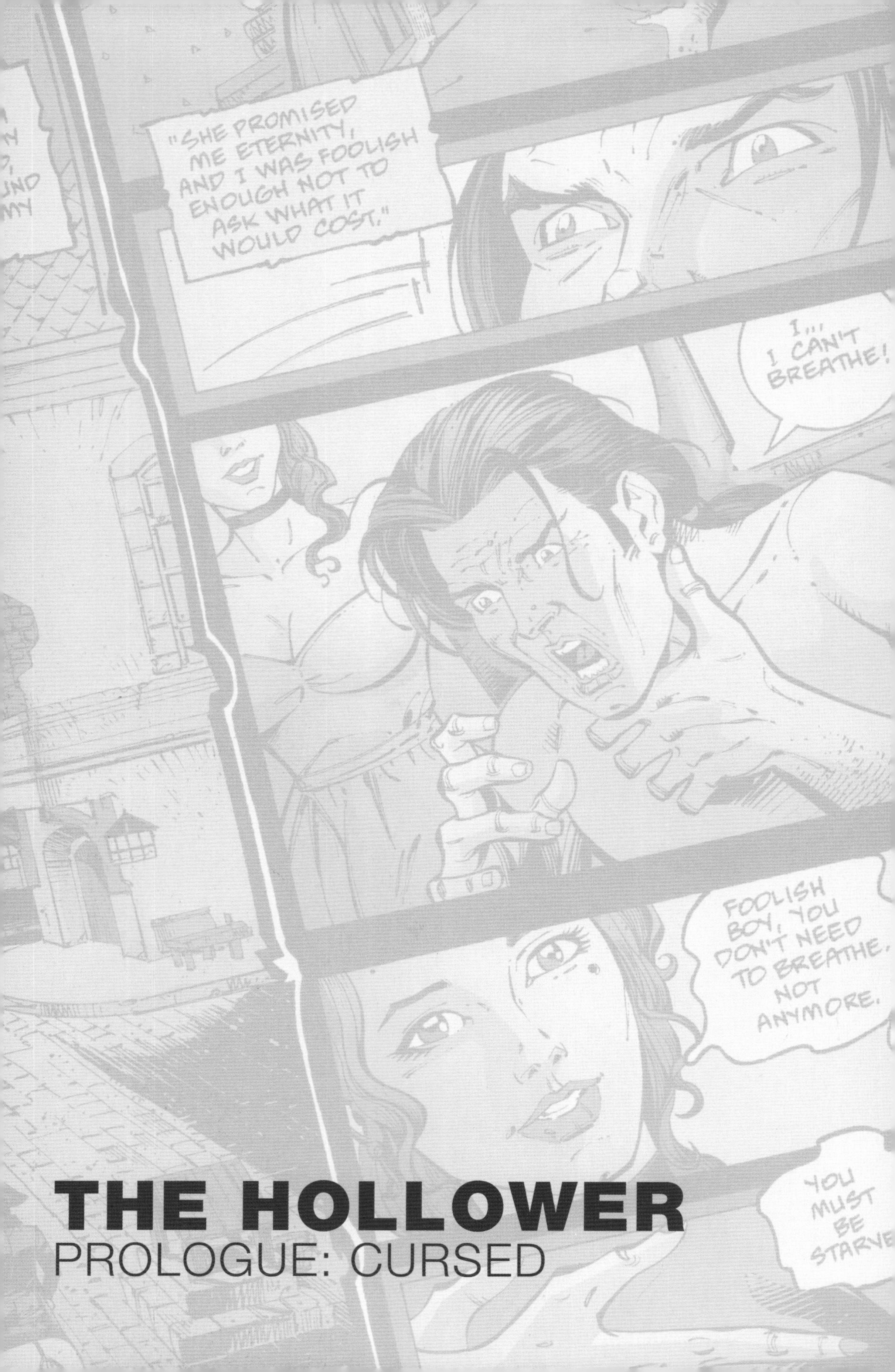
"SHE PROMISED ME ETERNITY, AND I WAS FOOLISH ENOUGH NOT TO ASK WHAT IT WOULD COST."
I... I CAN'T BREATHE!
FOOLISH BOY, YOU DON'T NEED TO BREATHE. NOT ANYMORE.
YOU MUST BE STARVE

THE HOLLOWER
PROLOGUE: CURSED

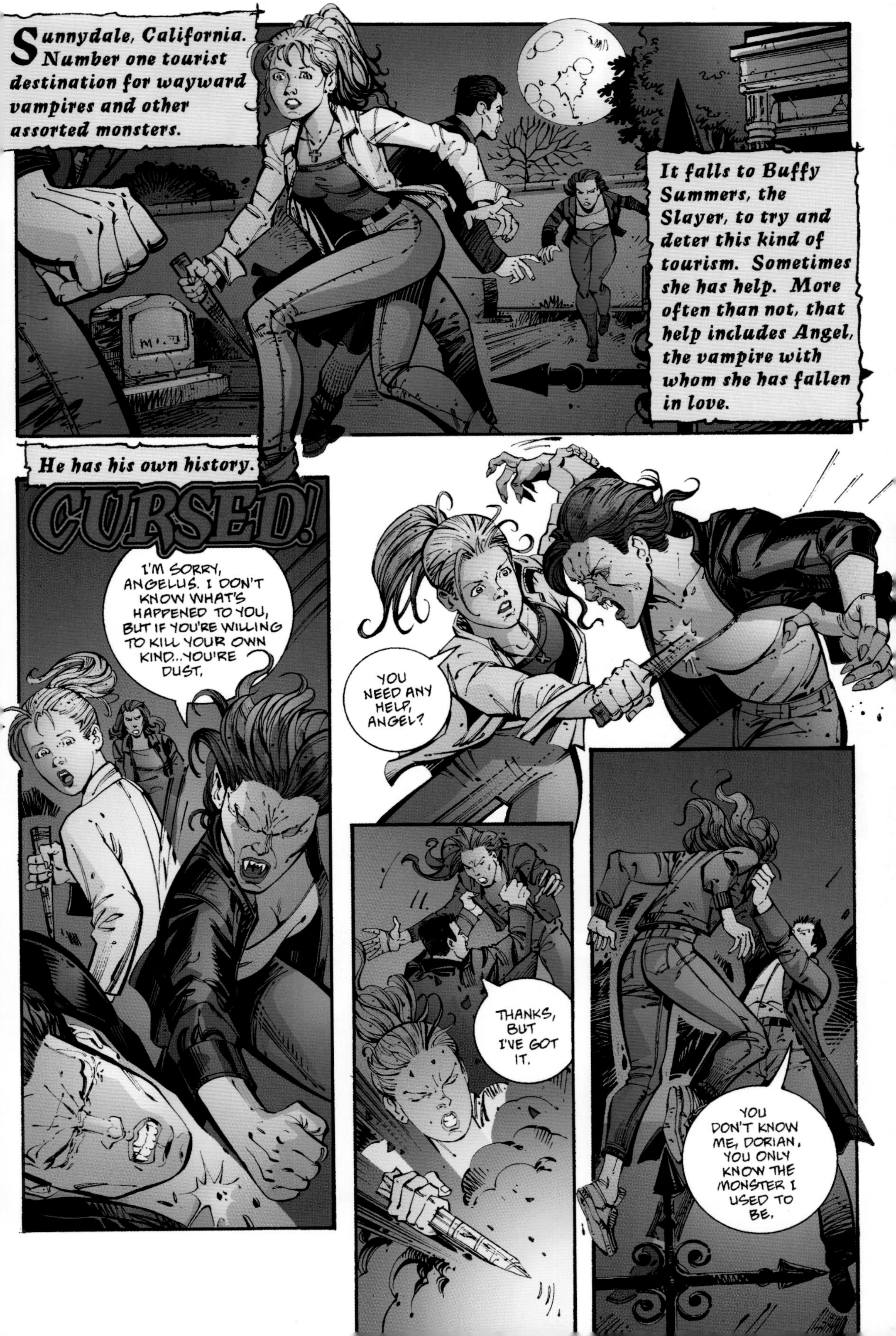
Sunnydale, California. Number one tourist destination for wayward vampires and other assorted monsters.
It falls to Buffy Summers, the Slayer, to try and deter this kind of tourism. Sometimes she has help. More often than not, that help includes Angel, the vampire with whom she has fallen in love.
He has his own history.
CURSED!
I'M SORRY, ANGELUS. I DON'T KNOW WHAT'S HAPPENED TO YOU, BUT IF YOU'RE WILLING TO KILL YOUR OWN KIND...YOU'RE DUST.
YOU NEED ANY HELP, ANGEL?
THANKS, BUT I'VE GOT IT.
YOU DON'T KNOW ME, DORIAN. YOU ONLY KNOW THE MONSTER I USED TO BE.

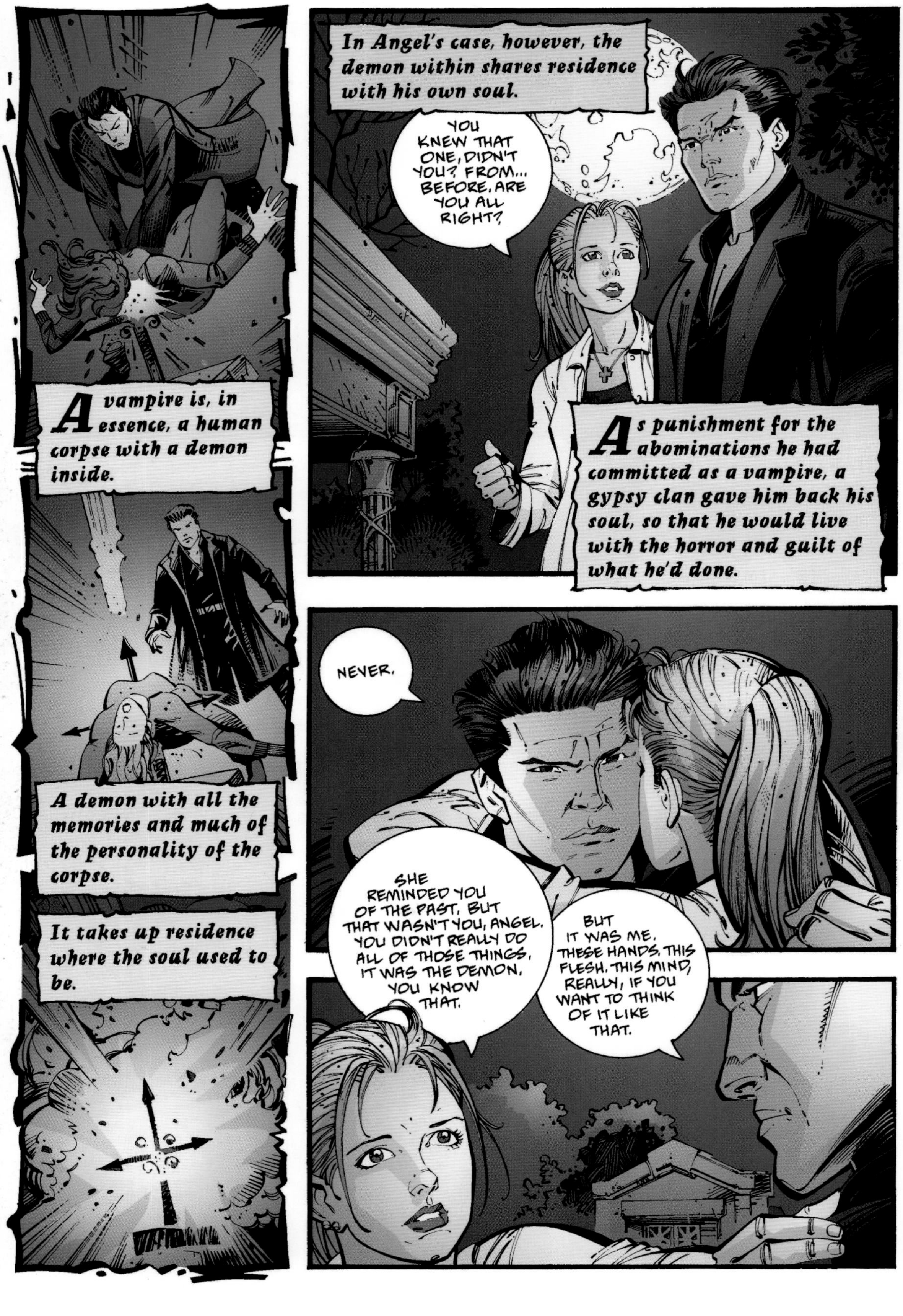

A vampire is, in essence, a human corpse with a demon inside.
A demon with all the memories and much of the personality of the corpse.
It takes up residence where the soul used to be.
In Angel's case, however, the demon within shares residence with his own soul.
YOU KNEW THAT ONE, DIDN'T YOU? FROM... BEFORE. ARE YOU ALL RIGHT?
As punishment for the abominations he had committed as a vampire, a gypsy clan gave him back his soul, so that he would live with the horror and guilt of what he'd done.
NEVER.
SHE REMINDED YOU OF THE PAST, BUT THAT WASN'T YOU, ANGEL. YOU DIDN'T REALLY DO ALL OF THOSE THINGS. IT WAS THE DEMON. YOU KNOW THAT.
BUT IT WAS ME. THESE HANDS, THIS FLESH, THIS MIND, REALLY, IF YOU WANT TO THINK OF IT LIKE THAT.

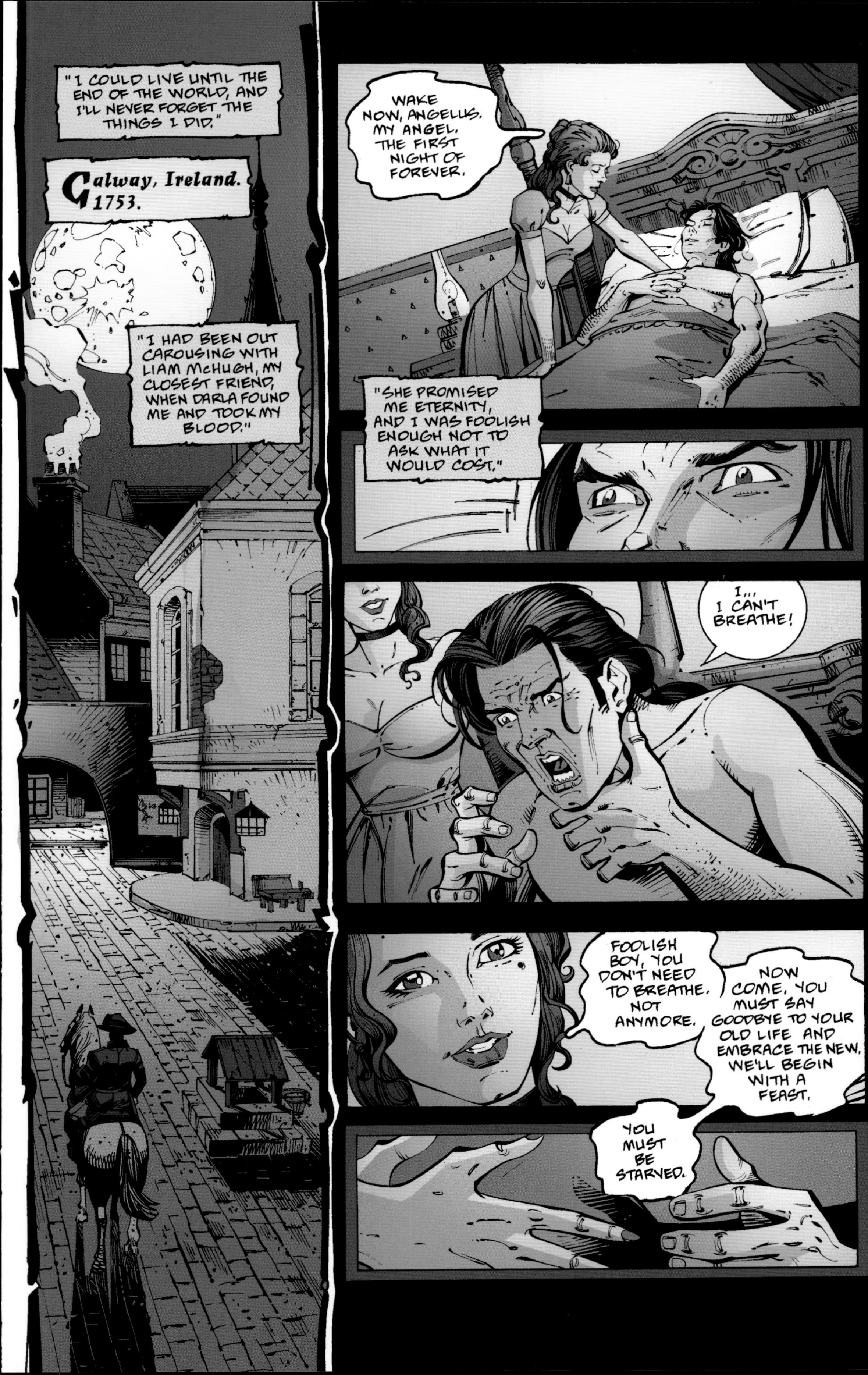
"I COULD LIVE UNTIL THE END OF THE WORLD, AND I'LL NEVER FORGET THE THINGS I DID."
Galway, Ireland. 1753.
"I HAD BEEN OUT CAROUSING WITH LIAM McHUGH, MY CLOSEST FRIEND, WHEN DARLA FOUND ME AND TOOK MY BLOOD."
WAKE NOW, ANGELUS, MY ANGEL, THE FIRST NIGHT OF FOREVER.
"SHE PROMISED ME ETERNITY, AND I WAS FOOLISH ENOUGH NOT TO ASK WHAT IT WOULD COST."
I... I CAN'T BREATHE!
FOOLISH BOY, YOU DON'T NEED TO BREATHE. NOT ANYMORE.
NOW COME, YOU MUST SAY GOODBYE TO YOUR OLD LIFE AND EMBRACE THE NEW. WE'LL BEGIN WITH A FEAST.
YOU MUST BE STARVED.

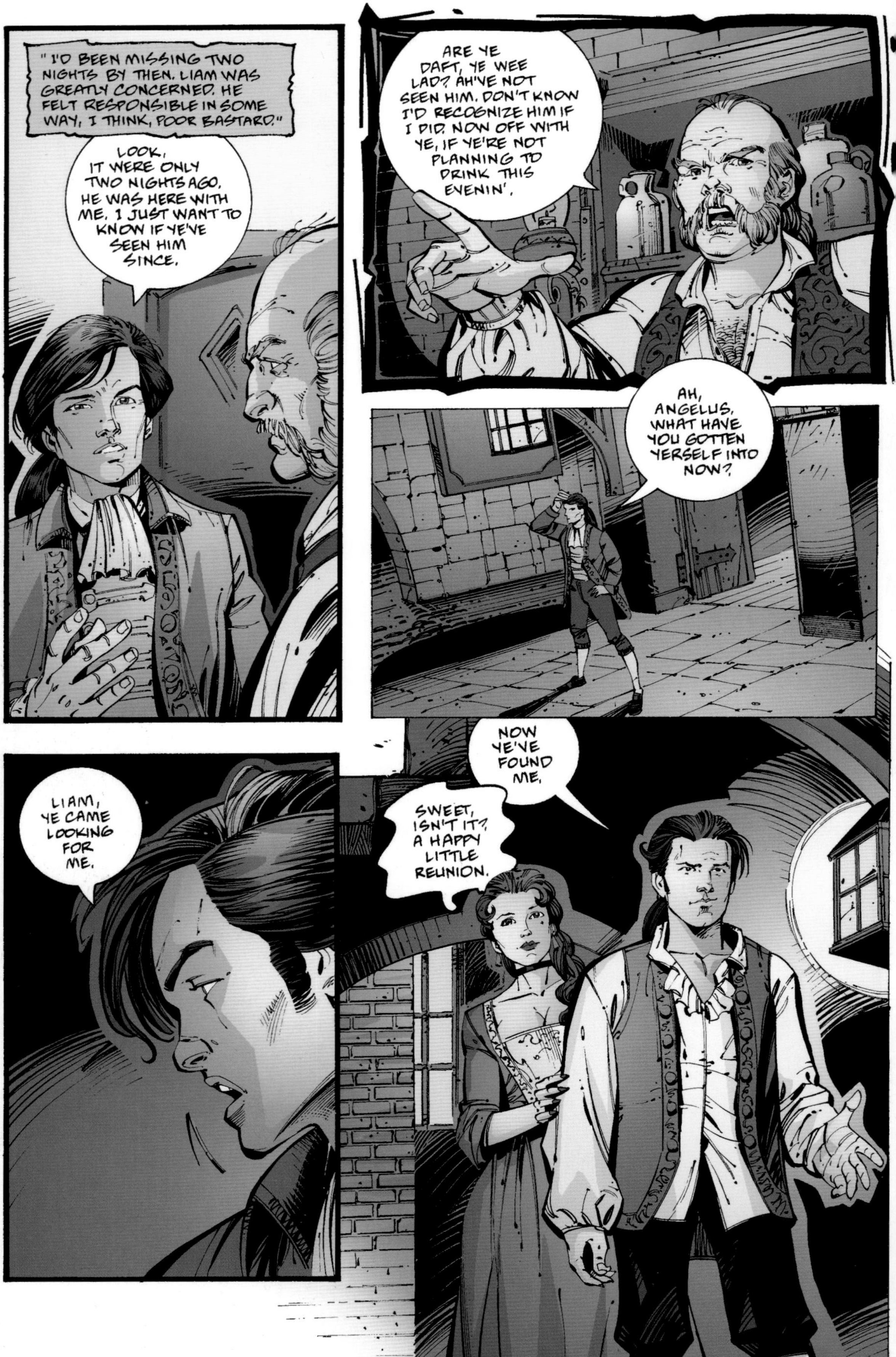
"I'D BEEN MISSING TWO NIGHTS BY THEN. LIAM WAS GREATLY CONCERNED. HE FELT RESPONSIBLE IN SOME WAY, I THINK, POOR BASTARD."
LOOK, IT WERE ONLY TWO NIGHTS AGO. HE WAS HERE WITH ME. I JUST WANT TO KNOW IF YE'VE SEEN HIM SINCE.
ARE YE DAFT, YE WEE LAD? AH'VE NOT SEEN HIM. DON'T KNOW I'D RECOGNIZE HIM IF I DID. NOW OFF WITH YE, IF YE'RE NOT PLANNING TO DRINK THIS EVENIN'.
AH, ANGELUS, WHAT HAVE YOU GOTTEN YERSELF INTO NOW?
LIAM, YE CAME LOOKING FOR ME.
NOW YE'VE FOUND ME.
SWEET, ISN'T IT? A HAPPY LITTLE REUNION.

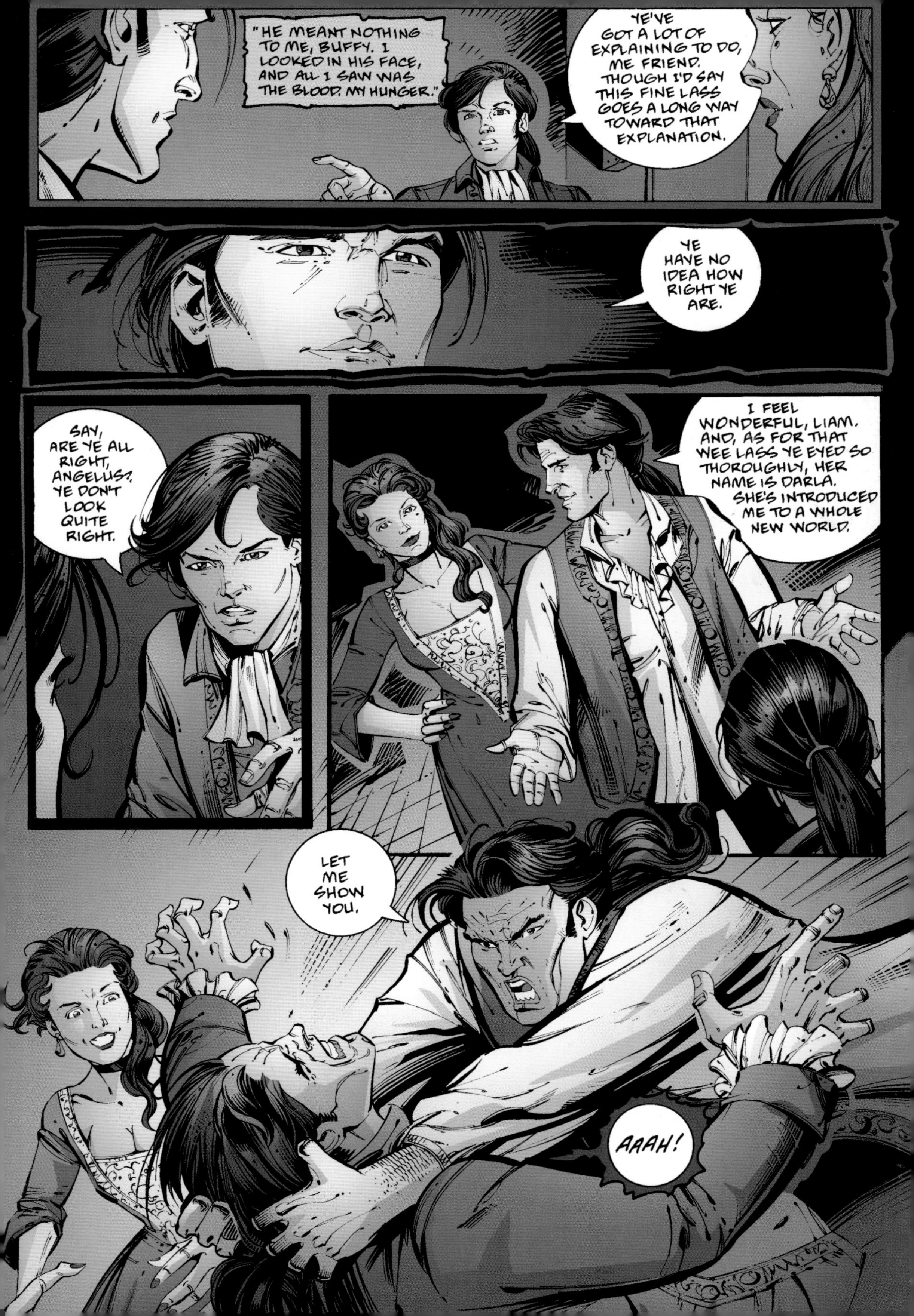
"HE MEANT NOTHING TO ME, BUFFY. I LOOKED IN HIS FACE, AND ALL I SAW WAS THE BLOOD. MY HUNGER."
YE'VE GOT A LOT OF EXPLAINING TO DO, ME FRIEND. THOUGH I'D SAY THIS FINE LASS GOES A LONG WAY TOWARD THAT EXPLANATION.
YE HAVE NO IDEA HOW RIGHT YE ARE.
SAY, ARE YE ALL RIGHT, ANGELUS? YE DON'T LOOK QUITE RIGHT.
I FEEL WONDERFUL, LIAM. AND, AS FOR THAT WEE LASS YE EYED SO THOROUGHLY, HER NAME IS DARLA. SHE'S INTRODUCED ME TO A WHOLE NEW WORLD.
LET ME SHOW YOU.
AAAH!

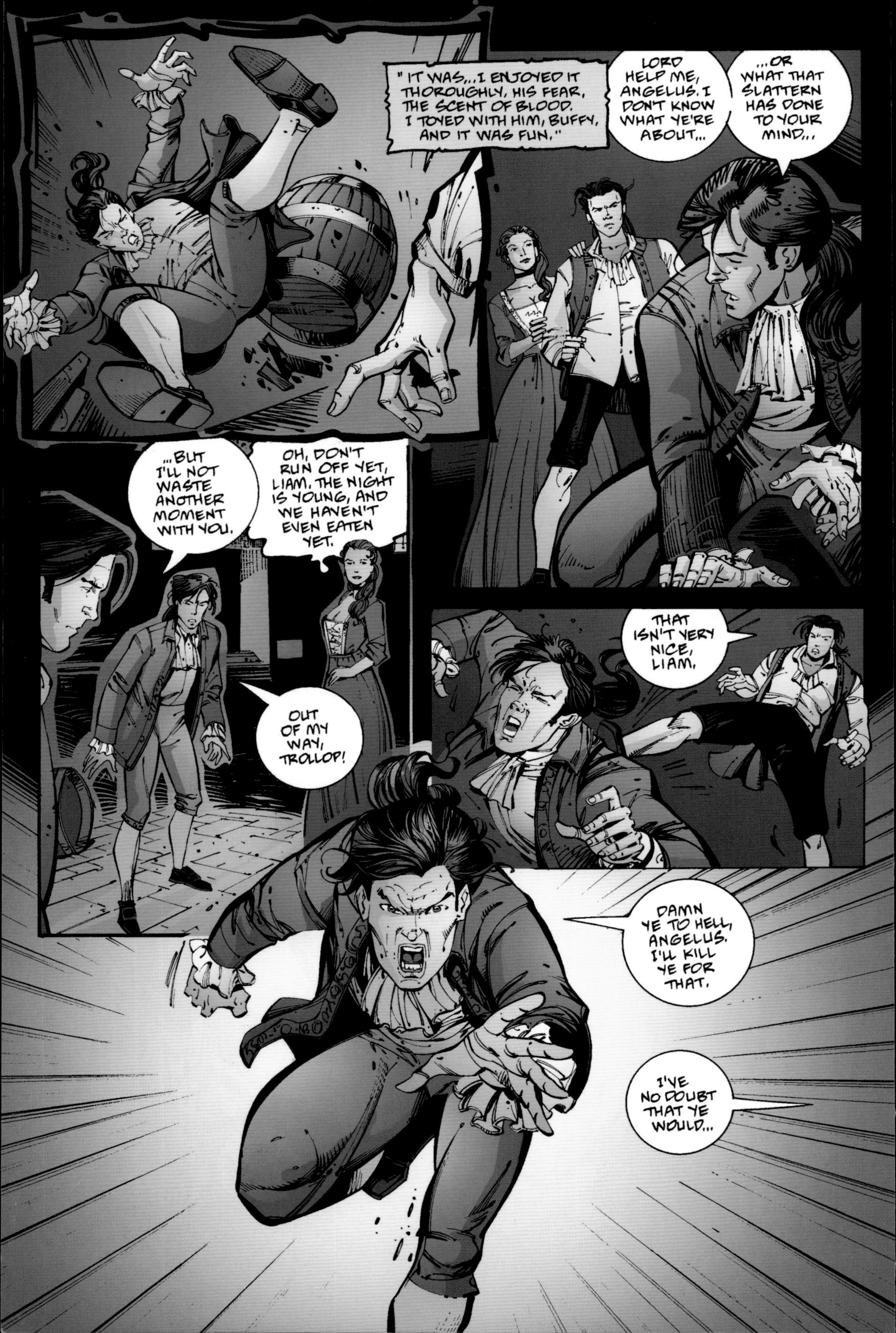
"IT WAS... I ENJOYED IT THOROUGHLY, HIS FEAR, THE SCENT OF BLOOD. I TOYED WITH HIM, BUFFY, AND IT WAS FUN."
LORD HELP ME, ANGELUS. I DON'T KNOW WHAT YE'RE ABOUT...
...OR WHAT THAT SLATTERN HAS DONE TO YOUR MIND...
...BUT I'LL NOT WASTE ANOTHER MOMENT WITH YOU.
OH, DON'T RUN OFF YET, LIAM. THE NIGHT IS YOUNG, AND WE HAVEN'T EVEN EATEN YET.
OUT OF MY WAY, TROLLOP!
THAT ISN'T VERY NICE, LIAM.
DAMN YE TO HELL, ANGELUS. I'LL KILL YE FOR THAT.
I'VE NO DOUBT THAT YE WOULD...

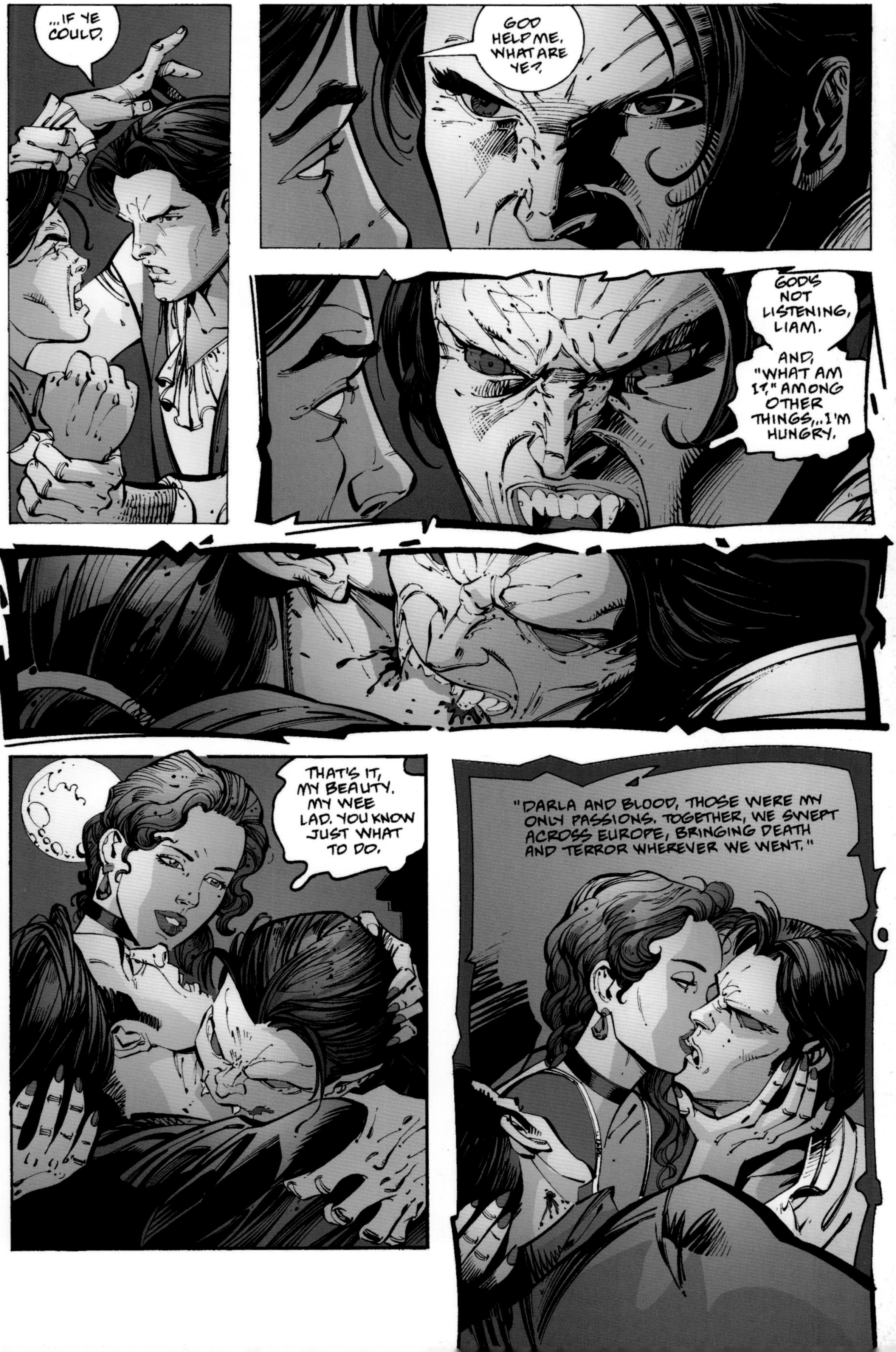
...IF YE COULD.
GOD HELP ME. WHAT ARE YE?
GOD'S NOT LISTENING, LIAM.
AND, "WHAT AM I?," AMONG OTHER THINGS... I'M HUNGRY.
THAT'S IT, MY BEAUTY. MY WEE LAD. YOU KNOW JUST WHAT TO DO.
"DARLA AND BLOOD, THOSE WERE MY ONLY PASSIONS. TOGETHER, WE SWEPT ACROSS EUROPE, BRINGING DEATH AND TERROR WHEREVER WE WENT."

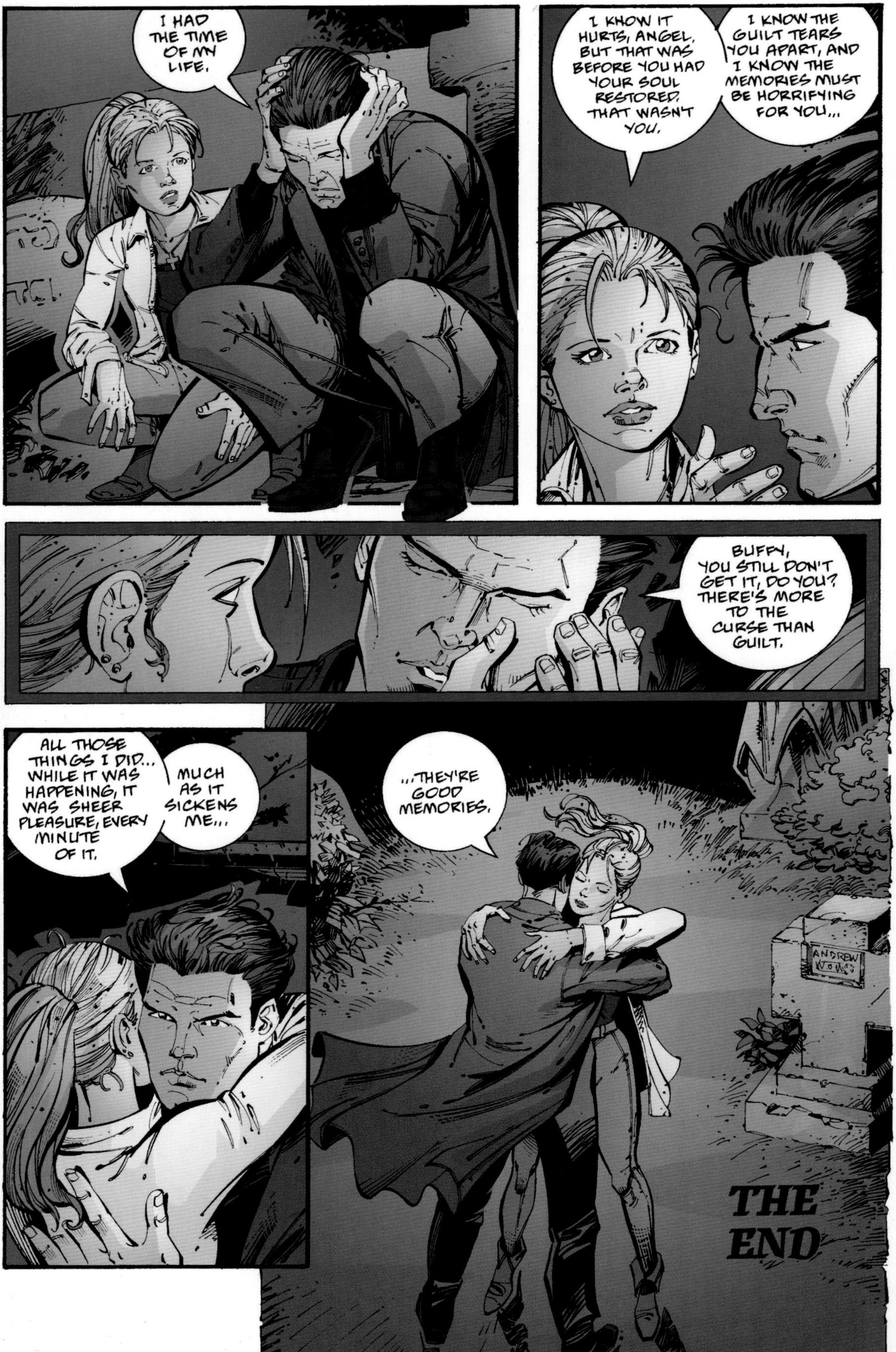
I HAD THE TIME OF MY LIFE.
I KNOW IT HURTS, ANGEL, BUT THAT WAS BEFORE YOU HAD YOUR SOUL RESTORED. THAT WASN'T YOU.
I KNOW THE GUILT TEARS YOU APART, AND I KNOW THE MEMORIES MUST BE HORRIFYING FOR YOU...
BUFFY, YOU STILL DON'T GET IT, DO YOU? THERE'S MORE TO THE CURSE THAN GUILT.
ALL THOSE THINGS I DID... WHILE IT WAS HAPPENING, IT WAS SHEER PLEASURE, EVERY MINUTE OF IT.
MUCH AS IT SICKENS ME...
...THEY'RE GOOD MEMORIES.
ANDREW
THE END

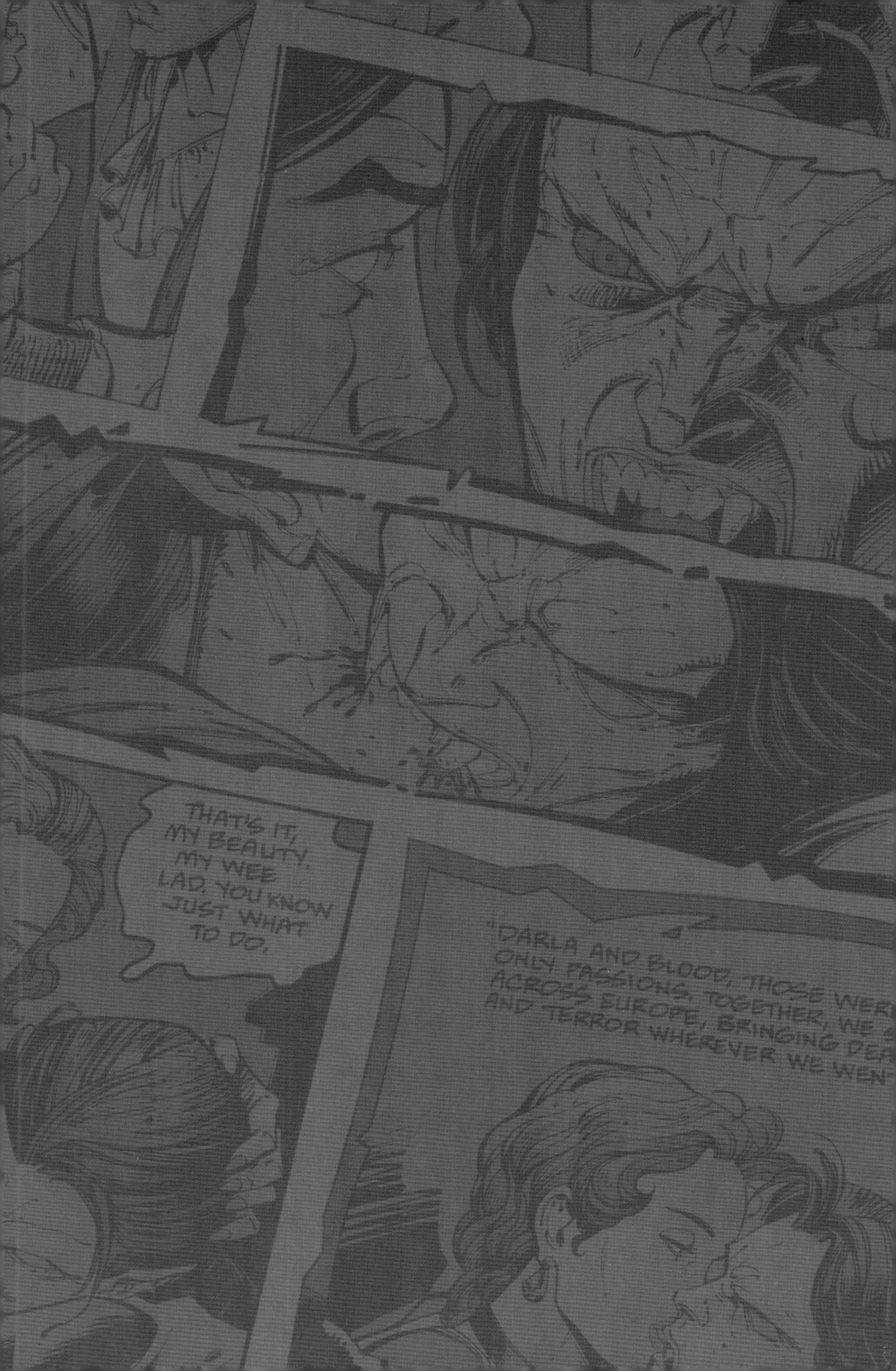
THAT'S IT, MY BEAUTY. MY WEE LAD. YOU KNOW JUST WHAT TO DO.
"DARLA AND BLOOD, THOSE WER
ONLY PASSIONS. TOGETHER, WE
ACROSS EUROPE, BRINGING DEA
AND TERROR WHEREVER WE WEN

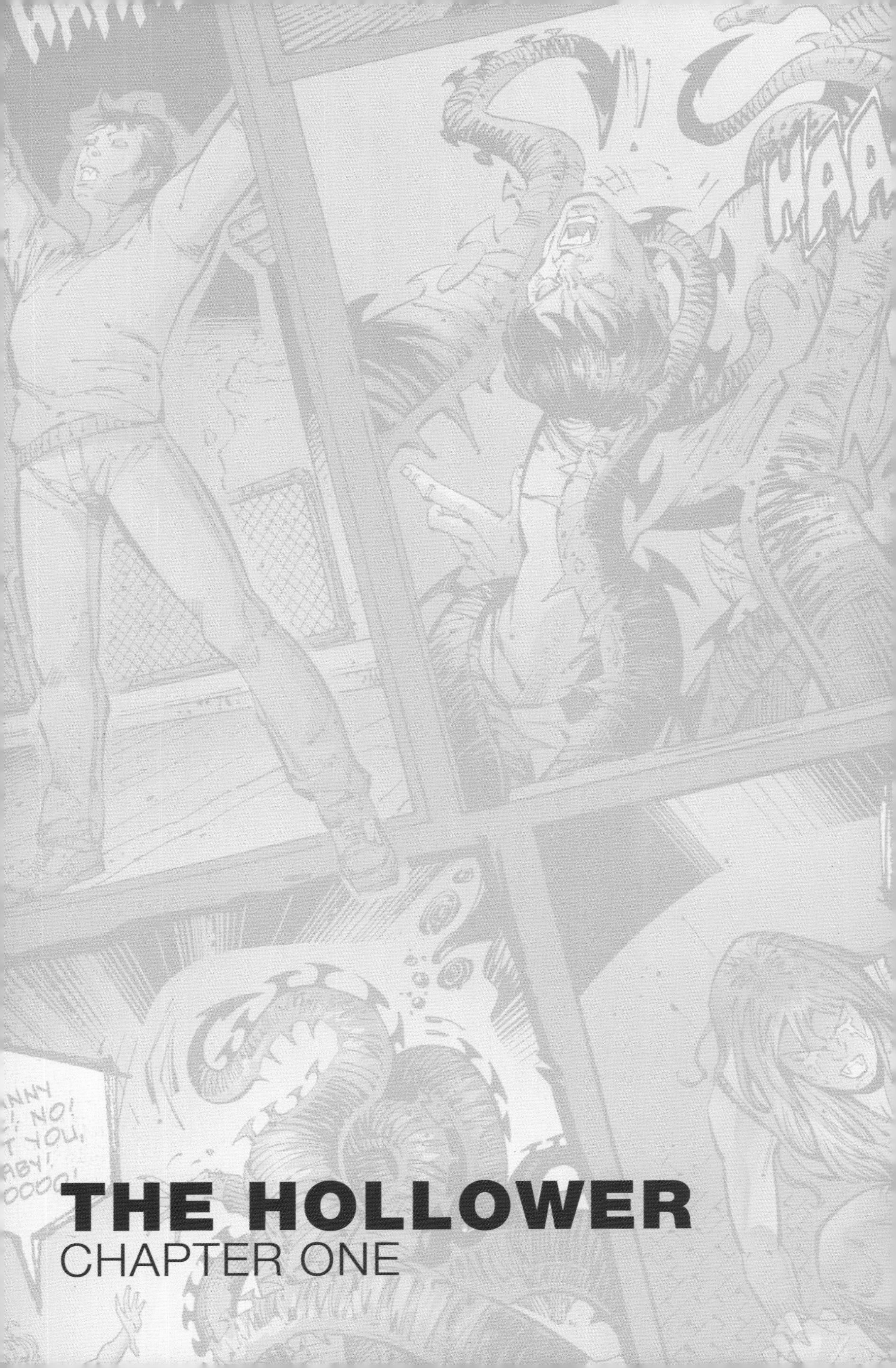

THE HOLLOWER
CHAPTER ONE

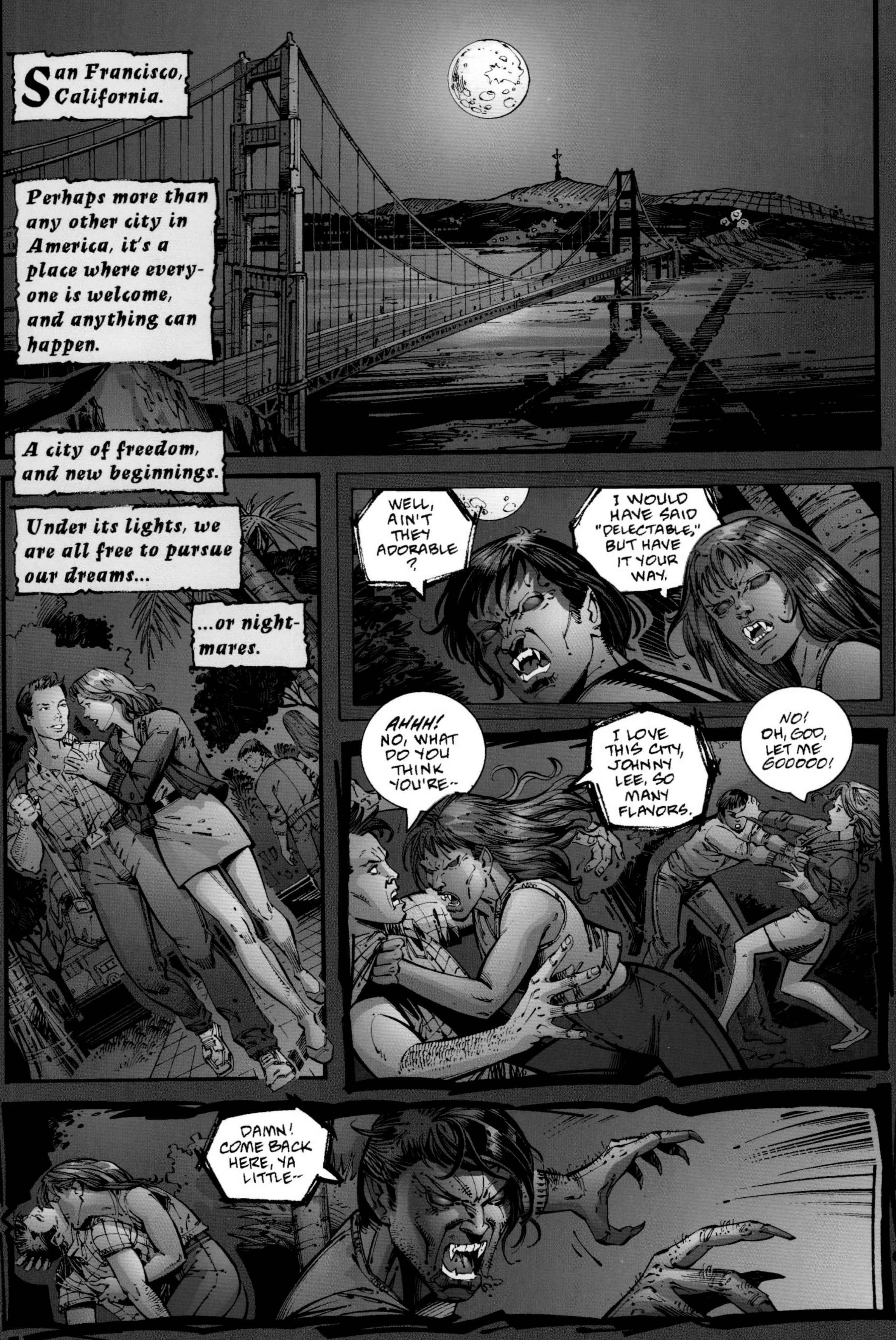
San Francisco, California.
Perhaps more than any other city in America, it's a place where everyone is welcome, and anything can happen.
A city of freedom, and new beginnings.
Under its lights, we are all free to pursue our dreams...
...or nightmares.
WELL, AIN'T THEY ADORABLE?
I WOULD HAVE SAID "DELECTABLE," BUT HAVE IT YOUR WAY.
AHHH! NO, WHAT DO YOU THINK YOU'RE--
I LOVE THIS CITY, JOHNNY LEE, SO MANY FLAVORS.
NO! OH, GOD, LET ME GOOOOO!
DAMN! COME BACK HERE, YA LITTLE--

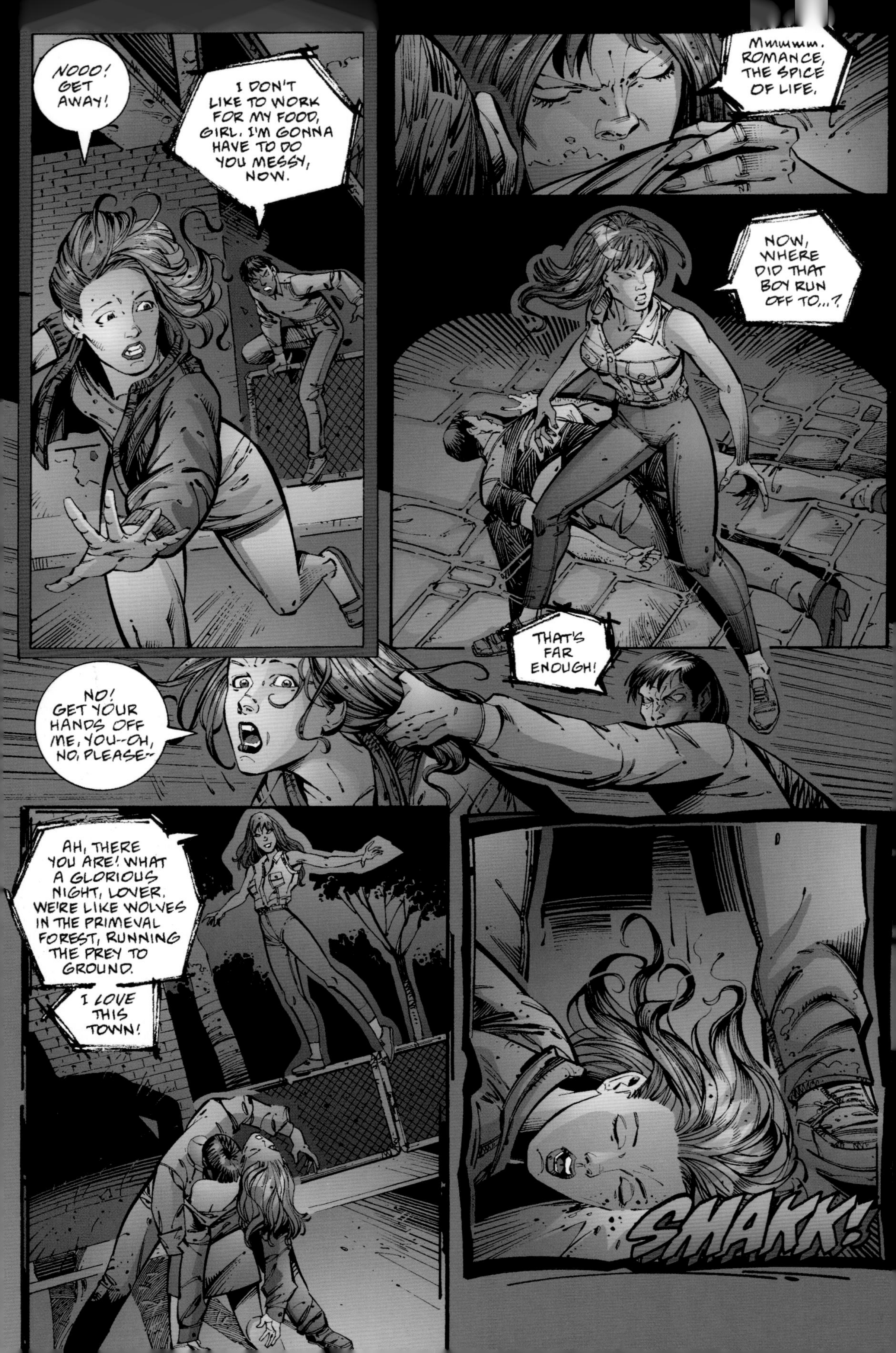

NOOO! GET AWAY!
I DON'T LIKE TO WORK FOR MY FOOD, GIRL. I'M GONNA HAVE TO DO YOU MESSY, NOW.
Mmmmm. ROMANCE, THE SPICE OF LIFE.
NOW, WHERE DID THAT BOY RUN OFF TO...?
THAT'S FAR ENOUGH!
NO! GET YOUR HANDS OFF ME, YOU--OH, NO, PLEASE--
AH, THERE YOU ARE! WHAT A GLORIOUS NIGHT, LOVER. WE'RE LIKE WOLVES IN THE PRIMEVAL FOREST, RUNNING THE PREY TO GROUND.
I LOVE THIS TOWN!
SHAKK!

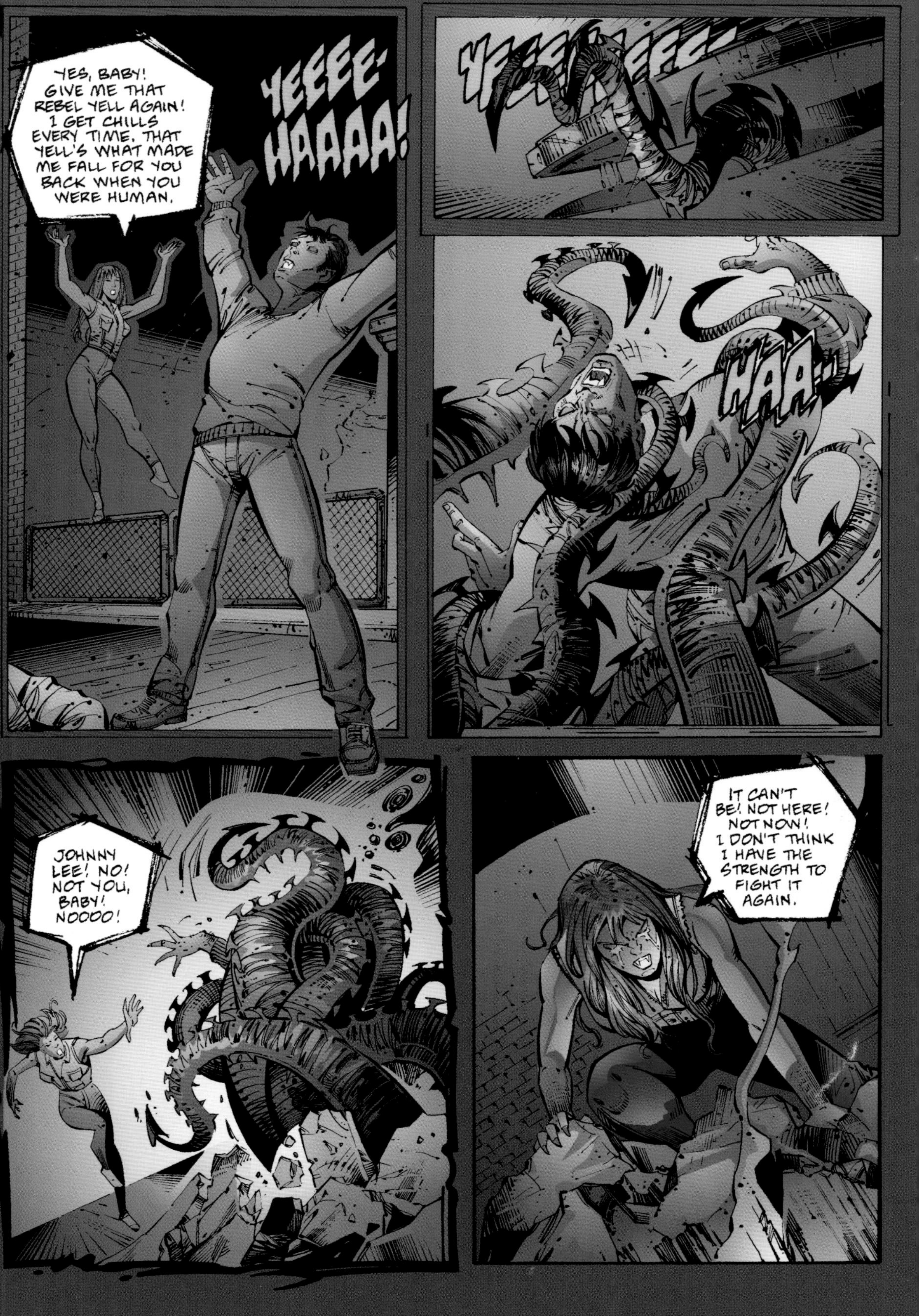
YES, BABY! GIVE ME THAT REBEL YELL AGAIN! I GET CHILLS EVERY TIME. THAT YELL'S WHAT MADE ME FALL FOR YOU BACK WHEN YOU WERE HUMAN.
YEEEE-HAAAA!
HAA-
JOHNNY LEE! NO! NOT YOU, BABY! NOOOO!
IT CAN'T BE! NOT HERE! NOT NOW! I DON'T THINK I HAVE THE STRENGTH TO FIGHT IT AGAIN.

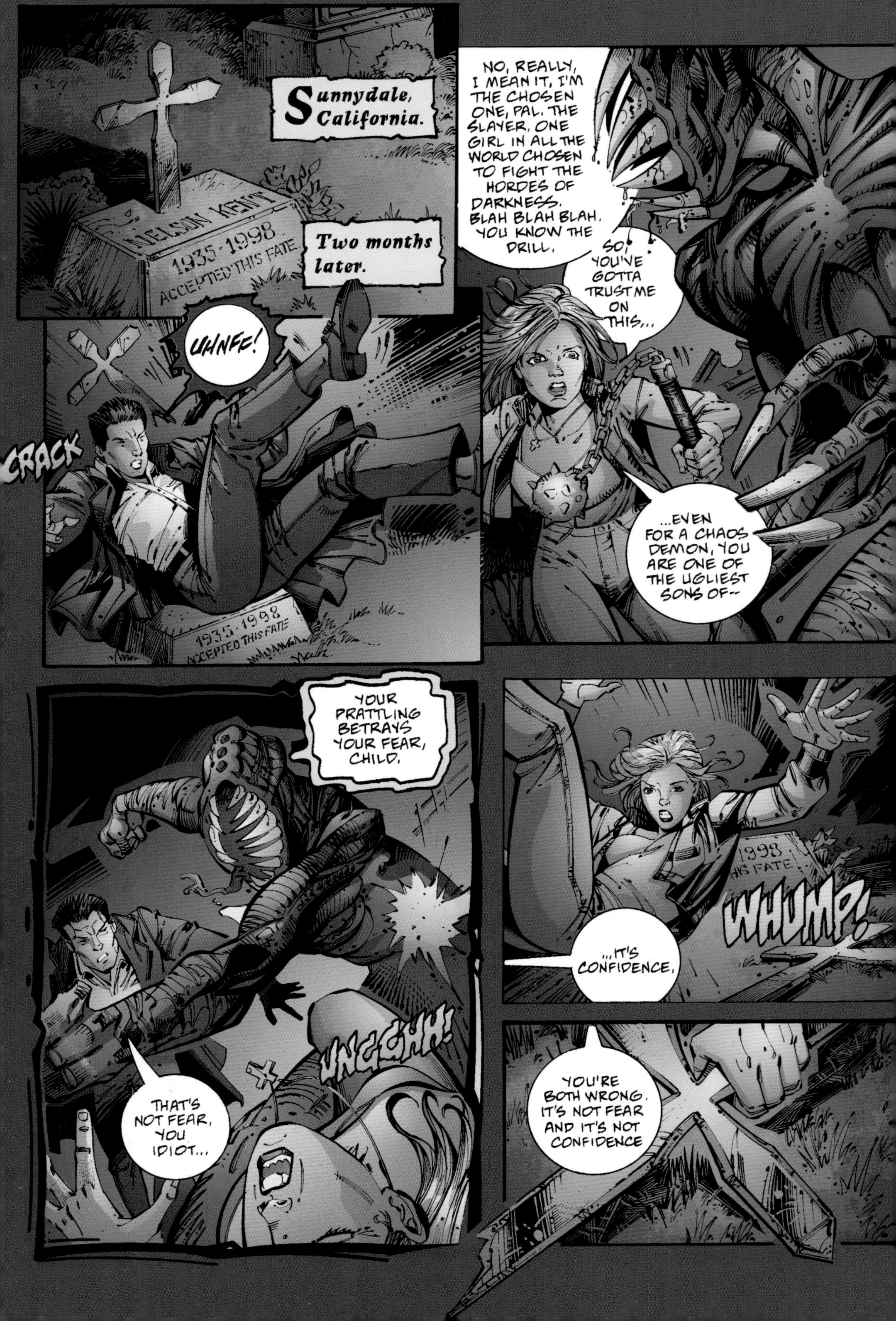
Sunnydale, California.
NELSON KENT 1935-1998 ACCEPTED THIS FATE
Two months later.
NO, REALLY, I MEAN IT, I'M THE CHOSEN ONE, PAL. THE SLAYER. ONE GIRL IN ALL THE WORLD CHOSEN TO FIGHT THE HORDES OF DARKNESS. BLAH BLAH BLAH. YOU KNOW THE DRILL.
SO, YOU'VE GOTTA TRUST ME ON THIS...
UHNFF!
CRACK
1935-1998 ACCEPTED THIS FATE
...EVEN FOR A CHAOS DEMON, YOU ARE ONE OF THE UGLIEST SONS OF--
YOUR PRATTLING BETRAYS YOUR FEAR, CHILD.
THAT'S NOT FEAR, YOU IDIOT...
UNGGHH!
WHUMP!
...IT'S CONFIDENCE.
YOU'RE BOTH WRONG. IT'S NOT FEAR AND IT'S NOT CONFIDENCE

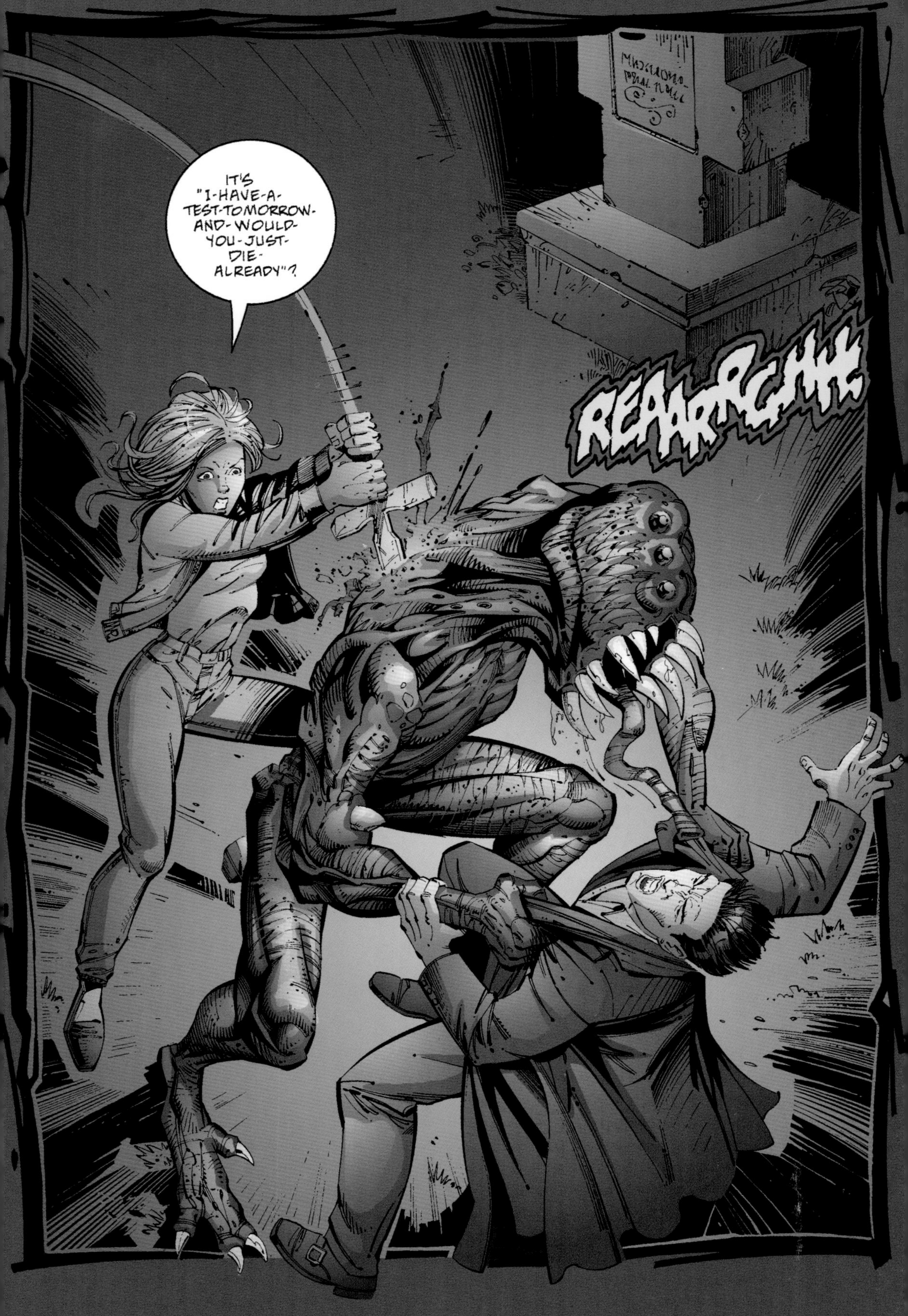
IT'S "I-HAVE-A-TEST-TOMORROW-AND-WOULD-YOU-JUST-DIE-ALREADY"?
REAARRGHH!

SKREEEEEEE...
HEK!!

YOU WANT TO TAKE CARE OF NEEDLE-FACE?

UNDER CONTROL.

SKRATCH!

WOULDN'T WANT THE CARETAKER FINDING THIS MESS IN THE MORNING. DON'T KNOW HOW THE COPS WOULD EXPLAIN THAT ONE AWAY.

FWOOOSH!!

THEY'D FIND A WAY, THEY ALWAYS DO.

SO, ARE YOU READY FOR THAT TEST TOMORROW?

I'LL BE ALL RIGHT...

...AS LONG AS NOTHING ELSE COMES UP.

Sunnydale High School.

Unlikely as it may seem, the strategies in the war against darkness are planned within these walls.

For each Slayer, there is a Watcher. A scholar learned in the mysteries of chaos, skilled in the ways of the warrior, assigned the venerable duty of training the Slayer.

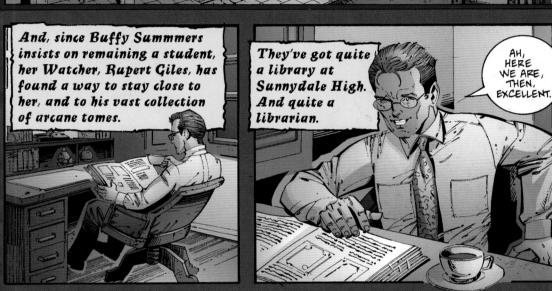

And, since Buffy Summmers insists on remaining a student, her Watcher, Rupert Giles, has found a way to stay close to her, and to his vast collection of arcane tomes.

They've got quite a library at Sunnydale High. And quite a librarian.

AH, HERE WE ARE, THEN, EXCELLENT.

...PLEASE ANGEL, OF COURSE HE'S STILL HERE I MEAN, HE'S GILES.

GILES? HIDEY-HO, NEIGHBOR, YOU ARE STILL HERE, RIGHT?

OF COURSE I'M STILL HERE, BUFFY, AFTER ALL, WHERE ELSE WOULD I GO?

I'M GILES.

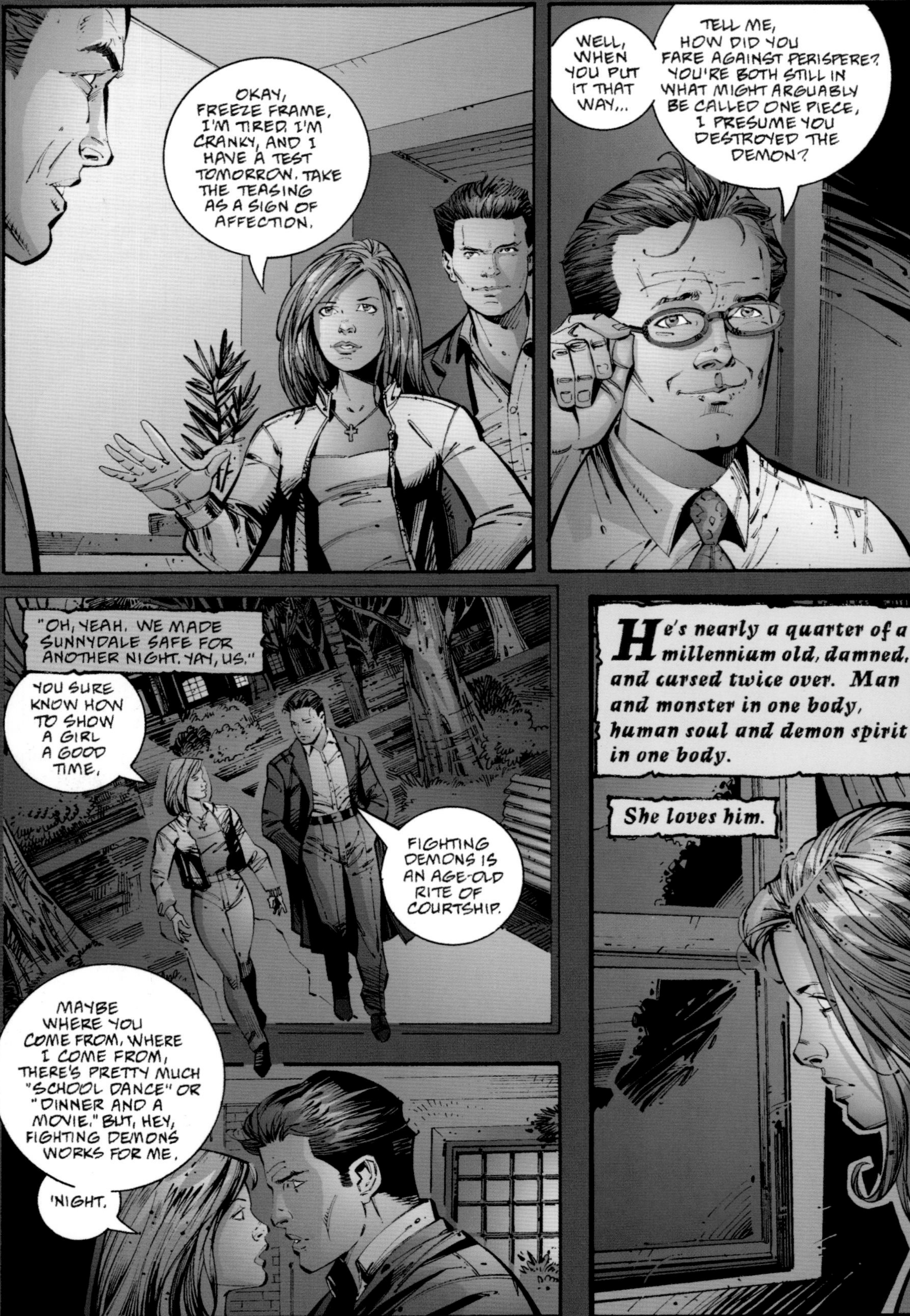

OKAY, FREEZE FRAME. I'M TIRED. I'M CRANKY, AND I HAVE A TEST TOMORROW. TAKE THE TEASING AS A SIGN OF AFFECTION.
WELL, WHEN YOU PUT IT THAT WAY...
TELL ME, HOW DID YOU FARE AGAINST PERISPERE? YOU'RE BOTH STILL IN WHAT MIGHT ARGUABLY BE CALLED ONE PIECE. I PRESUME YOU DESTROYED THE DEMON?
"OH, YEAH. WE MADE SUNNYDALE SAFE FOR ANOTHER NIGHT. YAY, US."
YOU SURE KNOW HOW TO SHOW A GIRL A GOOD TIME.
FIGHTING DEMONS IS AN AGE-OLD RITE OF COURTSHIP.
MAYBE WHERE YOU COME FROM. WHERE I COME FROM, THERE'S PRETTY MUCH "SCHOOL DANCE" OR "DINNER AND A MOVIE." BUT, HEY, FIGHTING DEMONS WORKS FOR ME.
'NIGHT.
He's nearly a quarter of a millennium old, damned, and cursed twice over. Man and monster in one body, human soul and demon spirit in one body.
She loves him.

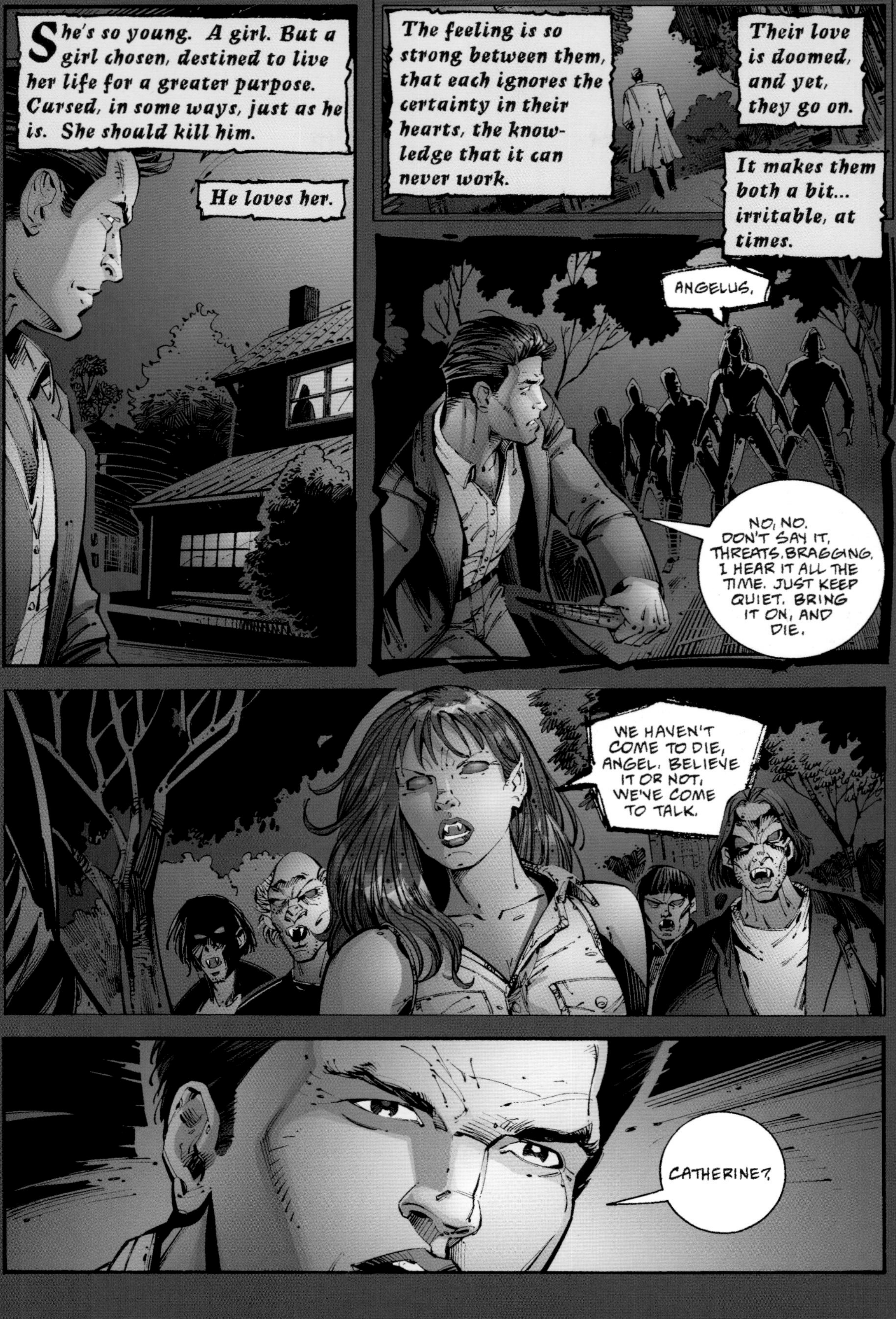
She's so young. A girl. But a girl chosen, destined to live her life for a greater purpose. Cursed, in some ways, just as he is. She should kill him.
He loves her.
The feeling is so strong between them, that each ignores the certainty in their hearts, the knowledge that it can never work.
Their love is doomed, and yet, they go on.
It makes them both a bit... irritable, at times.
ANGELUS.
NO, NO. DON'T SAY IT. THREATS, BRAGGING, I HEAR IT ALL THE TIME. JUST KEEP QUIET. BRING IT ON, AND DIE.
WE HAVEN'T COME TO DIE, ANGEL. BELIEVE IT OR NOT, WE'VE COME TO TALK.
CATHERINE?

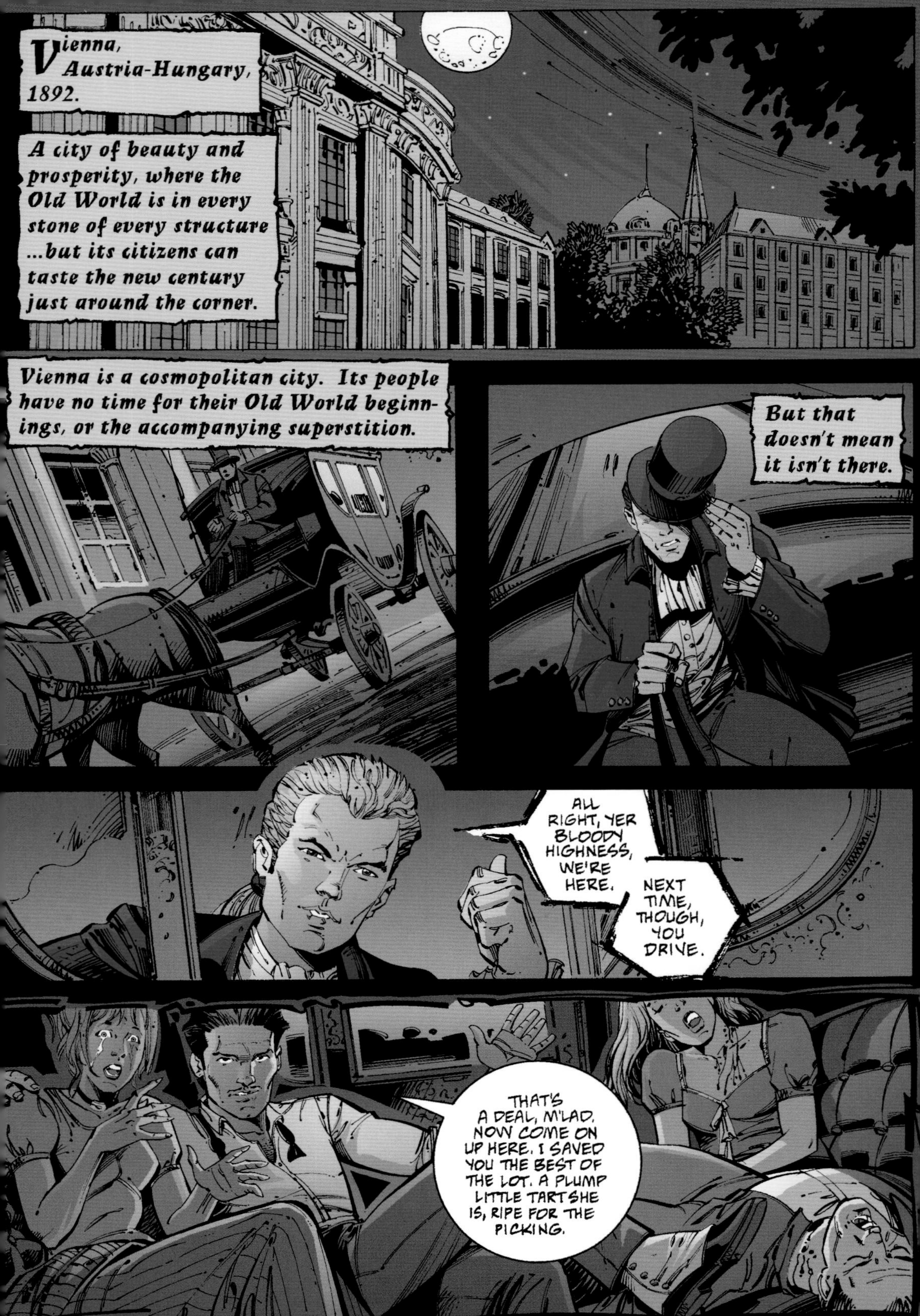
Vienna, Austria-Hungary, 1892.
A city of beauty and prosperity, where the Old World is in every stone of every structure ...but its citizens can taste the new century just around the corner.
Vienna is a cosmopolitan city. Its people have no time for their Old World beginnings, or the accompanying superstition.
But that doesn't mean it isn't there.
ALL RIGHT, YER BLOODY HIGHNESS, WE'RE HERE.
NEXT TIME, THOUGH, YOU DRIVE.
THAT'S A DEAL, M'LAD. NOW COME ON UP HERE. I SAVED YOU THE BEST OF THE LOT. A PLUMP LITTLE TART SHE IS, RIPE FOR THE PICKING.

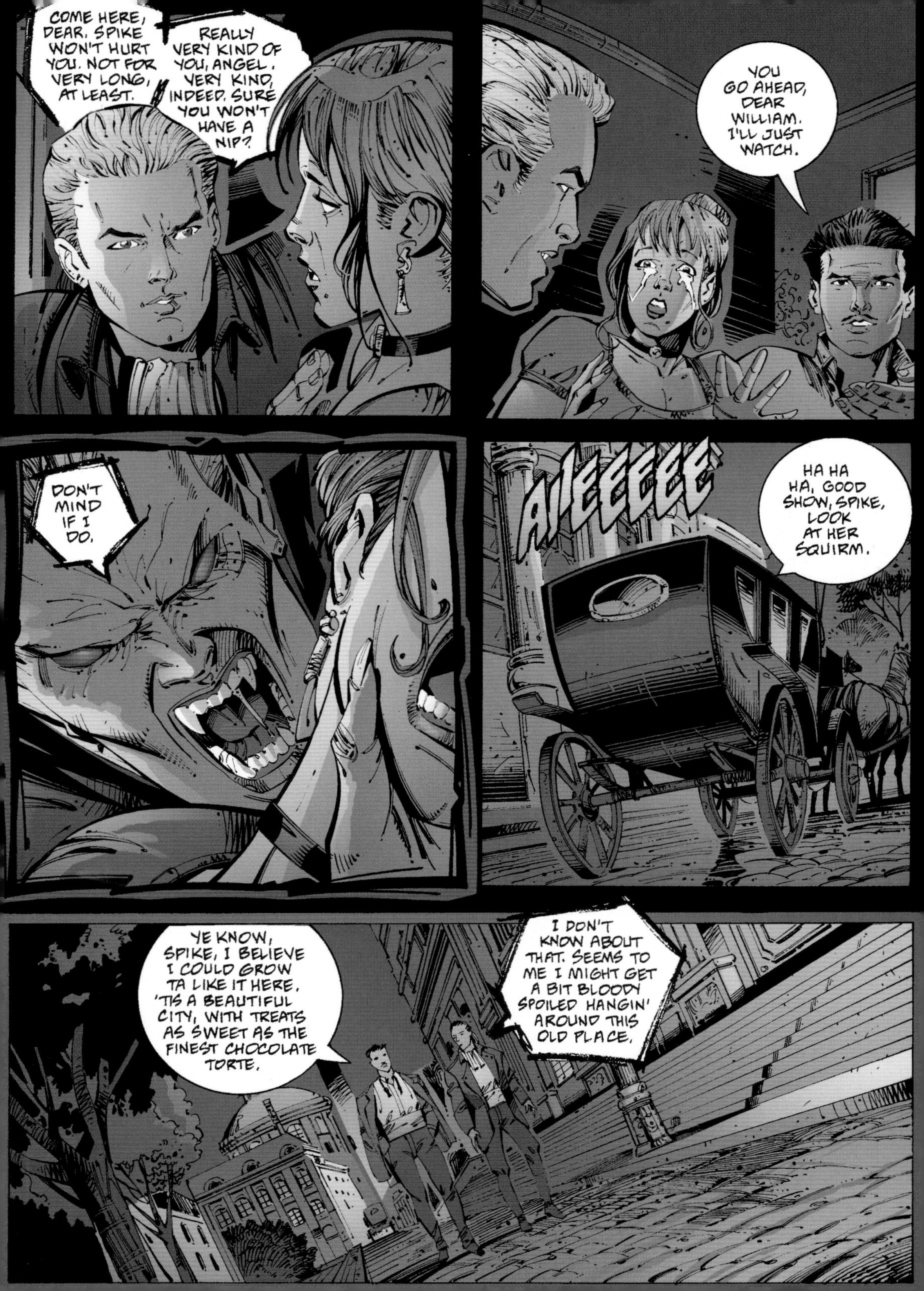

COME HERE, DEAR. SPIKE WON'T HURT YOU. NOT FOR VERY LONG, AT LEAST.
REALLY VERY KIND OF YOU, ANGEL. VERY KIND, INDEED. SURE YOU WON'T HAVE A NIP?
YOU GO AHEAD, DEAR WILLIAM. I'LL JUST WATCH.
DON'T MIND IF I DO.
AIEEEEE
HA HA HA, GOOD SHOW, SPIKE, LOOK AT HER SQUIRM.
YE KNOW, SPIKE, I BELIEVE I COULD GROW TA LIKE IT HERE. 'TIS A BEAUTIFUL CITY, WITH TREATS AS SWEET AS THE FINEST CHOCOLATE TORTE.
I DON'T KNOW ABOUT THAT. SEEMS TO ME I MIGHT GET A BIT BLOODY SPOILED HANGIN' AROUND THIS OLD PLACE.

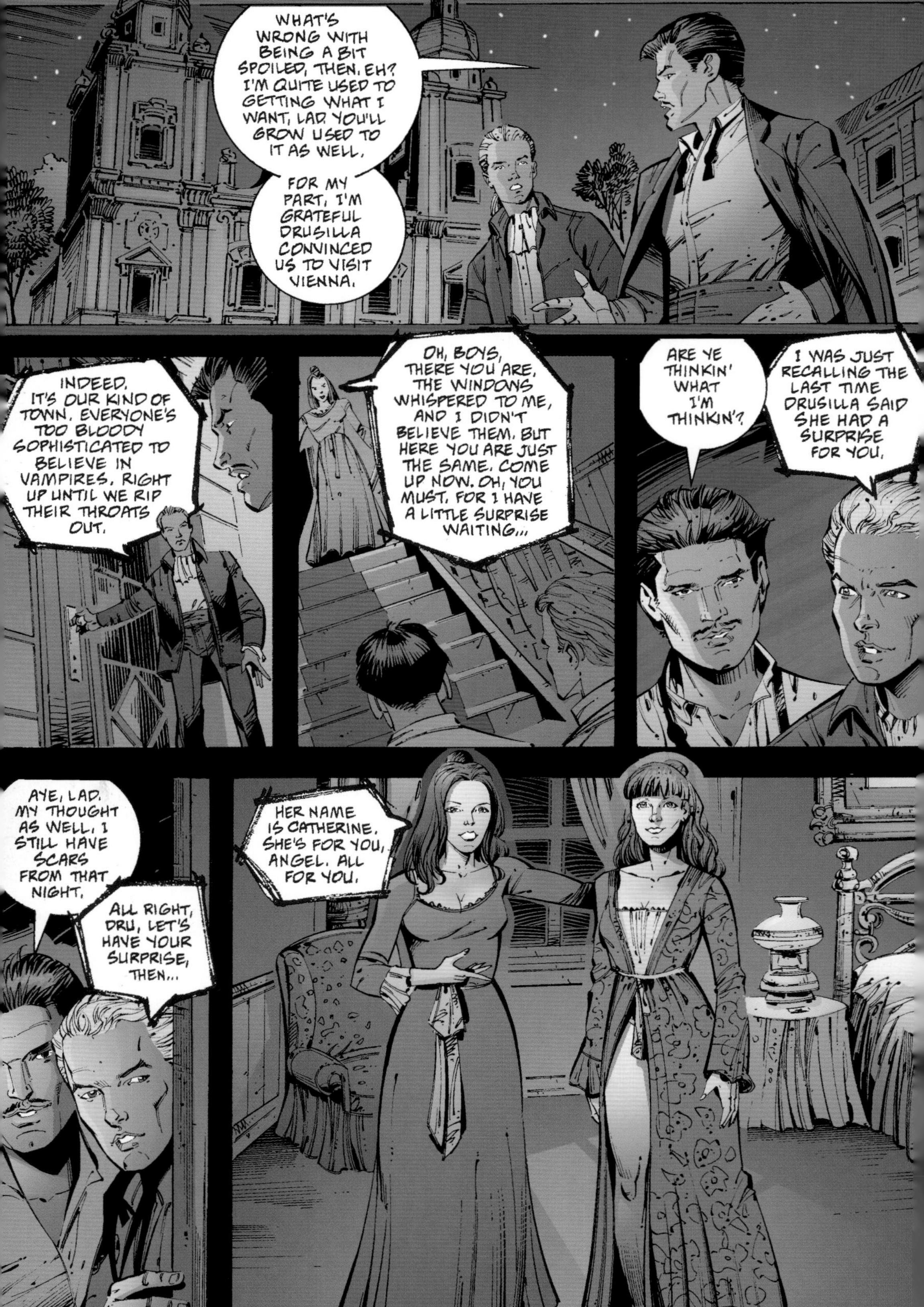
WHAT'S WRONG WITH BEING A BIT SPOILED, THEN, EH? I'M QUITE USED TO GETTING WHAT I WANT, LAD. YOU'LL GROW USED TO IT AS WELL.
FOR MY PART, I'M GRATEFUL DRUSILLA CONVINCED US TO VISIT VIENNA.
INDEED. IT'S OUR KIND OF TOWN. EVERYONE'S TOO BLOODY SOPHISTICATED TO BELIEVE IN VAMPIRES, RIGHT UP UNTIL WE RIP THEIR THROATS OUT.
OH, BOYS, THERE YOU ARE. THE WINDOWS WHISPERED TO ME, AND I DIDN'T BELIEVE THEM. BUT HERE YOU ARE JUST THE SAME. COME UP NOW. OH, YOU MUST, FOR I HAVE A LITTLE SURPRISE WAITING...
ARE YE THINKIN' WHAT I'M THINKIN'?
I WAS JUST RECALLING THE LAST TIME DRUSILLA SAID SHE HAD A SURPRISE FOR YOU.
AYE, LAD. MY THOUGHT AS WELL. I STILL HAVE SCARS FROM THAT NIGHT.
ALL RIGHT, DRU, LET'S HAVE YOUR SURPRISE, THEN...
HER NAME IS CATHERINE. SHE'S FOR YOU, ANGEL. ALL FOR YOU.

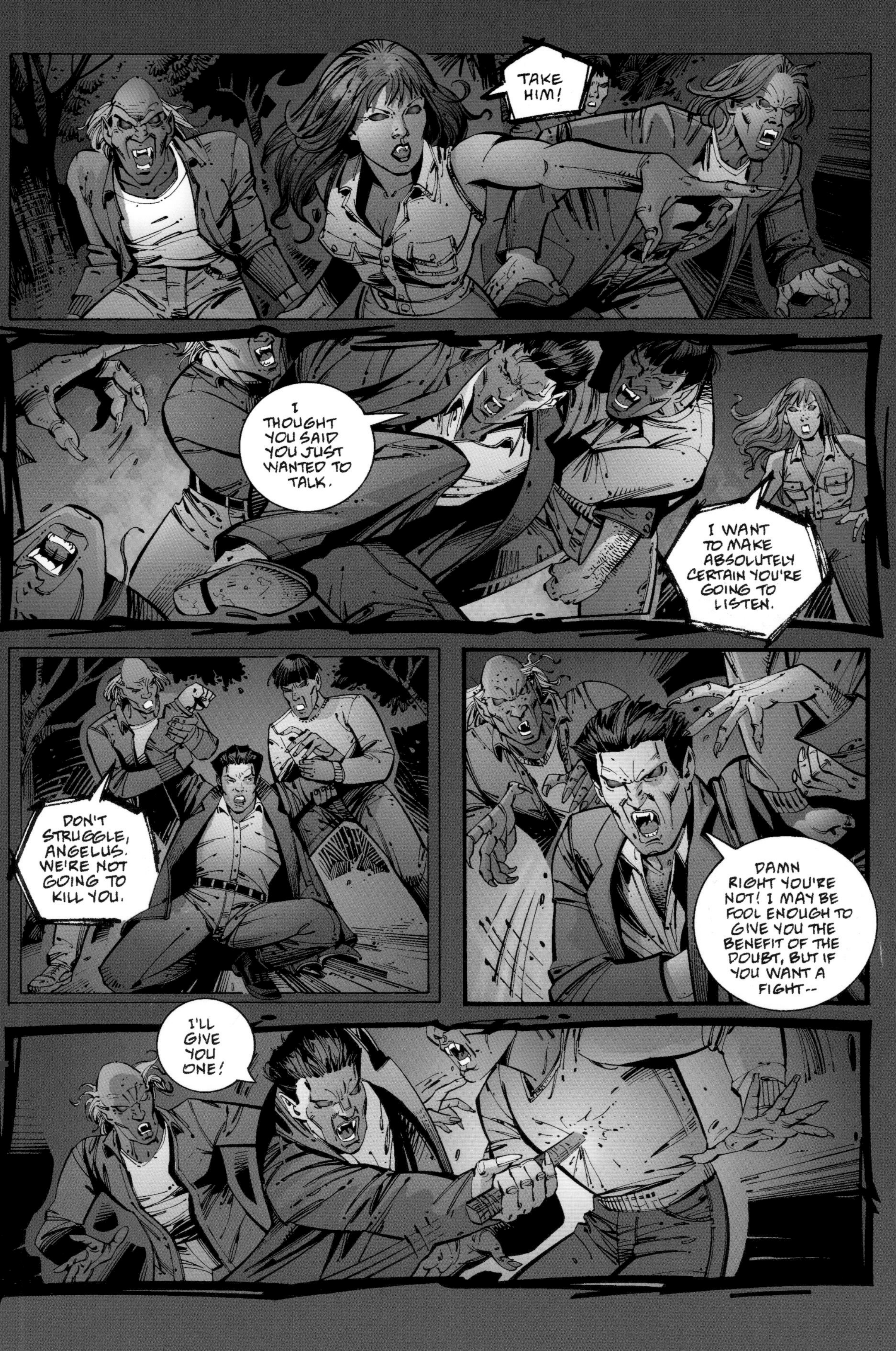
TAKE HIM!
I THOUGHT YOU SAID YOU JUST WANTED TO TALK.
I WANT TO MAKE ABSOLUTELY CERTAIN YOU'RE GOING TO LISTEN.
DON'T STRUGGLE, ANGELUS. WE'RE NOT GOING TO KILL YOU.
DAMN RIGHT YOU'RE NOT! I MAY BE FOOL ENOUGH TO GIVE YOU THE BENEFIT OF THE DOUBT, BUT IF YOU WANT A FIGHT--
I'LL GIVE YOU ONE!

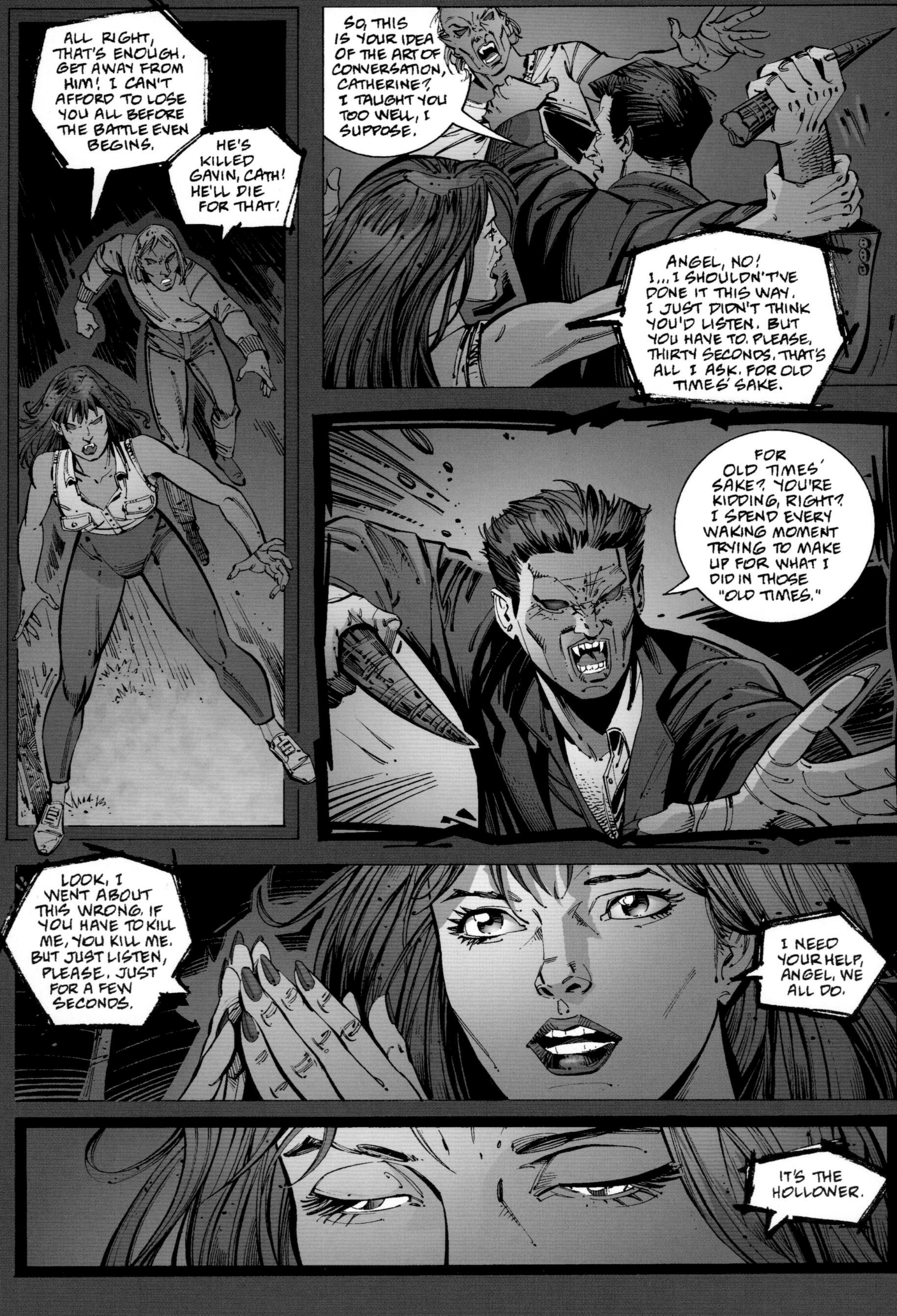

ALL RIGHT, THAT'S ENOUGH. GET AWAY FROM HIM! I CAN'T AFFORD TO LOSE YOU ALL BEFORE THE BATTLE EVEN BEGINS.
HE'S KILLED GAVIN, CATH! HE'LL DIE FOR THAT!
SO, THIS IS YOUR IDEA OF THE ART OF CONVERSATION, CATHERINE? I TAUGHT YOU TOO WELL, I SUPPOSE.
ANGEL, NO! I... I SHOULDN'T'VE DONE IT THIS WAY. I JUST DIDN'T THINK YOU'D LISTEN. BUT YOU HAVE TO. PLEASE. THIRTY SECONDS. THAT'S ALL I ASK. FOR OLD TIMES' SAKE.
FOR OLD TIMES' SAKE? YOU'RE KIDDING, RIGHT? I SPEND EVERY WAKING MOMENT TRYING TO MAKE UP FOR WHAT I DID IN THOSE "OLD TIMES."
LOOK, I WENT ABOUT THIS WRONG. IF YOU HAVE TO KILL ME, YOU KILL ME. BUT JUST LISTEN, PLEASE. JUST FOR A FEW SECONDS.
I NEED YOUR HELP, ANGEL. WE ALL DO.
IT'S THE HOLLOWER.

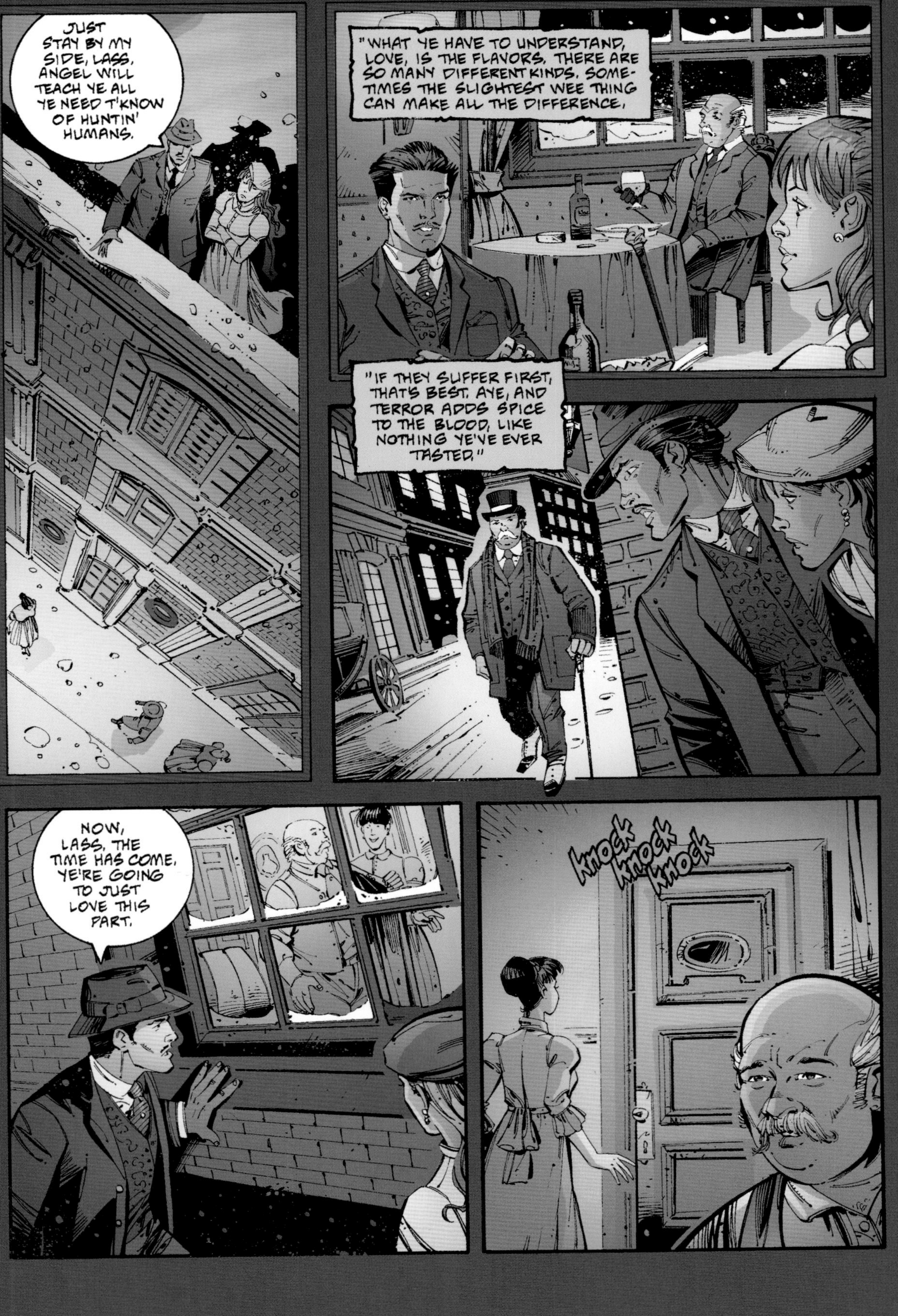
JUST STAY BY MY SIDE, LASS. ANGEL WILL TEACH YE ALL YE NEED T'KNOW OF HUNTIN' HUMANS.
"WHAT YE HAVE TO UNDERSTAND, LOVE, IS THE FLAVORS. THERE ARE SO MANY DIFFERENT KINDS. SOMETIMES THE SLIGHTEST WEE THING CAN MAKE ALL THE DIFFERENCE.
"IF THEY SUFFER FIRST, THAT'S BEST. AYE, AND TERROR ADDS SPICE TO THE BLOOD, LIKE NOTHING YE'VE EVER TASTED."
NOW, LASS, THE TIME HAS COME. YE'RE GOING TO JUST LOVE THIS PART.
knock knock knock

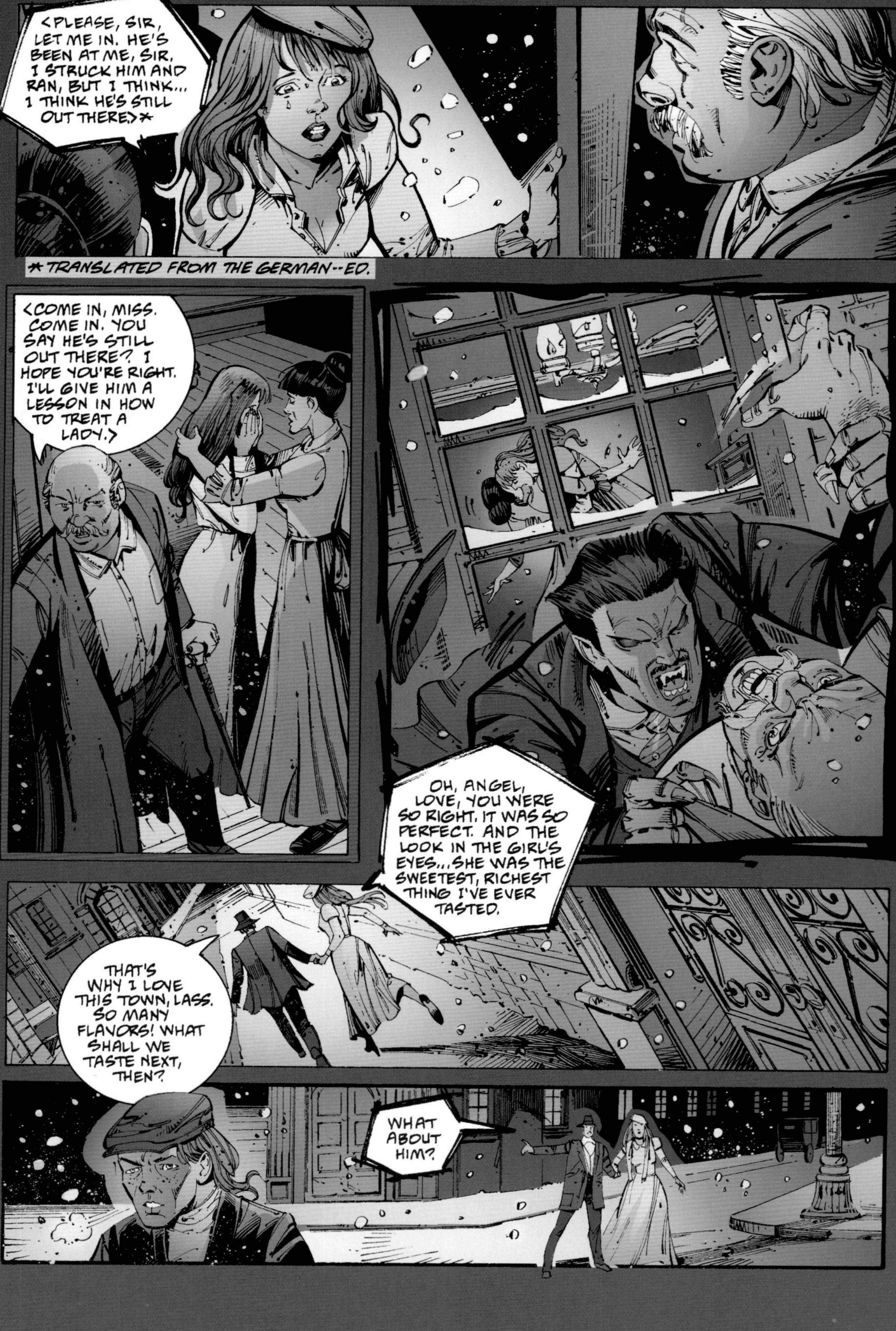
<PLEASE, SIR, LET ME IN. HE'S BEEN AT ME, SIR. I STRUCK HIM AND RAN, BUT I THINK... I THINK HE'S STILL OUT THERE.>*
*TRANSLATED FROM THE GERMAN--ED.
<COME IN, MISS. COME IN. YOU SAY HE'S STILL OUT THERE? I HOPE YOU'RE RIGHT. I'LL GIVE HIM A LESSON IN HOW TO TREAT A LADY.>
OH, ANGEL, LOVE, YOU WERE SO RIGHT. IT WAS SO PERFECT. AND THE LOOK IN THE GIRL'S EYES... SHE WAS THE SWEETEST, RICHEST THING I'VE EVER TASTED.
THAT'S WHY I LOVE THIS TOWN, LASS. SO MANY FLAVORS! WHAT SHALL WE TASTE NEXT, THEN?
WHAT ABOUT HIM?

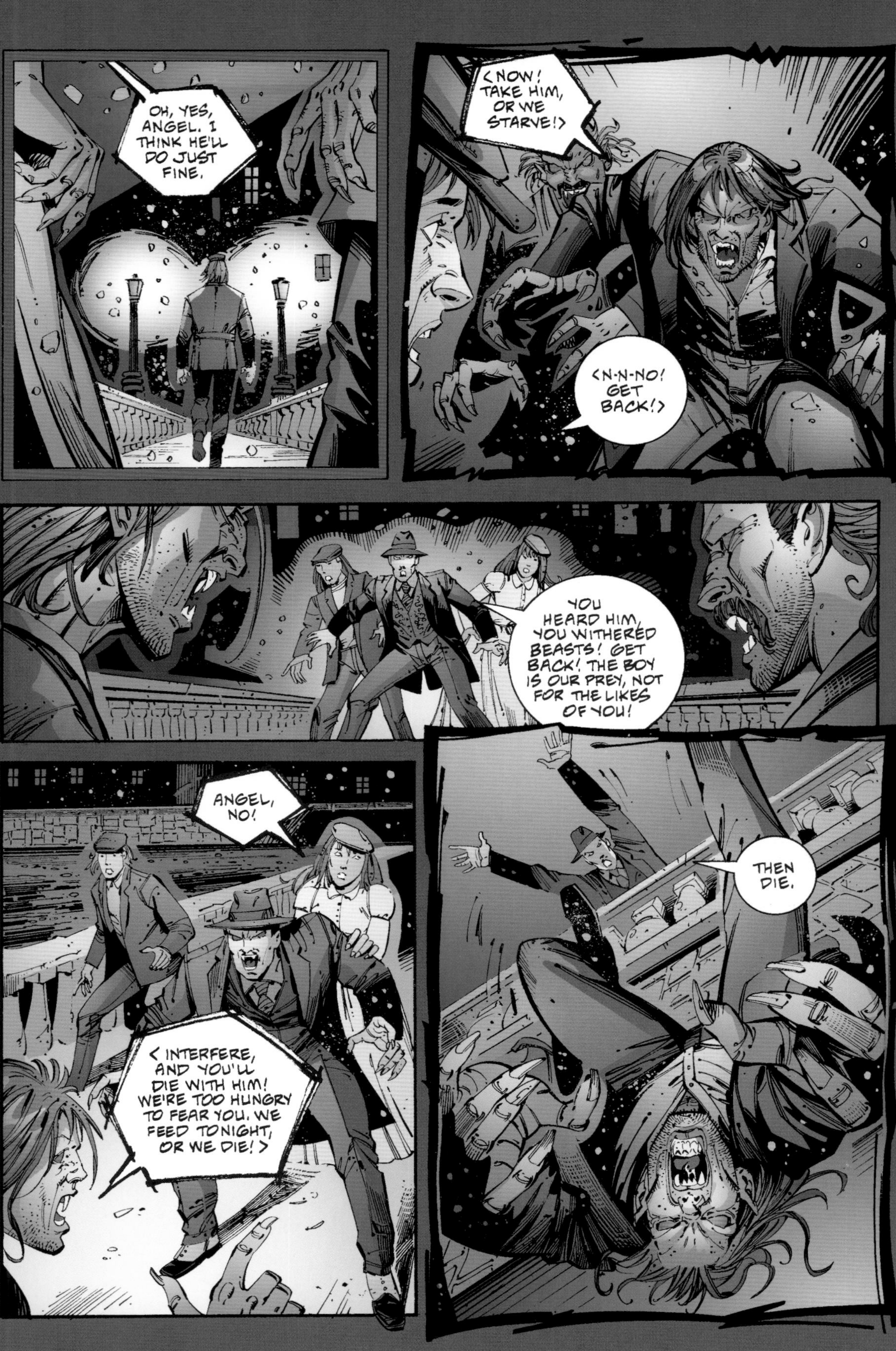
OH, YES, ANGEL. I THINK HE'LL DO JUST FINE.
<NOW! TAKE HIM, OR WE STARVE!>
<N-N-NO! GET BACK!>
YOU HEARD HIM, YOU WITHERED BEASTS! GET BACK! THE BOY IS OUR PREY, NOT FOR THE LIKES OF YOU!
ANGEL, NO!
< INTERFERE, AND YOU'LL DIE WITH HIM! WE'RE TOO HUNGRY TO FEAR YOU. WE FEED TONIGHT, OR WE DIE! >
THEN DIE.

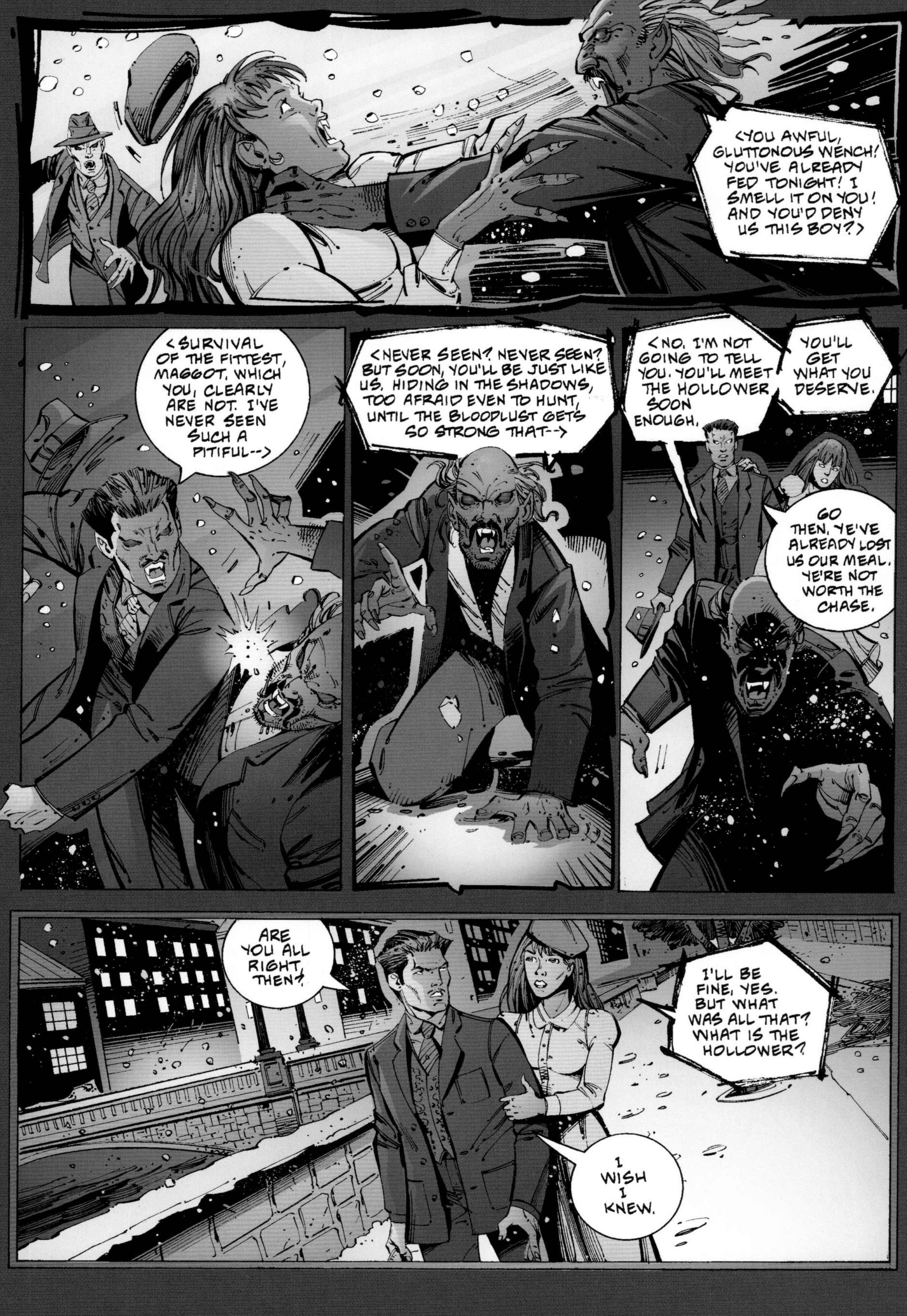
<YOU AWFUL, GLUTTONOUS WENCH! YOU'VE ALREADY FED TONIGHT! I SMELL IT ON YOU! AND YOU'D DENY US THIS BOY?>
<SURVIVAL OF THE FITTEST, MAGGOT, WHICH YOU, CLEARLY ARE NOT. I'VE NEVER SEEN SUCH A PITIFUL-->
<NEVER SEEN? NEVER SEEN? BUT SOON, YOU'LL BE JUST LIKE US, HIDING IN THE SHADOWS, TOO AFRAID EVEN TO HUNT, UNTIL THE BLOODLUST GETS SO STRONG THAT-->
<NO, I'M NOT GOING TO TELL YOU. YOU'LL MEET THE HOLLOWER SOON ENOUGH.
YOU'LL GET WHAT YOU DESERVE.
GO THEN, YE'VE ALREADY LOST US OUR MEAL. YE'RE NOT WORTH THE CHASE.
ARE YOU ALL RIGHT, THEN?
I'LL BE FINE, YES. BUT WHAT WAS ALL THAT? WHAT IS THE HOLLOWER?
I WISH I KNEW.

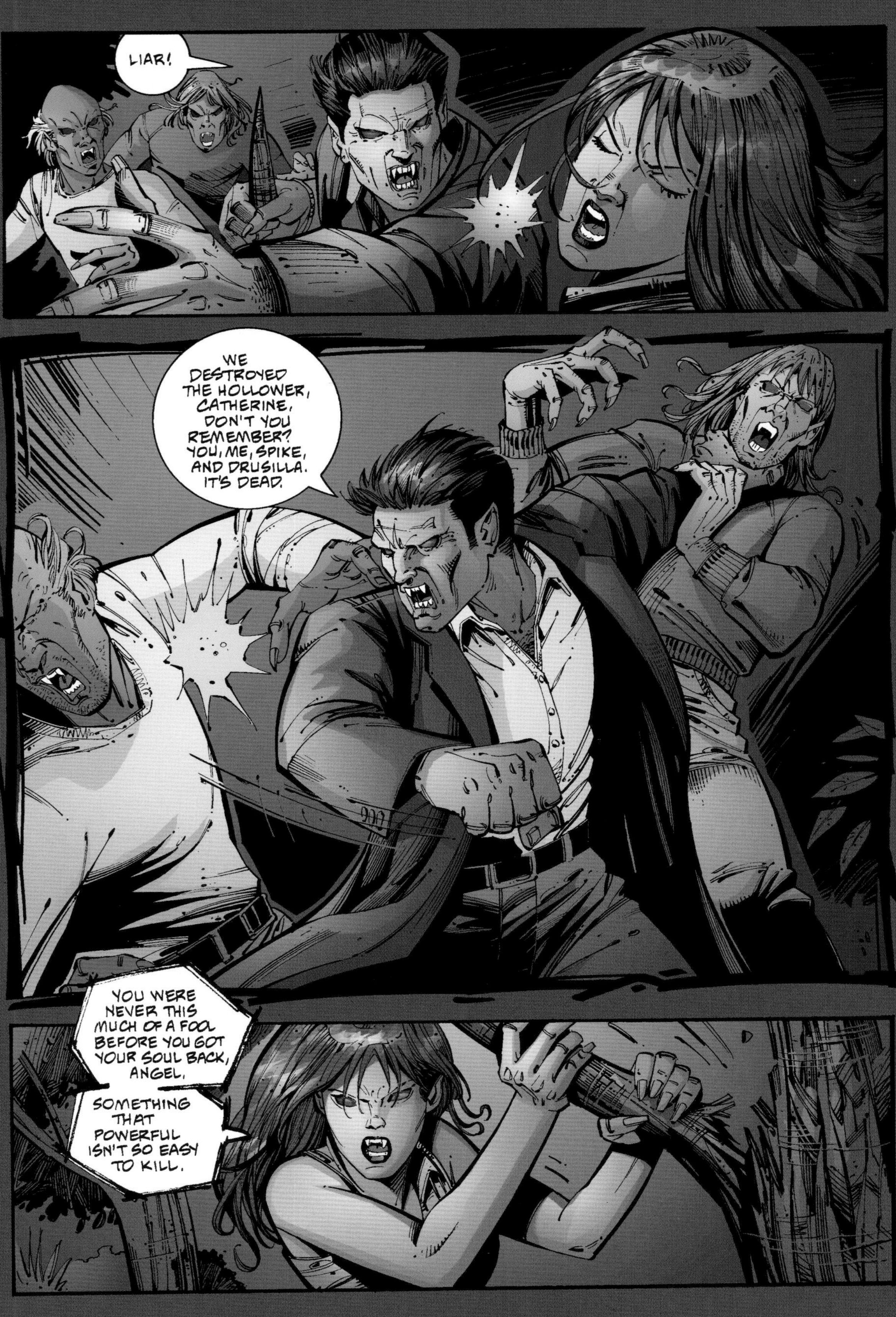
LIAR!
WE DESTROYED THE HOLLOWER, CATHERINE, DON'T YOU REMEMBER? YOU, ME, SPIKE, AND DRUSILLA. IT'S DEAD.
YOU WERE NEVER THIS MUCH OF A FOOL BEFORE YOU GOT YOUR SOUL BACK, ANGEL.
SOMETHING THAT POWERFUL ISN'T SO EASY TO KILL.

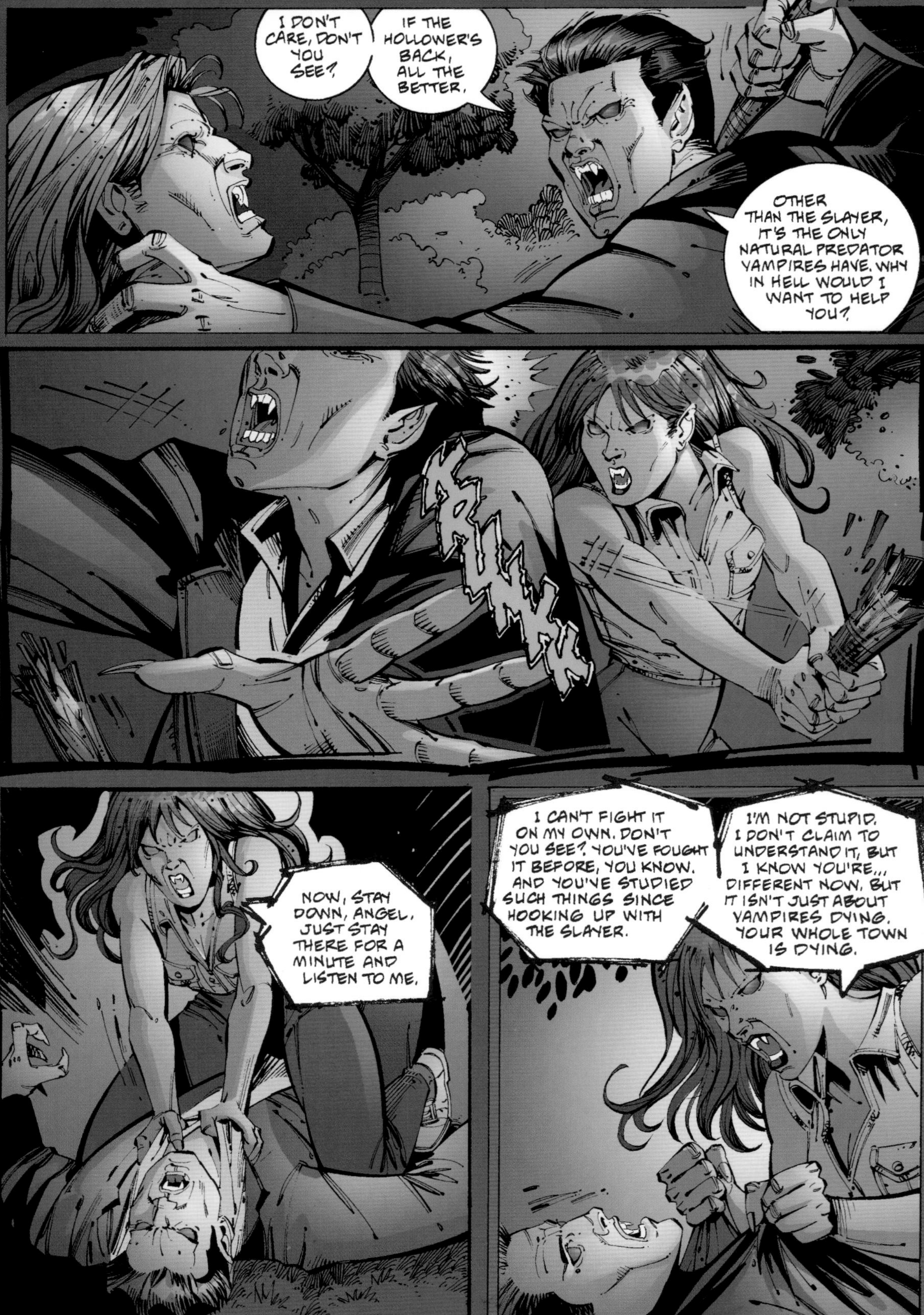
I DON'T CARE, DON'T YOU SEE?
IF THE HOLLOWER'S BACK, ALL THE BETTER.
OTHER THAN THE SLAYER, IT'S THE ONLY NATURAL PREDATOR VAMPIRES HAVE. WHY IN HELL WOULD I WANT TO HELP YOU?
NOW, STAY DOWN, ANGEL. JUST STAY THERE FOR A MINUTE AND LISTEN TO ME.
I CAN'T FIGHT IT ON MY OWN. DON'T YOU SEE? YOU'VE FOUGHT IT BEFORE, YOU KNOW. AND YOU'VE STUDIED SUCH THINGS SINCE HOOKING UP WITH THE SLAYER.
I'M NOT STUPID. I DON'T CLAIM TO UNDERSTAND IT, BUT I KNOW YOU'RE... DIFFERENT NOW. BUT IT ISN'T JUST ABOUT VAMPIRES DYING. YOUR WHOLE TOWN IS DYING.

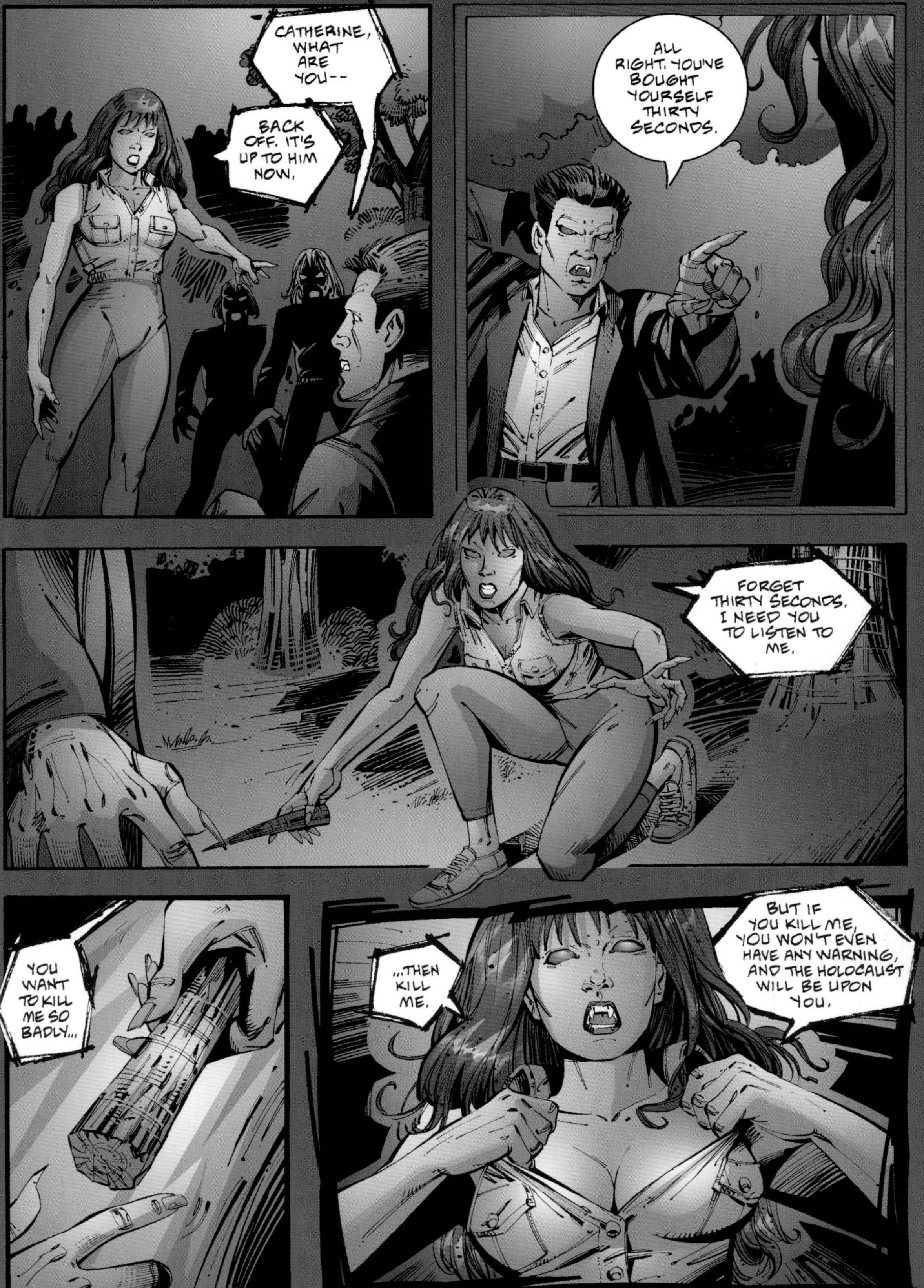
CATHERINE, WHAT ARE YOU--
BACK OFF. IT'S UP TO HIM NOW.
ALL RIGHT. YOU'VE BOUGHT YOURSELF THIRTY SECONDS.
FORGET THIRTY SECONDS. I NEED YOU TO LISTEN TO ME.
YOU WANT TO KILL ME SO BADLY...
...THEN KILL ME.
BUT IF YOU KILL ME, YOU WON'T EVEN HAVE ANY WARNING, AND THE HOLOCAUST WILL BE UPON YOU.

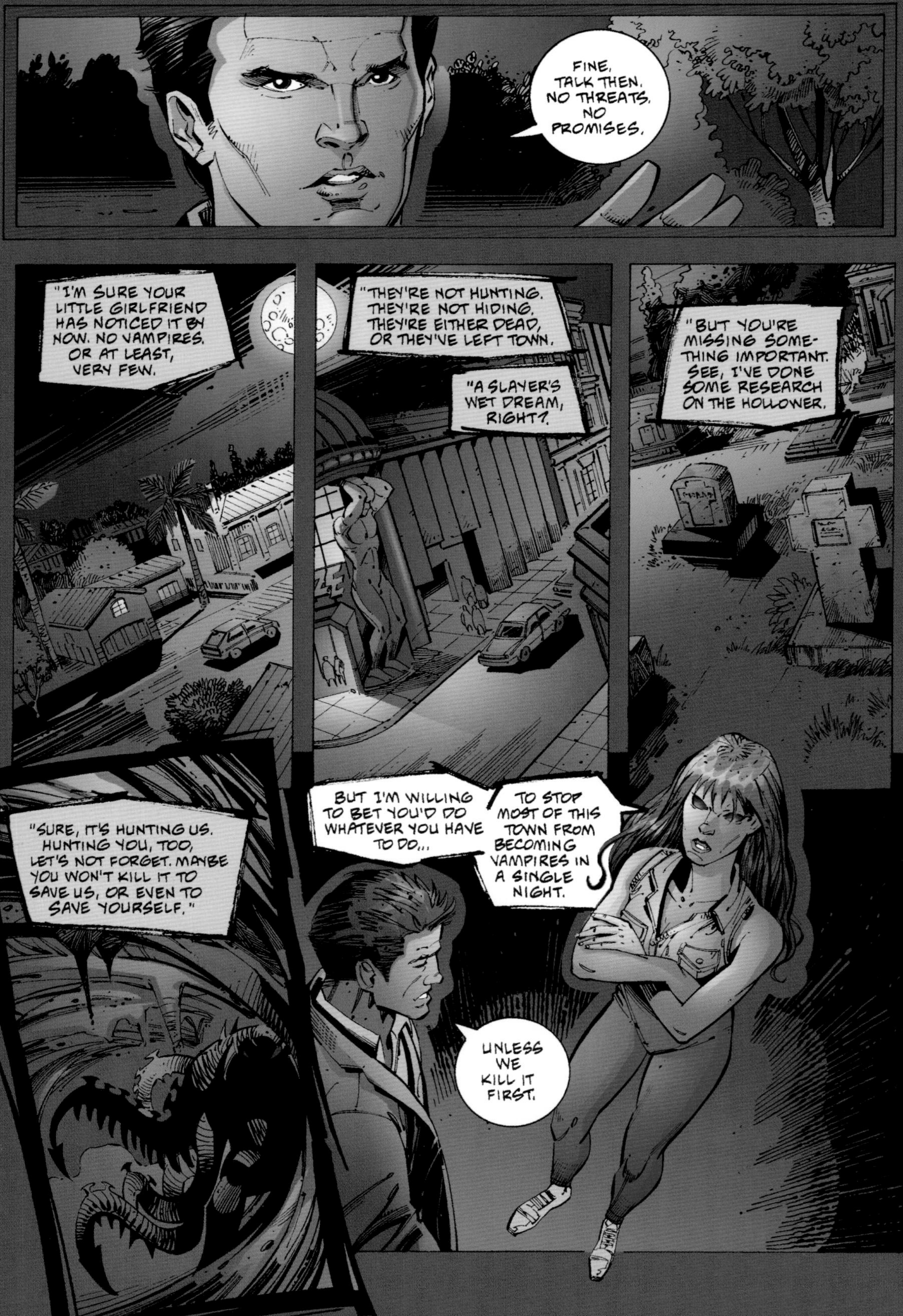
FINE, TALK THEN. NO THREATS, NO PROMISES.
"I'M SURE YOUR LITTLE GIRLFRIEND HAS NOTICED IT BY NOW. NO VAMPIRES. OR AT LEAST, VERY FEW.
"THEY'RE NOT HUNTING. THEY'RE NOT HIDING. THEY'RE EITHER DEAD, OR THEY'VE LEFT TOWN.
"A SLAYER'S WET DREAM, RIGHT?
"BUT YOU'RE MISSING SOME-THING IMPORTANT. SEE, I'VE DONE SOME RESEARCH ON THE HOLLOWER.
"SURE, IT'S HUNTING US. HUNTING YOU, TOO, LET'S NOT FORGET. MAYBE YOU WON'T KILL IT TO SAVE US, OR EVEN TO SAVE YOURSELF."
BUT I'M WILLING TO BET YOU'D DO WHATEVER YOU HAVE TO DO...
TO STOP MOST OF THIS TOWN FROM BECOMING VAMPIRES IN A SINGLE NIGHT.
UNLESS WE KILL IT FIRST.

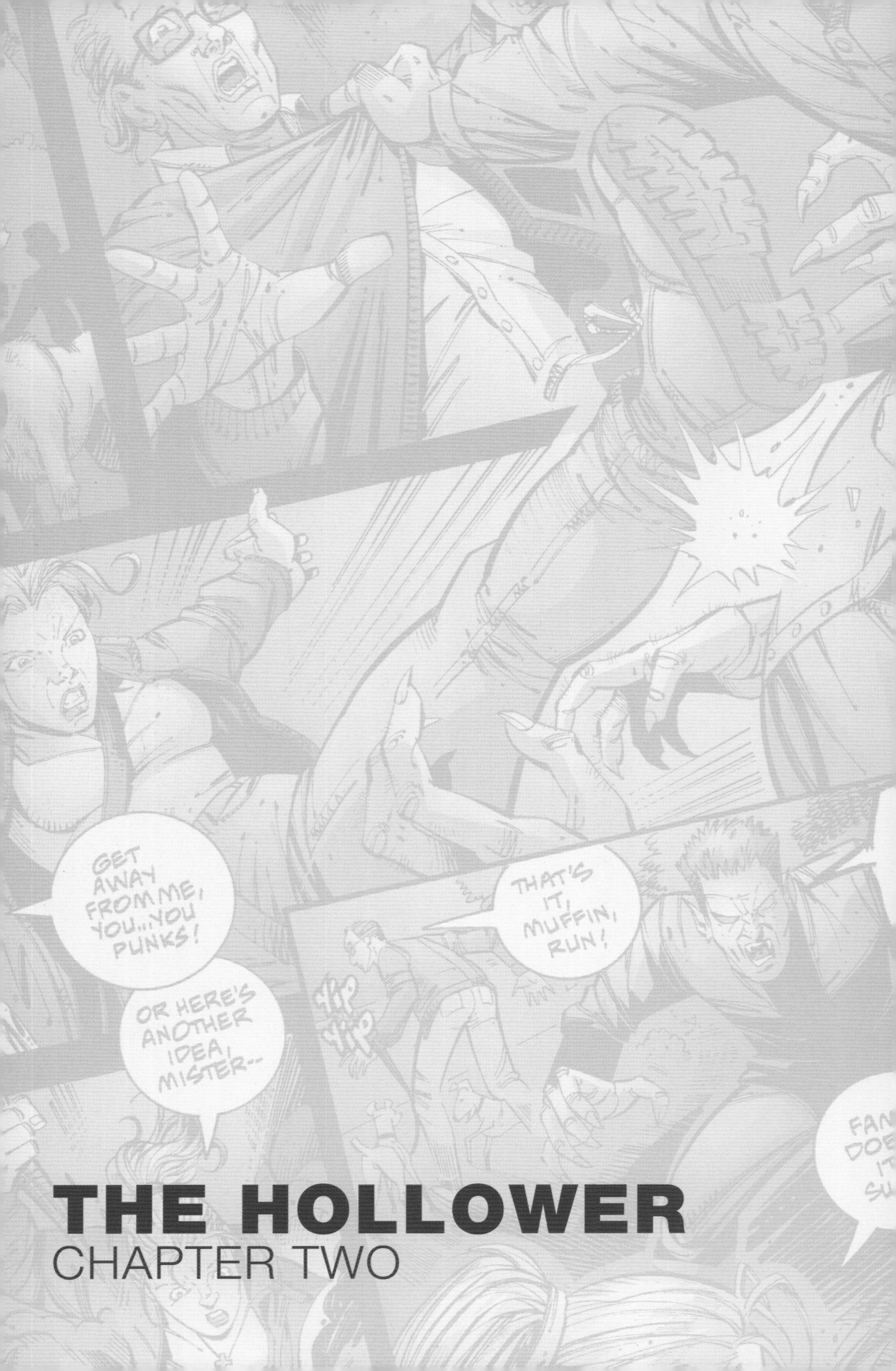
GET AWAY FROM ME, YOU...YOU PUNKS!
OR HERE'S ANOTHER IDEA, MISTER--
THAT'S IT, MUFFIN, RUN!

THE HOLLOWER
CHAPTER TWO

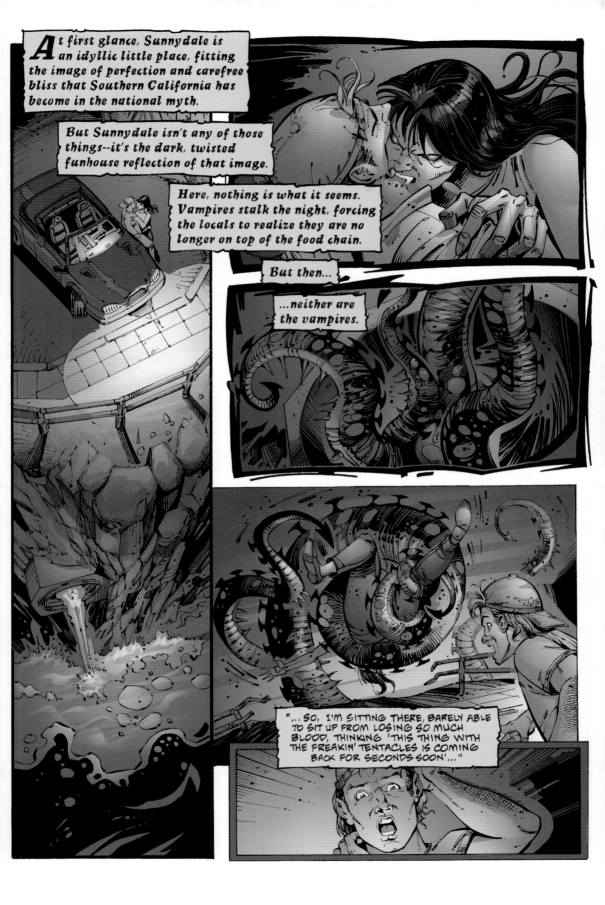

At first glance, Sunnydale is an idyllic little place, fitting the image of perfection and carefree bliss that Southern California has become in the national myth.

But Sunnydale isn't any of those things--it's the dark, twisted funhouse reflection of that image.

Here, nothing is what it seems. Vampires stalk the night, forcing the locals to realize they are no longer on top of the food chain.

But then...

...neither are the vampires.

"...SO, I'M SITTING THERE, BARELY ABLE TO SIT UP FROM LOSING SO MUCH BLOOD, THINKING 'THIS THING WITH THE FREAKIN' TENTACLES IS COMING BACK FOR SECONDS SOON',..."

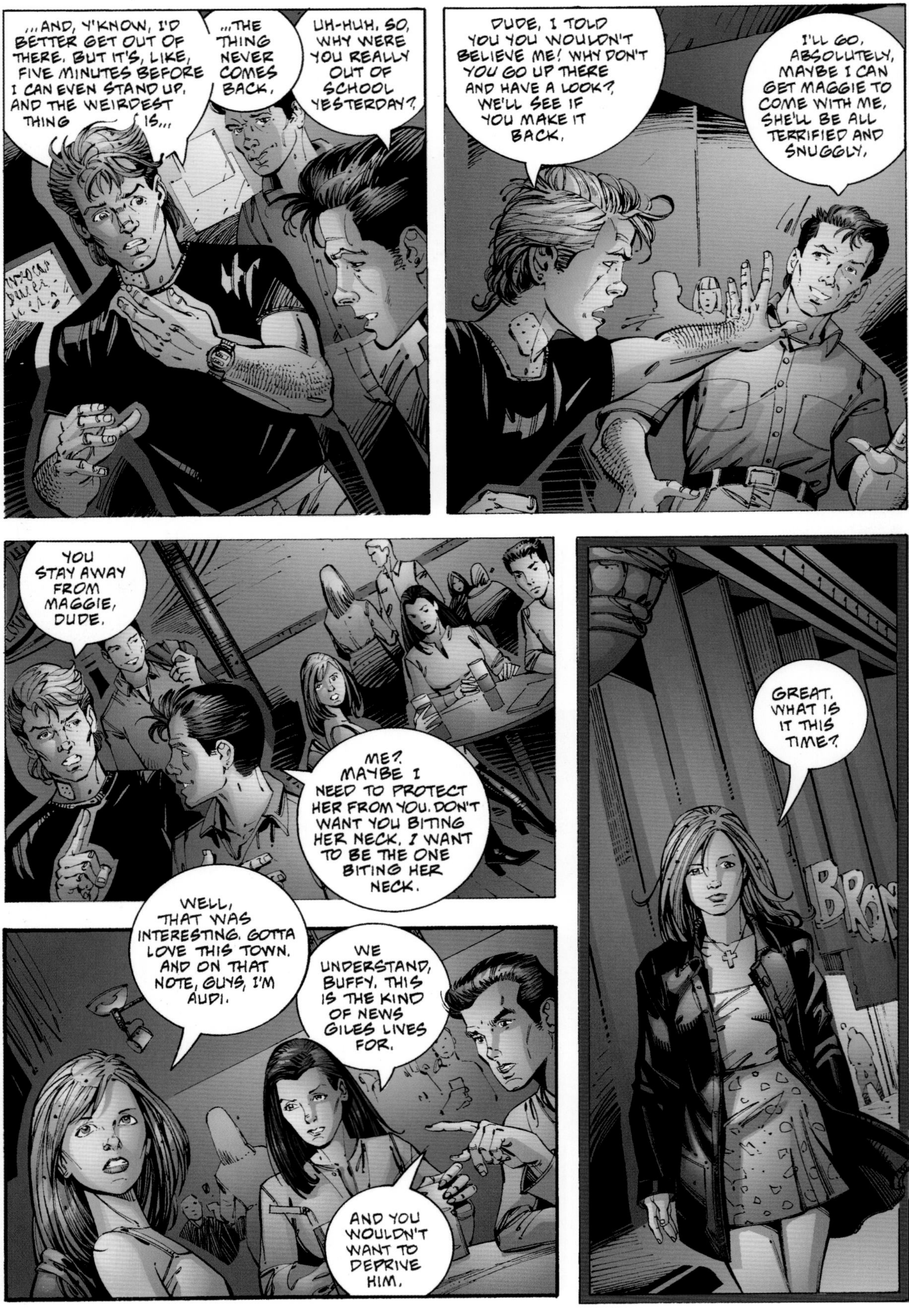
...AND, Y'KNOW, I'D BETTER GET OUT OF THERE. BUT IT'S, LIKE, FIVE MINUTES BEFORE I CAN EVEN STAND UP, AND THE WEIRDEST THING IS...
...THE THING NEVER COMES BACK.
UH-HUH. SO, WHY WERE YOU REALLY OUT OF SCHOOL YESTERDAY?
DUDE, I TOLD YOU YOU WOULDN'T BELIEVE ME! WHY DON'T YOU GO UP THERE AND HAVE A LOOK? WE'LL SEE IF YOU MAKE IT BACK.
I'LL GO, ABSOLUTELY. MAYBE I CAN GET MAGGIE TO COME WITH ME. SHE'LL BE ALL TERRIFIED AND SNUGGLY.
YOU STAY AWAY FROM MAGGIE, DUDE.
ME? MAYBE I NEED TO PROTECT HER FROM YOU. DON'T WANT YOU BITING HER NECK. I WANT TO BE THE ONE BITING HER NECK.
WELL, THAT WAS INTERESTING. GOTTA LOVE THIS TOWN. AND ON THAT NOTE, GUYS, I'M AUDI.
WE UNDERSTAND, BUFFY. THIS IS THE KIND OF NEWS GILES LIVES FOR.
AND YOU WOULDN'T WANT TO DEPRIVE HIM.
GREAT. WHAT IS IT THIS TIME?

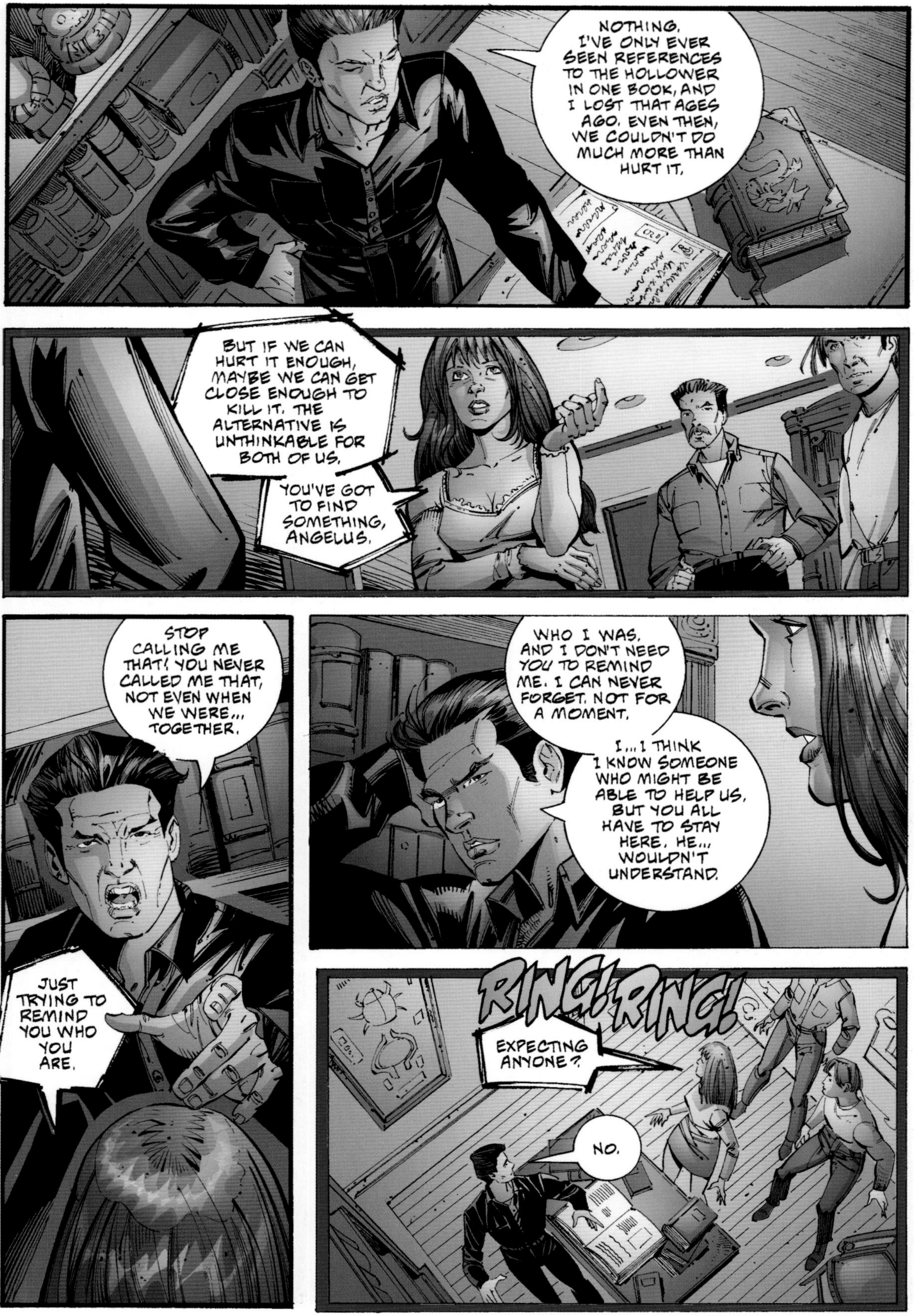
NOTHING. I'VE ONLY EVER SEEN REFERENCES TO THE HOLLOWER IN ONE BOOK, AND I LOST THAT AGES AGO. EVEN THEN, WE COULDN'T DO MUCH MORE THAN HURT IT.
BUT IF WE CAN HURT IT ENOUGH, MAYBE WE CAN GET CLOSE ENOUGH TO KILL IT. THE ALTERNATIVE IS UNTHINKABLE FOR BOTH OF US.
YOU'VE GOT TO FIND SOMETHING, ANGELUS.
STOP CALLING ME THAT! YOU NEVER CALLED ME THAT, NOT EVEN WHEN WE WERE... TOGETHER.
JUST TRYING TO REMIND YOU WHO YOU ARE.
WHO I WAS. AND I DON'T NEED YOU TO REMIND ME. I CAN NEVER FORGET. NOT FOR A MOMENT.
I... I THINK I KNOW SOMEONE WHO MIGHT BE ABLE TO HELP US. BUT YOU ALL HAVE TO STAY HERE. HE... WOULDN'T UNDERSTAND.
RING! RING!
EXPECTING ANYONE?
NO.

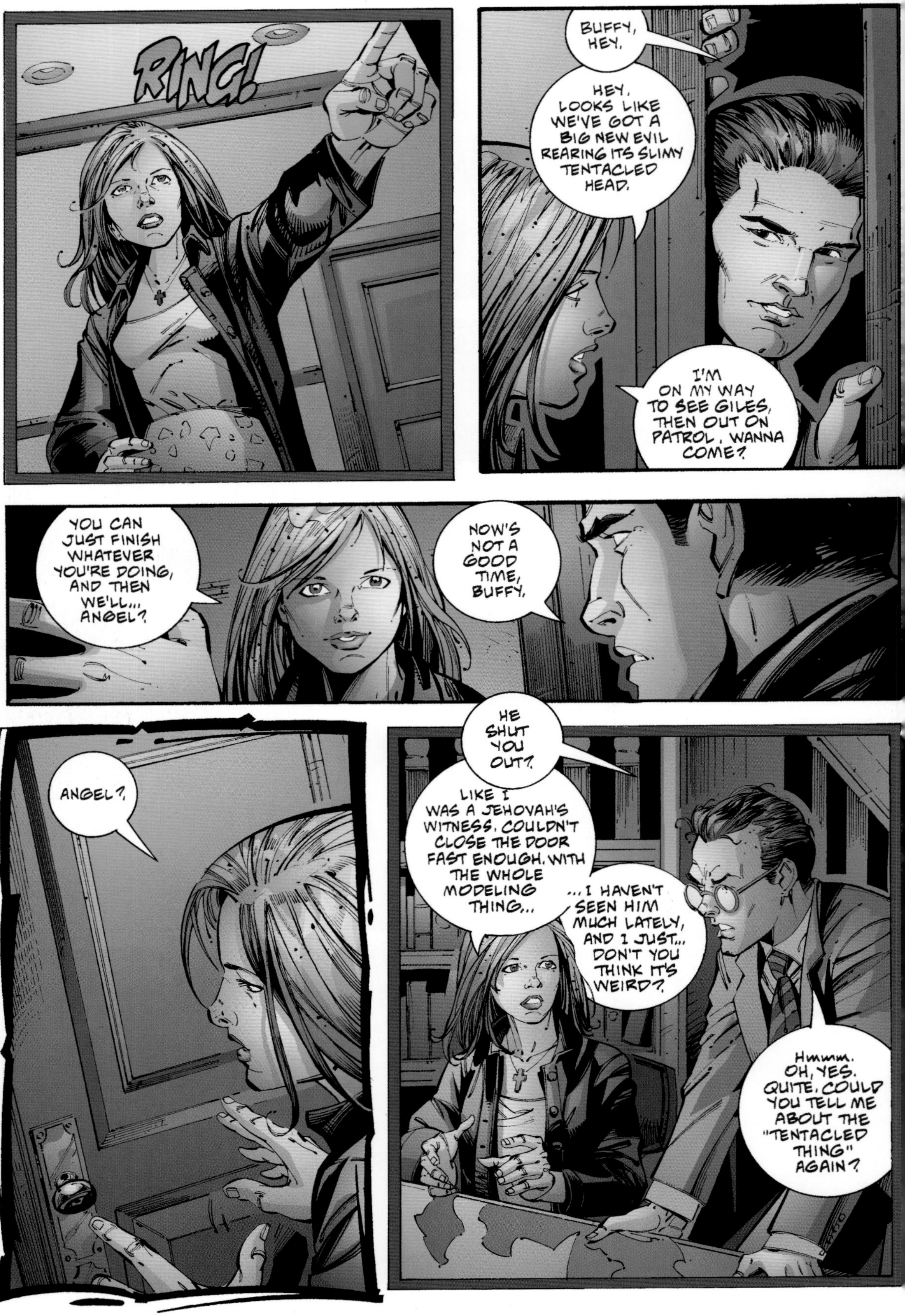
RING!
BUFFY, HEY.
HEY, LOOKS LIKE WE'VE GOT A BIG NEW EVIL REARING ITS SLIMY TENTACLED HEAD.
I'M ON MY WAY TO SEE GILES, THEN OUT ON PATROL, WANNA COME?
YOU CAN JUST FINISH WHATEVER YOU'RE DOING, AND THEN WE'LL... ANGEL?
NOW'S NOT A GOOD TIME, BUFFY.
ANGEL?
HE SHUT YOU OUT?
LIKE I WAS A JEHOVAH'S WITNESS. COULDN'T CLOSE THE DOOR FAST ENOUGH. WITH THE WHOLE MODELING THING...
...I HAVEN'T SEEN HIM MUCH LATELY, AND I JUST... DON'T YOU THINK IT'S WEIRD?
Hmmm. OH, YES. QUITE. COULD YOU TELL ME ABOUT THE "TENTACLED THING" AGAIN?

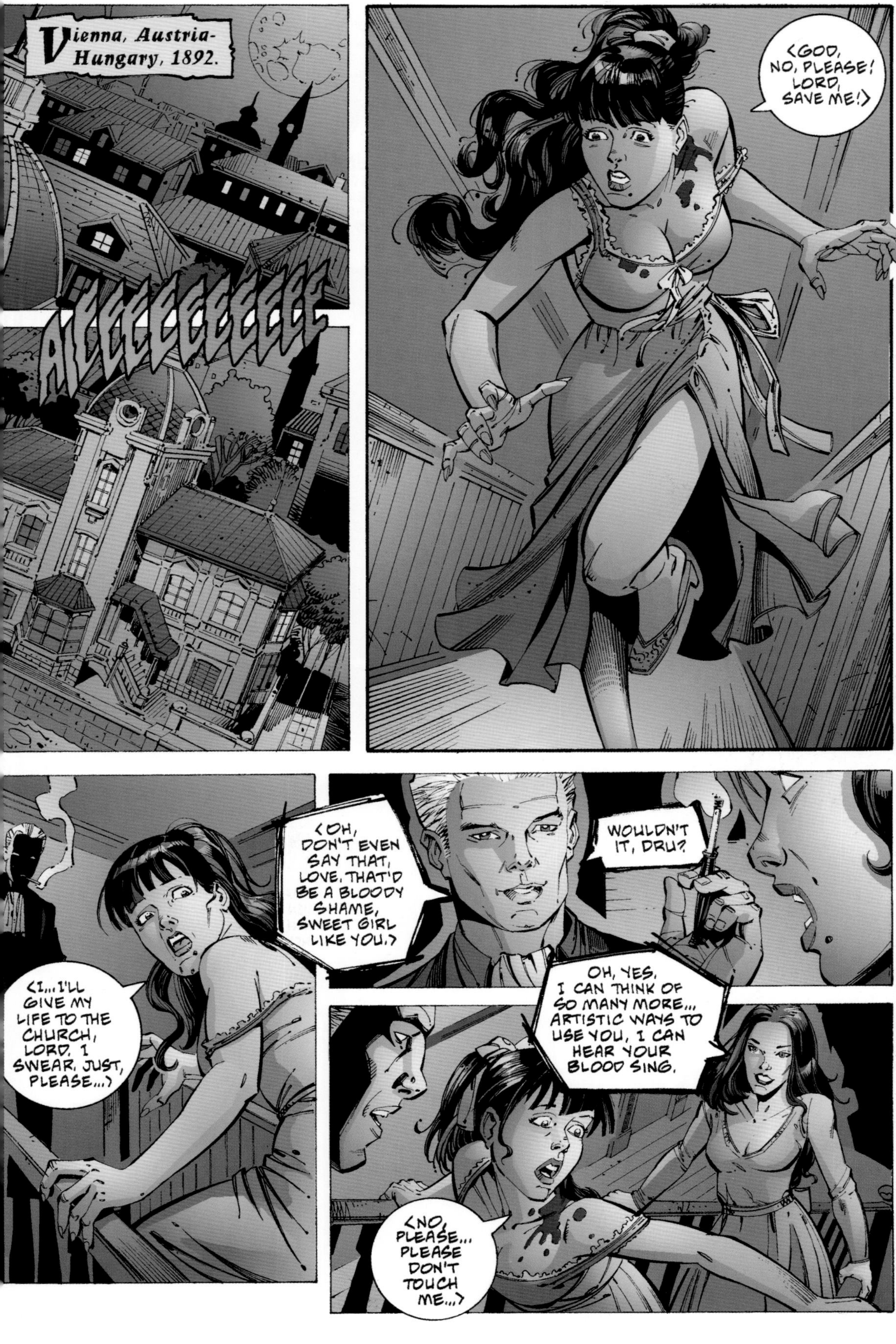
Vienna, Austria-Hungary, 1892.
AIEEEEEEEEE
<GOD, NO, PLEASE! LORD, SAVE ME!>
<OH, DON'T EVEN SAY THAT, LOVE. THAT'D BE A BLOODY SHAME, SWEET GIRL LIKE YOU.>
WOULDN'T IT, DRU?
<I... I'LL GIVE MY LIFE TO THE CHURCH, LORD. I SWEAR. JUST, PLEASE...>
OH, YES. I CAN THINK OF SO MANY MORE... ARTISTIC WAYS TO USE YOU. I CAN HEAR YOUR BLOOD SING.
<NO, PLEASE... PLEASE DON'T TOUCH ME...>

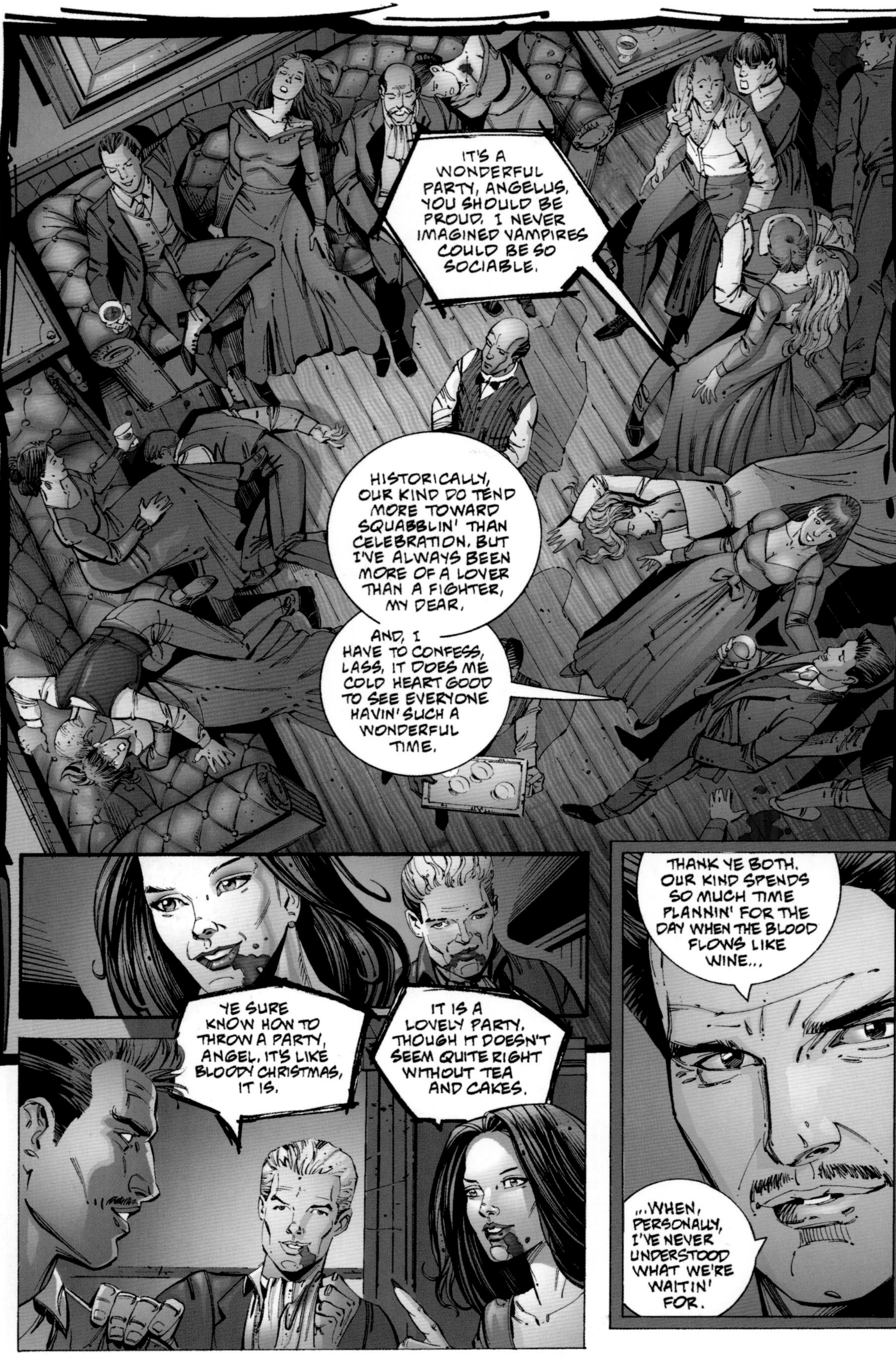
IT'S A WONDERFUL PARTY, ANGELUS, YOU SHOULD BE PROUD. I NEVER IMAGINED VAMPIRES COULD BE SO SOCIABLE.
HISTORICALLY, OUR KIND DO TEND MORE TOWARD SQUABBLIN' THAN CELEBRATION. BUT I'VE ALWAYS BEEN MORE OF A LOVER THAN A FIGHTER, MY DEAR.
AND, I HAVE TO CONFESS, LASS, IT DOES ME COLD HEART GOOD TO SEE EVERYONE HAVIN' SUCH A WONDERFUL TIME.
YE SURE KNOW HOW TO THROW A PARTY, ANGEL. IT'S LIKE BLOODY CHRISTMAS, IT IS.
IT IS A LOVELY PARTY, THOUGH IT DOESN'T SEEM QUITE RIGHT WITHOUT TEA AND CAKES.
THANK YE BOTH. OUR KIND SPENDS SO MUCH TIME PLANNIN' FOR THE DAY WHEN THE BLOOD FLOWS LIKE WINE...
...WHEN, PERSONALLY, I'VE NEVER UNDERSTOOD WHAT WE'RE WAITIN' FOR.

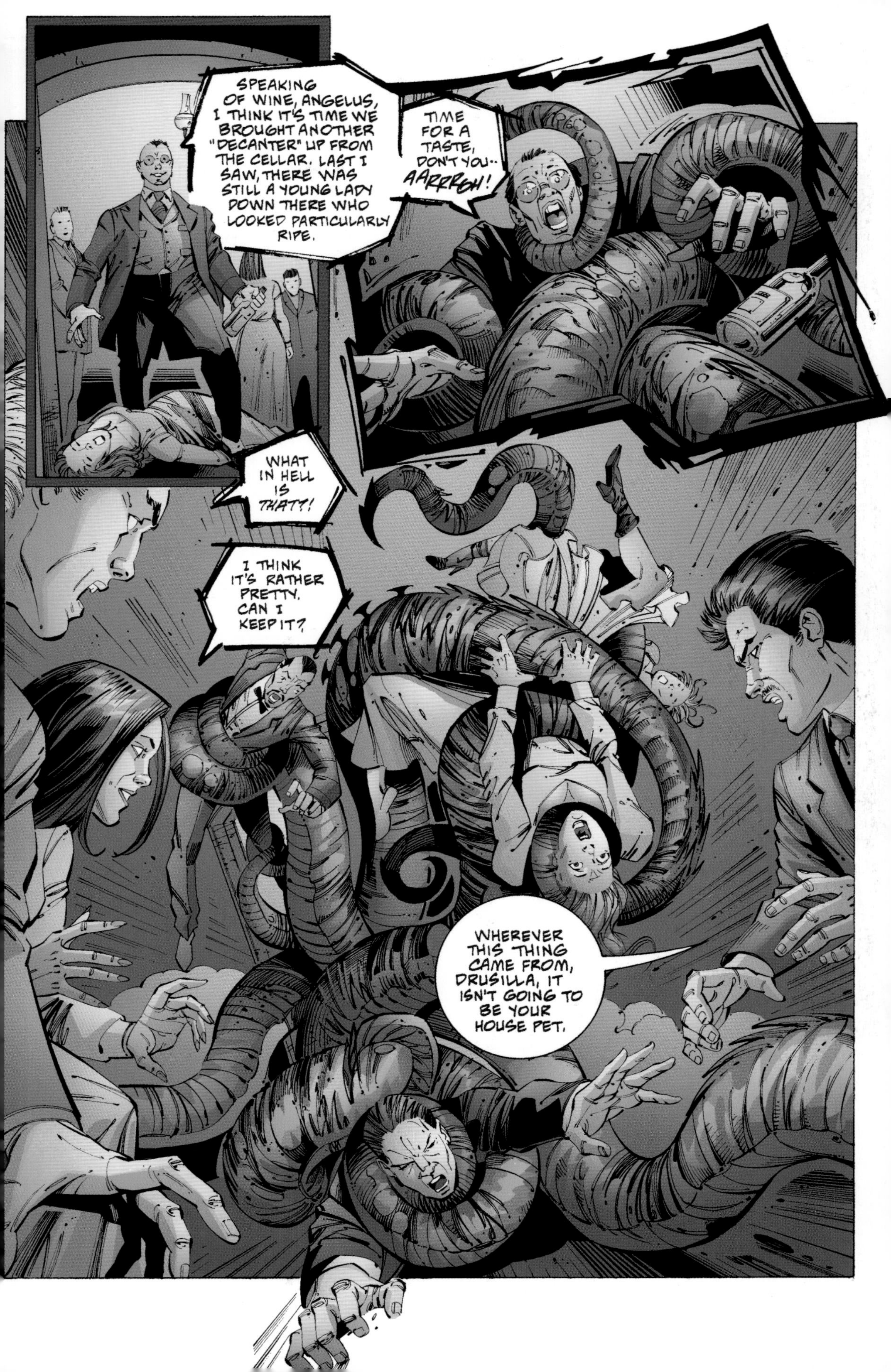
SPEAKING OF WINE, ANGELUS, I THINK IT'S TIME WE BROUGHT ANOTHER "DECANTER" UP FROM THE CELLAR. LAST I SAW, THERE WAS STILL A YOUNG LADY DOWN THERE WHO LOOKED PARTICULARLY RIPE.
TIME FOR A TASTE, DON'T YOU.. AARRRGH!
WHAT IN HELL IS THAT?!
I THINK IT'S RATHER PRETTY. CAN I KEEP IT?
WHEREVER THIS THING CAME FROM, DRUSILLA, IT ISN'T GOING TO BE YOUR HOUSE PET.

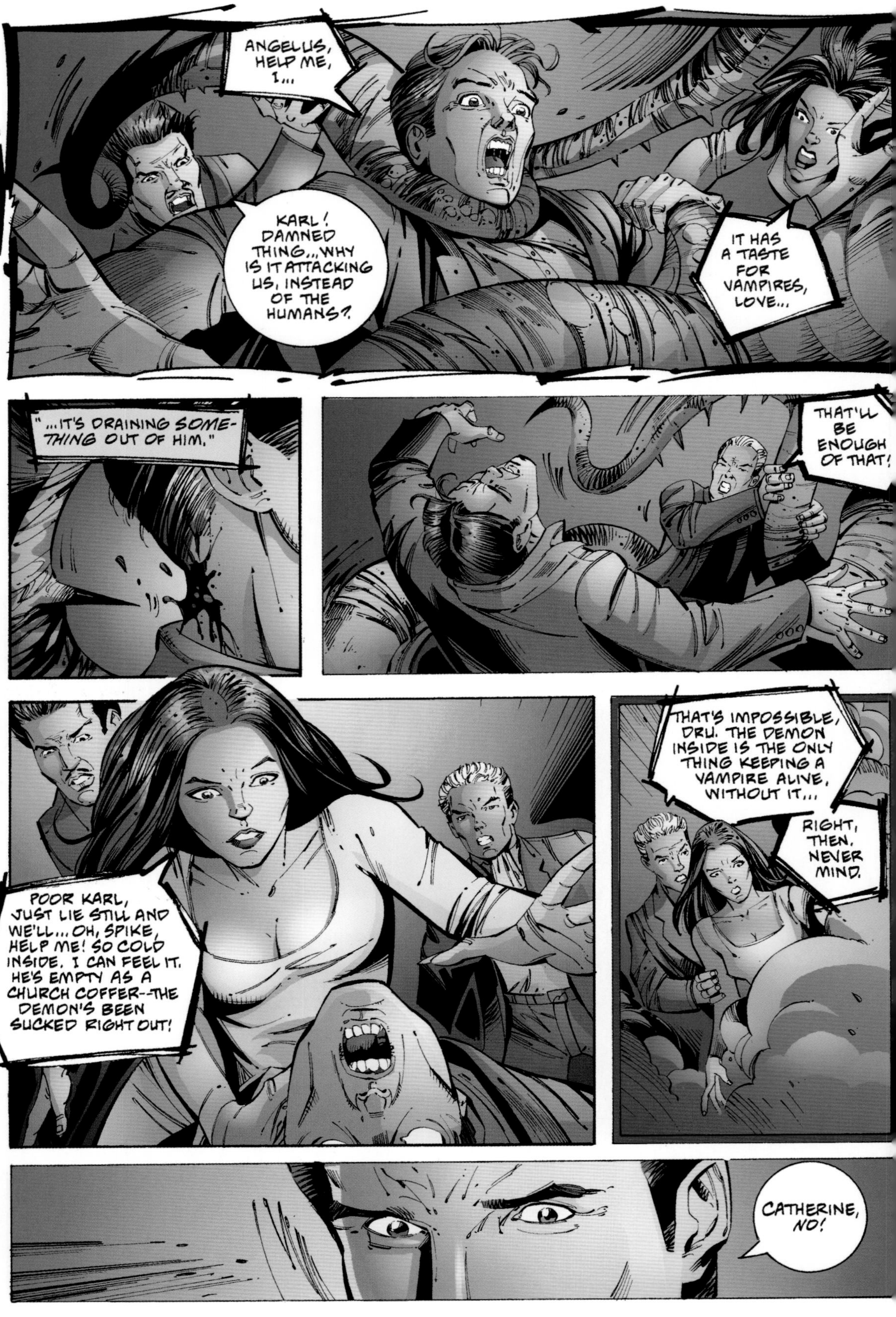
ANGELUS, HELP ME, I...
KARL! DAMNED THING... WHY IS IT ATTACKING US, INSTEAD OF THE HUMANS?
IT HAS A TASTE FOR VAMPIRES, LOVE...
"...IT'S DRAINING SOME-THING OUT OF HIM."
THAT'LL BE ENOUGH OF THAT!
POOR KARL, JUST LIE STILL AND WE'LL... OH, SPIKE, HELP ME! SO COLD INSIDE. I CAN FEEL IT. HE'S EMPTY AS A CHURCH COFFER--THE DEMON'S BEEN SUCKED RIGHT OUT!
THAT'S IMPOSSIBLE, DRU. THE DEMON INSIDE IS THE ONLY THING KEEPING A VAMPIRE ALIVE, WITHOUT IT...
RIGHT, THEN. NEVER MIND.
CATHERINE, NO!

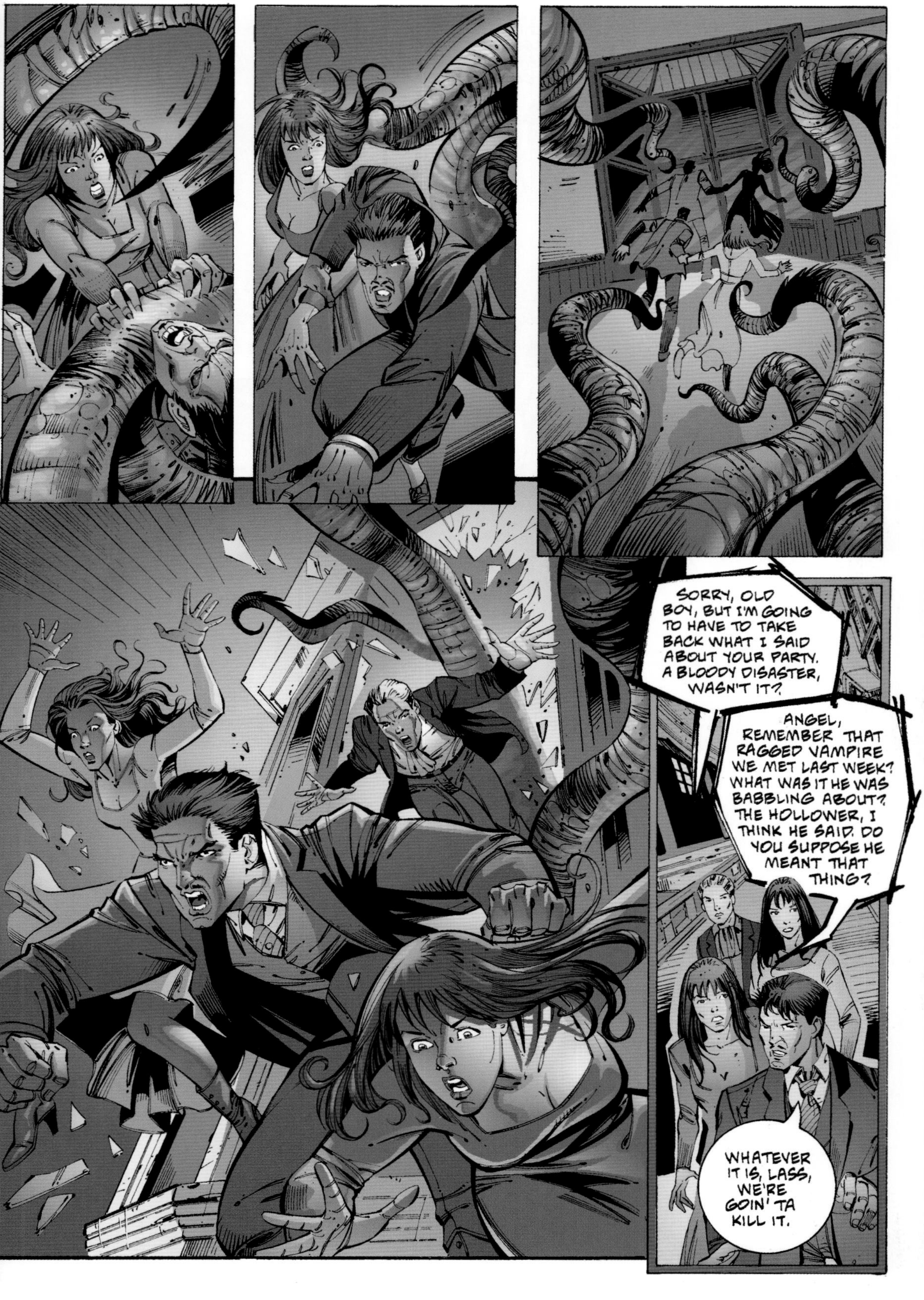
SORRY, OLD BOY, BUT I'M GOING TO HAVE TO TAKE BACK WHAT I SAID ABOUT YOUR PARTY. A BLOODY DISASTER, WASN'T IT?
ANGEL, REMEMBER THAT RAGGED VAMPIRE WE MET LAST WEEK? WHAT WAS IT HE WAS BABBLING ABOUT? THE HOLLOWER, I THINK HE SAID. DO YOU SUPPOSE HE MEANT THAT THING?
WHATEVER IT IS, LASS, WE'RE GOIN' TA KILL IT.

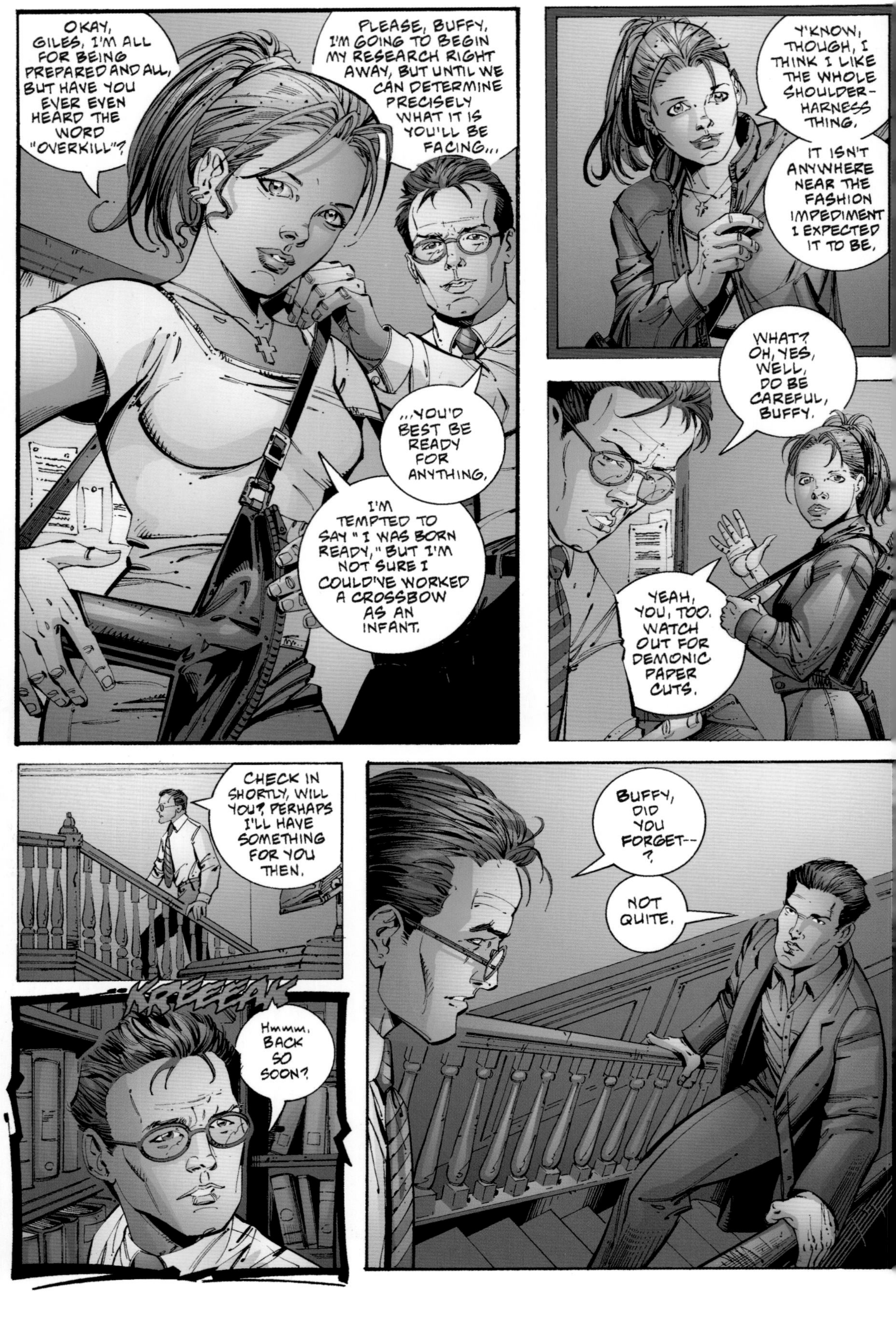
OKAY, GILES, I'M ALL FOR BEING PREPARED AND ALL, BUT HAVE YOU EVER EVEN HEARD THE WORD "OVERKILL"?
PLEASE, BUFFY, I'M GOING TO BEGIN MY RESEARCH RIGHT AWAY, BUT UNTIL WE CAN DETERMINE PRECISELY WHAT IT IS YOU'LL BE FACING...
...YOU'D BEST BE READY FOR ANYTHING.
I'M TEMPTED TO SAY "I WAS BORN READY," BUT I'M NOT SURE I COULD'VE WORKED A CROSSBOW AS AN INFANT.
Y'KNOW, THOUGH, I THINK I LIKE THE WHOLE SHOULDER-HARNESS THING.
IT ISN'T ANYWHERE NEAR THE FASHION IMPEDIMENT I EXPECTED IT TO BE.
WHAT? OH, YES, WELL, DO BE CAREFUL, BUFFY.
YEAH, YOU, TOO. WATCH OUT FOR DEMONIC PAPER CUTS.
CHECK IN SHORTLY, WILL YOU? PERHAPS I'LL HAVE SOMETHING FOR YOU THEN.
KREEEAK
HMMM. BACK SO SOON?
BUFFY, DID YOU FORGET--?
NOT QUITE.

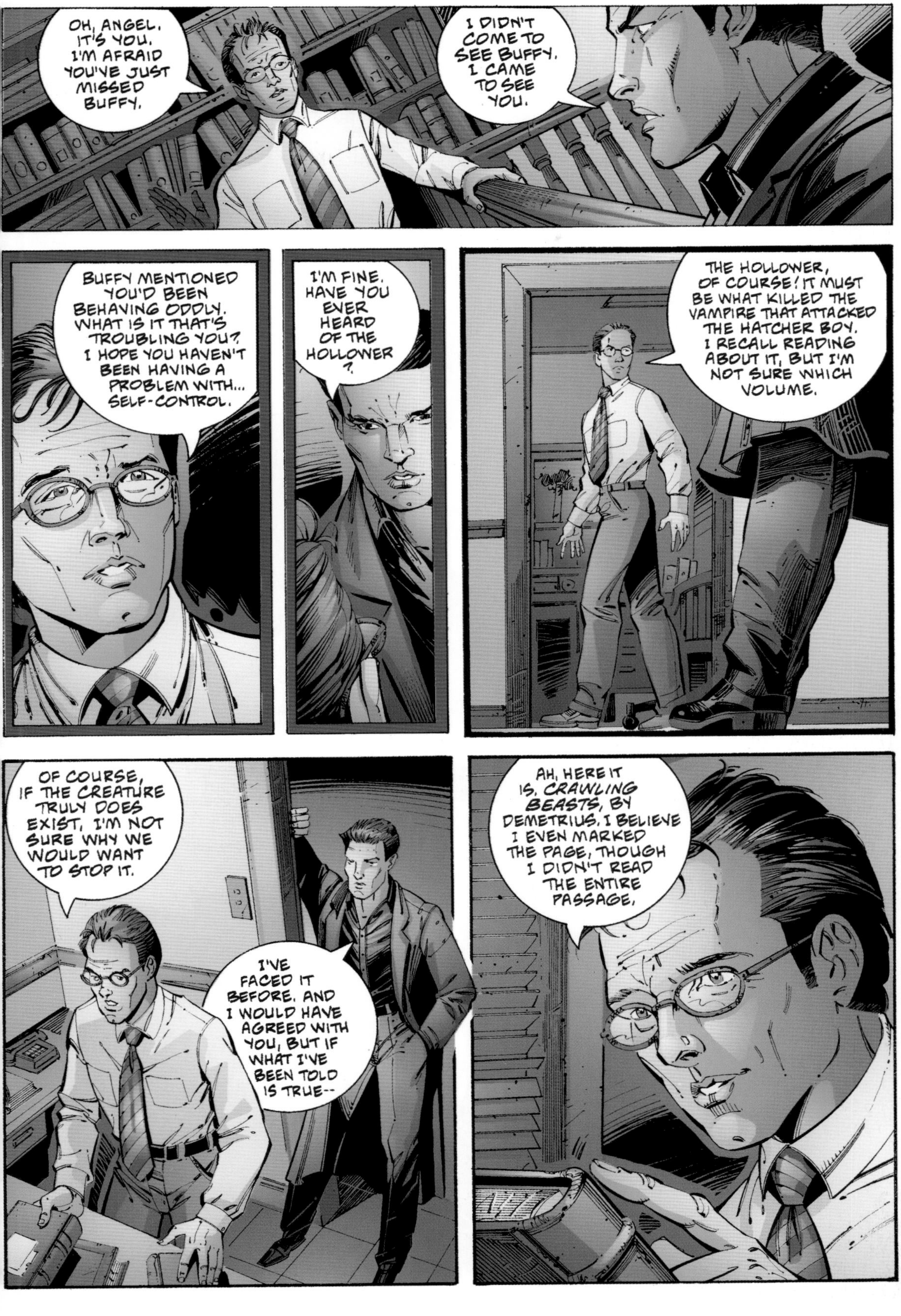
OH, ANGEL. IT'S YOU. I'M AFRAID YOU'VE JUST MISSED BUFFY.
I DIDN'T COME TO SEE BUFFY. I CAME TO SEE YOU.
BUFFY MENTIONED YOU'D BEEN BEHAVING ODDLY. WHAT IS IT THAT'S TROUBLING YOU? I HOPE YOU HAVEN'T BEEN HAVING A PROBLEM WITH... SELF-CONTROL.
I'M FINE. HAVE YOU EVER HEARD OF THE HOLLOWER?
THE HOLLOWER, OF COURSE! IT MUST BE WHAT KILLED THE VAMPIRE THAT ATTACKED THE HATCHER BOY. I RECALL READING ABOUT IT, BUT I'M NOT SURE WHICH VOLUME.
OF COURSE, IF THE CREATURE TRULY DOES EXIST, I'M NOT SURE WHY WE WOULD WANT TO STOP IT.
I'VE FACED IT BEFORE. AND I WOULD HAVE AGREED WITH YOU, BUT IF WHAT I'VE BEEN TOLD IS TRUE--
AH, HERE IT IS, CRAWLING BEASTS, BY DEMETRIUS. I BELIEVE I EVEN MARKED THE PAGE, THOUGH I DIDN'T READ THE ENTIRE PASSAGE.

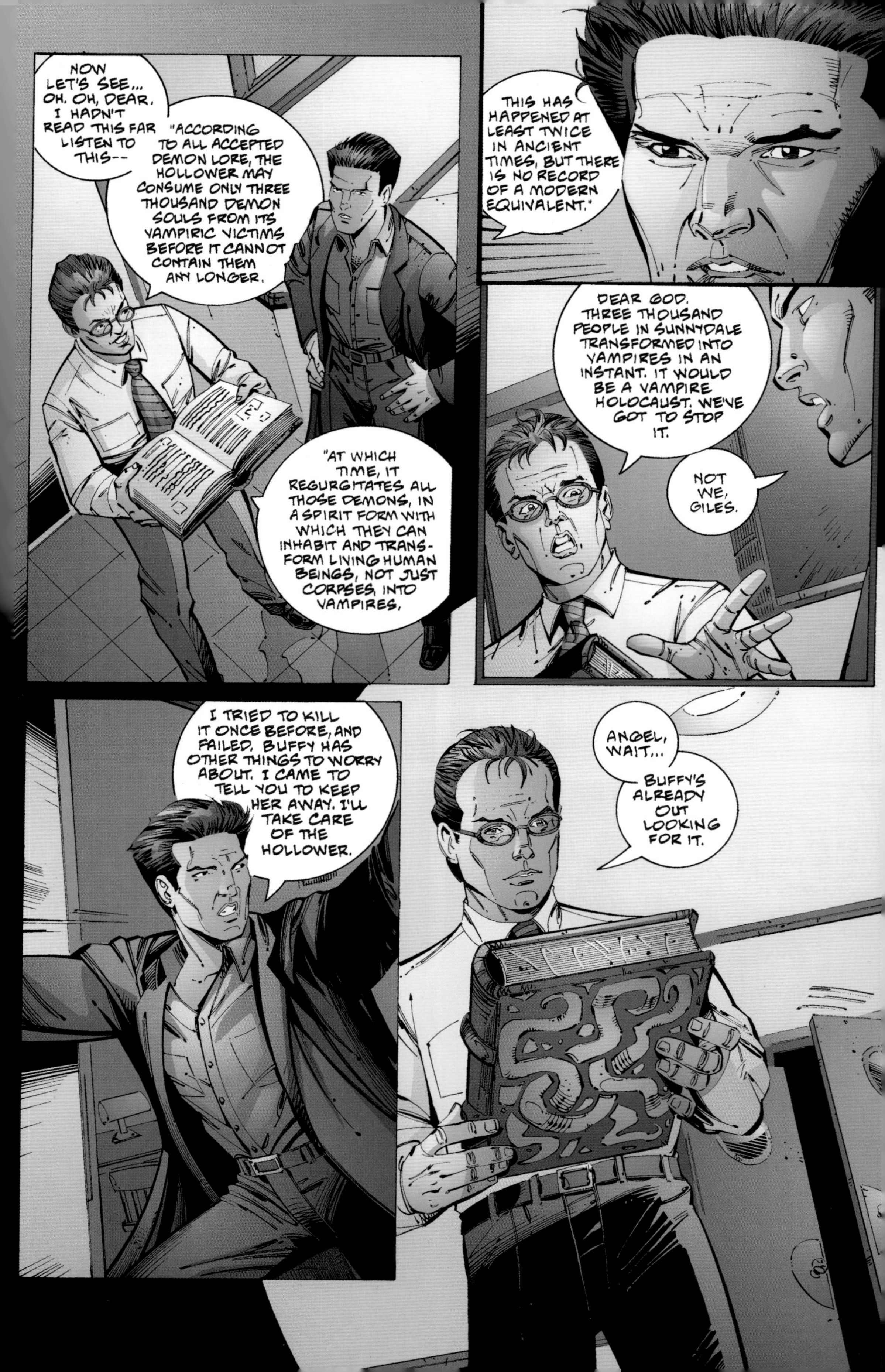
NOW LET'S SEE... OH. OH, DEAR. I HADN'T READ THIS FAR LISTEN TO THIS--
"ACCORDING TO ALL ACCEPTED DEMON LORE, THE HOLLOWER MAY CONSUME ONLY THREE THOUSAND DEMON SOULS FROM ITS VAMPIRIC VICTIMS BEFORE IT CANNOT CONTAIN THEM ANY LONGER.
"AT WHICH TIME, IT REGURGITATES ALL THOSE DEMONS, IN A SPIRIT FORM WITH WHICH THEY CAN INHABIT AND TRANS-FORM LIVING HUMAN BEINGS, NOT JUST CORPSES, INTO VAMPIRES.
THIS HAS HAPPENED AT LEAST TWICE IN ANCIENT TIMES, BUT THERE IS NO RECORD OF A MODERN EQUIVALENT."
DEAR GOD. THREE THOUSAND PEOPLE IN SUNNYDALE TRANSFORMED INTO VAMPIRES IN AN INSTANT. IT WOULD BE A VAMPIRE HOLOCAUST. WE'VE GOT TO STOP IT.
NOT WE, GILES.
I TRIED TO KILL IT ONCE BEFORE, AND FAILED. BUFFY HAS OTHER THINGS TO WORRY ABOUT. I CAME TO TELL YOU TO KEEP HER AWAY. I'LL TAKE CARE OF THE HOLLOWER.
ANGEL, WAIT...
BUFFY'S ALREADY OUT LOOKING FOR IT.

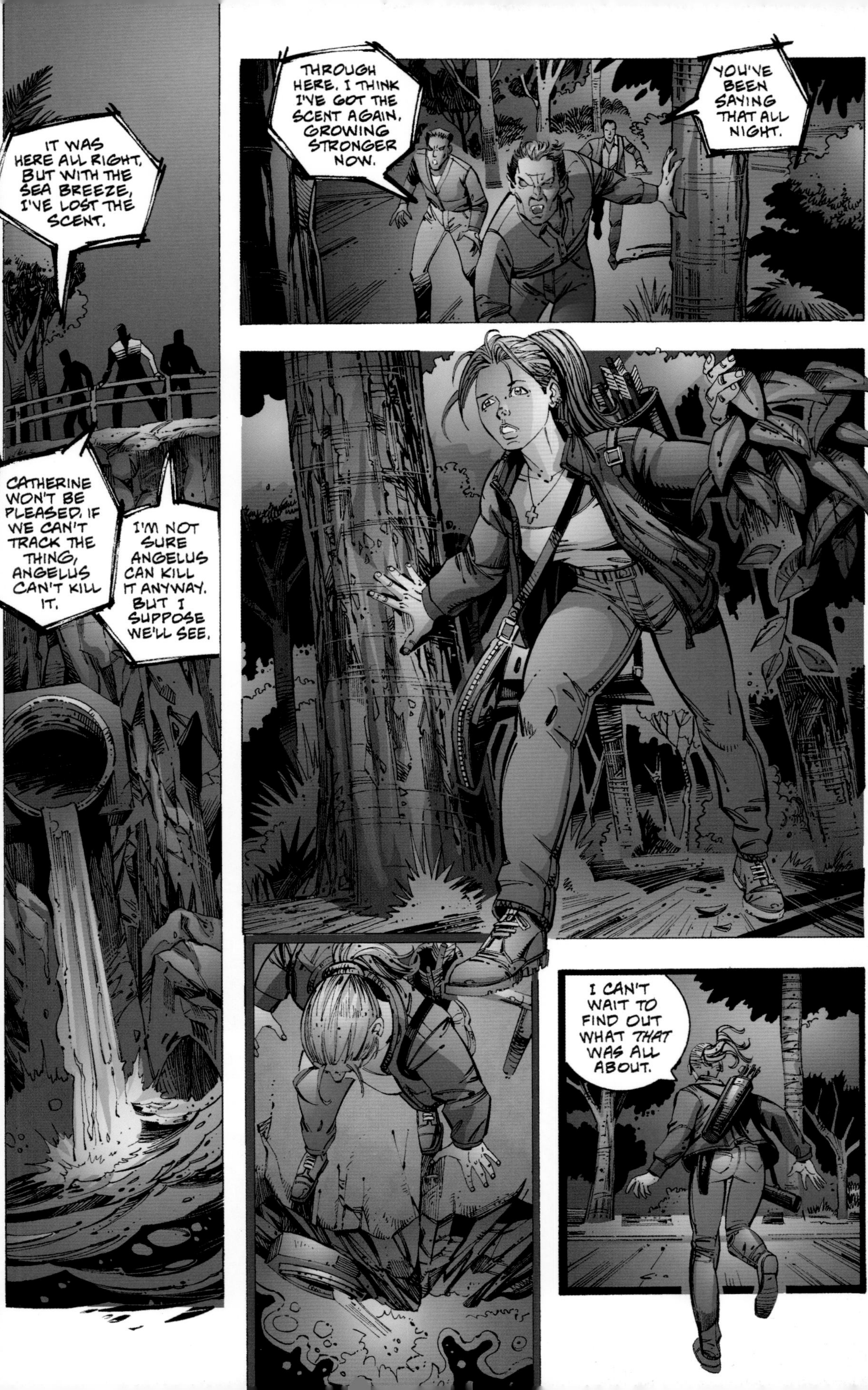
IT WAS HERE ALL RIGHT, BUT WITH THE SEA BREEZE, I'VE LOST THE SCENT.
CATHERINE WON'T BE PLEASED. IF WE CAN'T TRACK THE THING, ANGELUS CAN'T KILL IT.
I'M NOT SURE ANGELUS CAN KILL IT ANYWAY. BUT I SUPPOSE WE'LL SEE.
THROUGH HERE. I THINK I'VE GOT THE SCENT AGAIN, GROWING STRONGER NOW.
YOU'VE BEEN SAYING THAT ALL NIGHT.
I CAN'T WAIT TO FIND OUT WHAT *THAT* WAS ALL ABOUT.

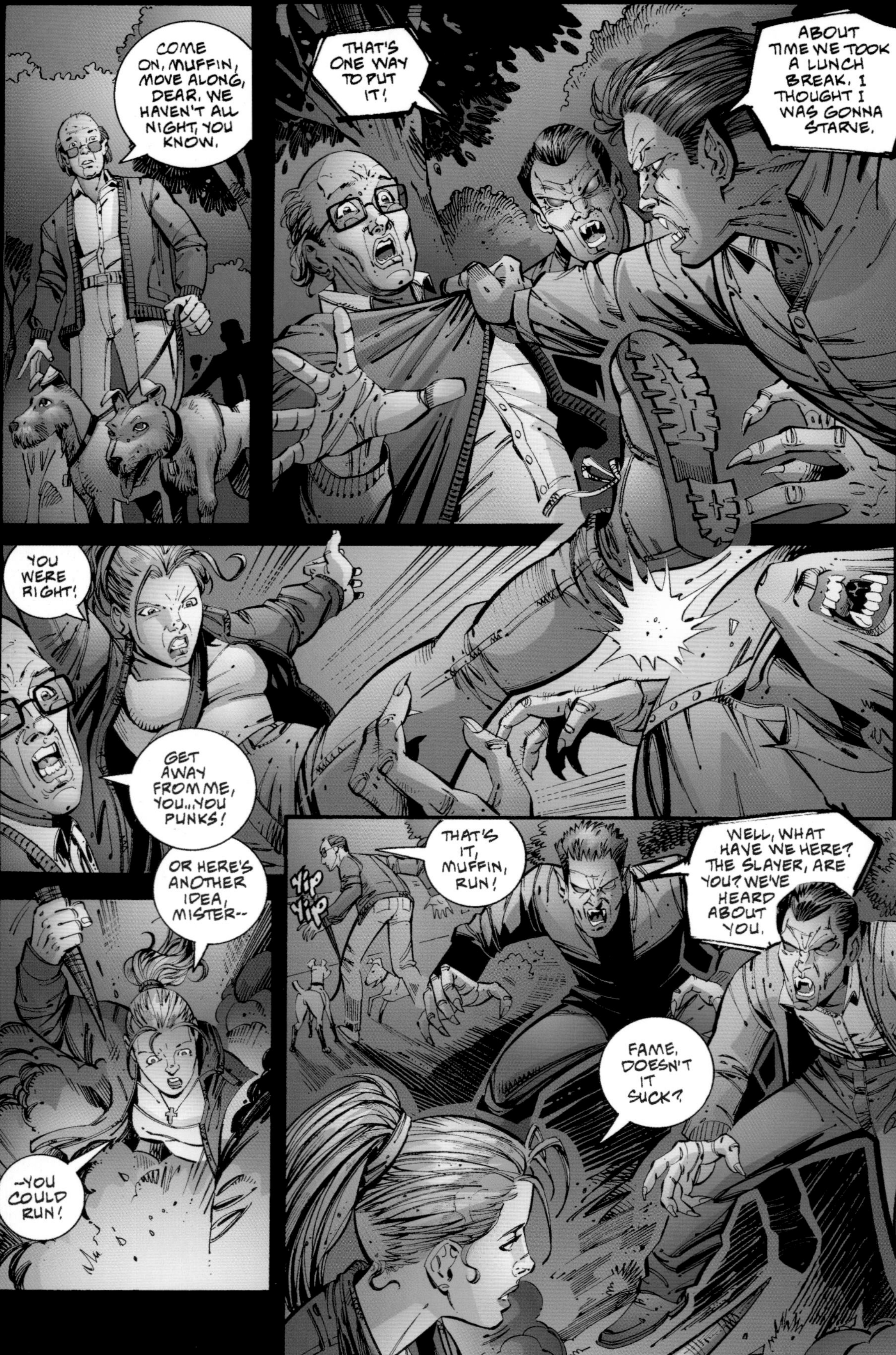
COME ON, MUFFIN, MOVE ALONG, DEAR. WE HAVEN'T ALL NIGHT, YOU KNOW.
THAT'S ONE WAY TO PUT IT!
ABOUT TIME WE TOOK A LUNCH BREAK. I THOUGHT I WAS GONNA STARVE.
YOU WERE RIGHT!
GET AWAY FROM ME, YOU...YOU PUNKS!
OR HERE'S ANOTHER IDEA, MISTER--
--YOU COULD RUN!
YIP YIP
THAT'S IT, MUFFIN, RUN!
WELL, WHAT HAVE WE HERE? THE SLAYER, ARE YOU? WE'VE HEARD ABOUT YOU.
FAME, DOESN'T IT SUCK?

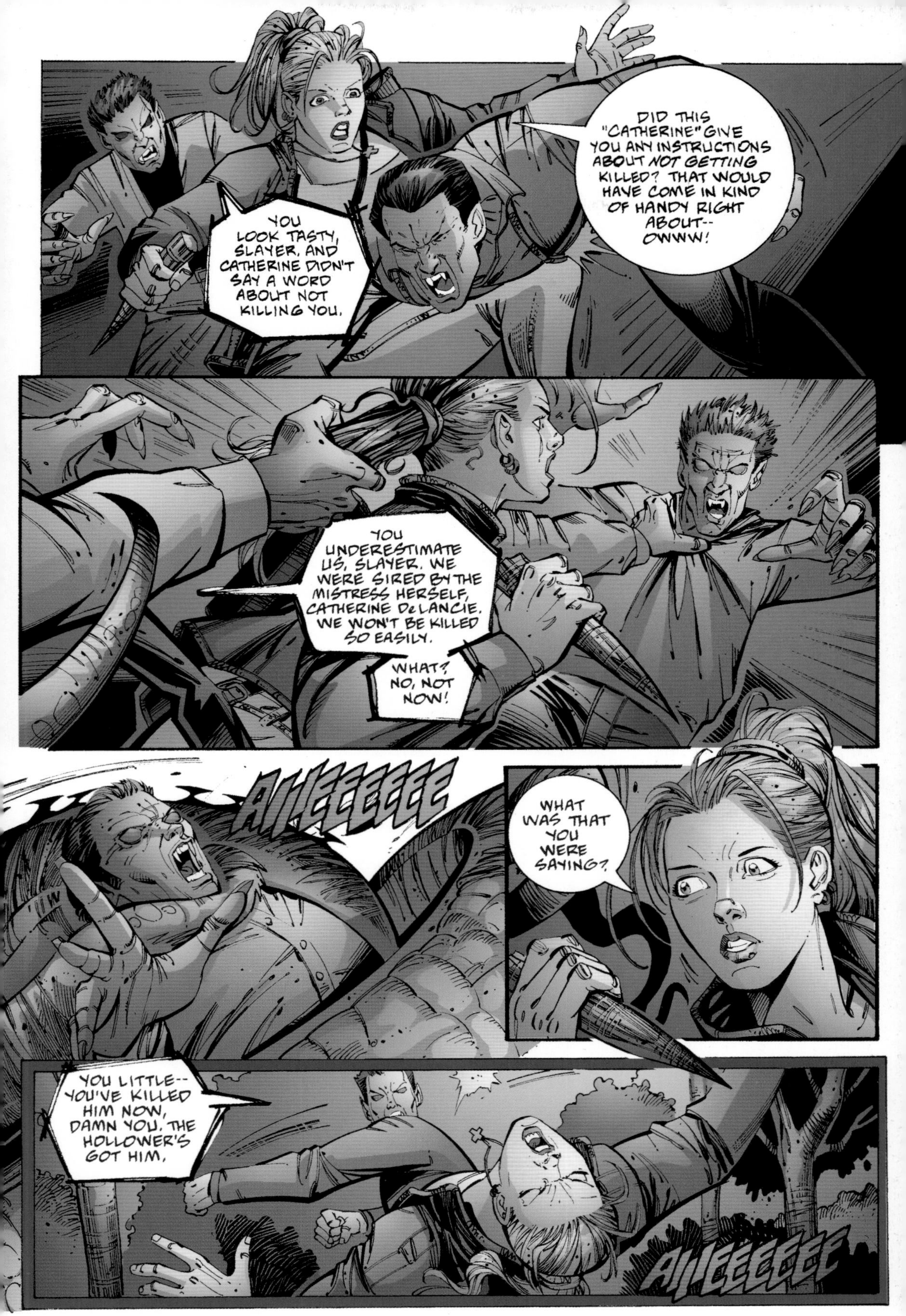
YOU LOOK TASTY, SLAYER, AND CATHERINE DIDN'T SAY A WORD ABOUT NOT KILLING YOU.
DID THIS "CATHERINE" GIVE YOU ANY INSTRUCTIONS ABOUT *NOT GETTING* KILLED? THAT WOULD HAVE COME IN KIND OF HANDY RIGHT ABOUT-- OWWW!
YOU UNDERESTIMATE US, SLAYER. WE WERE SIRED BY THE MISTRESS HERSELF, CATHERINE DeLANCIE. WE WON'T BE KILLED SO EASILY.
WHAT? NO, NOT NOW!
AIIEEEEEE
WHAT WAS THAT YOU WERE SAYING?
YOU LITTLE-- YOU'VE KILLED HIM NOW, DAMN YOU. THE HOLLOWER'S GOT HIM.
AIIEEEEE

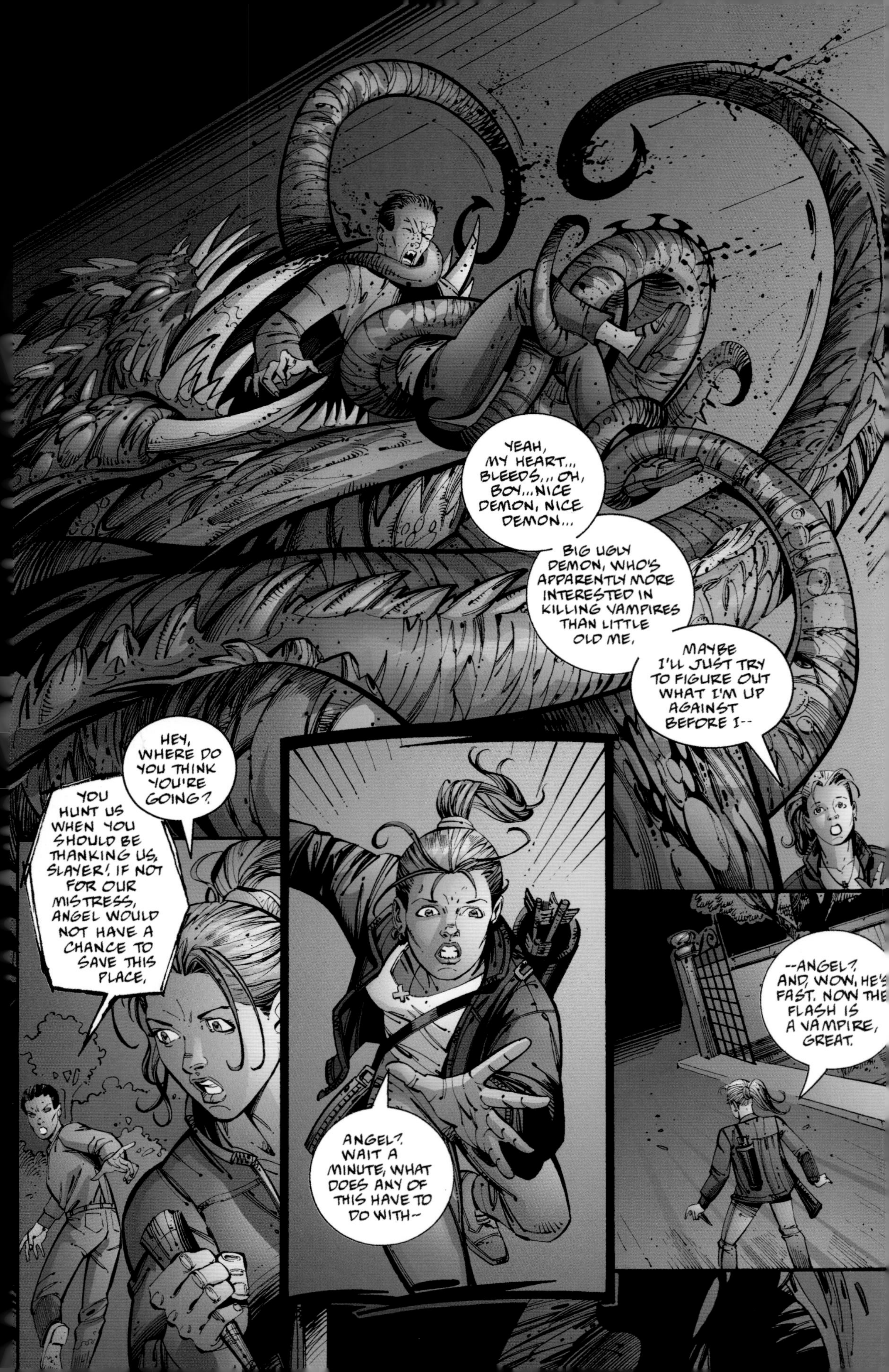
YEAH, MY HEART... BLEEDS... OH, BOY...NICE DEMON, NICE DEMON...
BIG UGLY DEMON, WHO'S APPARENTLY MORE INTERESTED IN KILLING VAMPIRES THAN LITTLE OLD ME.
MAYBE I'LL JUST TRY TO FIGURE OUT WHAT I'M UP AGAINST BEFORE I--
HEY, WHERE DO YOU THINK YOU'RE GOING?
YOU HUNT US WHEN YOU SHOULD BE THANKING US, SLAYER! IF NOT FOR OUR MISTRESS, ANGEL WOULD NOT HAVE A CHANCE TO SAVE THIS PLACE.
ANGEL? WAIT A MINUTE, WHAT DOES ANY OF THIS HAVE TO DO WITH-
--ANGEL? AND, WOW, HE'S FAST. NOW THE FLASH IS A VAMPIRE, GREAT.

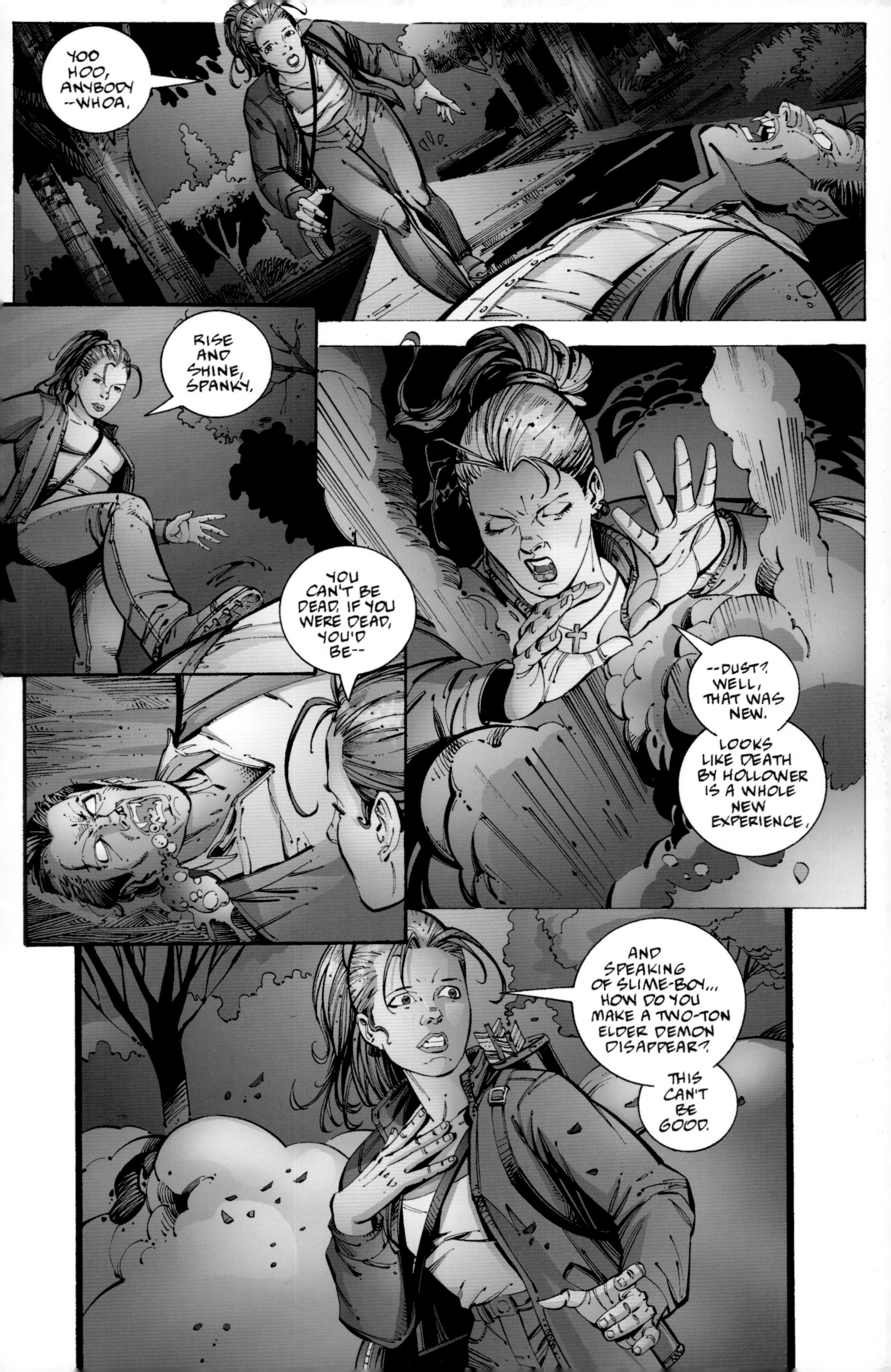
YOO HOO, ANYBODY --WHOA.
RISE AND SHINE, SPANKY.
YOU CAN'T BE DEAD. IF YOU WERE DEAD, YOU'D BE--
--DUST? WELL, THAT WAS NEW.
LOOKS LIKE DEATH BY HOLLOWER IS A WHOLE NEW EXPERIENCE.
AND SPEAKING OF SLIME-BOY... HOW DO YOU MAKE A TWO-TON ELDER DEMON DISAPPEAR?
THIS CAN'T BE GOOD.

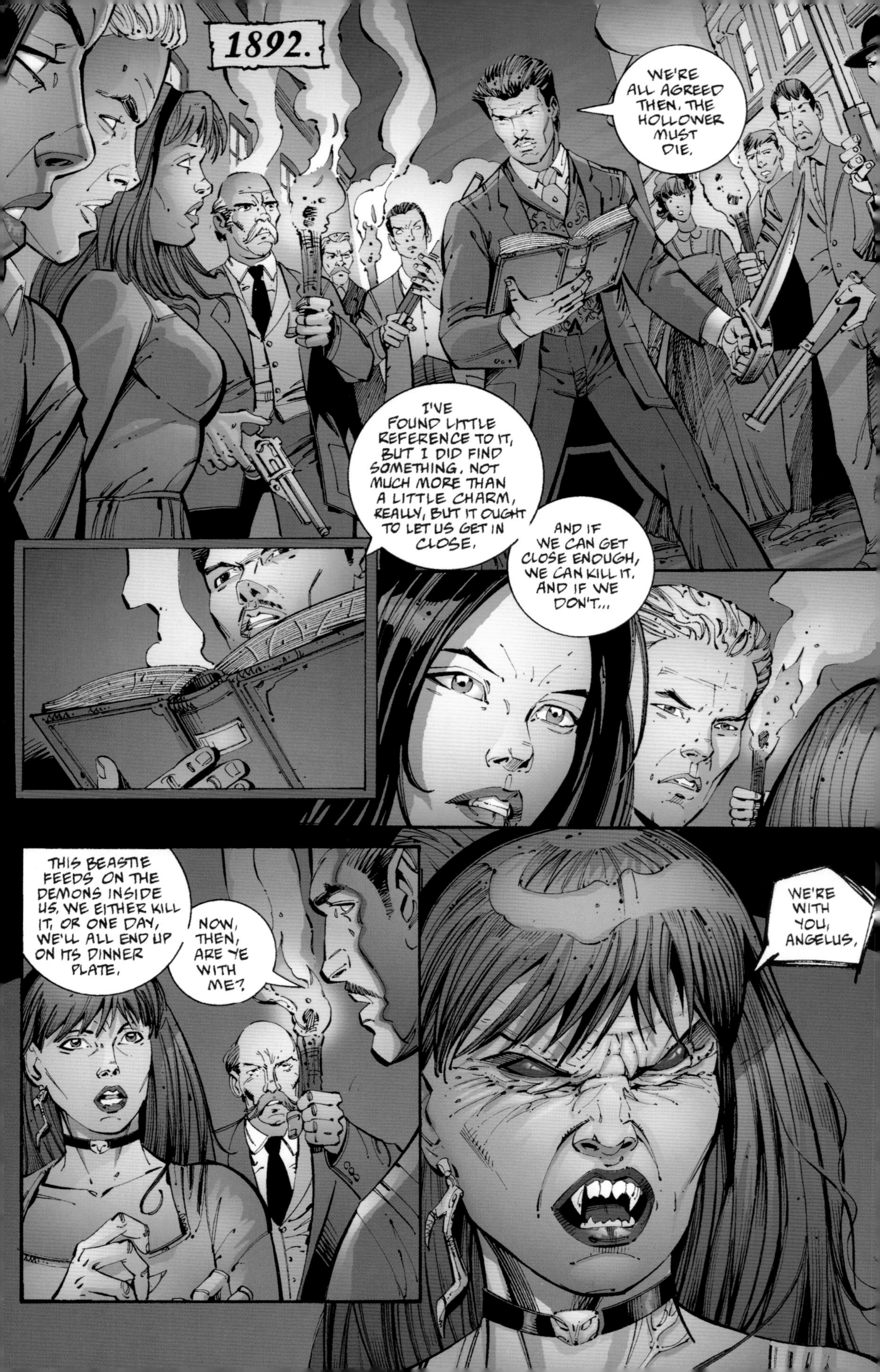
1892.
WE'RE ALL AGREED THEN. THE HOLLOWER MUST DIE.
I'VE FOUND LITTLE REFERENCE TO IT, BUT I DID FIND SOMETHING. NOT MUCH MORE THAN A LITTLE CHARM, REALLY, BUT IT OUGHT TO LET US GET IN CLOSE.
AND IF WE CAN GET CLOSE ENOUGH, WE CAN KILL IT. AND IF WE DON'T...
THIS BEASTIE FEEDS ON THE DEMONS INSIDE US. WE EITHER KILL IT, OR ONE DAY, WE'LL ALL END UP ON ITS DINNER PLATE.
NOW, THEN, ARE YE WITH ME?
WE'RE WITH YOU, ANGELUS.

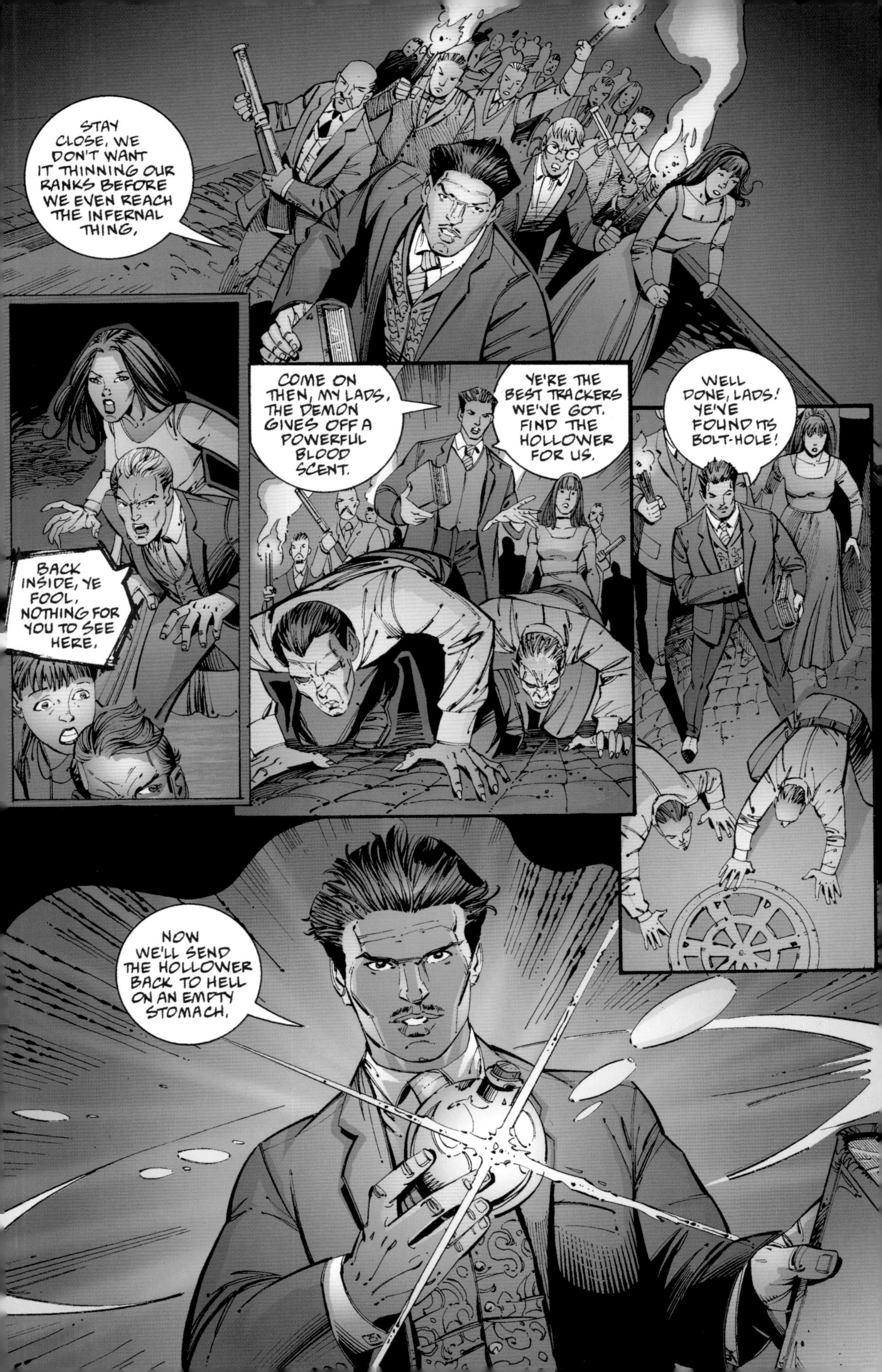
STAY CLOSE, WE DON'T WANT IT THINNING OUR RANKS BEFORE WE EVEN REACH THE INFERNAL THING,
BACK INSIDE, YE FOOL, NOTHING FOR YOU TO SEE HERE,
COME ON THEN, MY LADS, THE DEMON GIVES OFF A POWERFUL BLOOD SCENT.
YE'RE THE BEST TRACKERS WE'VE GOT. FIND THE HOLLOWER FOR US.
WELL DONE, LADS! YE'VE FOUND ITS BOLT-HOLE!
NOW WE'LL SEND THE HOLLOWER BACK TO HELL ON AN EMPTY STOMACH,

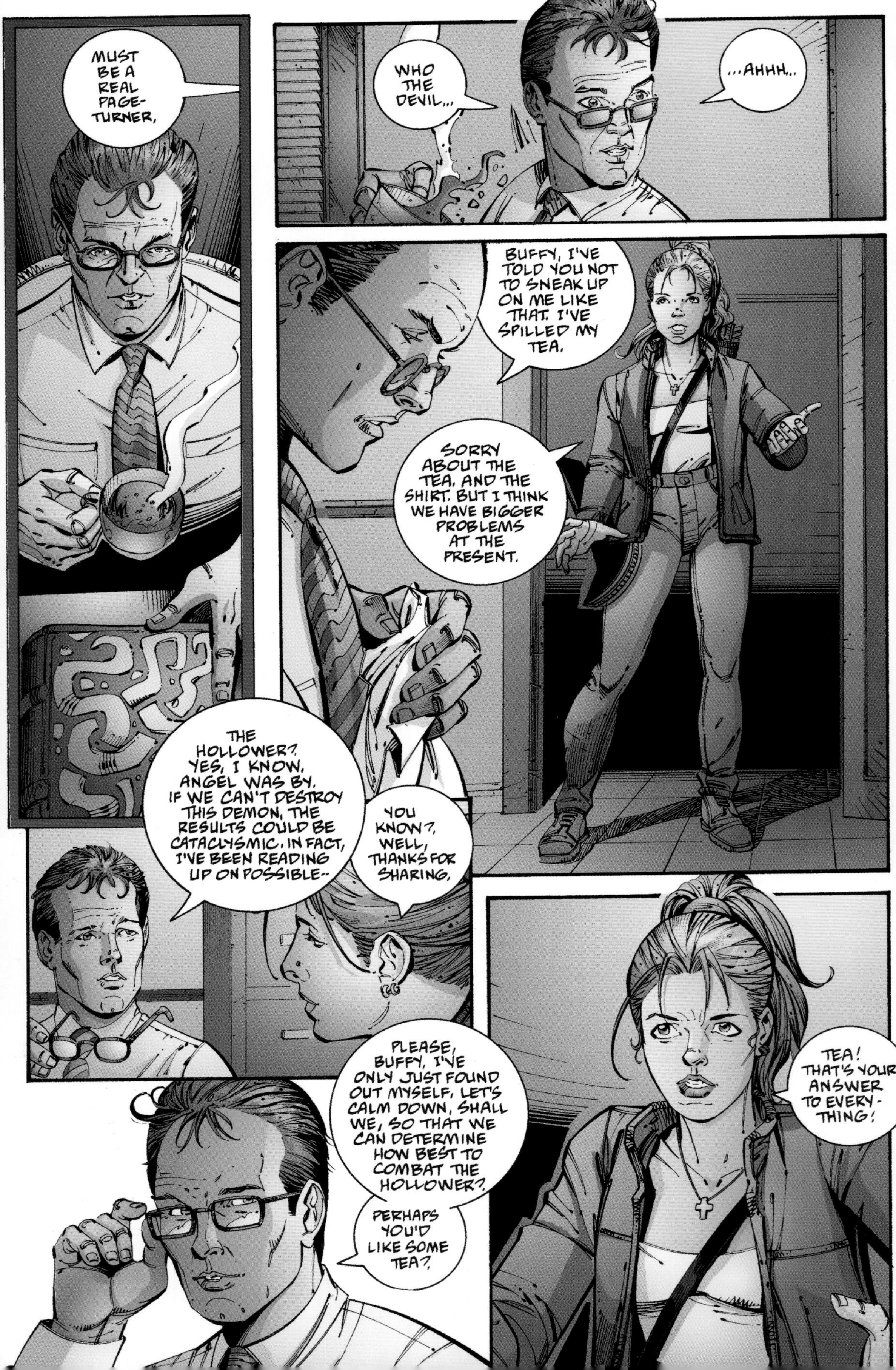
MUST BE A REAL PAGE-TURNER.
WHO THE DEVIL...
...AHHH...
BUFFY, I'VE TOLD YOU NOT TO SNEAK UP ON ME LIKE THAT. I'VE SPILLED MY TEA.
SORRY ABOUT THE TEA, AND THE SHIRT. BUT I THINK WE HAVE BIGGER PROBLEMS AT THE PRESENT.
THE HOLLOWER? YES, I KNOW. ANGEL WAS BY. IF WE CAN'T DESTROY THIS DEMON, THE RESULTS COULD BE CATACLYSMIC. IN FACT, I'VE BEEN READING UP ON POSSIBLE--
YOU KNOW? WELL, THANKS FOR SHARING.
PLEASE, BUFFY, I'VE ONLY JUST FOUND OUT MYSELF. LET'S CALM DOWN, SHALL WE, SO THAT WE CAN DETERMINE HOW BEST TO COMBAT THE HOLLOWER?
PERHAPS YOU'D LIKE SOME TEA?
TEA! THAT'S YOUR ANSWER TO EVERY-THING!

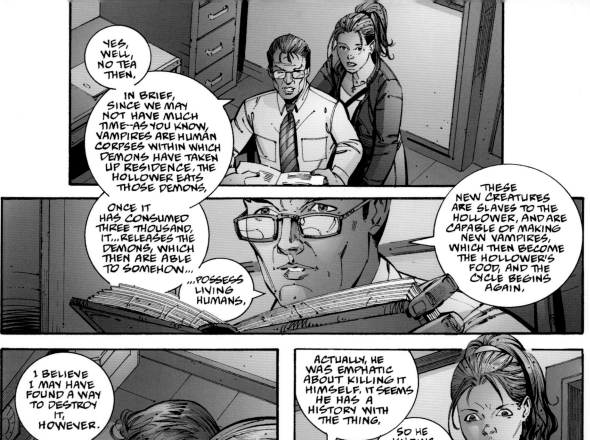

YES, WELL, NO TEA THEN.

IN BRIEF, SINCE WE MAY NOT HAVE MUCH TIME--AS YOU KNOW, VAMPIRES ARE HUMAN CORPSES WITHIN WHICH DEMONS HAVE TAKEN UP RESIDENCE, THE HOLLOWER EATS THOSE DEMONS.

ONCE IT HAS CONSUMED THREE THOUSAND, IT...RELEASES THE DEMONS, WHICH THEN ARE ABLE TO SOMEHOW...

...POSSESS LIVING HUMANS.

THESE NEW CREATURES ARE SLAVES TO THE HOLLOWER, AND ARE CAPABLE OF MAKING NEW VAMPIRES, WHICH THEN BECOME THE HOLLOWER'S FOOD, AND THE CYCLE BEGINS AGAIN.

I BELIEVE I MAY HAVE FOUND A WAY TO DESTROY IT, HOWEVER.

GILES, YOU'RE SAYING ANGEL KNEW ABOUT THIS THING, AND HE DIDN'T WAIT FOR ME? DIDN'T EVEN ASK FOR HELP?

ACTUALLY, HE WAS EMPHATIC ABOUT KILLING IT HIMSELF. IT SEEMS HE HAS A HISTORY WITH THE THING.

SO HE KNOWS WHAT IT DOES? HOW IT EATS?

OF COURSE HE DOES. DON'T WORRY, BUFFY, ANGEL'S GOING TO GET OUR HELP WHETHER HE WANTS IT OR NOT.

NO QUESTION, BUT THAT ISN'T WHAT'S BOTHERING ME. IT ISN'T LIKE ANGEL, GOING OFF ON SOME SOLO MISSION WHEN HE KNOWS WE COULD HELP.

MAKES ME WONDER IF THE REASON HE DOESN'T WANT OUR HELP IS BECAUSE HE HAS NO INTENTION OF KILLING THE HOLLOWER.

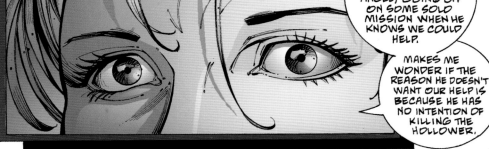

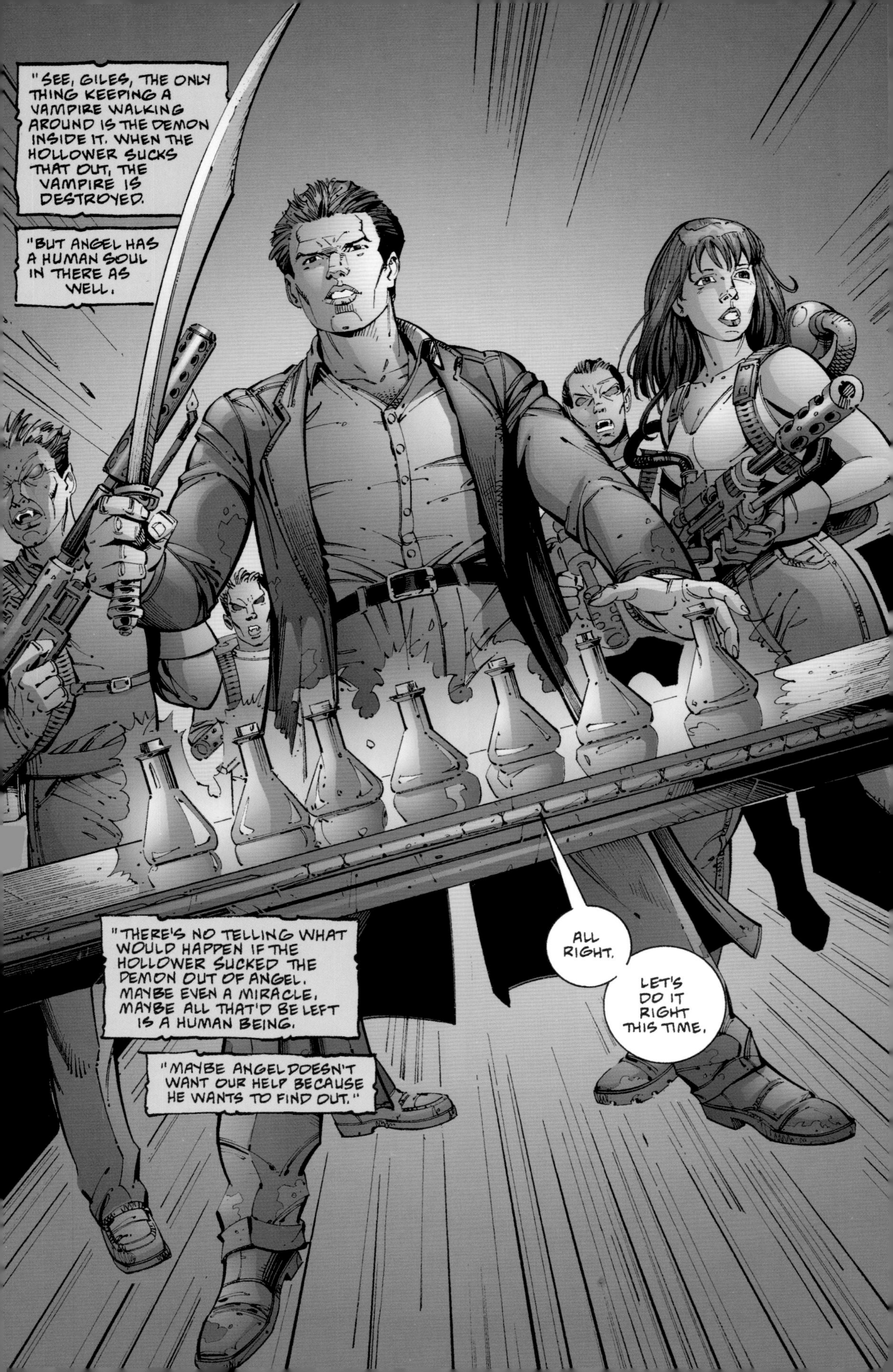
"SEE, GILES, THE ONLY THING KEEPING A VAMPIRE WALKING AROUND IS THE DEMON INSIDE IT. WHEN THE HOLLOWER SUCKS THAT OUT, THE VAMPIRE IS DESTROYED.
"BUT ANGEL HAS A HUMAN SOUL IN THERE AS WELL.
"THERE'S NO TELLING WHAT WOULD HAPPEN IF THE HOLLOWER SUCKED THE DEMON OUT OF ANGEL. MAYBE EVEN A MIRACLE. MAYBE ALL THAT'D BE LEFT IS A HUMAN BEING.
"MAYBE ANGEL DOESN'T WANT OUR HELP BECAUSE HE WANTS TO FIND OUT."
ALL RIGHT.
LET'S DO IT RIGHT THIS TIME.

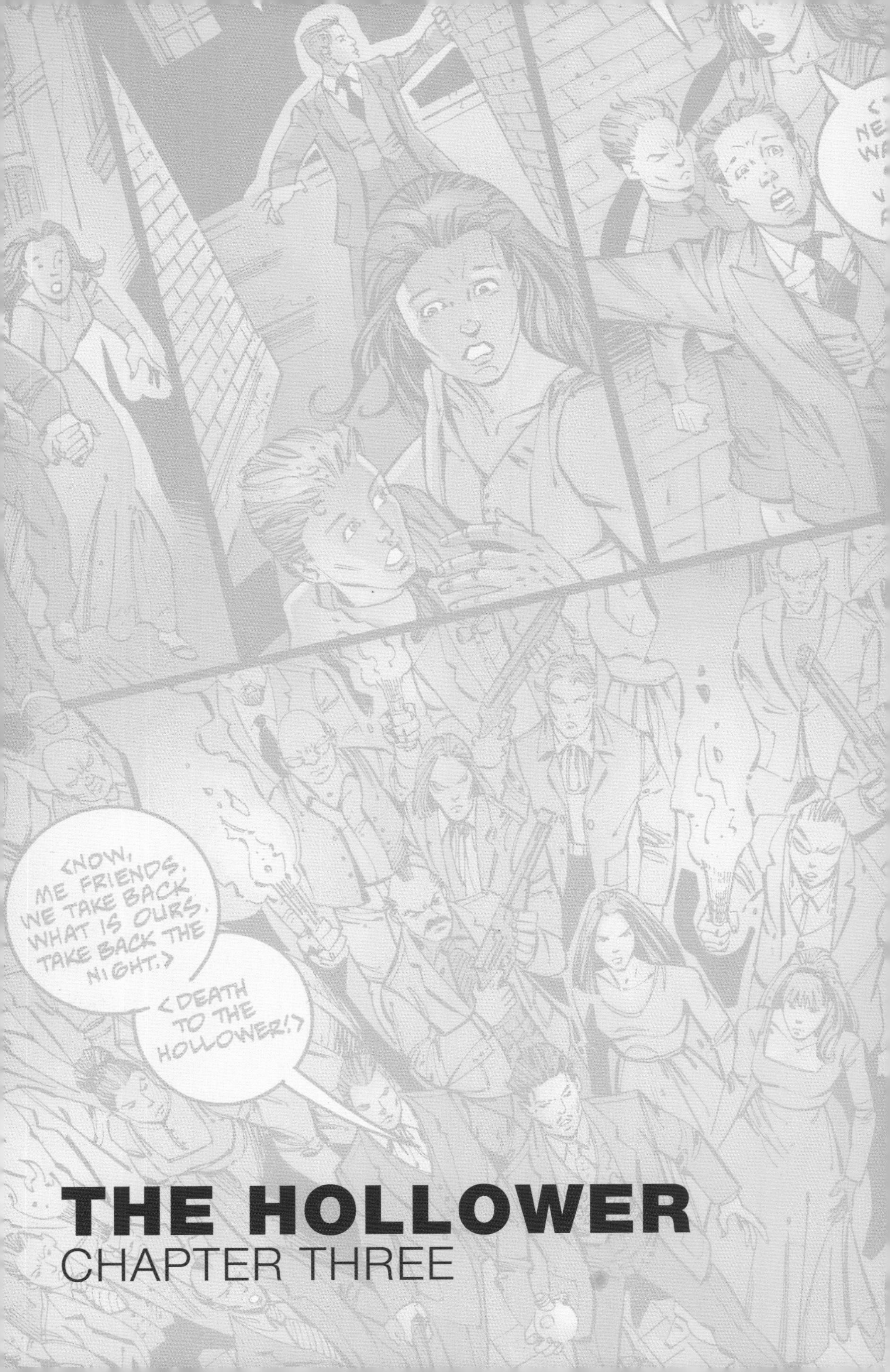
<NOW, ME FRIENDS, WE TAKE BACK WHAT IS OURS. TAKE BACK THE NIGHT.>
<DEATH TO THE HOLLOWER!>

THE HOLLOWER
CHAPTER THREE

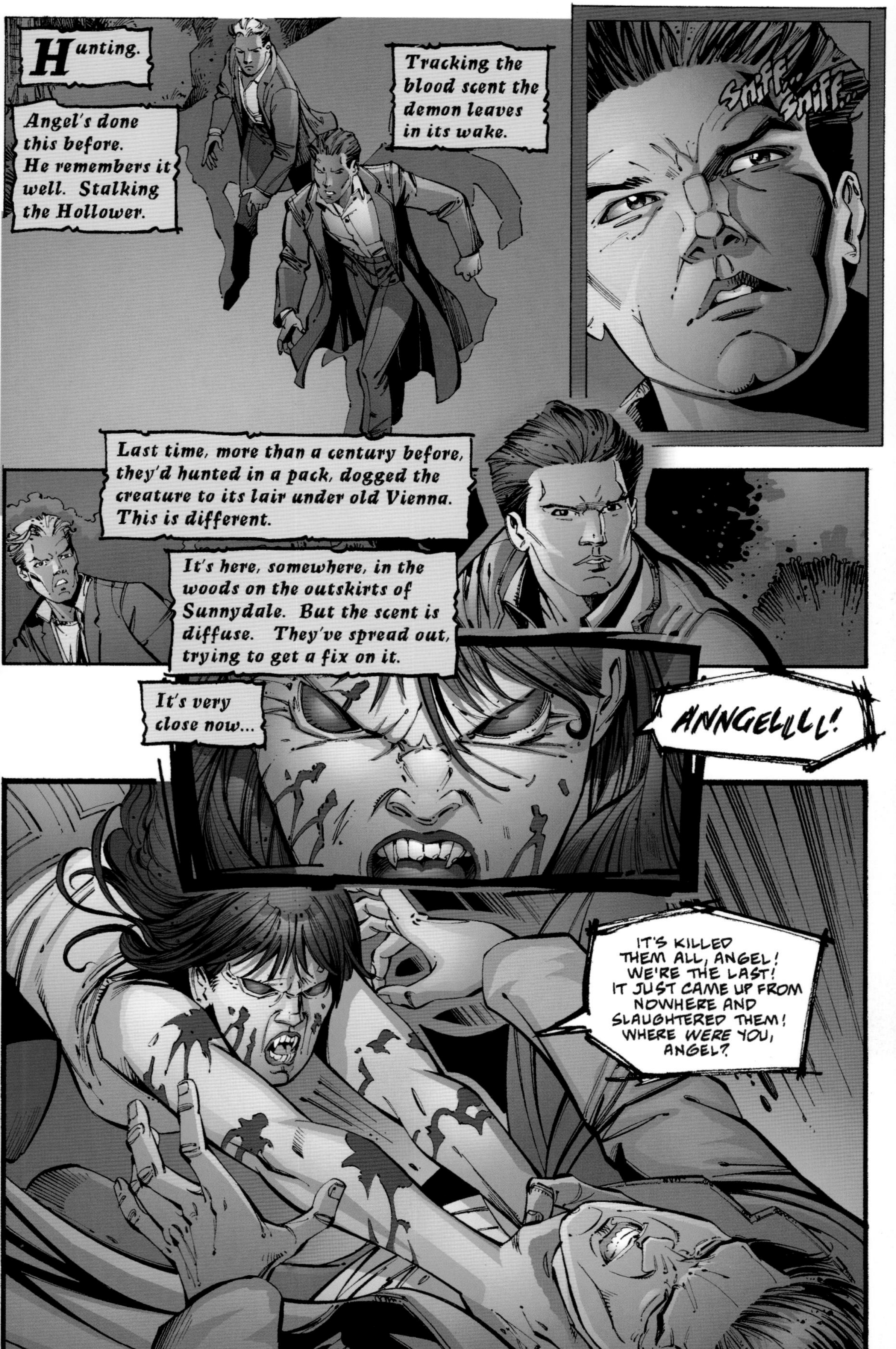
Hunting.
Angel's done this before. He remembers it well. Stalking the Hollower.
Tracking the blood scent the demon leaves in its wake.
SNIFF... SNIFF...
Last time, more than a century before, they'd hunted in a pack, dogged the creature to its lair under old Vienna. This is different.
It's here, somewhere, in the woods on the outskirts of Sunnydale. But the scent is diffuse. They've spread out, trying to get a fix on it.
It's very close now...
ANNGELLLL!
IT'S KILLED THEM ALL, ANGEL! WE'RE THE LAST! IT JUST CAME UP FROM NOWHERE AND SLAUGHTERED THEM! WHERE WERE YOU, ANGEL?

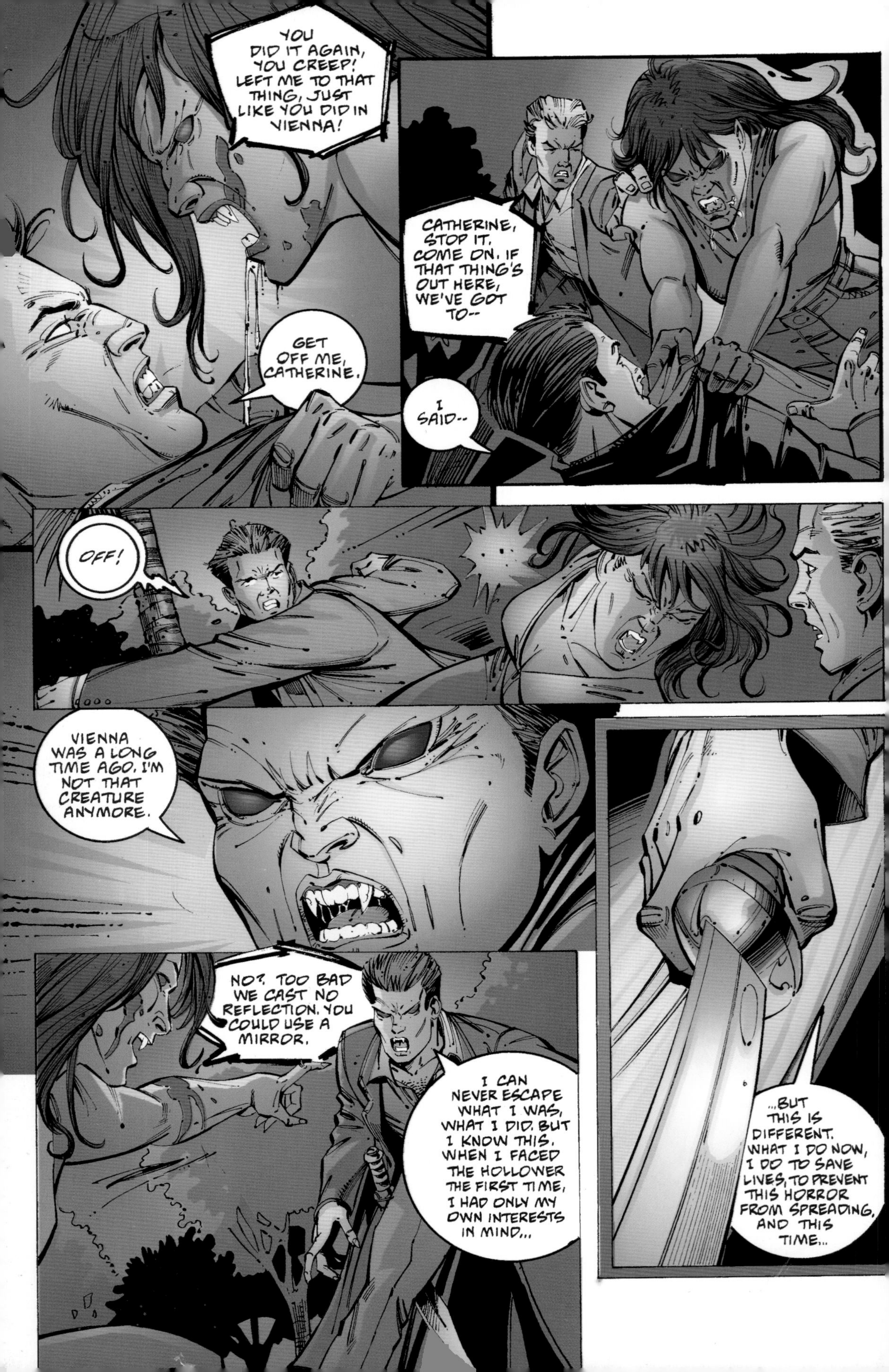
YOU DID IT AGAIN, YOU CREEP! LEFT ME TO THAT THING, JUST LIKE YOU DID IN VIENNA!
GET OFF ME, CATHERINE.
CATHERINE, STOP IT. COME ON. IF THAT THING'S OUT HERE, WE'VE GOT TO--
I SAID--
OFF!
VIENNA WAS A LONG TIME AGO. I'M NOT THAT CREATURE ANYMORE.
NO? TOO BAD WE CAST NO REFLECTION. YOU COULD USE A MIRROR.
I CAN NEVER ESCAPE WHAT I WAS, WHAT I DID. BUT I KNOW THIS. WHEN I FACED THE HOLLOWER THE FIRST TIME, I HAD ONLY MY OWN INTERESTS IN MIND...
...BUT THIS IS DIFFERENT. WHAT I DO NOW, I DO TO SAVE LIVES, TO PREVENT THIS HORROR FROM SPREADING, AND THIS TIME...

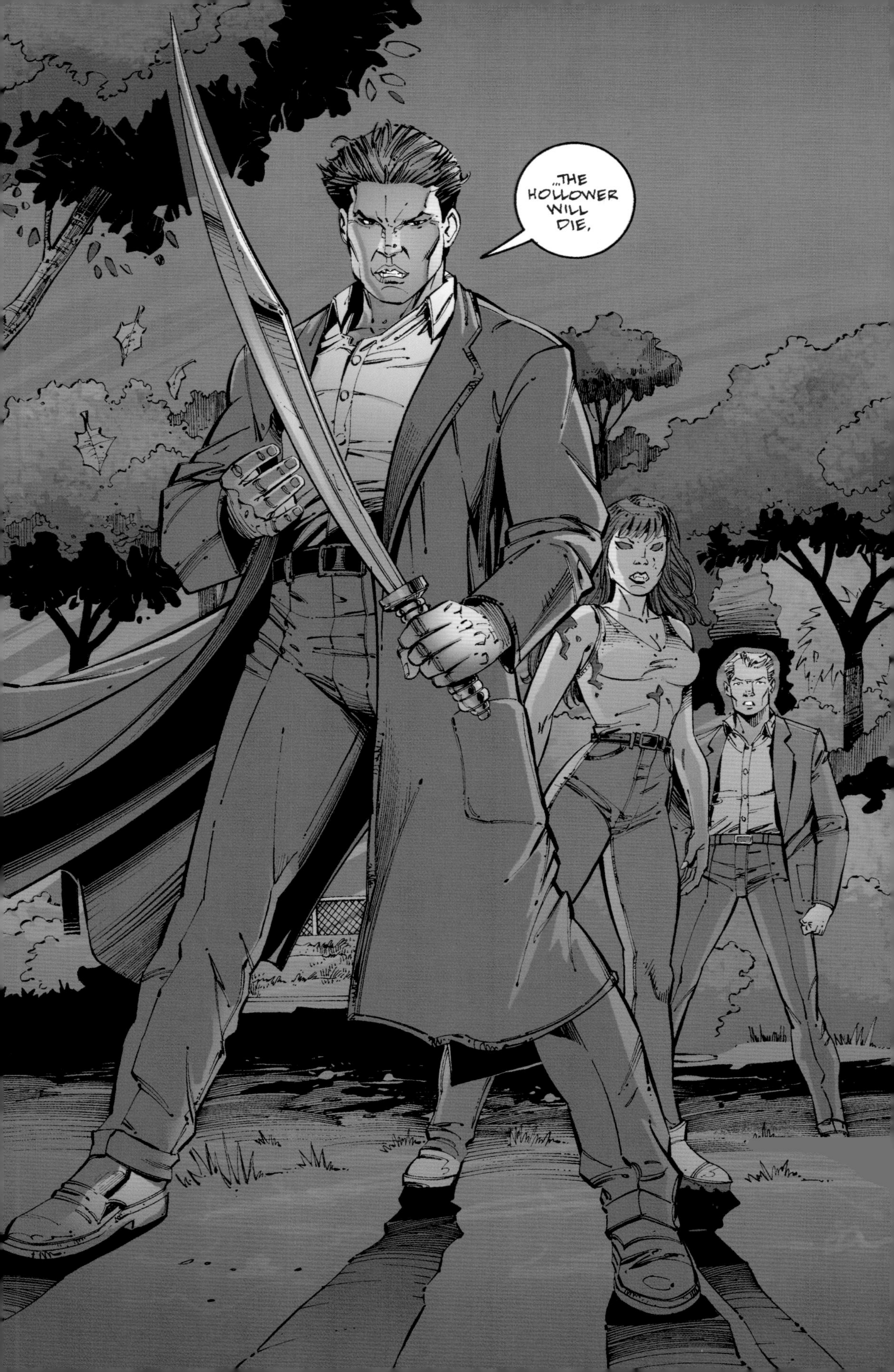
...THE HOLLOWER WILL DIE.

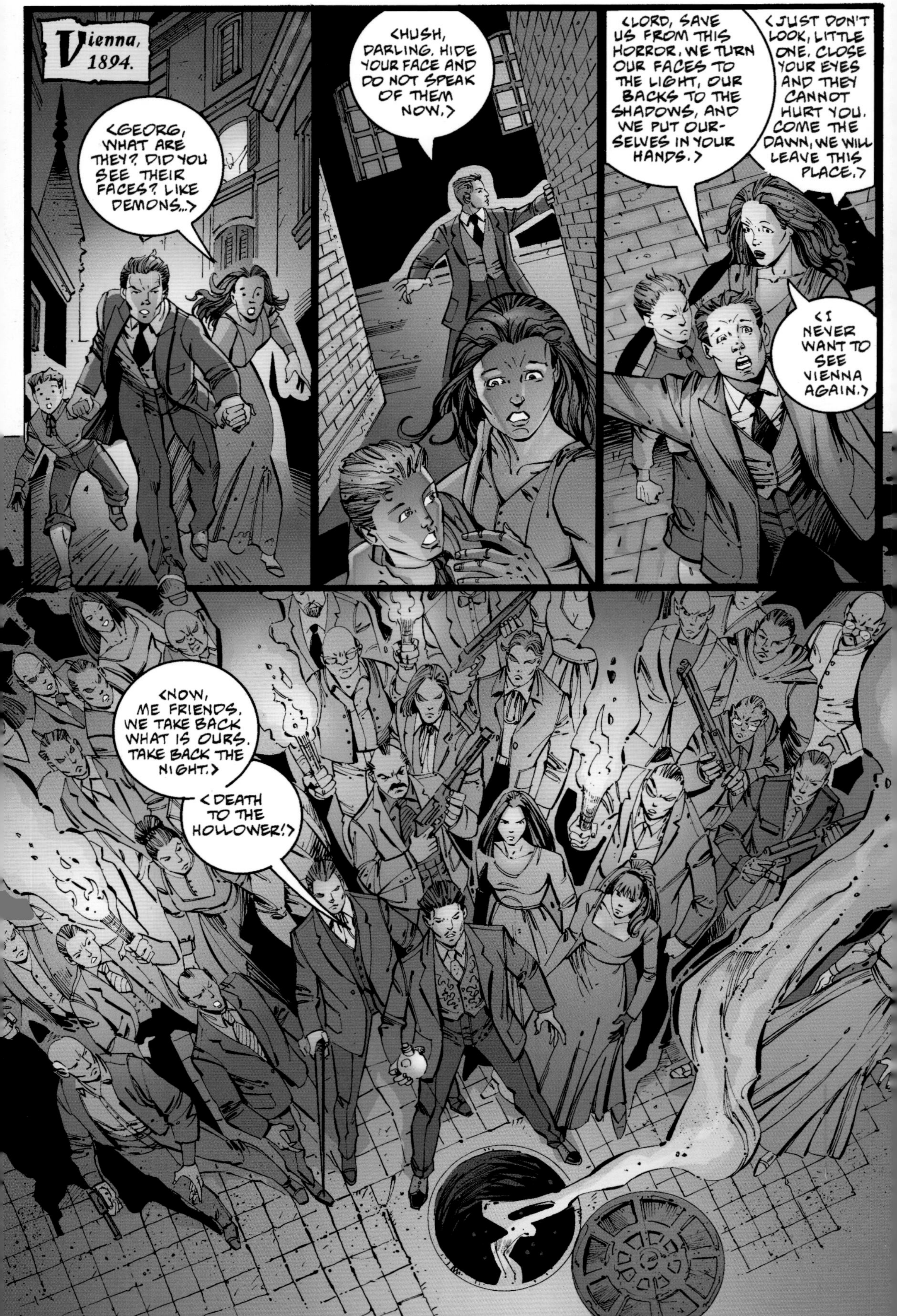
Vienna, 1894.
<GEORG, WHAT ARE THEY? DID YOU SEE THEIR FACES? LIKE DEMONS...>
<HUSH, DARLING. HIDE YOUR FACE AND DO NOT SPEAK OF THEM NOW.>
<LORD, SAVE US FROM THIS HORROR. WE TURN OUR FACES TO THE LIGHT, OUR BACKS TO THE SHADOWS, AND WE PUT OUR-SELVES IN YOUR HANDS.>
<JUST DON'T LOOK, LITTLE ONE. CLOSE YOUR EYES AND THEY CANNOT HURT YOU. COME THE DAWN, WE WILL LEAVE THIS PLACE.>
<I NEVER WANT TO SEE VIENNA AGAIN.>
<NOW, ME FRIENDS. WE TAKE BACK WHAT IS OURS. TAKE BACK THE NIGHT.>
<DEATH TO THE HOLLOWER!>

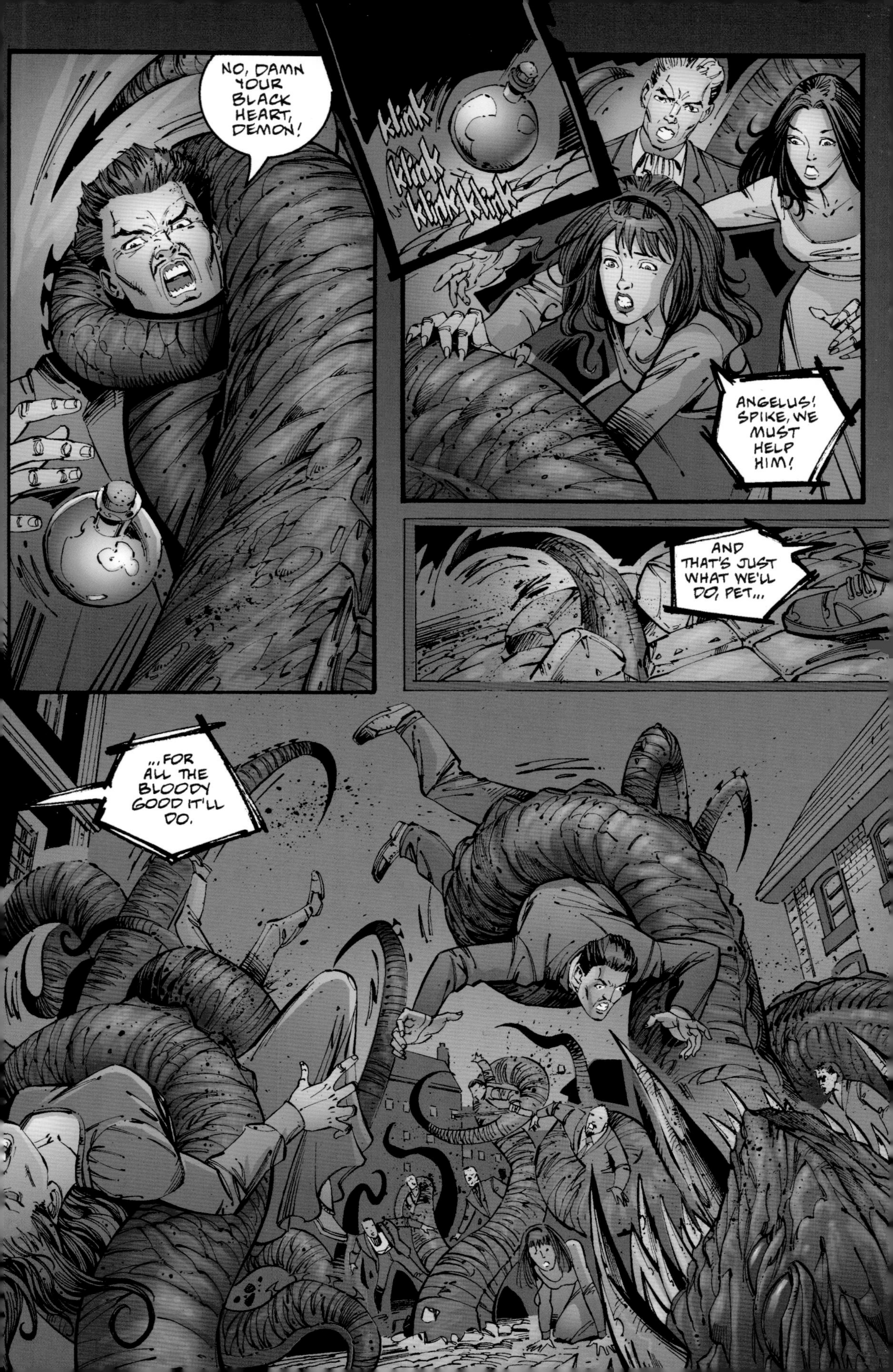
NO, DAMN YOUR BLACK HEART, DEMON!
klink
klink
klink klink klink
ANGELUS! SPIKE, WE MUST HELP HIM!
AND THAT'S JUST WHAT WE'LL DO, PET...
...FOR ALL THE BLOODY GOOD IT'LL DO.

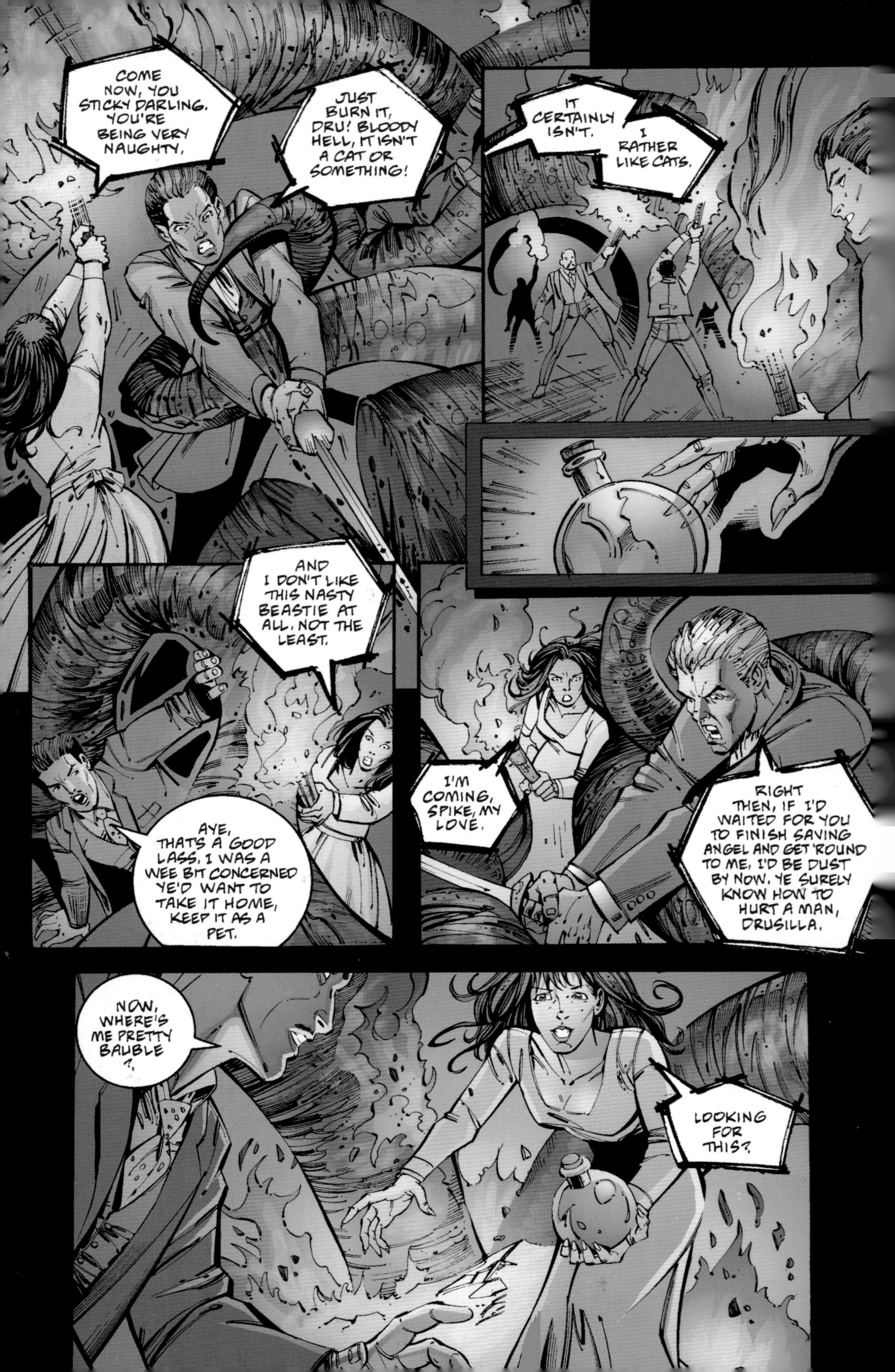
COME NOW, YOU STICKY DARLING. YOU'RE BEING VERY NAUGHTY.
JUST BURN IT, DRU! BLOODY HELL, IT ISN'T A CAT OR SOMETHING!
IT CERTAINLY ISN'T.
I RATHER LIKE CATS.
AND I DON'T LIKE THIS NASTY BEASTIE AT ALL. NOT THE LEAST.
AYE, THAT'S A GOOD LASS. I WAS A WEE BIT CONCERNED YE'D WANT TO TAKE IT HOME, KEEP IT AS A PET.
I'M COMING, SPIKE, MY LOVE.
RIGHT THEN, IF I'D WAITED FOR YOU TO FINISH SAVING ANGEL AND GET 'ROUND TO ME, I'D BE DUST BY NOW. YE SURELY KNOW HOW TO HURT A MAN, DRUSILLA.
NOW, WHERE'S ME PRETTY BAUBLE?
LOOKING FOR THIS?

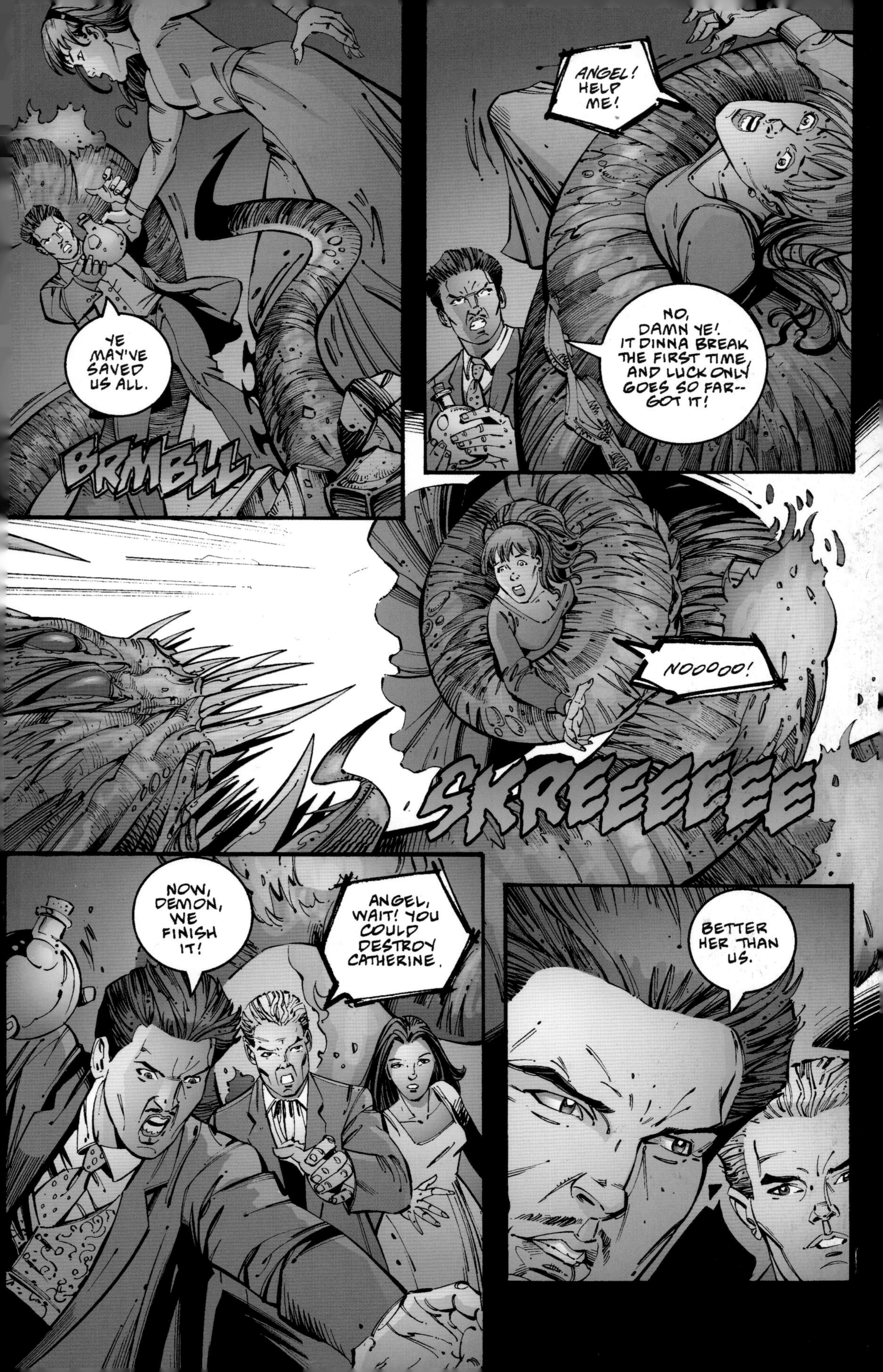
YE MAY'VE SAVED US ALL.
BRMBLL
ANGEL! HELP ME!
NO, DAMN YE! IT DINNA BREAK THE FIRST TIME, AND LUCK ONLY GOES SO FAR-- GOT IT!
NOOOOO!
SKREEEEEEE
NOW, DEMON, WE FINISH IT!
ANGEL, WAIT! YOU COULD DESTROY CATHERINE.
BETTER HER THAN US.

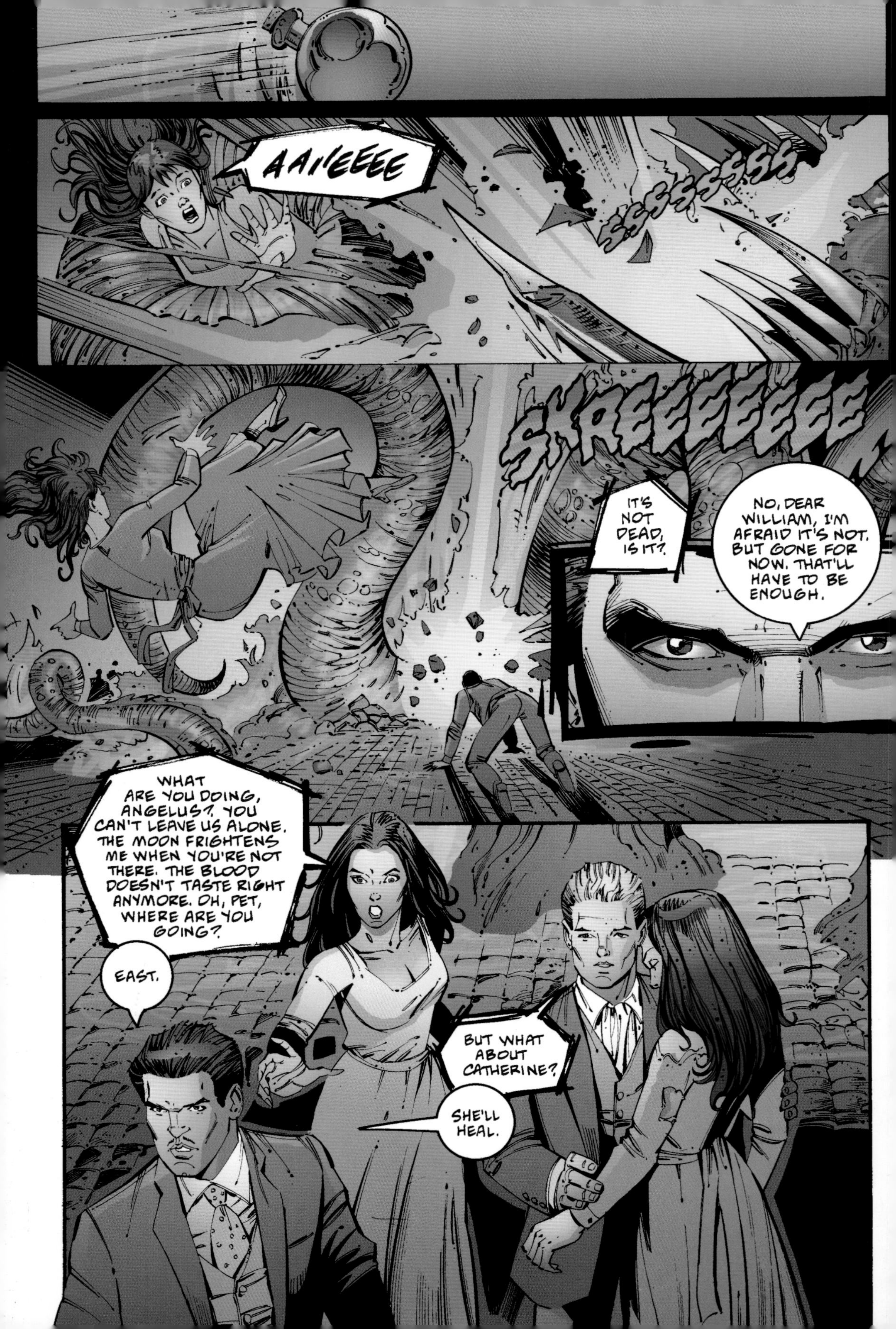
AAIIEEEE
SSSSSSSSS
SKREEEEEEEE
IT'S NOT DEAD, IS IT?
NO, DEAR WILLIAM, I'M AFRAID IT'S NOT. BUT GONE FOR NOW. THAT'LL HAVE TO BE ENOUGH.
WHAT ARE YOU DOING, ANGELUS? YOU CAN'T LEAVE US ALONE. THE MOON FRIGHTENS ME WHEN YOU'RE NOT THERE. THE BLOOD DOESN'T TASTE RIGHT ANYMORE. OH, PET, WHERE ARE YOU GOING?
EAST.
BUT WHAT ABOUT CATHERINE?
SHE'LL HEAL.

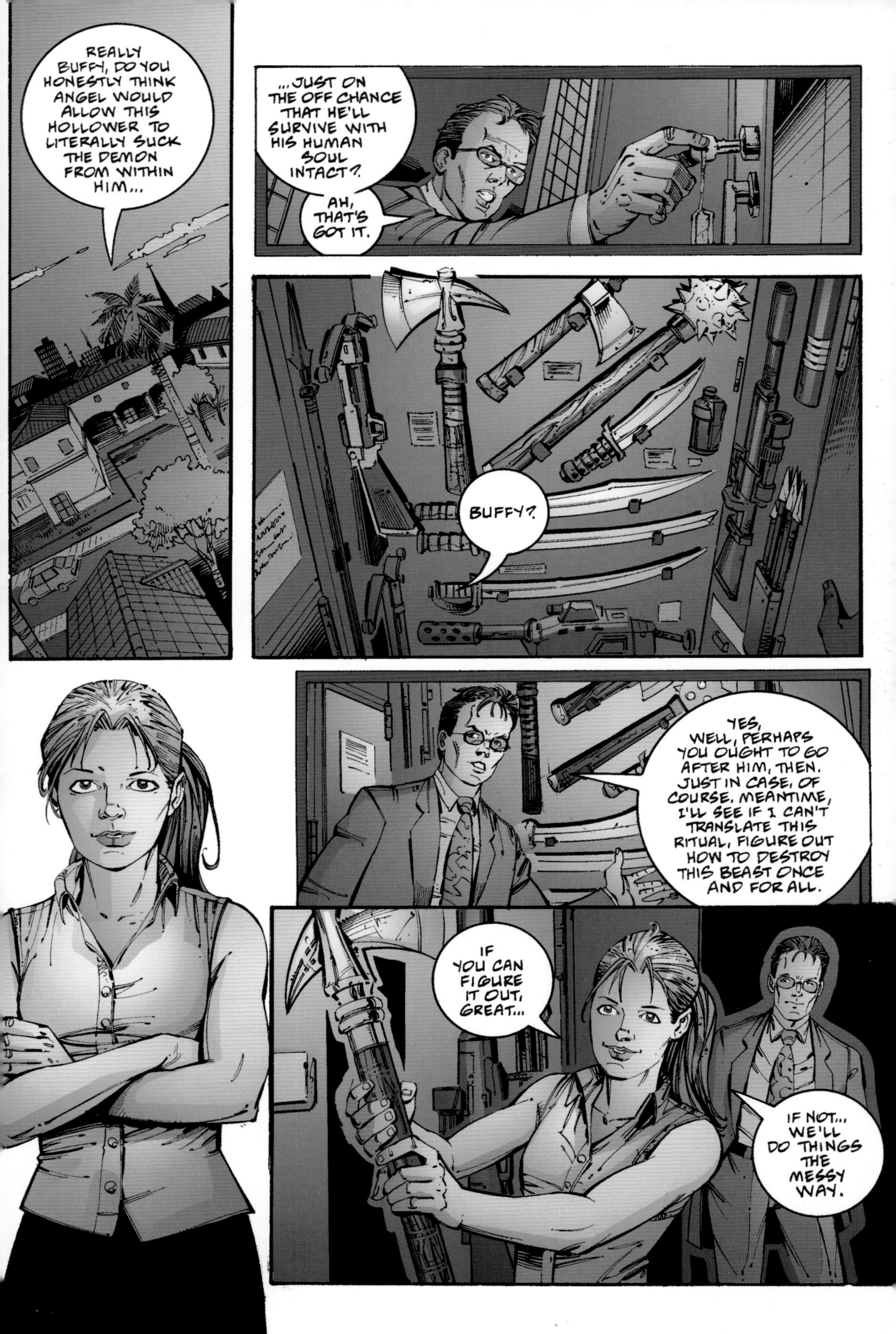
REALLY BUFFY, DO YOU HONESTLY THINK ANGEL WOULD ALLOW THIS HOLLOWER TO LITERALLY SUCK THE DEMON FROM WITHIN HIM...
...JUST ON THE OFF CHANCE THAT HE'LL SURVIVE WITH HIS HUMAN SOUL INTACT?.
AH, THAT'S GOT IT.
BUFFY?.
YES, WELL, PERHAPS YOU OUGHT TO GO AFTER HIM, THEN. JUST IN CASE, OF COURSE. MEANTIME, I'LL SEE IF I CAN'T TRANSLATE THIS RITUAL, FIGURE OUT HOW TO DESTROY THIS BEAST ONCE AND FOR ALL.
IF YOU CAN FIGURE IT OUT, GREAT...
IF NOT... WE'LL DO THINGS THE MESSY WAY.

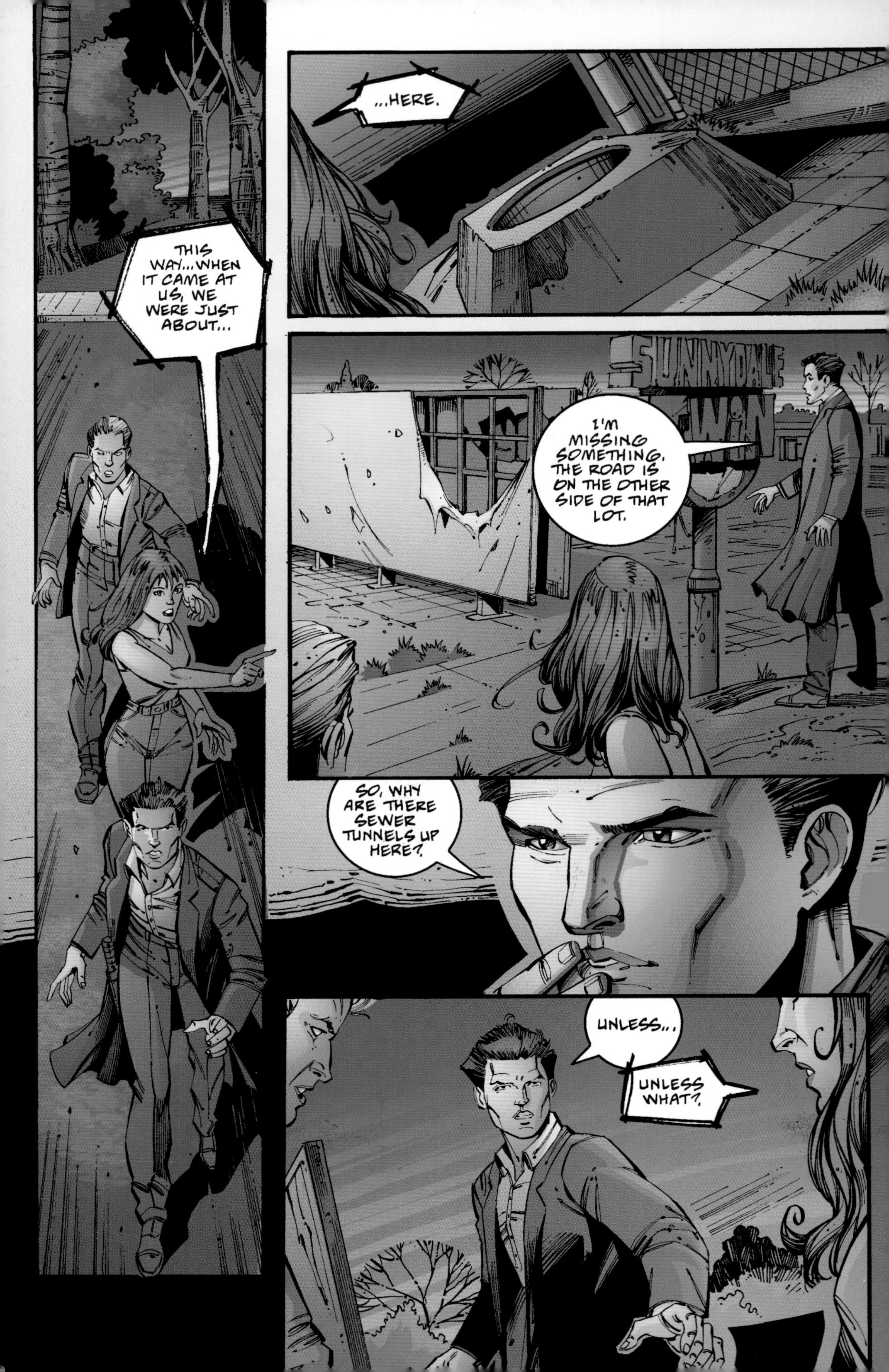
THIS WAY...WHEN IT CAME AT US, WE WERE JUST ABOUT...
...HERE.
SUNNYDALE
I'M MISSING SOMETHING. THE ROAD IS ON THE OTHER SIDE OF THAT LOT.
SO, WHY ARE THERE SEWER TUNNELS UP HERE?
UNLESS...
UNLESS WHAT?

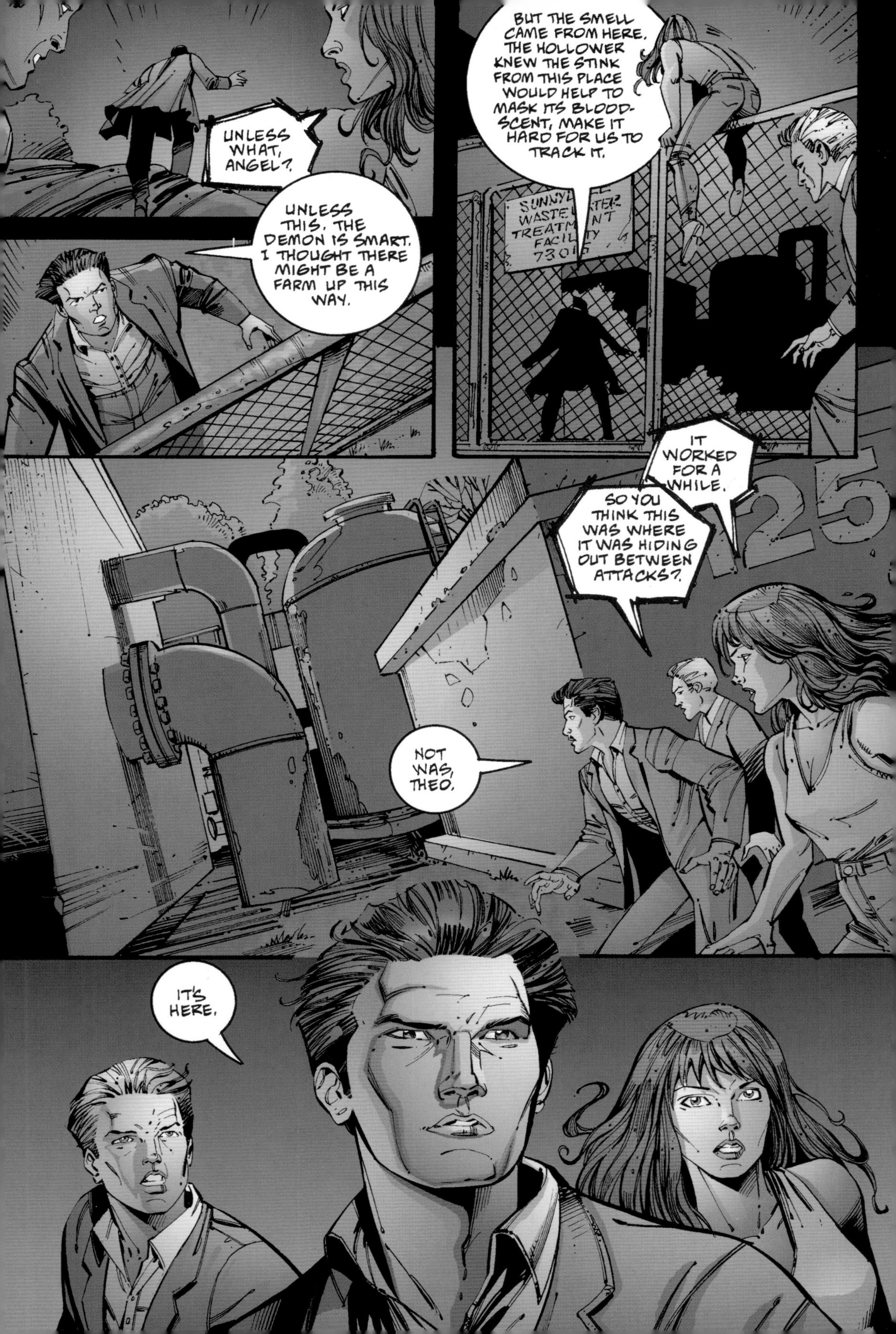
UNLESS WHAT, ANGEL?.
UNLESS THIS. THE DEMON IS SMART. I THOUGHT THERE MIGHT BE A FARM UP THIS WAY.
BUT THE SMELL CAME FROM HERE. THE HOLLOWER KNEW THE STINK FROM THIS PLACE WOULD HELP TO MASK ITS BLOOD-SCENT, MAKE IT HARD FOR US TO TRACK IT.
SO YOU THINK THIS WAS WHERE IT WAS HIDING OUT BETWEEN ATTACKS?.
IT WORKED FOR A WHILE.
NOT WAS, THEO.
IT'S HERE.

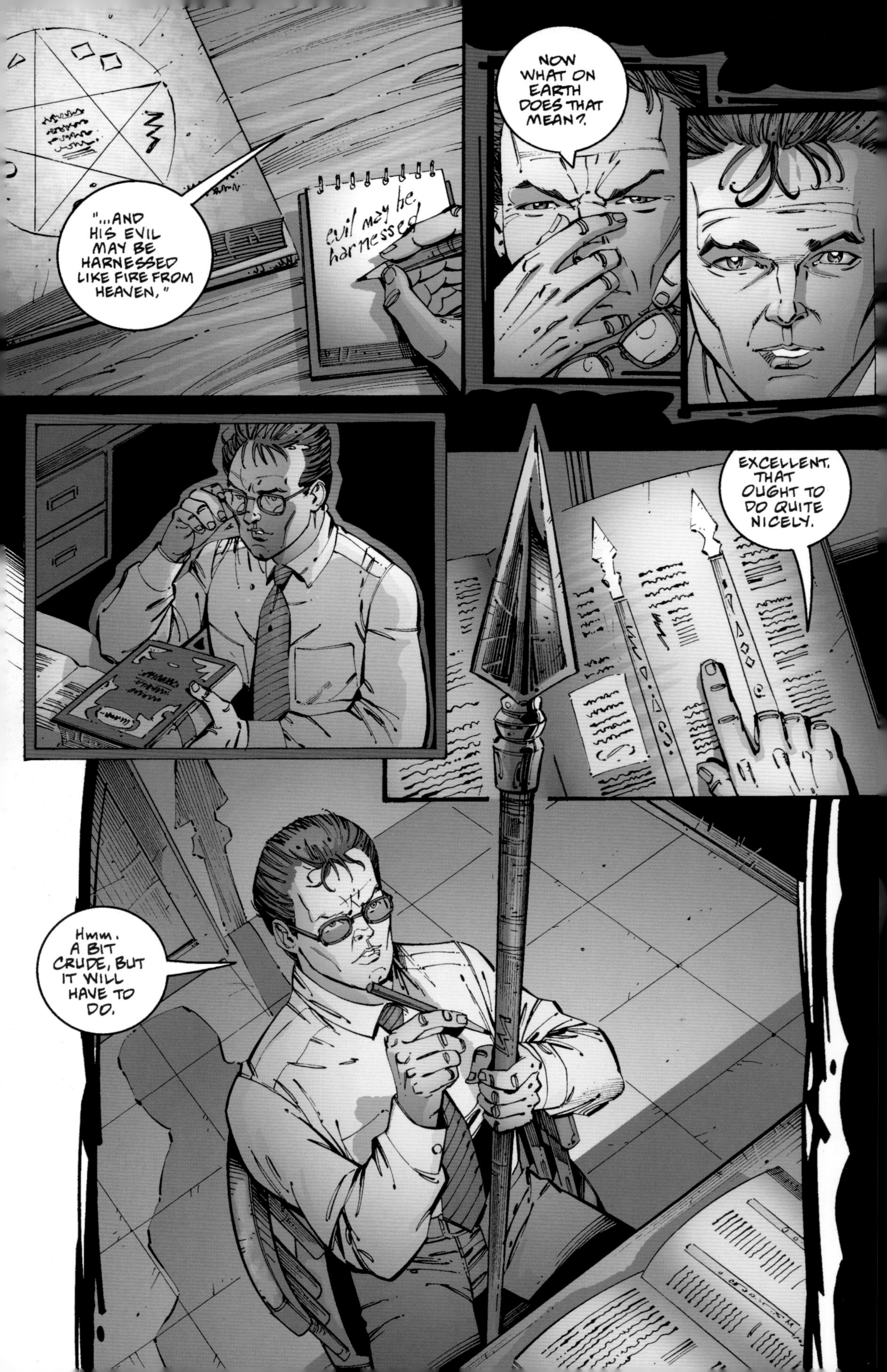
"...AND HIS EVIL MAY BE HARNESSED LIKE FIRE FROM HEAVEN."
evil may be harnessed
NOW WHAT ON EARTH DOES THAT MEAN?.
EXCELLENT. THAT OUGHT TO DO QUITE NICELY.
Hmm. A BIT CRUDE, BUT IT WILL HAVE TO DO.

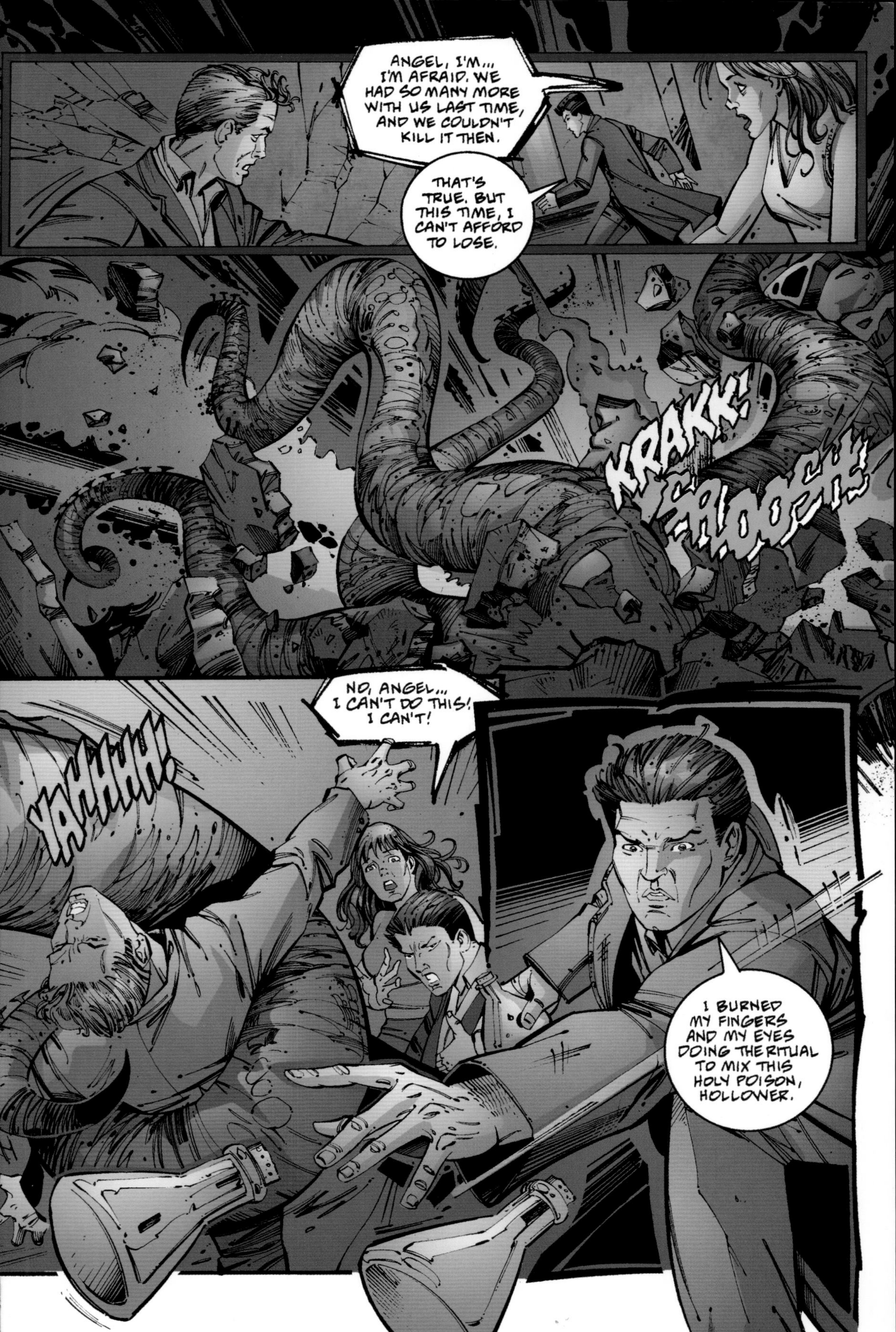

ANGEL, I'M... I'M AFRAID. WE HAD SO MANY MORE WITH US LAST TIME, AND WE COULDN'T KILL IT THEN.
THAT'S TRUE. BUT THIS TIME, I CAN'T AFFORD TO LOSE.
KRAKK!
SPLOOSH!
NO, ANGEL... I CAN'T DO THIS! I CAN'T!
YAHHHH!
I BURNED MY FINGERS AND MY EYES DOING THE RITUAL TO MIX THIS HOLY POISON, HOLLOWER.

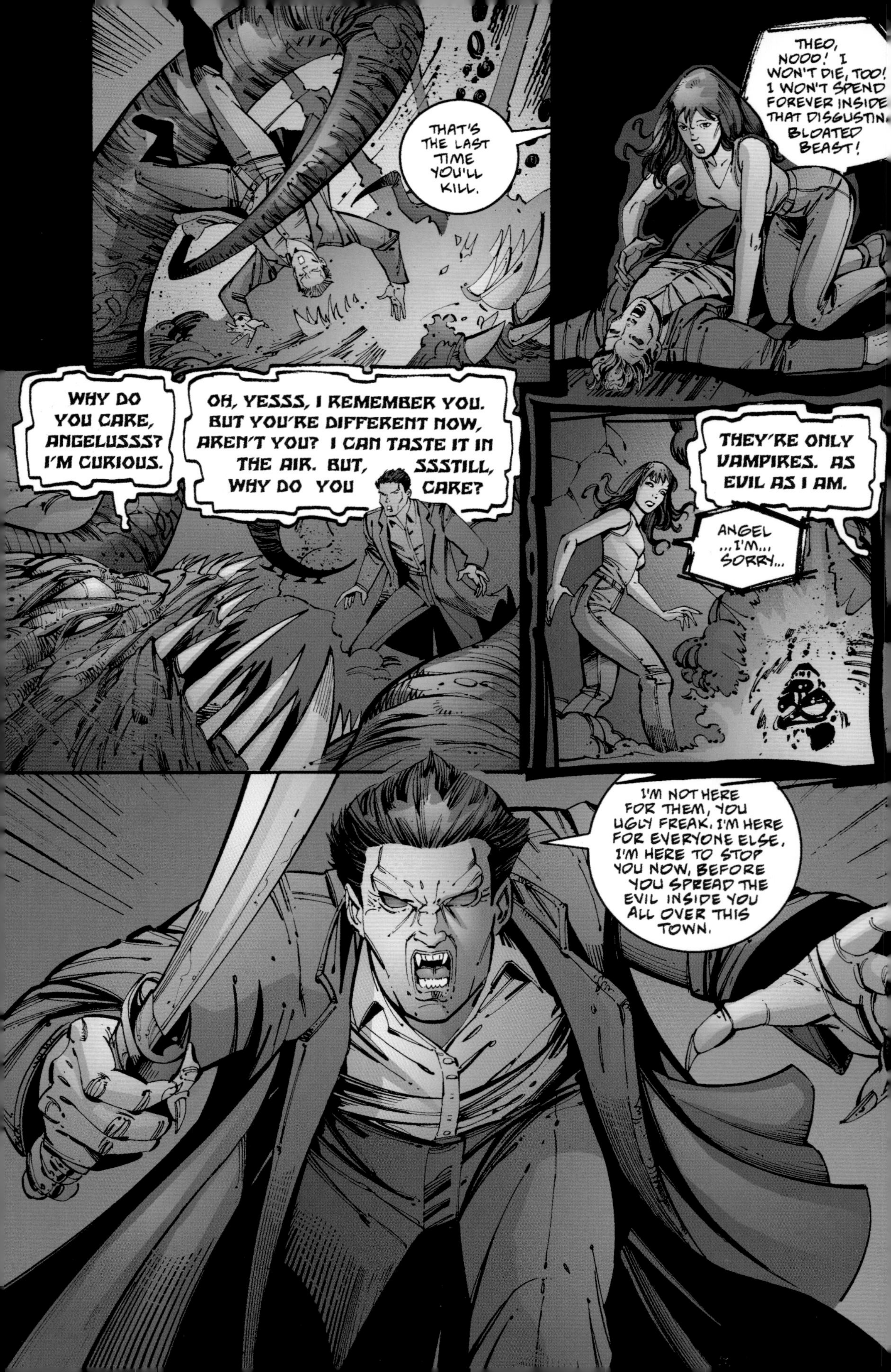
THAT'S THE LAST TIME YOU'LL KILL.
THEO, NOOO! I WON'T DIE, TOO! I WON'T SPEND FOREVER INSIDE THAT DISGUSTIN BLOATED BEAST!
WHY DO YOU CARE, ANGELUSSS? I'M CURIOUS.
OH, YESSS, I REMEMBER YOU. BUT YOU'RE DIFFERENT NOW, AREN'T YOU? I CAN TASTE IT IN THE AIR. BUT, SSSTILL, WHY DO YOU CARE?
THEY'RE ONLY VAMPIRES. AS EVIL AS I AM.
ANGEL ...I'M... SORRY...
I'M NOT HERE FOR THEM, YOU UGLY FREAK. I'M HERE FOR EVERYONE ELSE, I'M HERE TO STOP YOU NOW, BEFORE YOU SPREAD THE EVIL INSIDE YOU ALL OVER THIS TOWN.

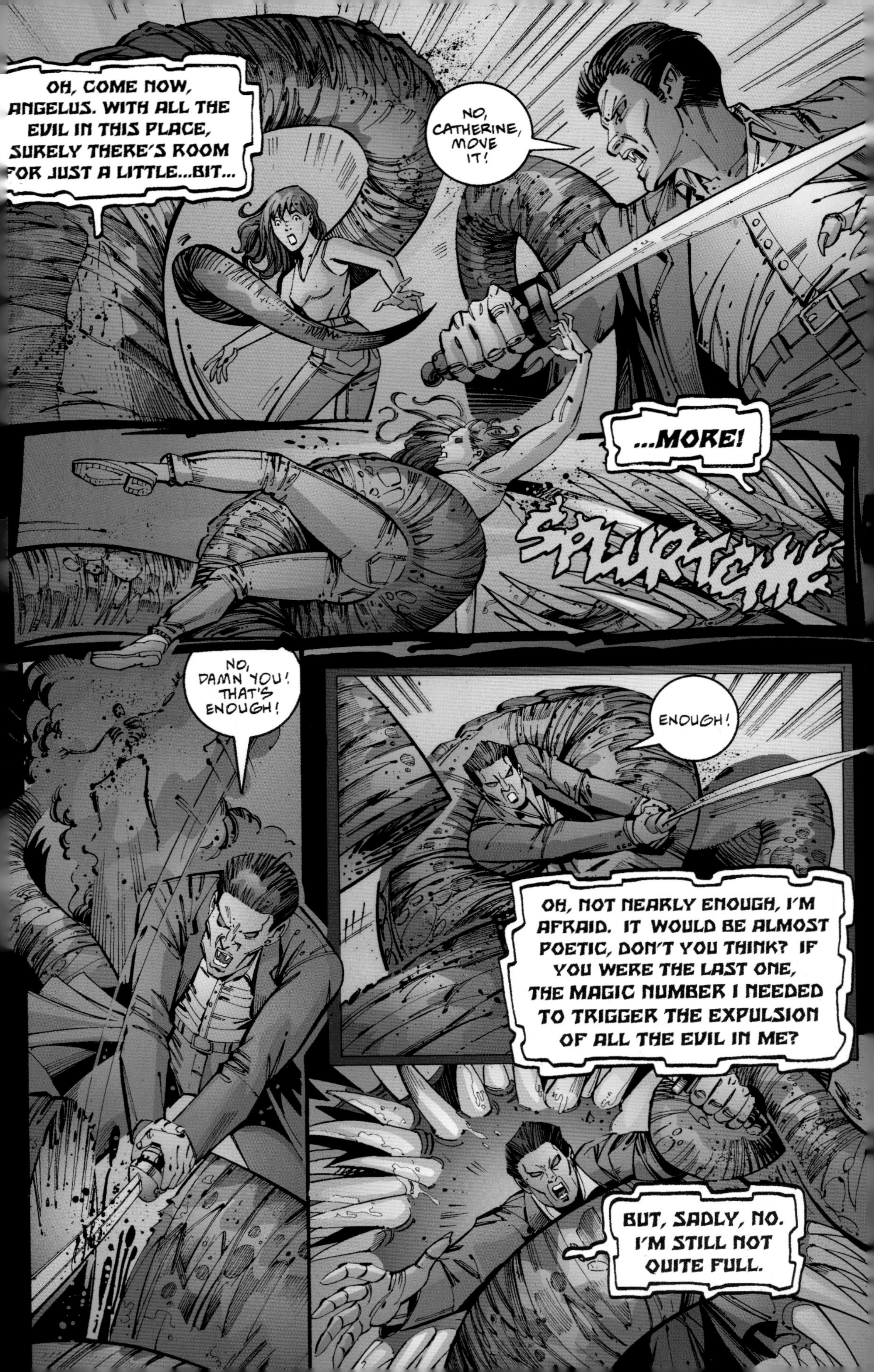
OH, COME NOW, ANGELUS. WITH ALL THE EVIL IN THIS PLACE, SURELY THERE'S ROOM FOR JUST A LITTLE...BIT...
NO, CATHERINE, MOVE IT!
...MORE!
SPLURTCHK
NO, DAMN YOU! THAT'S ENOUGH!
ENOUGH!
OH, NOT NEARLY ENOUGH, I'M AFRAID. IT WOULD BE ALMOST POETIC, DON'T YOU THINK? IF YOU WERE THE LAST ONE, THE MAGIC NUMBER I NEEDED TO TRIGGER THE EXPULSION OF ALL THE EVIL IN ME?
BUT, SADLY, NO. I'M STILL NOT QUITE FULL.

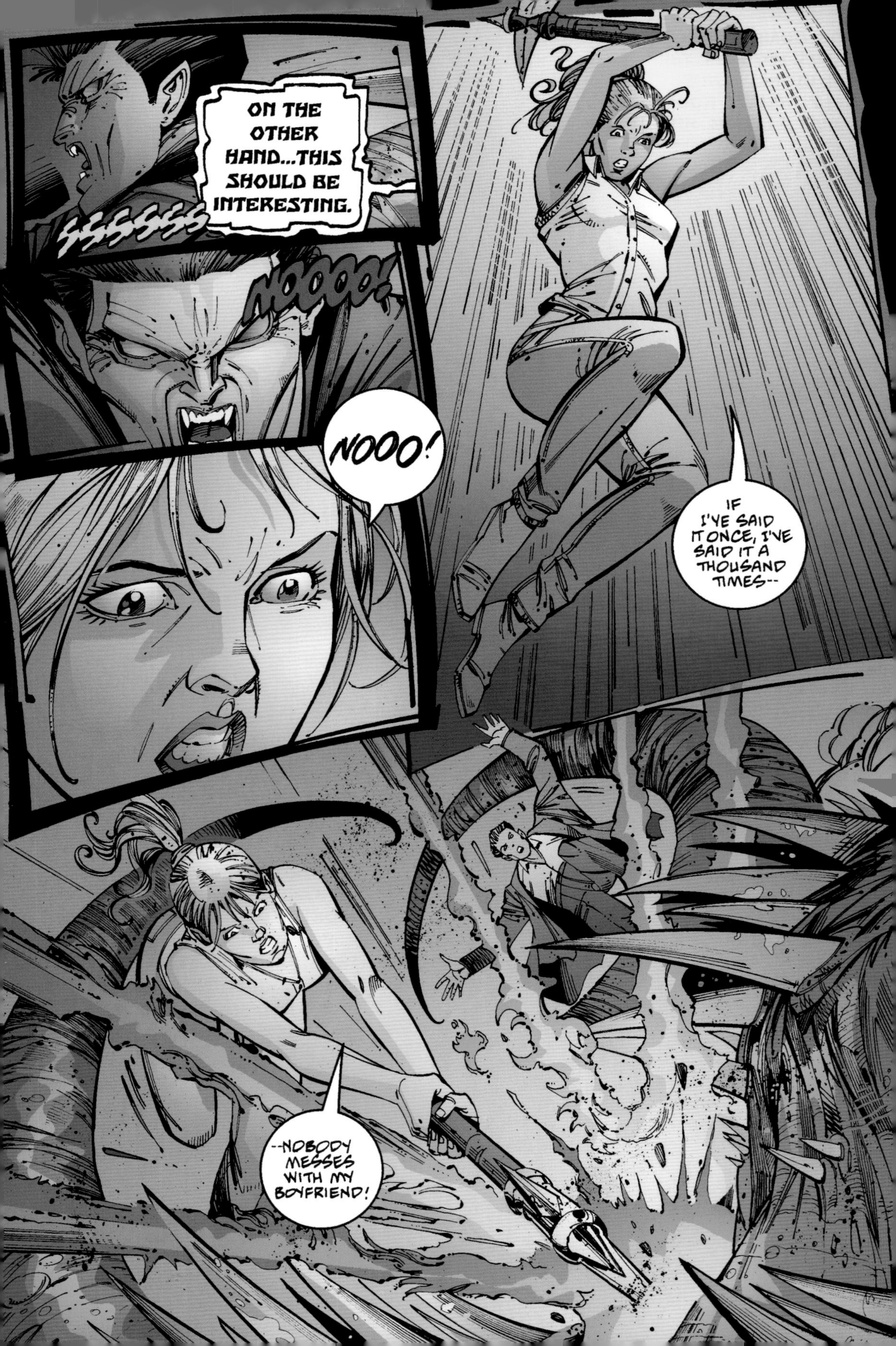

ON THE OTHER HAND...THIS SHOULD BE INTERESTING.
SSSSSS
NOOOO!
NOOO!
IF I'VE SAID IT ONCE, I'VE SAID IT A THOUSAND TIMES--
--NOBODY MESSES WITH MY BOYFRIEND!

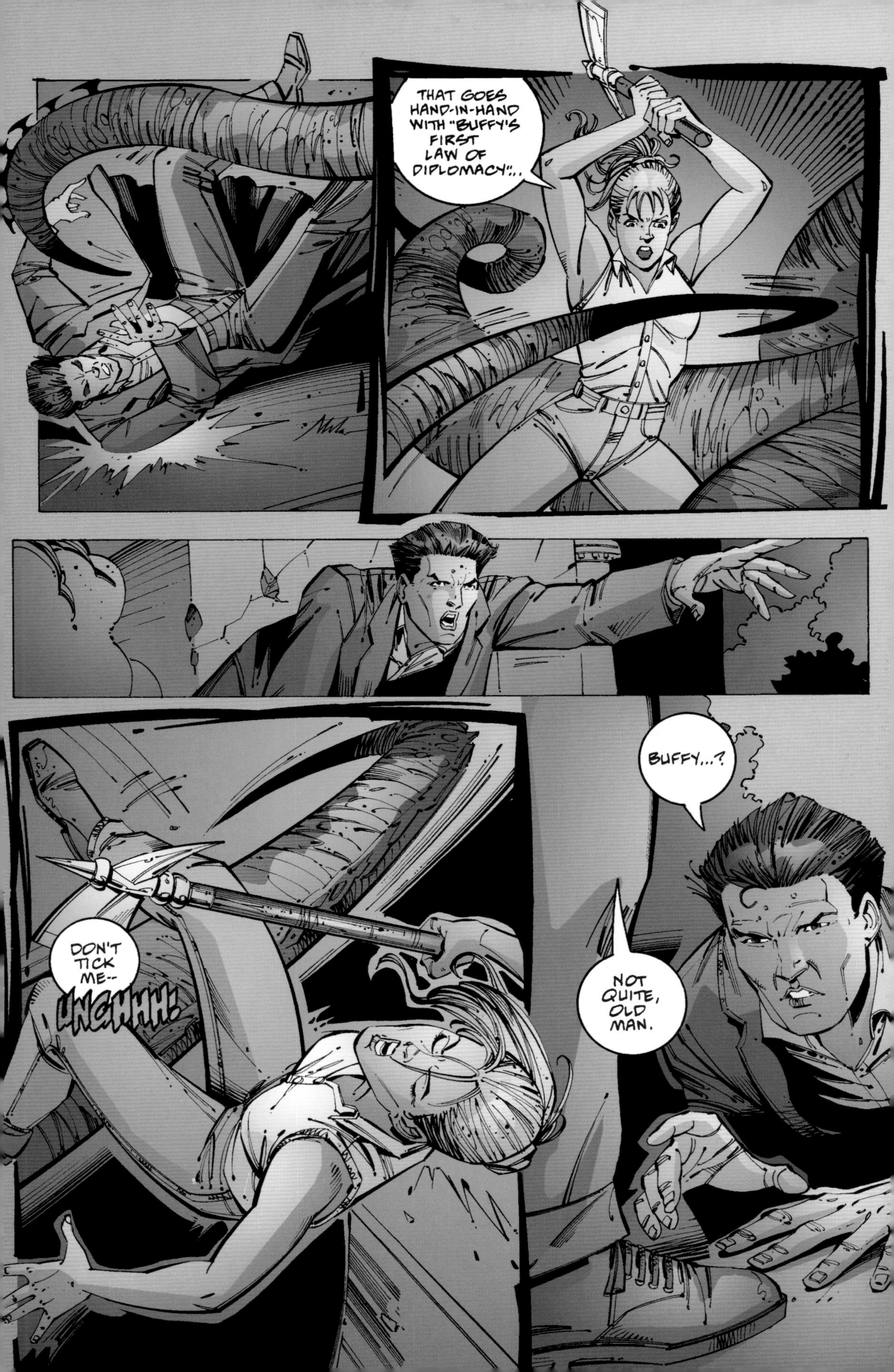
THAT GOES HAND-IN-HAND WITH "BUFFY'S FIRST LAW OF DIPLOMACY"...
BUFFY...?
DON'T TICK ME--
UNGHHH!
NOT QUITE, OLD MAN.

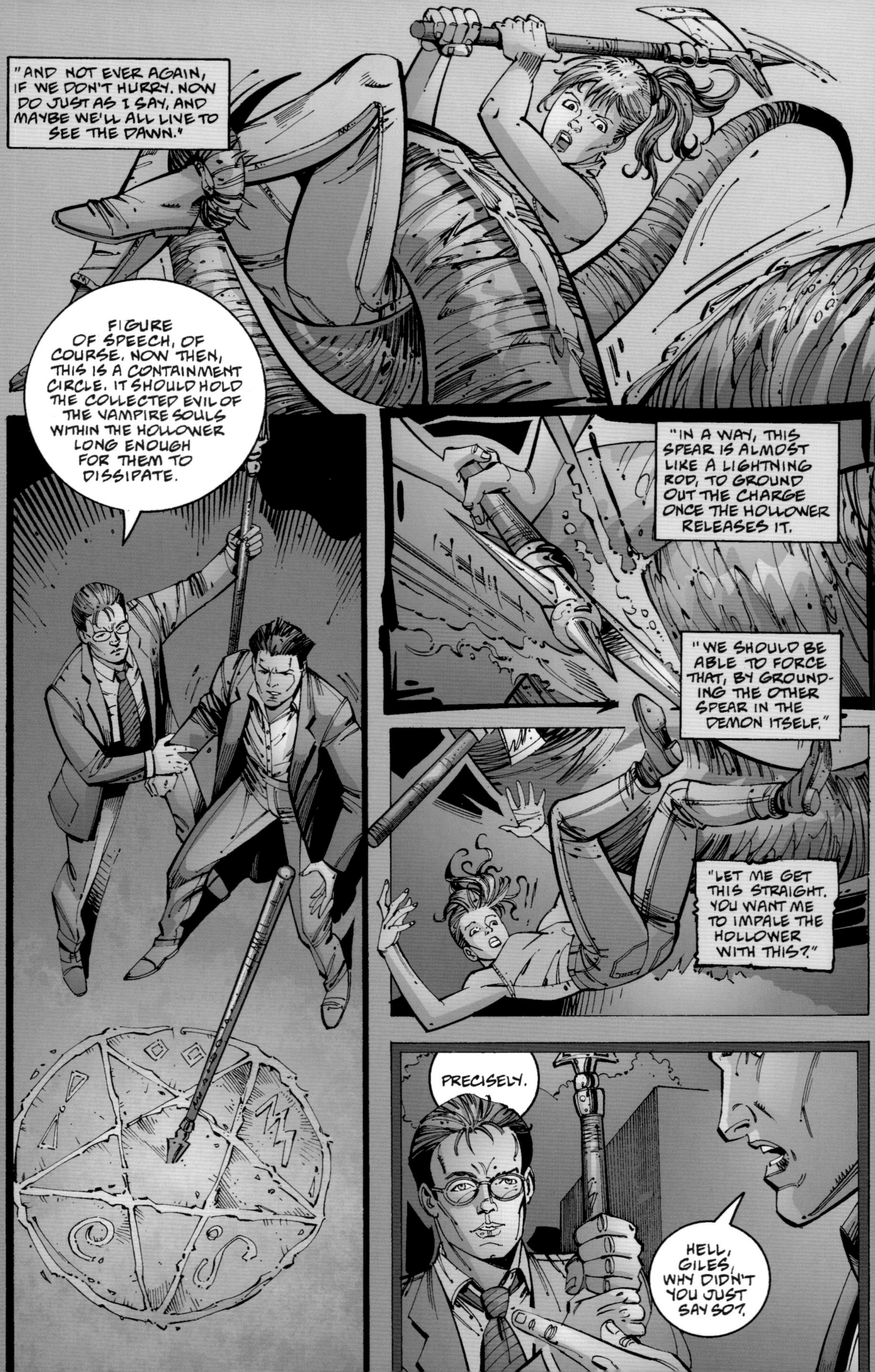
"AND NOT EVER AGAIN, IF WE DON'T HURRY. NOW DO JUST AS I SAY, AND MAYBE WE'LL ALL LIVE TO SEE THE DAWN."
FIGURE OF SPEECH, OF COURSE. NOW THEN, THIS IS A CONTAINMENT CIRCLE. IT SHOULD HOLD THE COLLECTED EVIL OF THE VAMPIRE SOULS WITHIN THE HOLLOWER LONG ENOUGH FOR THEM TO DISSIPATE.
"IN A WAY, THIS SPEAR IS ALMOST LIKE A LIGHTNING ROD, TO GROUND OUT THE CHARGE ONCE THE HOLLOWER RELEASES IT.
"WE SHOULD BE ABLE TO FORCE THAT, BY GROUNDING THE OTHER SPEAR IN THE DEMON ITSELF."
"LET ME GET THIS STRAIGHT. YOU WANT ME TO IMPALE THE HOLLOWER WITH THIS?"
PRECISELY.
HELL, GILES, WHY DIDN'T YOU JUST SAY SO?

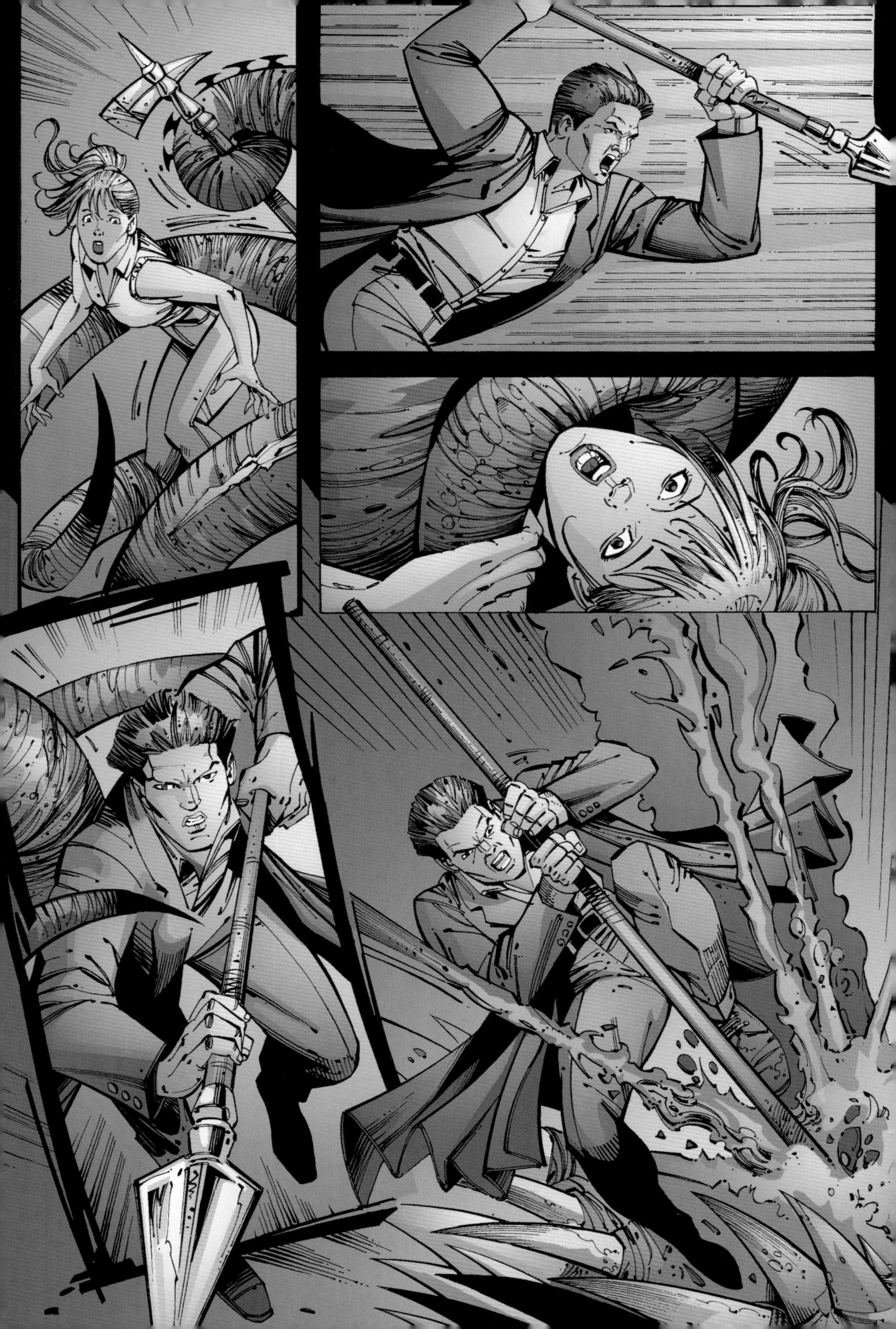

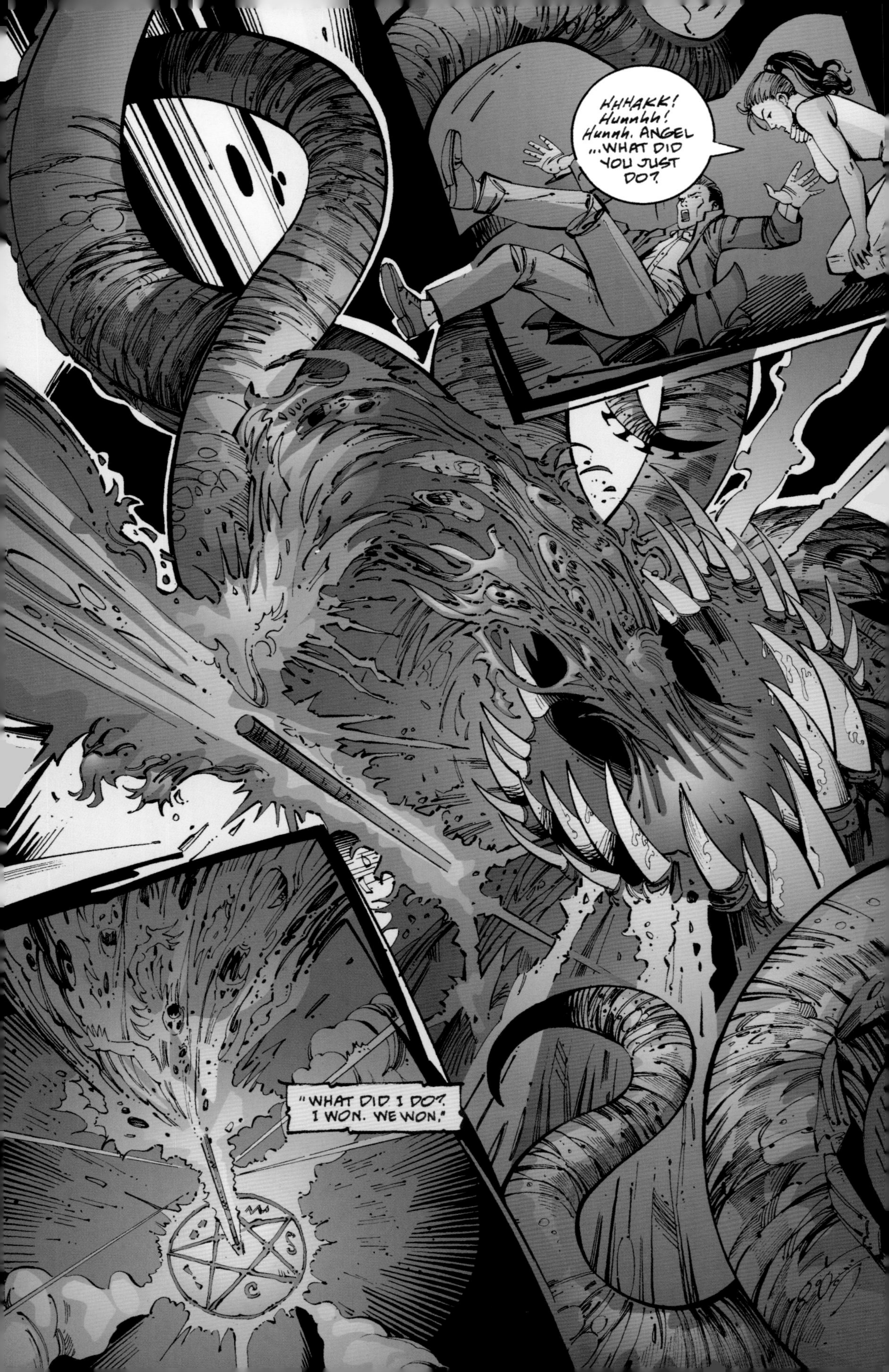
HHHAKK! Hunnhh! Hunnh. ANGEL ...WHAT DID YOU JUST DO?
"WHAT DID I DO? I WON. WE WON."

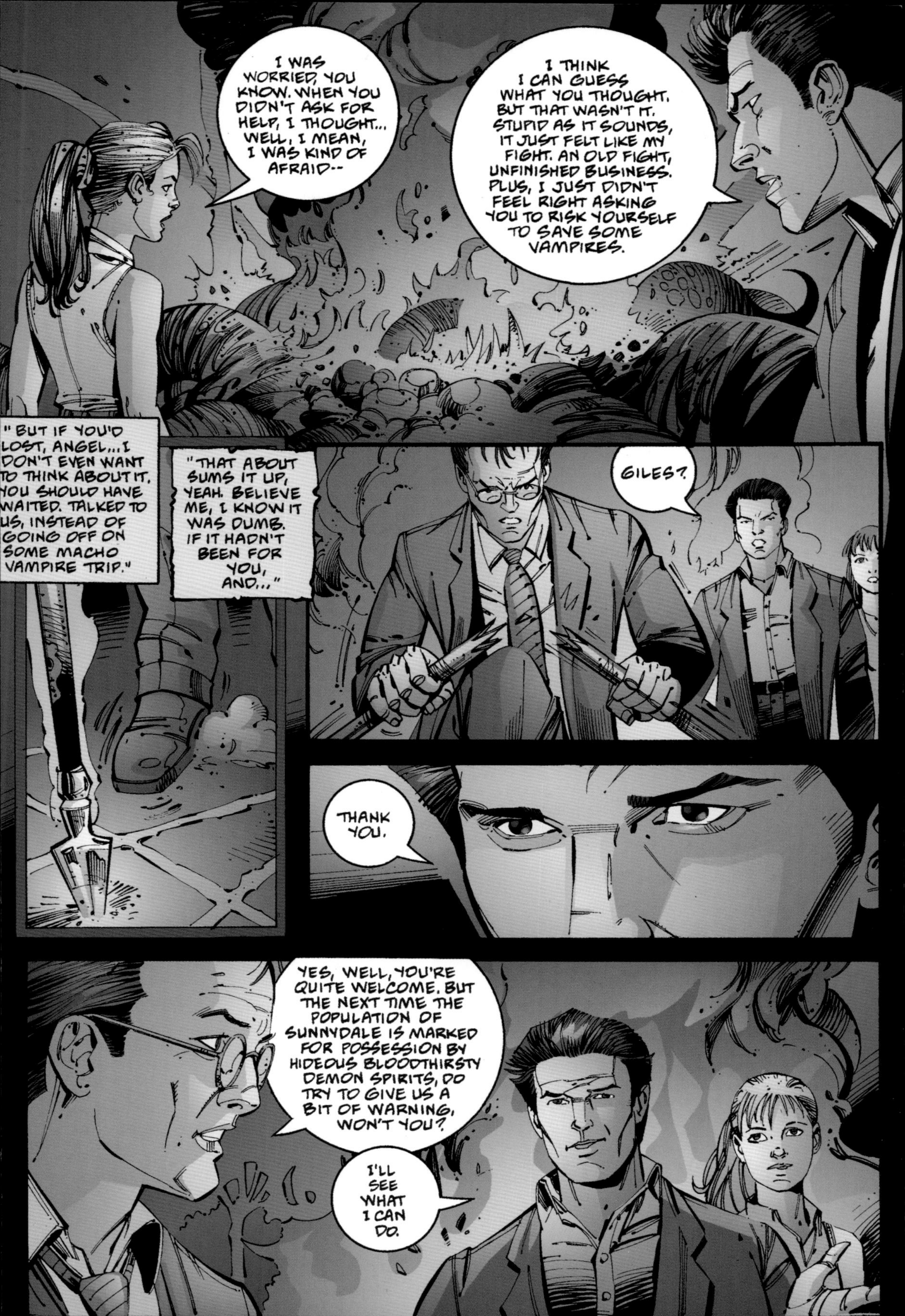
I WAS WORRIED, YOU KNOW. WHEN YOU DIDN'T ASK FOR HELP, I THOUGHT... WELL, I MEAN, I WAS KIND OF AFRAID--
I THINK I CAN GUESS WHAT YOU THOUGHT. BUT THAT WASN'T IT. STUPID AS IT SOUNDS, IT JUST FELT LIKE MY FIGHT. AN OLD FIGHT, UNFINISHED BUSINESS. PLUS, I JUST DIDN'T FEEL RIGHT ASKING YOU TO RISK YOURSELF TO SAVE SOME VAMPIRES.
"BUT IF YOU'D LOST, ANGEL... I DON'T EVEN WANT TO THINK ABOUT IT. YOU SHOULD HAVE WAITED. TALKED TO US, INSTEAD OF GOING OFF ON SOME MACHO VAMPIRE TRIP."
"THAT ABOUT SUMS IT UP, YEAH. BELIEVE ME, I KNOW IT WAS DUMB. IF IT HADN'T BEEN FOR YOU, AND..."
GILES?
THANK YOU.
YES, WELL, YOU'RE QUITE WELCOME. BUT THE NEXT TIME THE POPULATION OF SUNNYDALE IS MARKED FOR POSSESSION BY HIDEOUS BLOODTHIRSTY DEMON SPIRITS, DO TRY TO GIVE US A BIT OF WARNING, WON'T YOU?
I'LL SEE WHAT I CAN DO.

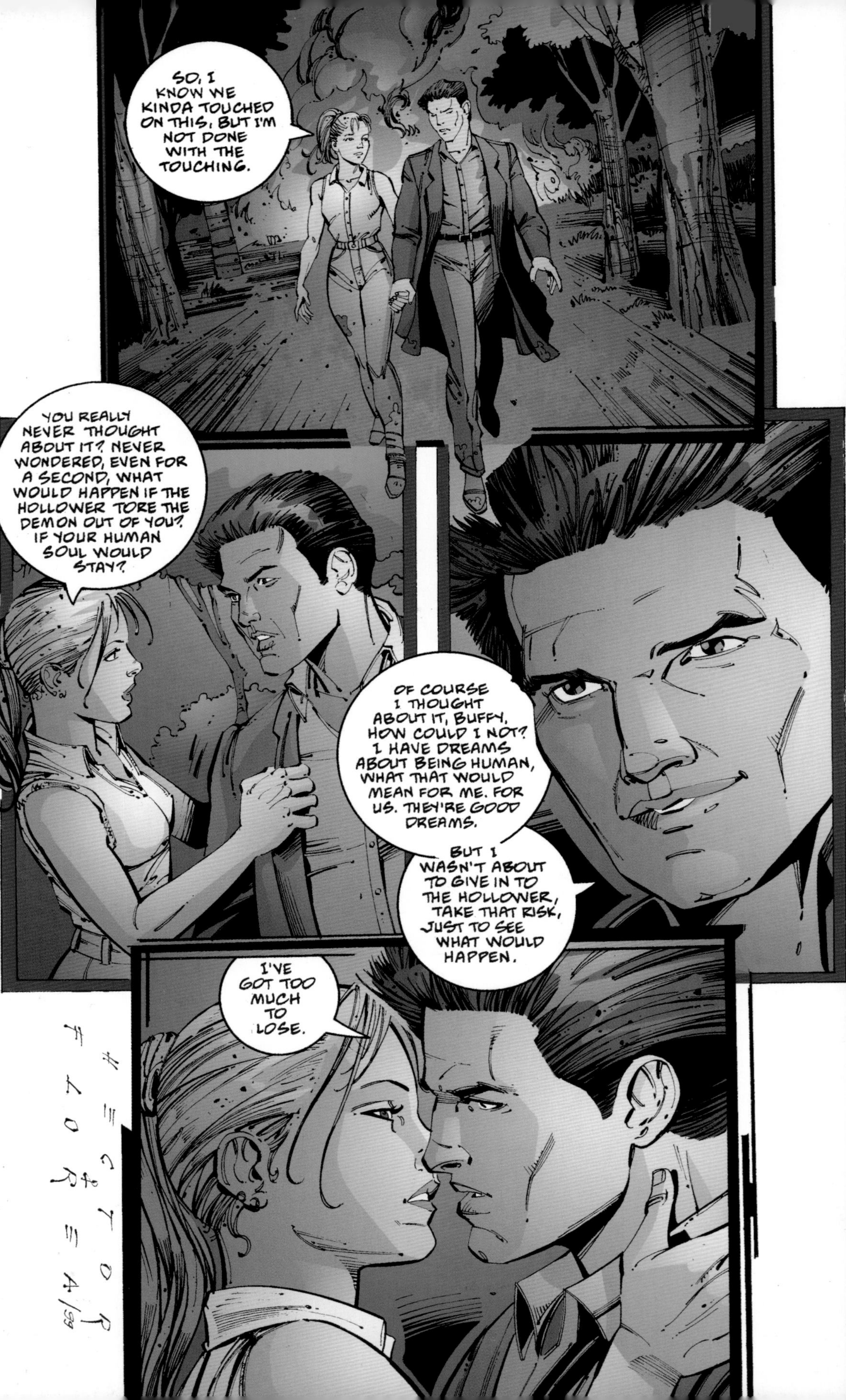
SO, I KNOW WE KINDA TOUCHED ON THIS, BUT I'M NOT DONE WITH THE TOUCHING.
YOU REALLY NEVER THOUGHT ABOUT IT? NEVER WONDERED, EVEN FOR A SECOND, WHAT WOULD HAPPEN IF THE HOLLOWER TORE THE DEMON OUT OF YOU? IF YOUR HUMAN SOUL WOULD STAY?
OF COURSE I THOUGHT ABOUT IT, BUFFY, HOW COULD I NOT? I HAVE DREAMS ABOUT BEING HUMAN, WHAT THAT WOULD MEAN FOR ME. FOR US. THEY'RE GOOD DREAMS.
BUT I WASN'T ABOUT TO GIVE IN TO THE HOLLOWER, TAKE THAT RISK, JUST TO SEE WHAT WOULD HAPPEN.
I'VE GOT TOO MUCH TO LOSE.

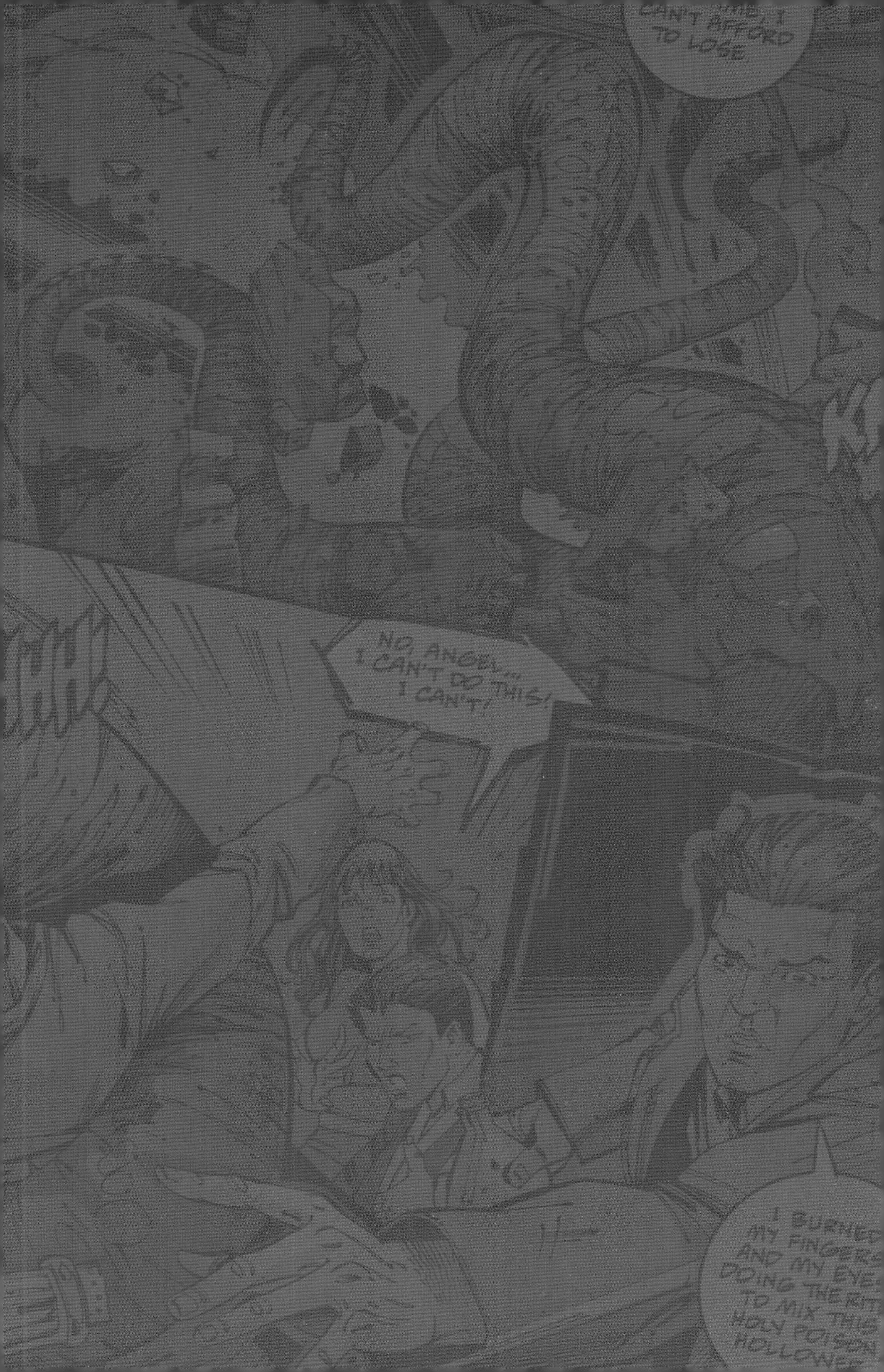
TO LOSE
NO, ANGEL... I CAN'T DO THIS! I CAN'T!
I
MY
AND MY
DOING
TO MIX
HOLY

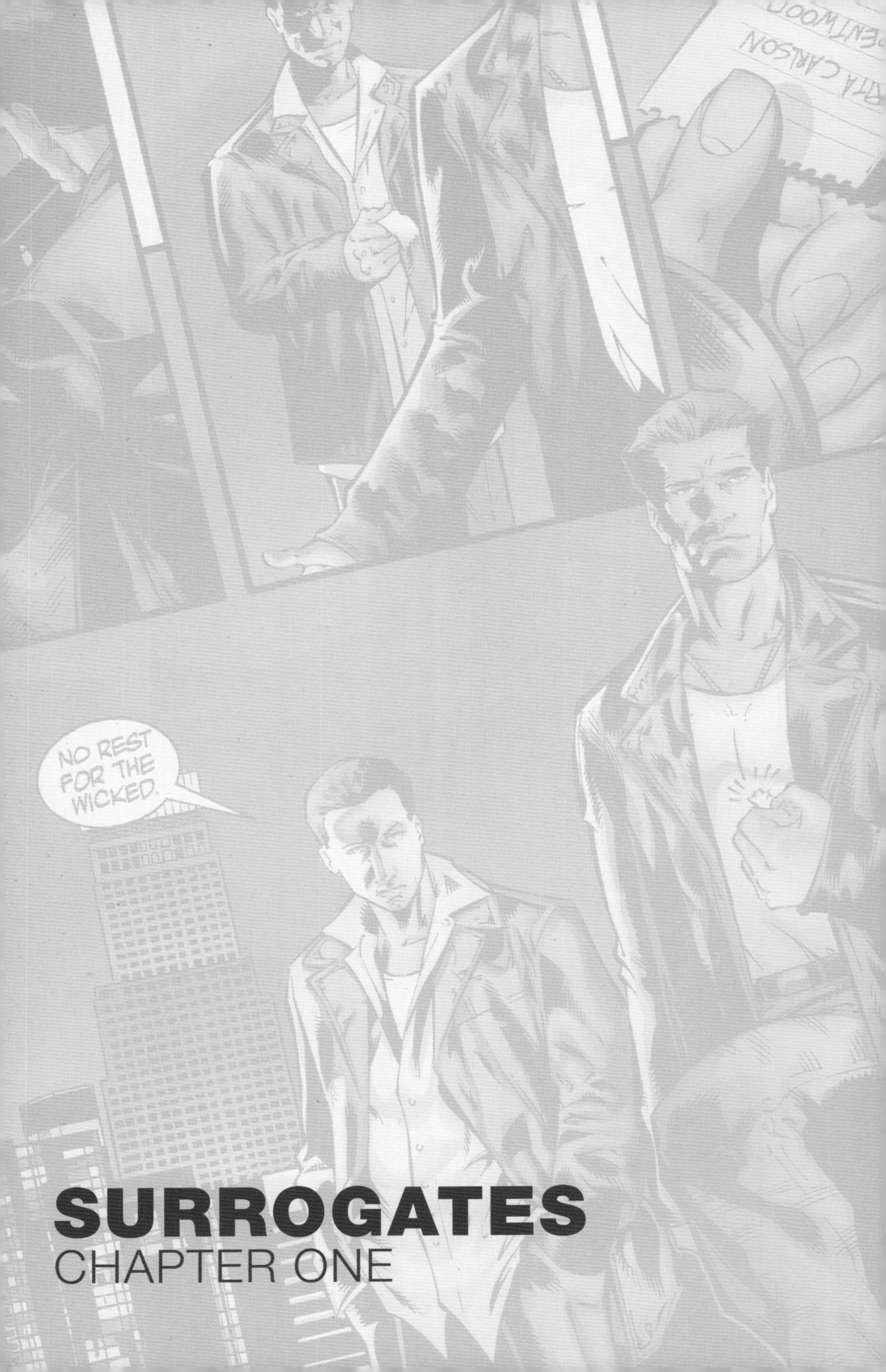
NO REST FOR THE WICKED.

SURROGATES
CHAPTER ONE

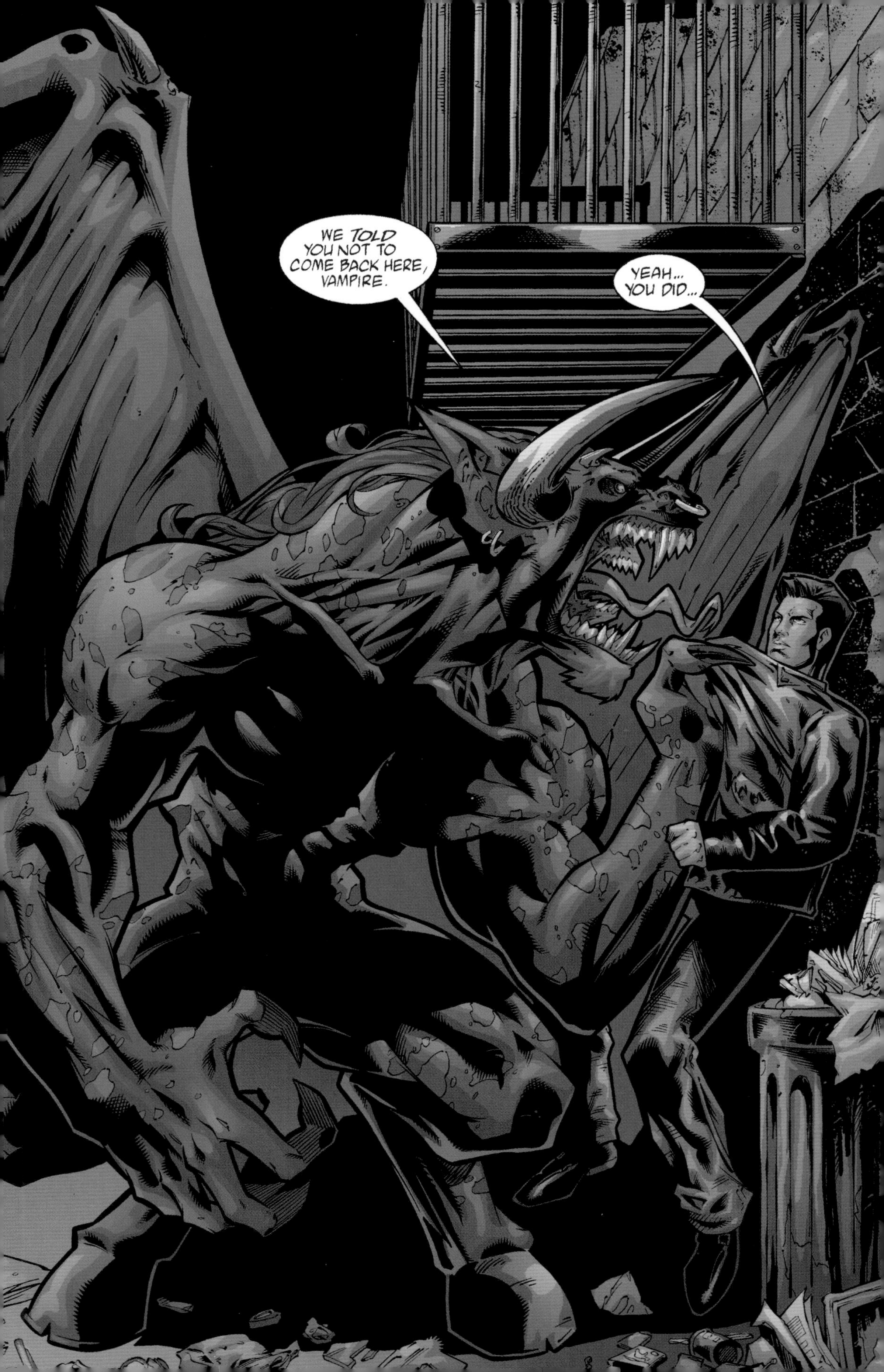
WE TOLD YOU NOT TO COME BACK HERE, VAMPIRE.
YEAH... YOU DID...

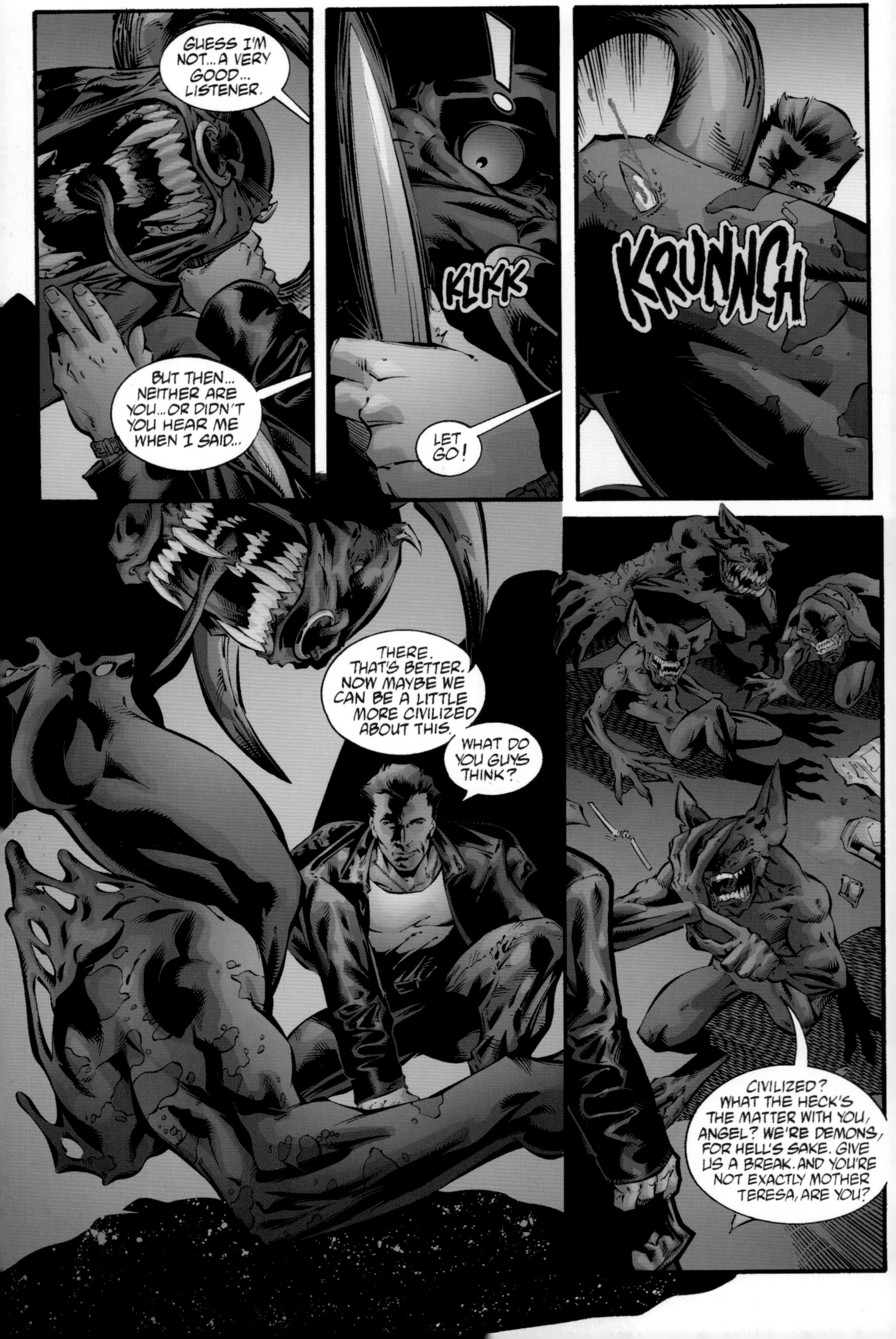
GUESS I'M NOT...A VERY GOOD... LISTENER.
BUT THEN... NEITHER ARE YOU...OR DIDN'T YOU HEAR ME WHEN I SAID...
KLIKK
LET GO!
KRUNNCH
THERE. THAT'S BETTER. NOW MAYBE WE CAN BE A LITTLE MORE CIVILIZED ABOUT THIS.
WHAT DO YOU GUYS THINK?
CIVILIZED? WHAT THE HECK'S THE MATTER WITH YOU, ANGEL? WE'RE DEMONS, FOR HELL'S SAKE. GIVE US A BREAK. AND YOU'RE NOT EXACTLY MOTHER TERESA, ARE YOU?

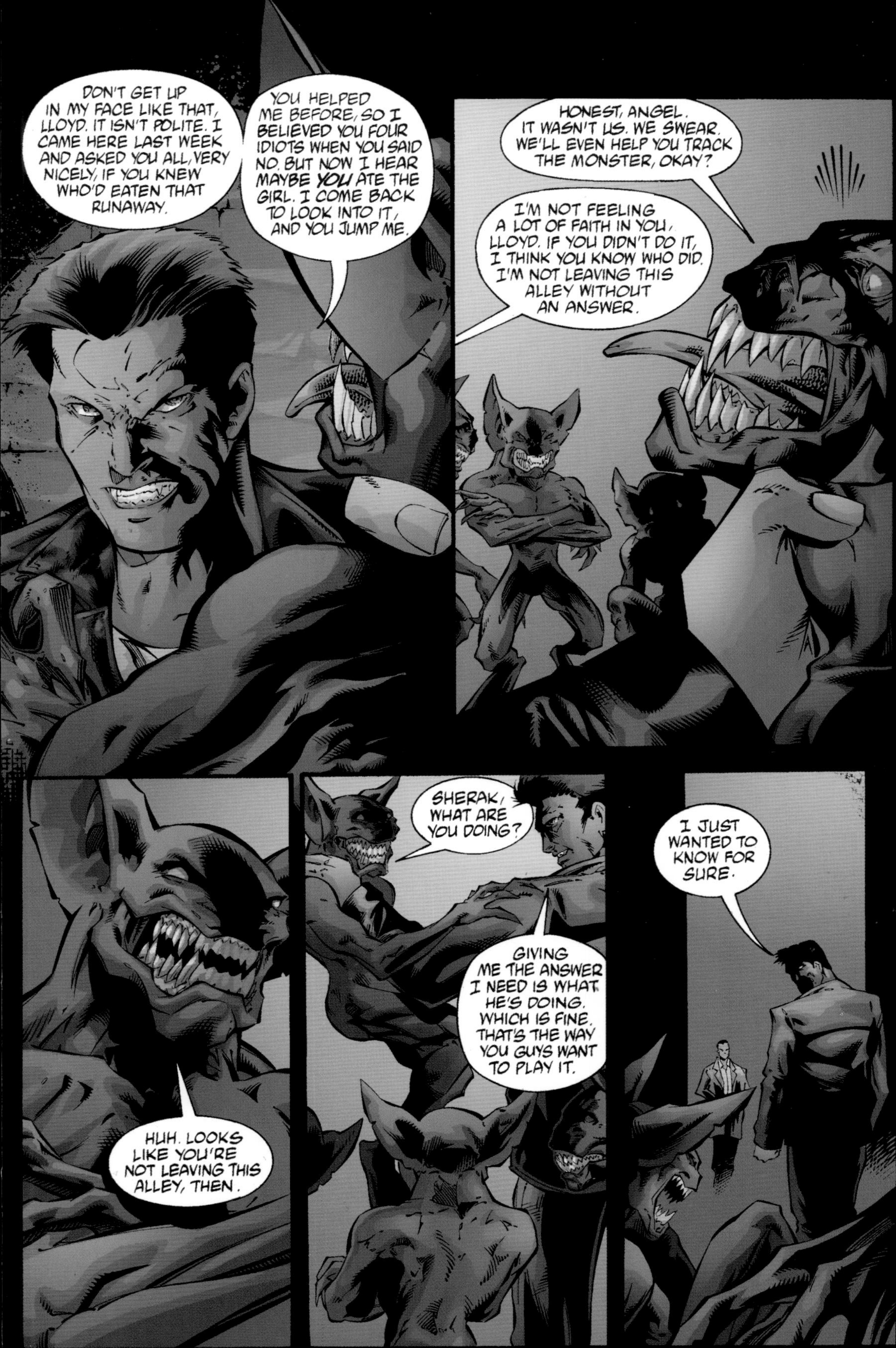
DON'T GET UP IN MY FACE LIKE THAT, LLOYD. IT ISN'T POLITE. I CAME HERE LAST WEEK AND ASKED YOU ALL, VERY NICELY, IF YOU KNEW WHO'D EATEN THAT RUNAWAY.
YOU HELPED ME BEFORE, SO I BELIEVED YOU FOUR IDIOTS WHEN YOU SAID NO. BUT NOW I HEAR MAYBE *YOU* ATE THE GIRL. I COME BACK TO LOOK INTO IT, AND YOU JUMP ME.
HONEST, ANGEL. IT WASN'T US. WE SWEAR. WE'LL EVEN HELP YOU TRACK THE MONSTER, OKAY?
I'M NOT FEELING A LOT OF FAITH IN YOU, LLOYD. IF YOU DIDN'T DO IT, I THINK YOU KNOW WHO DID. I'M NOT LEAVING THIS ALLEY WITHOUT AN ANSWER.
HUH. LOOKS LIKE YOU'RE NOT LEAVING THIS ALLEY, THEN.
SHERAK, WHAT ARE YOU DOING?
GIVING ME THE ANSWER I NEED IS WHAT HE'S DOING. WHICH IS FINE. THAT'S THE WAY YOU GUYS WANT TO PLAY IT.
I JUST WANTED TO KNOW FOR SURE.

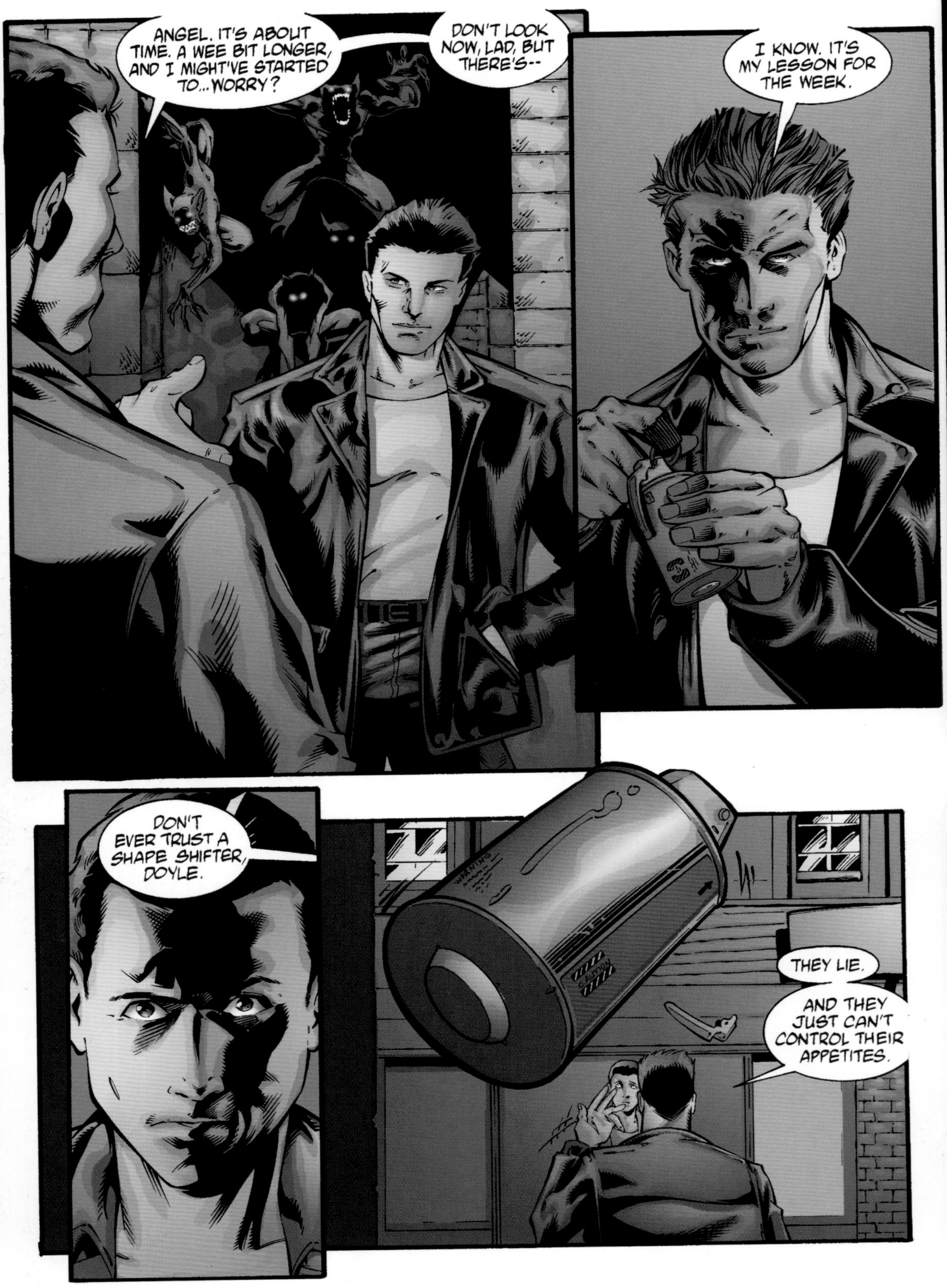

ANGEL. IT'S ABOUT TIME. A WEE BIT LONGER, AND I MIGHT'VE STARTED TO... WORRY?
DON'T LOOK NOW, LAD, BUT THERE'S--
I KNOW. IT'S MY LESSON FOR THE WEEK.
DON'T EVER TRUST A SHAPE SHIFTER, DOYLE.
THEY LIE.
AND THEY JUST CAN'T CONTROL THEIR APPETITES.

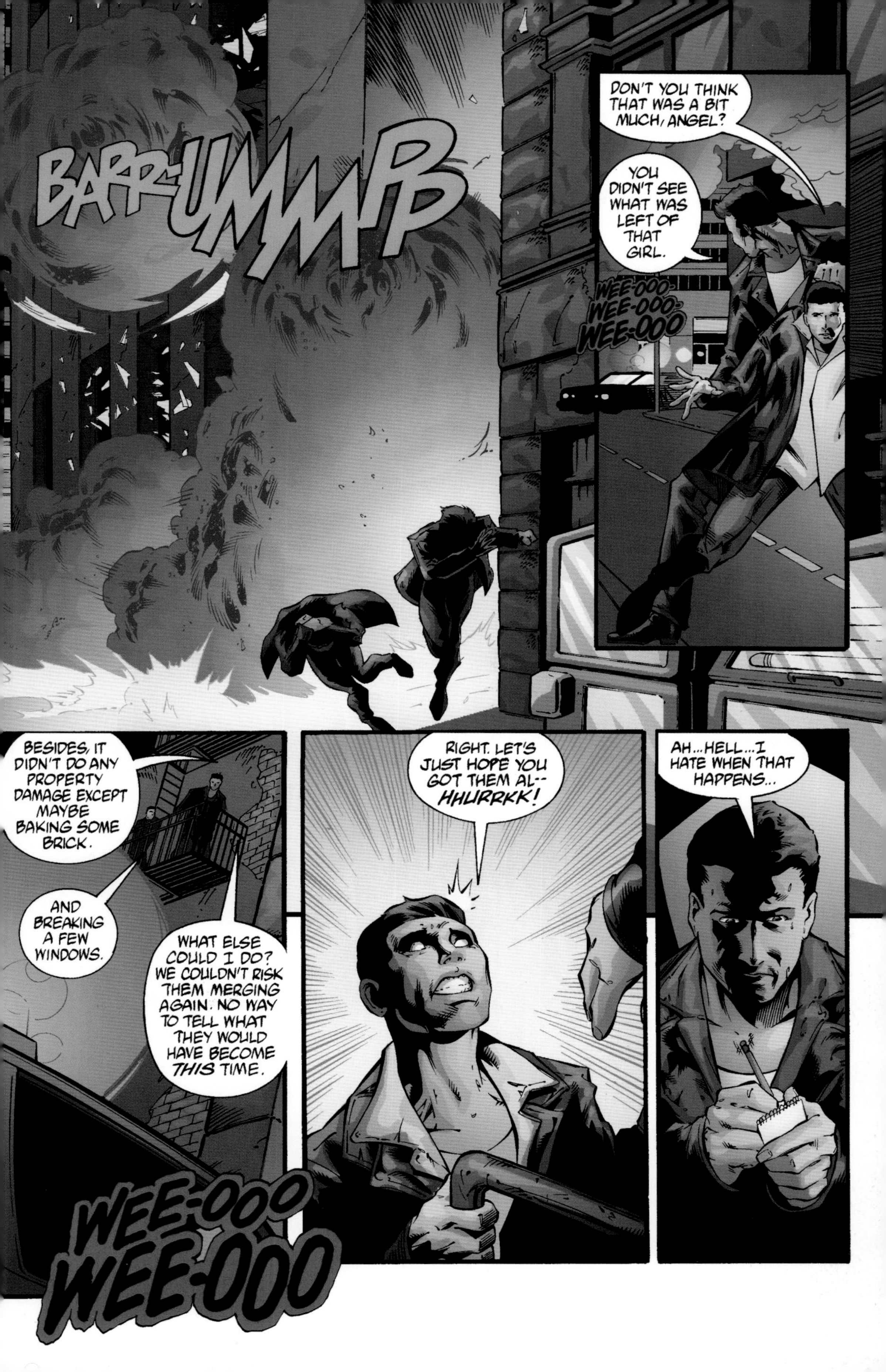
BARR-UMMPB
DON'T YOU THINK THAT WAS A BIT MUCH, ANGEL?
YOU DIDN'T SEE WHAT WAS LEFT OF THAT GIRL.
WEE-OOO-WEE-OOO-WEE-OOO
BESIDES, IT DIDN'T DO ANY PROPERTY DAMAGE EXCEPT MAYBE BAKING SOME BRICK.
AND BREAKING A FEW WINDOWS.
WHAT ELSE COULD I DO? WE COULDN'T RISK THEM MERGING AGAIN. NO WAY TO TELL WHAT THEY WOULD HAVE BECOME *THIS* TIME.
RIGHT. LET'S JUST HOPE YOU GOT THEM AL-- *HHURRKK!*
AH...HELL...I HATE WHEN THAT HAPPENS...
WEE-OOO WEE-OOO

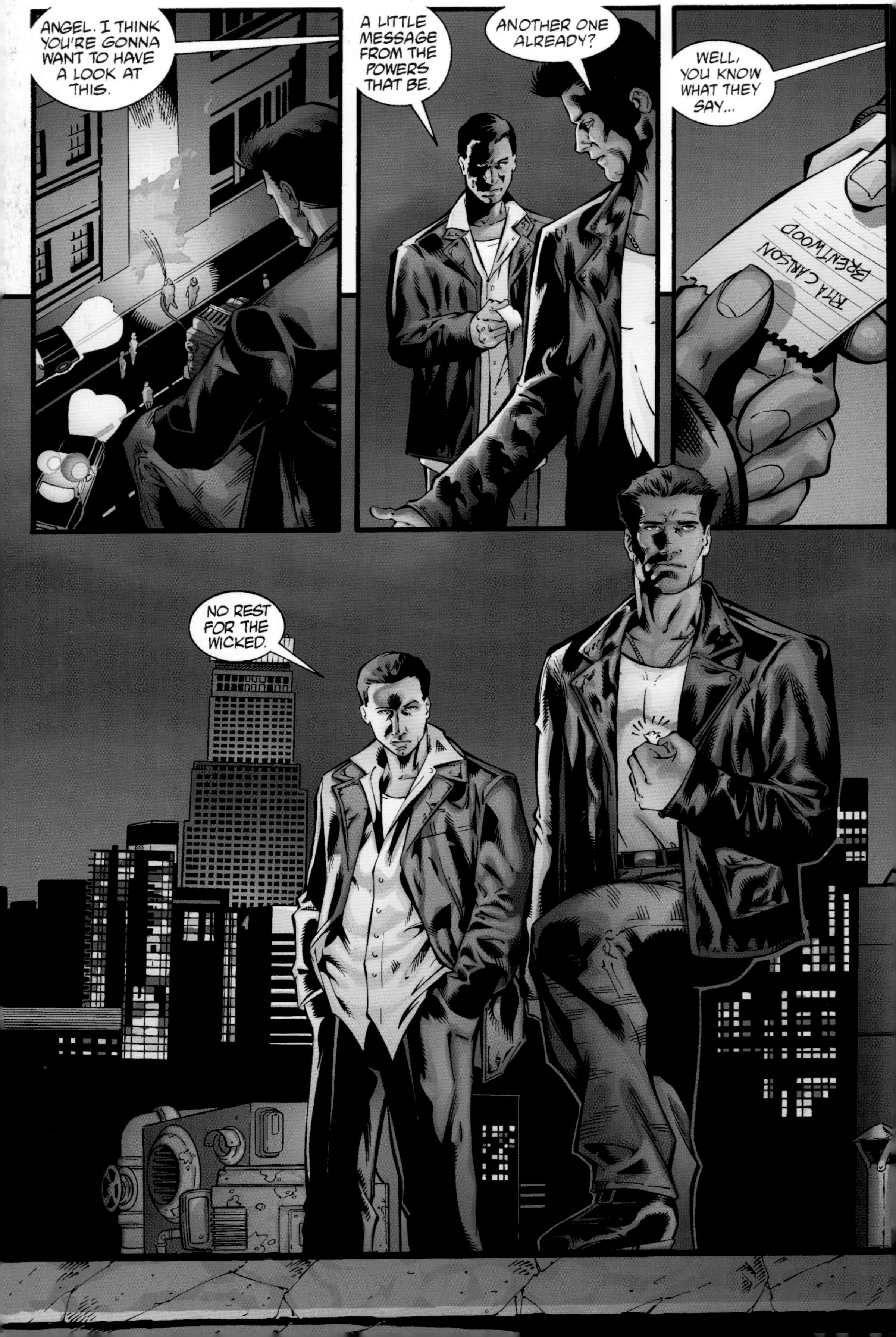
ANGEL. I THINK YOU'RE GONNA WANT TO HAVE A LOOK AT THIS.
A LITTLE MESSAGE FROM THE POWERS THAT BE.
ANOTHER ONE ALREADY?
WELL, YOU KNOW WHAT THEY SAY...
RITA CARLSON
BRENTWOOD
NO REST FOR THE WICKED.

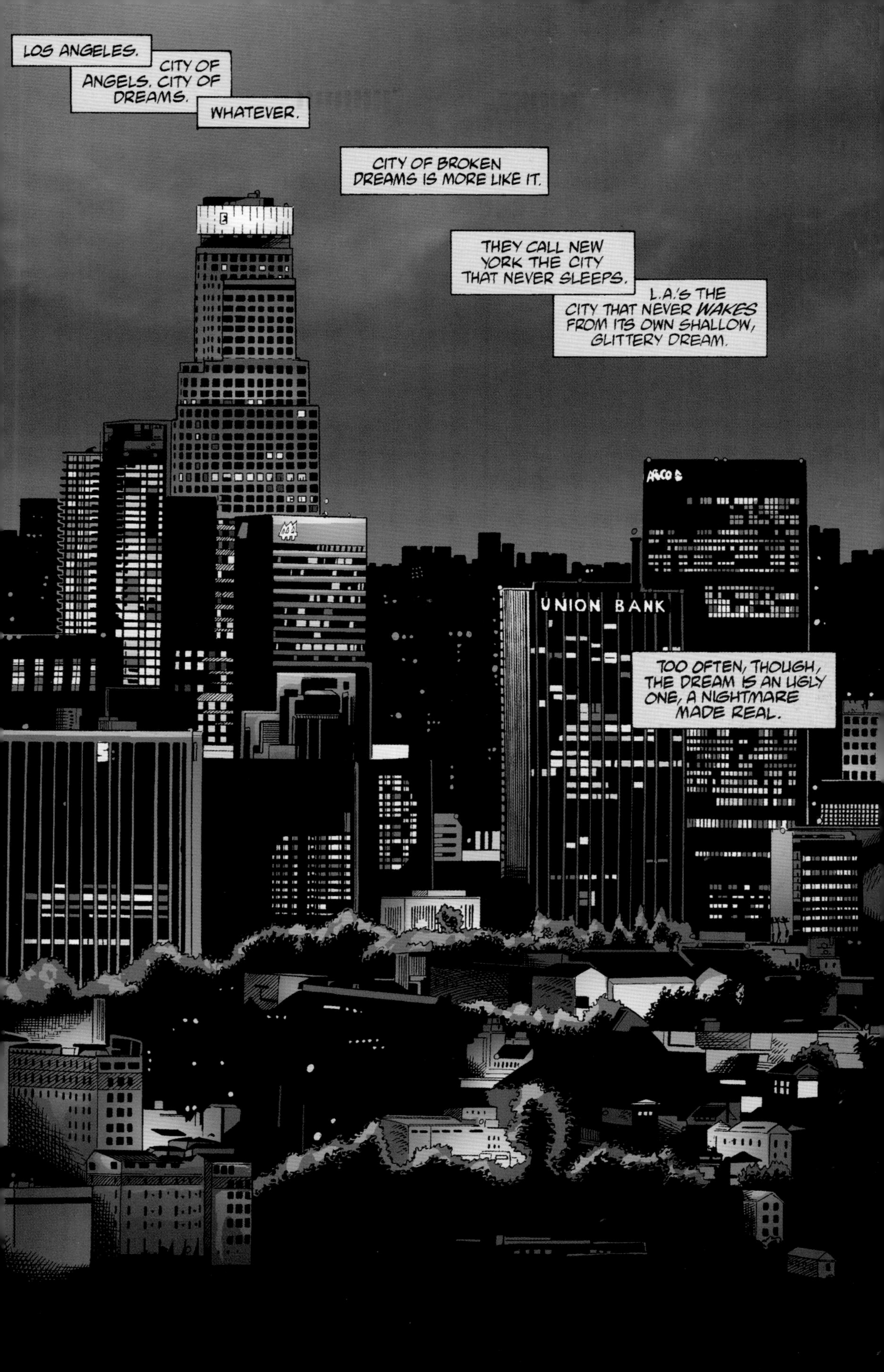
LOS ANGELES.
CITY OF ANGELS. CITY OF DREAMS.
WHATEVER.
CITY OF BROKEN DREAMS IS MORE LIKE IT.
THEY CALL NEW YORK THE CITY THAT NEVER SLEEPS.
L.A.'S THE CITY THAT NEVER WAKES FROM ITS OWN SHALLOW, GLITTERY DREAM.
UNION BANK
TOO OFTEN, THOUGH, THE DREAM IS AN UGLY ONE, A NIGHTMARE MADE REAL.

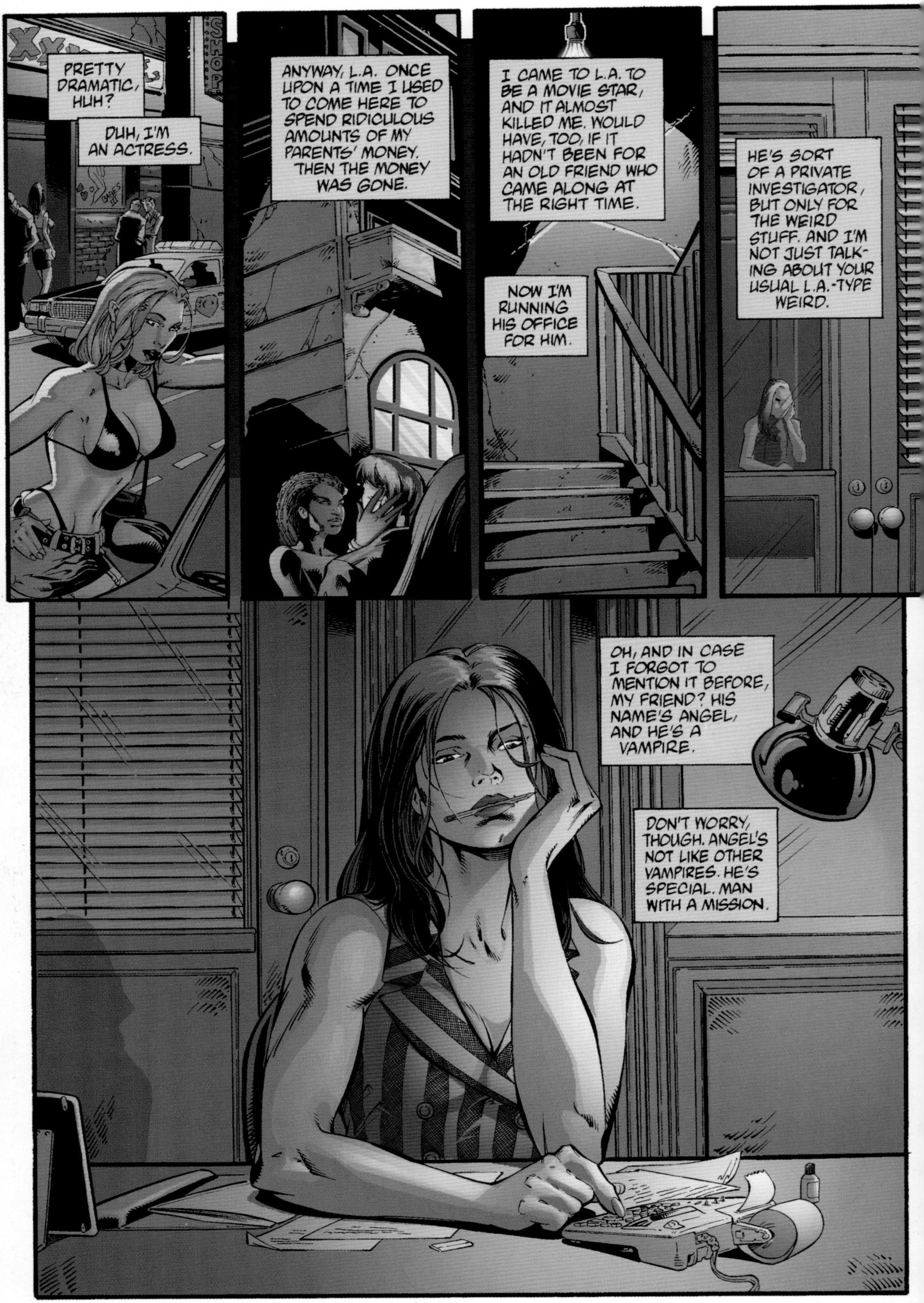
PRETTY DRAMATIC, HUH?
DUH, I'M AN ACTRESS.
ANYWAY, L.A. ONCE UPON A TIME I USED TO COME HERE TO SPEND RIDICULOUS AMOUNTS OF MY PARENTS' MONEY. THEN THE MONEY WAS GONE.
I CAME TO L.A. TO BE A MOVIE STAR, AND IT ALMOST KILLED ME. WOULD HAVE, TOO, IF IT HADN'T BEEN FOR AN OLD FRIEND WHO CAME ALONG AT THE RIGHT TIME.
NOW I'M RUNNING HIS OFFICE FOR HIM.
HE'S SORT OF A PRIVATE INVESTIGATOR, BUT ONLY FOR THE WEIRD STUFF. AND I'M NOT JUST TALKING ABOUT YOUR USUAL L.A.-TYPE WEIRD.
OH, AND IN CASE I FORGOT TO MENTION IT BEFORE, MY FRIEND? HIS NAME'S ANGEL, AND HE'S A VAMPIRE.
DON'T WORRY, THOUGH. ANGEL'S NOT LIKE OTHER VAMPIRES. HE'S SPECIAL. MAN WITH A MISSION.

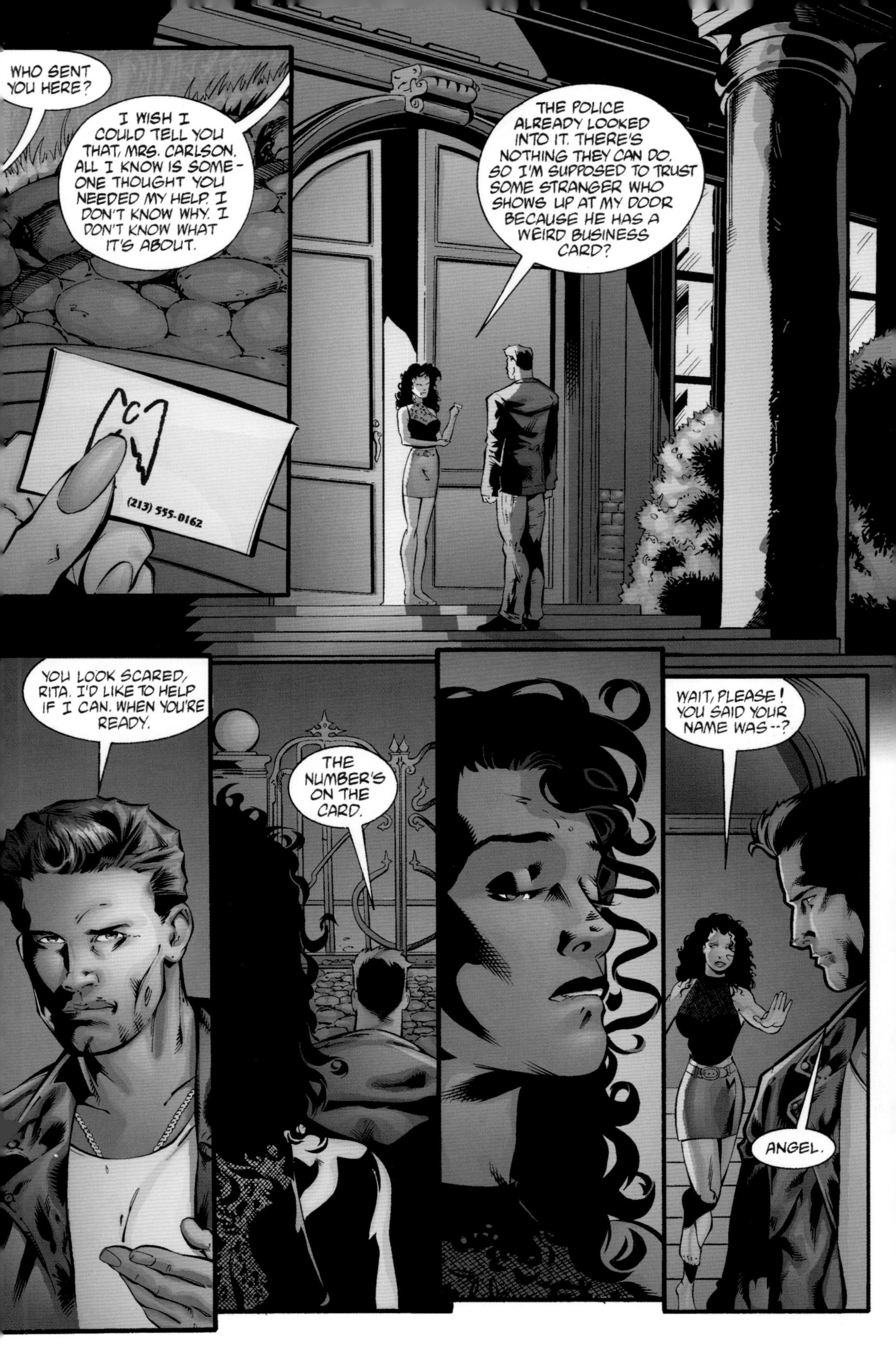
WHO SENT YOU HERE?
I WISH I COULD TELL YOU THAT, MRS. CARLSON. ALL I KNOW IS SOME-ONE THOUGHT YOU NEEDED MY HELP. I DON'T KNOW WHY. I DON'T KNOW WHAT IT'S ABOUT.
(213) 555-0162
THE POLICE ALREADY LOOKED INTO IT. THERE'S NOTHING THEY CAN DO. SO I'M SUPPOSED TO TRUST SOME STRANGER WHO SHOWS UP AT MY DOOR BECAUSE HE HAS A WEIRD BUSINESS CARD?
YOU LOOK SCARED, RITA. I'D LIKE TO HELP IF I CAN. WHEN YOU'RE READY.
THE NUMBER'S ON THE CARD.
WAIT, PLEASE! YOU SAID YOUR NAME WAS--?
ANGEL.

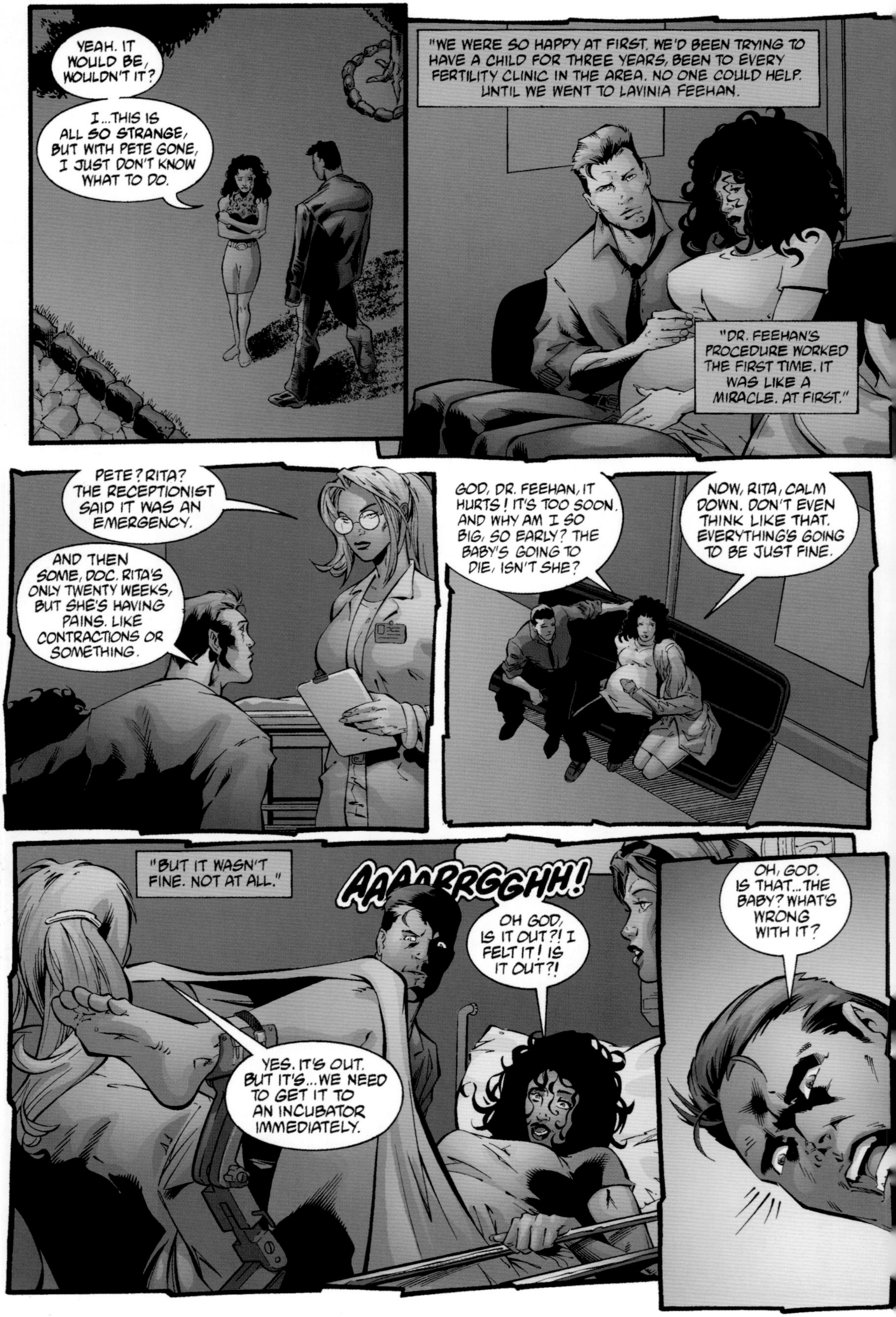
YEAH. IT WOULD BE, WOULDN'T IT?
I...THIS IS ALL SO STRANGE, BUT WITH PETE GONE, I JUST DON'T KNOW WHAT TO DO.
"WE WERE SO HAPPY AT FIRST. WE'D BEEN TRYING TO HAVE A CHILD FOR THREE YEARS, BEEN TO EVERY FERTILITY CLINIC IN THE AREA. NO ONE COULD HELP. UNTIL WE WENT TO LAVINIA FEEHAN.
"DR. FEEHAN'S PROCEDURE WORKED THE FIRST TIME. IT WAS LIKE A MIRACLE. AT FIRST."
PETE? RITA? THE RECEPTIONIST SAID IT WAS AN EMERGENCY.
AND THEN SOME, DOC. RITA'S ONLY TWENTY WEEKS, BUT SHE'S HAVING PAINS. LIKE CONTRACTIONS OR SOMETHING.
GOD, DR. FEEHAN, IT HURTS! IT'S TOO SOON. AND WHY AM I SO BIG, SO EARLY? THE BABY'S GOING TO DIE, ISN'T SHE?
NOW, RITA, CALM DOWN. DON'T EVEN THINK LIKE THAT. EVERYTHING'S GOING TO BE JUST FINE.
"BUT IT WASN'T FINE. NOT AT ALL."
AAAARRGGHH!
OH GOD, IS IT OUT?! I FELT IT! IS IT OUT?!
YES. IT'S OUT. BUT IT'S...WE NEED TO GET IT TO AN INCUBATOR IMMEDIATELY.
OH, GOD. IS THAT...THE BABY? WHAT'S WRONG WITH IT?

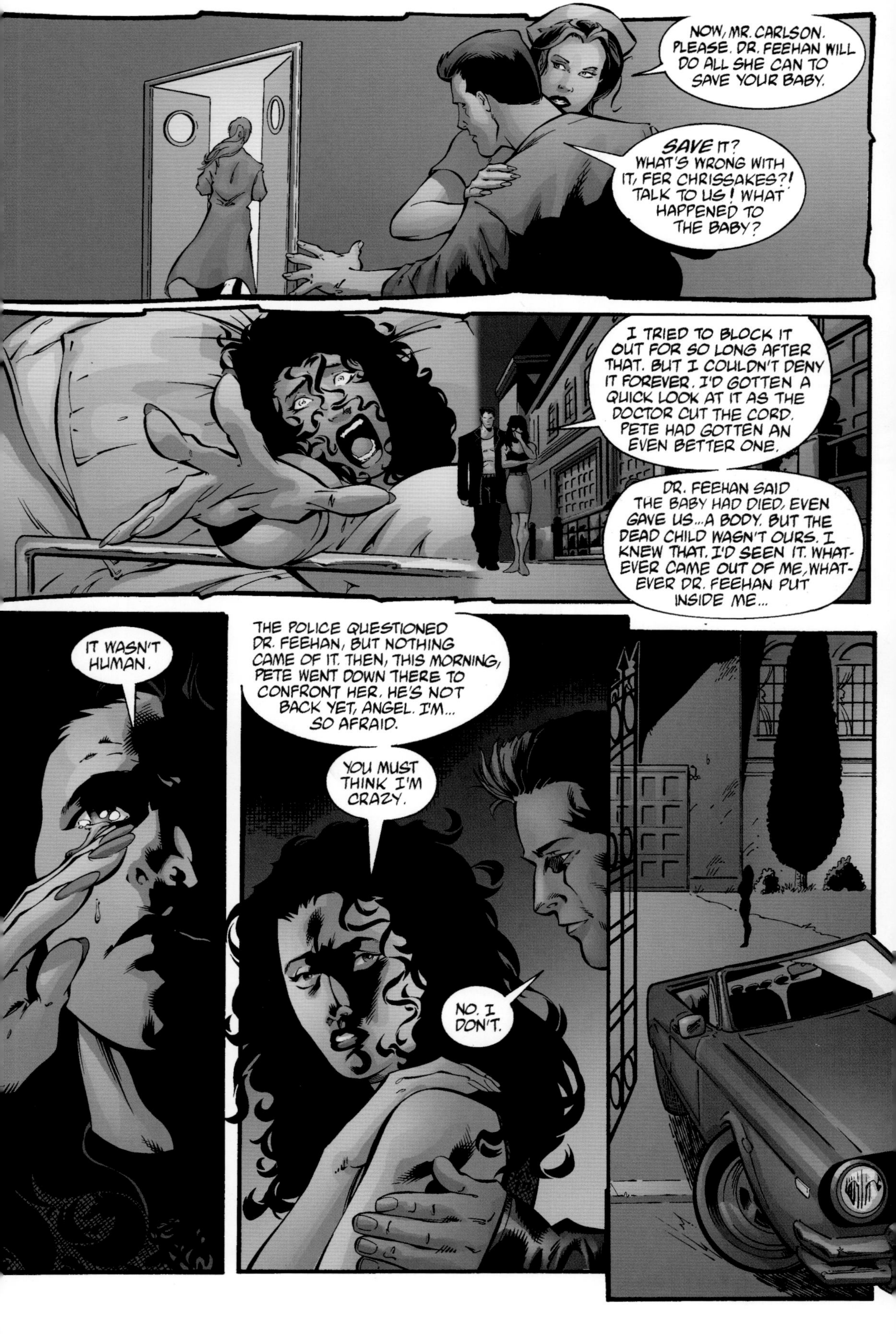

NOW, MR. CARLSON. PLEASE. DR. FEEHAN WILL DO ALL SHE CAN TO SAVE YOUR BABY.
SAVE IT? WHAT'S WRONG WITH IT, FER CHRISSAKES?! TALK TO US! WHAT HAPPENED TO THE BABY?
I TRIED TO BLOCK IT OUT FOR SO LONG AFTER THAT. BUT I COULDN'T DENY IT FOREVER. I'D GOTTEN A QUICK LOOK AT IT AS THE DOCTOR CUT THE CORD. PETE HAD GOTTEN AN EVEN BETTER ONE.
DR. FEEHAN SAID THE BABY HAD DIED, EVEN GAVE US...A BODY. BUT THE DEAD CHILD WASN'T OURS. I KNEW THAT. I'D SEEN IT. WHATEVER CAME OUT OF ME, WHATEVER DR. FEEHAN PUT INSIDE ME...
IT WASN'T HUMAN.
THE POLICE QUESTIONED DR. FEEHAN, BUT NOTHING CAME OF IT. THEN, THIS MORNING, PETE WENT DOWN THERE TO CONFRONT HER. HE'S NOT BACK YET, ANGEL. I'M... SO AFRAID.
YOU MUST THINK I'M CRAZY.
NO. I DON'T.

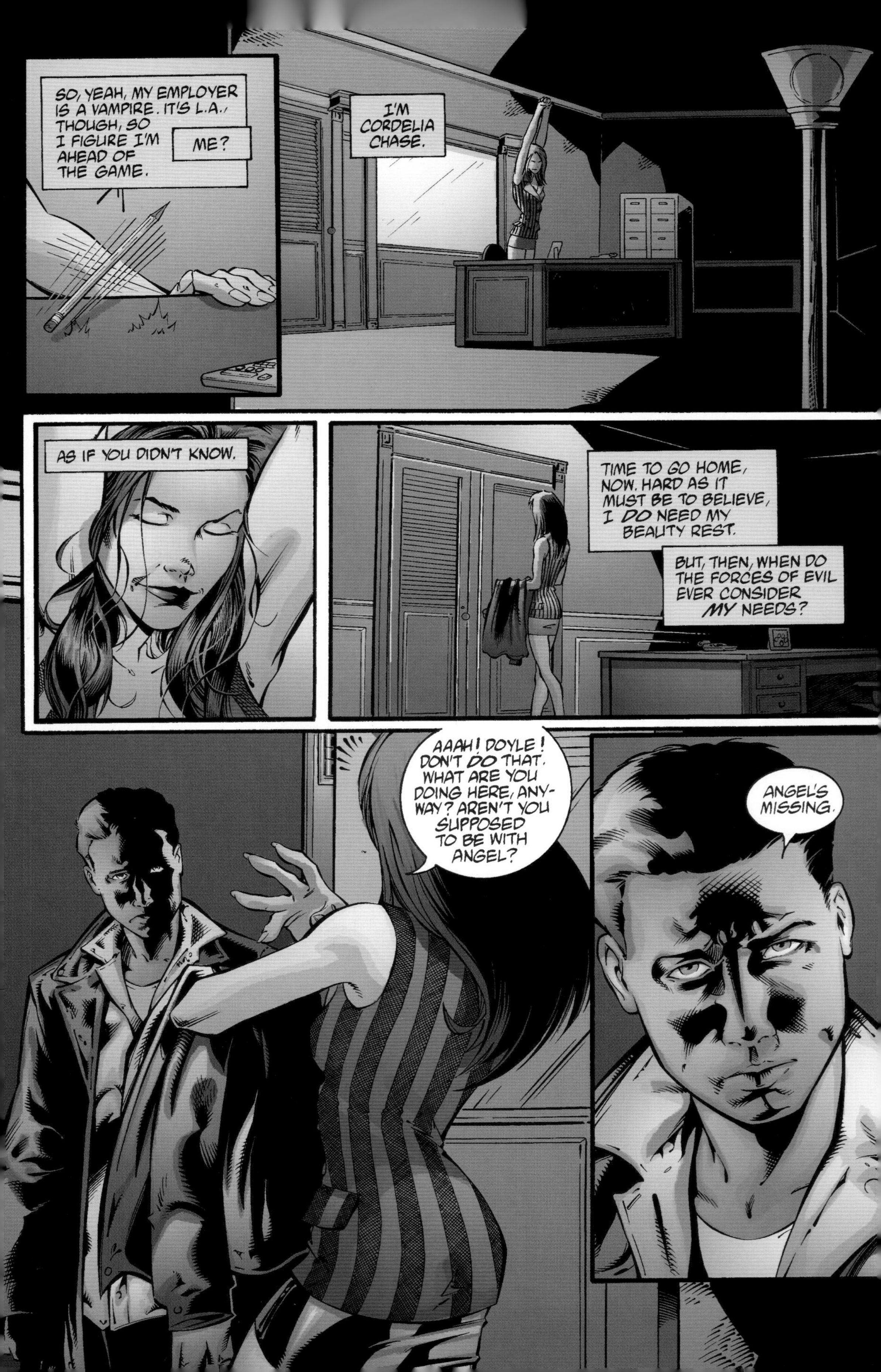
SO, YEAH, MY EMPLOYER IS A VAMPIRE. IT'S L.A., THOUGH, SO I FIGURE I'M AHEAD OF THE GAME.
ME?
I'M CORDELIA CHASE.
AS IF YOU DIDN'T KNOW.
TIME TO GO HOME, NOW. HARD AS IT MUST BE TO BELIEVE, I DO NEED MY BEAUTY REST.
BUT, THEN, WHEN DO THE FORCES OF EVIL EVER CONSIDER MY NEEDS?
AAAH! DOYLE! DON'T DO THAT. WHAT ARE YOU DOING HERE, ANY-WAY? AREN'T YOU SUPPOSED TO BE WITH ANGEL?
ANGEL'S MISSING.

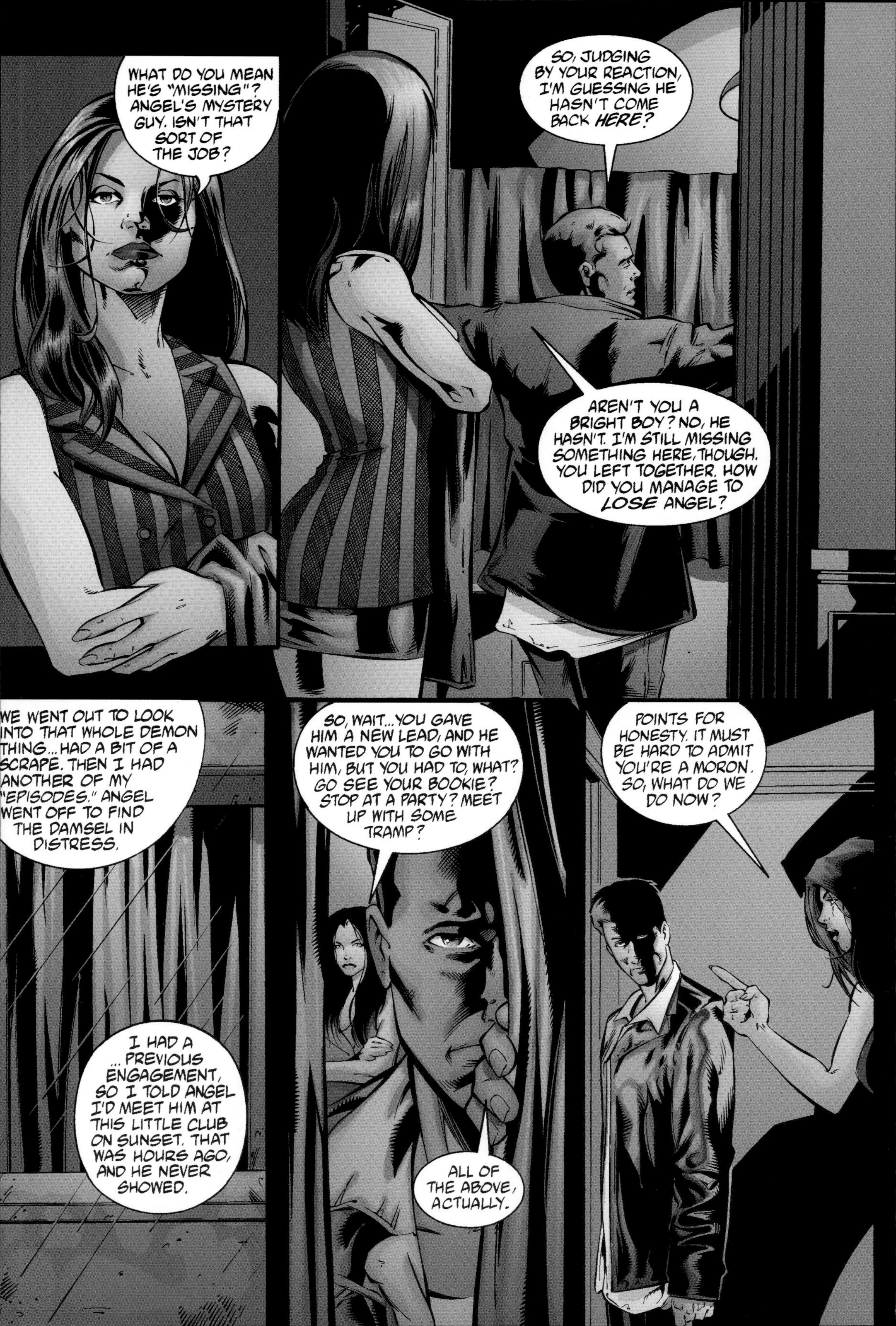
WHAT DO YOU MEAN HE'S "MISSING"? ANGEL'S MYSTERY GUY. ISN'T THAT SORT OF THE JOB?
SO, JUDGING BY YOUR REACTION, I'M GUESSING HE HASN'T COME BACK HERE?
AREN'T YOU A BRIGHT BOY? NO, HE HASN'T. I'M STILL MISSING SOMETHING HERE, THOUGH. YOU LEFT TOGETHER. HOW DID YOU MANAGE TO LOSE ANGEL?
WE WENT OUT TO LOOK INTO THAT WHOLE DEMON THING... HAD A BIT OF A SCRAPE. THEN I HAD ANOTHER OF MY "EPISODES." ANGEL WENT OFF TO FIND THE DAMSEL IN DISTRESS.
I HAD A ... PREVIOUS ENGAGEMENT, SO I TOLD ANGEL I'D MEET HIM AT THIS LITTLE CLUB ON SUNSET. THAT WAS HOURS AGO, AND HE NEVER SHOWED.
SO, WAIT... YOU GAVE HIM A NEW LEAD, AND HE WANTED YOU TO GO WITH HIM, BUT YOU HAD TO, WHAT? GO SEE YOUR BOOKIE? STOP AT A PARTY? MEET UP WITH SOME TRAMP?
ALL OF THE ABOVE, ACTUALLY.
POINTS FOR HONESTY. IT MUST BE HARD TO ADMIT YOU'RE A MORON. SO, WHAT DO WE DO NOW?

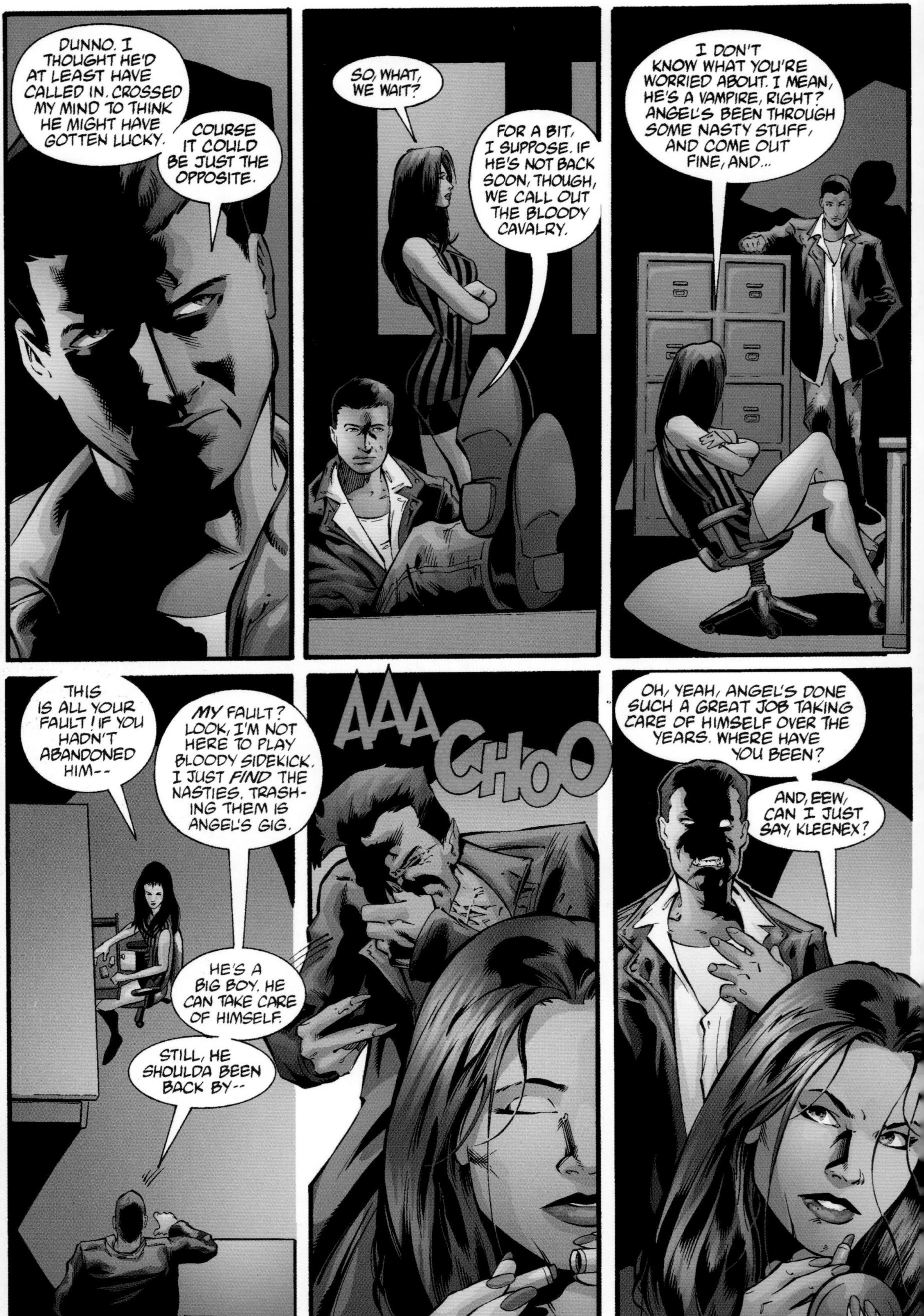
DUNNO. I THOUGHT HE'D AT LEAST HAVE CALLED IN. CROSSED MY MIND TO THINK HE MIGHT HAVE GOTTEN LUCKY.
COURSE IT COULD BE JUST THE OPPOSITE.
SO, WHAT, WE WAIT?
FOR A BIT, I SUPPOSE. IF HE'S NOT BACK SOON, THOUGH, WE CALL OUT THE BLOODY CAVALRY.
I DON'T KNOW WHAT YOU'RE WORRIED ABOUT. I MEAN, HE'S A VAMPIRE, RIGHT? ANGEL'S BEEN THROUGH SOME NASTY STUFF, AND COME OUT FINE, AND...
THIS IS ALL YOUR FAULT! IF YOU HADN'T ABANDONED HIM--
MY FAULT? LOOK, I'M NOT HERE TO PLAY BLOODY SIDEKICK. I JUST FIND THE NASTIES. TRASHING THEM IS ANGEL'S GIG.
HE'S A BIG BOY. HE CAN TAKE CARE OF HIMSELF.
STILL, HE SHOULDA BEEN BACK BY--
AAACHOO
OH, YEAH, ANGEL'S DONE SUCH A GREAT JOB TAKING CARE OF HIMSELF OVER THE YEARS. WHERE HAVE YOU BEEN?
AND, EEW, CAN I JUST SAY, KLEENEX?

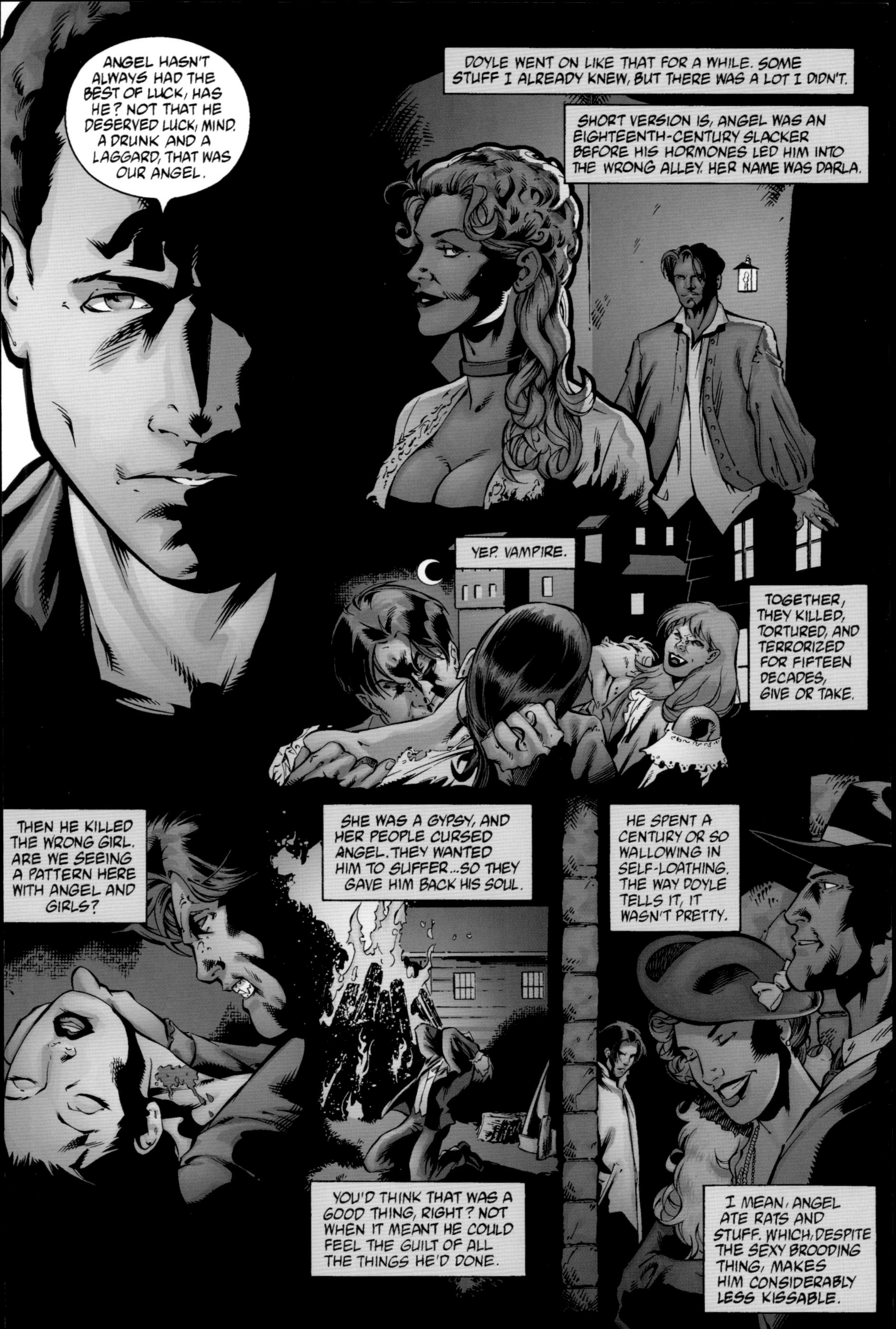

ANGEL HASN'T ALWAYS HAD THE BEST OF LUCK, HAS HE? NOT THAT HE DESERVED LUCK, MIND. A DRUNK AND A LAGGARD, THAT WAS OUR ANGEL.
DOYLE WENT ON LIKE THAT FOR A WHILE. SOME STUFF I ALREADY KNEW, BUT THERE WAS A LOT I DIDN'T.
SHORT VERSION IS, ANGEL WAS AN EIGHTEENTH-CENTURY SLACKER BEFORE HIS HORMONES LED HIM INTO THE WRONG ALLEY. HER NAME WAS DARLA.
YEP. VAMPIRE.
TOGETHER, THEY KILLED, TORTURED, AND TERRORIZED FOR FIFTEEN DECADES, GIVE OR TAKE.
THEN HE KILLED THE WRONG GIRL. ARE WE SEEING A PATTERN HERE WITH ANGEL AND GIRLS?
SHE WAS A GYPSY, AND HER PEOPLE CURSED ANGEL. THEY WANTED HIM TO SUFFER...SO THEY GAVE HIM BACK HIS SOUL.
YOU'D THINK THAT WAS A GOOD THING, RIGHT? NOT WHEN IT MEANT HE COULD FEEL THE GUILT OF ALL THE THINGS HE'D DONE.
HE SPENT A CENTURY OR SO WALLOWING IN SELF-LOATHING. THE WAY DOYLE TELLS IT, IT WASN'T PRETTY.
I MEAN, ANGEL ATE RATS AND STUFF. WHICH, DESPITE THE SEXY BROODING THING, MAKES HIM CONSIDERABLY LESS KISSABLE.

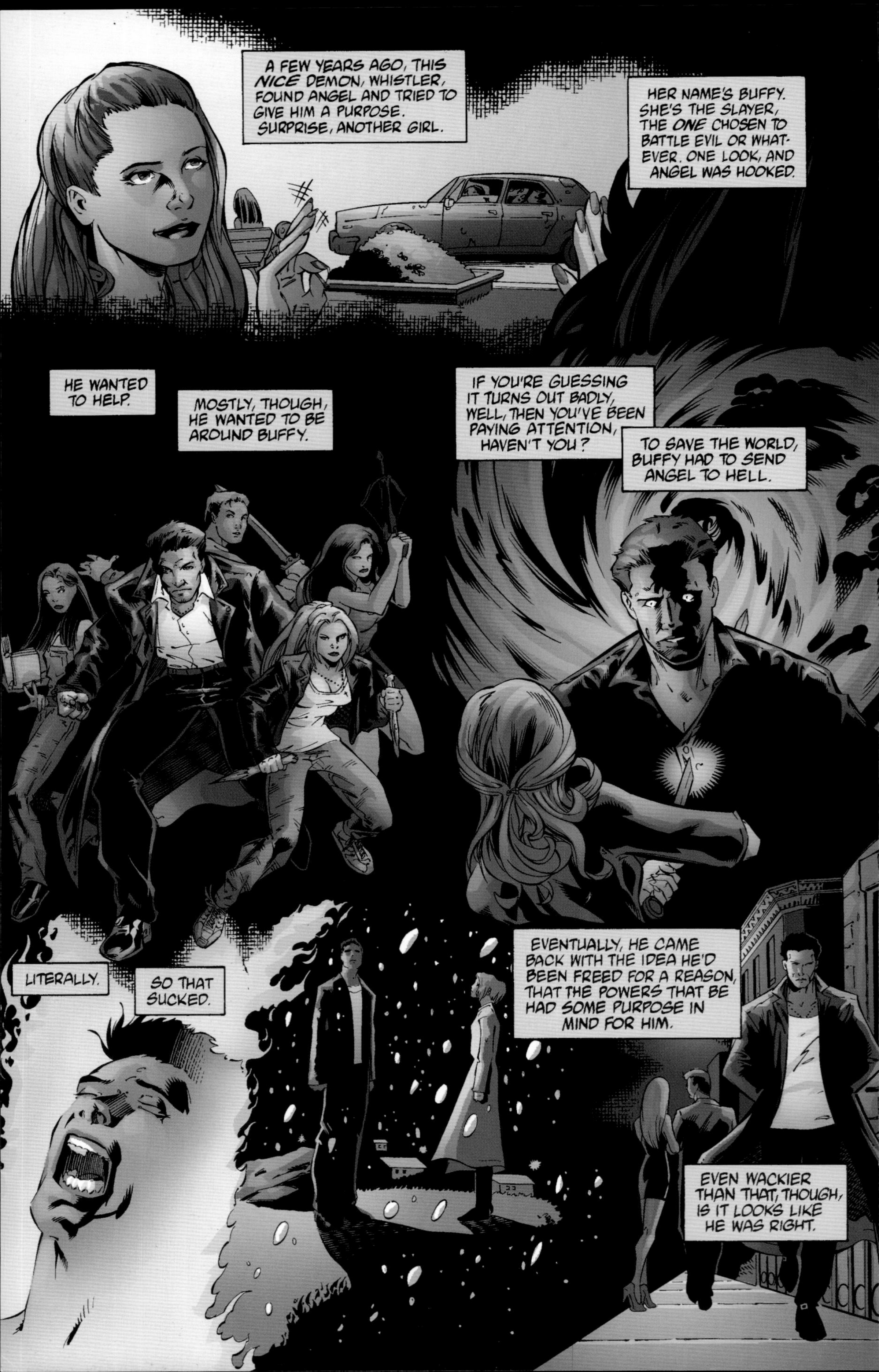
A FEW YEARS AGO, THIS NICE DEMON, WHISTLER, FOUND ANGEL AND TRIED TO GIVE HIM A PURPOSE. SURPRISE, ANOTHER GIRL.
HER NAME'S BUFFY. SHE'S THE SLAYER, THE ONE CHOSEN TO BATTLE EVIL OR WHAT-EVER. ONE LOOK, AND ANGEL WAS HOOKED.
HE WANTED TO HELP.
MOSTLY, THOUGH, HE WANTED TO BE AROUND BUFFY.
IF YOU'RE GUESSING IT TURNS OUT BADLY, WELL, THEN YOU'VE BEEN PAYING ATTENTION, HAVEN'T YOU?
TO SAVE THE WORLD, BUFFY HAD TO SEND ANGEL TO HELL.
LITERALLY.
SO THAT SUCKED.
EVENTUALLY, HE CAME BACK WITH THE IDEA HE'D BEEN FREED FOR A REASON, THAT THE POWERS THAT BE HAD SOME PURPOSE IN MIND FOR HIM.
EVEN WACKIER THAN THAT, THOUGH, IS IT LOOKS LIKE HE WAS RIGHT.

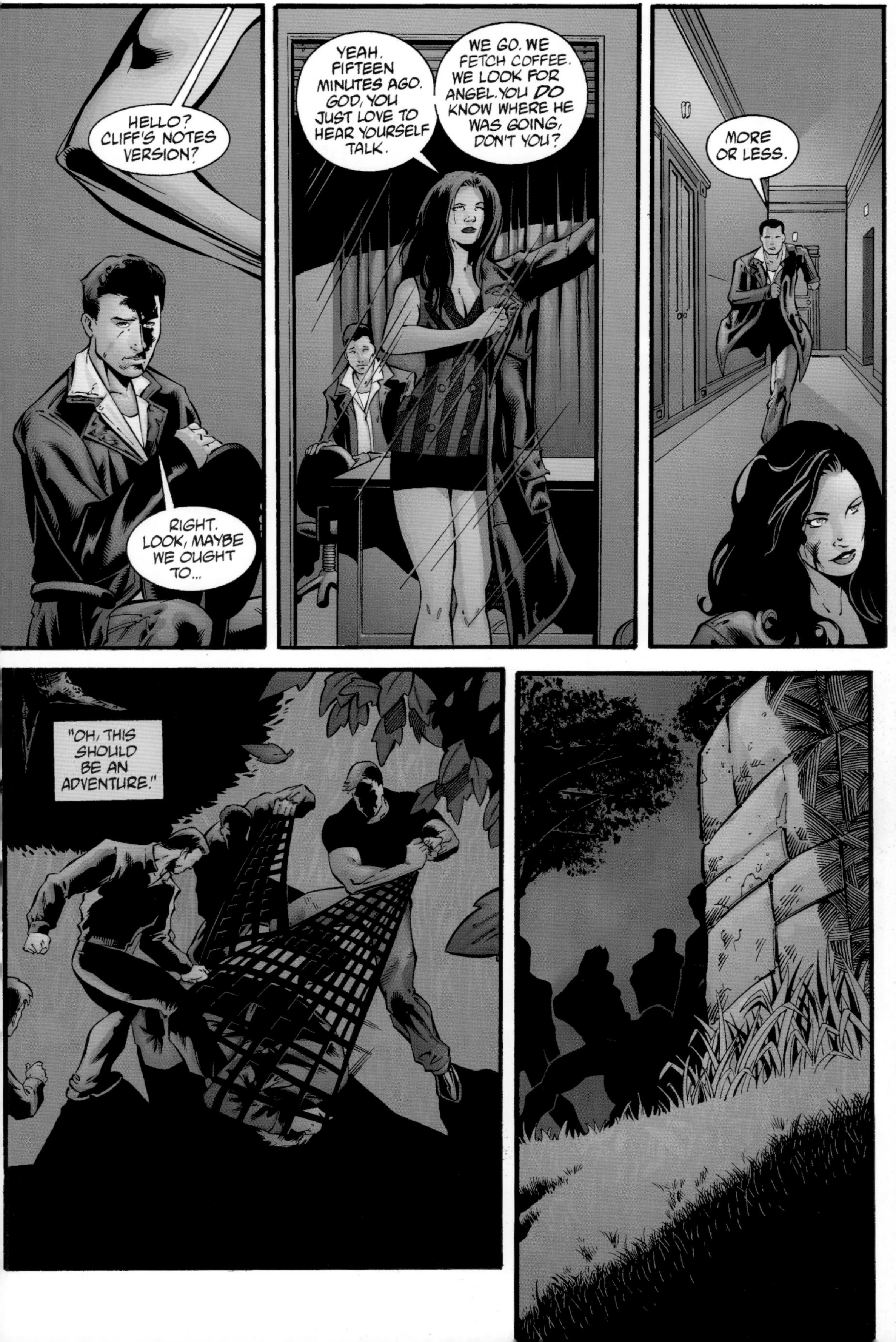
HELLO? CLIFF'S NOTES VERSION?
RIGHT. LOOK, MAYBE WE OUGHT TO...
YEAH. FIFTEEN MINUTES AGO. GOD, YOU JUST LOVE TO HEAR YOURSELF TALK.
WE GO. WE FETCH COFFEE. WE LOOK FOR ANGEL. YOU DO KNOW WHERE HE WAS GOING, DON'T YOU?
MORE OR LESS.
"OH, THIS SHOULD BE AN ADVENTURE."

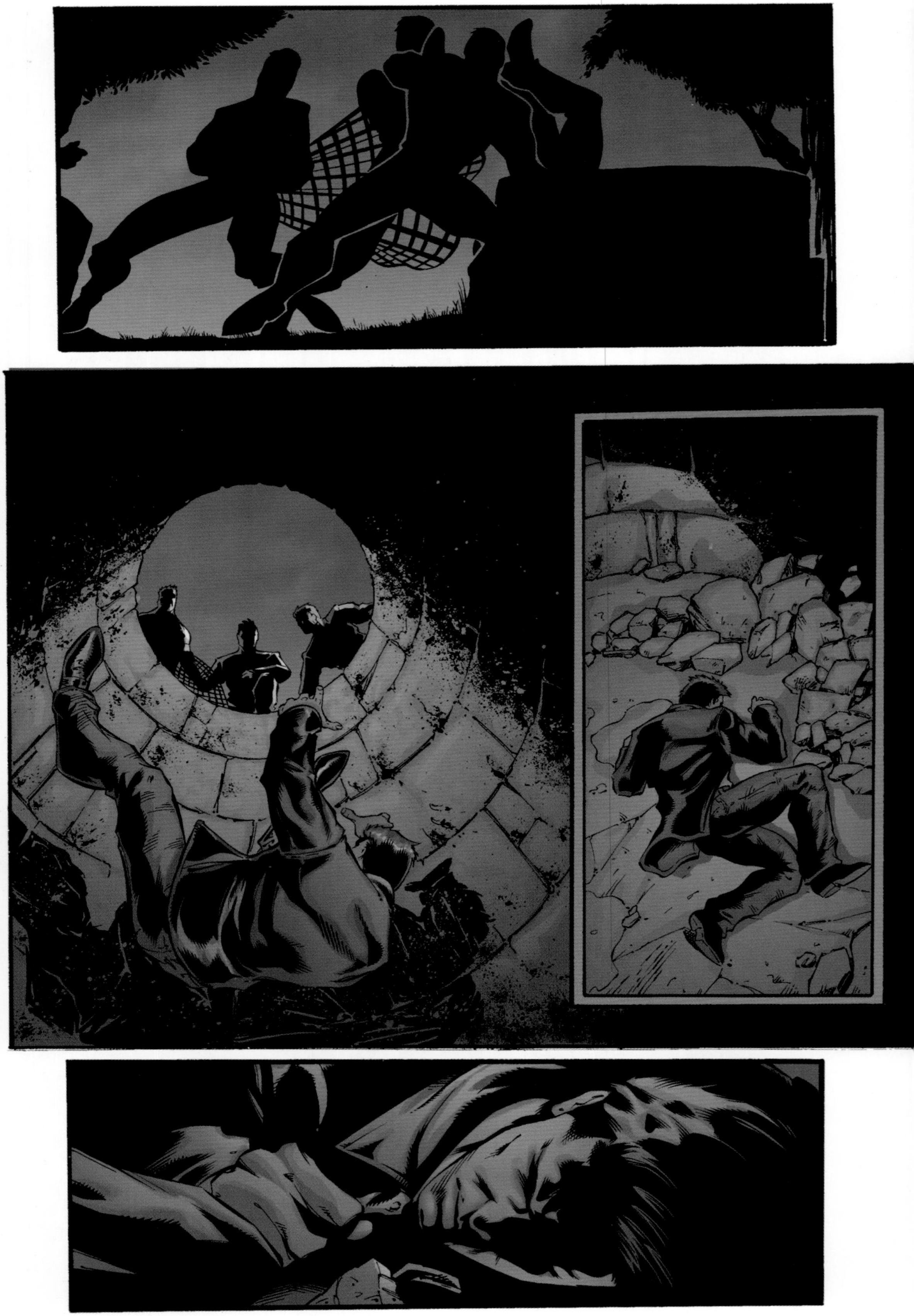

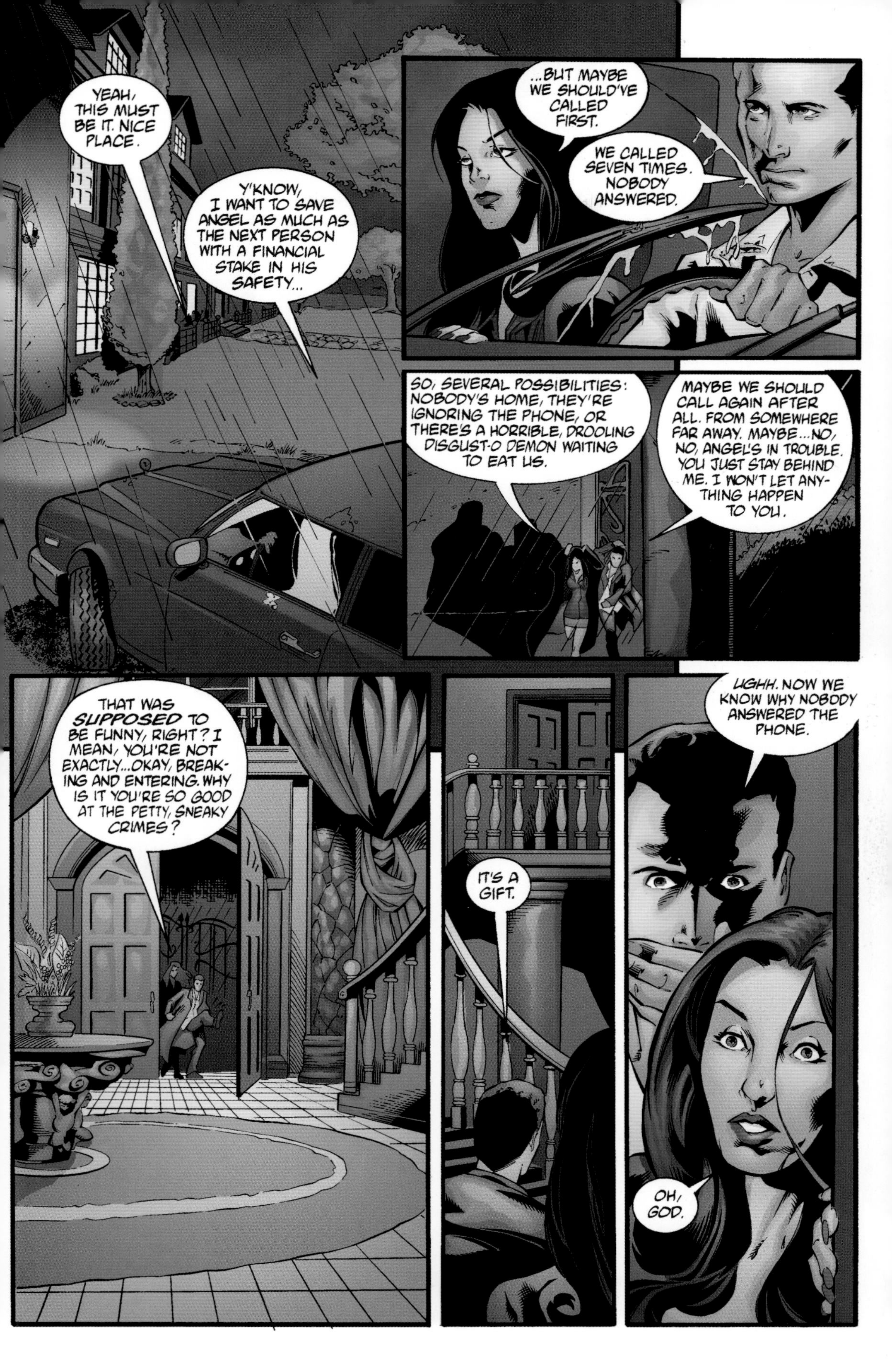
YEAH, THIS MUST BE IT. NICE PLACE.
Y'KNOW, I WANT TO SAVE ANGEL AS MUCH AS THE NEXT PERSON WITH A FINANCIAL STAKE IN HIS SAFETY...
...BUT MAYBE WE SHOULD'VE CALLED FIRST.
WE CALLED SEVEN TIMES. NOBODY ANSWERED.
SO, SEVERAL POSSIBILITIES: NOBODY'S HOME, THEY'RE IGNORING THE PHONE, OR THERE'S A HORRIBLE, DROOLING DISGUST-O DEMON WAITING TO EAT US.
MAYBE WE SHOULD CALL AGAIN AFTER ALL. FROM SOMEWHERE FAR AWAY. MAYBE...NO, NO, ANGEL'S IN TROUBLE. YOU JUST STAY BEHIND ME. I WON'T LET ANYTHING HAPPEN TO YOU.
THAT WAS SUPPOSED TO BE FUNNY, RIGHT? I MEAN, YOU'RE NOT EXACTLY...OKAY, BREAKING AND ENTERING. WHY IS IT YOU'RE SO GOOD AT THE PETTY, SNEAKY CRIMES?
IT'S A GIFT.
UGHH. NOW WE KNOW WHY NOBODY ANSWERED THE PHONE.
OH, GOD.

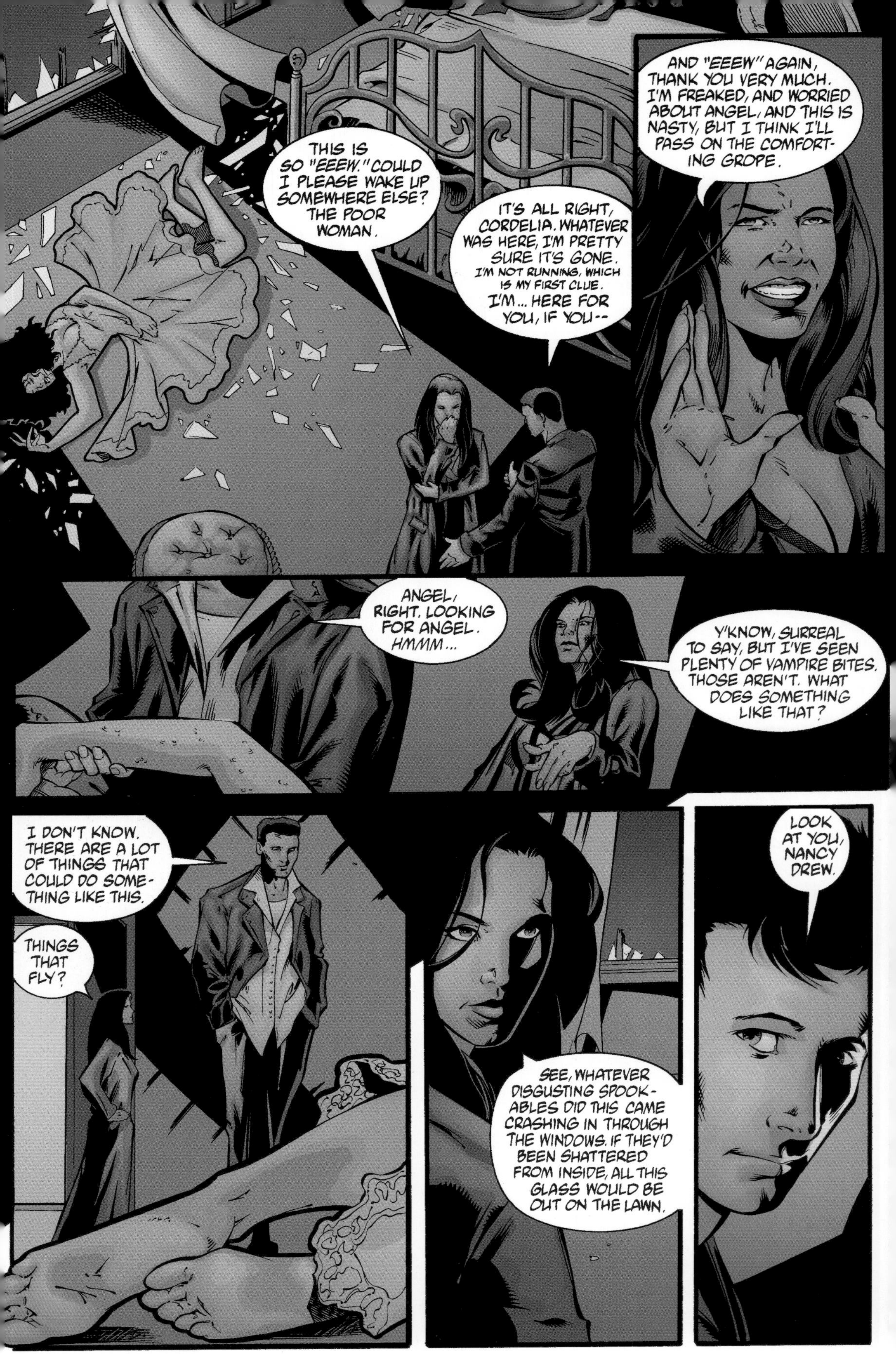
THIS IS SO "EEEW." COULD I PLEASE WAKE UP SOMEWHERE ELSE? THE POOR WOMAN.
IT'S ALL RIGHT, CORDELIA. WHATEVER WAS HERE, I'M PRETTY SURE IT'S GONE. I'M NOT RUNNING, WHICH IS MY FIRST CLUE. I'M... HERE FOR YOU, IF YOU--
AND "EEEW" AGAIN, THANK YOU VERY MUCH. I'M FREAKED, AND WORRIED ABOUT ANGEL, AND THIS IS NASTY, BUT I THINK I'LL PASS ON THE COMFORTING GROPE.
ANGEL, RIGHT. LOOKING FOR ANGEL. HMMM...
Y'KNOW, SURREAL TO SAY, BUT I'VE SEEN PLENTY OF VAMPIRE BITES. THOSE AREN'T. WHAT DOES SOMETHING LIKE THAT?
I DON'T KNOW. THERE ARE A LOT OF THINGS THAT COULD DO SOMETHING LIKE THIS.
THINGS THAT FLY?
SEE, WHATEVER DISGUSTING SPOOKABLES DID THIS CAME CRASHING IN THROUGH THE WINDOWS. IF THEY'D BEEN SHATTERED FROM INSIDE, ALL THIS GLASS WOULD BE OUT ON THE LAWN.
LOOK AT YOU, NANCY DREW.

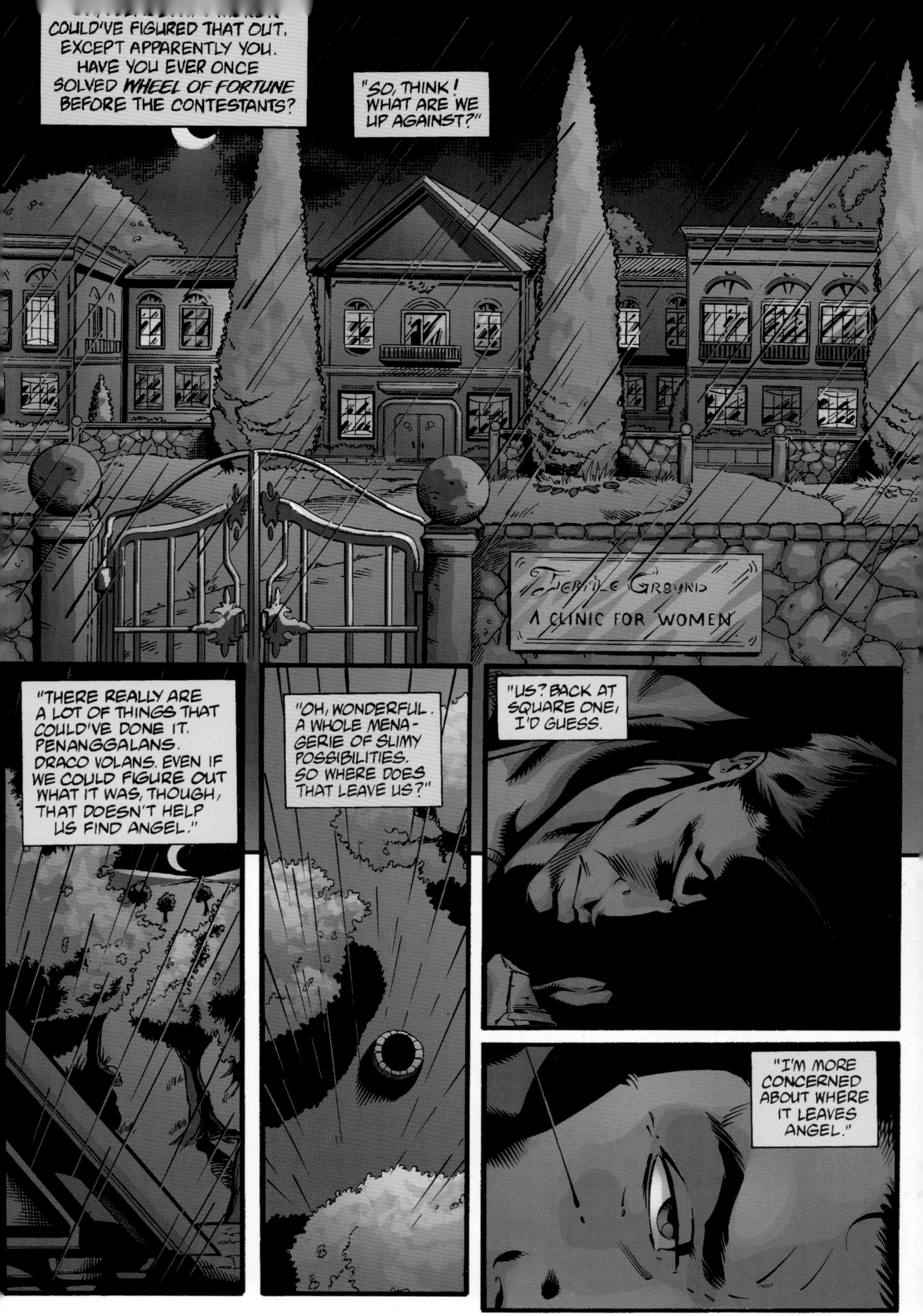
COULD'VE FIGURED THAT OUT. EXCEPT APPARENTLY YOU. HAVE YOU EVER ONCE SOLVED WHEEL OF FORTUNE BEFORE THE CONTESTANTS?
"SO, THINK! WHAT ARE WE UP AGAINST?"
FERTILE GROUND
A CLINIC FOR WOMEN
"THERE REALLY ARE A LOT OF THINGS THAT COULD'VE DONE IT. PENANGGALANS. DRACO VOLANS. EVEN IF WE COULD FIGURE OUT WHAT IT WAS, THOUGH, THAT DOESN'T HELP US FIND ANGEL."
"OH, WONDERFUL. A WHOLE MENAGERIE OF SLIMY POSSIBILITIES. SO WHERE DOES THAT LEAVE US?"
"US? BACK AT SQUARE ONE, I'D GUESS.
"I'M MORE CONCERNED ABOUT WHERE IT LEAVES ANGEL."

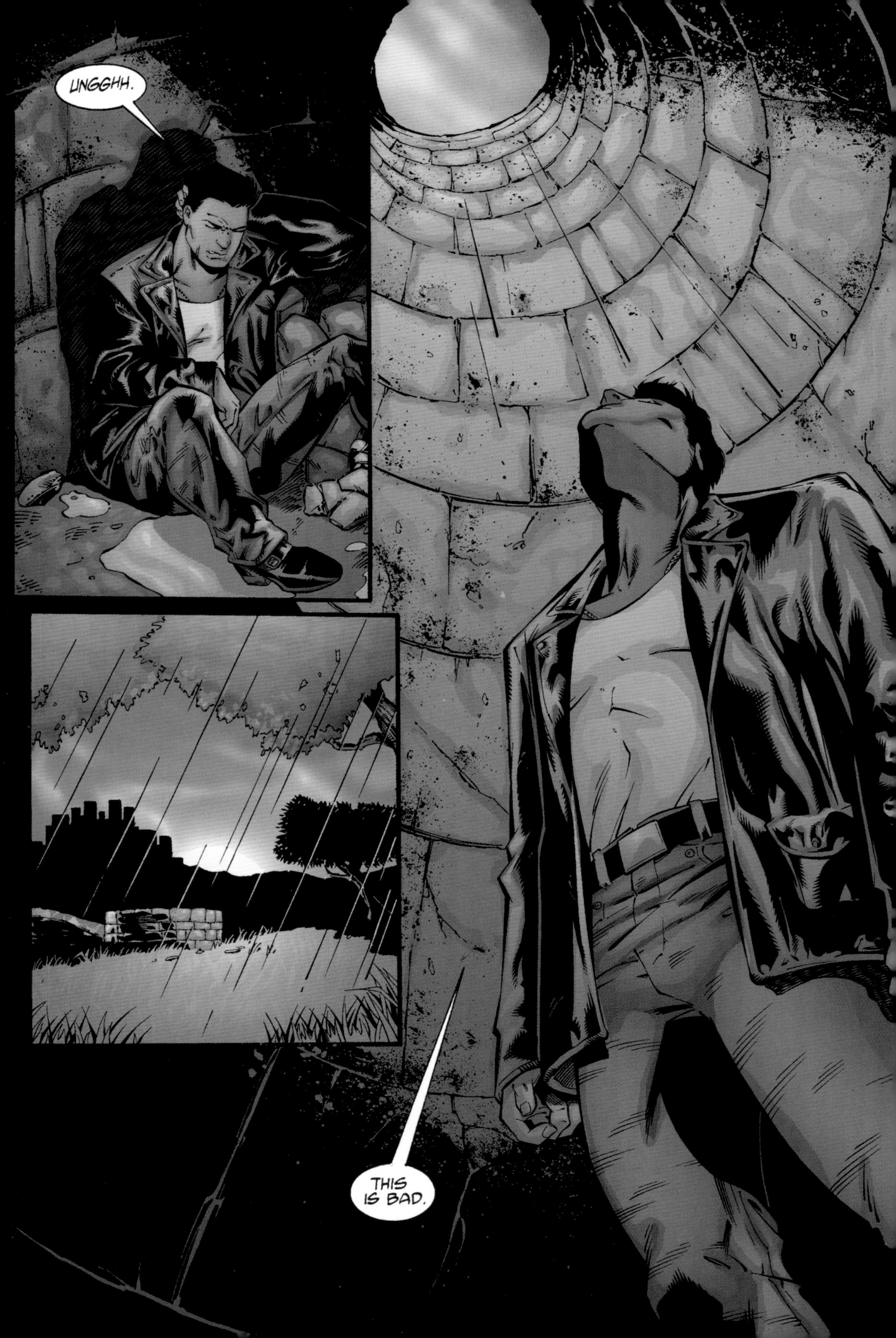
UNGGHH.
THIS IS BAD.

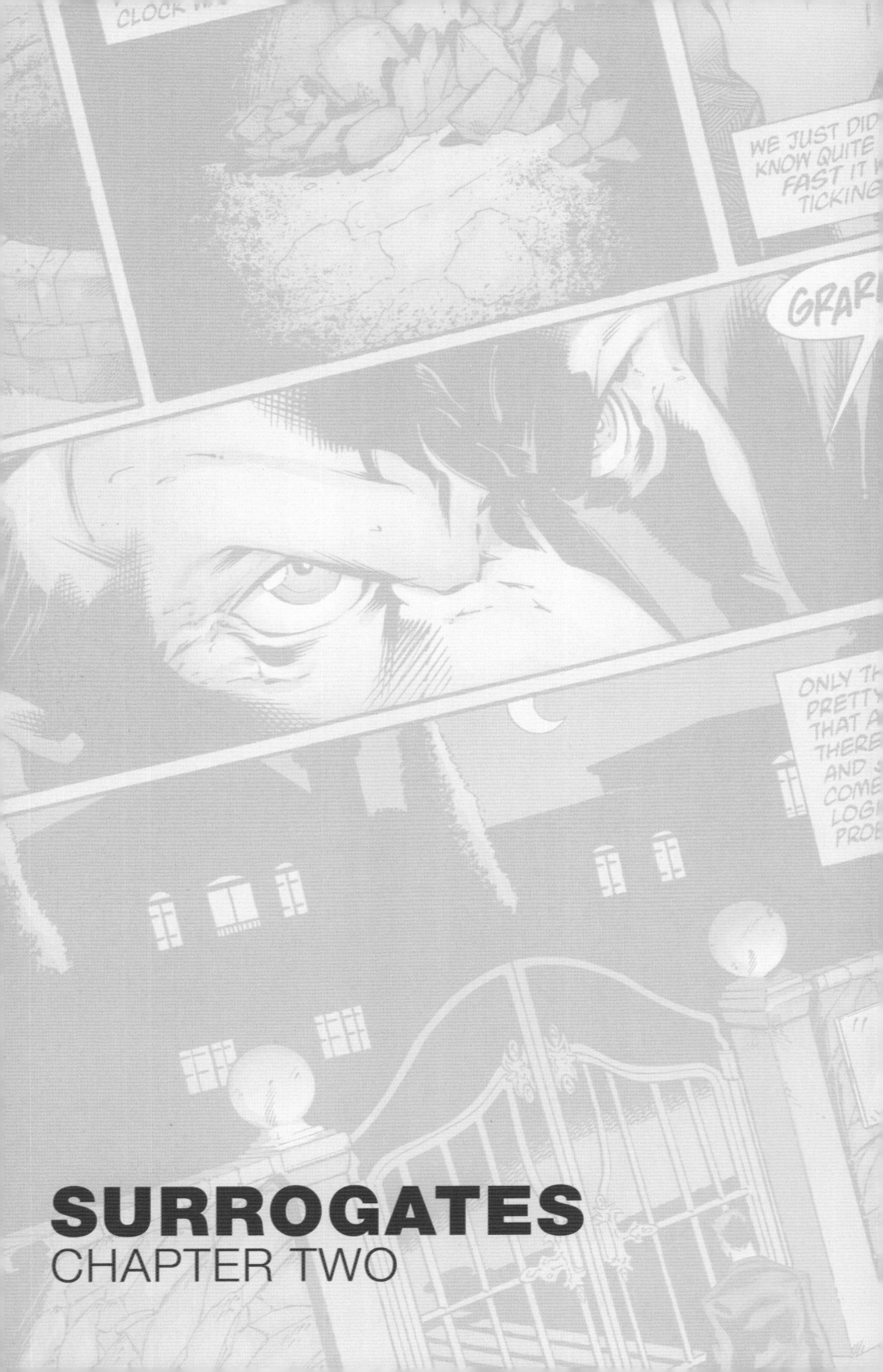

CLOCK
WE JUST
KNOW QUITE
FAST IT

SURROGATES
CHAPTER TWO

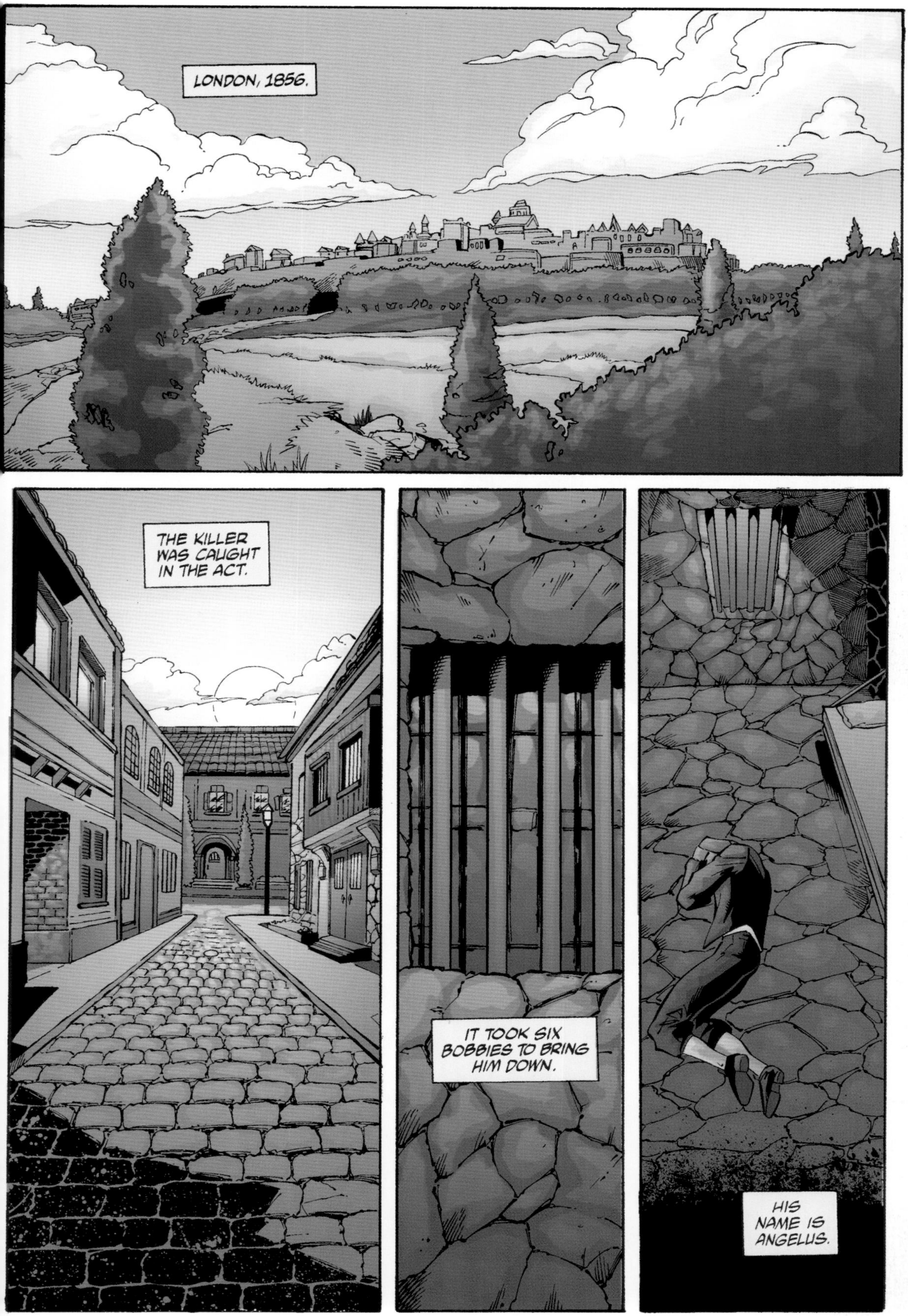
LONDON, 1856.
THE KILLER WAS CAUGHT IN THE ACT.
IT TOOK SIX BOBBIES TO BRING HIM DOWN.
HIS NAME IS ANGELUS.

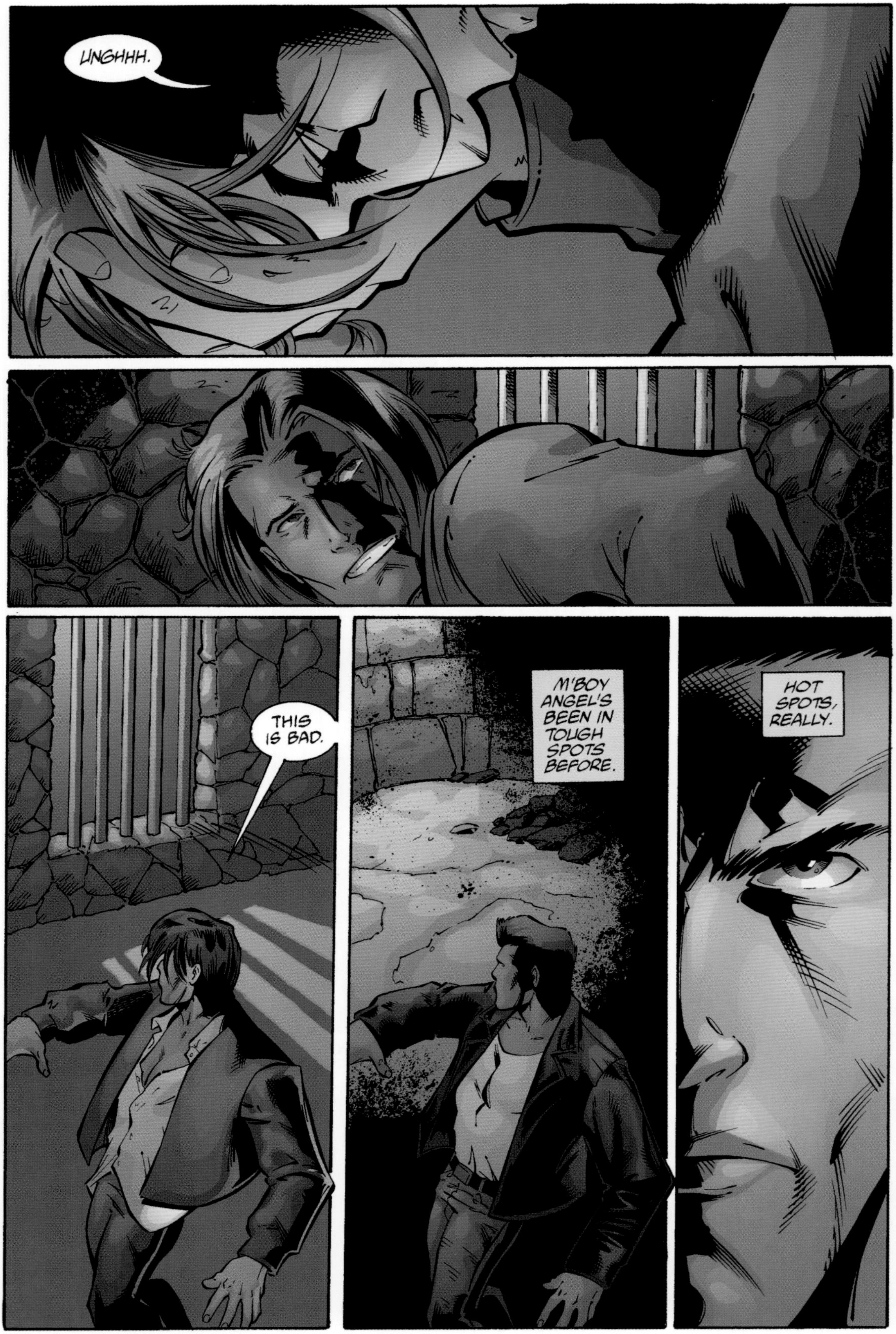
UNGHHH.
THIS IS BAD.
M'BOY ANGEL'S BEEN IN TOUGH SPOTS BEFORE.
HOT SPOTS, REALLY.

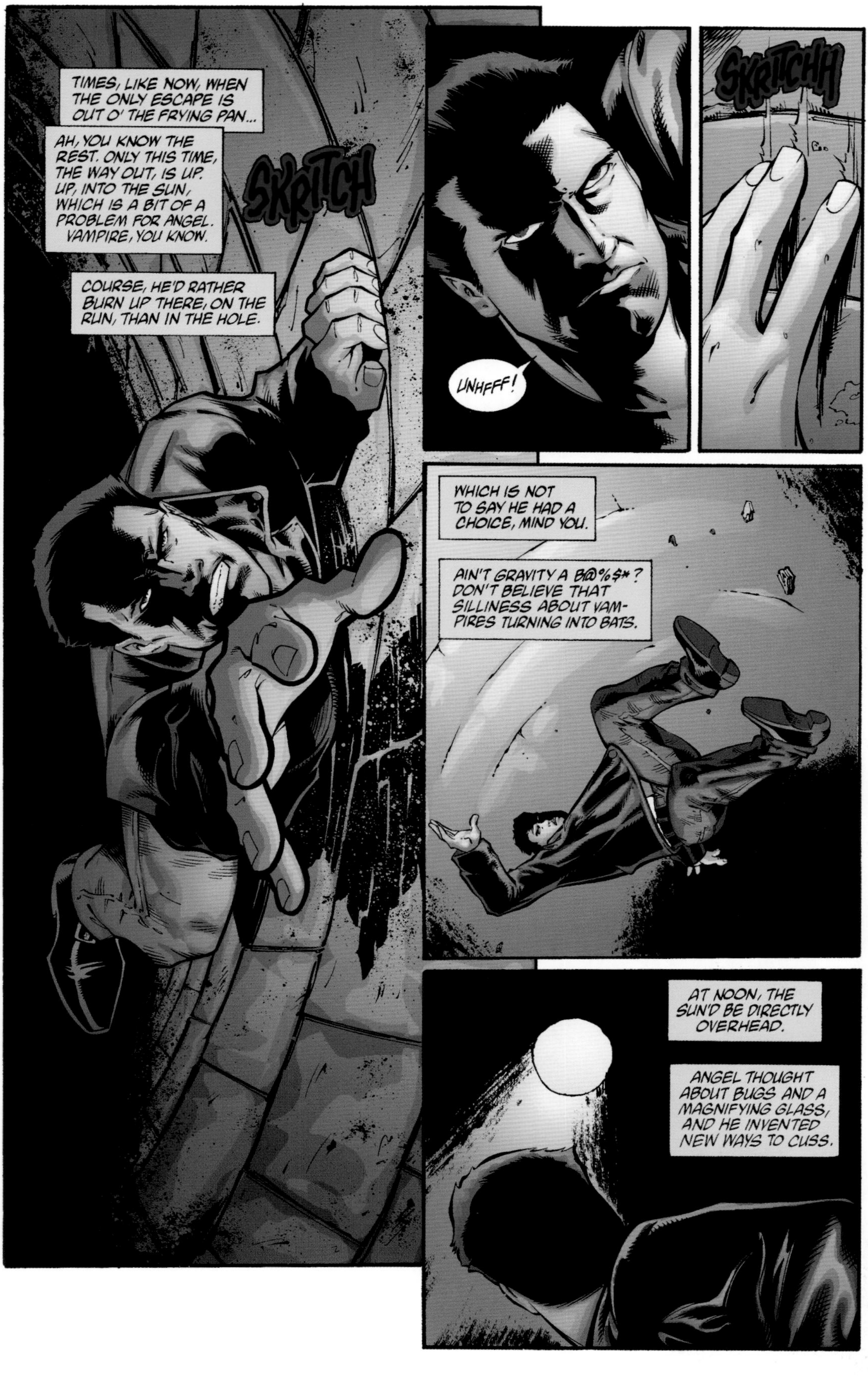
TIMES, LIKE NOW, WHEN THE ONLY ESCAPE IS OUT O' THE FRYING PAN...
AH, YOU KNOW THE REST. ONLY THIS TIME, THE WAY OUT, IS UP. UP, INTO THE SUN, WHICH IS A BIT OF A PROBLEM FOR ANGEL. VAMPIRE, YOU KNOW.
SKRITCH
COURSE, HE'D RATHER BURN UP THERE, ON THE RUN, THAN IN THE HOLE.
UNHFFF!
SKRITCHH
WHICH IS NOT TO SAY HE HAD A CHOICE, MIND YOU.
AIN'T GRAVITY A B@%$*? DON'T BELIEVE THAT SILLINESS ABOUT VAMPIRES TURNING INTO BATS.
AT NOON, THE SUN'D BE DIRECTLY OVERHEAD.
ANGEL THOUGHT ABOUT BUGS AND A MAGNIFYING GLASS, AND HE INVENTED NEW WAYS TO CUSS.

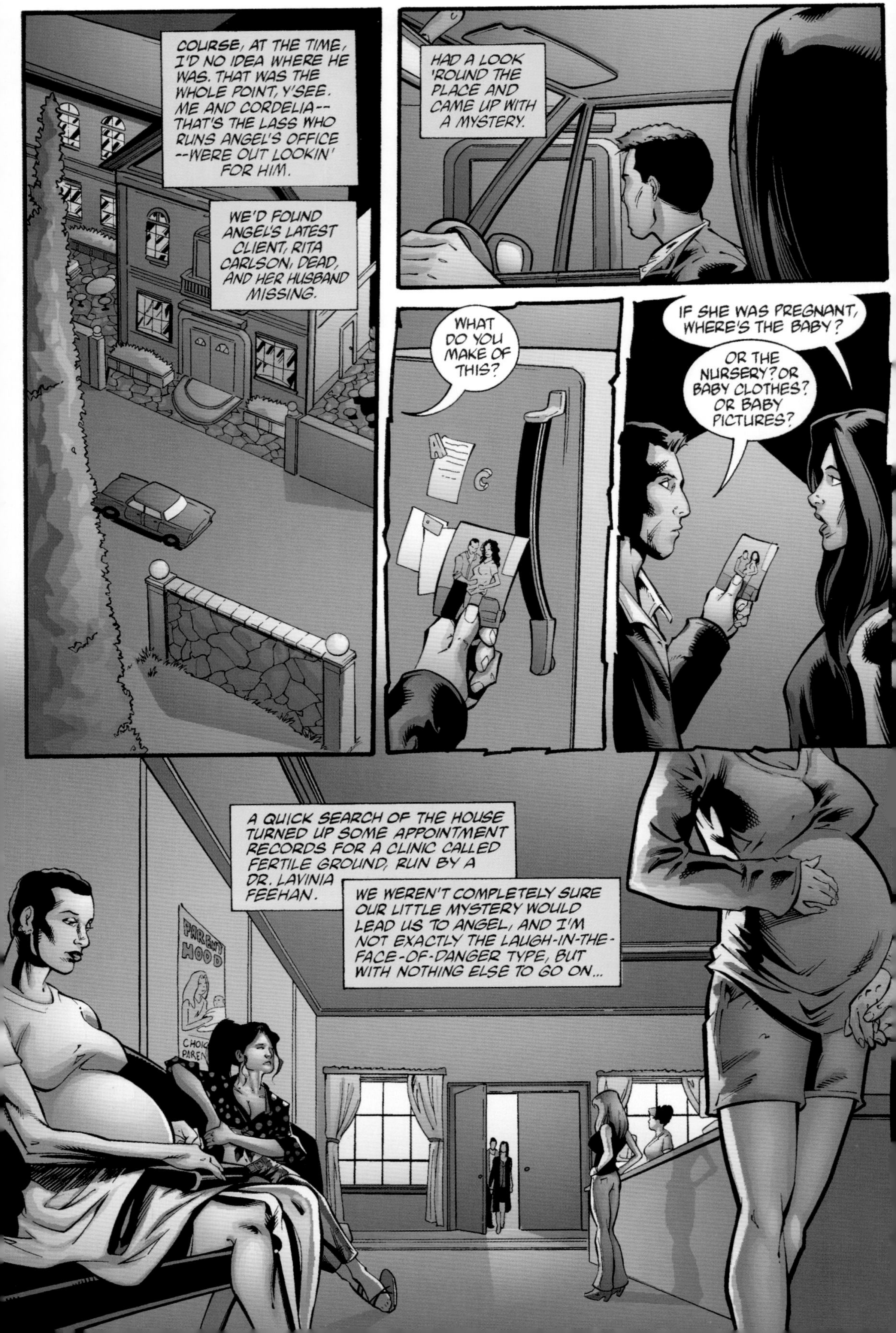
COURSE, AT THE TIME, I'D NO IDEA WHERE HE WAS. THAT WAS THE WHOLE POINT, Y'SEE. ME AND CORDELIA-- THAT'S THE LASS WHO RUNS ANGEL'S OFFICE --WERE OUT LOOKIN' FOR HIM.
WE'D FOUND ANGEL'S LATEST CLIENT, RITA CARLSON, DEAD, AND HER HUSBAND MISSING.
HAD A LOOK 'ROUND THE PLACE AND CAME UP WITH A MYSTERY.
WHAT DO YOU MAKE OF THIS?
IF SHE WAS PREGNANT, WHERE'S THE BABY?
OR THE NURSERY? OR BABY CLOTHES? OR BABY PICTURES?
A QUICK SEARCH OF THE HOUSE TURNED UP SOME APPOINTMENT RECORDS FOR A CLINIC CALLED FERTILE GROUND, RUN BY A DR. LAVINIA FEEHAN.
WE WEREN'T COMPLETELY SURE OUR LITTLE MYSTERY WOULD LEAD US TO ANGEL, AND I'M NOT EXACTLY THE LAUGH-IN-THE-FACE-OF-DANGER TYPE, BUT WITH NOTHING ELSE TO GO ON...
PARENTHOOD

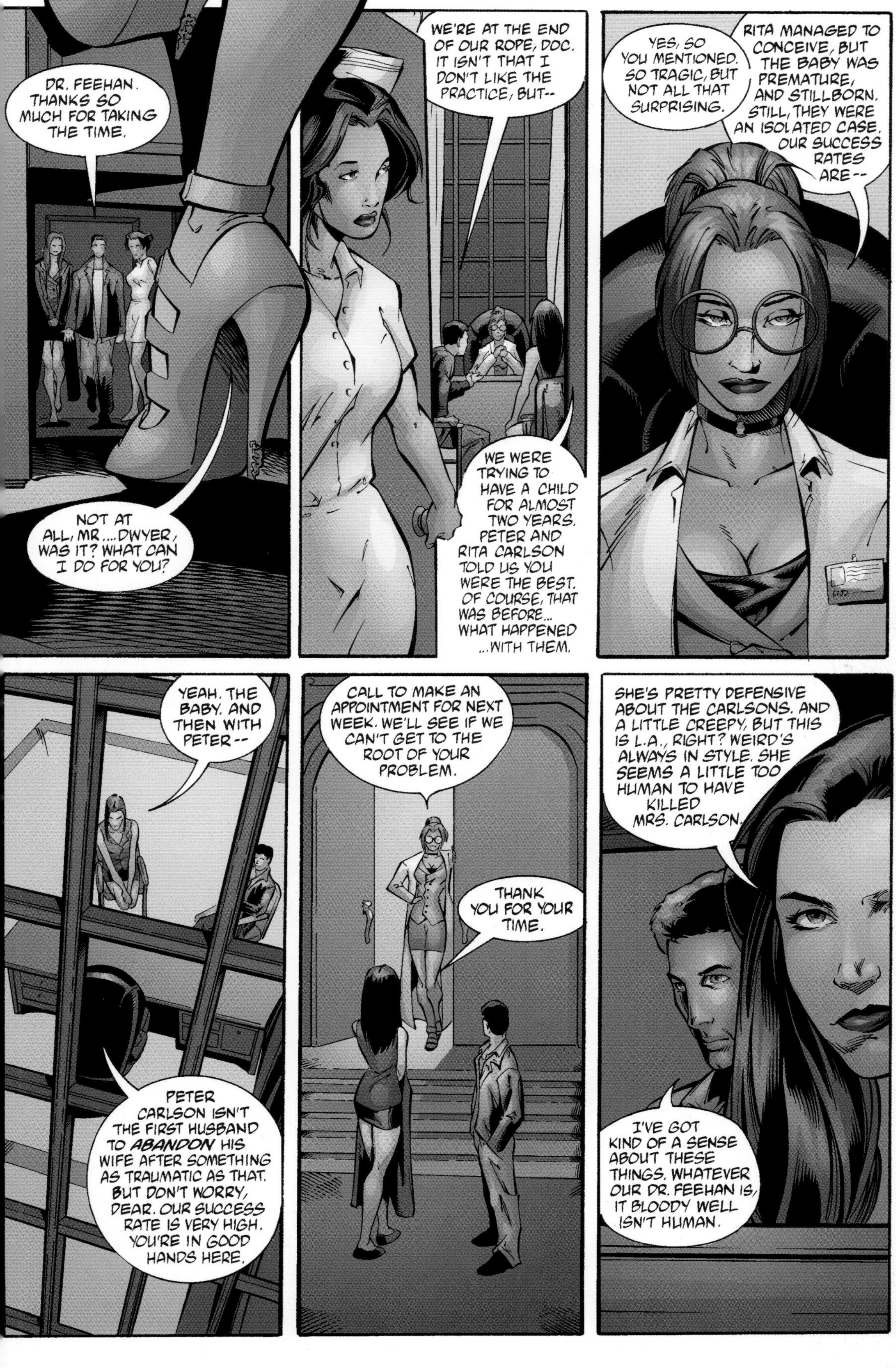
DR. FEEHAN. THANKS SO MUCH FOR TAKING THE TIME.
NOT AT ALL, MR....DWYER, WAS IT? WHAT CAN I DO FOR YOU?
WE'RE AT THE END OF OUR ROPE, DOC. IT ISN'T THAT I DON'T LIKE THE PRACTICE, BUT--
WE WERE TRYING TO HAVE A CHILD FOR ALMOST TWO YEARS. PETER AND RITA CARLSON TOLD US YOU WERE THE BEST. OF COURSE, THAT WAS BEFORE... WHAT HAPPENED ...WITH THEM.
YES, SO YOU MENTIONED. SO TRAGIC, BUT NOT ALL THAT SURPRISING.
RITA MANAGED TO CONCEIVE, BUT THE BABY WAS PREMATURE, AND STILLBORN. STILL, THEY WERE AN ISOLATED CASE. OUR SUCCESS RATES ARE--
YEAH. THE BABY. AND THEN WITH PETER--
PETER CARLSON ISN'T THE FIRST HUSBAND TO ABANDON HIS WIFE AFTER SOMETHING AS TRAUMATIC AS THAT. BUT DON'T WORRY, DEAR. OUR SUCCESS RATE IS VERY HIGH. YOU'RE IN GOOD HANDS HERE.
CALL TO MAKE AN APPOINTMENT FOR NEXT WEEK. WE'LL SEE IF WE CAN'T GET TO THE ROOT OF YOUR PROBLEM.
THANK YOU FOR YOUR TIME.
SHE'S PRETTY DEFENSIVE ABOUT THE CARLSONS. AND A LITTLE CREEPY, BUT THIS IS L.A., RIGHT? WEIRD'S ALWAYS IN STYLE. SHE SEEMS A LITTLE TOO HUMAN TO HAVE KILLED MRS. CARLSON.
I'VE GOT KIND OF A SENSE ABOUT THESE THINGS. WHATEVER OUR DR. FEEHAN IS, IT BLOODY WELL ISN'T HUMAN.

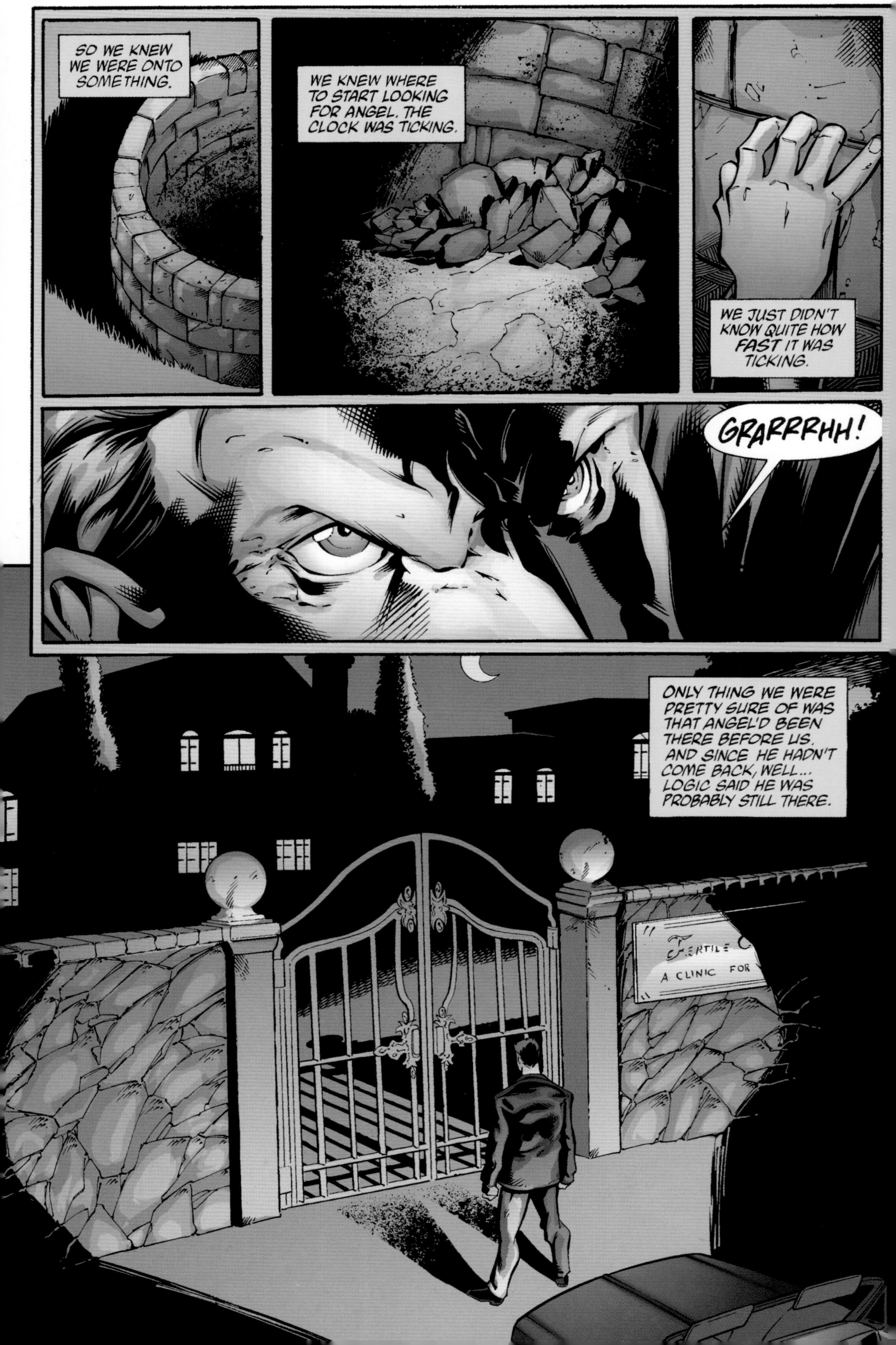
SO WE KNEW WE WERE ONTO SOMETHING.
WE KNEW WHERE TO START LOOKING FOR ANGEL. THE CLOCK WAS TICKING.
WE JUST DIDN'T KNOW QUITE HOW FAST IT WAS TICKING.
GRARRRHH!
ONLY THING WE WERE PRETTY SURE OF WAS THAT ANGEL'D BEEN THERE BEFORE US. AND SINCE HE HADN'T COME BACK, WELL... LOGIC SAID HE WAS PROBABLY STILL THERE.
A CLINIC FOR

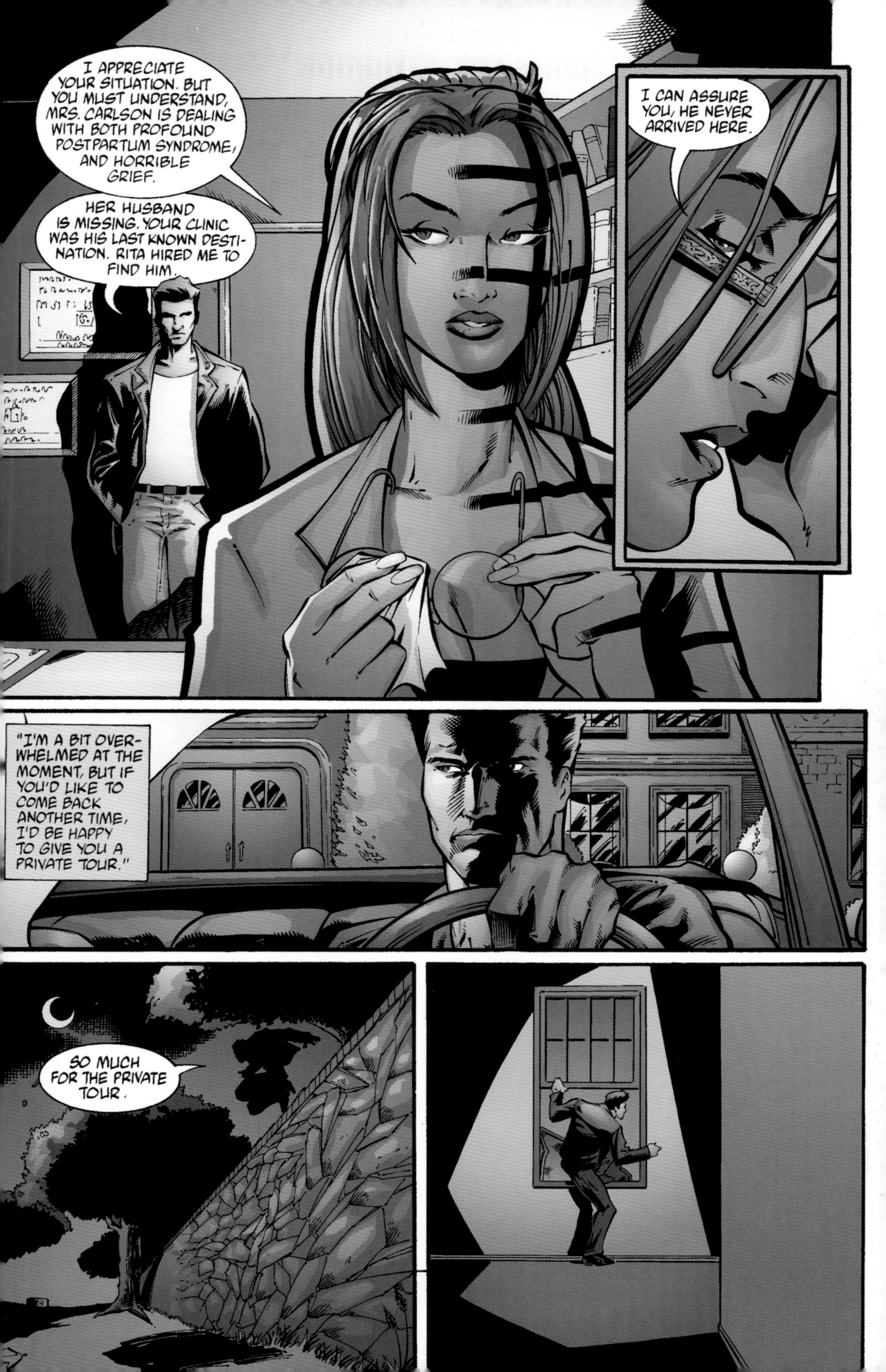

I APPRECIATE YOUR SITUATION. BUT YOU MUST UNDERSTAND, MRS. CARLSON IS DEALING WITH BOTH PROFOUND POSTPARTUM SYNDROME, AND HORRIBLE GRIEF.
HER HUSBAND IS MISSING. YOUR CLINIC WAS HIS LAST KNOWN DESTINATION. RITA HIRED ME TO FIND HIM.
I CAN ASSURE YOU, HE NEVER ARRIVED HERE.
"I'M A BIT OVERWHELMED AT THE MOMENT, BUT IF YOU'D LIKE TO COME BACK ANOTHER TIME, I'D BE HAPPY TO GIVE YOU A PRIVATE TOUR."
SO MUCH FOR THE PRIVATE TOUR.

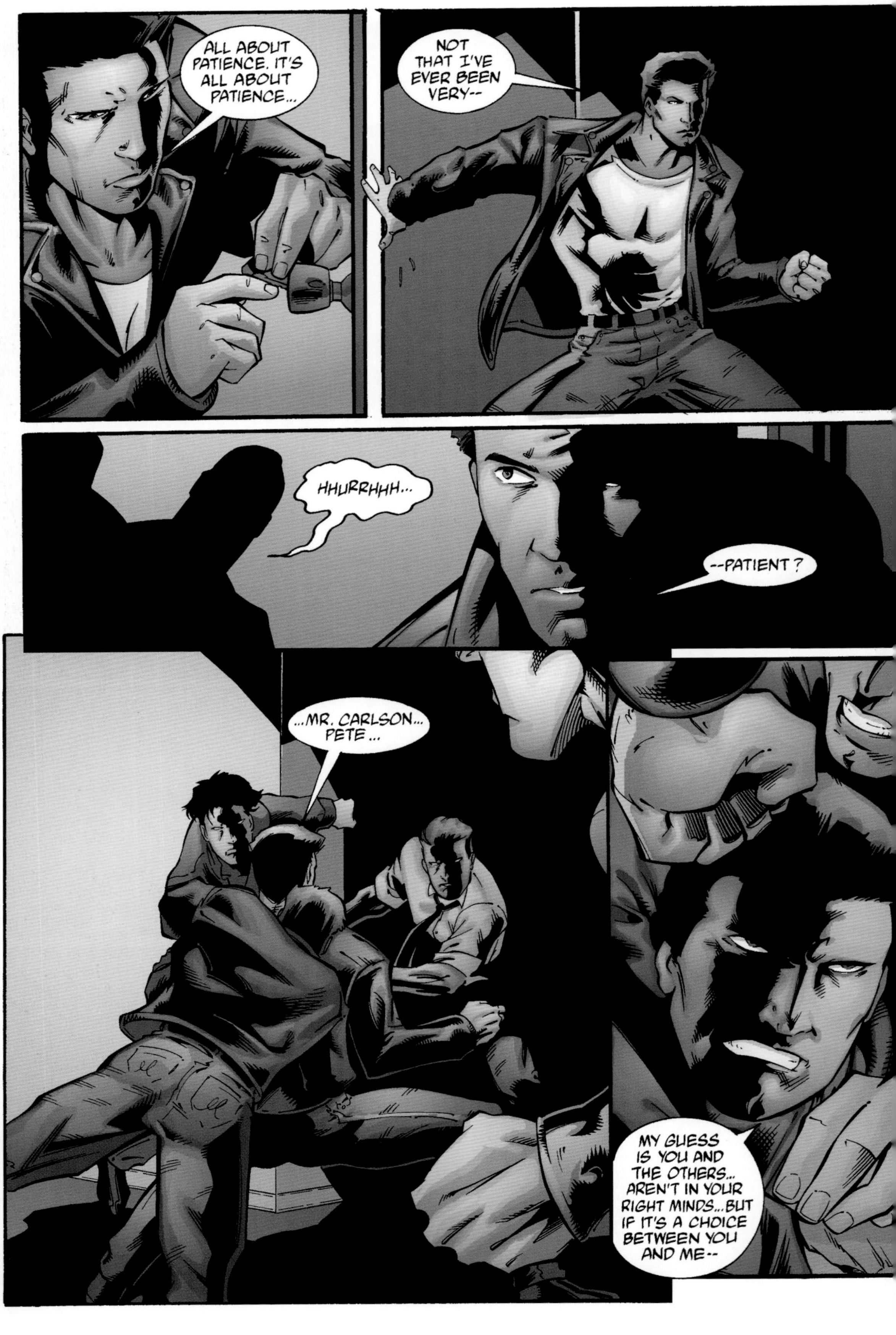
ALL ABOUT PATIENCE. IT'S ALL ABOUT PATIENCE...
NOT THAT I'VE EVER BEEN VERY--
HHURRHHH...
--PATIENT?
...MR. CARLSON... PETE...
MY GUESS IS YOU AND THE OTHERS... AREN'T IN YOUR RIGHT MINDS...BUT IF IT'S A CHOICE BETWEEN YOU AND ME--

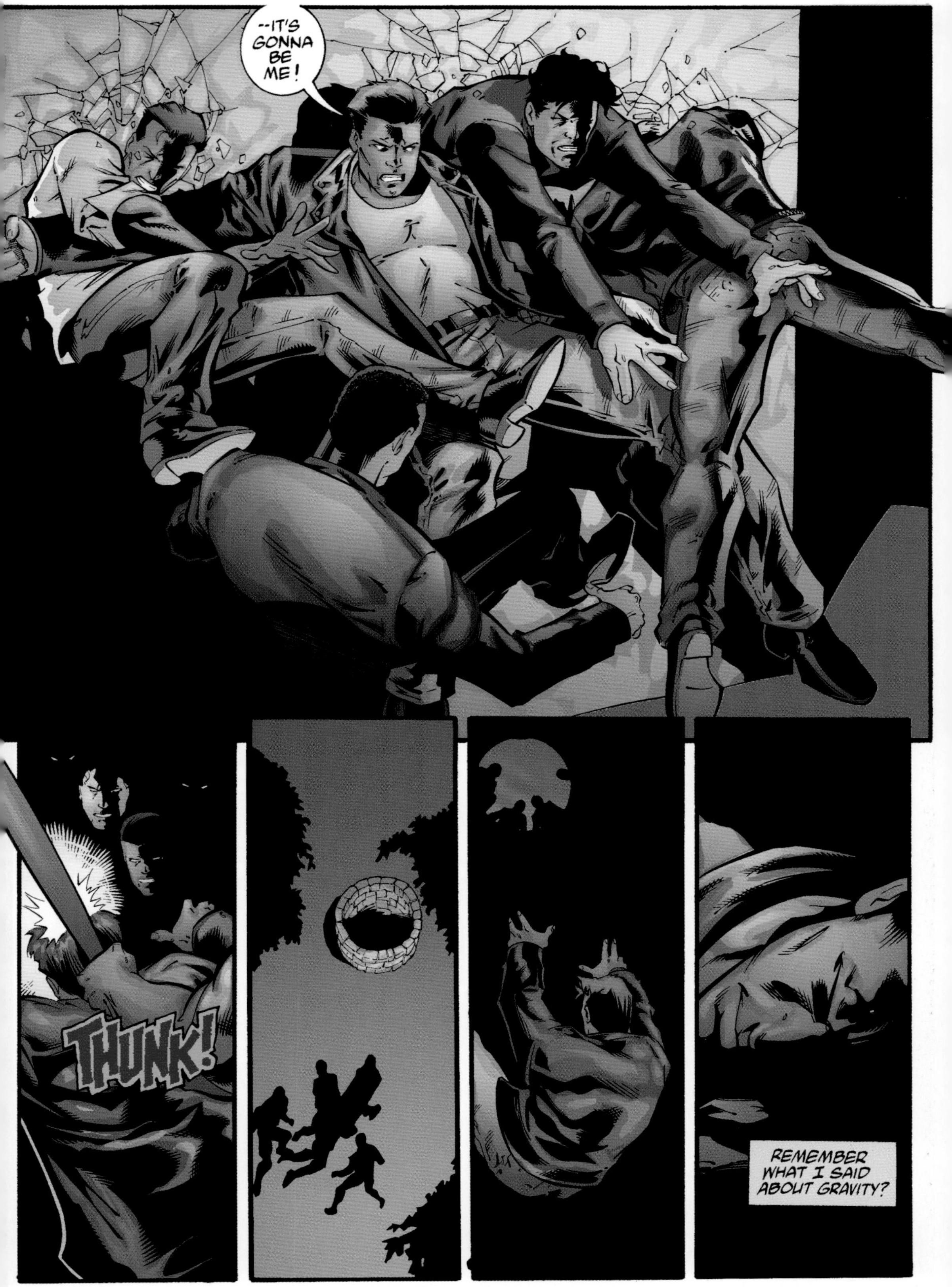
--IT'S GONNA BE ME!
THUNK!
REMEMBER WHAT I SAID ABOUT GRAVITY?

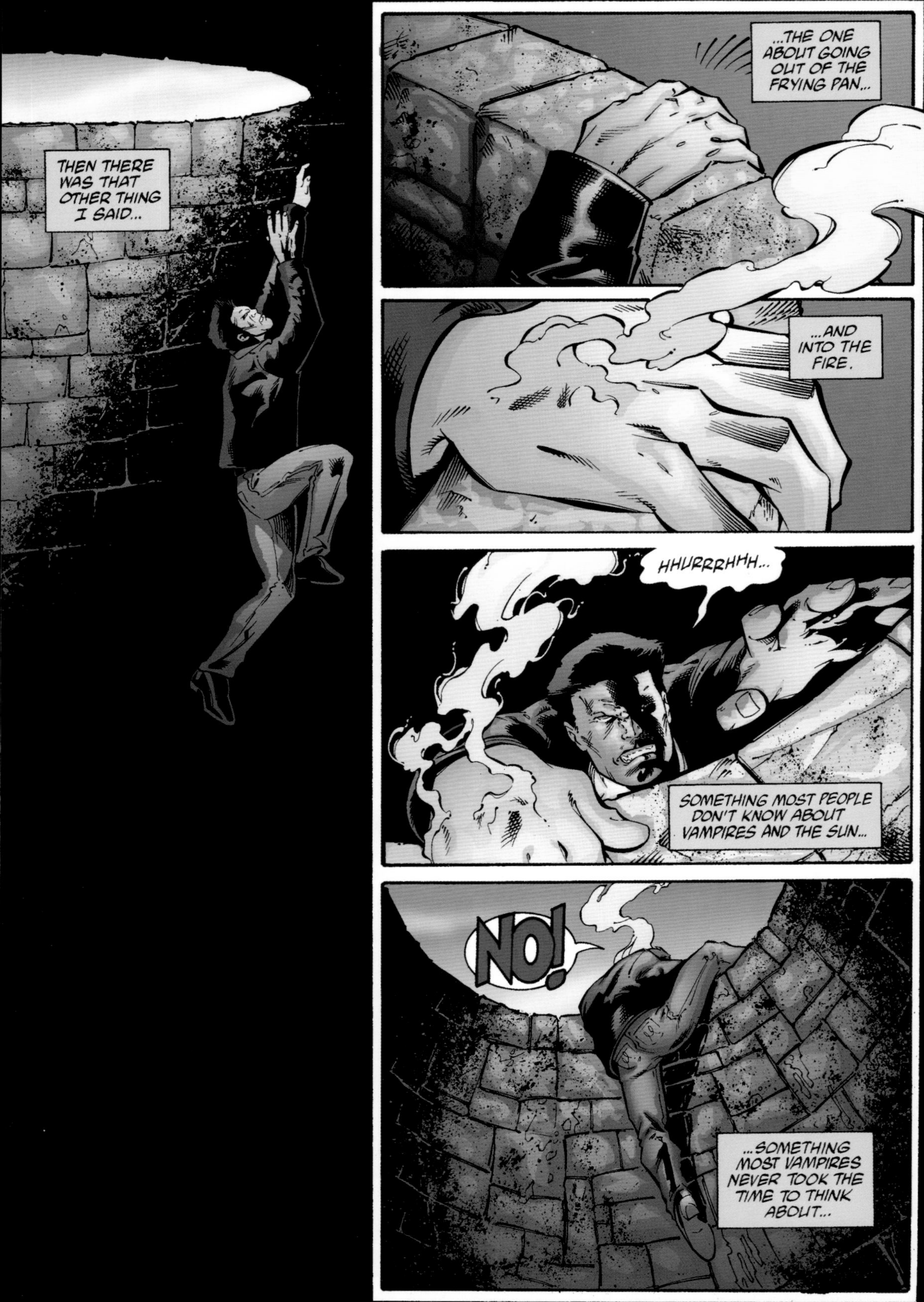
THEN THERE WAS THAT OTHER THING I SAID...
...THE ONE ABOUT GOING OUT OF THE FRYING PAN...
...AND INTO THE FIRE.
HHURRRHHH...
SOMETHING MOST PEOPLE DON'T KNOW ABOUT VAMPIRES AND THE SUN...
NO!
...SOMETHING MOST VAMPIRES NEVER TOOK THE TIME TO THINK ABOUT...

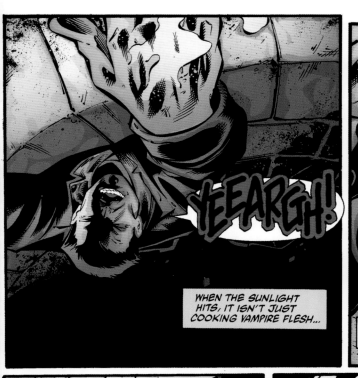

YEEARGH!

WHEN THE SUNLIGHT HITS, IT ISN'T JUST COOKING VAMPIRE FLESH...

...IT'S BURNING THE DEMON WITHIN.

AND MAYBE THAT'S WHAT THE DEMONS DESERVE. EVEN THE ONES WHO MEAN WELL.

BUT NOT TODAY.

NOT ANGEL.

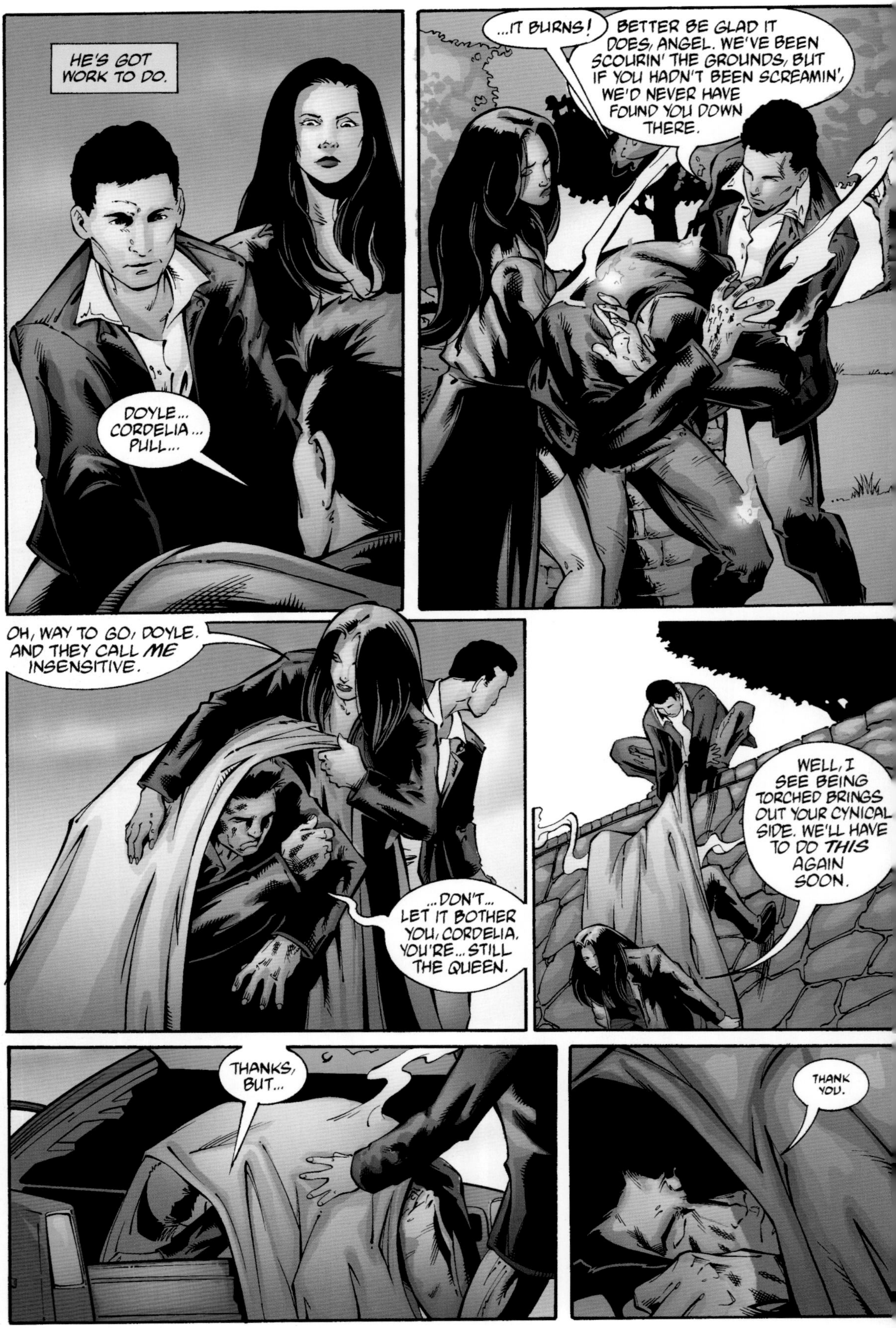
HE'S GOT WORK TO DO.
DOYLE... CORDELIA... PULL...
...IT BURNS!
BETTER BE GLAD IT DOES, ANGEL. WE'VE BEEN SCOURIN' THE GROUNDS, BUT IF YOU HADN'T BEEN SCREAMIN', WE'D NEVER HAVE FOUND YOU DOWN THERE.
OH, WAY TO GO, DOYLE. AND THEY CALL ME INSENSITIVE.
...DON'T... LET IT BOTHER YOU, CORDELIA. YOU'RE... STILL THE QUEEN.
WELL, I SEE BEING TORCHED BRINGS OUT YOUR CYNICAL SIDE. WE'LL HAVE TO DO THIS AGAIN SOON.
THANKS, BUT...
THANK YOU.

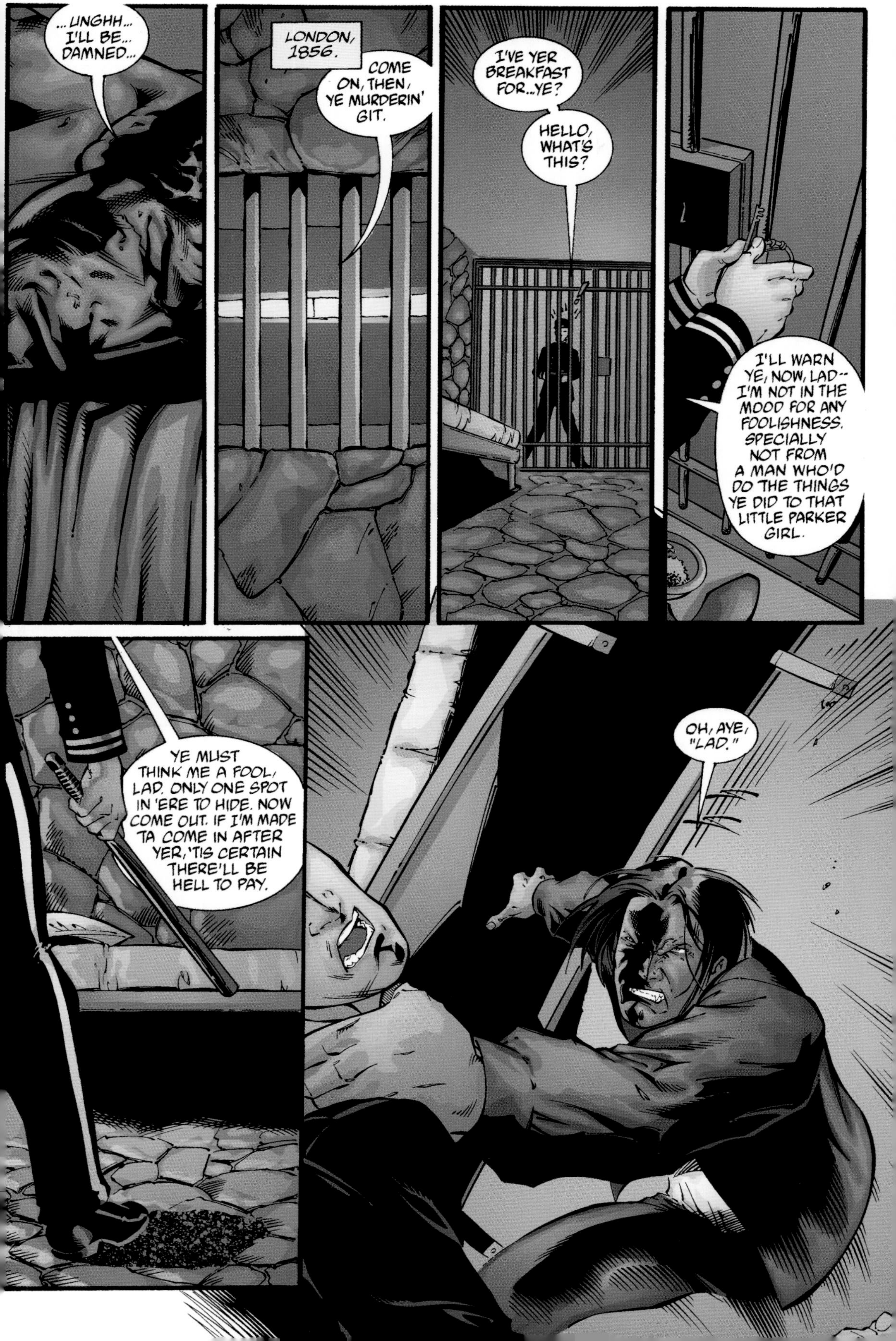
...UNGHH... I'LL BE... DAMNED...
LONDON, 1856.
COME ON, THEN, YE MURDERIN' GIT.
I'VE YER BREAKFAST FOR...YE?
HELLO, WHAT'S THIS?
I'LL WARN YE, NOW, LAD-- I'M NOT IN THE MOOD FOR ANY FOOLISHNESS. SPECIALLY NOT FROM A MAN WHO'D DO THE THINGS YE DID TO THAT LITTLE PARKER GIRL.
YE MUST THINK ME A FOOL, LAD. ONLY ONE SPOT IN 'ERE TO HIDE. NOW COME OUT. IF I'M MADE TA COME IN AFTER YER, 'TIS CERTAIN THERE'LL BE HELL TO PAY.
OH, AYE, "LAD."

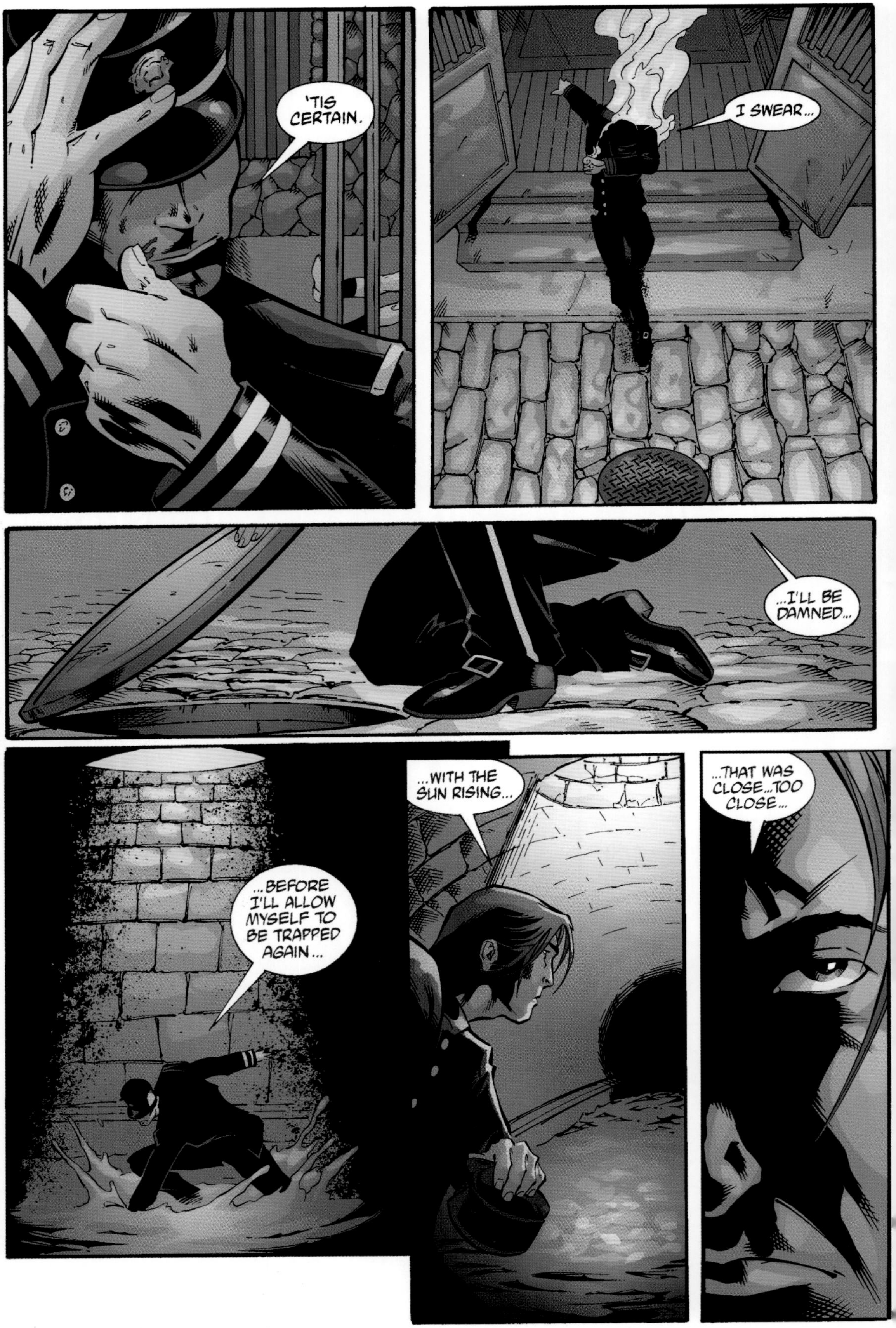
'TIS CERTAIN.
I SWEAR...
...I'LL BE DAMNED...
...BEFORE I'LL ALLOW MYSELF TO BE TRAPPED AGAIN...
...WITH THE SUN RISING...
...THAT WAS CLOSE...TOO CLOSE...

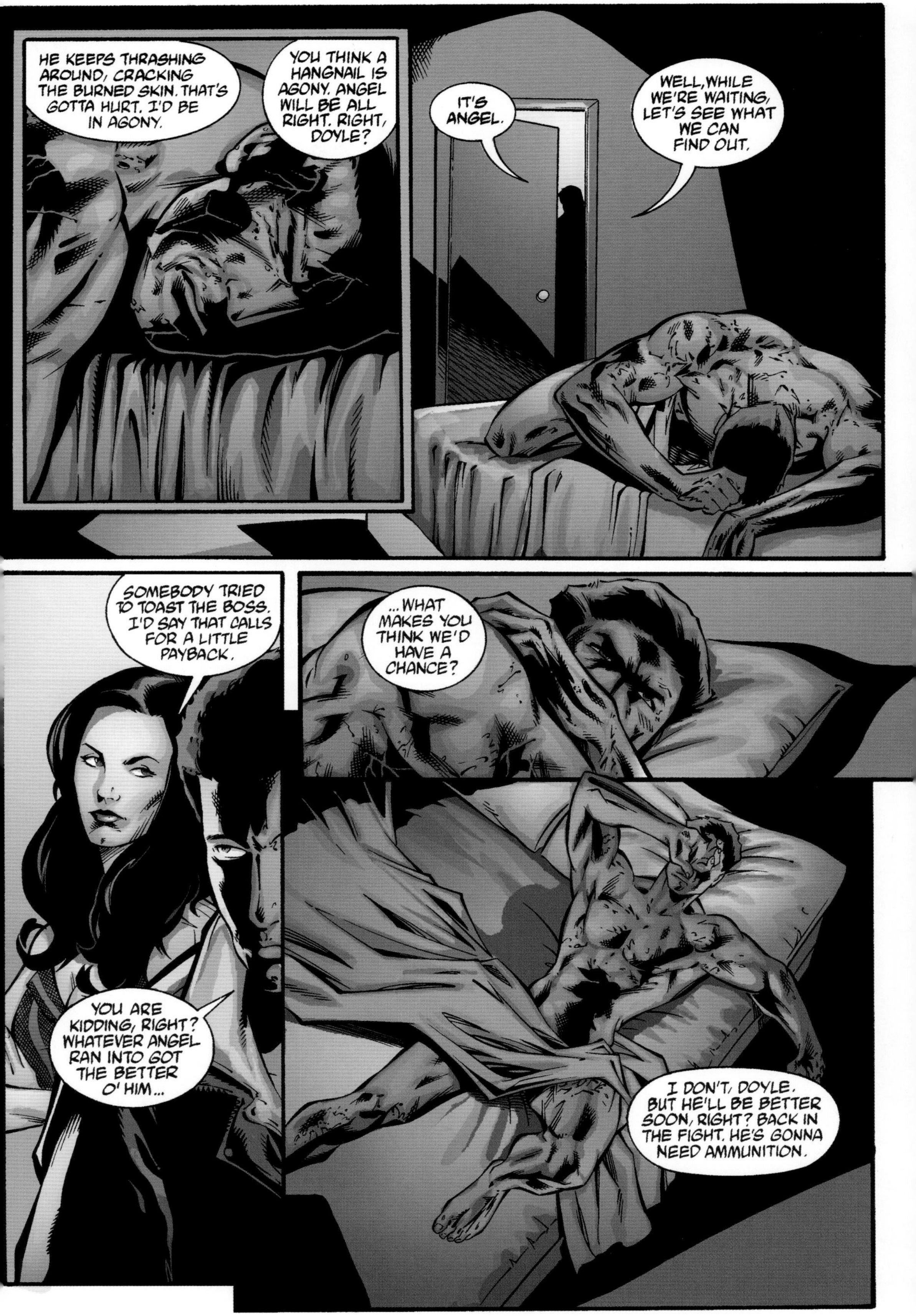
HE KEEPS THRASHING AROUND, CRACKING THE BURNED SKIN. THAT'S GOTTA HURT. I'D BE IN AGONY.
YOU THINK A HANGNAIL IS AGONY. ANGEL WILL BE ALL RIGHT. RIGHT, DOYLE?
IT'S ANGEL.
WELL, WHILE WE'RE WAITING, LET'S SEE WHAT WE CAN FIND OUT.
SOMEBODY TRIED TO TOAST THE BOSS. I'D SAY THAT CALLS FOR A LITTLE PAYBACK.
...WHAT MAKES YOU THINK WE'D HAVE A CHANCE?
YOU ARE KIDDING, RIGHT? WHATEVER ANGEL RAN INTO GOT THE BETTER O' HIM...
I DON'T, DOYLE. BUT HE'LL BE BETTER SOON, RIGHT? BACK IN THE FIGHT. HE'S GONNA NEED AMMUNITION.

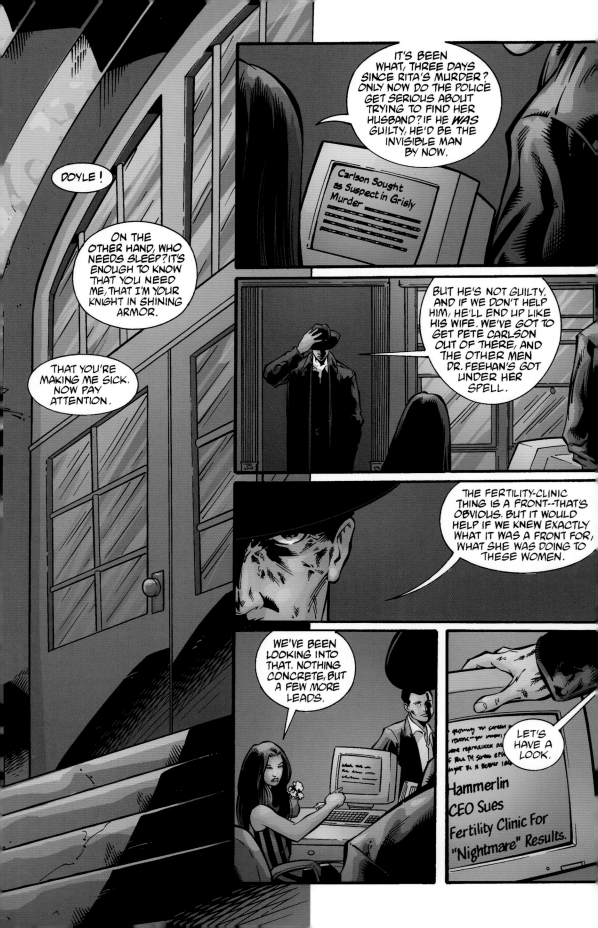

IT'S BEEN WHAT, THREE DAYS SINCE RITA'S MURDER? ONLY NOW DO THE POLICE GET SERIOUS ABOUT TRYING TO FIND HER HUSBAND? IF HE *WAS* GUILTY, HE'D BE THE INVISIBLE MAN BY NOW.

Carlson Sought as Suspect in Grisly Murder

DOYLE!

ON THE OTHER HAND, WHO NEEDS SLEEP? IT'S ENOUGH TO KNOW THAT YOU NEED ME, THAT I'M YOUR KNIGHT IN SHINING ARMOR.

THAT YOU'RE MAKING ME SICK. NOW PAY ATTENTION.

BUT HE'S NOT GUILTY, AND IF WE DON'T HELP HIM, HE'LL END UP LIKE HIS WIFE. WE'VE GOT TO GET PETE CARLSON OUT OF THERE, AND THE OTHER MEN DR. FEEHAN'S GOT UNDER HER SPELL.

THE FERTILITY-CLINIC THING IS A FRONT--THAT'S OBVIOUS. BUT IT WOULD HELP IF WE KNEW EXACTLY WHAT IT WAS A FRONT FOR, WHAT SHE WAS DOING TO THESE WOMEN.

WE'VE BEEN LOOKING INTO THAT. NOTHING CONCRETE, BUT A FEW MORE LEADS.

LET'S HAVE A LOOK.

Hammerlin CEO Sues Fertility Clinic For "Nightmare" Results.

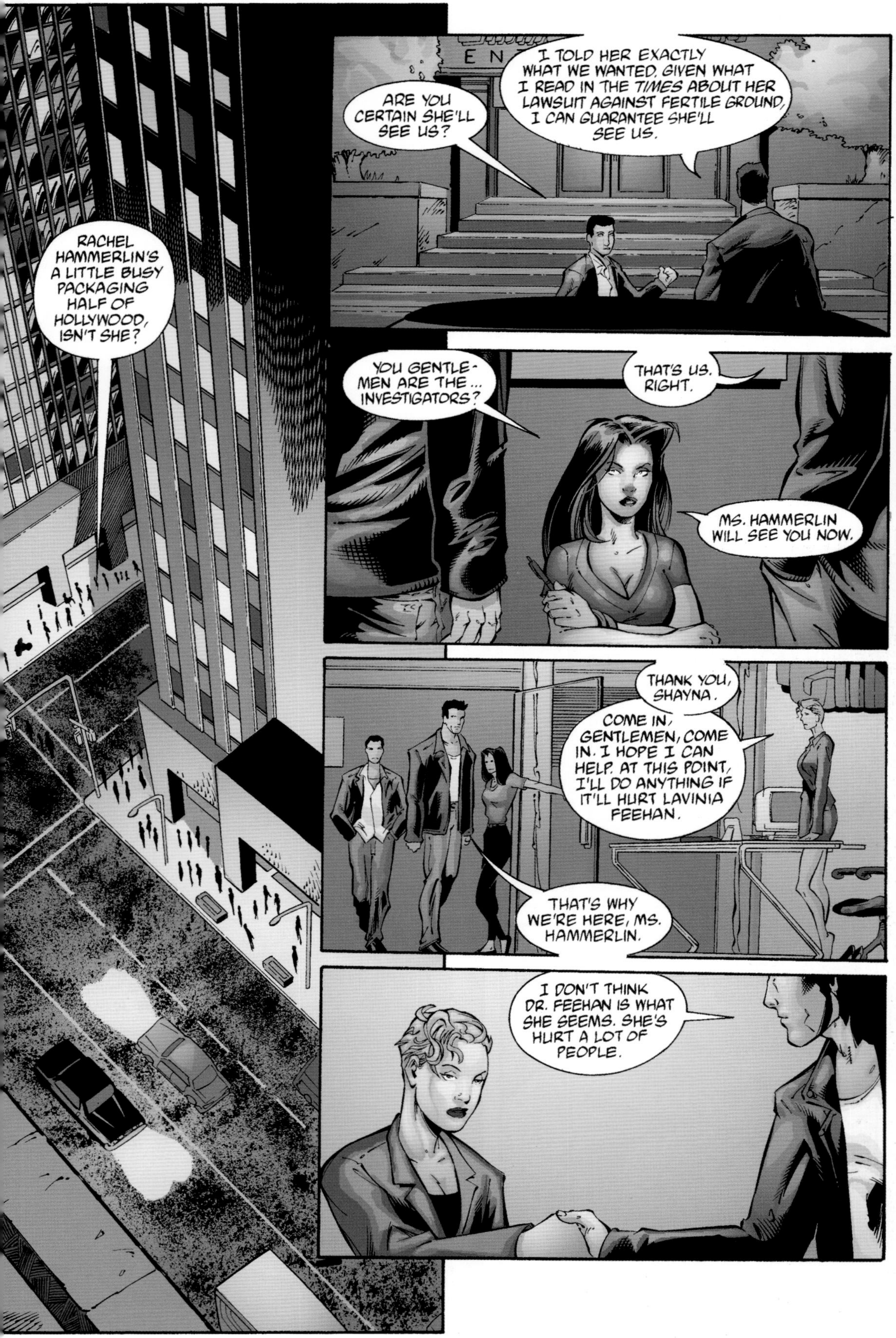
RACHEL HAMMERLIN'S A LITTLE BUSY PACKAGING HALF OF HOLLYWOOD, ISN'T SHE?
ARE YOU CERTAIN SHE'LL SEE US?
I TOLD HER EXACTLY WHAT WE WANTED. GIVEN WHAT I READ IN THE *TIMES* ABOUT HER LAWSUIT AGAINST FERTILE GROUND, I CAN GUARANTEE SHE'LL SEE US.
YOU GENTLEMEN ARE THE... INVESTIGATORS?
THAT'S US. RIGHT.
MS. HAMMERLIN WILL SEE YOU NOW.
THANK YOU, SHAYNA.
COME IN, GENTLEMEN, COME IN. I HOPE I CAN HELP. AT THIS POINT, I'LL DO ANYTHING IF IT'LL HURT LAVINIA FEEHAN.
THAT'S WHY WE'RE HERE, MS. HAMMERLIN.
I DON'T THINK DR. FEEHAN IS WHAT SHE SEEMS. SHE'S HURT A LOT OF PEOPLE.

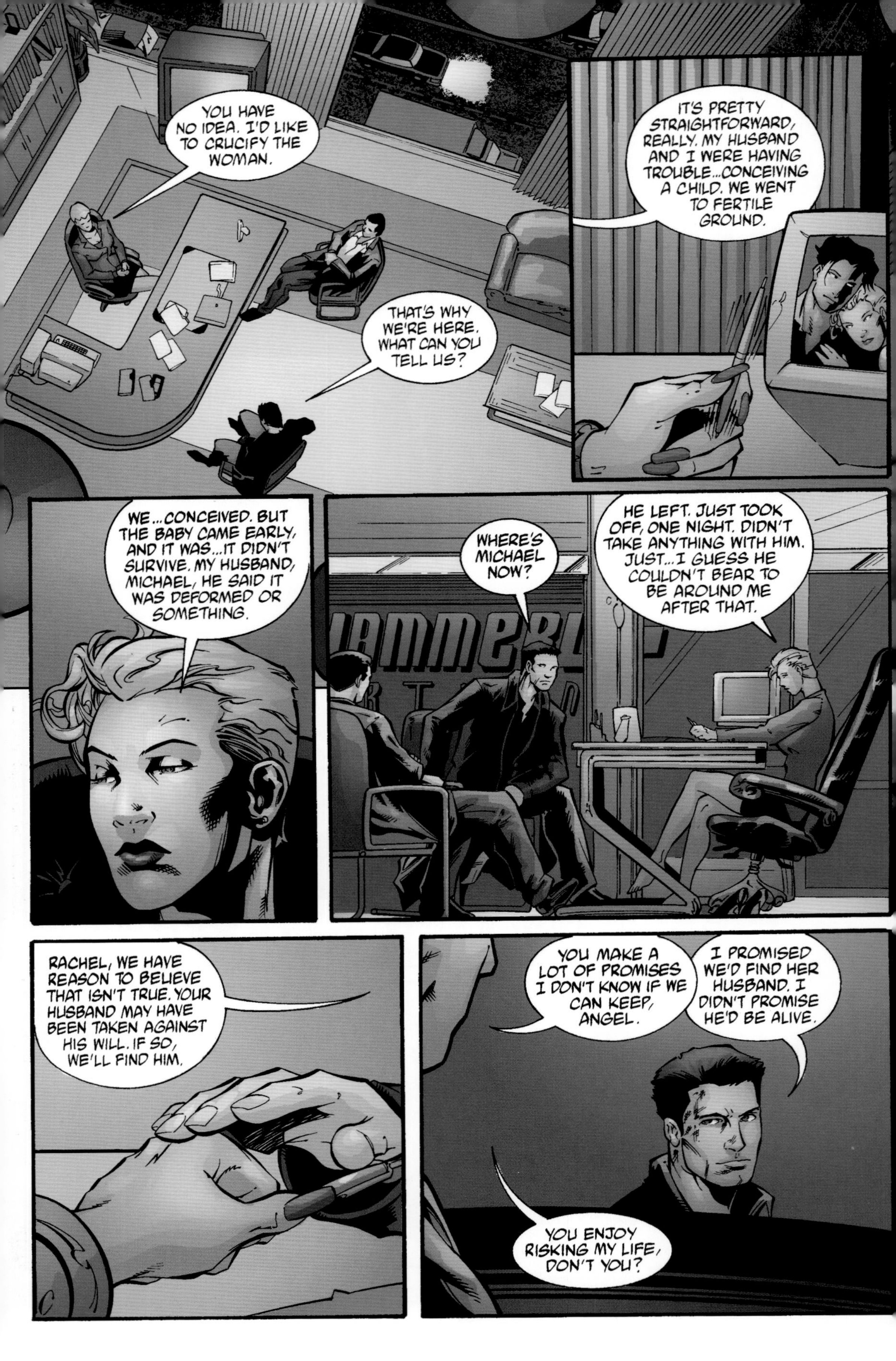

YOU HAVE NO IDEA. I'D LIKE TO CRUCIFY THE WOMAN.
THAT'S WHY WE'RE HERE. WHAT CAN YOU TELL US?
IT'S PRETTY STRAIGHTFORWARD, REALLY. MY HUSBAND AND I WERE HAVING TROUBLE...CONCEIVING A CHILD. WE WENT TO FERTILE GROUND.
WE...CONCEIVED. BUT THE BABY CAME EARLY, AND IT WAS...IT DIDN'T SURVIVE. MY HUSBAND, MICHAEL, HE SAID IT WAS DEFORMED OR SOMETHING.
WHERE'S MICHAEL NOW?
HE LEFT. JUST TOOK OFF, ONE NIGHT. DIDN'T TAKE ANYTHING WITH HIM. JUST...I GUESS HE COULDN'T BEAR TO BE AROUND ME AFTER THAT.
RACHEL, WE HAVE REASON TO BELIEVE THAT ISN'T TRUE. YOUR HUSBAND MAY HAVE BEEN TAKEN AGAINST HIS WILL. IF SO, WE'LL FIND HIM.
YOU MAKE A LOT OF PROMISES I DON'T KNOW IF WE CAN KEEP, ANGEL.
I PROMISED WE'D FIND HER HUSBAND. I DIDN'T PROMISE HE'D BE ALIVE.
YOU ENJOY RISKING MY LIFE, DON'T YOU?

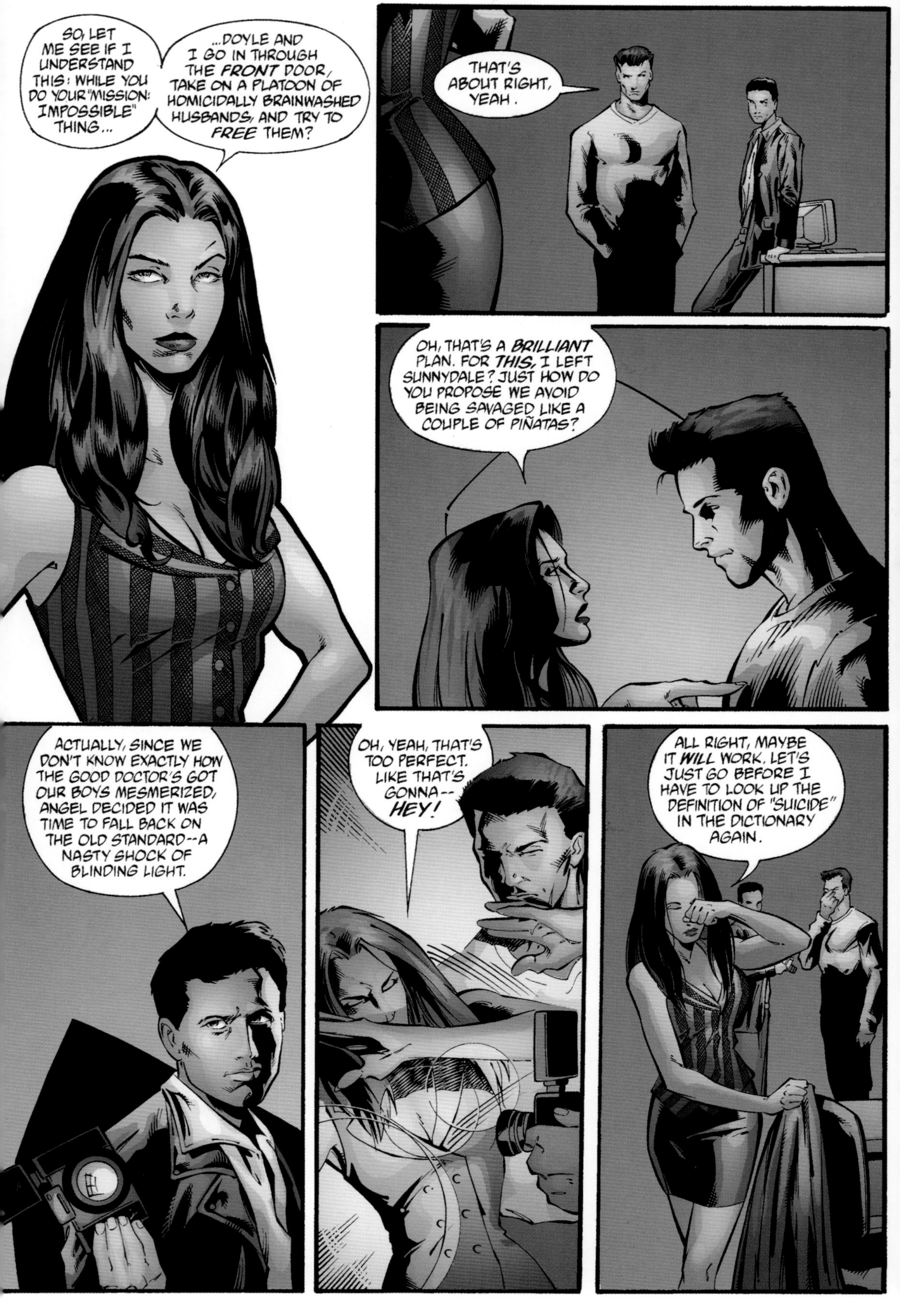
SO, LET ME SEE IF I UNDERSTAND THIS: WHILE YOU DO YOUR "MISSION: IMPOSSIBLE" THING...
...DOYLE AND I GO IN THROUGH THE FRONT DOOR, TAKE ON A PLATOON OF HOMICIDALLY BRAINWASHED HUSBANDS, AND TRY TO FREE THEM?
THAT'S ABOUT RIGHT, YEAH.
OH, THAT'S A BRILLIANT PLAN. FOR THIS, I LEFT SUNNYDALE? JUST HOW DO YOU PROPOSE WE AVOID BEING SAVAGED LIKE A COUPLE OF PIÑATAS?
ACTUALLY, SINCE WE DON'T KNOW EXACTLY HOW THE GOOD DOCTOR'S GOT OUR BOYS MESMERIZED, ANGEL DECIDED IT WAS TIME TO FALL BACK ON THE OLD STANDARD--A NASTY SHOCK OF BLINDING LIGHT.
OH, YEAH, THAT'S TOO PERFECT. LIKE THAT'S GONNA-- HEY!
ALL RIGHT, MAYBE IT WILL WORK. LET'S JUST GO BEFORE I HAVE TO LOOK UP THE DEFINITION OF "SUICIDE" IN THE DICTIONARY AGAIN.

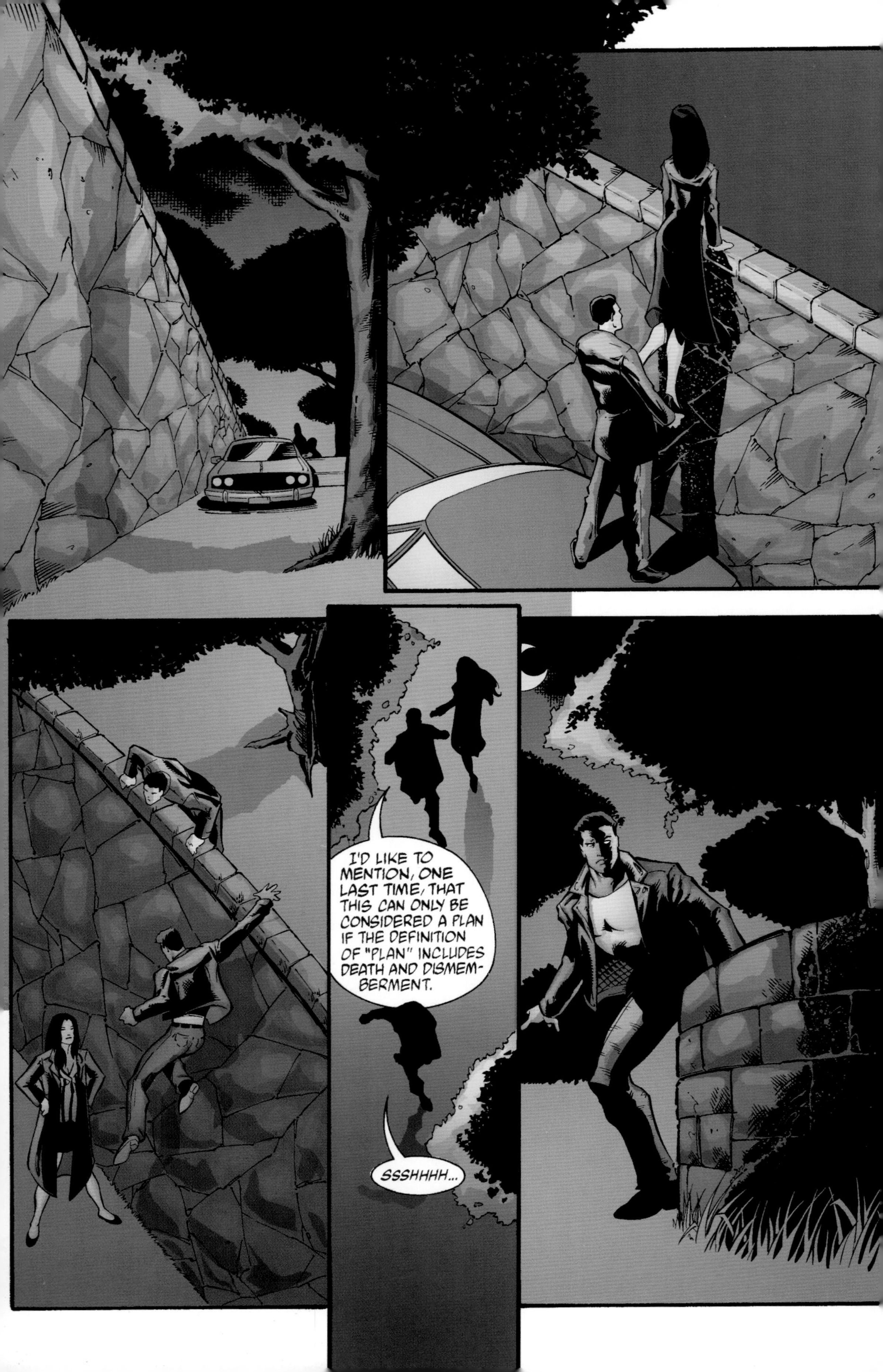
I'D LIKE TO MENTION, ONE LAST TIME, THAT THIS CAN ONLY BE CONSIDERED A PLAN IF THE DEFINITION OF "PLAN" INCLUDES DEATH AND DISMEMBERMENT.
SSSHHHH...

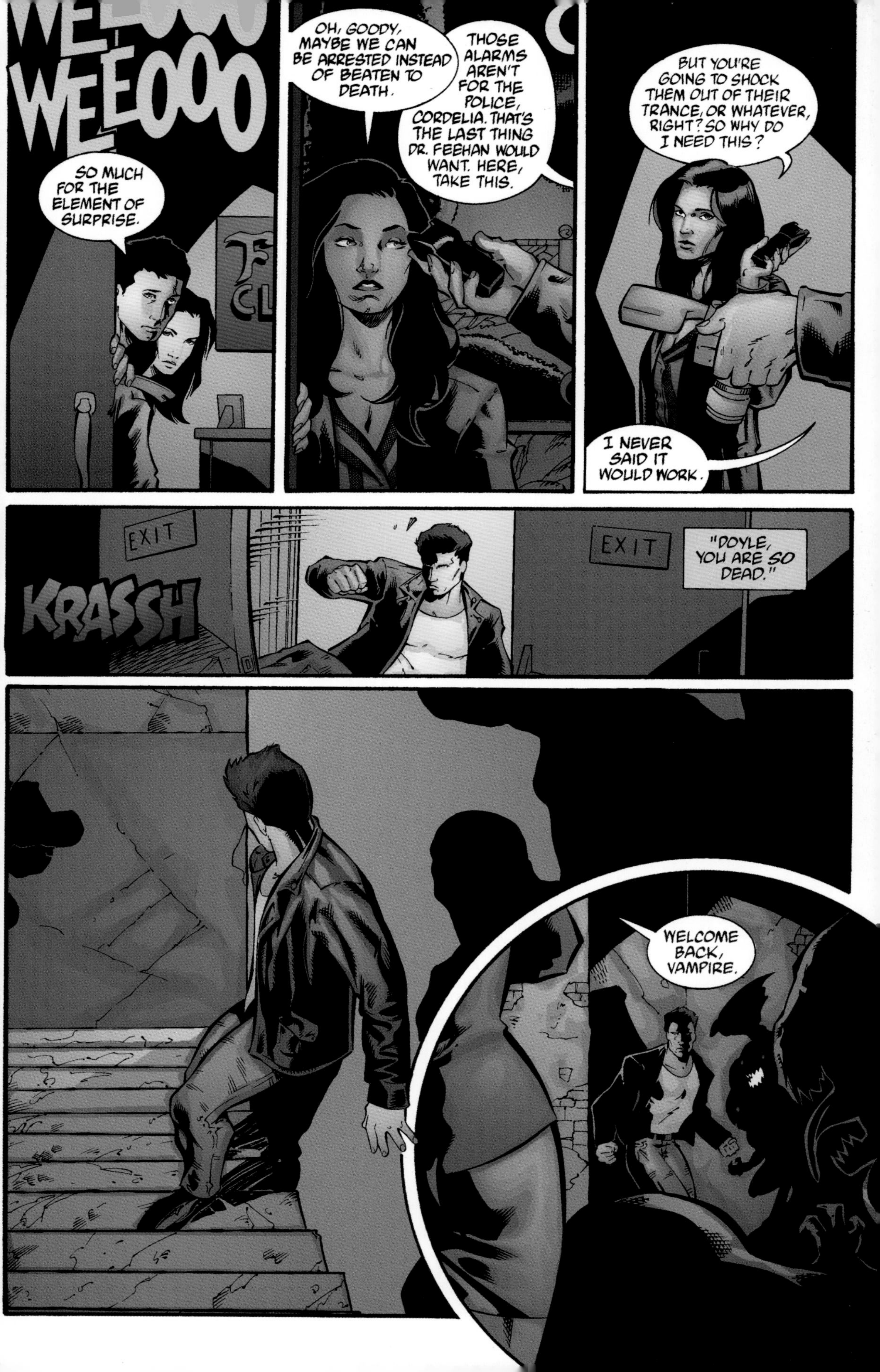
WEEOOO
SO MUCH FOR THE ELEMENT OF SURPRISE.
OH, GOODY, MAYBE WE CAN BE ARRESTED INSTEAD OF BEATEN TO DEATH.
THOSE ALARMS AREN'T FOR THE POLICE, CORDELIA. THAT'S THE LAST THING DR. FEEHAN WOULD WANT. HERE, TAKE THIS.
BUT YOU'RE GOING TO SHOCK THEM OUT OF THEIR TRANCE, OR WHATEVER, RIGHT? SO WHY DO I NEED THIS?
I NEVER SAID IT WOULD WORK.
EXIT
KRASSH
EXIT
"DOYLE, YOU ARE SO DEAD."
WELCOME BACK, VAMPIRE.

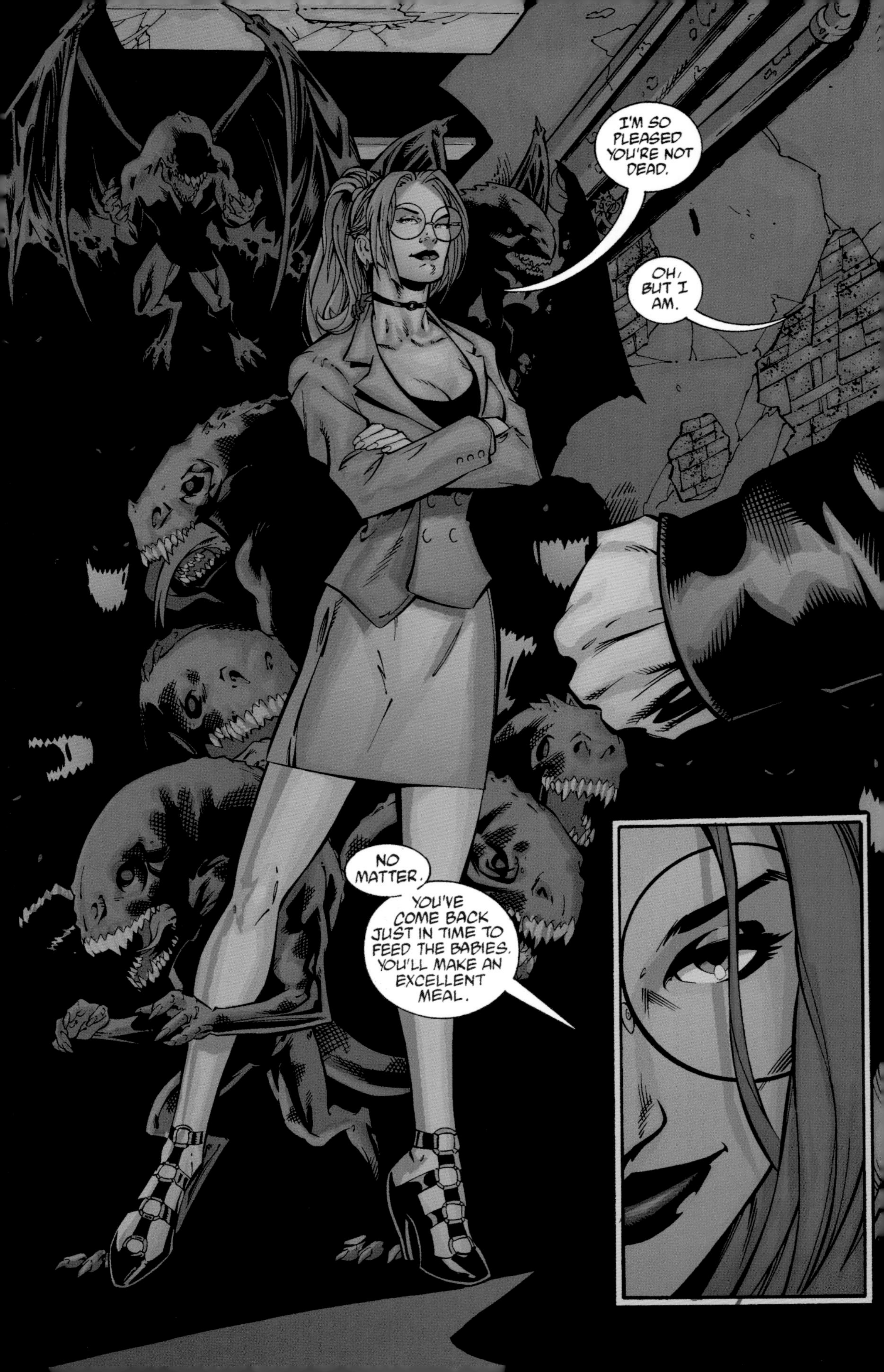
I'M SO PLEASED YOU'RE NOT DEAD.
OH, BUT I AM.
NO MATTER.
YOU'VE COME BACK JUST IN TIME TO FEED THE BABIES. YOU'LL MAKE AN EXCELLENT MEAL.

YEEARGH!
WHEN THE SUNLIGHT HITS, IT ISN'T JUST COOKING VAMPIRE FLESH...
...IT'S BURNING THE DEMON WITHIN.
AND MAYBE THAT'S WHAT THE DEMONS DESERVE.
EVEN THE ONES WHO MEAN WELL.
BUT NOT TODAY.

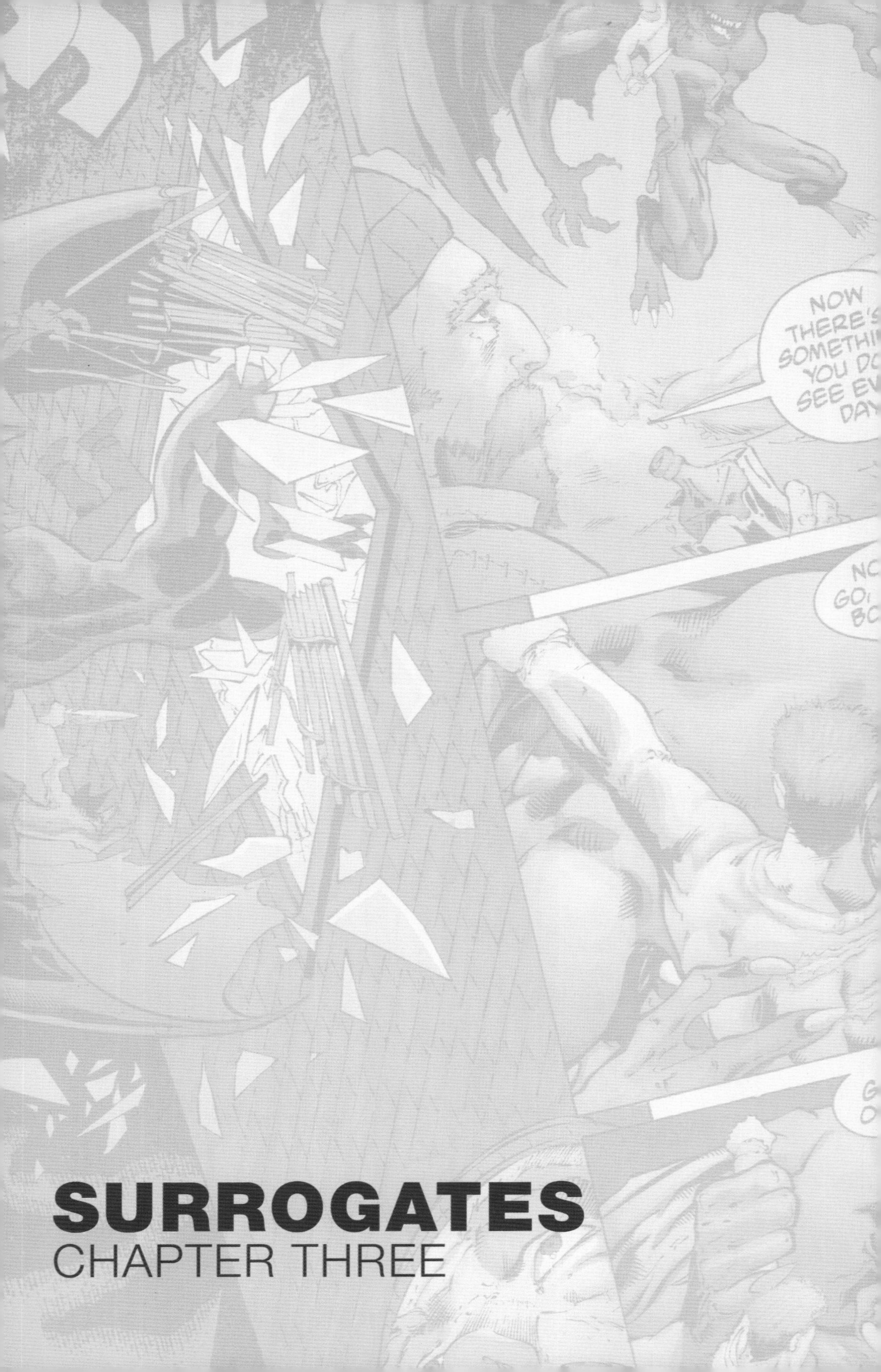

SURROGATES
CHAPTER THREE

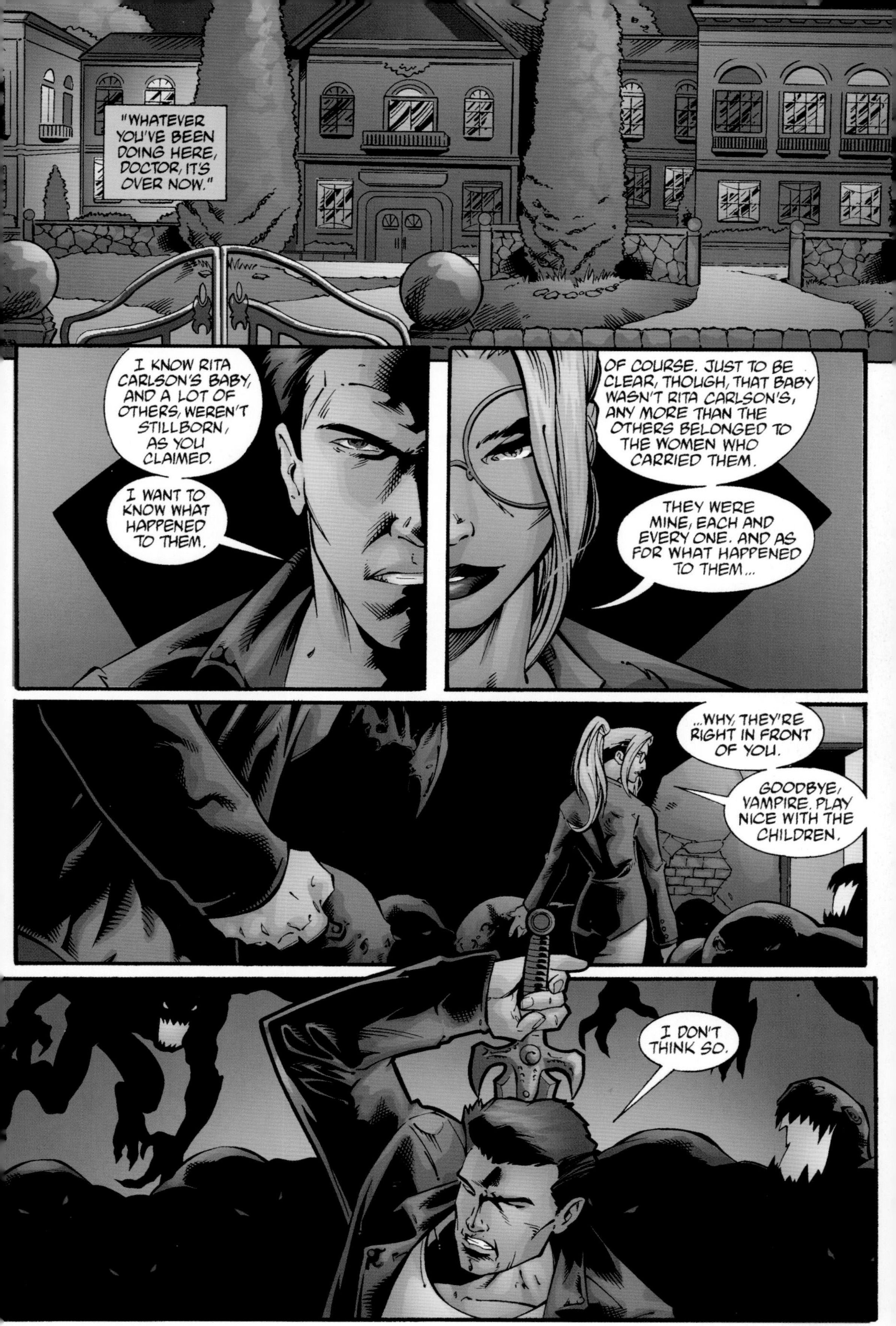
"WHATEVER YOU'VE BEEN DOING HERE, DOCTOR, IT'S OVER NOW."
I KNOW RITA CARLSON'S BABY, AND A LOT OF OTHERS, WEREN'T STILLBORN, AS YOU CLAIMED.
I WANT TO KNOW WHAT HAPPENED TO THEM.
OF COURSE. JUST TO BE CLEAR, THOUGH, THAT BABY WASN'T RITA CARLSON'S, ANY MORE THAN THE OTHERS BELONGED TO THE WOMEN WHO CARRIED THEM.
THEY WERE MINE, EACH AND EVERY ONE. AND AS FOR WHAT HAPPENED TO THEM...
...WHY, THEY'RE RIGHT IN FRONT OF YOU.
GOODBYE, VAMPIRE. PLAY NICE WITH THE CHILDREN.
I DON'T THINK SO.

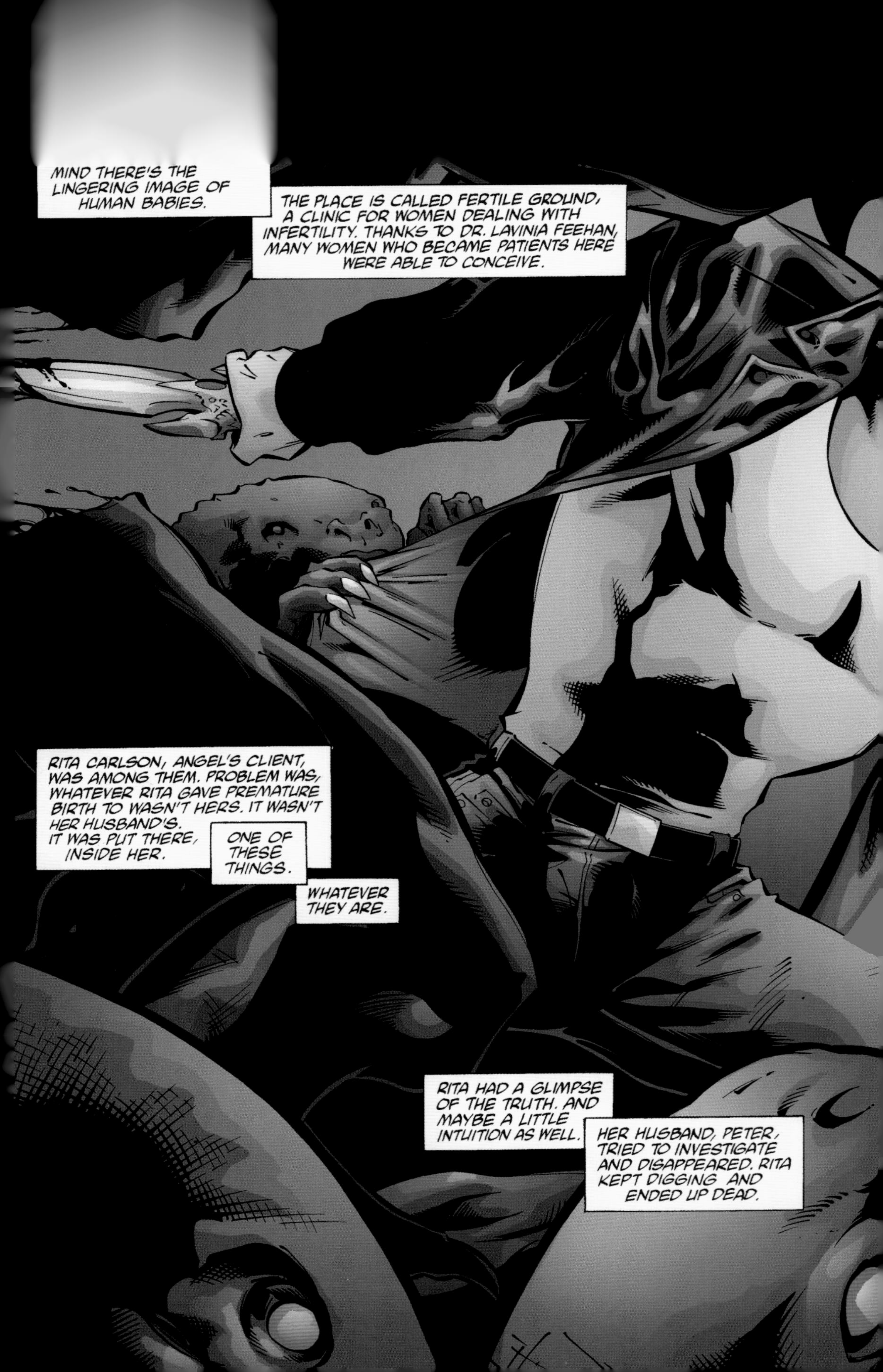
MIND THERE'S THE LINGERING IMAGE OF HUMAN BABIES.
THE PLACE IS CALLED FERTILE GROUND, A CLINIC FOR WOMEN DEALING WITH INFERTILITY. THANKS TO DR. LAVINIA FEEHAN, MANY WOMEN WHO BECAME PATIENTS HERE WERE ABLE TO CONCEIVE.
RITA CARLSON, ANGEL'S CLIENT, WAS AMONG THEM. PROBLEM WAS, WHATEVER RITA GAVE PREMATURE BIRTH TO WASN'T HERS. IT WASN'T HER HUSBAND'S. IT WAS PUT THERE, INSIDE HER.
ONE OF THESE THINGS.
WHATEVER THEY ARE.
RITA HAD A GLIMPSE OF THE TRUTH. AND MAYBE A LITTLE INTUITION AS WELL.
HER HUSBAND, PETER, TRIED TO INVESTIGATE AND DISAPPEARED. RITA KEPT DIGGING AND ENDED UP DEAD.

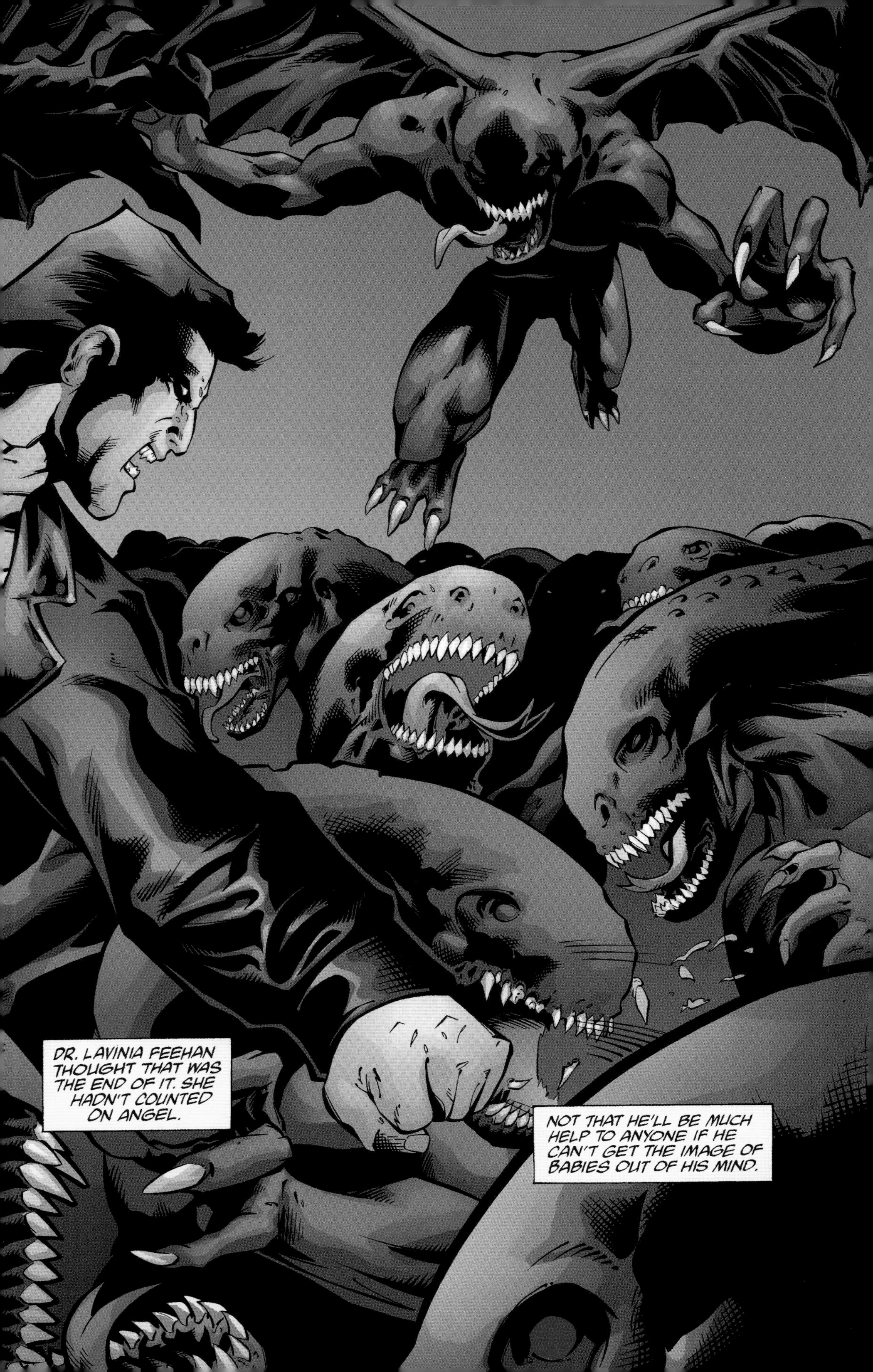
DR. LAVINIA FEEHAN THOUGHT THAT WAS THE END OF IT. SHE HADN'T COUNTED ON ANGEL.
NOT THAT HE'LL BE MUCH HELP TO ANYONE IF HE CAN'T GET THE IMAGE OF BABIES OUT OF HIS MIND.

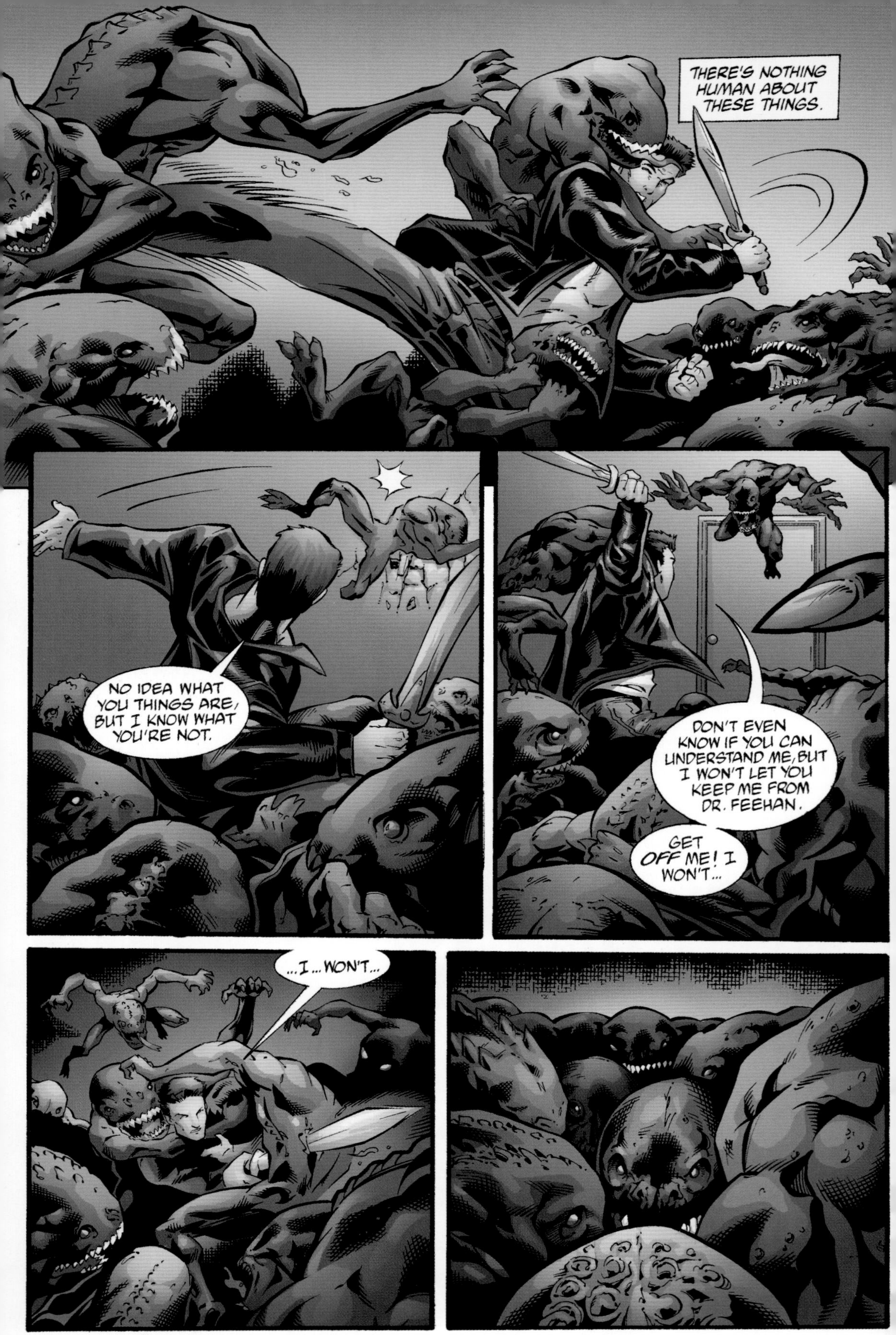
THERE'S NOTHING HUMAN ABOUT THESE THINGS.
NO IDEA WHAT YOU THINGS ARE, BUT I KNOW WHAT YOU'RE NOT.
DON'T EVEN KNOW IF YOU CAN UNDERSTAND ME, BUT I WON'T LET YOU KEEP ME FROM DR. FEEHAN.
GET OFF ME! I WON'T...
...I...WON'T...

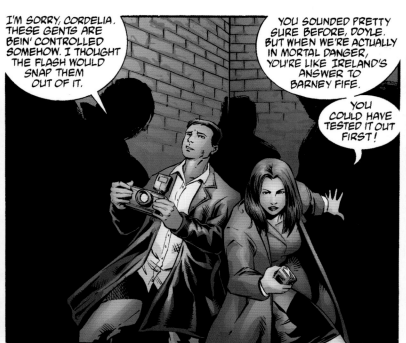

SOME-BODY'S GONNA DIE!

I'M SORRY, CORDELIA. THESE GENTS ARE BEIN' CONTROLLED SOMEHOW. I THOUGHT THE FLASH WOULD SNAP THEM OUT OF IT.

YOU SOUNDED PRETTY SURE BEFORE, DOYLE. BUT WHEN WE'RE ACTUALLY IN MORTAL DANGER, YOU'RE LIKE IRELAND'S ANSWER TO BARNEY FIFE.

YOU COULD HAVE TESTED IT OUT FIRST!

WHAT'S WRONG WITH NOW?

OTHER THAN THE WHOLE BLINDNESS THING?

DO I EVEN NEED TO ANSWER THAT?

YOU WOULDN'T BE SO SMUG IF IT'D WORKED.

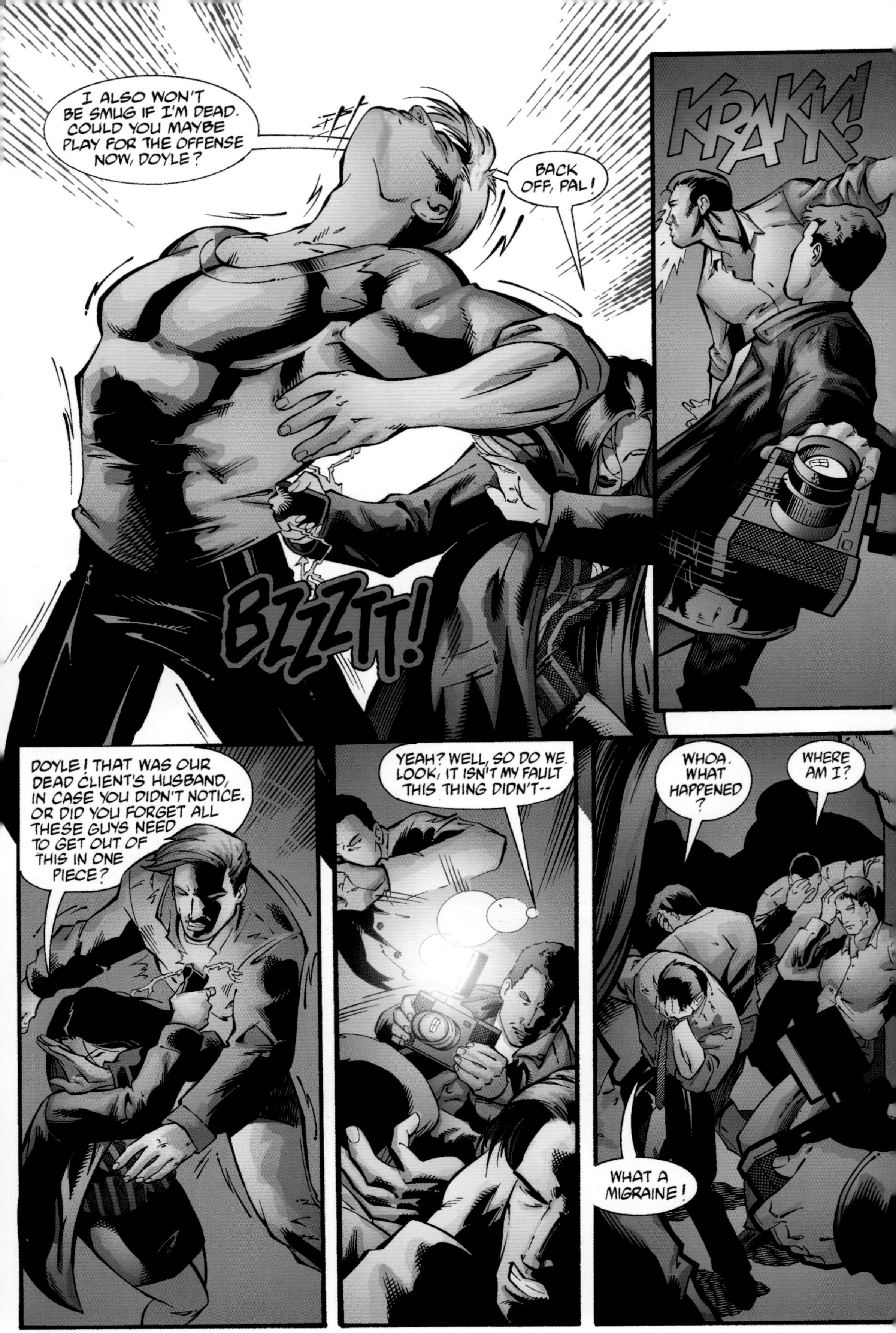
I ALSO WON'T BE SMUG IF I'M DEAD. COULD YOU MAYBE PLAY FOR THE OFFENSE NOW, DOYLE?
BACK OFF, PAL!
BZZZTT!
KRAKK!
DOYLE! THAT WAS OUR DEAD CLIENT'S HUSBAND, IN CASE YOU DIDN'T NOTICE. OR DID YOU FORGET ALL THESE GUYS NEED TO GET OUT OF THIS IN ONE PIECE?
YEAH? WELL, SO DO WE. LOOK, IT ISN'T MY FAULT THIS THING DIDN'T--
WHOA. WHAT HAPPENED?
WHERE AM I?
WHAT A MIGRAINE!

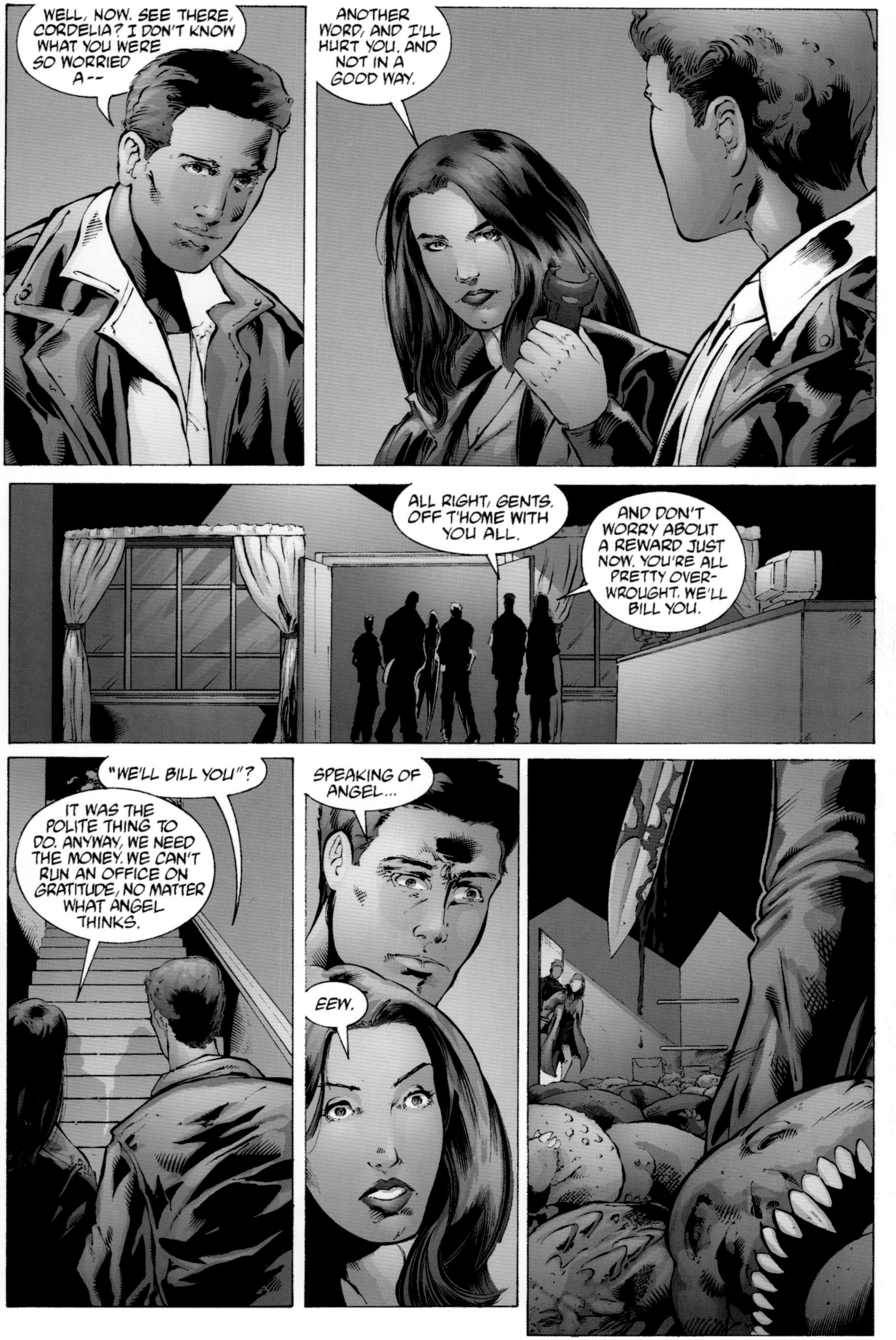
WELL, NOW. SEE THERE, CORDELIA? I DON'T KNOW WHAT YOU WERE SO WORRIED A--
ANOTHER WORD, AND I'LL HURT YOU. AND NOT IN A GOOD WAY.
ALL RIGHT, GENTS. OFF T'HOME WITH YOU ALL.
AND DON'T WORRY ABOUT A REWARD JUST NOW. YOU'RE ALL PRETTY OVER-WROUGHT. WE'LL BILL YOU.
"WE'LL BILL YOU"?
IT WAS THE POLITE THING TO DO. ANYWAY, WE NEED THE MONEY. WE CAN'T RUN AN OFFICE ON GRATITUDE, NO MATTER WHAT ANGEL THINKS.
SPEAKING OF ANGEL...
EEW.

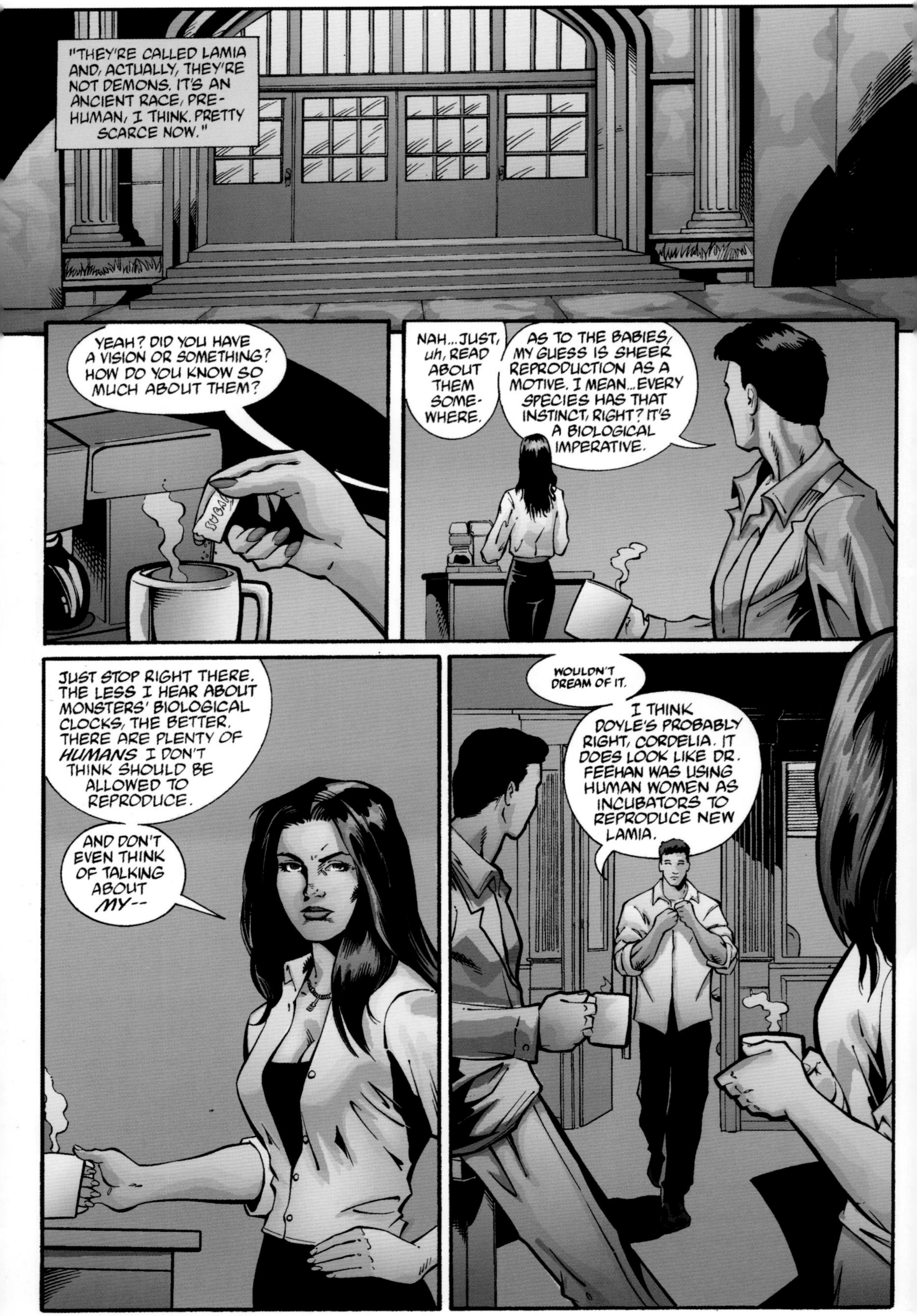
"THEY'RE CALLED LAMIA AND, ACTUALLY, THEY'RE NOT DEMONS. IT'S AN ANCIENT RACE, PRE-HUMAN, I THINK. PRETTY SCARCE NOW."
YEAH? DID YOU HAVE A VISION OR SOMETHING? HOW DO YOU KNOW SO MUCH ABOUT THEM?
SUGAR
NAH... JUST, uh, READ ABOUT THEM SOME-WHERE.
AS TO THE BABIES, MY GUESS IS SHEER REPRODUCTION AS A MOTIVE. I MEAN... EVERY SPECIES HAS THAT INSTINCT, RIGHT? IT'S A BIOLOGICAL IMPERATIVE.
JUST STOP RIGHT THERE. THE LESS I HEAR ABOUT MONSTERS' BIOLOGICAL CLOCKS, THE BETTER. THERE ARE PLENTY OF HUMANS I DON'T THINK SHOULD BE ALLOWED TO REPRODUCE.
AND DON'T EVEN THINK OF TALKING ABOUT MY--
WOULDN'T DREAM OF IT.
I THINK DOYLE'S PROBABLY RIGHT, CORDELIA. IT DOES LOOK LIKE DR. FEEHAN WAS USING HUMAN WOMEN AS INCUBATORS TO REPRODUCE NEW LAMIA.

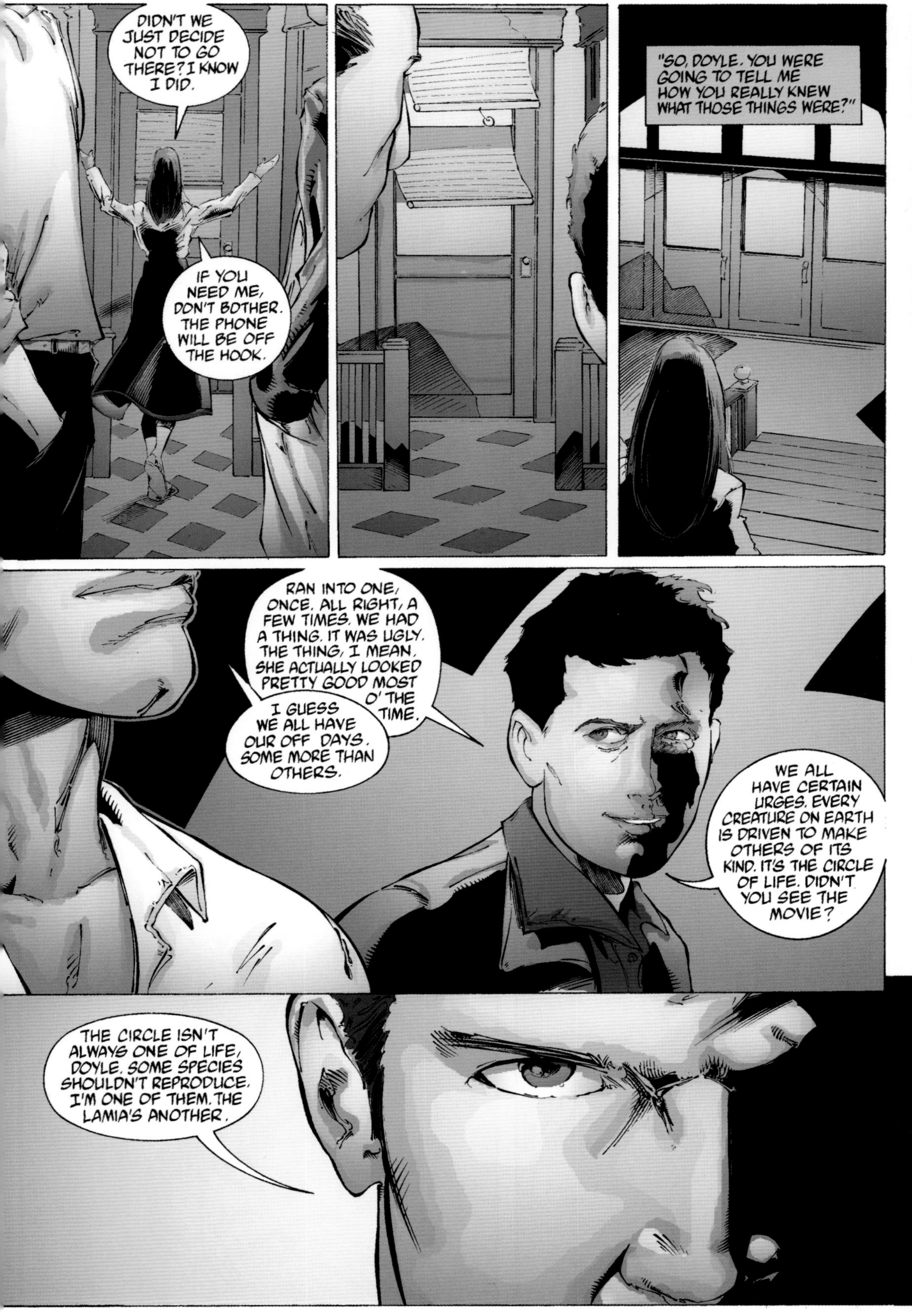
DIDN'T WE JUST DECIDE NOT TO GO THERE? I KNOW I DID.
IF YOU NEED ME, DON'T BOTHER. THE PHONE WILL BE OFF THE HOOK.
"SO, DOYLE. YOU WERE GOING TO TELL ME HOW YOU REALLY KNEW WHAT THOSE THINGS WERE?"
RAN INTO ONE, ONCE. ALL RIGHT, A FEW TIMES. WE HAD A THING. IT WAS UGLY. THE THING, I MEAN. SHE ACTUALLY LOOKED PRETTY GOOD MOST O' THE TIME.
I GUESS WE ALL HAVE OUR OFF DAYS. SOME MORE THAN OTHERS.
WE ALL HAVE CERTAIN URGES. EVERY CREATURE ON EARTH IS DRIVEN TO MAKE OTHERS OF ITS KIND. IT'S THE CIRCLE OF LIFE. DIDN'T YOU SEE THE MOVIE?
THE CIRCLE ISN'T ALWAYS ONE OF LIFE, DOYLE. SOME SPECIES SHOULDN'T REPRODUCE. I'M ONE OF THEM. THE LAMIA'S ANOTHER.

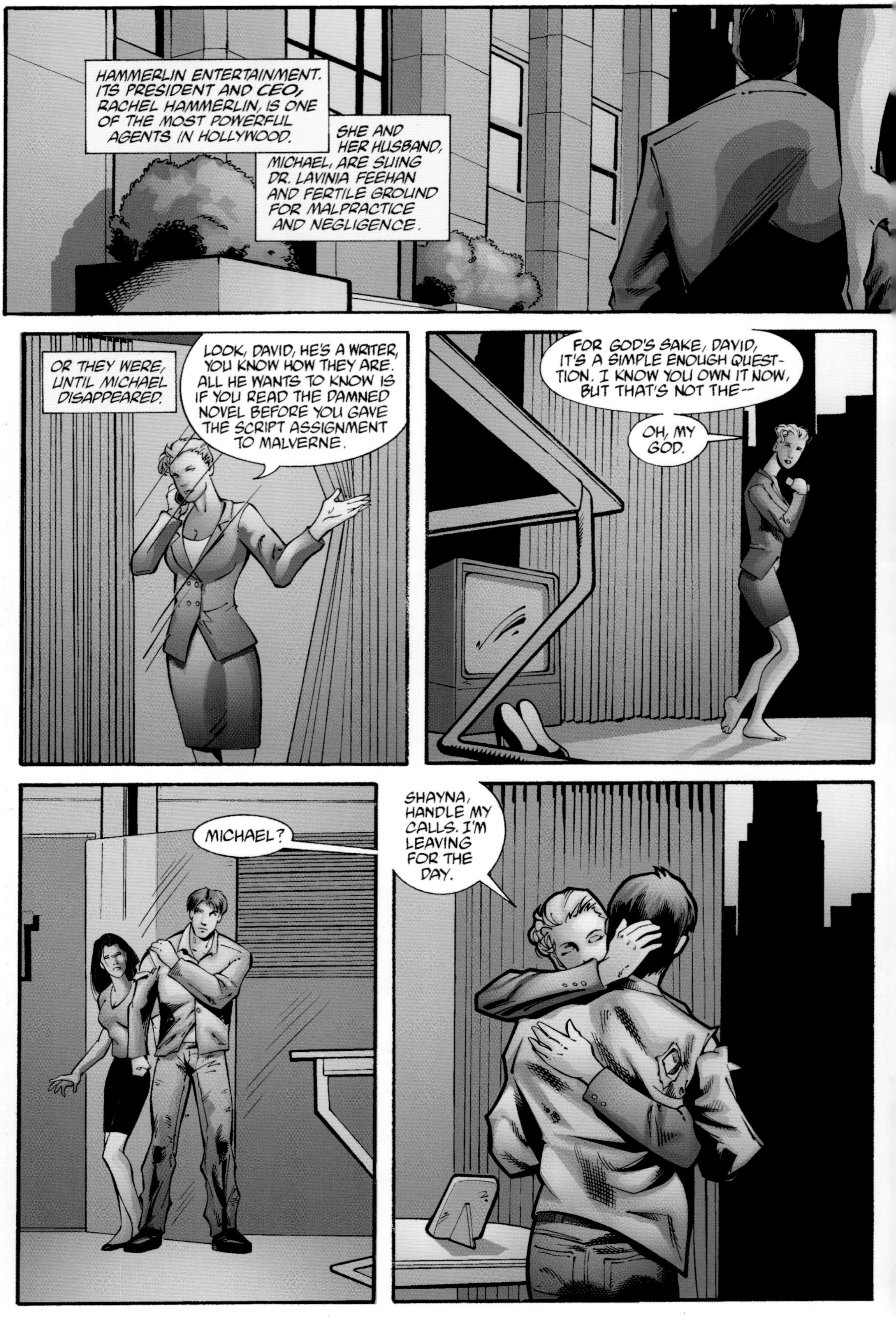

HAMMERLIN ENTERTAINMENT. ITS PRESIDENT AND CEO, RACHEL HAMMERLIN, IS ONE OF THE MOST POWERFUL AGENTS IN HOLLYWOOD.
SHE AND HER HUSBAND, MICHAEL, ARE SUING DR. LAVINIA FEEHAN AND FERTILE GROUND FOR MALPRACTICE AND NEGLIGENCE.
OR THEY WERE, UNTIL MICHAEL DISAPPEARED.
LOOK, DAVID, HE'S A WRITER, YOU KNOW HOW THEY ARE. ALL HE WANTS TO KNOW IS IF YOU READ THE DAMNED NOVEL BEFORE YOU GAVE THE SCRIPT ASSIGNMENT TO MALVERNE.
FOR GOD'S SAKE, DAVID, IT'S A SIMPLE ENOUGH QUESTION. I KNOW YOU OWN IT NOW, BUT THAT'S NOT THE--
OH, MY GOD.
MICHAEL?
SHAYNA, HANDLE MY CALLS. I'M LEAVING FOR THE DAY.

YOU LOOK... YOU LOOK LIKE HELL, MICHAEL. WHAT HAPPENED TO YOU?

SO INSANE...RACHEL...NEVER BELIEVE IT. I...STARTED DIGGING INTO FEEHAN'S CREDENTIALS.

SO THEN THEY JUST TOLD US TO GO HOME. BUT I CAME HERE FIRST.

GUESS WE BOTH HAD THE SAME IDEA.

EXCUSE ME, MISS HAMMERLIN. I WAS HOPING I COULD ASK YOU A FAVOR.

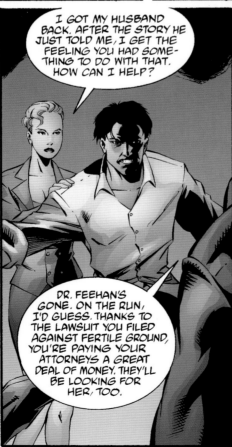

I GOT MY HUSBAND BACK. AFTER THE STORY HE JUST TOLD ME, I GET THE FEELING YOU HAD SOMETHING TO DO WITH THAT. HOW CAN I HELP?

DR. FEEHAN'S GONE. ON THE RUN, I'D GUESS. THANKS TO THE LAWSUIT YOU FILED AGAINST FERTILE GROUND, YOU'RE PAYING YOUR ATTORNEYS A GREAT DEAL OF MONEY. THEY'LL BE LOOKING FOR HER, TOO.

"AND YOU WANT ME TO CALL YOU IF MY LAWYERS TRACK HER DOWN? I CAN DO THAT. I TOLD YOU ONCE BEFORE, I'LL DO WHATEVER I CAN TO HURT LAVINIA FEEHAN. DO YOU REALLY THINK YOU'LL FIND HER NOW, THOUGH?"

"I WISH I KNEW."

EXIT

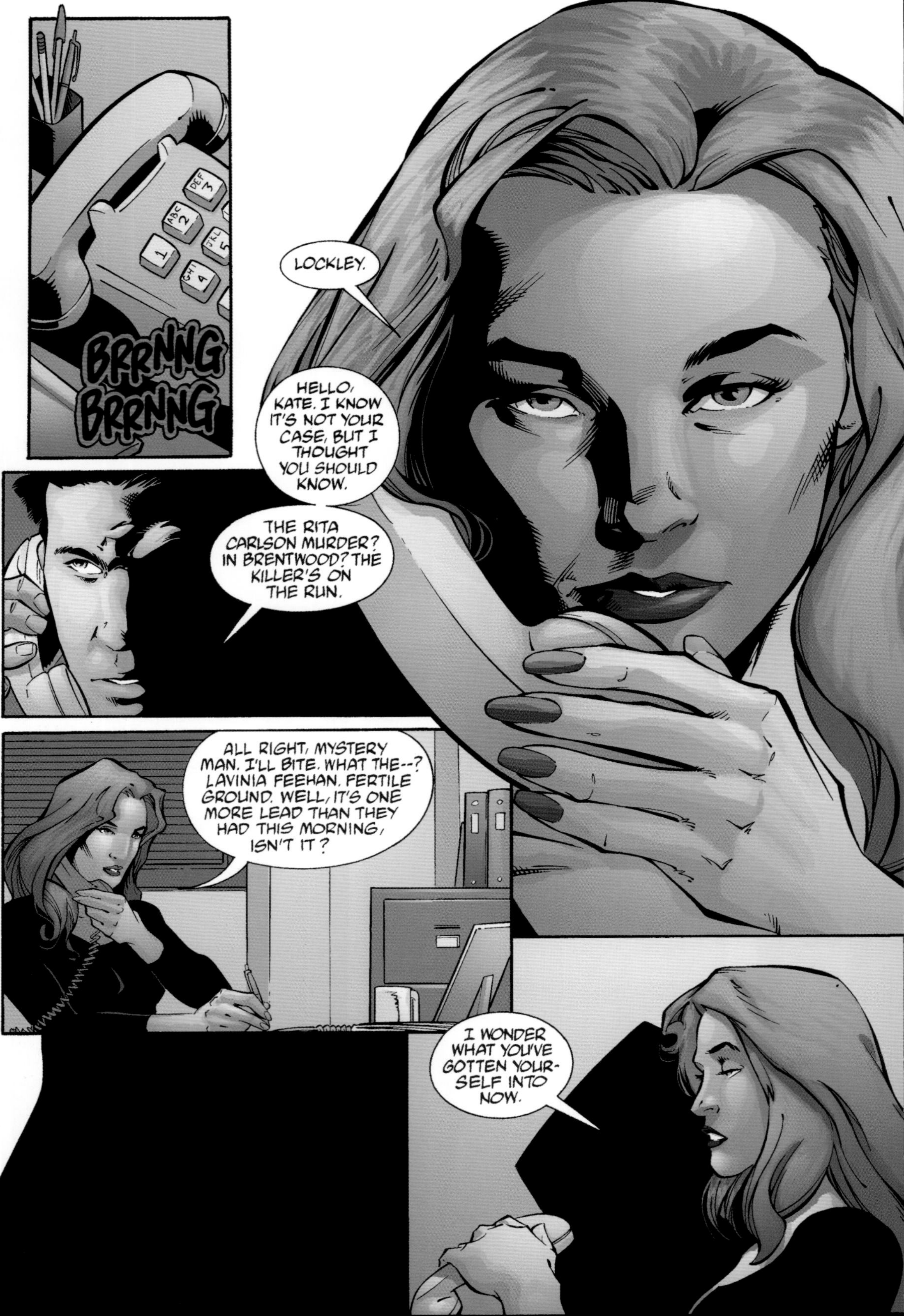
BRRNNG BRRNNG
LOCKLEY.
HELLO, KATE. I KNOW IT'S NOT YOUR CASE, BUT I THOUGHT YOU SHOULD KNOW.
THE RITA CARLSON MURDER? IN BRENTWOOD? THE KILLER'S ON THE RUN.
ALL RIGHT, MYSTERY MAN. I'LL BITE. WHAT THE--? LAVINIA FEEHAN. FERTILE GROUND. WELL, IT'S ONE MORE LEAD THAN THEY HAD THIS MORNING, ISN'T IT?
I WONDER WHAT YOU'VE GOTTEN YOURSELF INTO NOW.

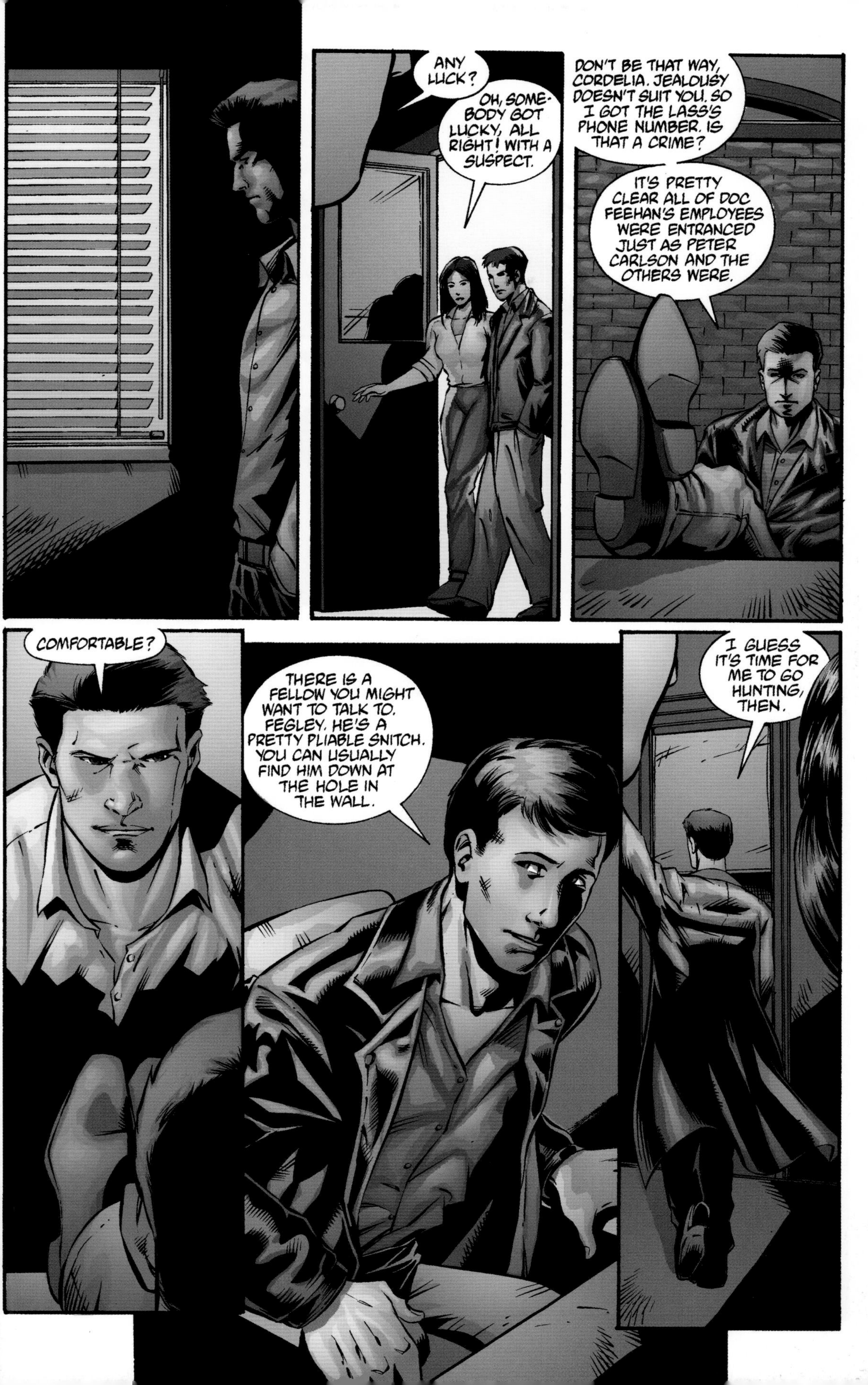
ANY LUCK?
OH, SOMEBODY GOT LUCKY, ALL RIGHT! WITH A SUSPECT.
DON'T BE THAT WAY, CORDELIA. JEALOUSY DOESN'T SUIT YOU. SO I GOT THE LASS'S PHONE NUMBER. IS THAT A CRIME?
IT'S PRETTY CLEAR ALL OF DOC FEEHAN'S EMPLOYEES WERE ENTRANCED JUST AS PETER CARLSON AND THE OTHERS WERE.
COMFORTABLE?
THERE IS A FELLOW YOU MIGHT WANT TO TALK TO. FEGLEY. HE'S A PRETTY PLIABLE SNITCH. YOU CAN USUALLY FIND HIM DOWN AT THE HOLE IN THE WALL.
I GUESS IT'S TIME FOR ME TO GO HUNTING, THEN.

YOU FEGLEY?

WHO'S ASKING?

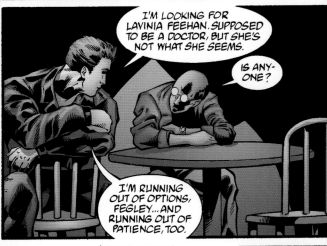

I'M LOOKING FOR LAVINIA FEEHAN. SUPPOSED TO BE A DOCTOR, BUT SHE'S NOT WHAT SHE SEEMS.

IS ANY-ONE?

I'M RUNNING OUT OF OPTIONS, FEGLEY... AND RUNNING OUT OF PATIENCE, TOO.

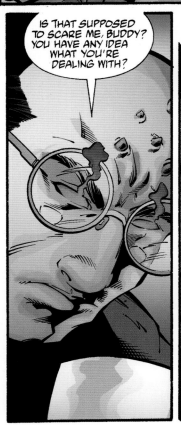

IS THAT SUPPOSED TO SCARE ME, BUDDY? YOU HAVE ANY IDEA WHAT YOU'RE DEALING WITH?

DO YOU? THE NAME'S ANGEL.

...OH...RIGHT... ANGELUS, KILLED MORE EUROPEANS THAN THE PLAGUE. SO...I HEAR ANY-THING, I'LL GET IT TO YOU, RIGHT AWAY. I SWEAR.

YOU DO THAT. AND BRUSH UP ON THE EVIL GLARE. MAYBE CURL THE LIP A LITTLE MORE, NOT ENOUGH MENACE.

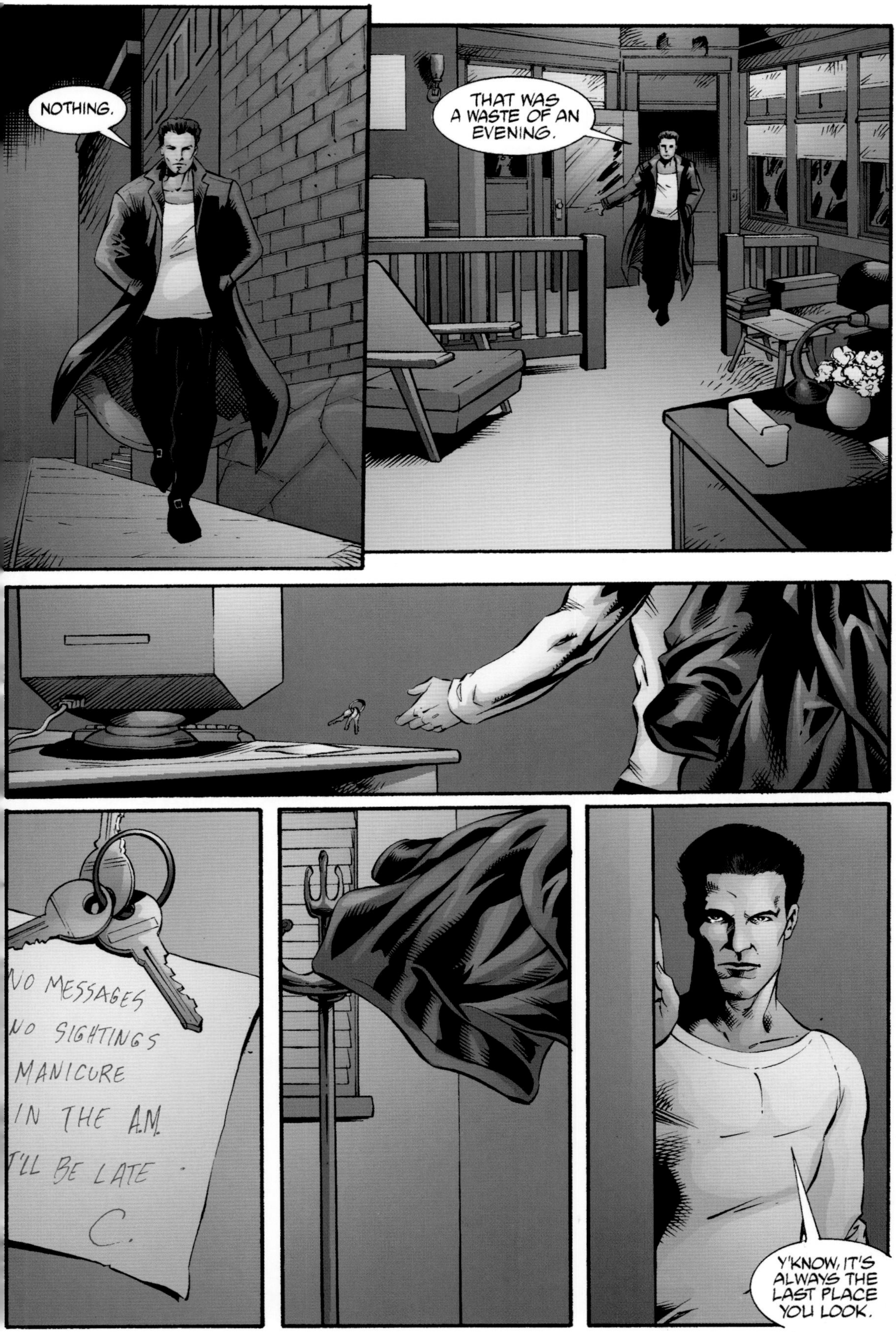
NOTHING.
THAT WAS A WASTE OF AN EVENING.
NO MESSAGES
NO SIGHTINGS
MANICURE
IN THE A.M.
I'LL BE LATE
C.
Y'KNOW, IT'S ALWAYS THE LAST PLACE YOU LOOK.

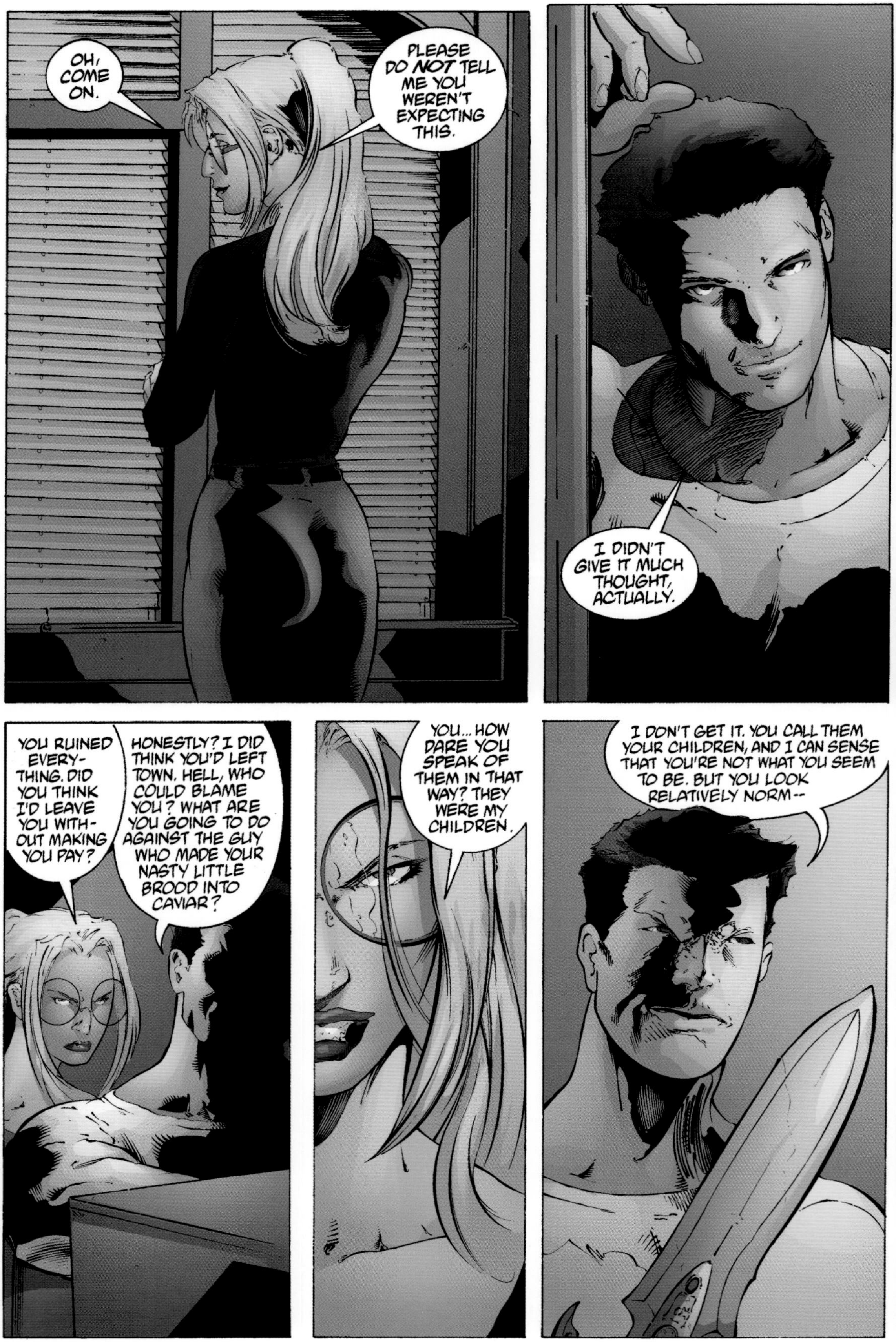
OH, COME ON.
PLEASE DO NOT TELL ME YOU WEREN'T EXPECTING THIS.
I DIDN'T GIVE IT MUCH THOUGHT, ACTUALLY.
YOU RUINED EVERYTHING. DID YOU THINK I'D LEAVE YOU WITHOUT MAKING YOU PAY?
HONESTLY? I DID THINK YOU'D LEFT TOWN. HELL, WHO COULD BLAME YOU? WHAT ARE YOU GOING TO DO AGAINST THE GUY WHO MADE YOUR NASTY LITTLE BROOD INTO CAVIAR?
YOU... HOW DARE YOU SPEAK OF THEM IN THAT WAY? THEY WERE MY CHILDREN.
I DON'T GET IT. YOU CALL THEM YOUR CHILDREN, AND I CAN SENSE THAT YOU'RE NOT WHAT YOU SEEM TO BE. BUT YOU LOOK RELATIVELY NORM--

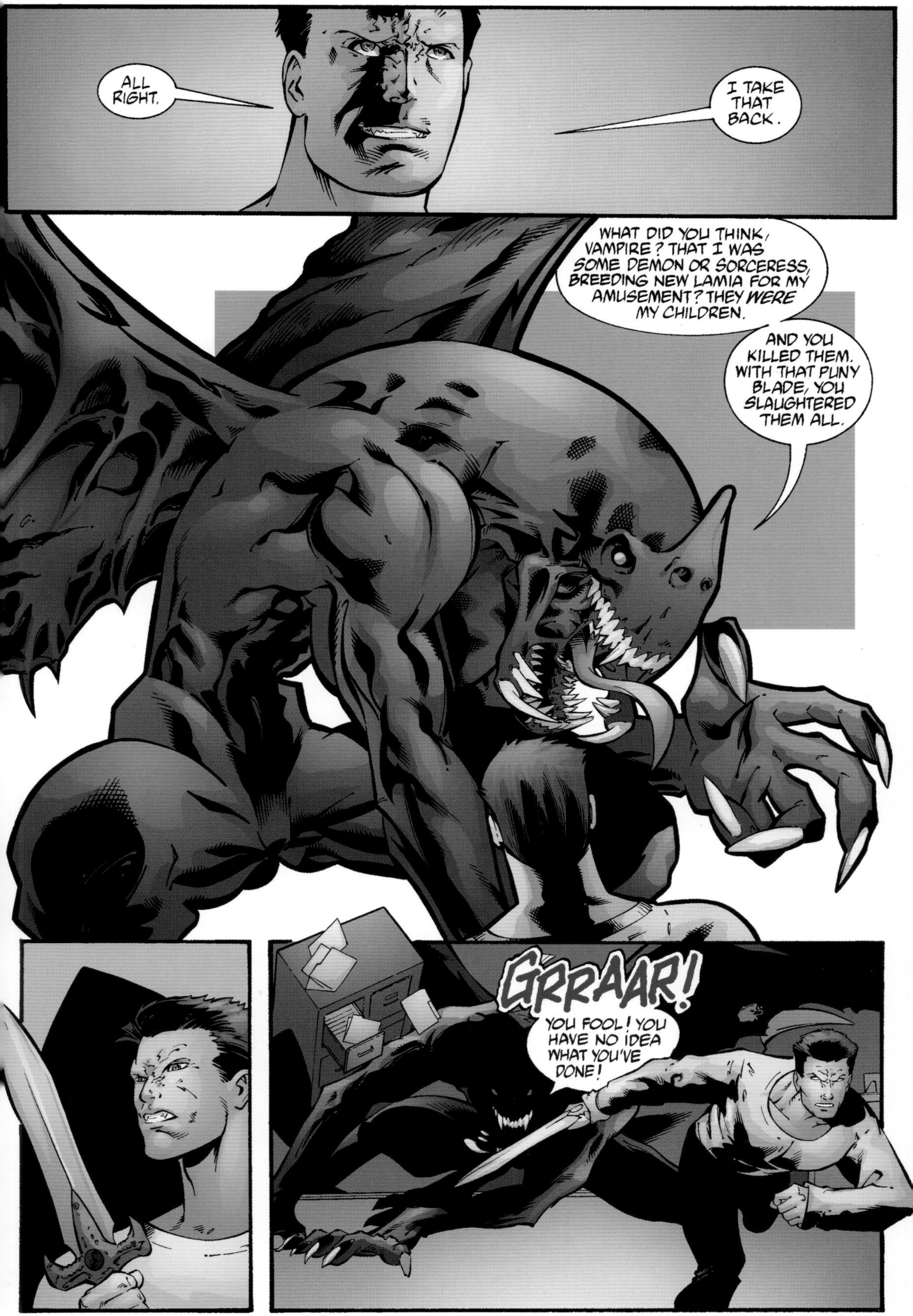
ALL RIGHT.
I TAKE THAT BACK.
WHAT DID YOU THINK, VAMPIRE? THAT I WAS SOME DEMON OR SORCERESS, BREEDING NEW LAMIA FOR MY AMUSEMENT? THEY *WERE* MY CHILDREN.
AND YOU KILLED THEM. WITH THAT PUNY BLADE, YOU SLAUGHTERED THEM ALL.
GRRAAR!
YOU FOOL! YOU HAVE NO IDEA WHAT YOU'VE DONE!

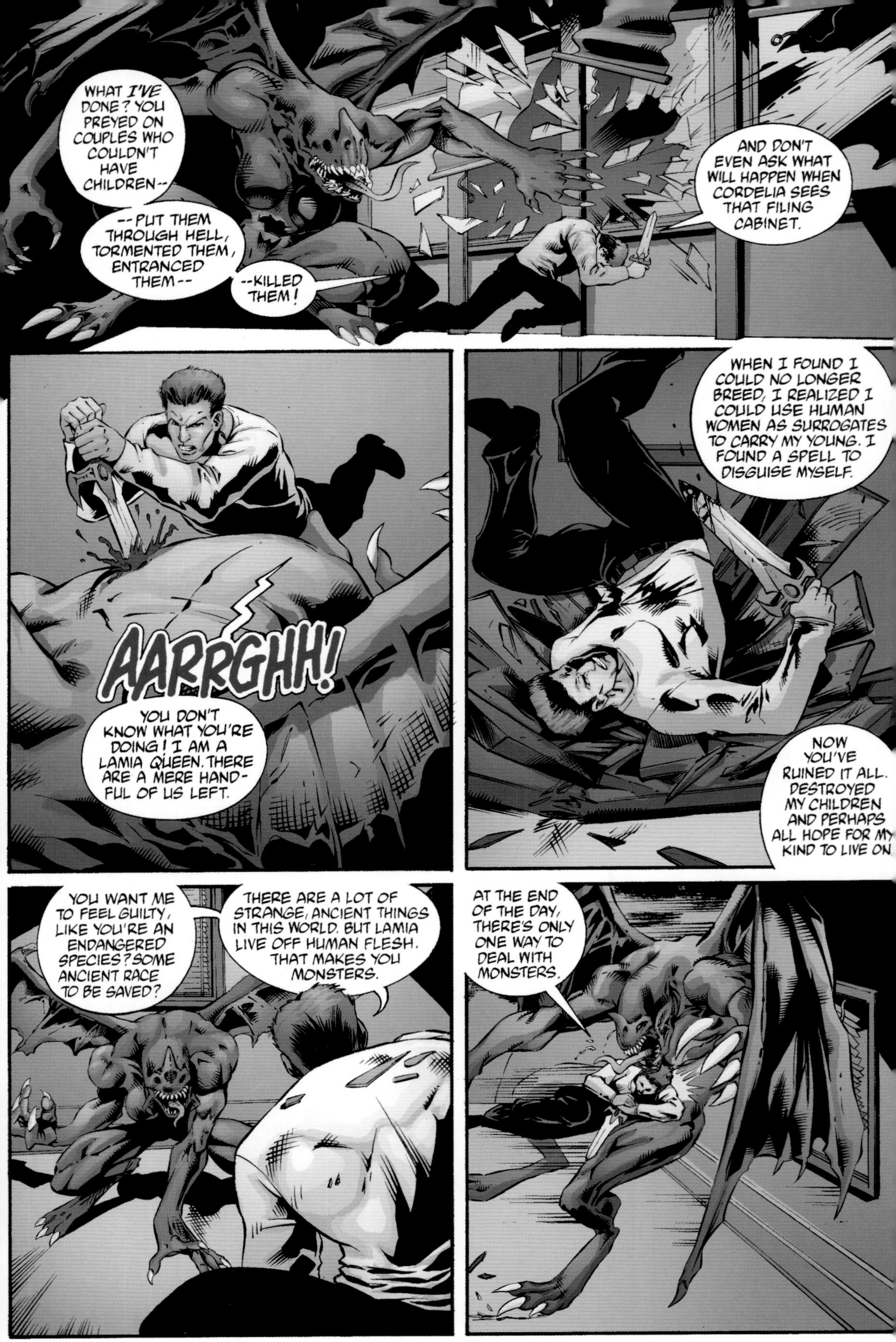
WHAT I'VE DONE? YOU PREYED ON COUPLES WHO COULDN'T HAVE CHILDREN--
--PUT THEM THROUGH HELL, TORMENTED THEM, ENTRANCED THEM--
--KILLED THEM!
AND DON'T EVEN ASK WHAT WILL HAPPEN WHEN CORDELIA SEES THAT FILING CABINET.
AARRGHH!
YOU DON'T KNOW WHAT YOU'RE DOING! I AM A LAMIA QUEEN. THERE ARE A MERE HANDFUL OF US LEFT.
WHEN I FOUND I COULD NO LONGER BREED, I REALIZED I COULD USE HUMAN WOMEN AS SURROGATES TO CARRY MY YOUNG. I FOUND A SPELL TO DISGUISE MYSELF.
NOW YOU'VE RUINED IT ALL. DESTROYED MY CHILDREN AND PERHAPS ALL HOPE FOR MY KIND TO LIVE ON
YOU WANT ME TO FEEL GUILTY, LIKE YOU'RE AN ENDANGERED SPECIES? SOME ANCIENT RACE TO BE SAVED?
THERE ARE A LOT OF STRANGE, ANCIENT THINGS IN THIS WORLD. BUT LAMIA LIVE OFF HUMAN FLESH. THAT MAKES YOU MONSTERS.
AT THE END OF THE DAY, THERE'S ONLY ONE WAY TO DEAL WITH MONSTERS.

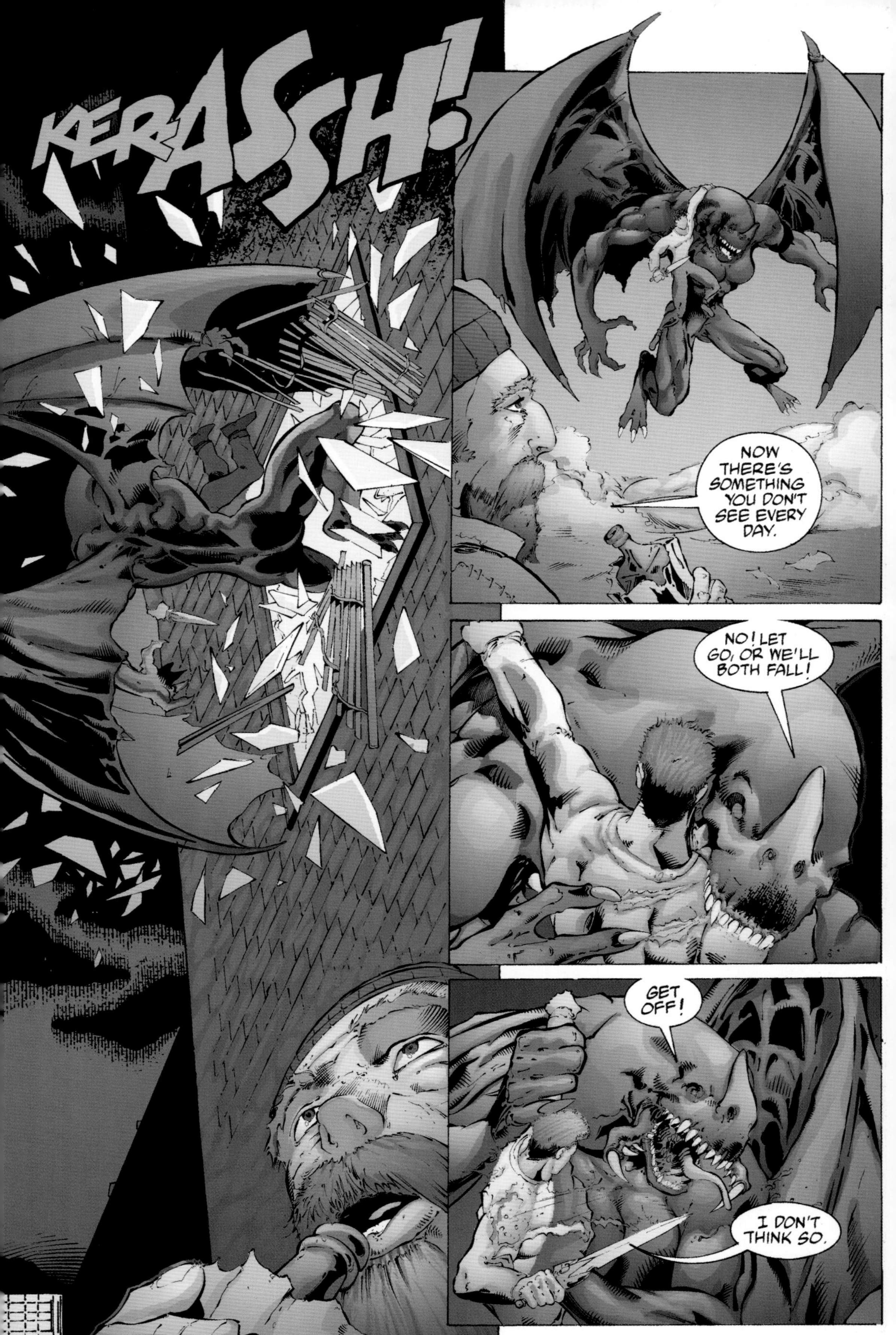
KERASH!
NOW THERE'S SOMETHING YOU DON'T SEE EVERY DAY.
NO! LET GO, OR WE'LL BOTH FALL!
GET OFF!
I DON'T THINK SO.

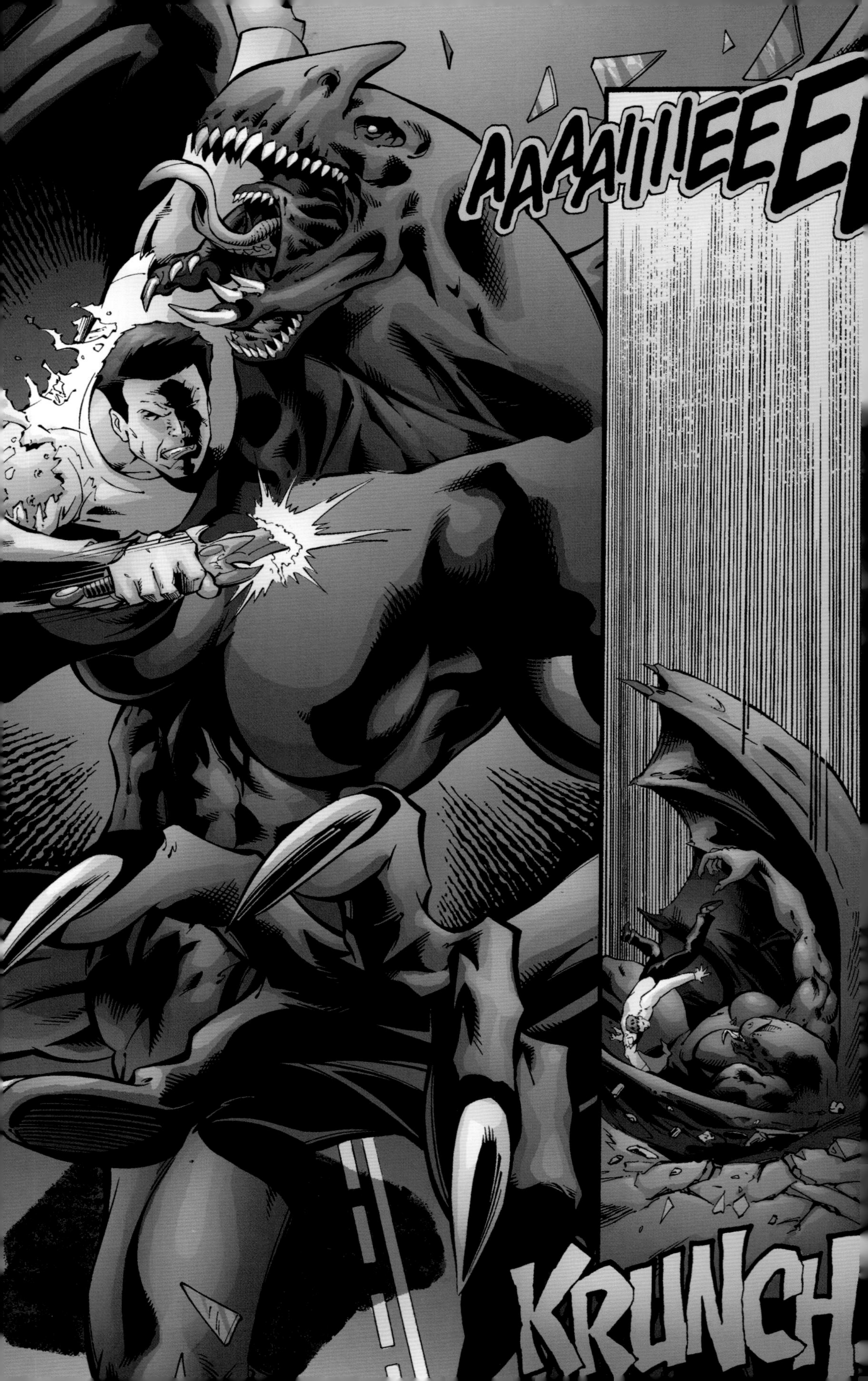
AAAAIIIEEE
KRUNCH

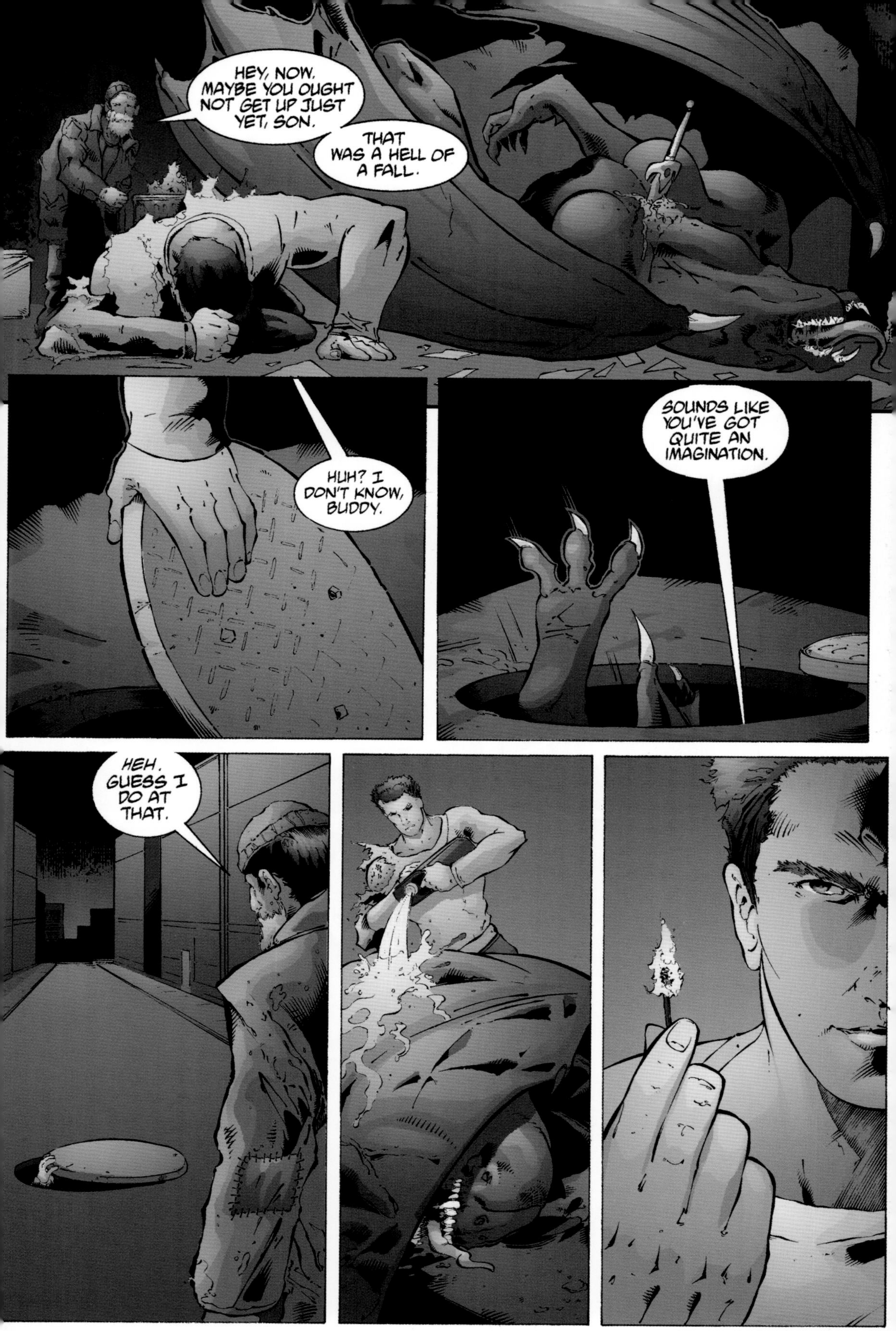
HEY, NOW. MAYBE YOU OUGHT NOT GET UP JUST YET, SON.
THAT WAS A HELL OF A FALL.
HUH? I DON'T KNOW, BUDDY.
SOUNDS LIKE YOU'VE GOT QUITE AN IMAGINATION.
HEH. GUESS I DO AT THAT.

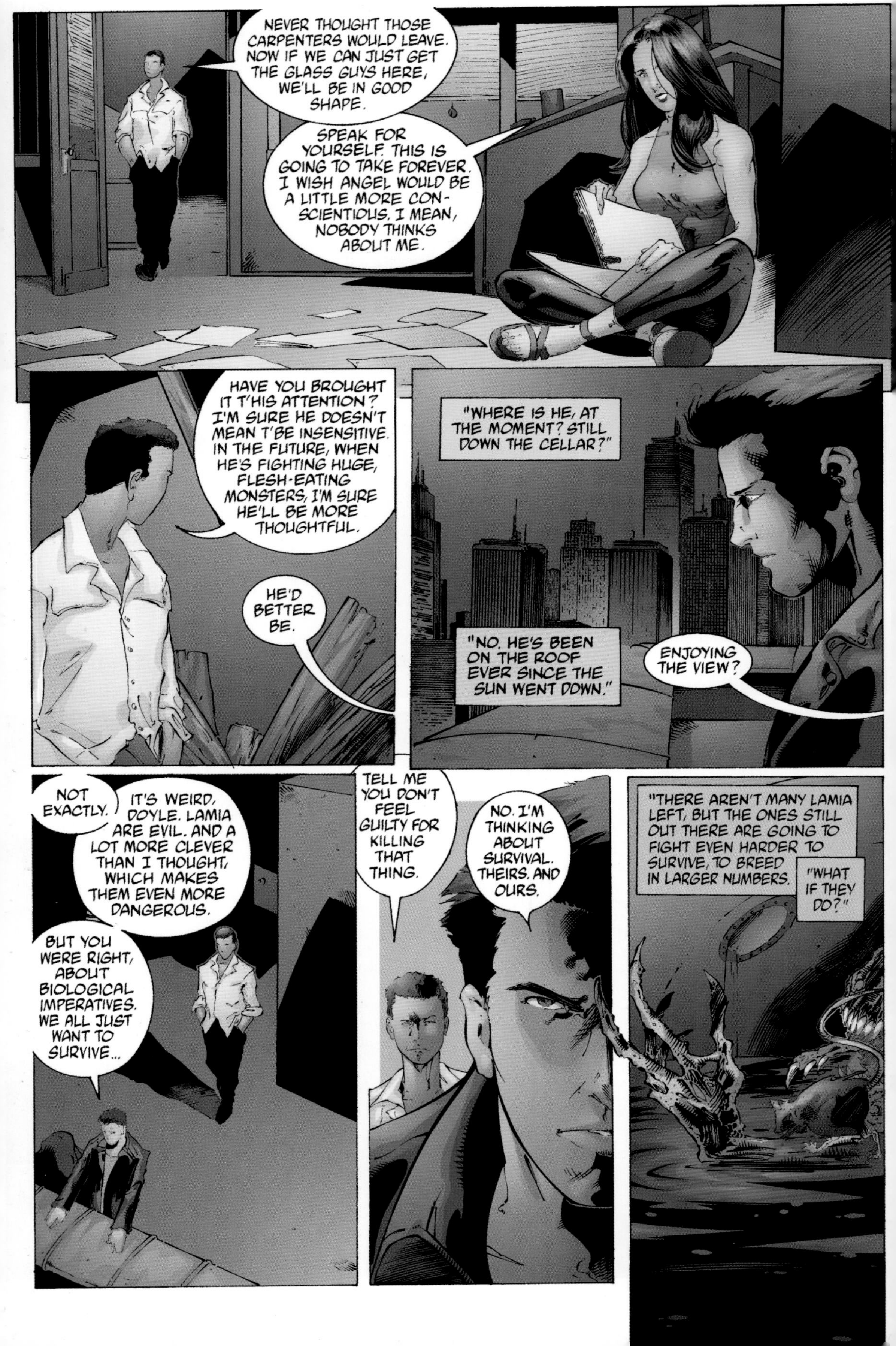
NEVER THOUGHT THOSE CARPENTERS WOULD LEAVE. NOW IF WE CAN JUST GET THE GLASS GUYS HERE, WE'LL BE IN GOOD SHAPE.
SPEAK FOR YOURSELF. THIS IS GOING TO TAKE FOREVER. I WISH ANGEL WOULD BE A LITTLE MORE CON-SCIENTIOUS. I MEAN, NOBODY THINKS ABOUT ME.
HAVE YOU BROUGHT IT T'HIS ATTENTION? I'M SURE HE DOESN'T MEAN T'BE INSENSITIVE. IN THE FUTURE, WHEN HE'S FIGHTING HUGE, FLESH-EATING MONSTERS, I'M SURE HE'LL BE MORE THOUGHTFUL.
HE'D BETTER BE.
"WHERE IS HE, AT THE MOMENT? STILL DOWN THE CELLAR?"
"NO. HE'S BEEN ON THE ROOF EVER SINCE THE SUN WENT DOWN."
ENJOYING THE VIEW?
NOT EXACTLY.
IT'S WEIRD, DOYLE. LAMIA ARE EVIL. AND A LOT MORE CLEVER THAN I THOUGHT, WHICH MAKES THEM EVEN MORE DANGEROUS.
BUT YOU WERE RIGHT, ABOUT BIOLOGICAL IMPERATIVES. WE ALL JUST WANT TO SURVIVE...
TELL ME YOU DON'T FEEL GUILTY FOR KILLING THAT THING.
NO. I'M THINKING ABOUT SURVIVAL. THEIRS. AND OURS.
"THERE AREN'T MANY LAMIA LEFT, BUT THE ONES STILL OUT THERE ARE GOING TO FIGHT EVEN HARDER TO SURVIVE, TO BREED IN LARGER NUMBERS.
"WHAT IF THEY DO?"

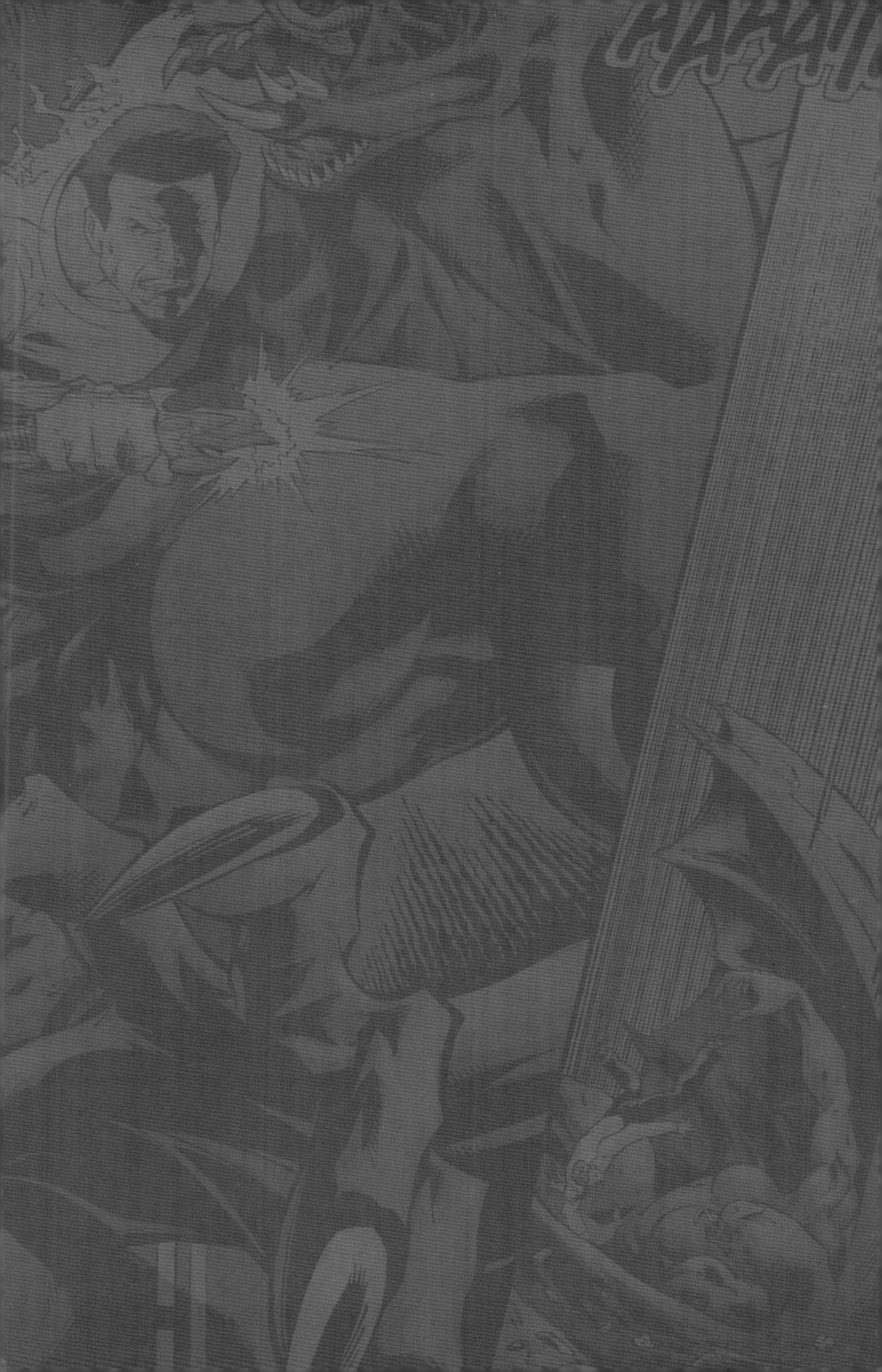

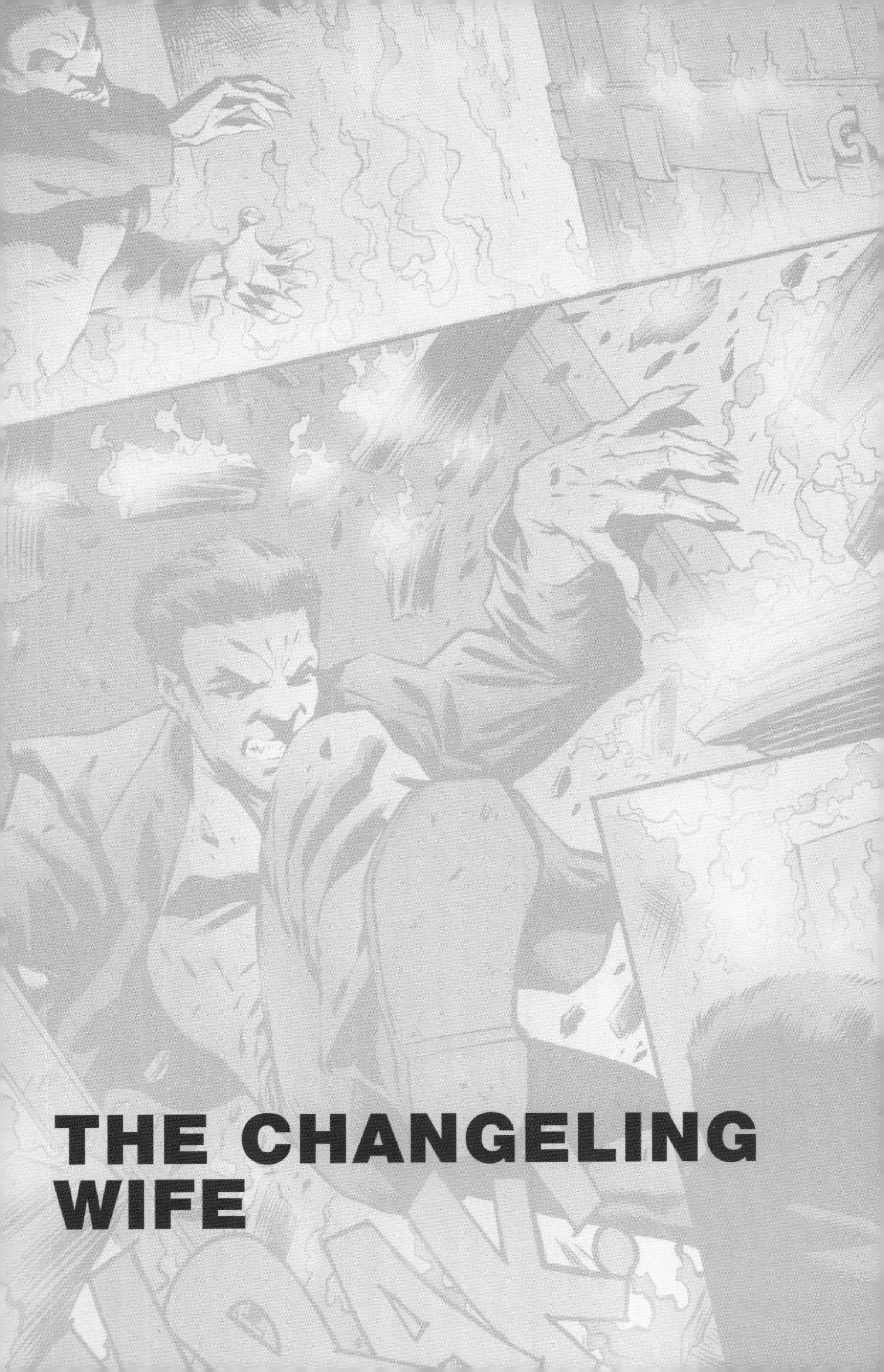

THE CHANGELING WIFE

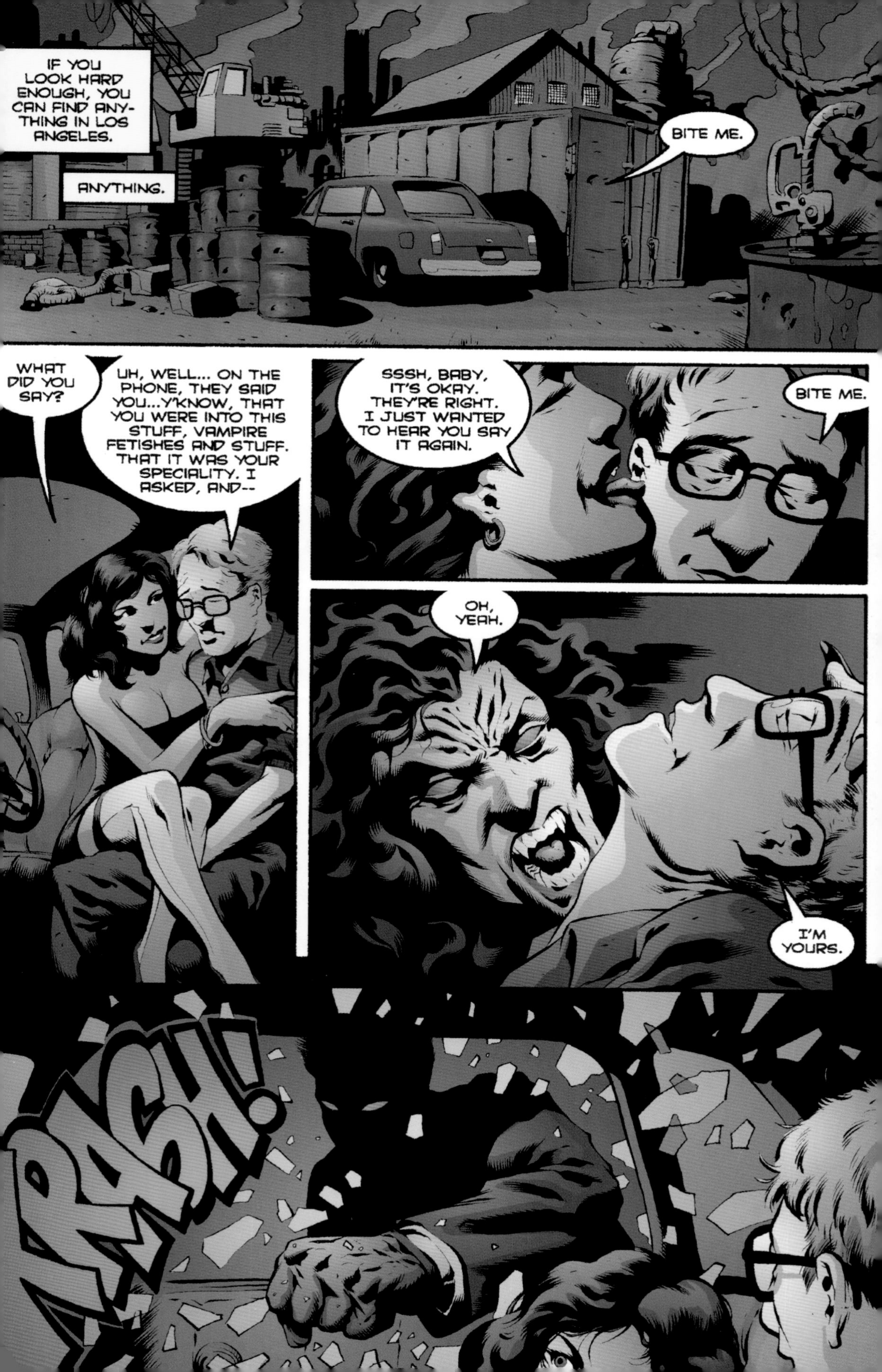
IF YOU LOOK HARD ENOUGH, YOU CAN FIND ANY-THING IN LOS ANGELES.
ANYTHING.
BITE ME.
WHAT DID YOU SAY?
UH, WELL... ON THE PHONE, THEY SAID YOU...Y'KNOW, THAT YOU WERE INTO THIS STUFF, VAMPIRE FETISHES AND STUFF. THAT IT WAS YOUR SPECIALITY. I ASKED, AND--
SSSH, BABY, IT'S OKAY. THEY'RE RIGHT. I JUST WANTED TO HEAR YOU SAY IT AGAIN.
BITE ME.
OH, YEAH.
I'M YOURS.
KRASH!!

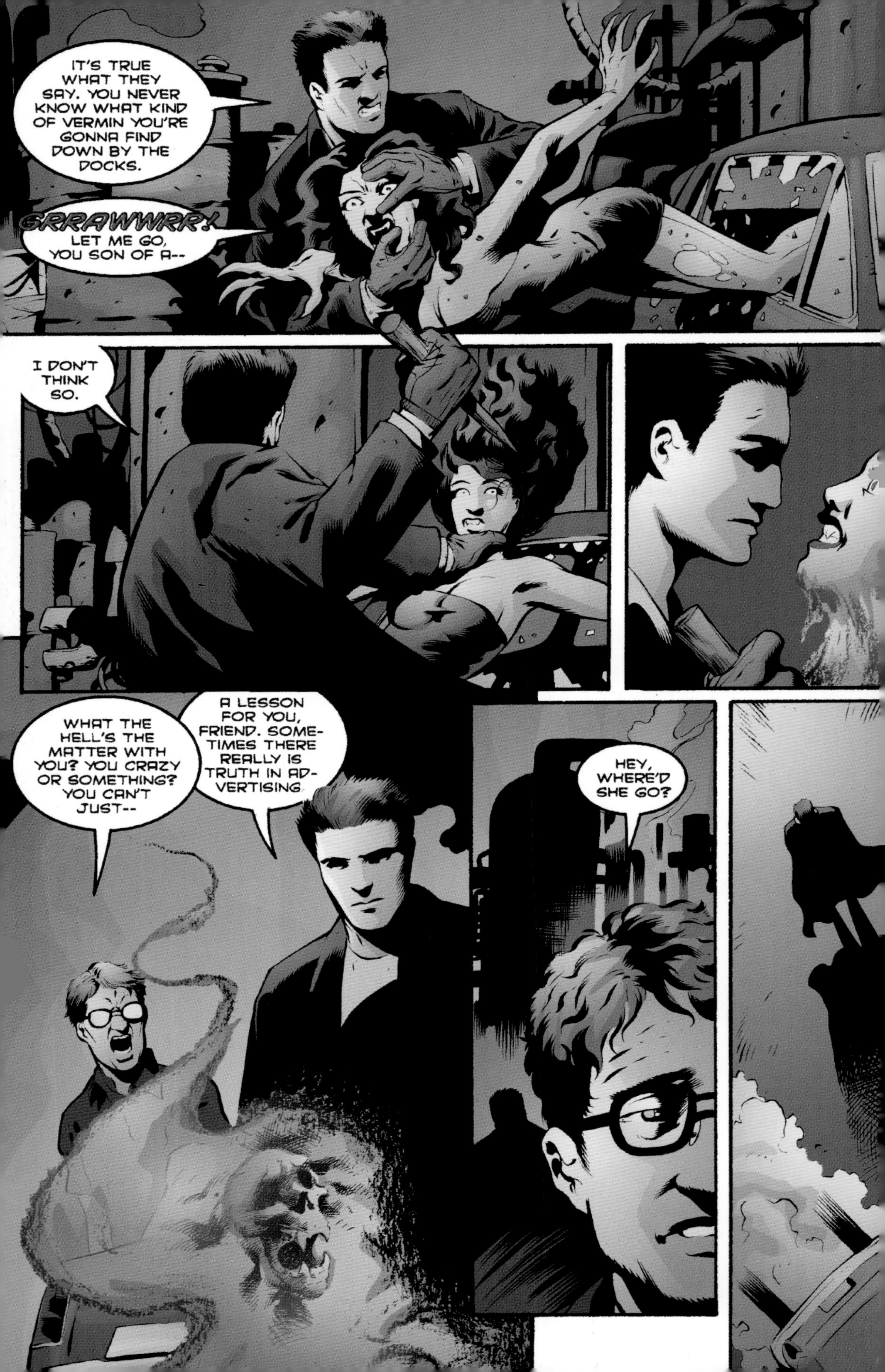
IT'S TRUE WHAT THEY SAY. YOU NEVER KNOW WHAT KIND OF VERMIN YOU'RE GONNA FIND DOWN BY THE DOCKS.
GRRAWWRR!
LET ME GO, YOU SON OF A--
I DON'T THINK SO.
WHAT THE HELL'S THE MATTER WITH YOU? YOU CRAZY OR SOMETHING? YOU CAN'T JUST--
A LESSON FOR YOU, FRIEND. SOMETIMES THERE REALLY IS TRUTH IN ADVERTISING.
HEY, WHERE'D SHE GO?

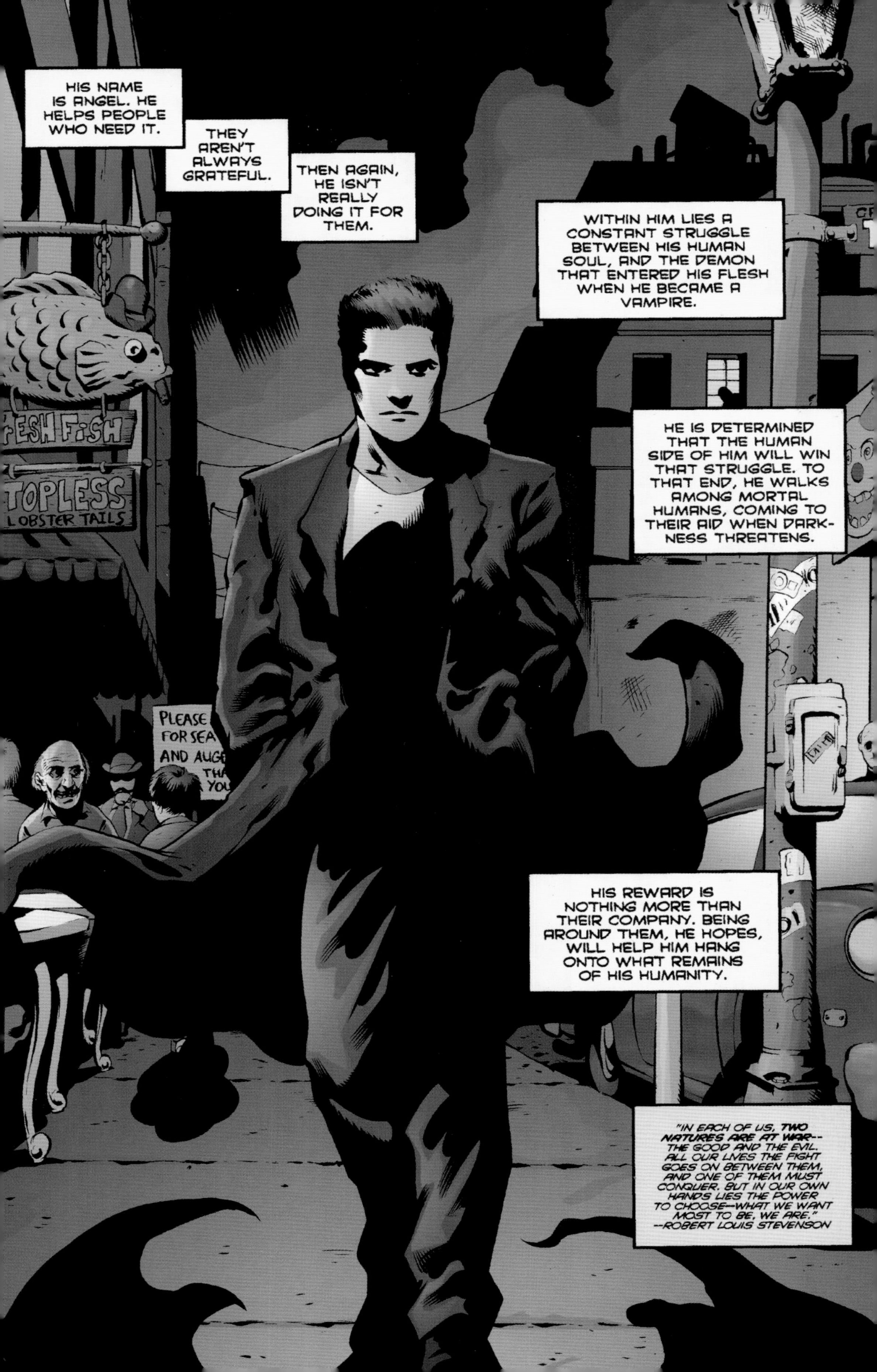
HIS NAME IS ANGEL. HE HELPS PEOPLE WHO NEED IT.
THEY AREN'T ALWAYS GRATEFUL.
THEN AGAIN, HE ISN'T REALLY DOING IT FOR THEM.
WITHIN HIM LIES A CONSTANT STRUGGLE BETWEEN HIS HUMAN SOUL, AND THE DEMON THAT ENTERED HIS FLESH WHEN HE BECAME A VAMPIRE.
HE IS DETERMINED THAT THE HUMAN SIDE OF HIM WILL WIN THAT STRUGGLE. TO THAT END, HE WALKS AMONG MORTAL HUMANS, COMING TO THEIR AID WHEN DARKNESS THREATENS.
HIS REWARD IS NOTHING MORE THAN THEIR COMPANY. BEING AROUND THEM, HE HOPES, WILL HELP HIM HANG ONTO WHAT REMAINS OF HIS HUMANITY.
"IN EACH OF US, TWO NATURES ARE AT WAR-- THE GOOD AND THE EVIL. ALL OUR LIVES THE FIGHT GOES ON BETWEEN THEM, AND ONE OF THEM MUST CONQUER. BUT IN OUR OWN HANDS LIES THE POWER TO CHOOSE--WHAT WE WANT MOST TO BE, WE ARE." --ROBERT LOUIS STEVENSON
TOPLESS
LOBSTER TAILS

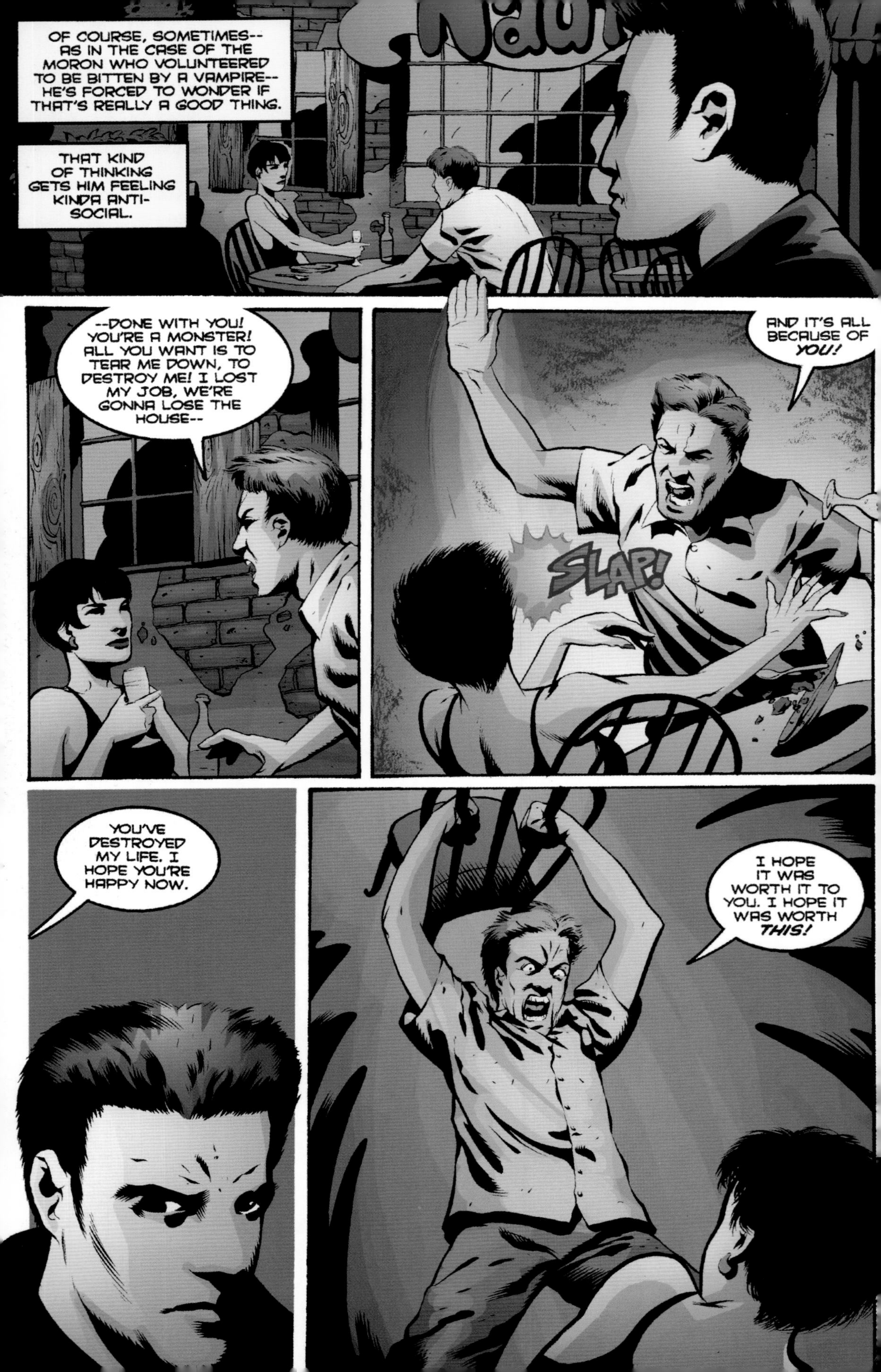

OF COURSE, SOMETIMES-- AS IN THE CASE OF THE MORON WHO VOLUNTEERED TO BE BITTEN BY A VAMPIRE-- HE'S FORCED TO WONDER IF THAT'S REALLY A GOOD THING.
THAT KIND OF THINKING GETS HIM FEELING KINDA ANTI-SOCIAL.
--DONE WITH YOU! YOU'RE A MONSTER! ALL YOU WANT IS TO TEAR ME DOWN, TO DESTROY ME! I LOST MY JOB, WE'RE GONNA LOSE THE HOUSE--
AND IT'S ALL BECAUSE OF *YOU!*
SLAP!
YOU'VE DESTROYED MY LIFE. I HOPE YOU'RE HAPPY NOW.
I HOPE IT WAS WORTH IT TO YOU. I HOPE IT WAS WORTH *THIS!*

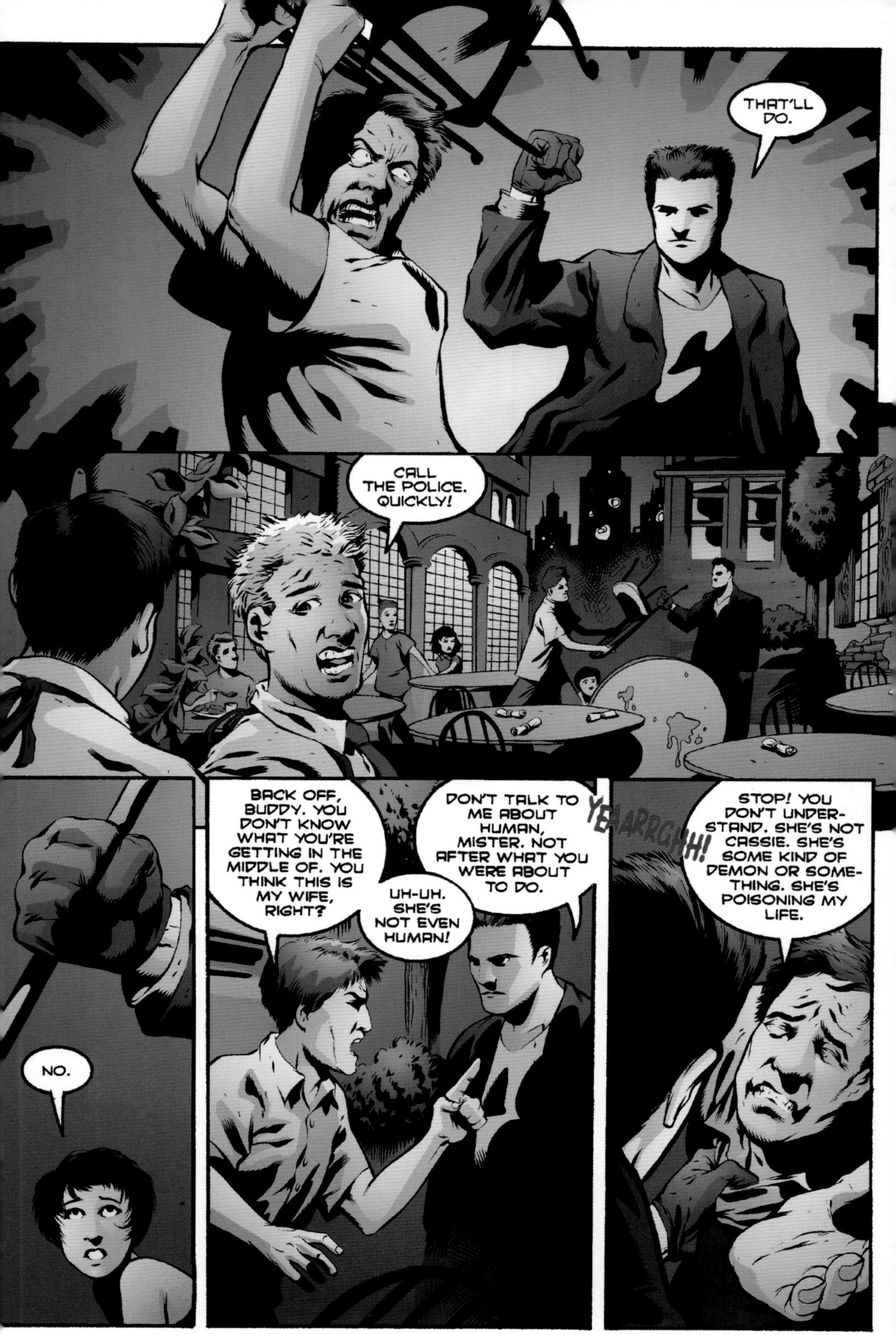
THAT'LL DO.
CALL THE POLICE. QUICKLY!
NO.
BACK OFF, BUDDY. YOU DON'T KNOW WHAT YOU'RE GETTING IN THE MIDDLE OF. YOU THINK THIS IS MY WIFE, RIGHT?
UH-UH. SHE'S NOT EVEN HUMAN!
DON'T TALK TO ME ABOUT HUMAN, MISTER. NOT AFTER WHAT YOU WERE ABOUT TO DO.
YEAARRGHH!
STOP! YOU DON'T UNDER-STAND. SHE'S NOT CASSIE. SHE'S SOME KIND OF DEMON OR SOME-THING. SHE'S POISONING MY LIFE.

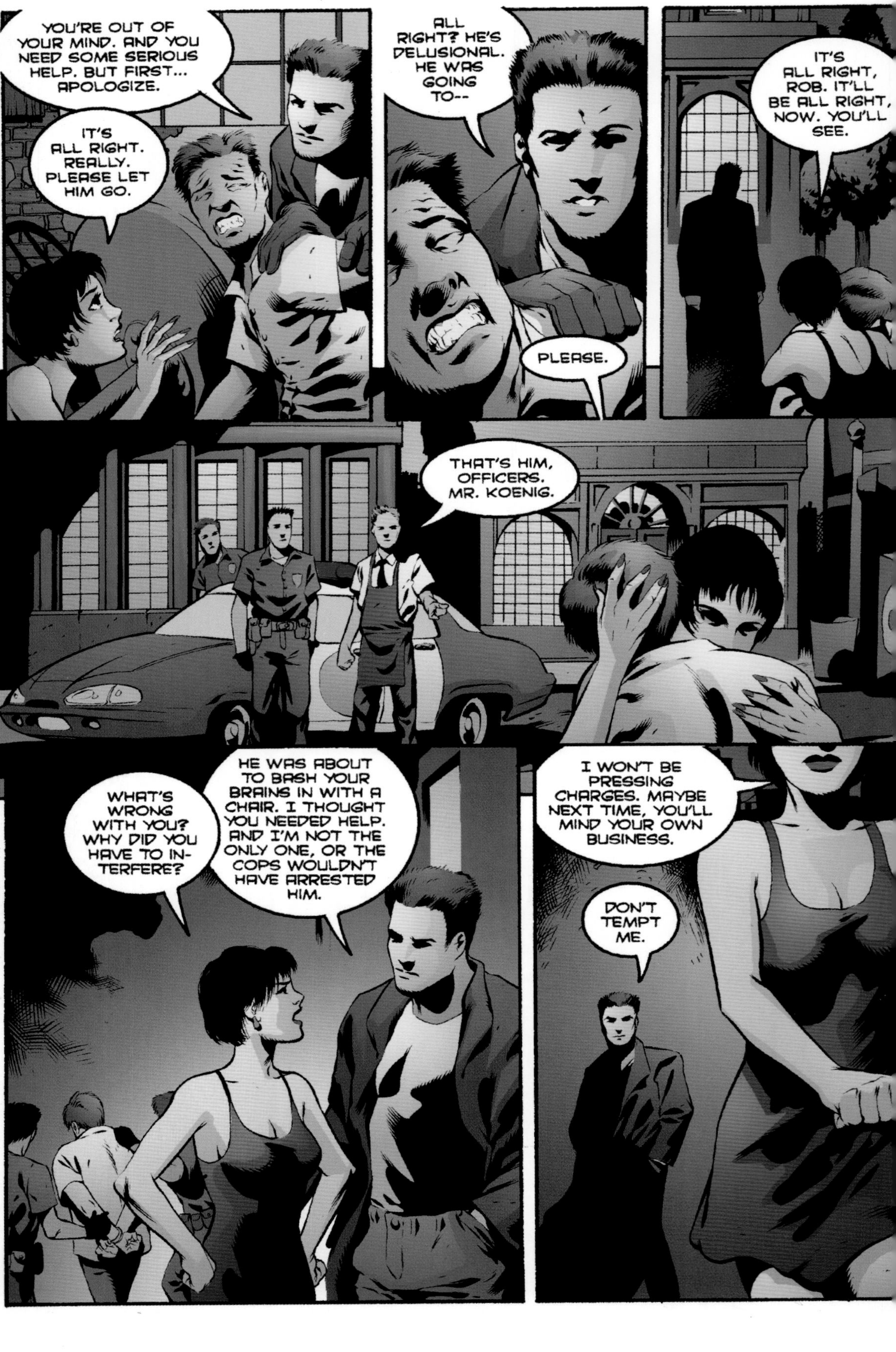
YOU'RE OUT OF YOUR MIND. AND YOU NEED SOME SERIOUS HELP. BUT FIRST... APOLOGIZE.
IT'S ALL RIGHT. REALLY. PLEASE LET HIM GO.
ALL RIGHT? HE'S DELUSIONAL. HE WAS GOING TO--
PLEASE.
IT'S ALL RIGHT, ROB. IT'LL BE ALL RIGHT, NOW. YOU'LL SEE.
THAT'S HIM, OFFICERS. MR. KOENIG.
WHAT'S WRONG WITH YOU? WHY DID YOU HAVE TO INTERFERE?
HE WAS ABOUT TO BASH YOUR BRAINS IN WITH A CHAIR. I THOUGHT YOU NEEDED HELP. AND I'M NOT THE ONLY ONE, OR THE COPS WOULDN'T HAVE ARRESTED HIM.
I WON'T BE PRESSING CHARGES. MAYBE NEXT TIME, YOU'LL MIND YOUR OWN BUSINESS.
DON'T TEMPT ME.

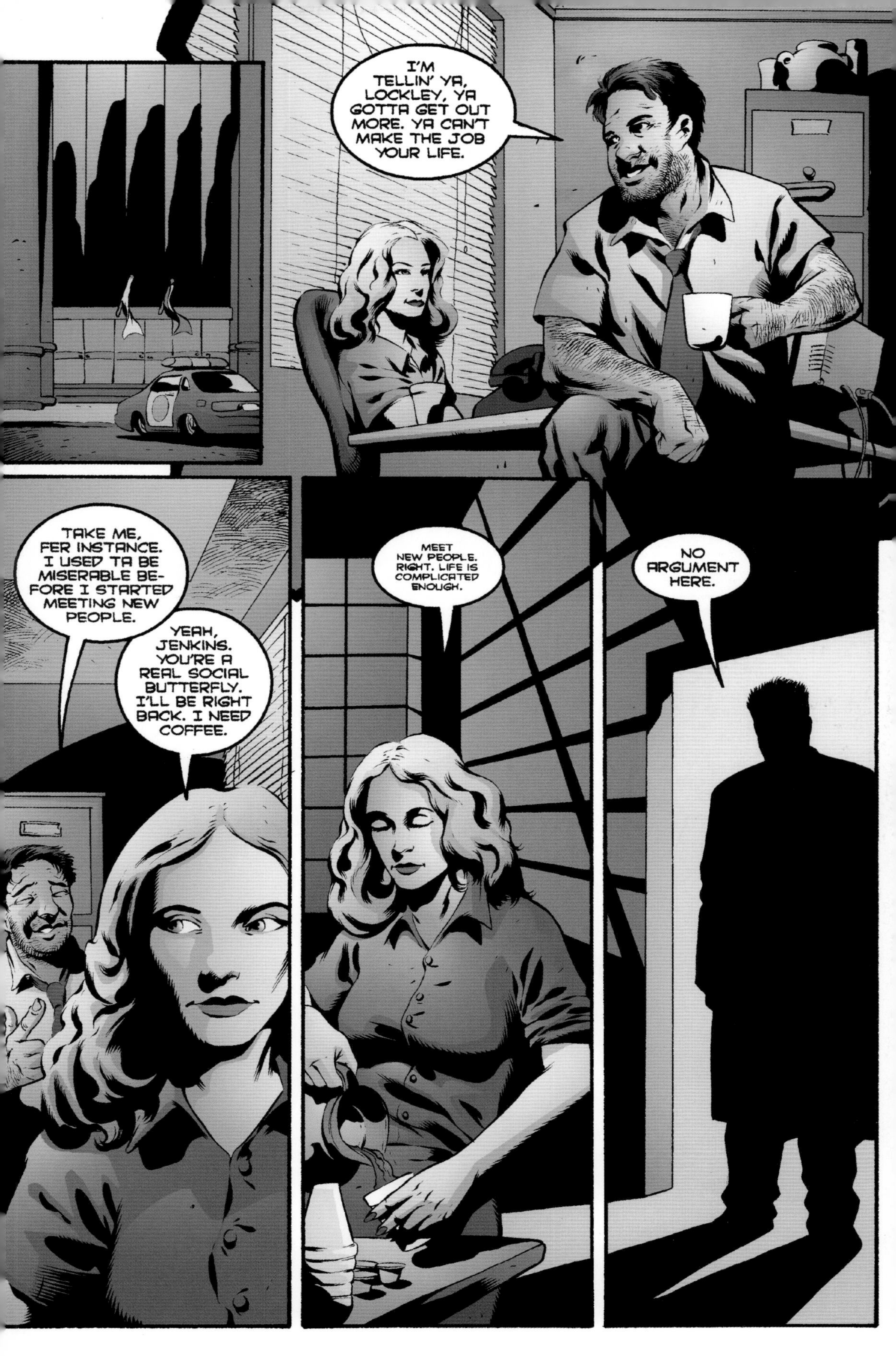
I'M TELLIN' YA, LOCKLEY, YA GOTTA GET OUT MORE. YA CAN'T MAKE THE JOB YOUR LIFE.
TAKE ME, FER INSTANCE. I USED TA BE MISERABLE BEFORE I STARTED MEETING NEW PEOPLE.
YEAH, JENKINS. YOU'RE A REAL SOCIAL BUTTERFLY. I'LL BE RIGHT BACK. I NEED COFFEE.
MEET NEW PEOPLE. RIGHT. LIFE IS COMPLICATED ENOUGH.
NO ARGUMENT HERE.

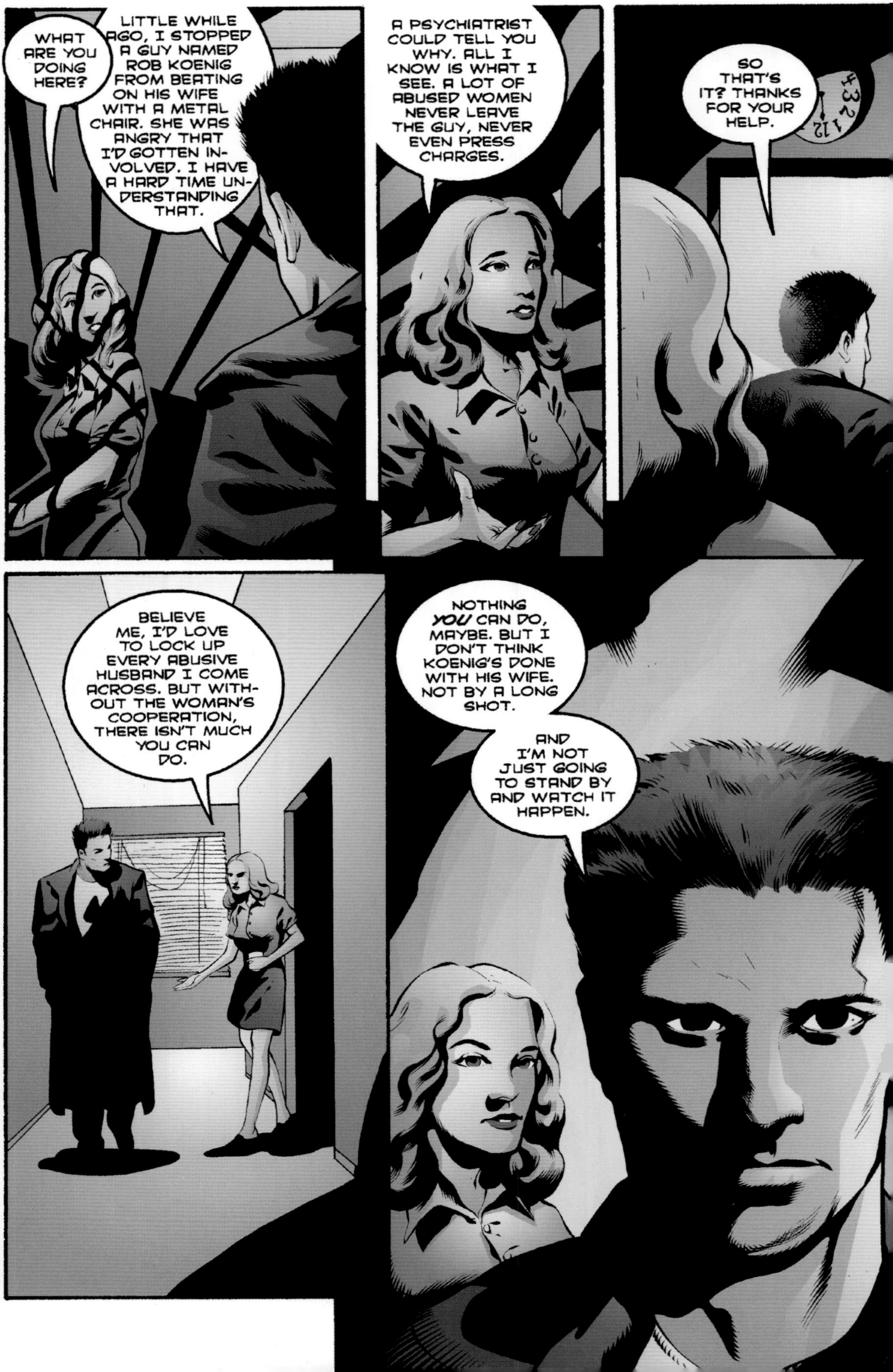
WHAT ARE YOU DOING HERE?
LITTLE WHILE AGO, I STOPPED A GUY NAMED ROB KOENIG FROM BEATING ON HIS WIFE WITH A METAL CHAIR. SHE WAS ANGRY THAT I'D GOTTEN INVOLVED. I HAVE A HARD TIME UNDERSTANDING THAT.
A PSYCHIATRIST COULD TELL YOU WHY. ALL I KNOW IS WHAT I SEE. A LOT OF ABUSED WOMEN NEVER LEAVE THE GUY, NEVER EVEN PRESS CHARGES.
SO THAT'S IT? THANKS FOR YOUR HELP.
BELIEVE ME, I'D LOVE TO LOCK UP EVERY ABUSIVE HUSBAND I COME ACROSS. BUT WITHOUT THE WOMAN'S COOPERATION, THERE ISN'T MUCH YOU CAN DO.
NOTHING *YOU* CAN DO, MAYBE. BUT I DON'T THINK KOENIG'S DONE WITH HIS WIFE. NOT BY A LONG SHOT.
AND I'M NOT JUST GOING TO STAND BY AND WATCH IT HAPPEN.

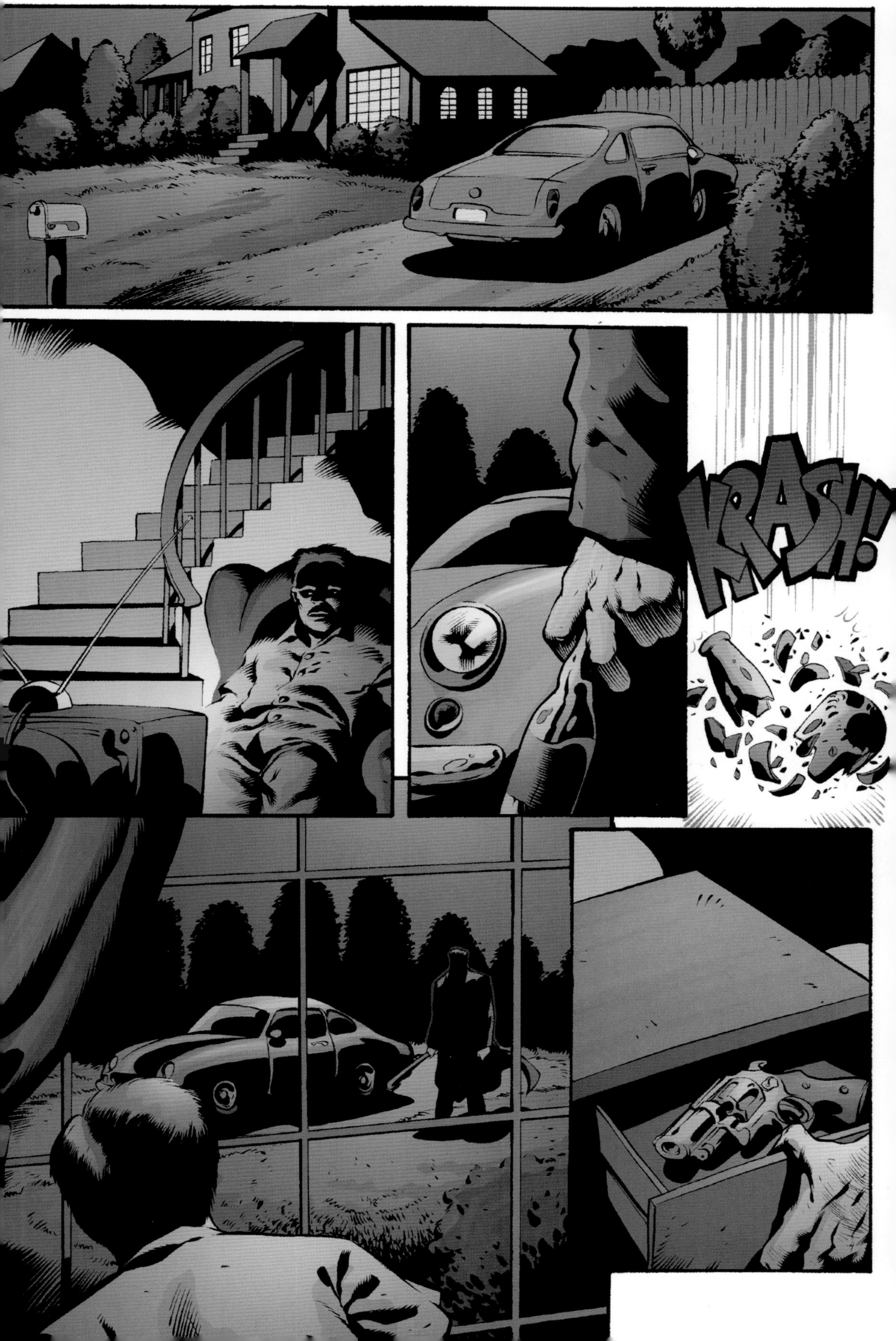
KRASH!

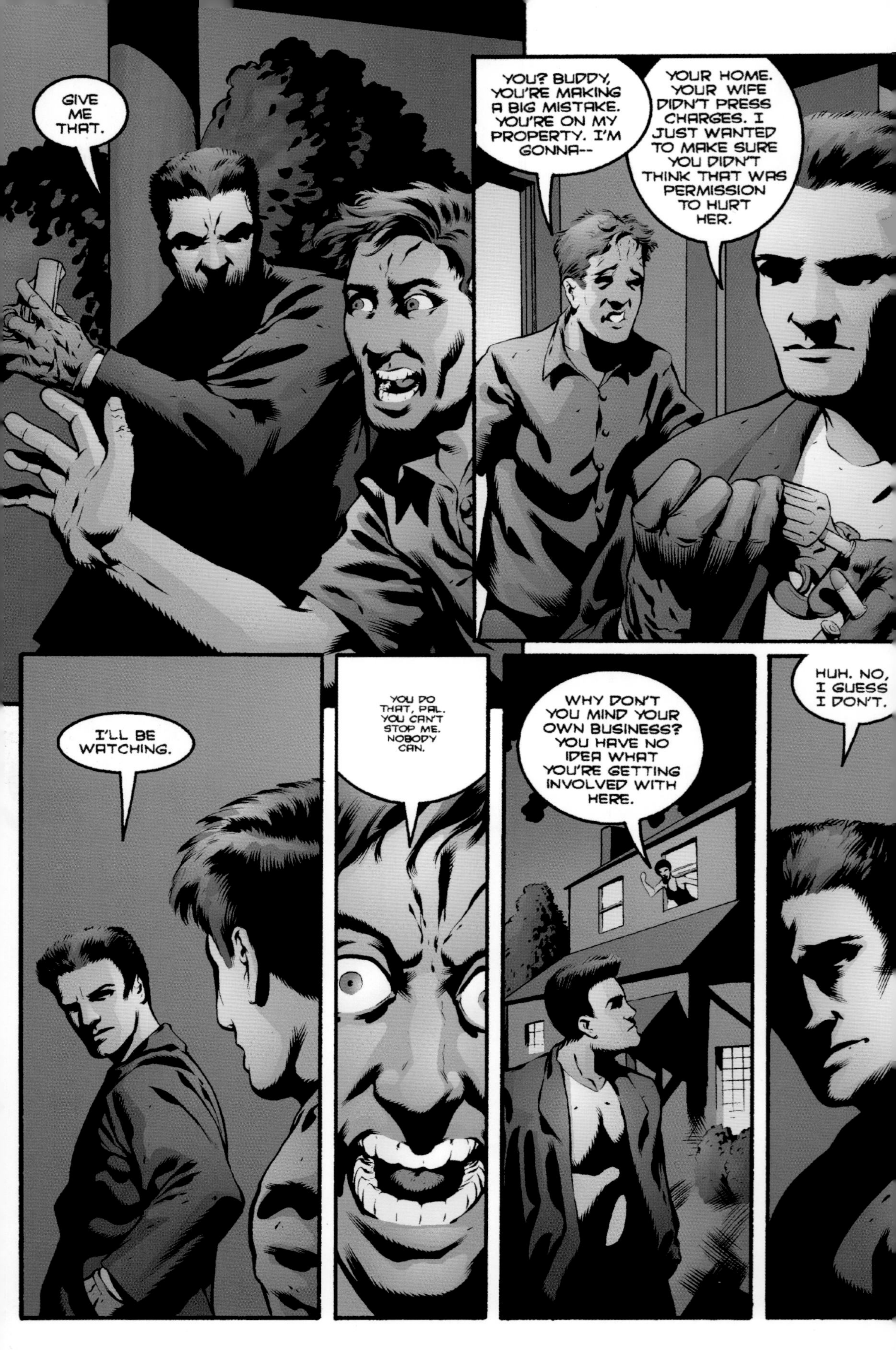
GIVE ME THAT.
YOU? BUDDY, YOU'RE MAKING A BIG MISTAKE. YOU'RE ON MY PROPERTY. I'M GONNA--
YOUR HOME. YOUR WIFE DIDN'T PRESS CHARGES. I JUST WANTED TO MAKE SURE YOU DIDN'T THINK THAT WAS PERMISSION TO HURT HER.
I'LL BE WATCHING.
YOU DO THAT, PAL. YOU CAN'T STOP ME. NOBODY CAN.
WHY DON'T YOU MIND YOUR OWN BUSINESS? YOU HAVE NO IDEA WHAT YOU'RE GETTING INVOLVED WITH HERE.
HUH. NO, I GUESS I DON'T.

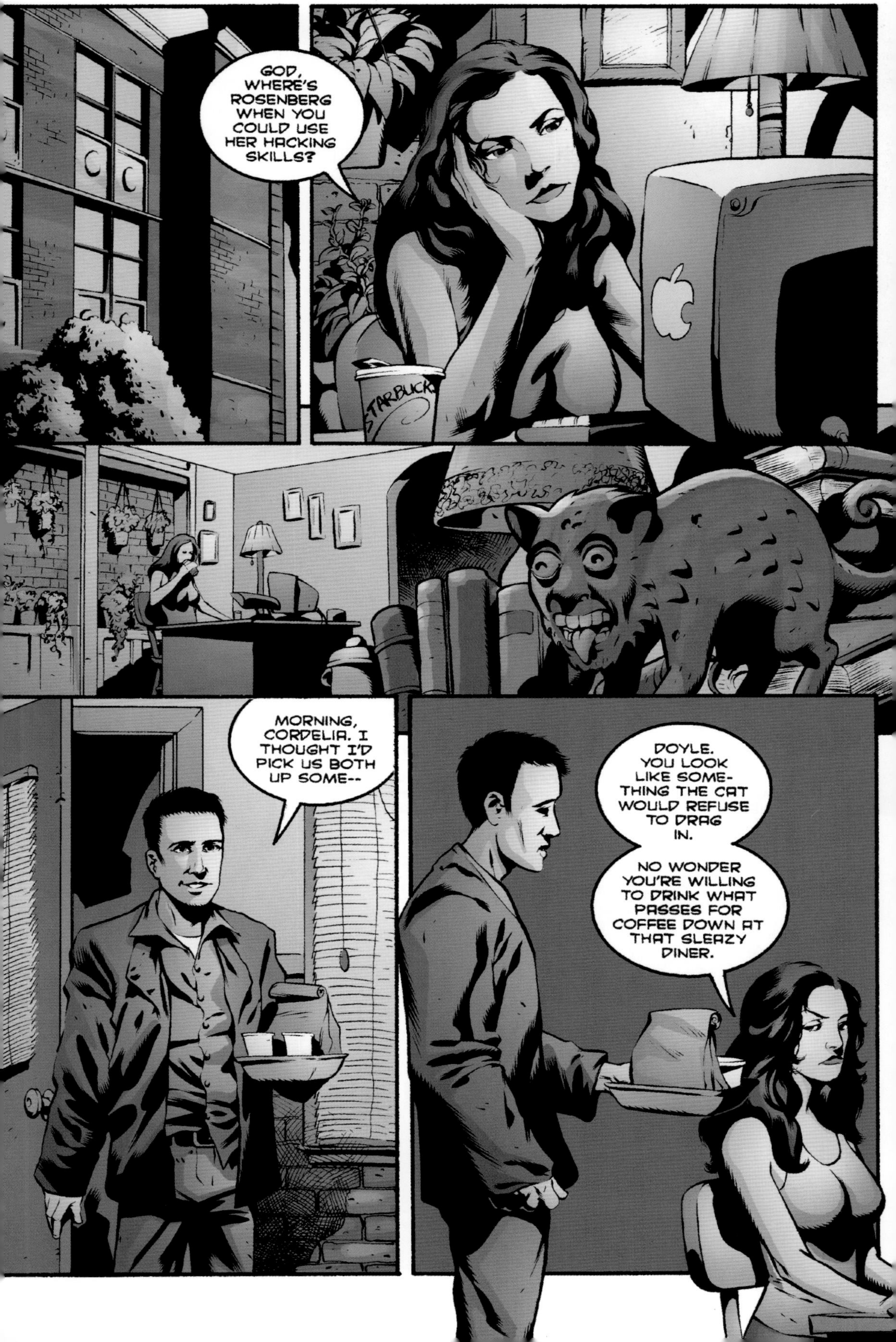
GOD, WHERE'S ROSENBERG WHEN YOU COULD USE HER HACKING SKILLS?
STARBUCKS
MORNING, CORDELIA. I THOUGHT I'D PICK US BOTH UP SOME--
DOYLE. YOU LOOK LIKE SOME-THING THE CAT WOULD REFUSE TO DRAG IN.
NO WONDER YOU'RE WILLING TO DRINK WHAT PASSES FOR COFFEE DOWN AT THAT SLEAZY DINER.

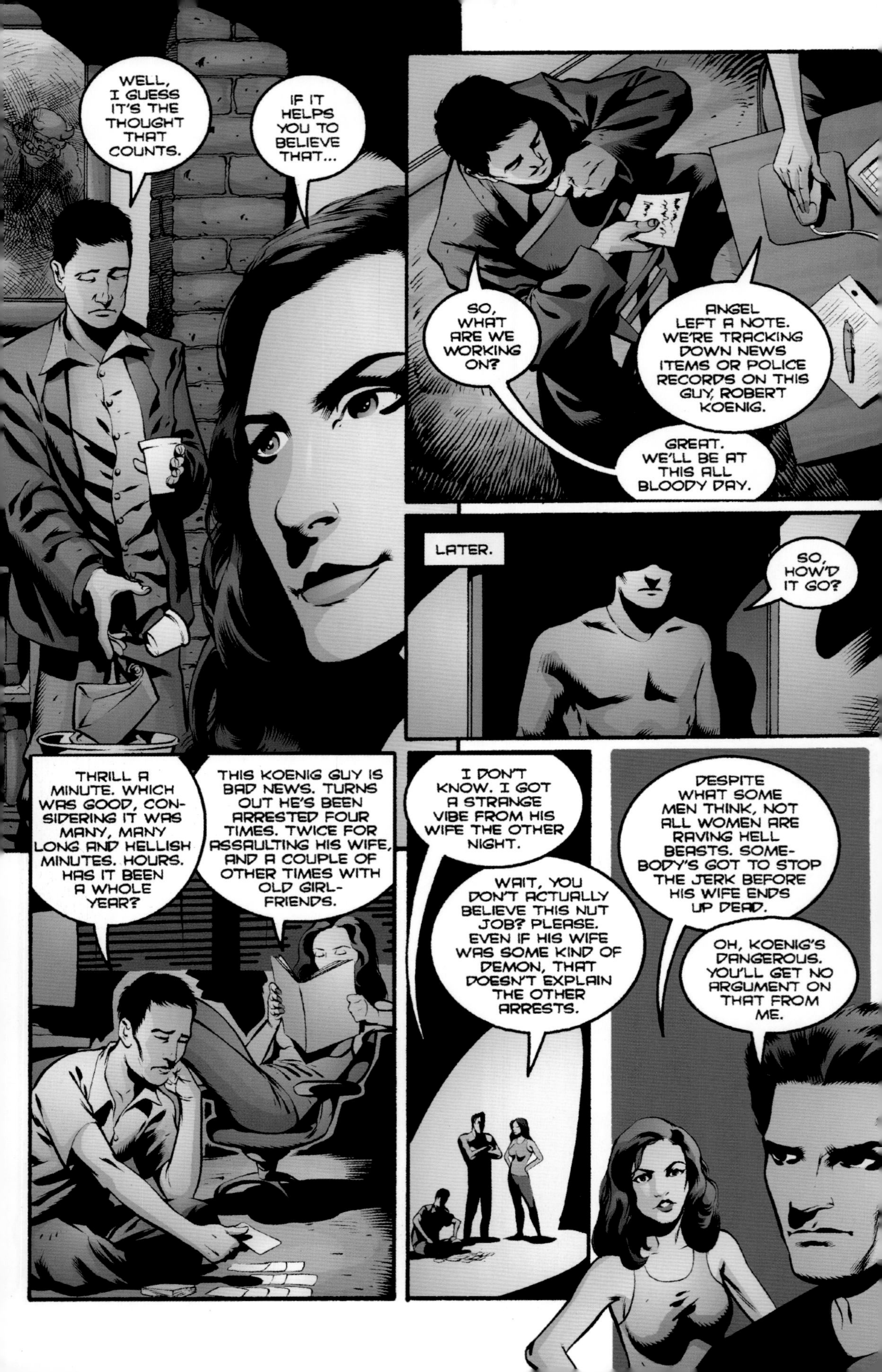
WELL, I GUESS IT'S THE THOUGHT THAT COUNTS.
IF IT HELPS YOU TO BELIEVE THAT...
SO, WHAT ARE WE WORKING ON?
ANGEL LEFT A NOTE. WE'RE TRACKING DOWN NEWS ITEMS OR POLICE RECORDS ON THIS GUY, ROBERT KOENIG.
GREAT. WE'LL BE AT THIS ALL BLOODY DAY.
LATER.
SO, HOW'D IT GO?
THRILL A MINUTE. WHICH WAS GOOD, CONSIDERING IT WAS MANY, MANY LONG AND HELLISH MINUTES. HOURS. HAS IT BEEN A WHOLE YEAR?
THIS KOENIG GUY IS BAD NEWS. TURNS OUT HE'S BEEN ARRESTED FOUR TIMES. TWICE FOR ASSAULTING HIS WIFE, AND A COUPLE OF OTHER TIMES WITH OLD GIRLFRIENDS.
I DON'T KNOW. I GOT A STRANGE VIBE FROM HIS WIFE THE OTHER NIGHT.
WAIT, YOU DON'T ACTUALLY BELIEVE THIS NUT JOB? PLEASE. EVEN IF HIS WIFE WAS SOME KIND OF DEMON, THAT DOESN'T EXPLAIN THE OTHER ARRESTS.
DESPITE WHAT SOME MEN THINK, NOT ALL WOMEN ARE RAVING HELL BEASTS. SOMEBODY'S GOT TO STOP THE JERK BEFORE HIS WIFE ENDS UP DEAD.
OH, KOENIG'S DANGEROUS. YOU'LL GET NO ARGUMENT ON THAT FROM ME.

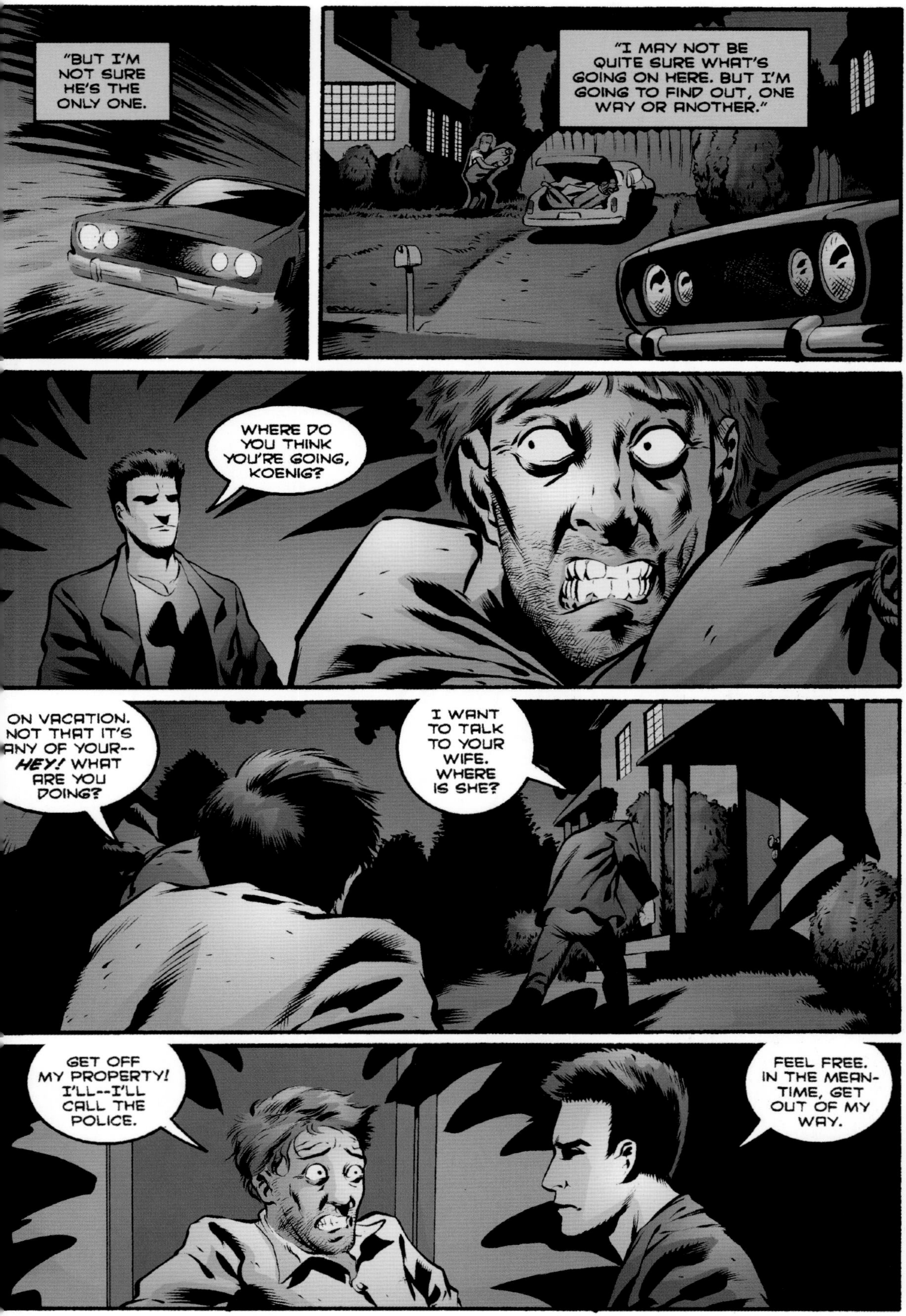
"BUT I'M NOT SURE HE'S THE ONLY ONE.
"I MAY NOT BE QUITE SURE WHAT'S GOING ON HERE. BUT I'M GOING TO FIND OUT, ONE WAY OR ANOTHER."
WHERE DO YOU THINK YOU'RE GOING, KOENIG?
ON VACATION. NOT THAT IT'S ANY OF YOUR-- *HEY!* WHAT ARE YOU DOING?
I WANT TO TALK TO YOUR WIFE. WHERE IS SHE?
GET OFF MY PROPERTY! I'LL--I'LL CALL THE POLICE.
FEEL FREE. IN THE MEAN-TIME, GET OUT OF MY WAY.

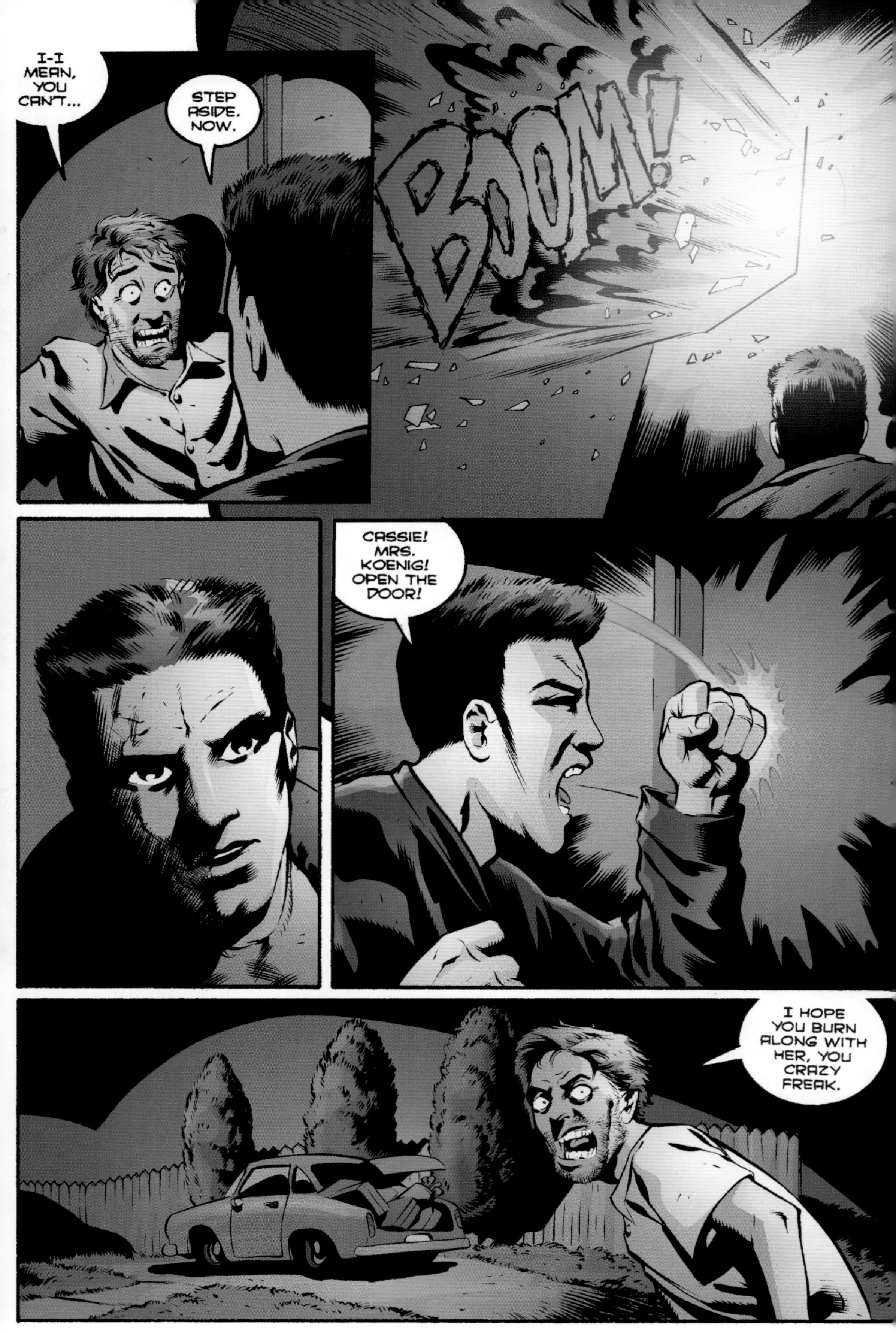
I-I MEAN, YOU CAN'T...
STEP ASIDE. NOW.
BOOM!
CASSIE! MRS. KOENIG! OPEN THE DOOR!
I HOPE YOU BURN ALONG WITH HER, YOU CRAZY FREAK.

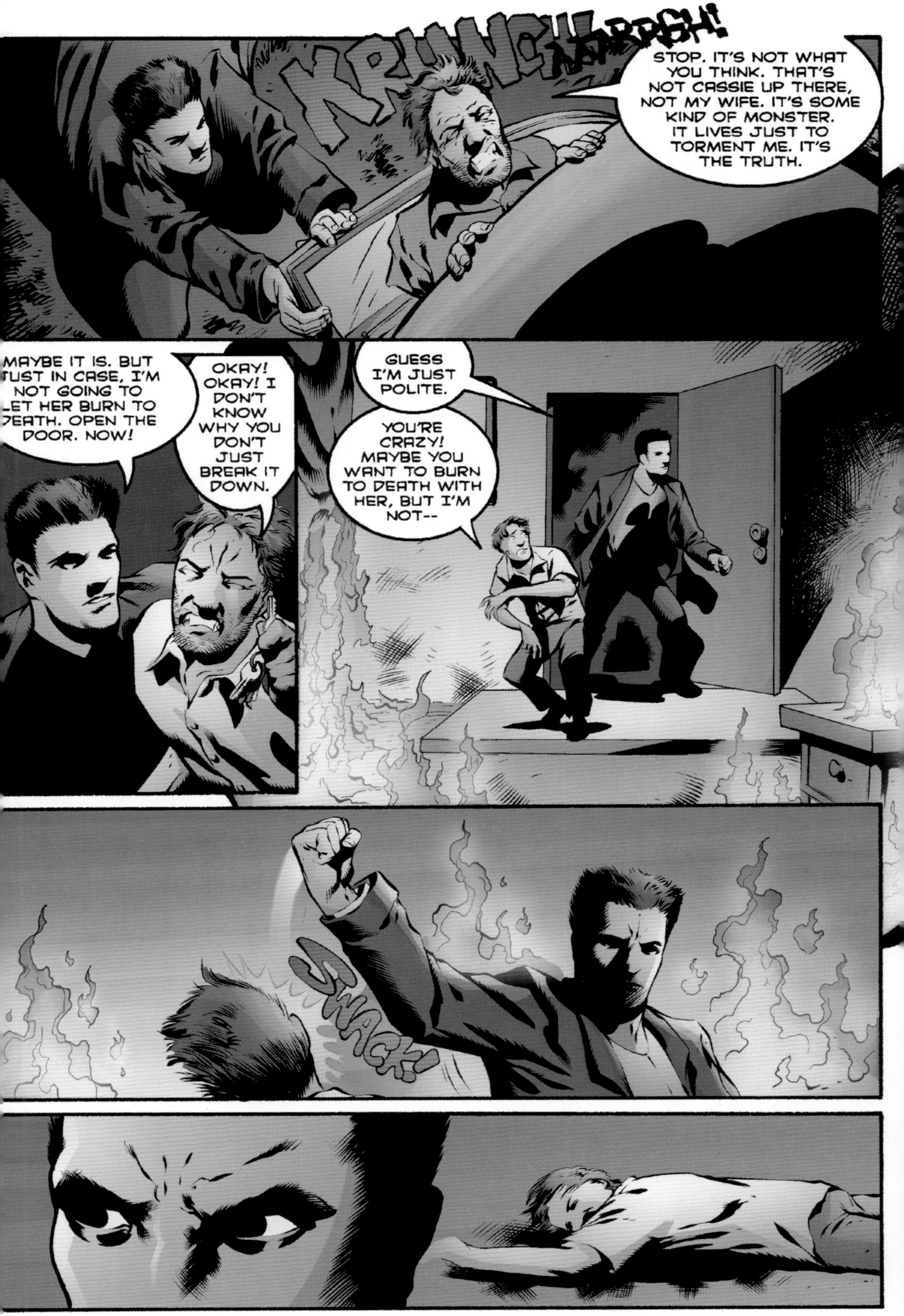
KRUNCH!
AAARRGH!
STOP. IT'S NOT WHAT YOU THINK. THAT'S NOT CASSIE UP THERE, NOT MY WIFE. IT'S SOME KIND OF MONSTER. IT LIVES JUST TO TORMENT ME. IT'S THE TRUTH.
MAYBE IT IS. BUT JUST IN CASE, I'M NOT GOING TO LET HER BURN TO DEATH. OPEN THE DOOR. NOW!
OKAY! OKAY! I DON'T KNOW WHY YOU DON'T JUST BREAK IT DOWN.
GUESS I'M JUST POLITE.
YOU'RE CRAZY! MAYBE YOU WANT TO BURN TO DEATH WITH HER, BUT I'M NOT--
SWACK!

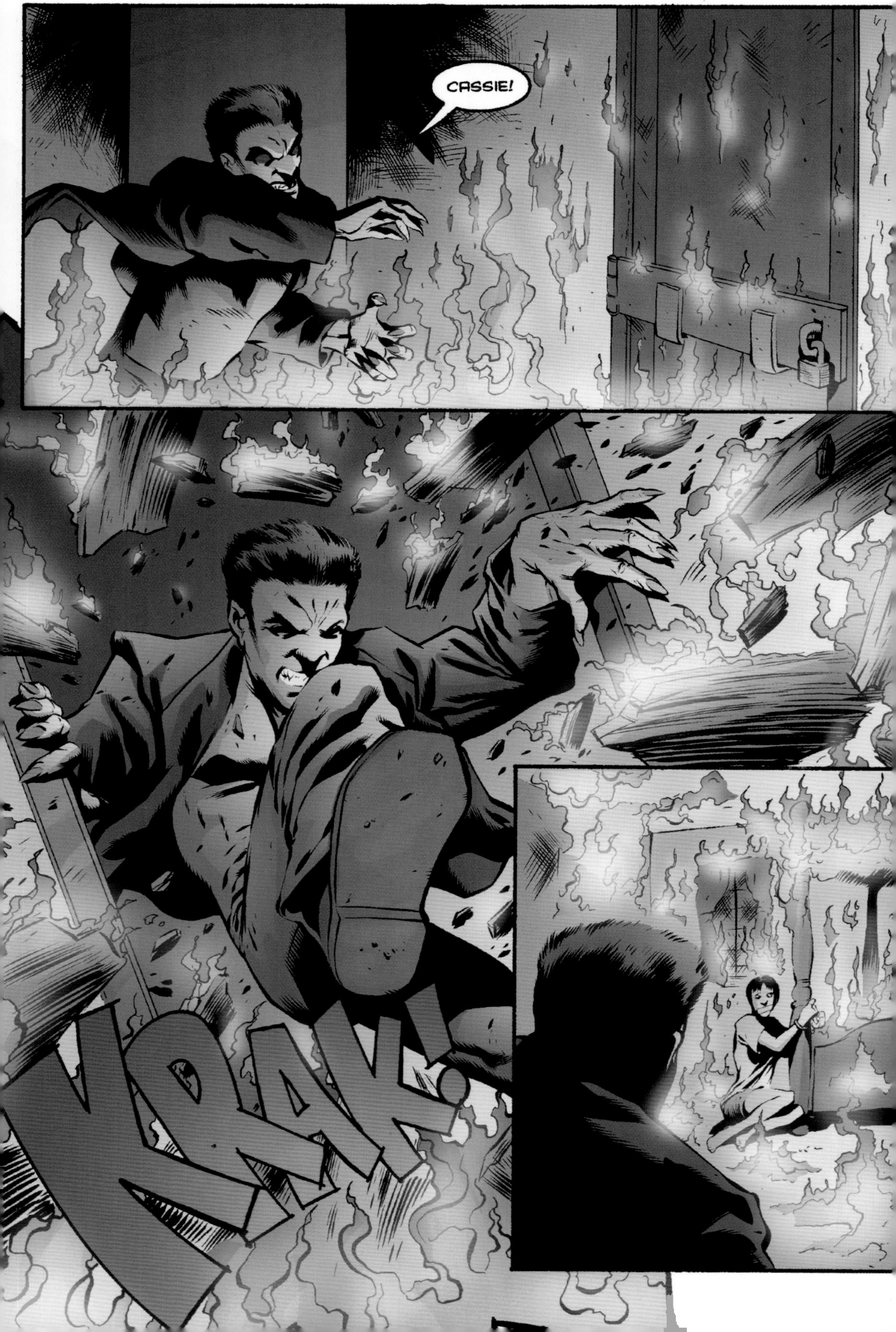
CASSIE!
KRAK!

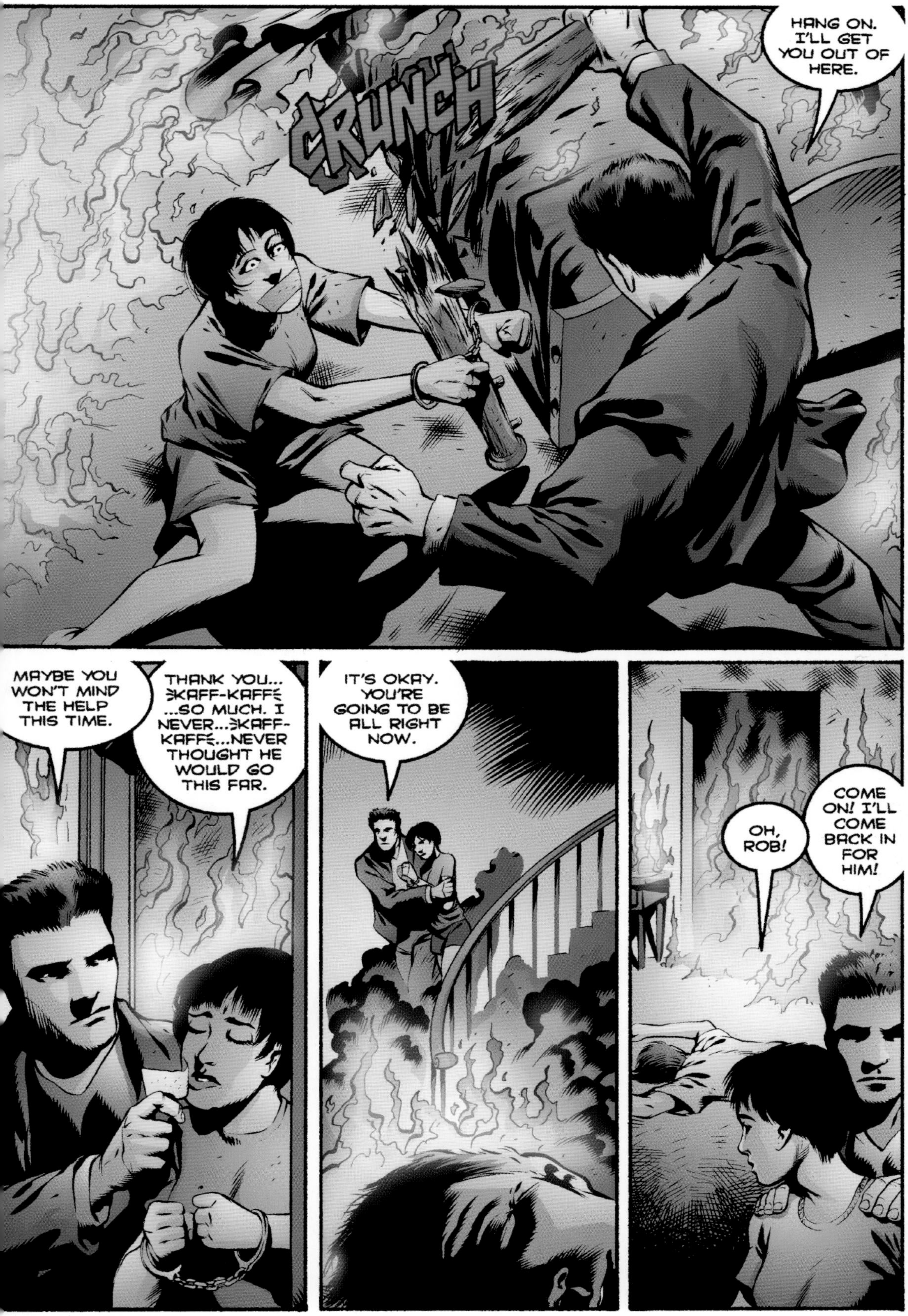
CRUNCH
HANG ON. I'LL GET YOU OUT OF HERE.
MAYBE YOU WON'T MIND THE HELP THIS TIME.
THANK YOU... KAFF-KAFF ...SO MUCH. I NEVER... KAFF-KAFF ...NEVER THOUGHT HE WOULD GO THIS FAR.
IT'S OKAY. YOU'RE GOING TO BE ALL RIGHT NOW.
OH, ROB!
COME ON! I'LL COME BACK IN FOR HIM!

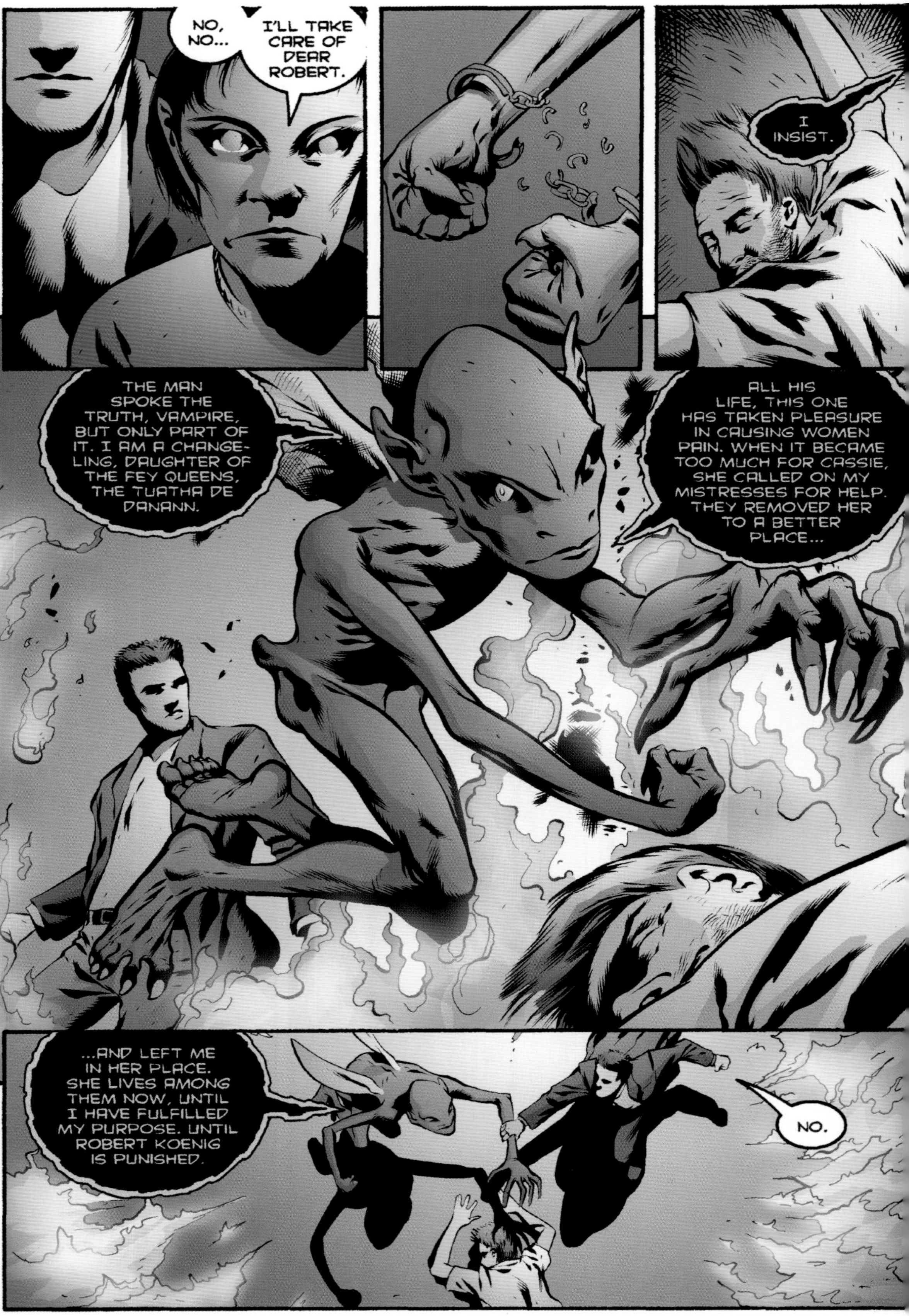
NO, NO...
I'LL TAKE CARE OF DEAR ROBERT.
I INSIST.
THE MAN SPOKE THE TRUTH, VAMPIRE, BUT ONLY PART OF IT. I AM A CHANGE-LING, DAUGHTER OF THE FEY QUEENS, THE TUATHA DE DANANN.
ALL HIS LIFE, THIS ONE HAS TAKEN PLEASURE IN CAUSING WOMEN PAIN. WHEN IT BECAME TOO MUCH FOR CASSIE, SHE CALLED ON MY MISTRESSES FOR HELP. THEY REMOVED HER TO A BETTER PLACE...
...AND LEFT ME IN HER PLACE. SHE LIVES AMONG THEM NOW, UNTIL I HAVE FULFILLED MY PURPOSE. UNTIL ROBERT KOENIG IS PUNISHED.
NO.

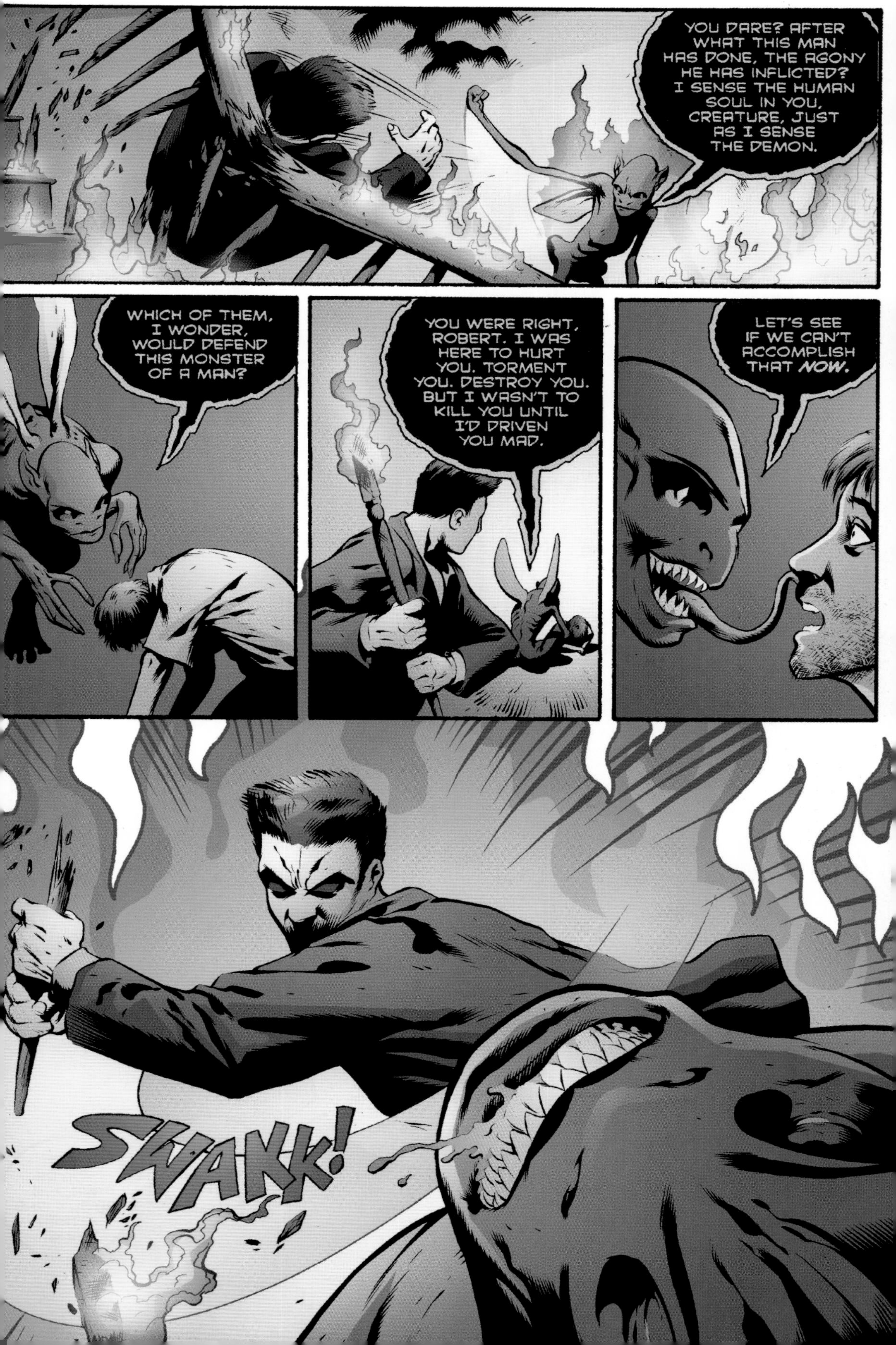
YOU DARE? AFTER WHAT THIS MAN HAS DONE, THE AGONY HE HAS INFLICTED? I SENSE THE HUMAN SOUL IN YOU, CREATURE, JUST AS I SENSE THE DEMON.
WHICH OF THEM, I WONDER, WOULD DEFEND THIS MONSTER OF A MAN?
YOU WERE RIGHT, ROBERT. I WAS HERE TO HURT YOU. TORMENT YOU. DESTROY YOU. BUT I WASN'T TO KILL YOU UNTIL I'D DRIVEN YOU MAD.
LET'S SEE IF WE CAN'T ACCOMPLISH THAT *NOW*.
SWAKK!

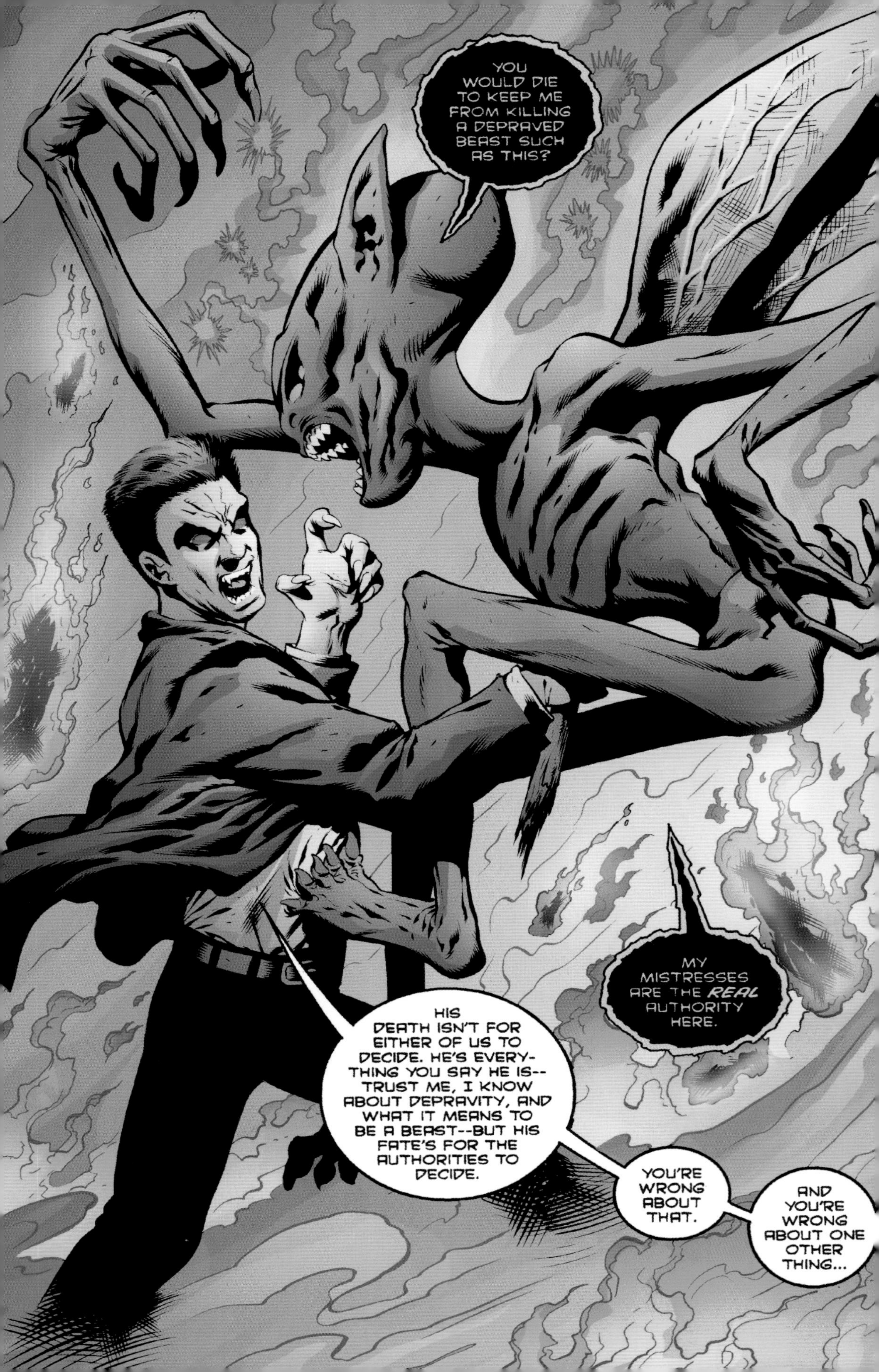
YOU WOULD DIE TO KEEP ME FROM KILLING A DEPRAVED BEAST SUCH AS THIS?
HIS DEATH ISN'T FOR EITHER OF US TO DECIDE. HE'S EVERYTHING YOU SAY HE IS-- TRUST ME, I KNOW ABOUT DEPRAVITY, AND WHAT IT MEANS TO BE A BEAST--BUT HIS FATE'S FOR THE AUTHORITIES TO DECIDE.
MY MISTRESSES ARE THE *REAL* AUTHORITY HERE.
YOU'RE WRONG ABOUT THAT.
AND YOU'RE WRONG ABOUT ONE OTHER THING...

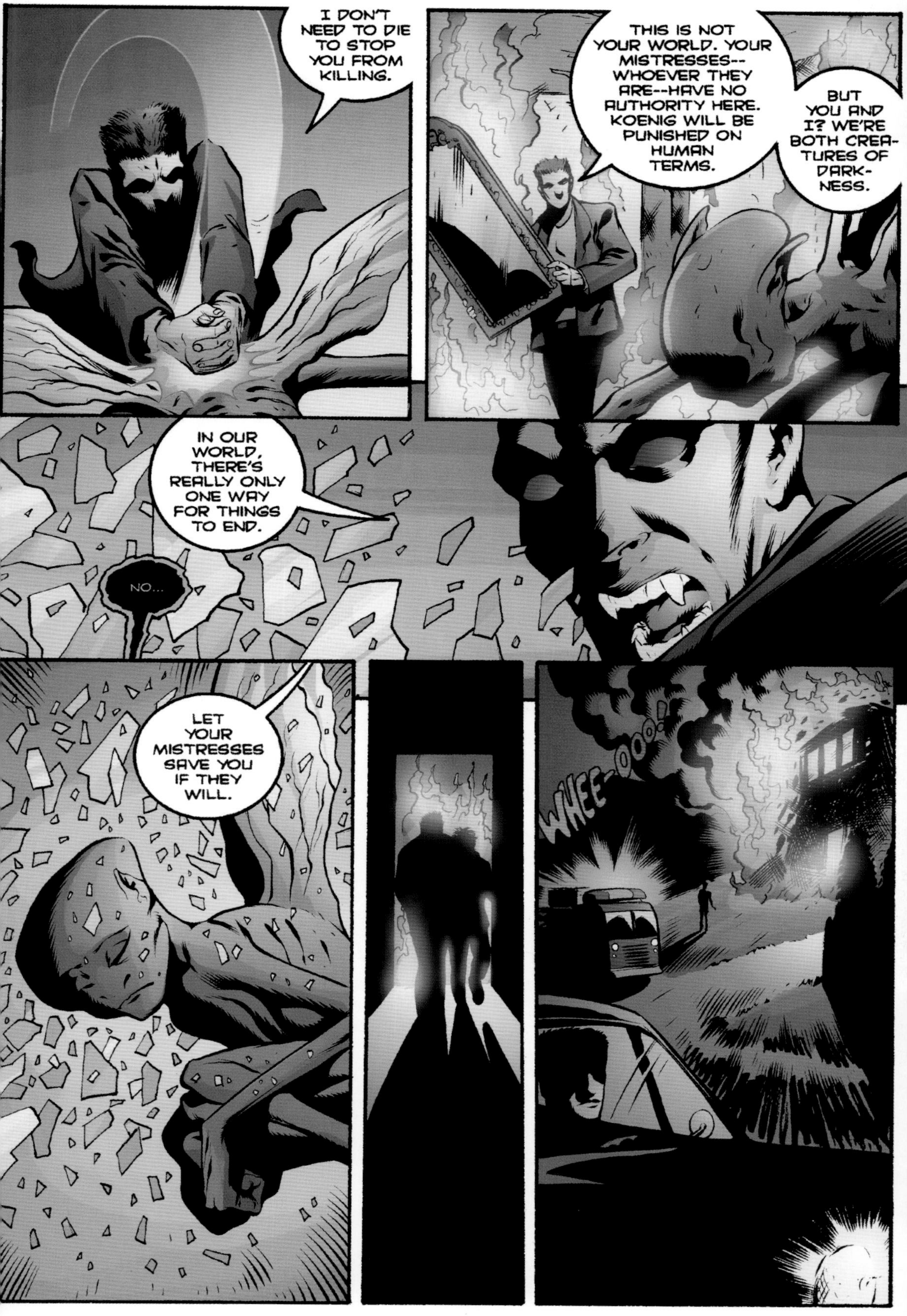
I DON'T NEED TO DIE TO STOP YOU FROM KILLING.
THIS IS NOT YOUR WORLD. YOUR MISTRESSES-- WHOEVER THEY ARE--HAVE NO AUTHORITY HERE. KOENIG WILL BE PUNISHED ON HUMAN TERMS.
BUT YOU AND I? WE'RE BOTH CREA-TURES OF DARK-NESS.
IN OUR WORLD, THERE'S REALLY ONLY ONE WAY FOR THINGS TO END.
NO...
LET YOUR MISTRESSES SAVE YOU IF THEY WILL.
WHEE-OOO!

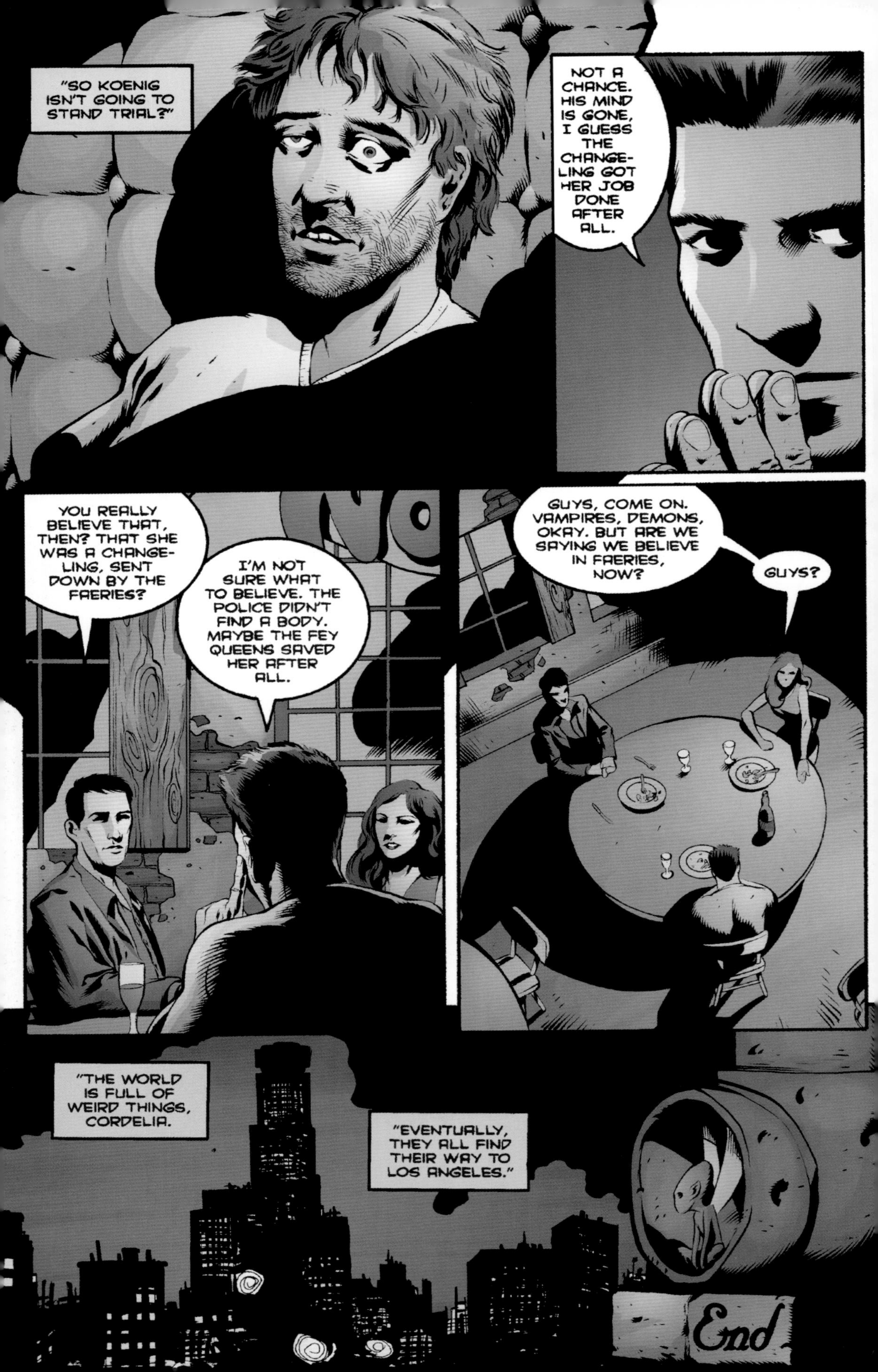
"SO KOENIG ISN'T GOING TO STAND TRIAL?"
NOT A CHANCE. HIS MIND IS GONE, I GUESS THE CHANGE-LING GOT HER JOB DONE AFTER ALL.
YOU REALLY BELIEVE THAT, THEN? THAT SHE WAS A CHANGE-LING, SENT DOWN BY THE FAERIES?
I'M NOT SURE WHAT TO BELIEVE. THE POLICE DIDN'T FIND A BODY. MAYBE THE FEY QUEENS SAVED HER AFTER ALL.
GUYS, COME ON. VAMPIRES, DEMONS, OKAY. BUT ARE WE SAYING WE BELIEVE IN FAERIES, NOW?
GUYS?
"THE WORLD IS FULL OF WEIRD THINGS, CORDELIA.
"EVENTUALLY, THEY ALL FIND THEIR WAY TO LOS ANGELES."
End

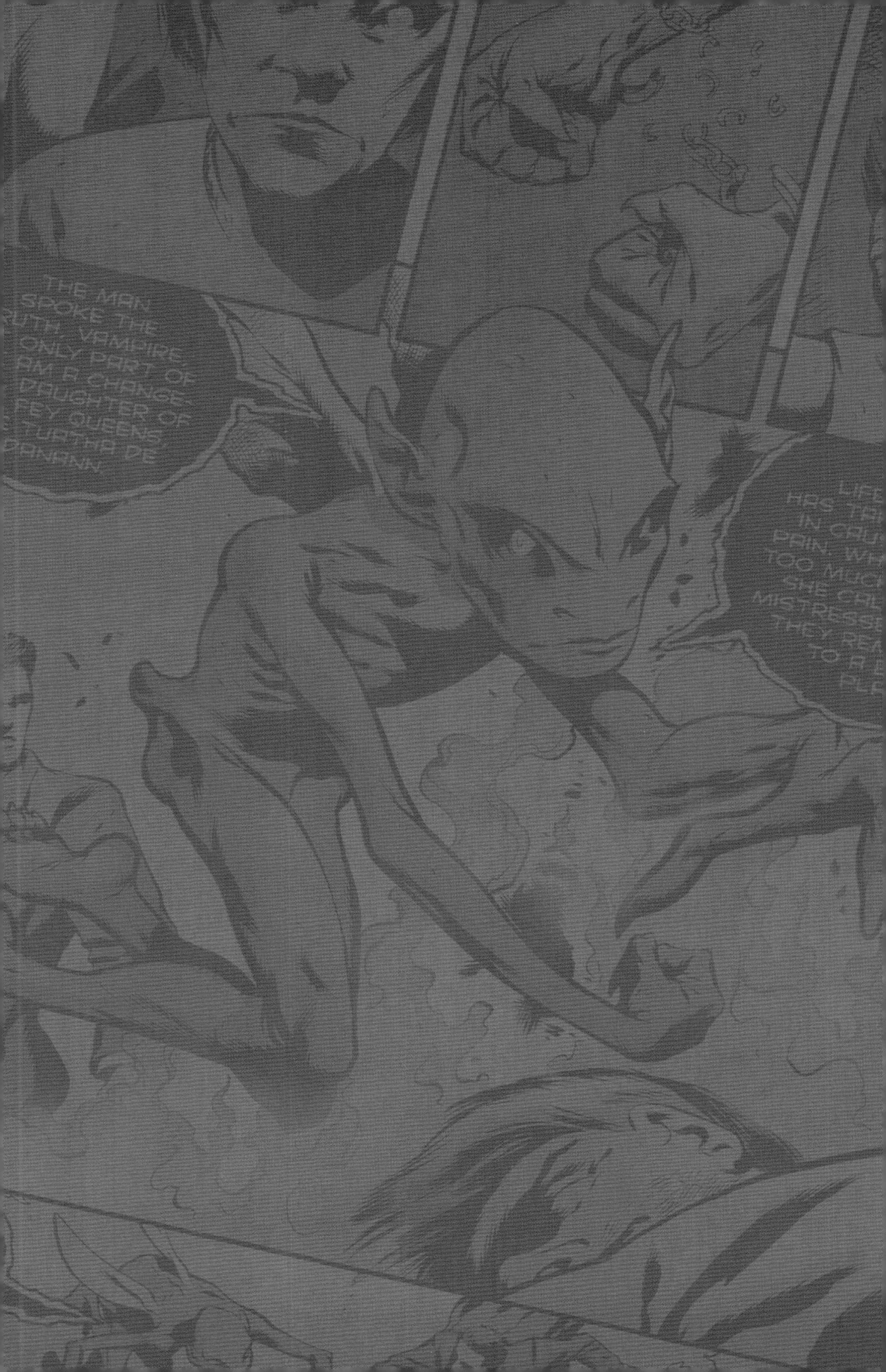
THE MAN
SPOKE THE
RUTH, VAMPIRE.
ONLY PART OF
AM A CHANGE-
DAUGHTER OF
FEY QUEENS,
TUATHA DE
DANANN.
LIFE
HAS TR
IN CRU
PAIN. WH
TOO MUC
SHE CH
MISTRESSE
THEY REM
TO A
PLE

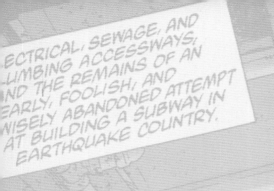

ELECTRICAL, SEWAGE, AND PLUMBING ACCESSWAYS, AND THE REMAINS OF AN EARLY, FOOLISH, AND WISELY ABANDONED ATTEMPT AT BUILDING A SUBWAY IN EARTHQUAKE COUNTRY.

ROUTES POSSIBLE FOR A DETERMINED INDIVIDUAL TO MAKE THEIR WAY AROUND L.A. WITHOUT EVER SEEING THE SUN.

PERFECT FOR VAMPIRES.

AMONG OTHER

NEVER KNOW WHA YOU'RE GOING TO INTO DOWN THER

BUT THAT STORY F ANOTHER

EARTHLY
POSSESSIONS
CHAPTER ONE

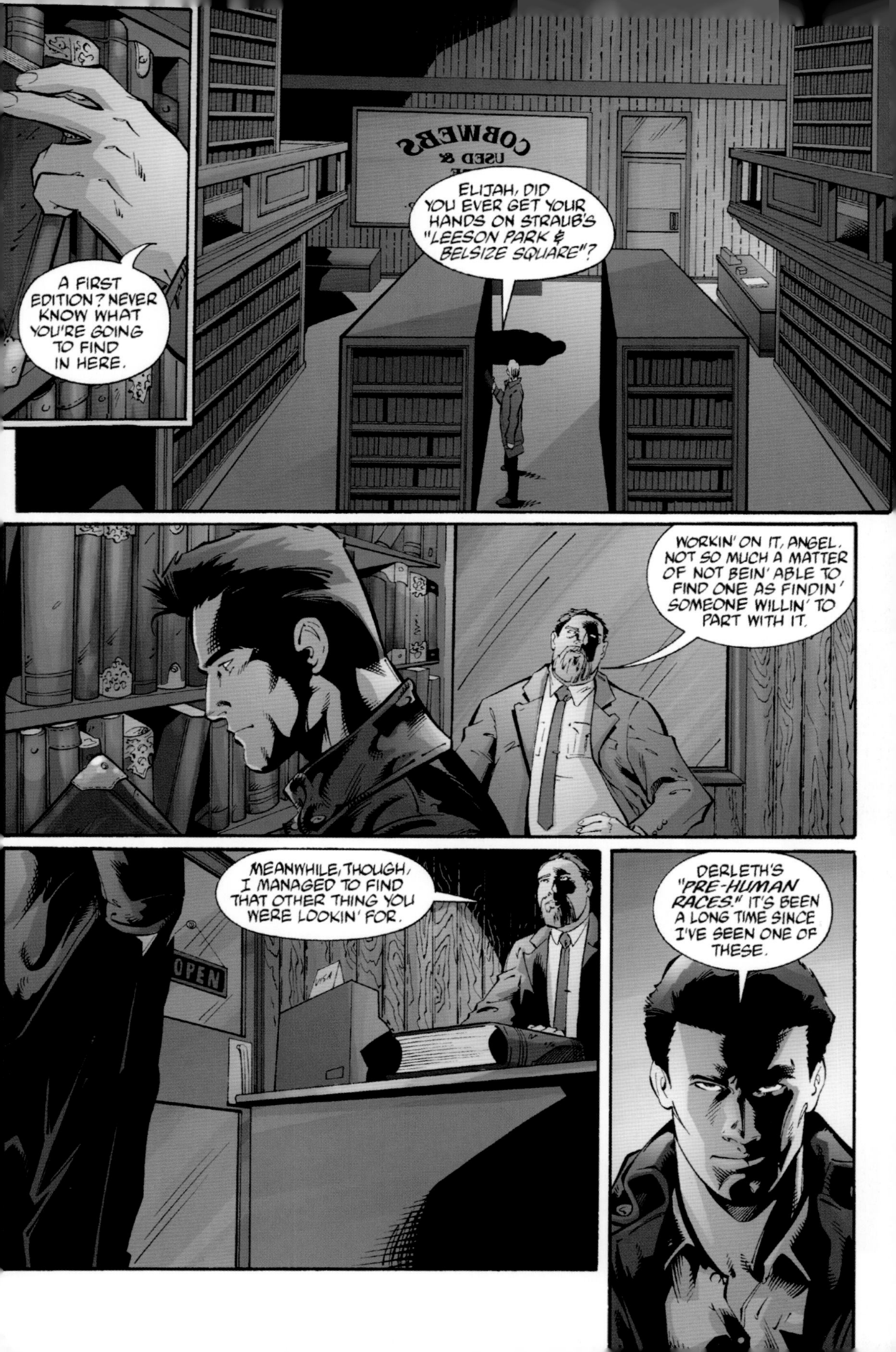
ELIJAH, DID YOU EVER GET YOUR HANDS ON STRAUB'S "LEESON PARK & BELSIZE SQUARE"?
A FIRST EDITION? NEVER KNOW WHAT YOU'RE GOING TO FIND IN HERE.
WORKIN' ON IT, ANGEL. NOT SO MUCH A MATTER OF NOT BEIN' ABLE TO FIND ONE AS FINDIN' SOMEONE WILLIN' TO PART WITH IT.
MEANWHILE, THOUGH, I MANAGED TO FIND THAT OTHER THING YOU WERE LOOKIN' FOR.
OPEN
DERLETH'S "PRE-HUMAN RACES." IT'S BEEN A LONG TIME SINCE I'VE SEEN ONE OF THESE.

YOU MAY HAVE RETIRED, ELIJAH, BUT YOU'RE STILL A MAGICIAN.

COBWEBS

USED & RARE BOOKS

E.J. Carnegie, Prop

"NO MAGIC IN IT, ANGEL. JUST PERSISTENCE. GOOD NIGHT, LAD."

COME ON NOW! THERE'S NO NEED FOR--

AAGGHH!

DOYLE...

THUNK

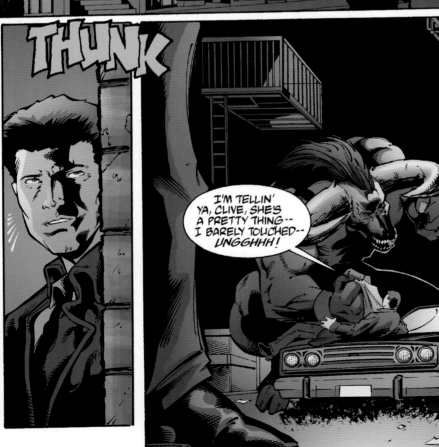

I'M TELLIN' YA, CLIVE, SHE'S A PRETTY THING-- I BARELY TOUCHED-- UNGGHHH!

LET HIM GO.

YOU. I FIGURED YOU WERE AROUND HERE SOMEWHERE. THIS AIN'T YOUR CONCERN. DOYLE'S BEEN MESSING WITH MY GIRL. HE DIES.

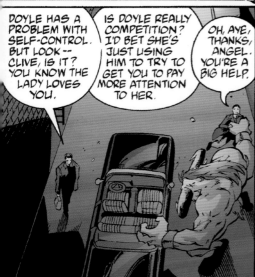

DOYLE HAS A PROBLEM WITH SELF-CONTROL. BUT LOOK -- CLIVE, IS IT? YOU KNOW THE LADY LOVES YOU.

IS DOYLE REALLY COMPETITION? I'D BET SHE'S JUST USING HIM TO TRY TO GET YOU TO PAY MORE ATTENTION TO HER.

OH, AYE, THANKS, ANGEL. YOU'RE A BIG HELP.

I RECOGNIZE YOUR MARKINGS. YOU'RE A YAZI. YOUR KIND IS PRETTY SOCIALIZED. IT DOESN'T HAVE TO GET UGLY FROM HERE.

THING IS, CLIVE, DOYLE'S WITH ME. SO I'M ASKING YOU TO PUT HIM DOWN, AND STEP AWAY FROM MY CAR. YOU'VE DONE ENOUGH DAMAGE ALREADY.

YOU WANT HIM? HERE YA GO!

WHUMP

ALL RIGHT! THAT'S ENOUGH OF THAT!

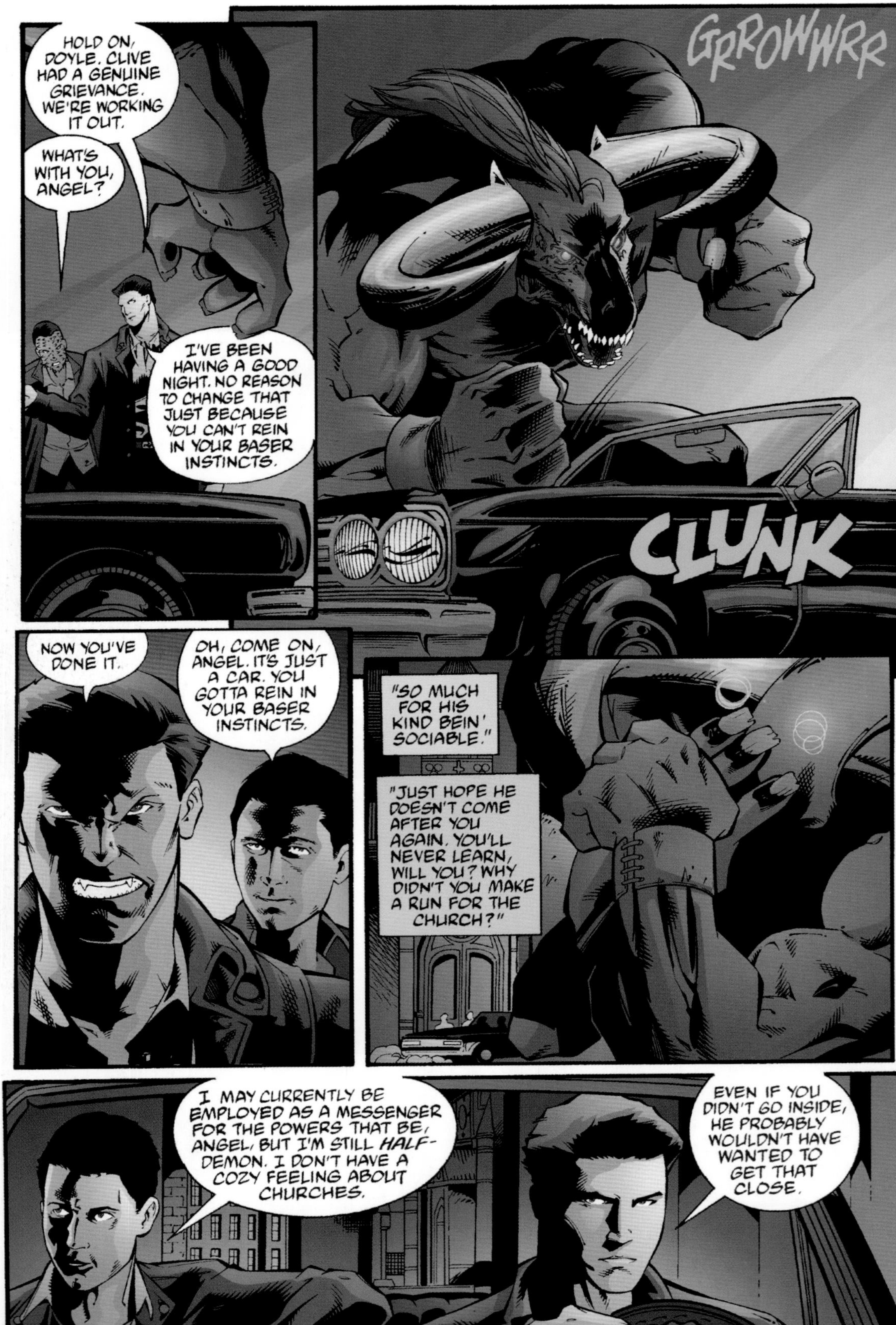
HOLD ON, DOYLE. CLIVE HAD A GENUINE GRIEVANCE. WE'RE WORKING IT OUT.
WHAT'S WITH YOU, ANGEL?
I'VE BEEN HAVING A GOOD NIGHT. NO REASON TO CHANGE THAT JUST BECAUSE YOU CAN'T REIN IN YOUR BASER INSTINCTS.
GRROWWRR
CLUNK
NOW YOU'VE DONE IT.
OH, COME ON, ANGEL. IT'S JUST A CAR. YOU GOTTA REIN IN YOUR BASER INSTINCTS.
"SO MUCH FOR HIS KIND BEIN' SOCIABLE."
"JUST HOPE HE DOESN'T COME AFTER YOU AGAIN. YOU'LL NEVER LEARN, WILL YOU? WHY DIDN'T YOU MAKE A RUN FOR THE CHURCH?"
I MAY CURRENTLY BE EMPLOYED AS A MESSENGER FOR THE POWERS THAT BE, ANGEL, BUT I'M STILL HALF-DEMON. I DON'T HAVE A COZY FEELING ABOUT CHURCHES.
EVEN IF YOU DIDN'T GO INSIDE, HE PROBABLY WOULDN'T HAVE WANTED TO GET THAT CLOSE.

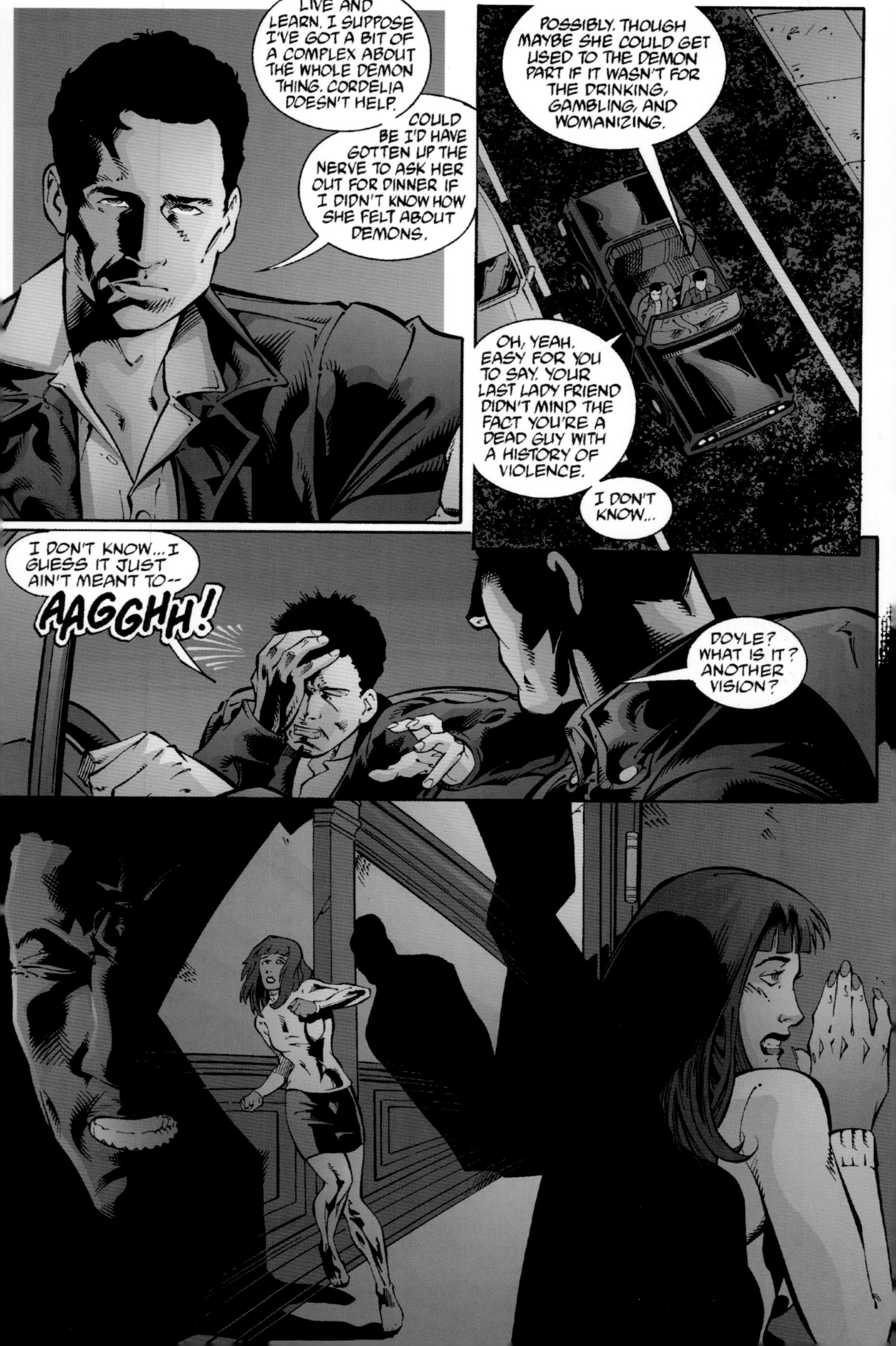
LIVE AND LEARN. I SUPPOSE I'VE GOT A BIT OF A COMPLEX ABOUT THE WHOLE DEMON THING. CORDELIA DOESN'T HELP.
COULD BE I'D HAVE GOTTEN UP THE NERVE TO ASK HER OUT FOR DINNER IF I DIDN'T KNOW HOW SHE FELT ABOUT DEMONS.
POSSIBLY. THOUGH MAYBE SHE COULD GET USED TO THE DEMON PART IF IT WASN'T FOR THE DRINKING, GAMBLING, AND WOMANIZING.
OH, YEAH. EASY FOR YOU TO SAY. YOUR LAST LADY FRIEND DIDN'T MIND THE FACT YOU'RE A DEAD GUY WITH A HISTORY OF VIOLENCE.
I DON'T KNOW...
I DON'T KNOW... I GUESS IT JUST AIN'T MEANT TO--
AAGGHH!
DOYLE? WHAT IS IT? ANOTHER VISION?

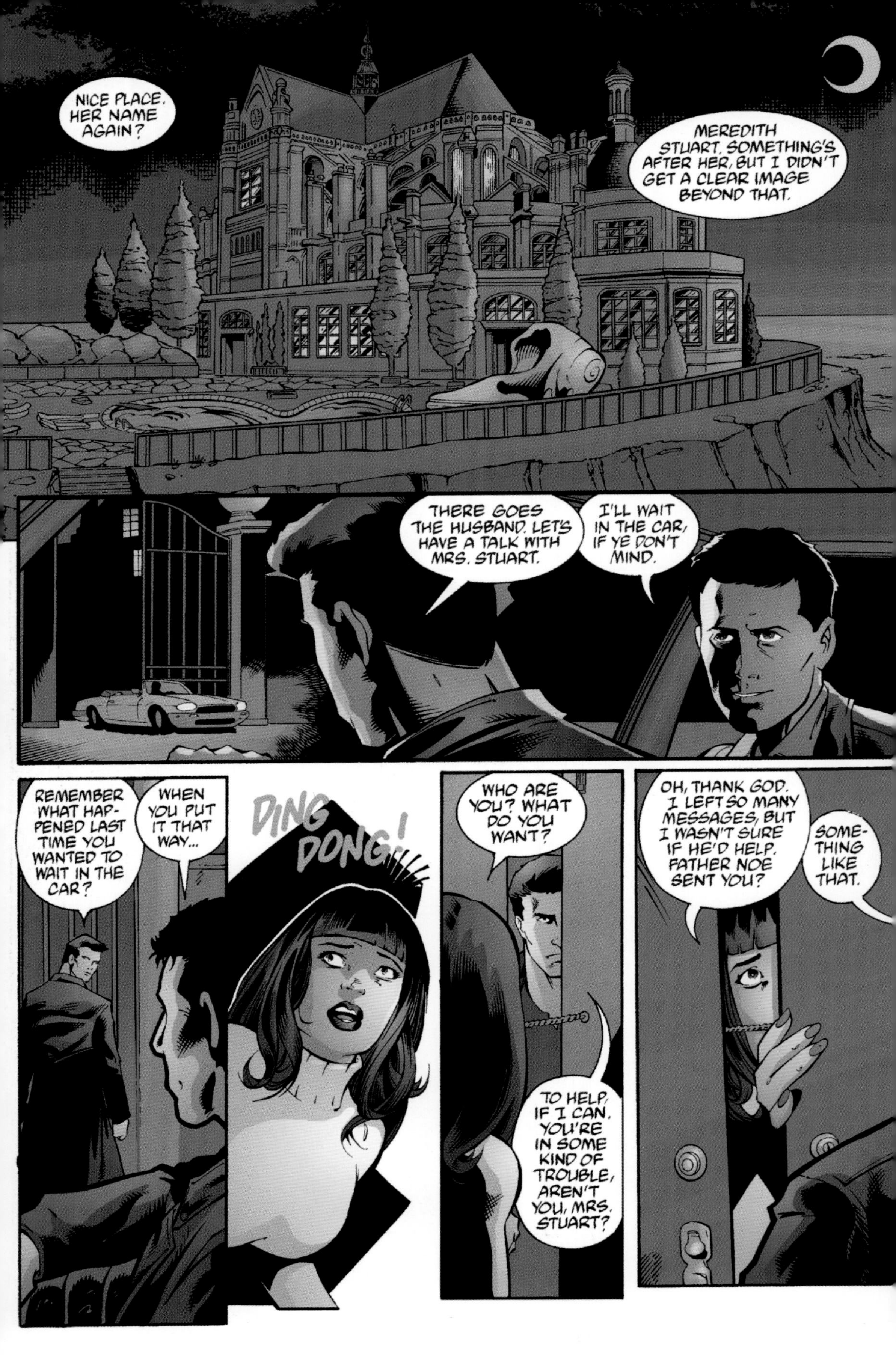
NICE PLACE. HER NAME AGAIN?
MEREDITH STUART. SOMETHING'S AFTER HER, BUT I DIDN'T GET A CLEAR IMAGE BEYOND THAT.
THERE GOES THE HUSBAND. LET'S HAVE A TALK WITH MRS. STUART.
I'LL WAIT IN THE CAR, IF YE DON'T MIND.
REMEMBER WHAT HAP-PENED LAST TIME YOU WANTED TO WAIT IN THE CAR?
WHEN YOU PUT IT THAT WAY...
DING DONG!
WHO ARE YOU? WHAT DO YOU WANT?
TO HELP, IF I CAN. YOU'RE IN SOME KIND OF TROUBLE, AREN'T YOU, MRS. STUART?
OH, THANK GOD. I LEFT SO MANY MESSAGES, BUT I WASN'T SURE IF HE'D HELP. FATHER NOE SENT YOU?
SOME-THING LIKE THAT.

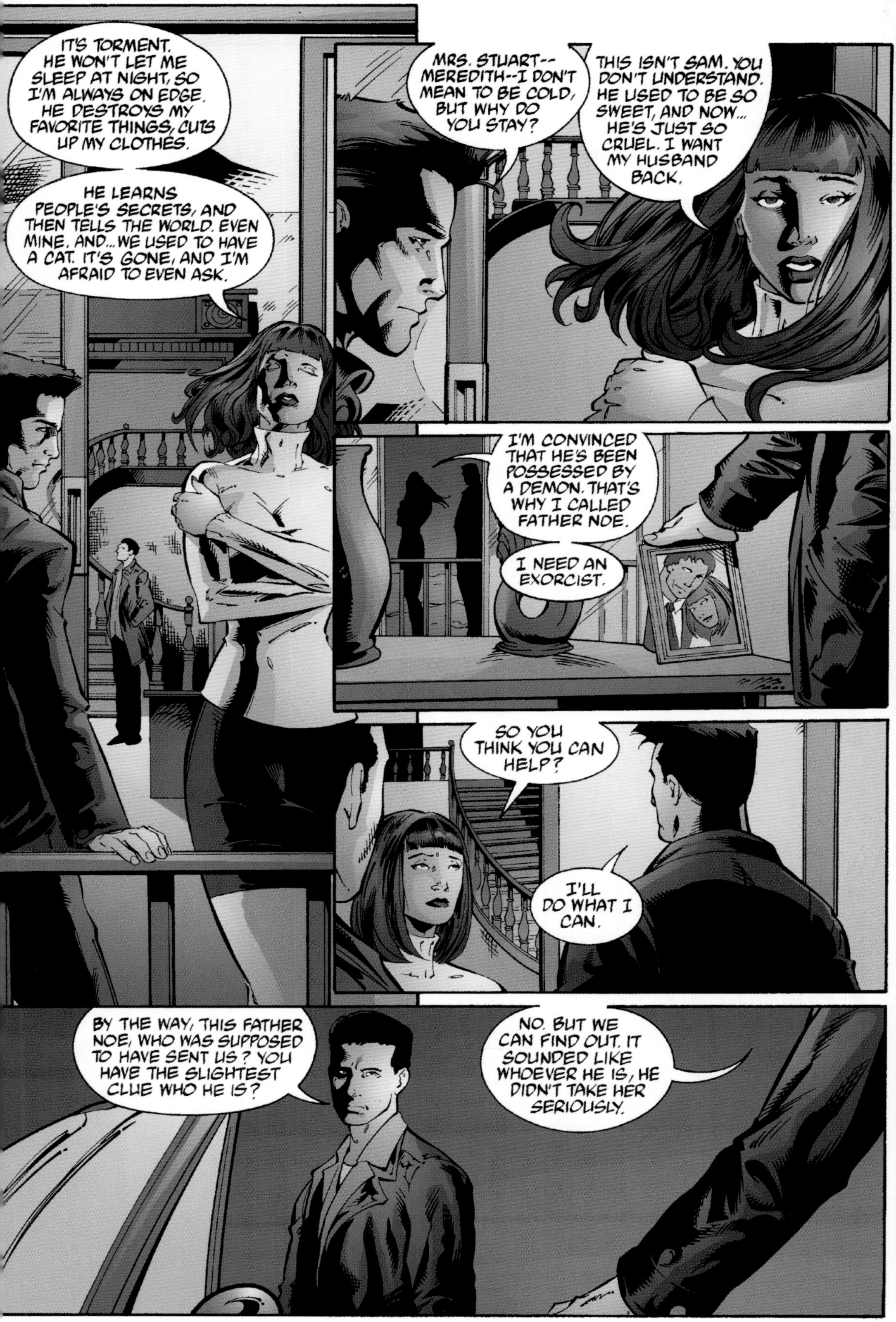
IT'S TORMENT. HE WON'T LET ME SLEEP AT NIGHT, SO I'M ALWAYS ON EDGE. HE DESTROYS MY FAVORITE THINGS, CUTS UP MY CLOTHES.
HE LEARNS PEOPLE'S SECRETS, AND THEN TELLS THE WORLD. EVEN MINE. AND...WE USED TO HAVE A CAT. IT'S GONE, AND I'M AFRAID TO EVEN ASK.
MRS. STUART--MEREDITH--I DON'T MEAN TO BE COLD, BUT WHY DO YOU STAY?
THIS ISN'T SAM. YOU DON'T UNDERSTAND. HE USED TO BE SO SWEET, AND NOW... HE'S JUST SO CRUEL. I WANT MY HUSBAND BACK.
I'M CONVINCED THAT HE'S BEEN POSSESSED BY A DEMON. THAT'S WHY I CALLED FATHER NOE.
I NEED AN EXORCIST.
SO YOU THINK YOU CAN HELP?
I'LL DO WHAT I CAN.
BY THE WAY, THIS FATHER NOE, WHO WAS SUPPOSED TO HAVE SENT US? YOU HAVE THE SLIGHTEST CLUE WHO HE IS?
NO. BUT WE CAN FIND OUT. IT SOUNDED LIKE WHOEVER HE IS, HE DIDN'T TAKE HER SERIOUSLY.

"DO YOU? BELIEVE HER, I MEAN. HELL, HE'S A LAWYER, AFTER ALL. JUST 'CAUSE HE ACTS LIKE A DEMON, THAT DOESN'T MEAN HE IS ONE."

"WE'LL HAVE TO SEE ABOUT THAT."

LADIES AND GENTLEMEN, I SHARE YOUR DISGUST. MY CLIENT IS DESPICABLE. I'M NOT HERE TO ARGUE THAT.

HE TOOK LURID VIDEOTAPES OF A FORMER LOVER, AND WITHOUT HER CONSENT, HE PUT THEM ON THE INTERNET. OF THAT, HE IS MOST CERTAINLY GUILTY.

BUT HE'S NOT A MURDERER. THE DECEASED, ENRAGED OVER WHAT MY CLIENT HAD DONE, ATTACKED HIM.

THE GUN WAS HERS. SHE BROUGHT IT WITH HER. *SHE* SHOT *HIM*. IN THE STRUGGLE THAT ENSUED, SHE ALSO WAS SHOT.

IS IT TRAGIC THAT SHE DIED? OF COURSE. WAS IT MURDER? NO.

THE DECEASED ATTEMPTED TO MURDER MY CLIENT. WHILE HE WAS DEFENDING HIMSELF, SHE SUSTAINED A FATAL INJURY.

LOOK AT THE EVIDENCE, LADIES AND GENTLEMEN.

HE MAY BE A MONSTER, BUT HE'S NOT A MURDERER.

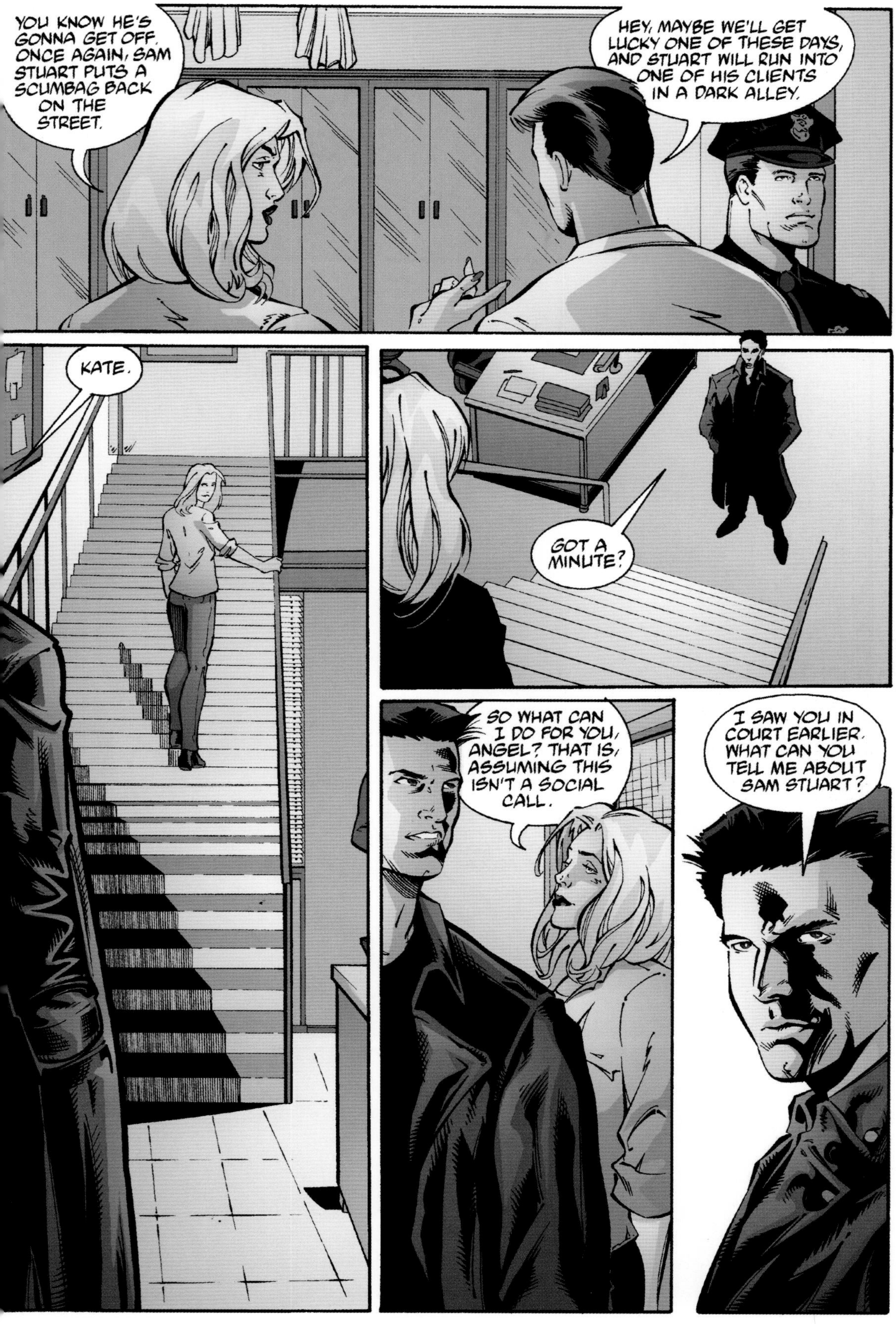
YOU KNOW HE'S GONNA GET OFF. ONCE AGAIN, SAM STUART PUTS A SCUMBAG BACK ON THE STREET.
HEY, MAYBE WE'LL GET LUCKY ONE OF THESE DAYS, AND STUART WILL RUN INTO ONE OF HIS CLIENTS IN A DARK ALLEY.
KATE.
GOT A MINUTE?
SO WHAT CAN I DO FOR YOU, ANGEL? THAT IS, ASSUMING THIS ISN'T A SOCIAL CALL.
I SAW YOU IN COURT EARLIER. WHAT CAN YOU TELL ME ABOUT SAM STUART?

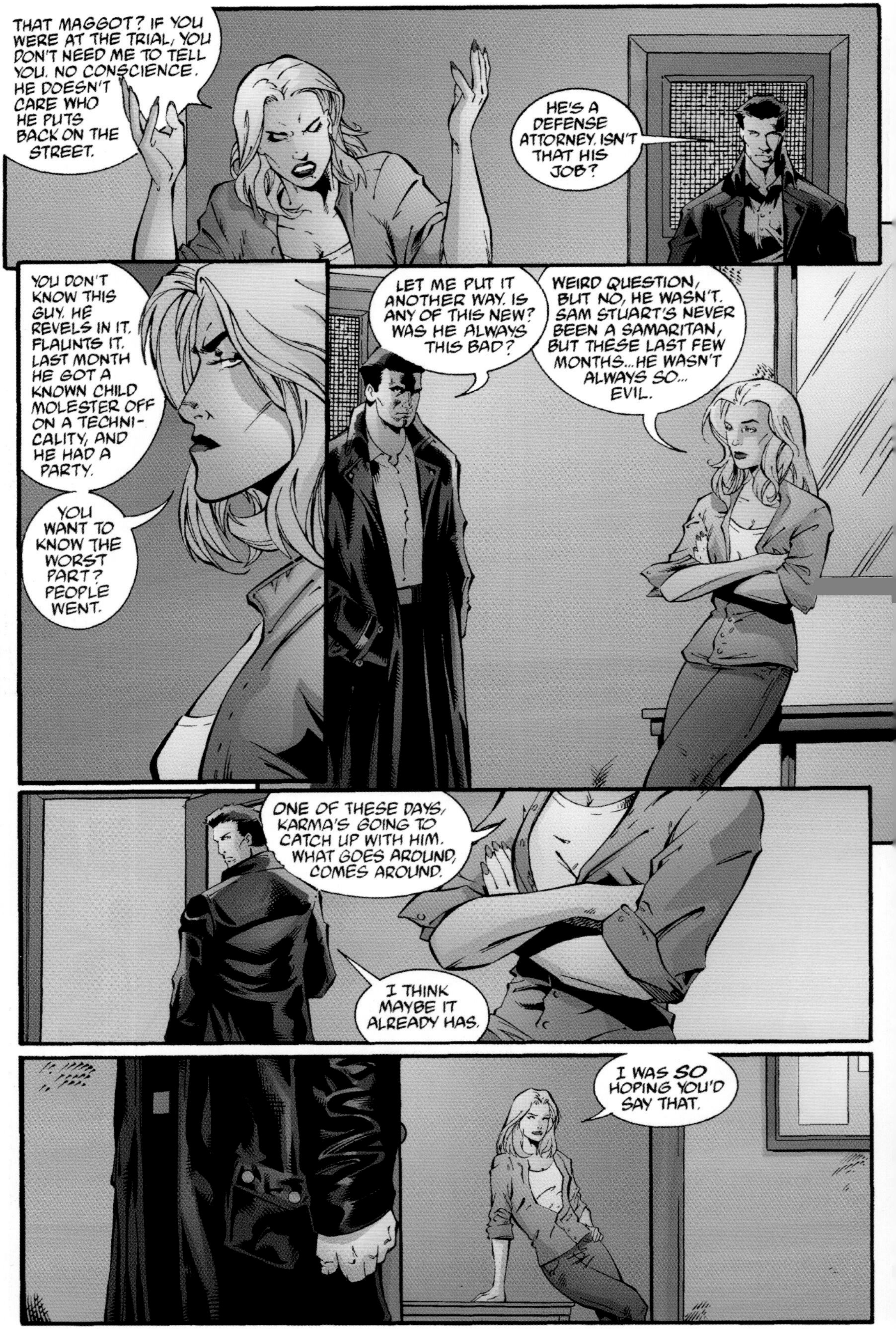
THAT MAGGOT? IF YOU WERE AT THE TRIAL, YOU DON'T NEED ME TO TELL YOU. NO CONSCIENCE. HE DOESN'T CARE WHO HE PUTS BACK ON THE STREET.
HE'S A DEFENSE ATTORNEY. ISN'T THAT HIS JOB?
YOU DON'T KNOW THIS GUY. HE REVELS IN IT. FLAUNTS IT. LAST MONTH HE GOT A KNOWN CHILD MOLESTER OFF ON A TECHNICALITY, AND HE HAD A PARTY.
YOU WANT TO KNOW THE WORST PART? PEOPLE WENT.
LET ME PUT IT ANOTHER WAY. IS ANY OF THIS NEW? WAS HE ALWAYS THIS BAD?
WEIRD QUESTION, BUT NO, HE WASN'T. SAM STUART'S NEVER BEEN A SAMARITAN, BUT THESE LAST FEW MONTHS...HE WASN'T ALWAYS SO... EVIL.
ONE OF THESE DAYS, KARMA'S GOING TO CATCH UP WITH HIM. WHAT GOES AROUND, COMES AROUND.
I THINK MAYBE IT ALREADY HAS.
I WAS SO HOPING YOU'D SAY THAT.

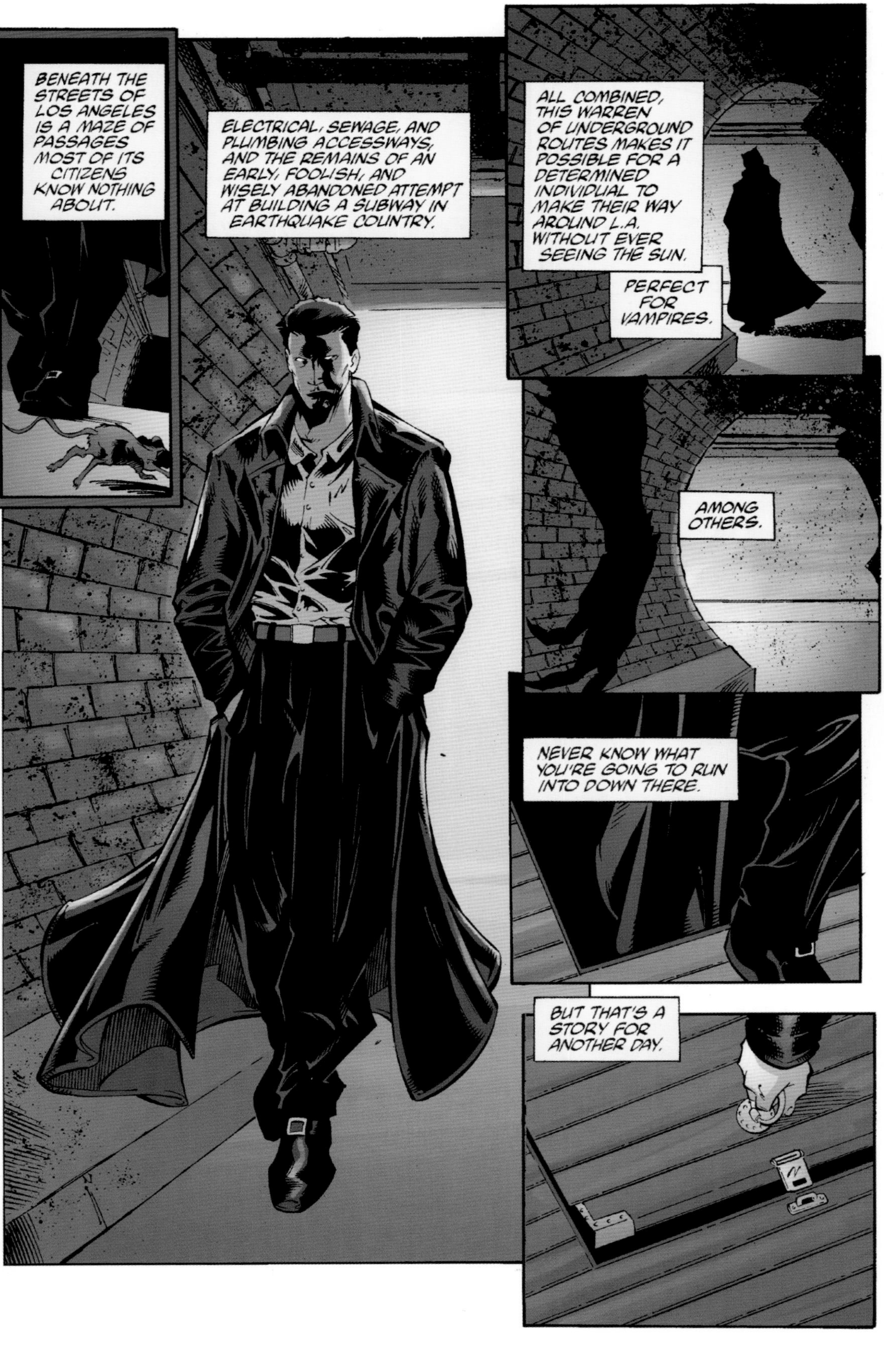
BENEATH THE STREETS OF LOS ANGELES IS A MAZE OF PASSAGES MOST OF ITS CITIZENS KNOW NOTHING ABOUT.
ELECTRICAL, SEWAGE, AND PLUMBING ACCESSWAYS, AND THE REMAINS OF AN EARLY, FOOLISH, AND WISELY ABANDONED ATTEMPT AT BUILDING A SUBWAY IN EARTHQUAKE COUNTRY.
ALL COMBINED, THIS WARREN OF UNDERGROUND ROUTES MAKES IT POSSIBLE FOR A DETERMINED INDIVIDUAL TO MAKE THEIR WAY AROUND L.A. WITHOUT EVER SEEING THE SUN.
PERFECT FOR VAMPIRES.
AMONG OTHERS.
NEVER KNOW WHAT YOU'RE GOING TO RUN INTO DOWN THERE.
BUT THAT'S A STORY FOR ANOTHER DAY.

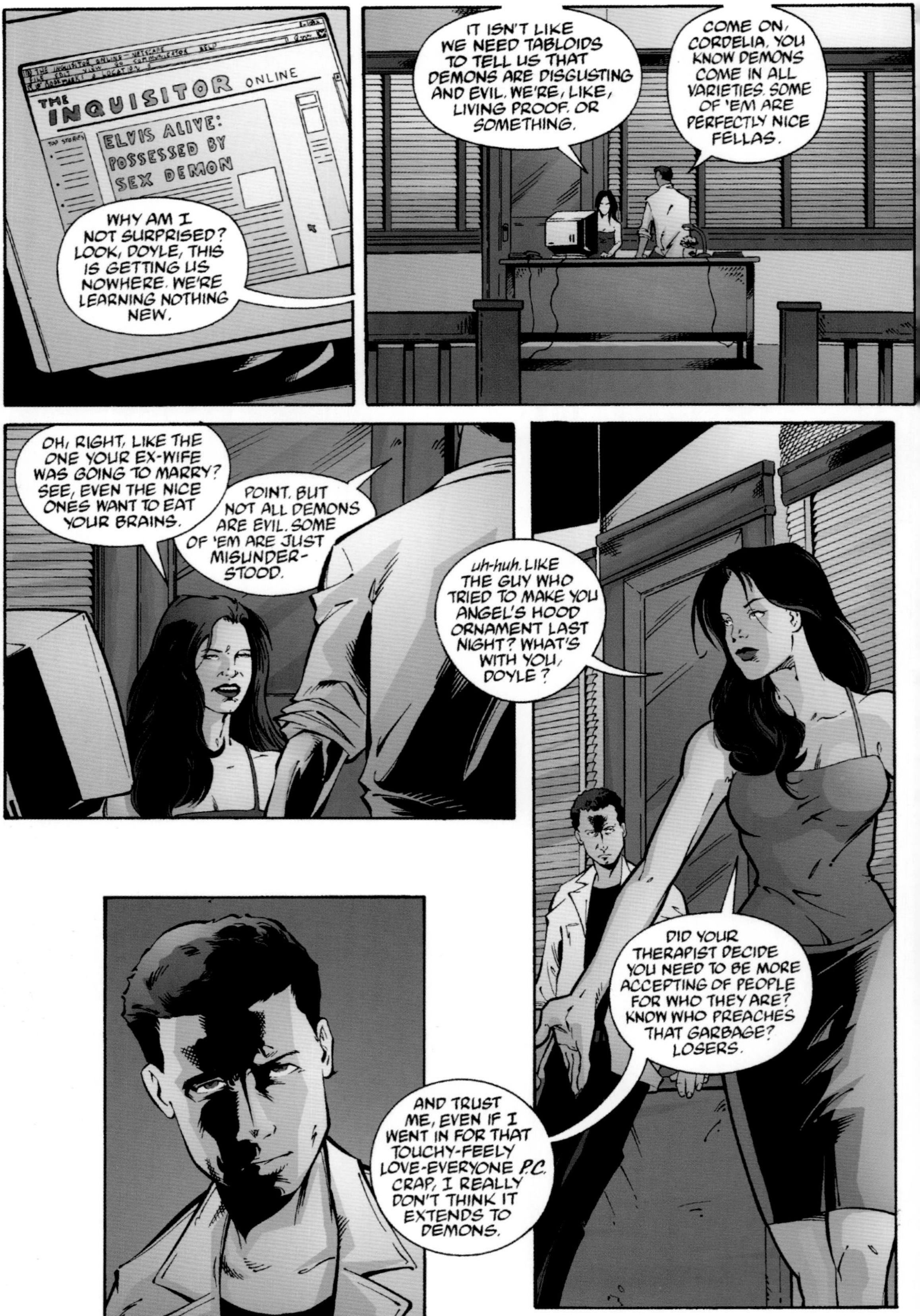
THE INQUISITOR ONLINE
ELVIS ALIVE: POSSESSED BY SEX DEMON
WHY AM I NOT SURPRISED? LOOK, DOYLE, THIS IS GETTING US NOWHERE. WE'RE LEARNING NOTHING NEW.
IT ISN'T LIKE WE NEED TABLOIDS TO TELL US THAT DEMONS ARE DISGUSTING AND EVIL. WE'RE, LIKE, LIVING PROOF. OR SOMETHING.
COME ON, CORDELIA, YOU KNOW DEMONS COME IN ALL VARIETIES. SOME OF 'EM ARE PERFECTLY NICE FELLAS.
OH, RIGHT, LIKE THE ONE YOUR EX-WIFE WAS GOING TO MARRY? SEE, EVEN THE NICE ONES WANT TO EAT YOUR BRAINS.
POINT. BUT NOT ALL DEMONS ARE EVIL. SOME OF 'EM ARE JUST MISUNDER-STOOD.
uh-huh. LIKE THE GUY WHO TRIED TO MAKE YOU ANGEL'S HOOD ORNAMENT LAST NIGHT? WHAT'S WITH YOU, DOYLE?
DID YOUR THERAPIST DECIDE YOU NEED TO BE MORE ACCEPTING OF PEOPLE FOR WHO THEY ARE? KNOW WHO PREACHES THAT GARBAGE? LOSERS.
AND TRUST ME, EVEN IF I WENT IN FOR THAT TOUCHY-FEELY LOVE-EVERYONE P.C. CRAP, I REALLY DON'T THINK IT EXTENDS TO DEMONS.

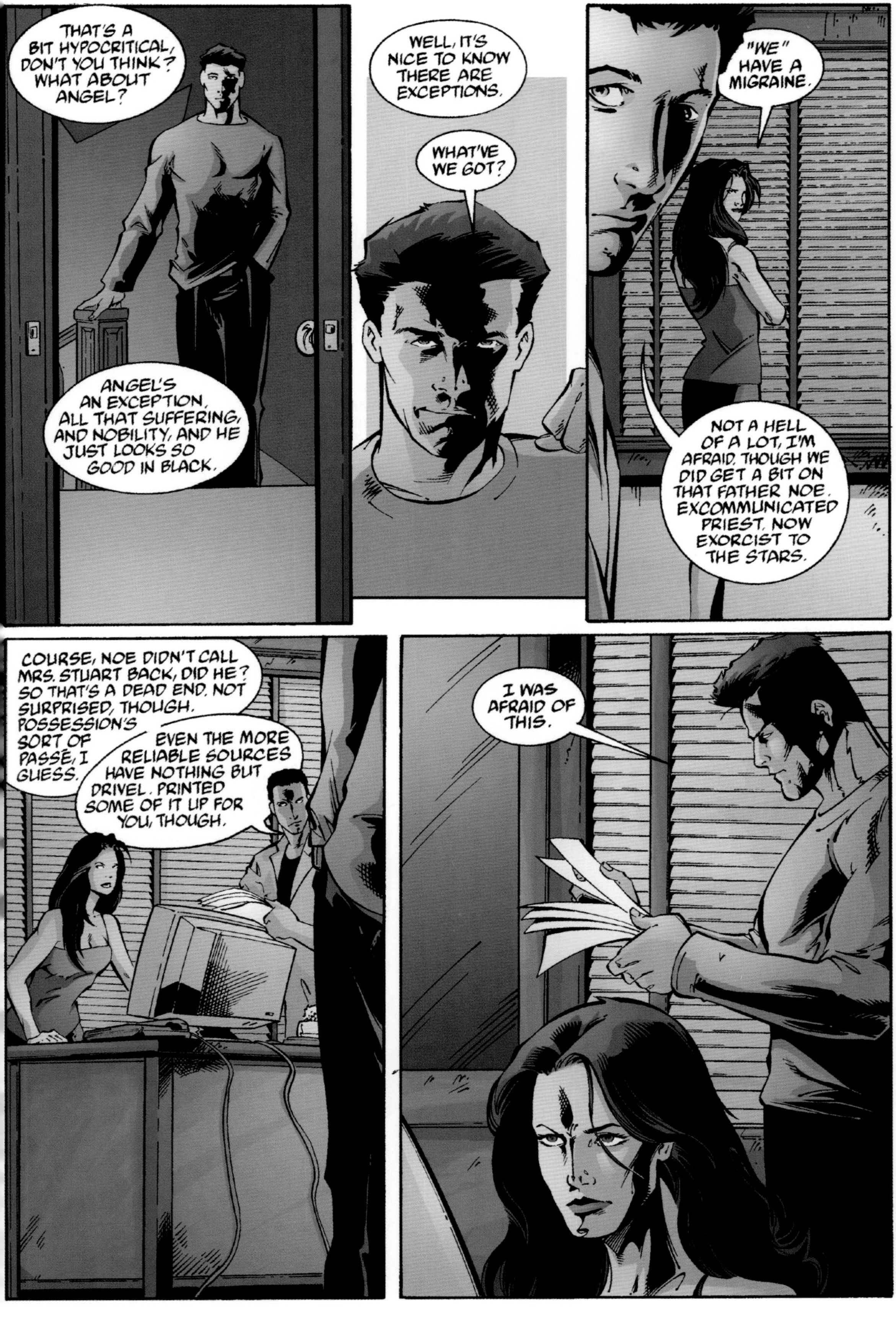
THAT'S A BIT HYPOCRITICAL, DON'T YOU THINK? WHAT ABOUT ANGEL?
ANGEL'S AN EXCEPTION. ALL THAT SUFFERING, AND NOBILITY, AND HE JUST LOOKS SO GOOD IN BLACK.
WELL, IT'S NICE TO KNOW THERE ARE EXCEPTIONS.
WHAT'VE WE GOT?
"WE" HAVE A MIGRAINE.
NOT A HELL OF A LOT, I'M AFRAID, THOUGH WE DID GET A BIT ON THAT FATHER NOE. EXCOMMUNICATED PRIEST, NOW EXORCIST TO THE STARS.
COURSE, NOE DIDN'T CALL MRS. STUART BACK, DID HE? SO THAT'S A DEAD END. NOT SURPRISED, THOUGH. POSSESSION'S SORT OF PASSÉ, I GUESS.
EVEN THE MORE RELIABLE SOURCES HAVE NOTHING BUT DRIVEL. PRINTED SOME OF IT UP FOR YOU, THOUGH.
I WAS AFRAID OF THIS.

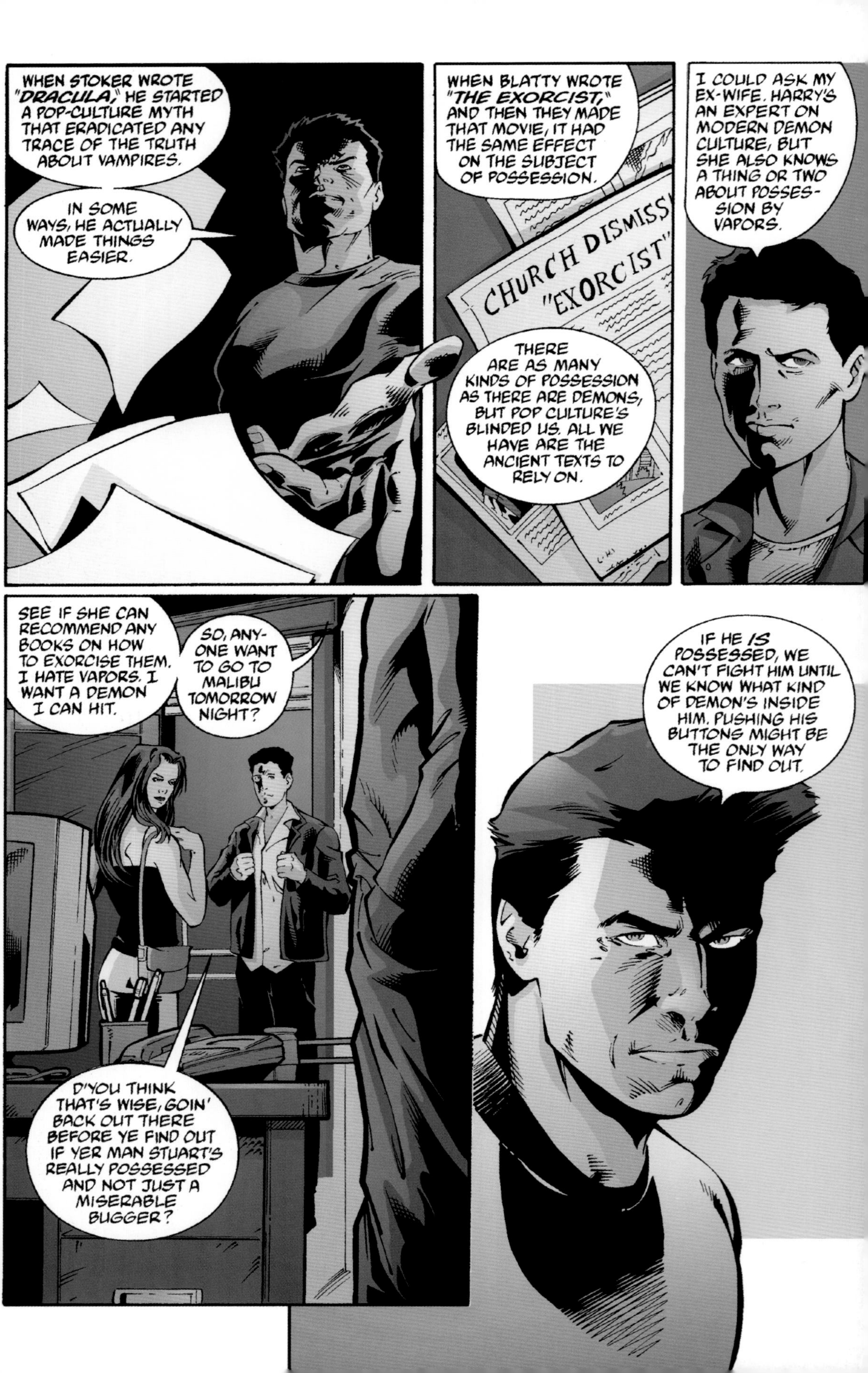
WHEN STOKER WROTE "DRACULA," HE STARTED A POP-CULTURE MYTH THAT ERADICATED ANY TRACE OF THE TRUTH ABOUT VAMPIRES.
IN SOME WAYS, HE ACTUALLY MADE THINGS EASIER.
WHEN BLATTY WROTE "THE EXORCIST," AND THEN THEY MADE THAT MOVIE, IT HAD THE SAME EFFECT ON THE SUBJECT OF POSSESSION.
CHURCH DISMISS "EXORCIST"
THERE ARE AS MANY KINDS OF POSSESSION AS THERE ARE DEMONS, BUT POP CULTURE'S BLINDED US. ALL WE HAVE ARE THE ANCIENT TEXTS TO RELY ON.
I COULD ASK MY EX-WIFE. HARRY'S AN EXPERT ON MODERN DEMON CULTURE, BUT SHE ALSO KNOWS A THING OR TWO ABOUT POSSES-SION BY VAPORS.
SEE IF SHE CAN RECOMMEND ANY BOOKS ON HOW TO EXORCISE THEM. I HATE VAPORS. I WANT A DEMON I CAN HIT.
SO, ANY-ONE WANT TO GO TO MALIBU TOMORROW NIGHT?
D'YOU THINK THAT'S WISE, GOIN' BACK OUT THERE BEFORE YE FIND OUT IF YER MAN STUART'S REALLY POSSESSED AND NOT JUST A MISERABLE BUGGER?
IF HE IS POSSESSED, WE CAN'T FIGHT HIM UNTIL WE KNOW WHAT KIND OF DEMON'S INSIDE HIM. PUSHING HIS BUTTONS MIGHT BE THE ONLY WAY TO FIND OUT.

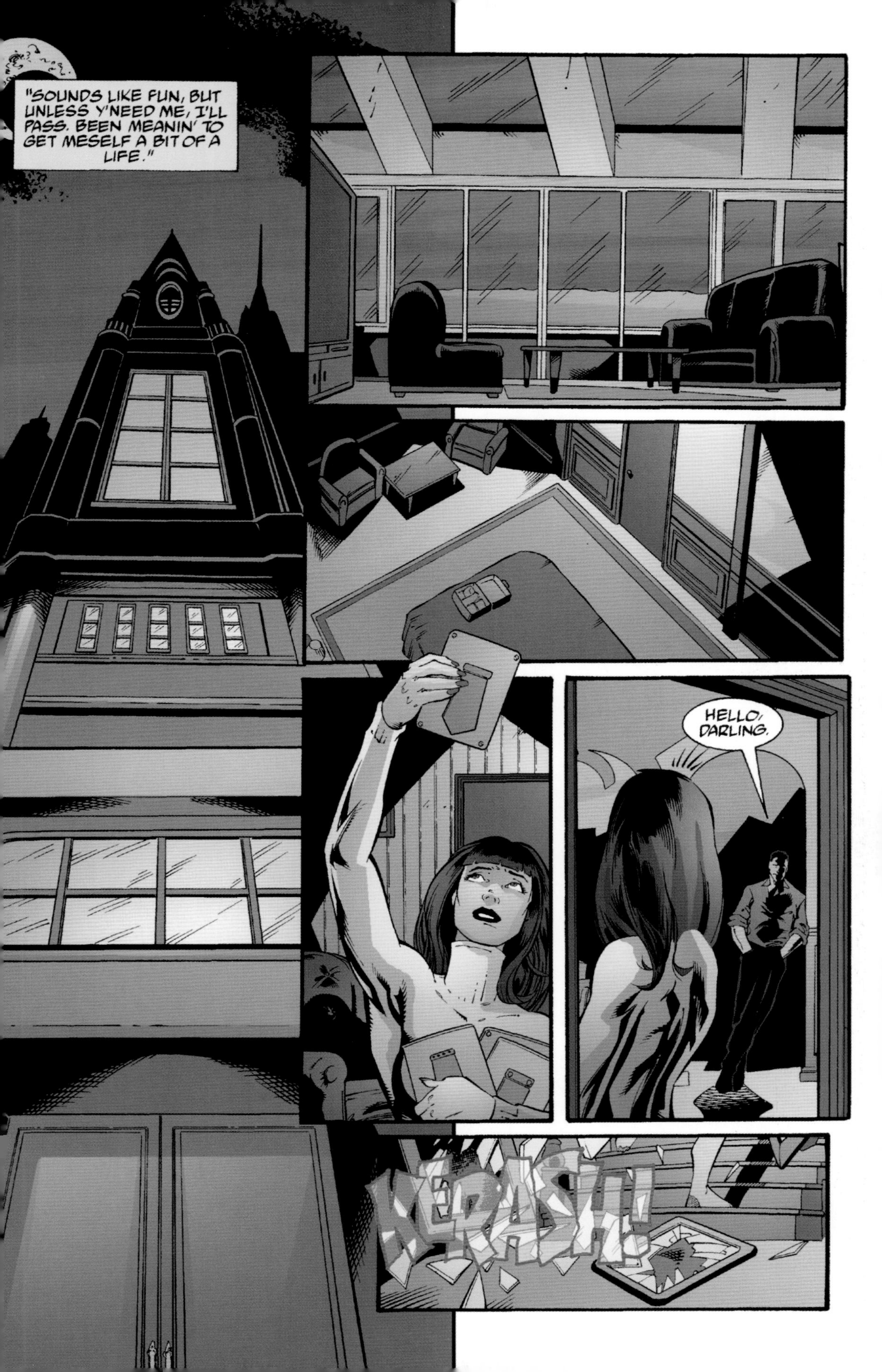
"SOUNDS LIKE FUN, BUT UNLESS Y'NEED ME, I'LL PASS. BEEN MEANIN' TO GET MESELF A BIT OF A LIFE."
HELLO, DARLING.
KERASH!

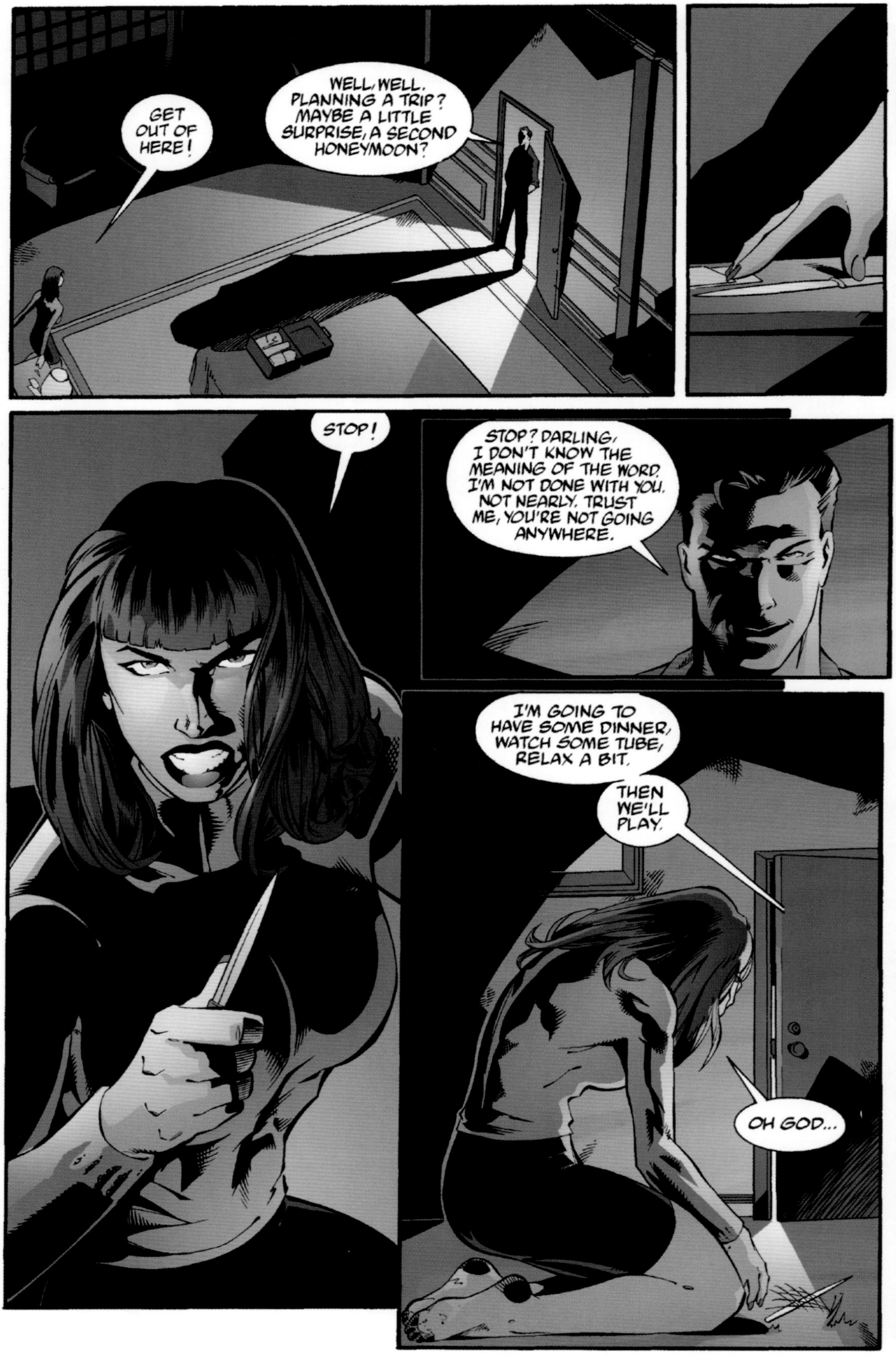
GET OUT OF HERE!
WELL, WELL. PLANNING A TRIP? MAYBE A LITTLE SURPRISE, A SECOND HONEYMOON?
STOP!
STOP? DARLING, I DON'T KNOW THE MEANING OF THE WORD. I'M NOT DONE WITH YOU. NOT NEARLY. TRUST ME, YOU'RE NOT GOING ANYWHERE.
I'M GOING TO HAVE SOME DINNER, WATCH SOME TUBE, RELAX A BIT.
THEN WE'LL PLAY.
OH GOD...

HEH-HEH.
THAT KRAMER, WHAT
A GOOF.

KLIK

...BE BRAVE...JUST
GO...WALK RIGHT
OUT AND--

MEREDITH.

OH!

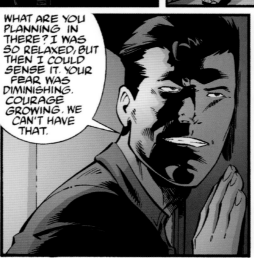

WHAT ARE YOU
PLANNING IN
THERE? I WAS
SO RELAXED, BUT
THEN I COULD
SENSE IT. YOUR
FEAR WAS
DIMINISHING.
COURAGE
GROWING. WE
CAN'T HAVE
THAT.

DINGDONG!

NOW, WHO
COULD...ARE
YOU EXPECTING
SOMEONE,
DARLING?

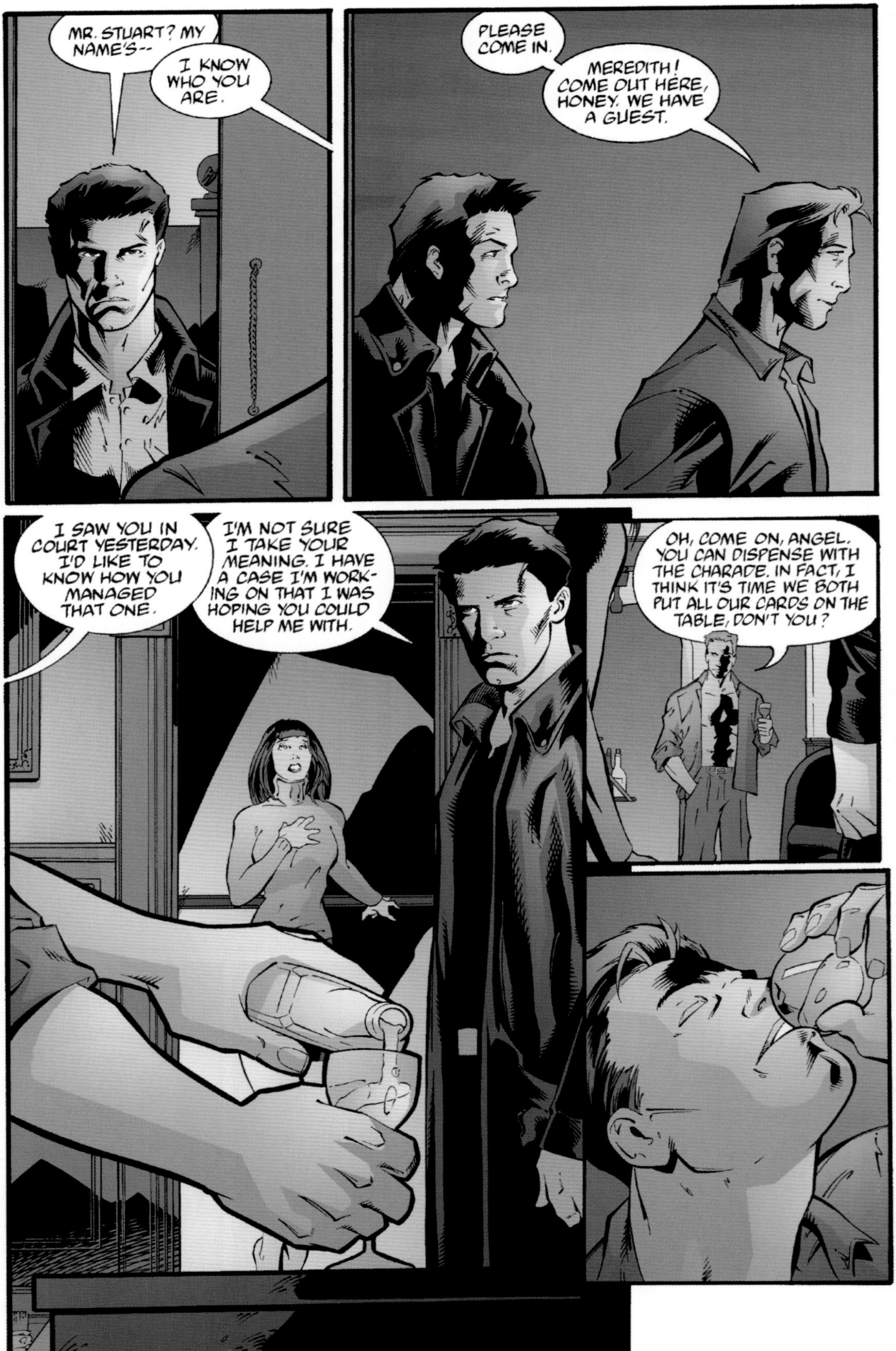
MR. STUART? MY NAME'S--
I KNOW WHO YOU ARE.
PLEASE COME IN.
MEREDITH! COME OUT HERE, HONEY. WE HAVE A GUEST.
I SAW YOU IN COURT YESTERDAY. I'D LIKE TO KNOW HOW YOU MANAGED THAT ONE.
I'M NOT SURE I TAKE YOUR MEANING. I HAVE A CASE I'M WORKING ON THAT I WAS HOPING YOU COULD HELP ME WITH.
OH, COME ON, ANGEL. YOU CAN DISPENSE WITH THE CHARADE. IN FACT, I THINK IT'S TIME WE BOTH PUT ALL OUR CARDS ON THE TABLE, DON'T YOU?

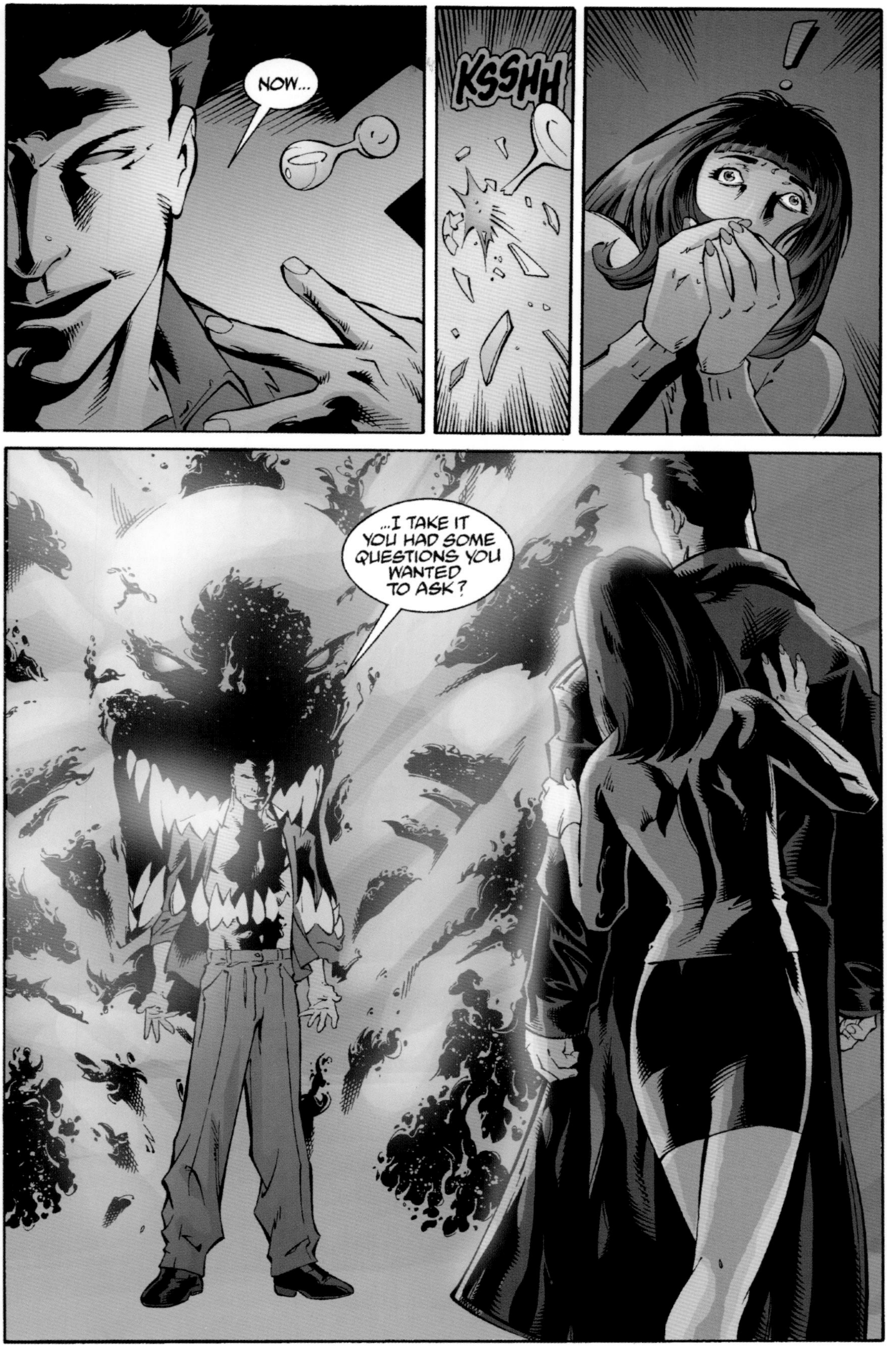
NOW...
KSSHH
!
...I TAKE IT YOU HAD SOME QUESTIONS YOU WANTED TO ASK?

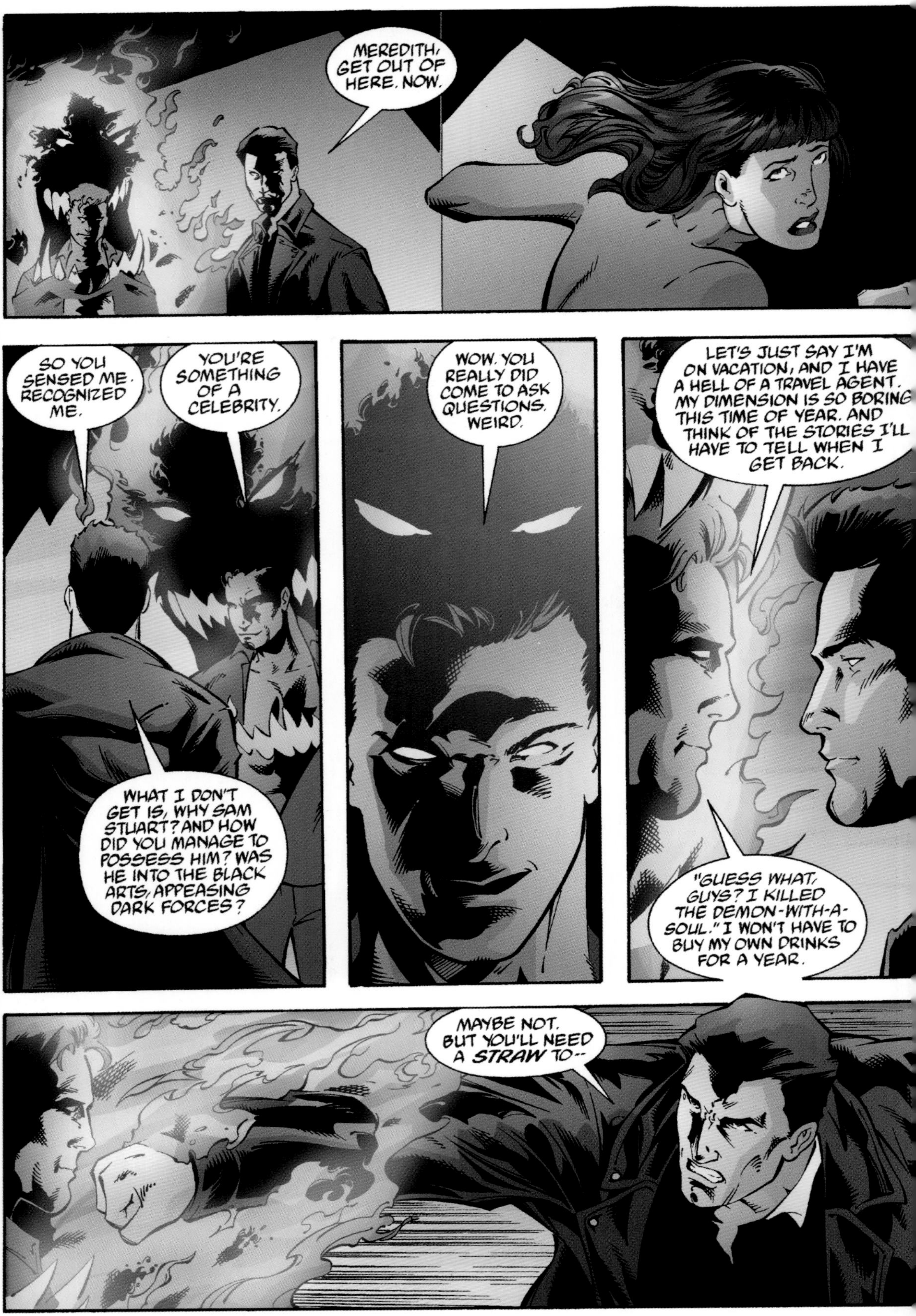
MEREDITH, GET OUT OF HERE. NOW.
SO YOU SENSED ME. RECOGNIZED ME.
YOU'RE SOMETHING OF A CELEBRITY.
WHAT I DON'T GET IS, WHY SAM STUART? AND HOW DID YOU MANAGE TO POSSESS HIM? WAS HE INTO THE BLACK ARTS, APPEASING DARK FORCES?
WOW. YOU REALLY DID COME TO ASK QUESTIONS. WEIRD.
LET'S JUST SAY I'M ON VACATION, AND I HAVE A HELL OF A TRAVEL AGENT. MY DIMENSION IS SO BORING THIS TIME OF YEAR. AND THINK OF THE STORIES I'LL HAVE TO TELL WHEN I GET BACK.
"GUESS WHAT, GUYS? I KILLED THE DEMON-WITH-A-SOUL." I WON'T HAVE TO BUY MY OWN DRINKS FOR A YEAR.
MAYBE NOT. BUT YOU'LL NEED A *STRAW* TO--

AARRH!

OH, THAT LOOKS LIKE IT SMARTS. LET ME HELP YOU PUT THAT *OUT!*

KRASH

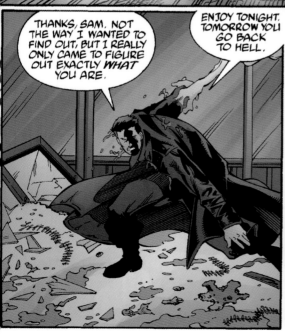

THANKS, SAM. NOT THE WAY I WANTED TO FIND OUT, BUT I REALLY ONLY CAME TO FIGURE OUT EXACTLY *WHAT* YOU ARE.

ENJOY TONIGHT. TOMORROW YOU GO BACK TO HELL.

AWW, AND JUST WHEN WE WERE STARTING TO HAVE FUN. COME ON, WON'T YOU STAY A WHILE LONGER?

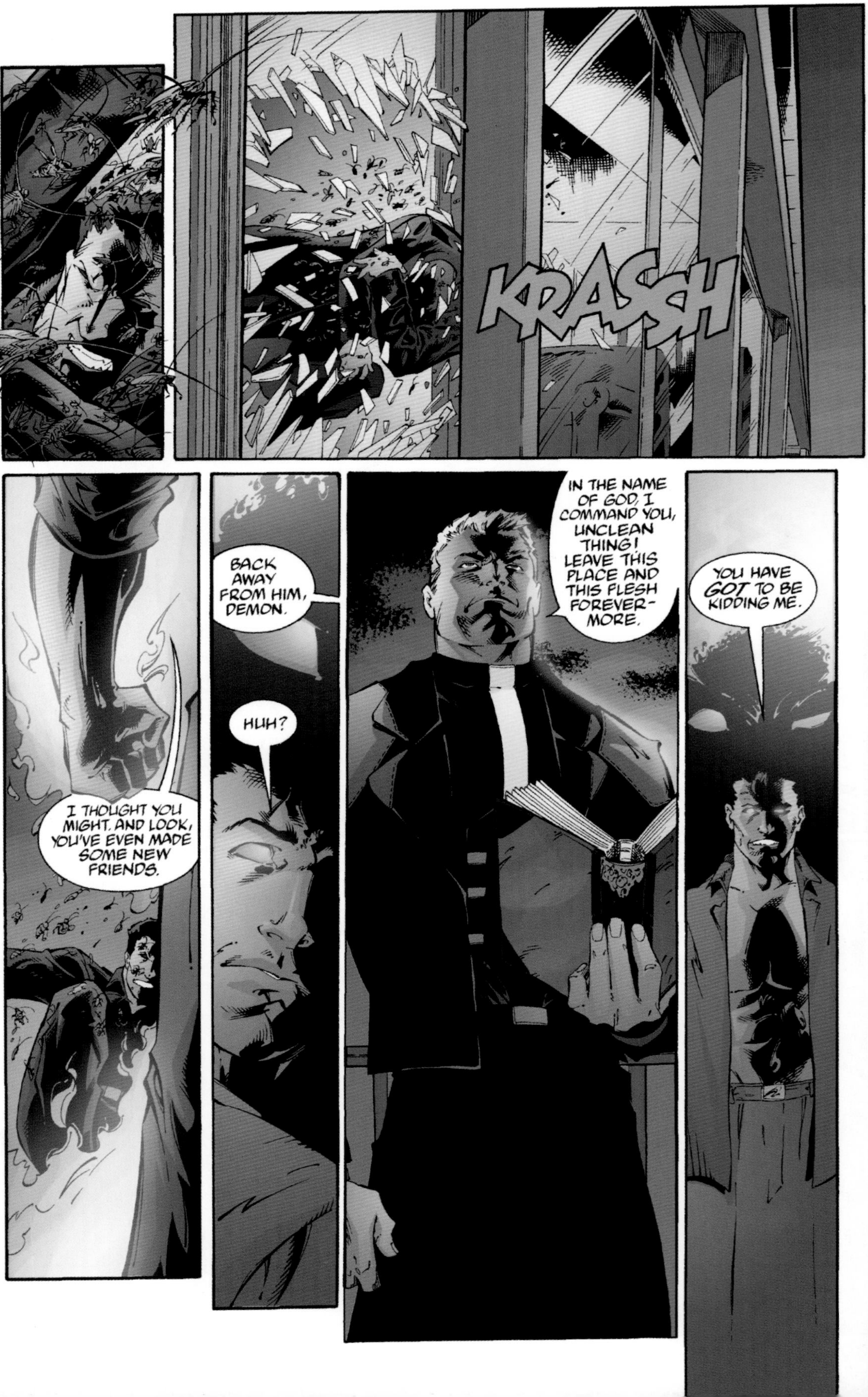
KRASSH
I THOUGHT YOU MIGHT. AND LOOK, YOU'VE EVEN MADE SOME NEW FRIENDS.
BACK AWAY FROM HIM, DEMON.
HUH?
IN THE NAME OF GOD, I COMMAND YOU, UNCLEAN THING! LEAVE THIS PLACE AND THIS FLESH FOREVER-MORE.
YOU HAVE GOT TO BE KIDDING ME.

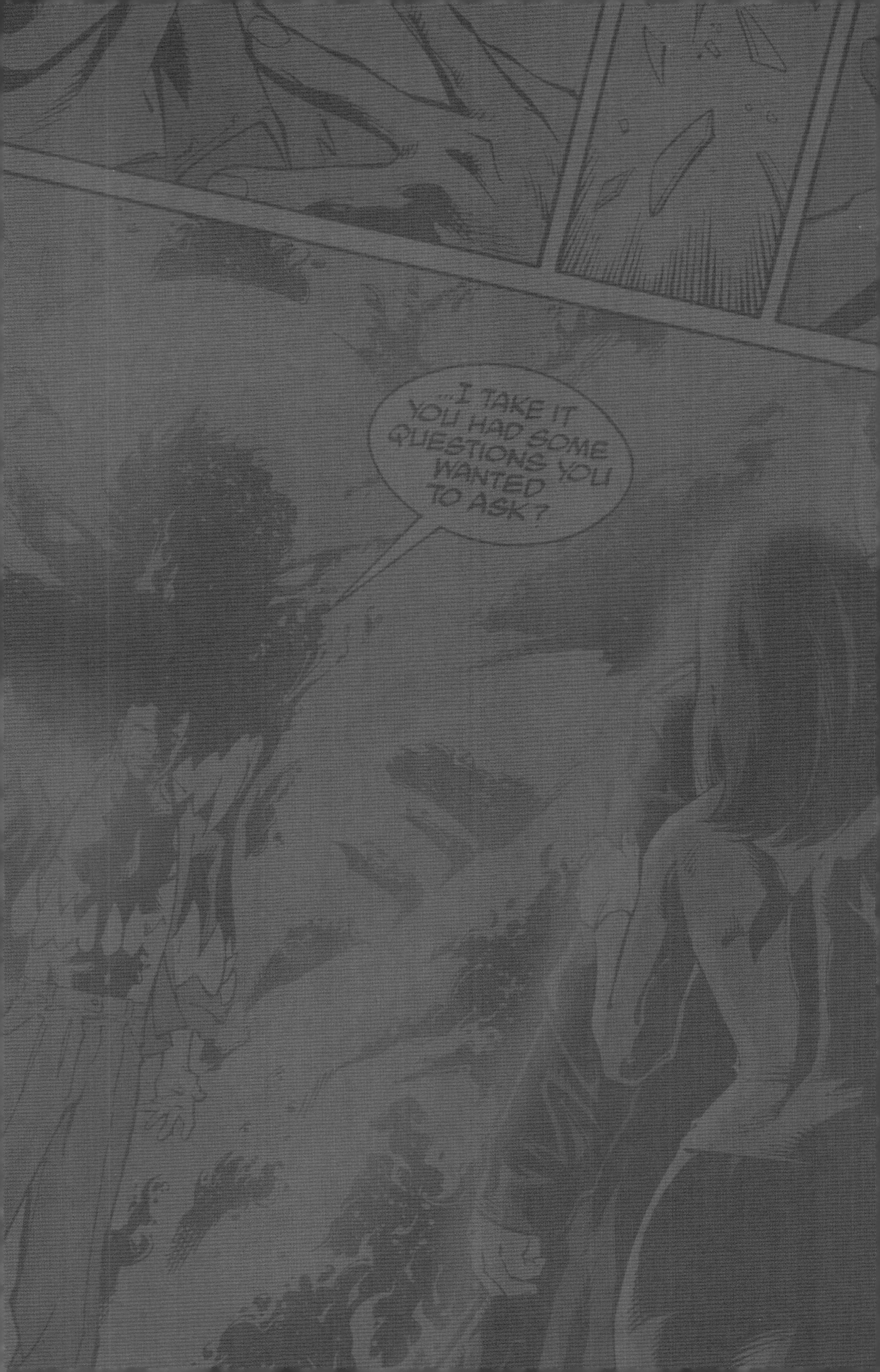
...I TAKE IT YOU HAD SOME QUESTIONS YOU WANTED TO ASK?

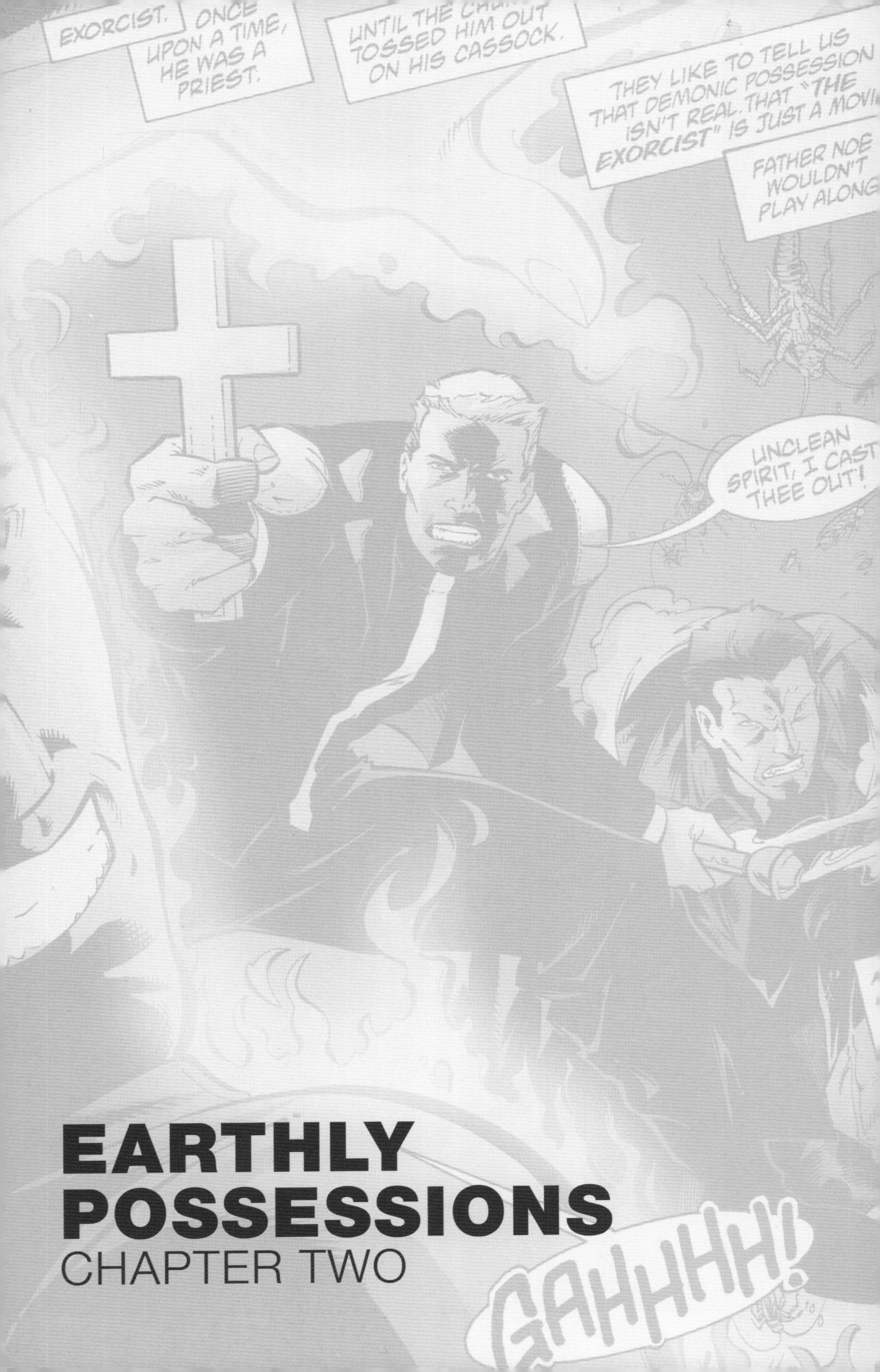
EXORCIST.
ONCE UPON A TIME, HE WAS A PRIEST.
TOSSED HIM OUT ON HIS CASSOCK.
THEY LIKE TO TELL US THAT DEMONIC POSSESSION ISN'T REAL. THAT "THE EXORCIST" IS JUST A
WOULDN'T PLAY ALONG
UNCLEAN SPIRIT, I CAST THEE OUT!
GAHHHH!

EARTHLY POSSESSIONS
CHAPTER TWO

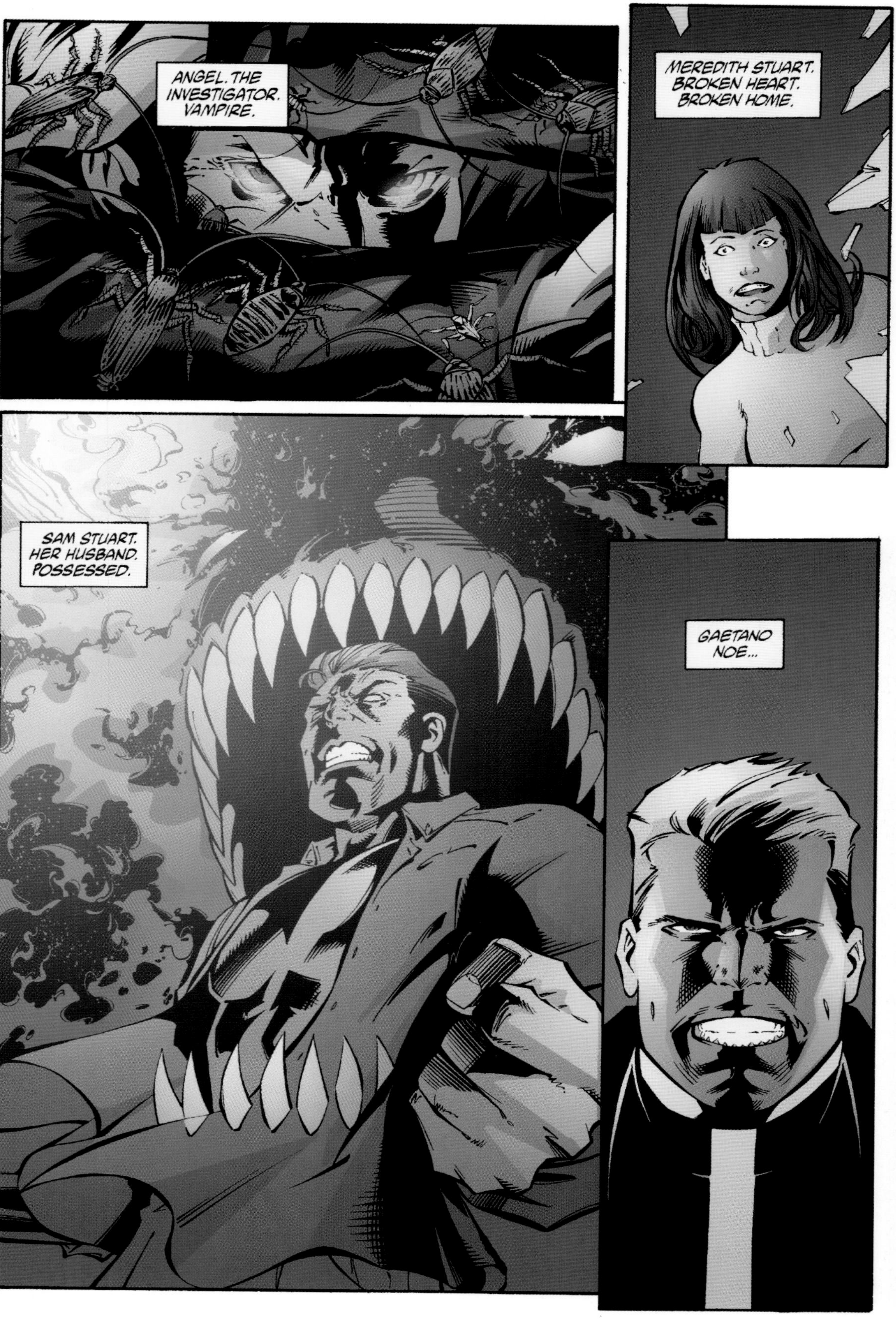
ANGEL. THE INVESTIGATOR. VAMPIRE.
MEREDITH STUART. BROKEN HEART. BROKEN HOME.
SAM STUART. HER HUSBAND. POSSESSED.
GAETANO NOE...

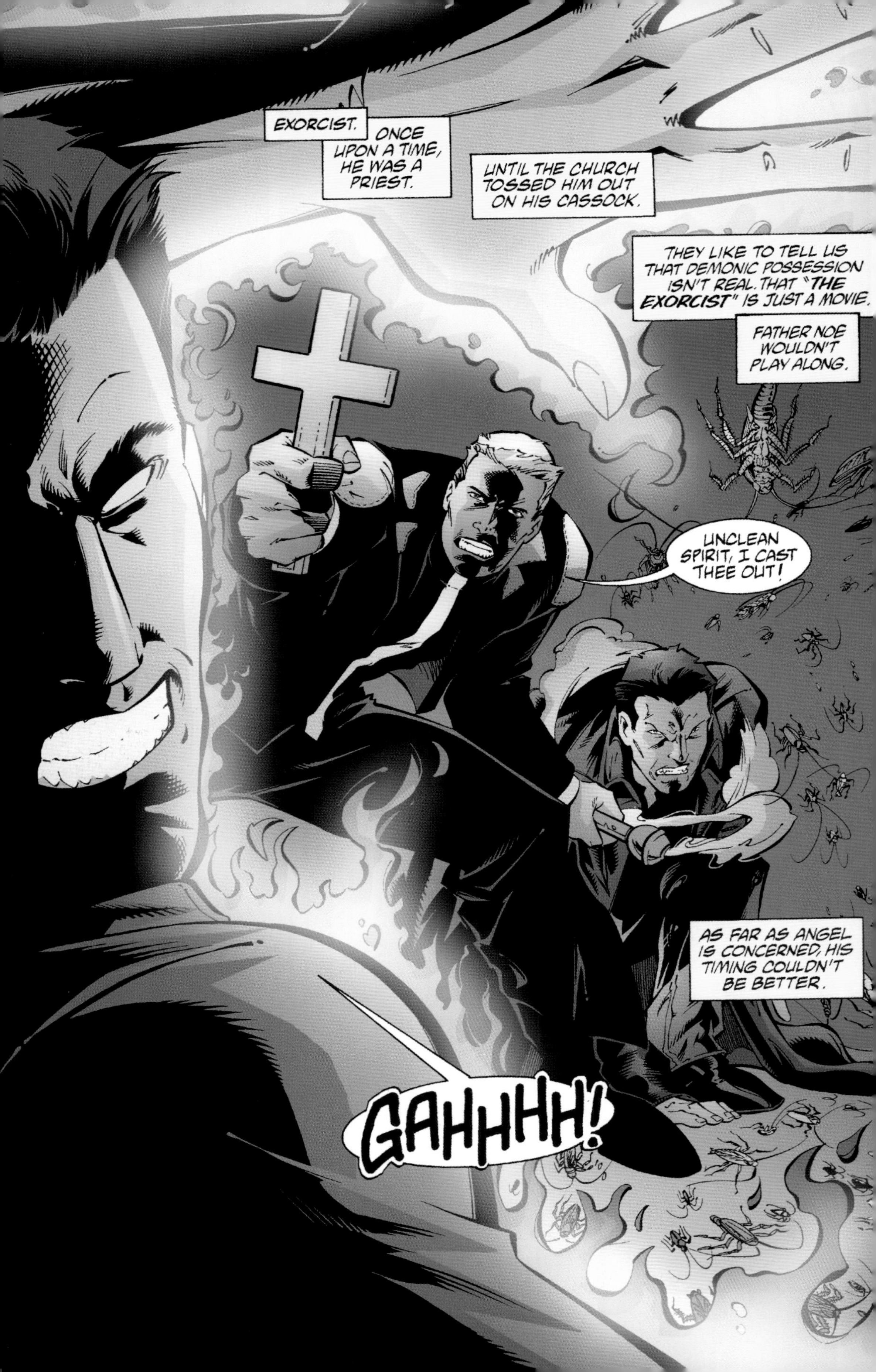
EXORCIST.
ONCE UPON A TIME, HE WAS A PRIEST.
UNTIL THE CHURCH TOSSED HIM OUT ON HIS CASSOCK.
THEY LIKE TO TELL US THAT DEMONIC POSSESSION ISN'T REAL. THAT "THE EXORCIST" IS JUST A MOVIE.
FATHER NOE WOULDN'T PLAY ALONG.
UNCLEAN SPIRIT, I CAST THEE OUT!
AS FAR AS ANGEL IS CONCERNED, HIS TIMING COULDN'T BE BETTER.
GAHHHH!

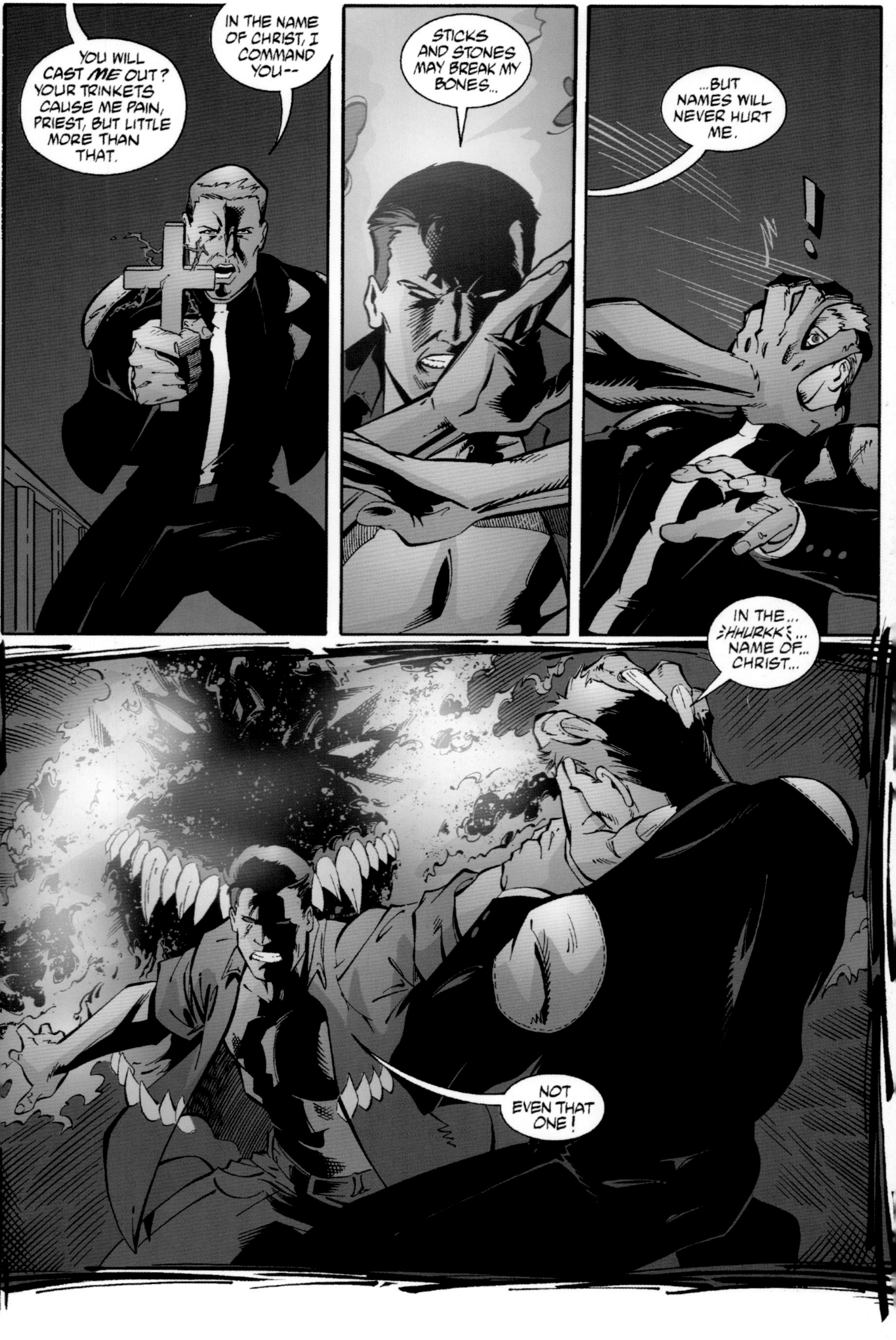
YOU WILL CAST ME OUT? YOUR TRINKETS CAUSE ME PAIN, PRIEST, BUT LITTLE MORE THAN THAT.
IN THE NAME OF CHRIST, I COMMAND YOU--
STICKS AND STONES MAY BREAK MY BONES...
...BUT NAMES WILL NEVER HURT ME.
!
IN THE... HHURKK... NAME OF... CHRIST...
NOT EVEN THAT ONE!

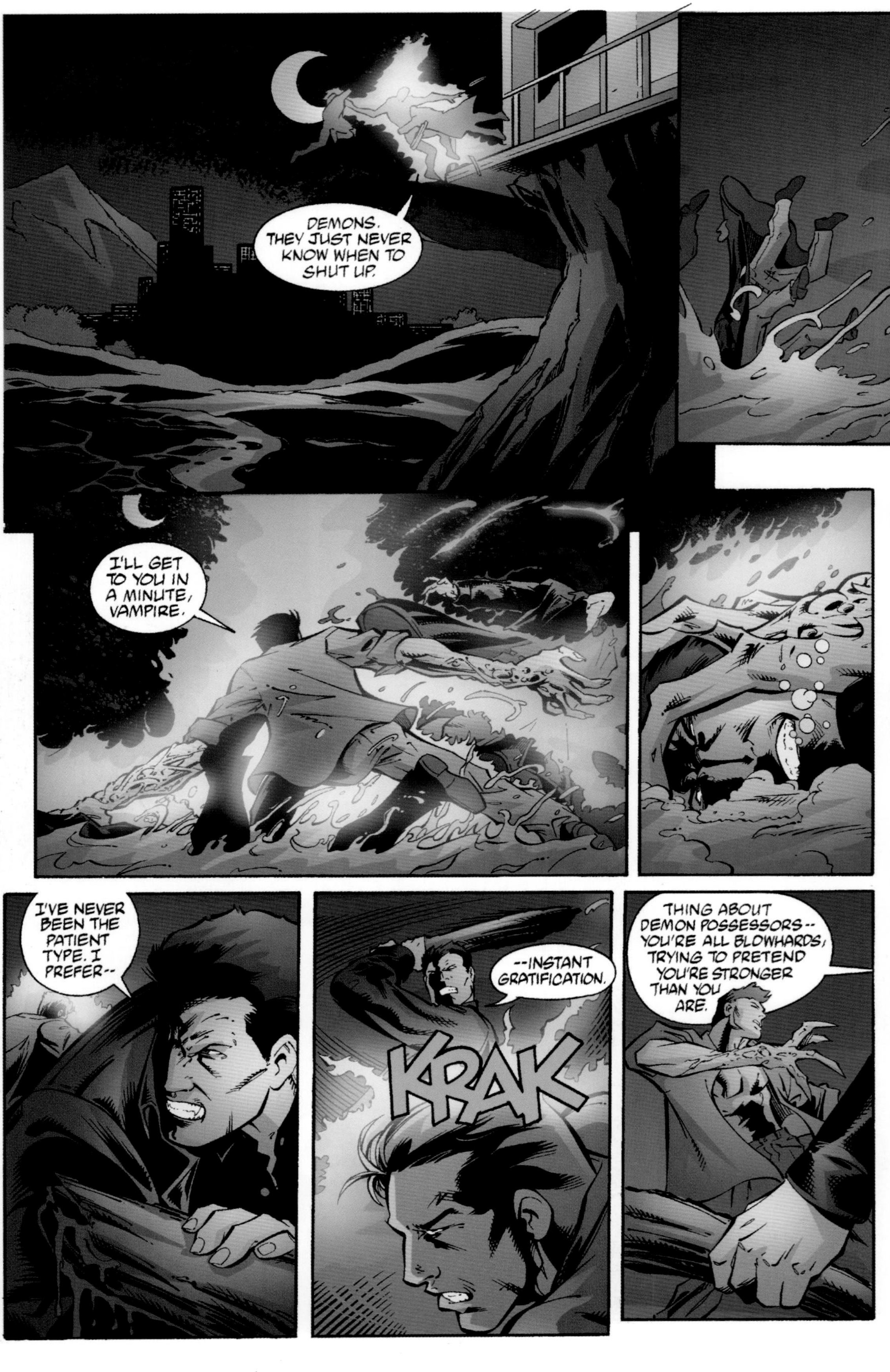
DEMONS. THEY JUST NEVER KNOW WHEN TO SHUT UP.
I'LL GET TO YOU IN A MINUTE, VAMPIRE.
I'VE NEVER BEEN THE PATIENT TYPE. I PREFER--
--INSTANT GRATIFICATION.
KRAK
THING ABOUT DEMON POSSESSORS--YOU'RE ALL BLOWHARDS, TRYING TO PRETEND YOU'RE STRONGER THAN YOU ARE.

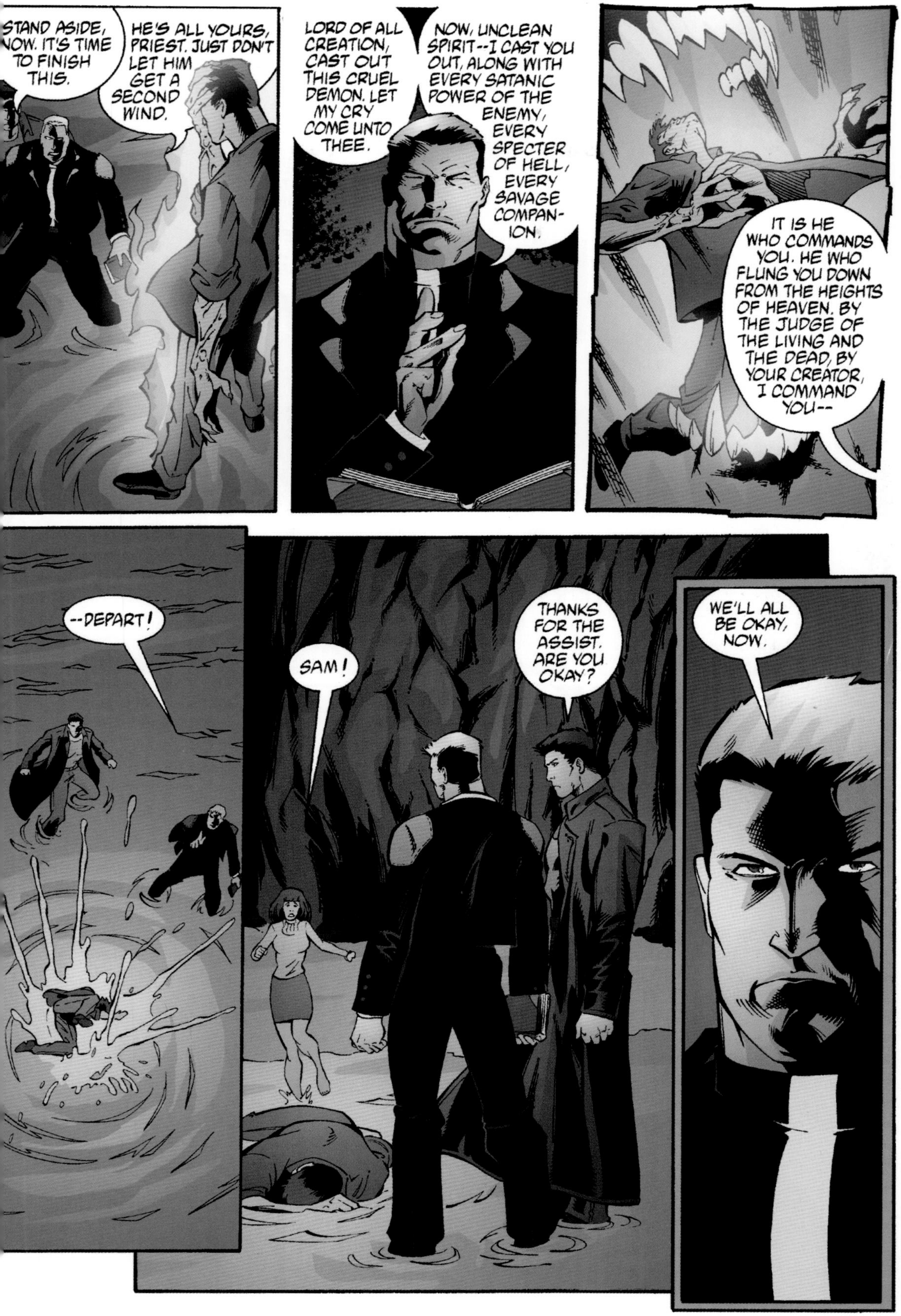
STAND ASIDE, NOW. IT'S TIME TO FINISH THIS.
HE'S ALL YOURS, PRIEST. JUST DON'T LET HIM GET A SECOND WIND.
LORD OF ALL CREATION, CAST OUT THIS CRUEL DEMON. LET MY CRY COME UNTO THEE.
NOW, UNCLEAN SPIRIT--I CAST YOU OUT, ALONG WITH EVERY SATANIC POWER OF THE ENEMY, EVERY SPECTER OF HELL, EVERY SAVAGE COMPANION.
IT IS HE WHO COMMANDS YOU. HE WHO FLUNG YOU DOWN FROM THE HEIGHTS OF HEAVEN. BY THE JUDGE OF THE LIVING AND THE DEAD, BY YOUR CREATOR, I COMMAND YOU--
--DEPART!
SAM!
THANKS FOR THE ASSIST. ARE YOU OKAY?
WE'LL ALL BE OKAY, NOW.

SO MRS. STUART PAID THIS NOE A LOT OF MONEY, AND HE JUST TOOK IT, LIKE IT WAS HIS DUE.

NOT TO PUT TOO FINE A POINT ON IT, LAD, BUT SHE PAID US TOO, DIDN'T SHE? AND IF I RECALL, IT WAS A LOT OF MONEY.

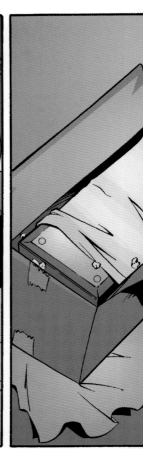

ANGEL'S USED TO STARVING HIMSELF, DOYLE. SOMETIMES HE DOESN'T GET THAT THE REST OF US NEED TO EAT.

THIS CHECK WILL COVER *LAST* MONTH'S BILLS, AND THERE'S STILL ENOUGH LEFT OVER FOR THE NEW LEATHER PANTS I'VE BEEN EYEING.

T'HELL WITH THE BILLS. *THAT'S* MONEY WELL SPENT.

YES, I TOOK THE MONEY. BUT AT LEAST I HAD THE DECENCY TO FEEL AWKWARD ABOUT IT. HER HUSBAND WAS POSSESSED. SHE NEEDED OUR HELP. TAKING MONEY MAKES ME FEEL LIKE A PREDATOR.

OH, AYE, AND THAT'S NOT A FAMILIAR FEELING FOR YOU, ANGEL?

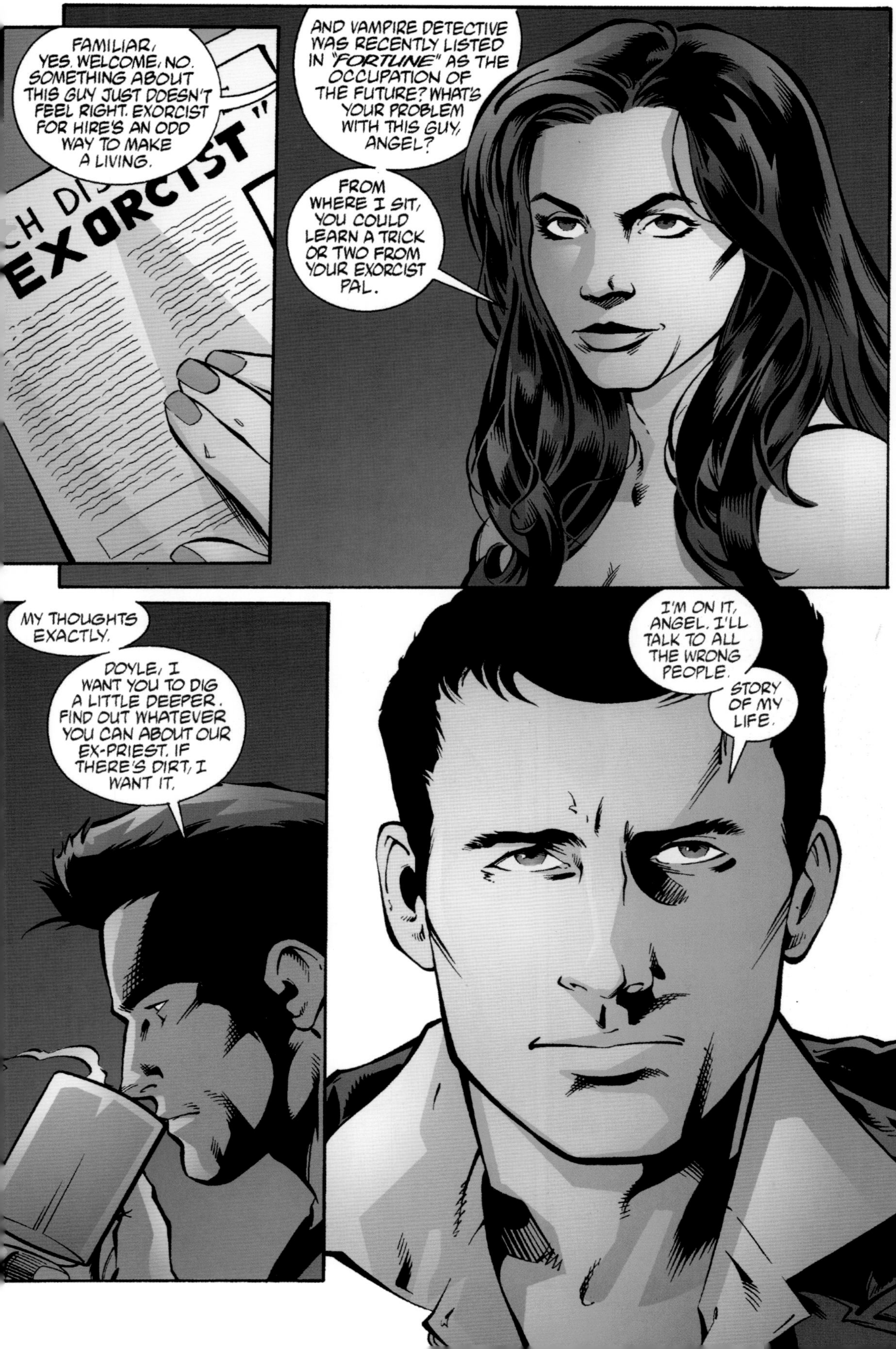
FAMILIAR, YES. WELCOME, NO. SOMETHING ABOUT THIS GUY JUST DOESN'T FEEL RIGHT. EXORCIST FOR HIRE'S AN ODD WAY TO MAKE A LIVING.
EXORCIST
AND VAMPIRE DETECTIVE WAS RECENTLY LISTED IN "FORTUNE" AS THE OCCUPATION OF THE FUTURE? WHAT'S YOUR PROBLEM WITH THIS GUY, ANGEL?
FROM WHERE I SIT, YOU COULD LEARN A TRICK OR TWO FROM YOUR EXORCIST PAL.
MY THOUGHTS EXACTLY.
DOYLE, I WANT YOU TO DIG A LITTLE DEEPER. FIND OUT WHATEVER YOU CAN ABOUT OUR EX-PRIEST. IF THERE'S DIRT, I WANT IT.
I'M ON IT, ANGEL. I'LL TALK TO ALL THE WRONG PEOPLE.
STORY OF MY LIFE.

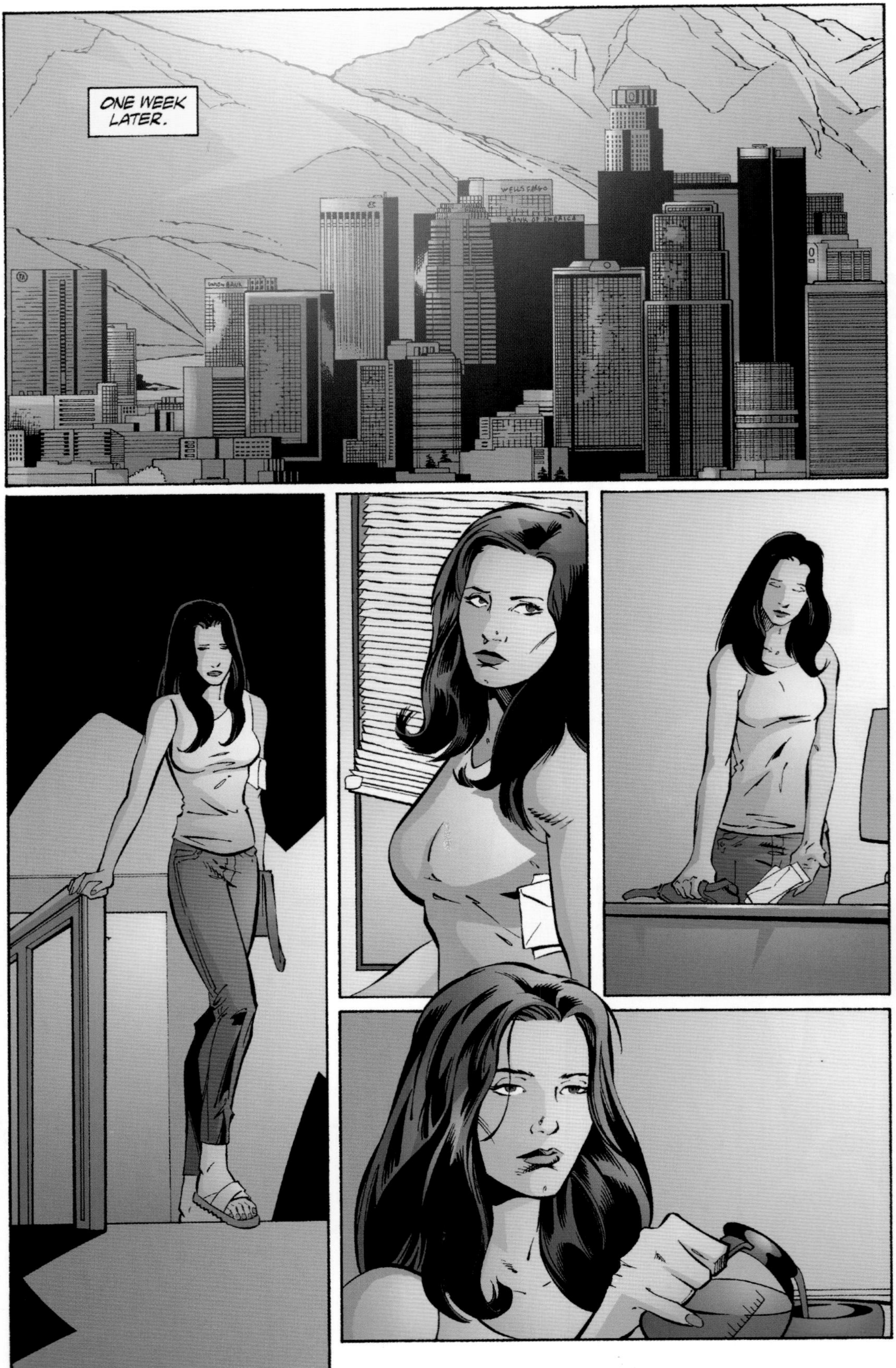
ONE WEEK LATER.

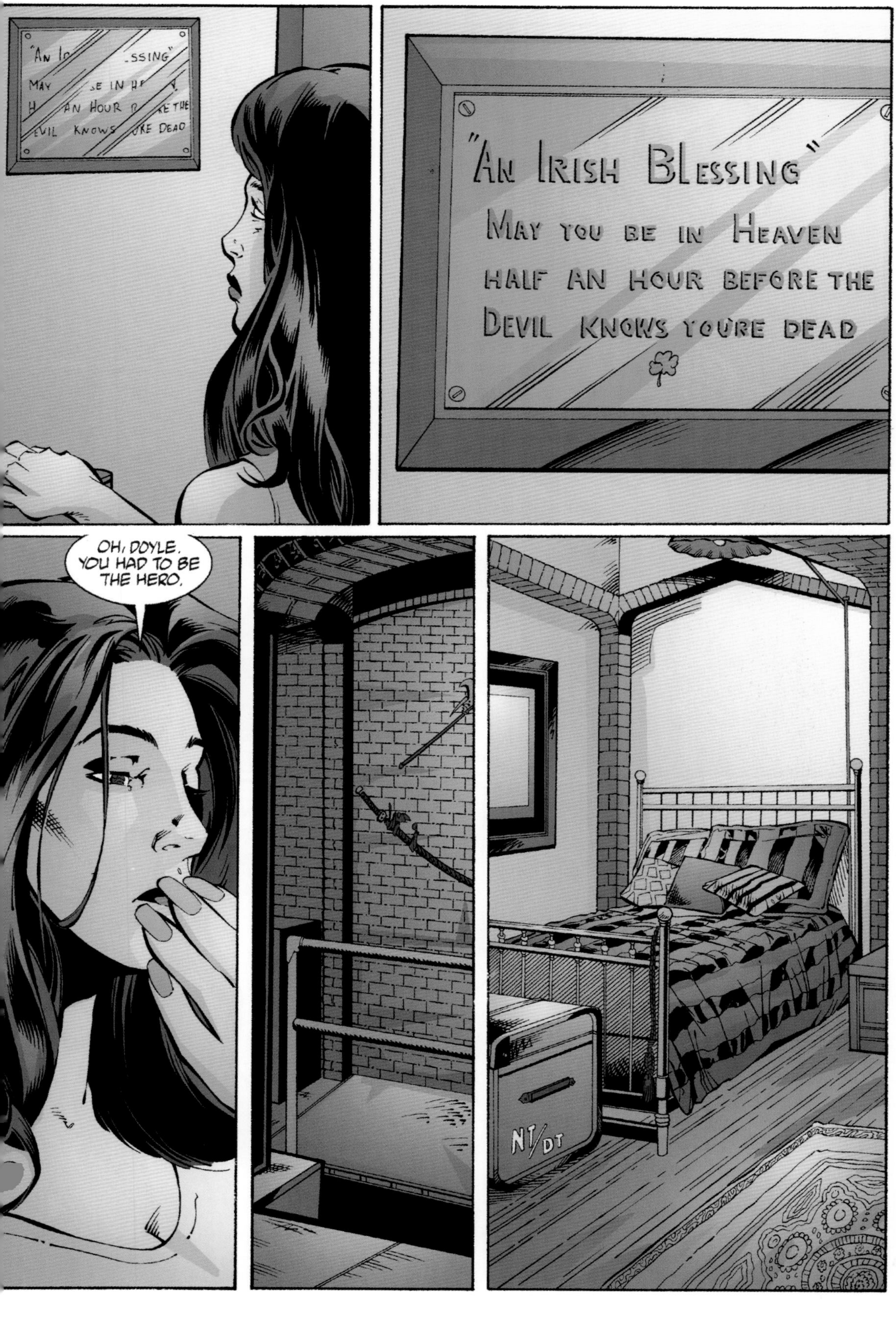
"AN IRISH BLESSING"
MAY YOU BE IN HEAVEN
HALF AN HOUR BEFORE THE
DEVIL KNOWS YOU'RE DEAD
OH, DOYLE. YOU HAD TO BE THE HERO.
NT/DT

"DO NOT GO GENTLE INTO THAT GOOD NIGHT."

Do not go gentle into that good night

Old age should bu rave at close of day

e rage against of the

"OLD AGE SHOULD BURN AND RAVE AT CLOSE OF DAY."

"RAGE, RAGE AGAINST THE DYING OF THE LIGHT."

BRRRINGG!
BRRRINGG!
BRRRINGG!
BRRRINGG!

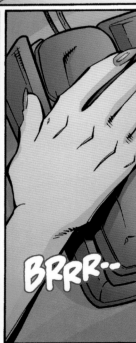

BRRR--

ANGEL INVESTIGATIONS.

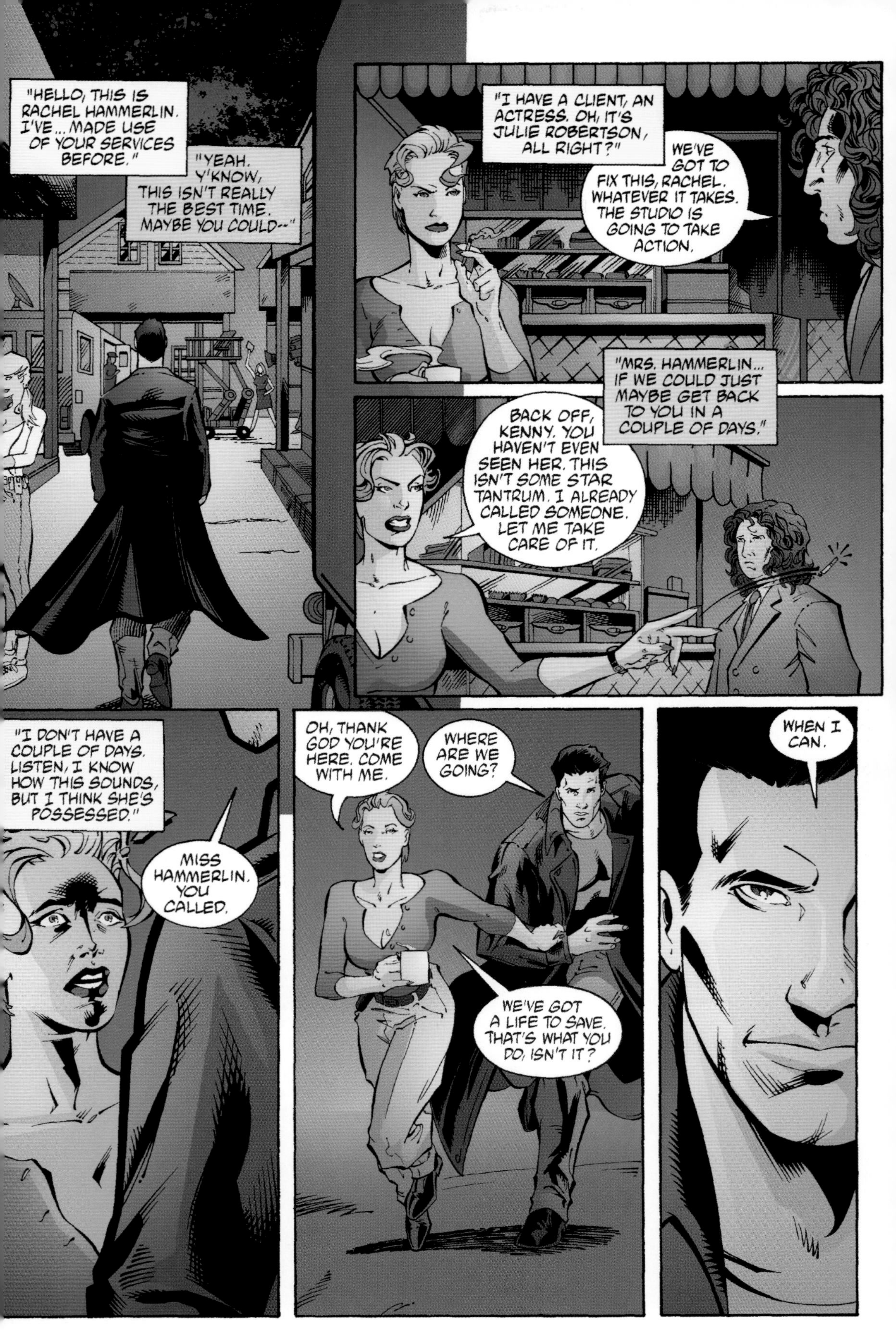
"HELLO, THIS IS RACHEL HAMMERLIN. I'VE... MADE USE OF YOUR SERVICES BEFORE."
"YEAH. Y'KNOW, THIS ISN'T REALLY THE BEST TIME. MAYBE YOU COULD--"
"I HAVE A CLIENT, AN ACTRESS. OH, IT'S JULIE ROBERTSON, ALL RIGHT?"
WE'VE GOT TO FIX THIS, RACHEL. WHATEVER IT TAKES. THE STUDIO IS GOING TO TAKE ACTION.
"MRS. HAMMERLIN... IF WE COULD JUST MAYBE GET BACK TO YOU IN A COUPLE OF DAYS."
BACK OFF, KENNY. YOU HAVEN'T EVEN SEEN HER. THIS ISN'T SOME STAR TANTRUM. I ALREADY CALLED SOMEONE. LET ME TAKE CARE OF IT.
"I DON'T HAVE A COUPLE OF DAYS. LISTEN, I KNOW HOW THIS SOUNDS, BUT I THINK SHE'S POSSESSED."
MISS HAMMERLIN. YOU CALLED.
OH, THANK GOD YOU'RE HERE. COME WITH ME.
WHERE ARE WE GOING?
WE'VE GOT A LIFE TO SAVE. THAT'S WHAT YOU DO, ISN'T IT?
WHEN I CAN.

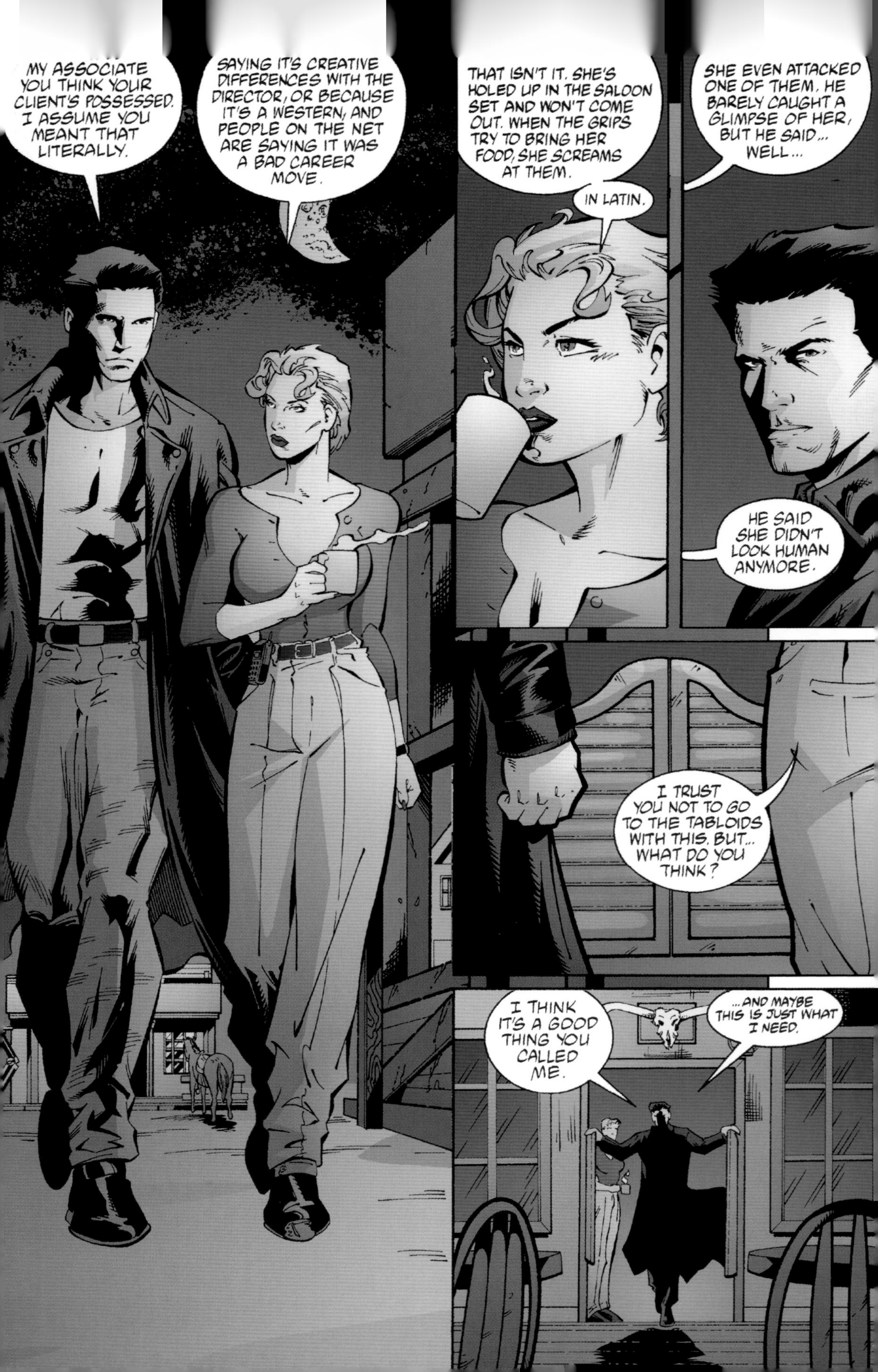
MY ASSOCIATE YOU THINK YOUR CLIENT'S POSSESSED. I ASSUME YOU MEANT THAT LITERALLY.
SAYING IT'S CREATIVE DIFFERENCES WITH THE DIRECTOR, OR BECAUSE IT'S A WESTERN, AND PEOPLE ON THE NET ARE SAYING IT WAS A BAD CAREER MOVE.
THAT ISN'T IT. SHE'S HOLED UP IN THE SALOON SET AND WON'T COME OUT. WHEN THE GRIPS TRY TO BRING HER FOOD, SHE SCREAMS AT THEM.
IN LATIN.
SHE EVEN ATTACKED ONE OF THEM. HE BARELY CAUGHT A GLIMPSE OF HER, BUT HE SAID... WELL...
HE SAID SHE DIDN'T LOOK HUMAN ANYMORE.
I TRUST YOU NOT TO GO TO THE TABLOIDS WITH THIS. BUT... WHAT DO YOU THINK?
I THINK IT'S A GOOD THING YOU CALLED ME.
...AND MAYBE THIS IS JUST WHAT I NEED.

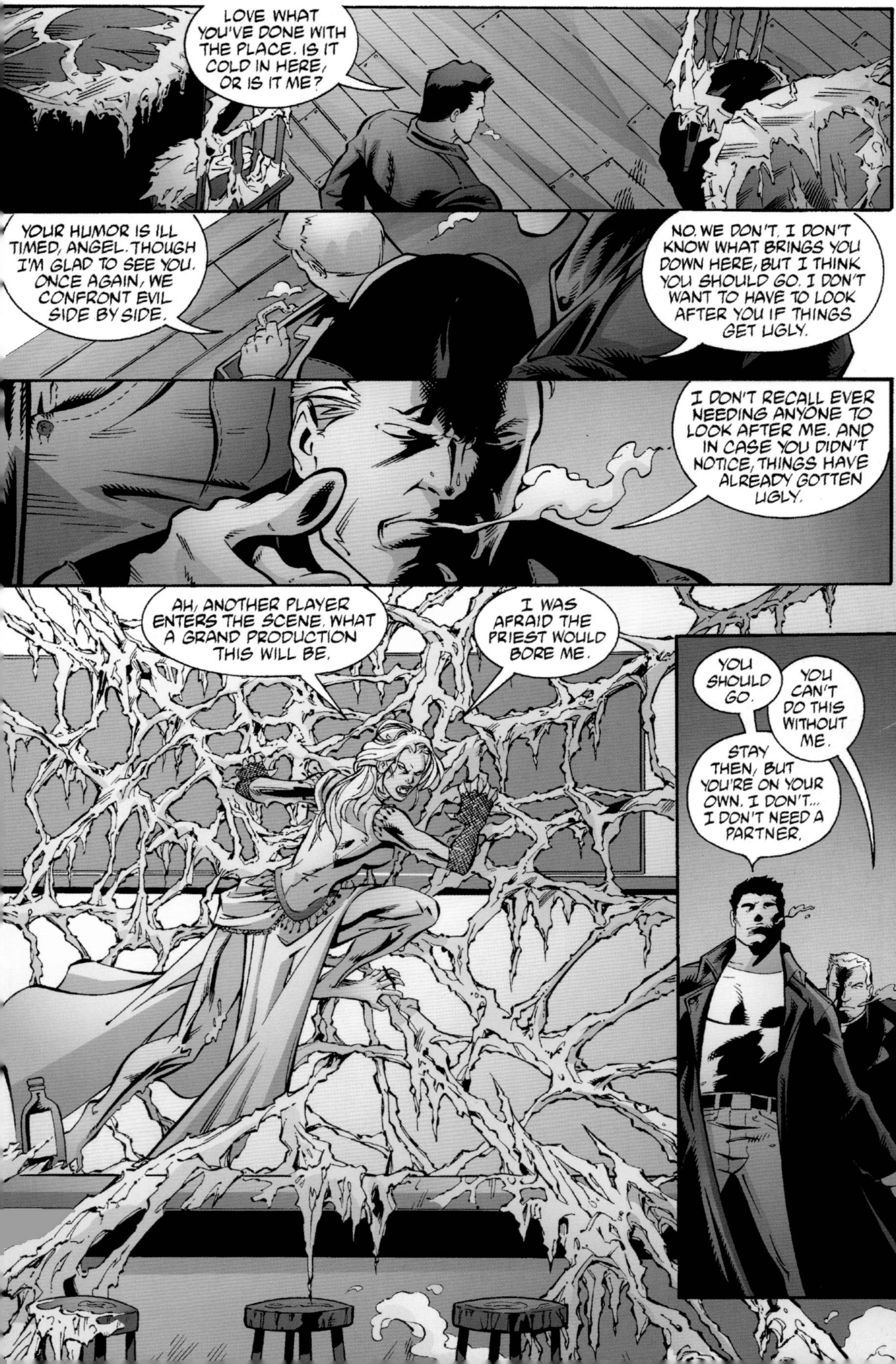
LOVE WHAT YOU'VE DONE WITH THE PLACE. IS IT COLD IN HERE, OR IS IT ME?
YOUR HUMOR IS ILL TIMED, ANGEL. THOUGH I'M GLAD TO SEE YOU. ONCE AGAIN, WE CONFRONT EVIL SIDE BY SIDE.
NO, WE DON'T. I DON'T KNOW WHAT BRINGS YOU DOWN HERE, BUT I THINK YOU SHOULD GO. I DON'T WANT TO HAVE TO LOOK AFTER YOU IF THINGS GET UGLY.
I DON'T RECALL EVER NEEDING ANYONE TO LOOK AFTER ME. AND IN CASE YOU DIDN'T NOTICE, THINGS HAVE ALREADY GOTTEN UGLY.
AH, ANOTHER PLAYER ENTERS THE SCENE. WHAT A GRAND PRODUCTION THIS WILL BE.
I WAS AFRAID THE PRIEST WOULD BORE ME.
YOU SHOULD GO.
YOU CAN'T DO THIS WITHOUT ME.
STAY THEN, BUT YOU'RE ON YOUR OWN. I DON'T... I DON'T NEED A PARTNER.

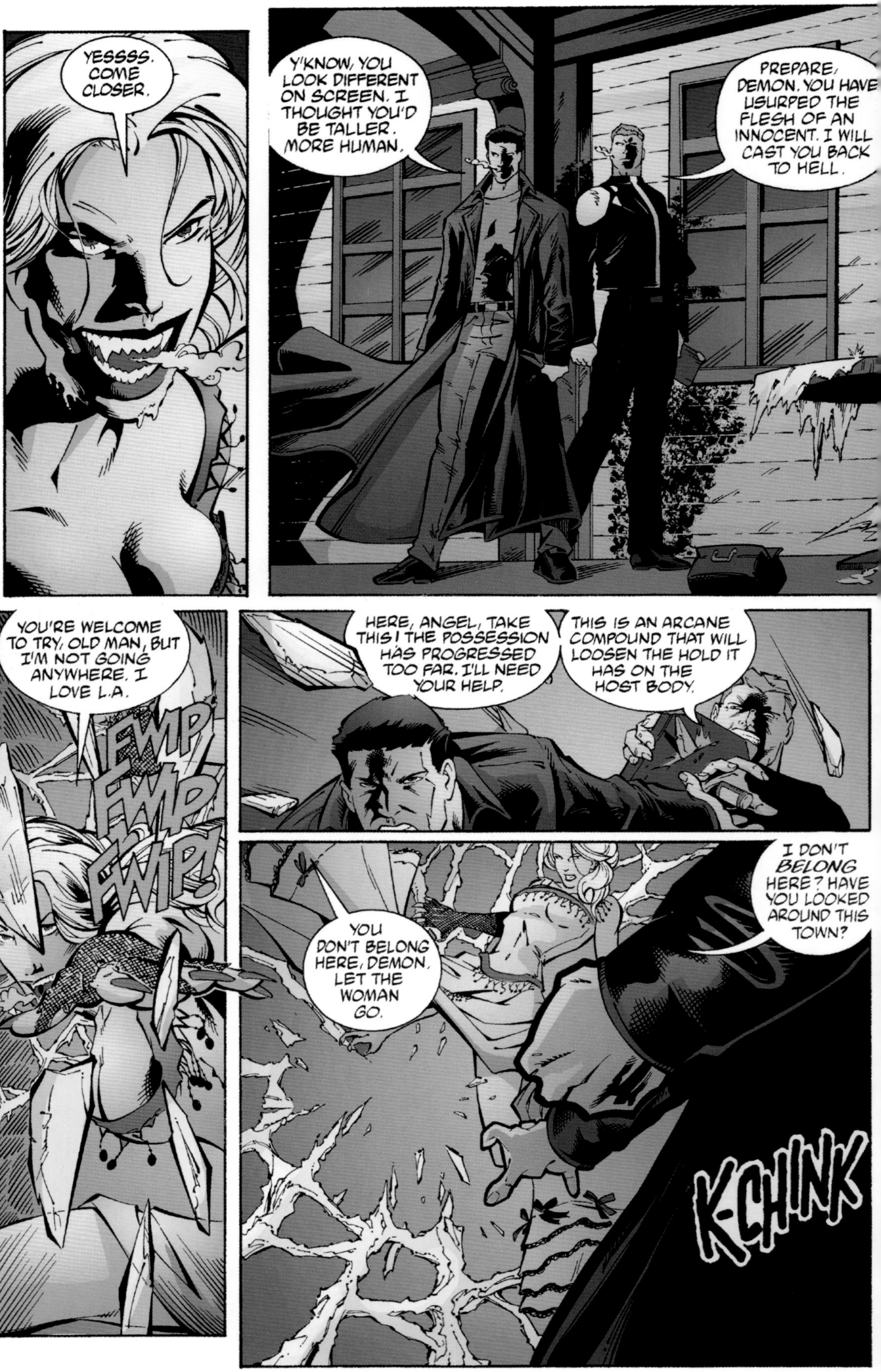
YESSSS. COME CLOSER.
Y'KNOW, YOU LOOK DIFFERENT ON SCREEN. I THOUGHT YOU'D BE TALLER. MORE HUMAN.
PREPARE, DEMON. YOU HAVE USURPED THE FLESH OF AN INNOCENT. I WILL CAST YOU BACK TO HELL.
YOU'RE WELCOME TO TRY, OLD MAN, BUT I'M NOT GOING ANYWHERE. I LOVE L.A.
FWIP FWIP FWIP!
HERE, ANGEL, TAKE THIS! THE POSSESSION HAS PROGRESSED TOO FAR. I'LL NEED YOUR HELP.
THIS IS AN ARCANE COMPOUND THAT WILL LOOSEN THE HOLD IT HAS ON THE HOST BODY.
YOU DON'T BELONG HERE, DEMON. LET THE WOMAN GO.
I DON'T *BELONG* HERE? HAVE YOU LOOKED AROUND THIS TOWN?
K-CHINK

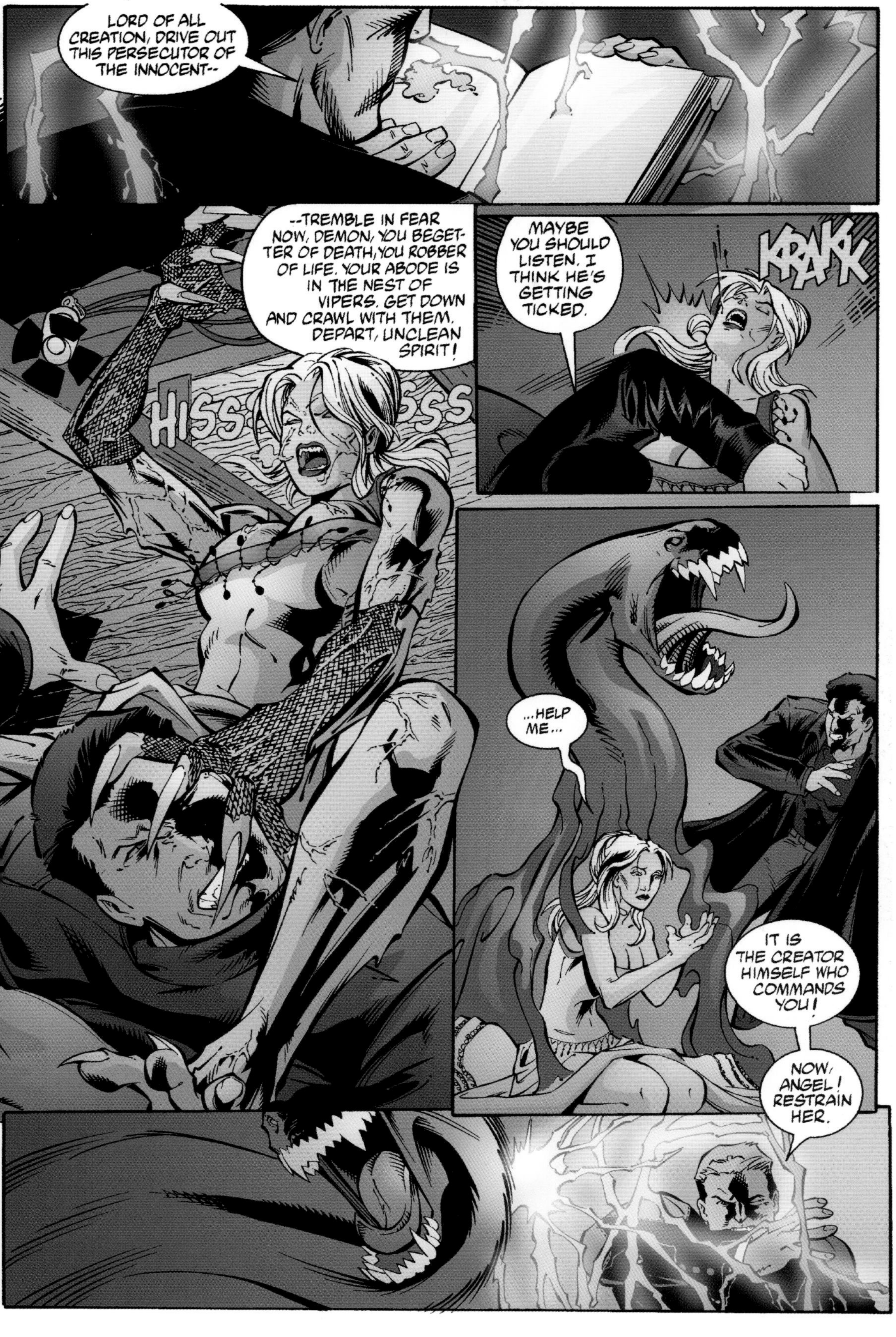
LORD OF ALL CREATION, DRIVE OUT THIS PERSECUTOR OF THE INNOCENT--
--TREMBLE IN FEAR NOW, DEMON, YOU BEGETTER OF DEATH, YOU ROBBER OF LIFE. YOUR ABODE IS IN THE NEST OF VIPERS. GET DOWN AND CRAWL WITH THEM. DEPART, UNCLEAN SPIRIT!
HISSSSS
MAYBE YOU SHOULD LISTEN. I THINK HE'S GETTING TICKED.
KRAKK
...HELP ME...
IT IS THE CREATOR HIMSELF WHO COMMANDS YOU!
NOW, ANGEL! RESTRAIN HER.

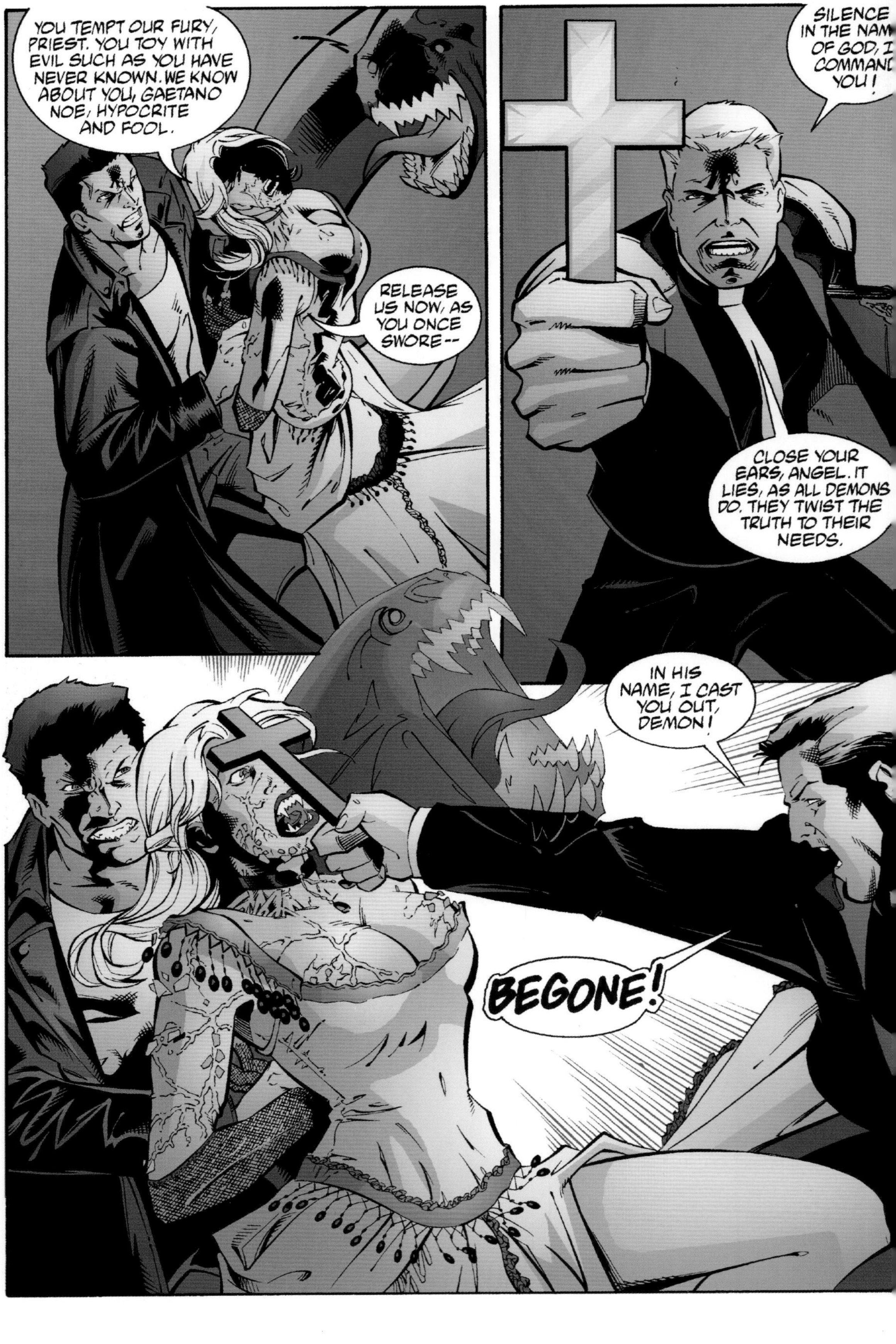
YOU TEMPT OUR FURY, PRIEST. YOU TOY WITH EVIL SUCH AS YOU HAVE NEVER KNOWN. WE KNOW ABOUT YOU, GAETANO NOE, HYPOCRITE AND FOOL.
RELEASE US NOW, AS YOU ONCE SWORE--
SILENCE IN THE NAM OF GOD, I COMMAND YOU!
CLOSE YOUR EARS, ANGEL. IT LIES, AS ALL DEMONS DO. THEY TWIST THE TRUTH TO THEIR NEEDS.
IN HIS NAME, I CAST YOU OUT, DEMON!
BEGONE!

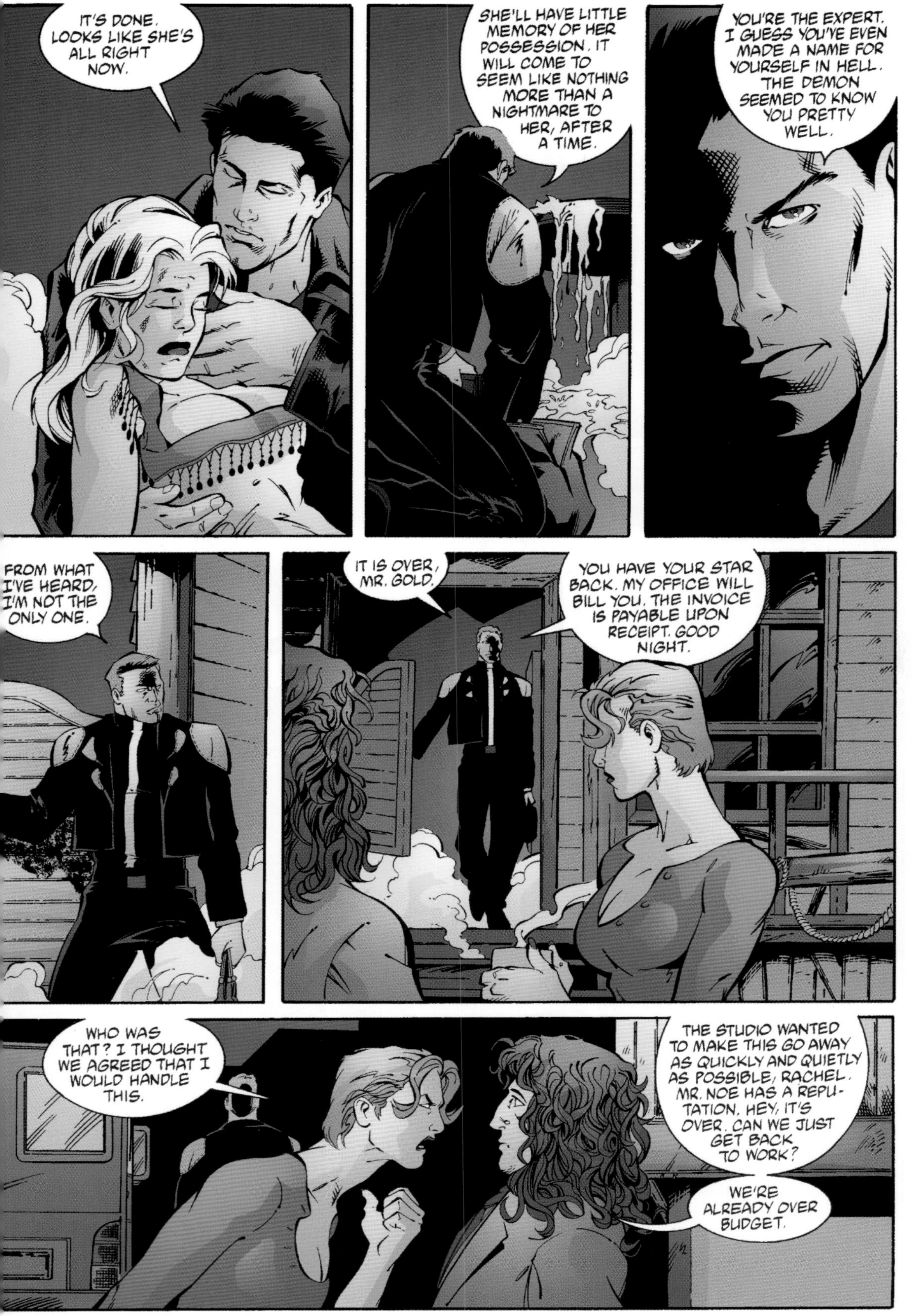
IT'S DONE. LOOKS LIKE SHE'S ALL RIGHT NOW.
SHE'LL HAVE LITTLE MEMORY OF HER POSSESSION. IT WILL COME TO SEEM LIKE NOTHING MORE THAN A NIGHTMARE TO HER, AFTER A TIME.
YOU'RE THE EXPERT. I GUESS YOU'VE EVEN MADE A NAME FOR YOURSELF IN HELL. THE DEMON SEEMED TO KNOW YOU PRETTY WELL.
FROM WHAT I'VE HEARD, I'M NOT THE ONLY ONE.
IT IS OVER, MR. GOLD.
YOU HAVE YOUR STAR BACK. MY OFFICE WILL BILL YOU. THE INVOICE IS PAYABLE UPON RECEIPT. GOOD NIGHT.
WHO WAS THAT? I THOUGHT WE AGREED THAT I WOULD HANDLE THIS.
THE STUDIO WANTED TO MAKE THIS GO AWAY AS QUICKLY AND QUIETLY AS POSSIBLE, RACHEL. MR. NOE HAS A REPU-TATION. HEY, IT'S OVER. CAN WE JUST GET BACK TO WORK?
WE'RE ALREADY OVER BUDGET.

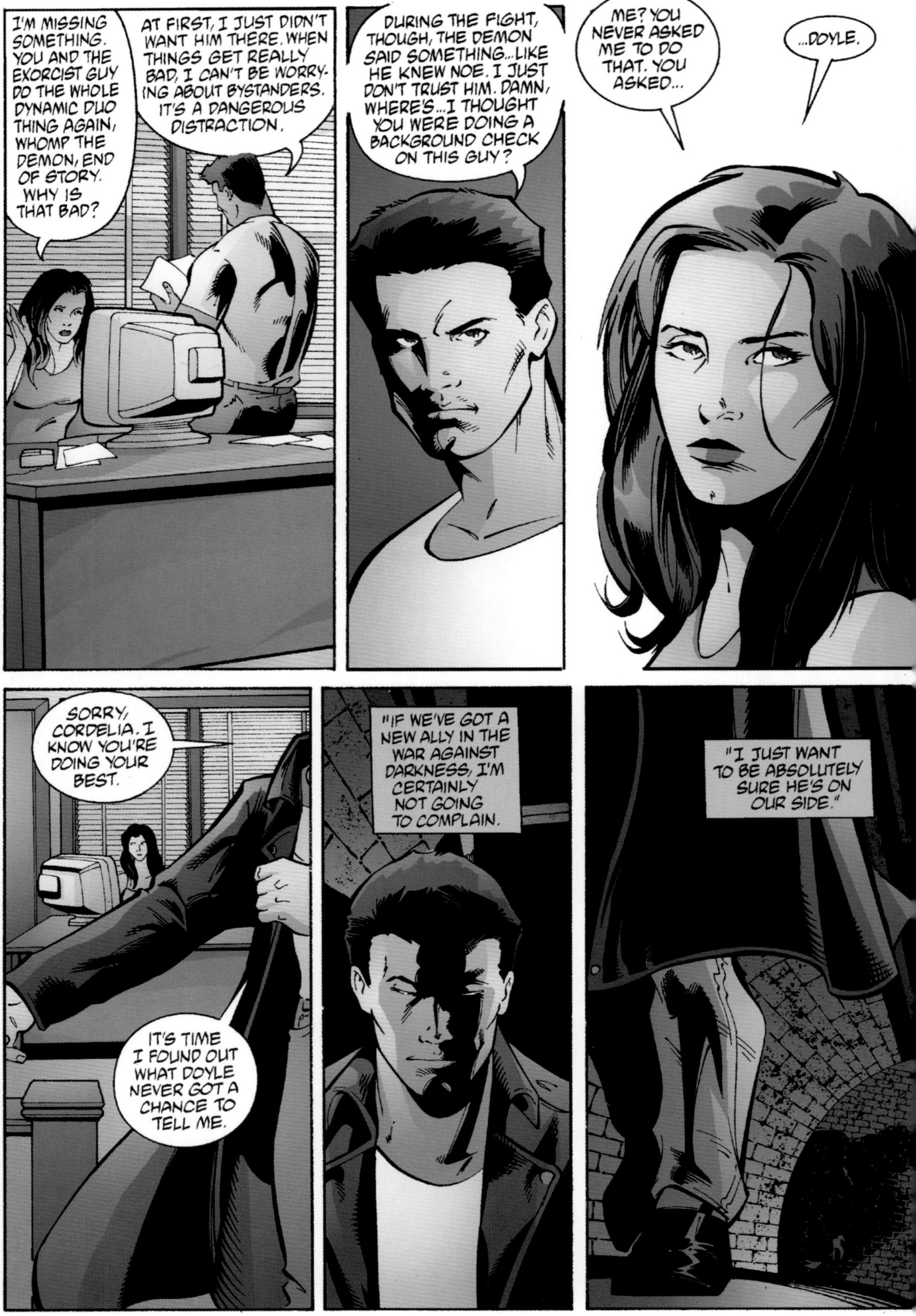

I'M MISSING SOMETHING. YOU AND THE EXORCIST GUY DO THE WHOLE DYNAMIC DUO THING AGAIN, WHOMP THE DEMON, END OF STORY. WHY IS THAT BAD?
AT FIRST, I JUST DIDN'T WANT HIM THERE. WHEN THINGS GET REALLY BAD, I CAN'T BE WORRYING ABOUT BYSTANDERS. IT'S A DANGEROUS DISTRACTION.
DURING THE FIGHT, THOUGH, THE DEMON SAID SOMETHING...LIKE HE KNEW NOE. I JUST DON'T TRUST HIM. DAMN, WHERE'S...I THOUGHT YOU WERE DOING A BACKGROUND CHECK ON THIS GUY?
ME? YOU NEVER ASKED ME TO DO THAT. YOU ASKED...
...DOYLE.
SORRY, CORDELIA. I KNOW YOU'RE DOING YOUR BEST.
IT'S TIME I FOUND OUT WHAT DOYLE NEVER GOT A CHANCE TO TELL ME.
"IF WE'VE GOT A NEW ALLY IN THE WAR AGAINST DARKNESS, I'M CERTAINLY NOT GOING TO COMPLAIN.
"I JUST WANT TO BE ABSOLUTELY SURE HE'S ON OUR SIDE."

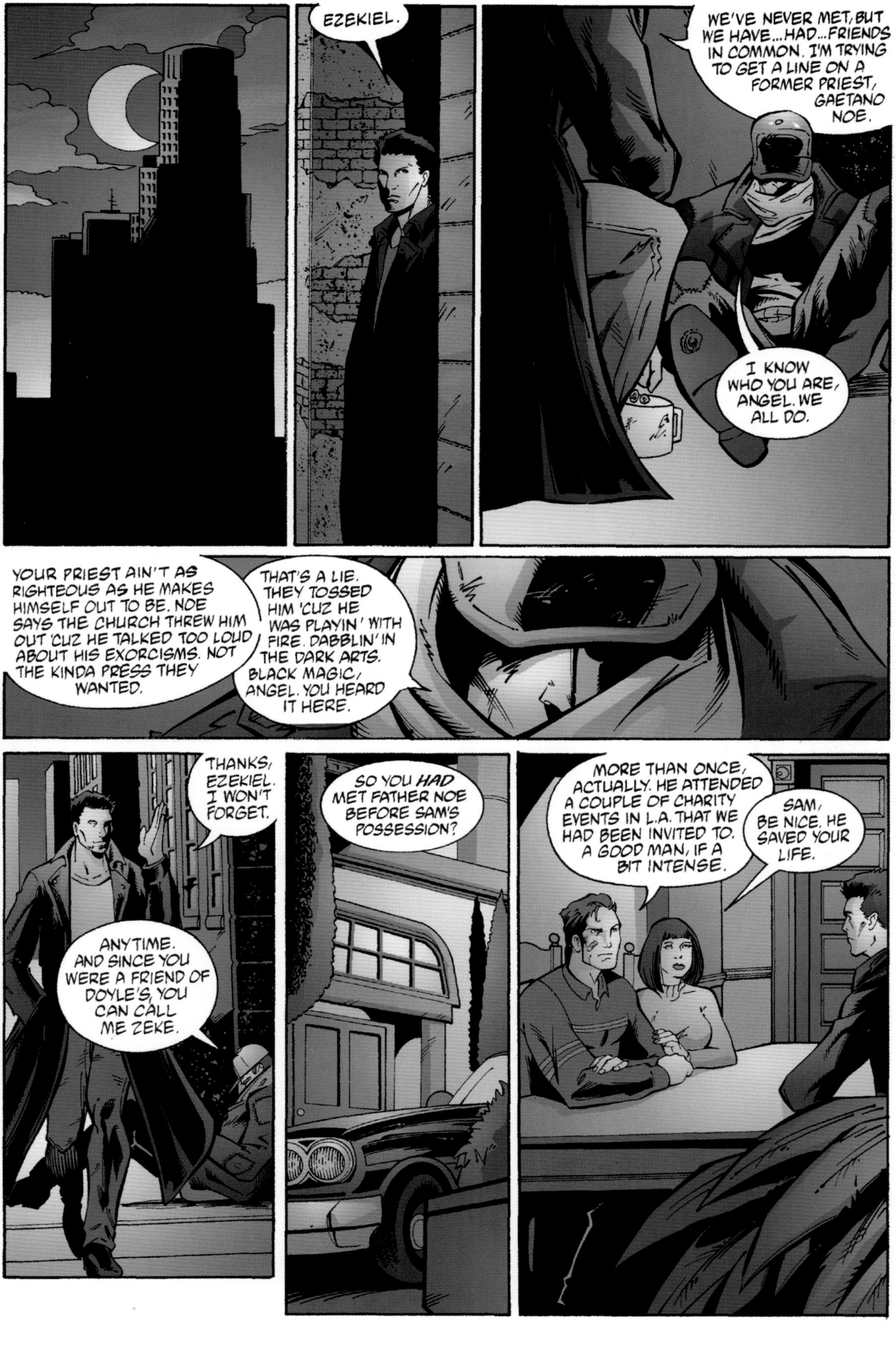
EZEKIEL.
WE'VE NEVER MET, BUT WE HAVE... HAD... FRIENDS IN COMMON. I'M TRYING TO GET A LINE ON A FORMER PRIEST, GAETANO NOE.
I KNOW WHO YOU ARE, ANGEL. WE ALL DO.
YOUR PRIEST AIN'T AS RIGHTEOUS AS HE MAKES HIMSELF OUT TO BE. NOE SAYS THE CHURCH THREW HIM OUT 'CUZ HE TALKED TOO LOUD ABOUT HIS EXORCISMS. NOT THE KINDA PRESS THEY WANTED.
THAT'S A LIE. THEY TOSSED HIM 'CUZ HE WAS PLAYIN' WITH FIRE. DABBLIN' IN THE DARK ARTS. BLACK MAGIC, ANGEL. YOU HEARD IT HERE.
THANKS, EZEKIEL. I WON'T FORGET.
ANYTIME. AND SINCE YOU WERE A FRIEND OF DOYLE'S, YOU CAN CALL ME ZEKE.
SO YOU *HAD* MET FATHER NOE BEFORE SAM'S POSSESSION?
MORE THAN ONCE, ACTUALLY. HE ATTENDED A COUPLE OF CHARITY EVENTS IN L.A. THAT WE HAD BEEN INVITED TO. A GOOD MAN, IF A BIT INTENSE.
SAM, BE NICE. HE SAVED YOUR LIFE.

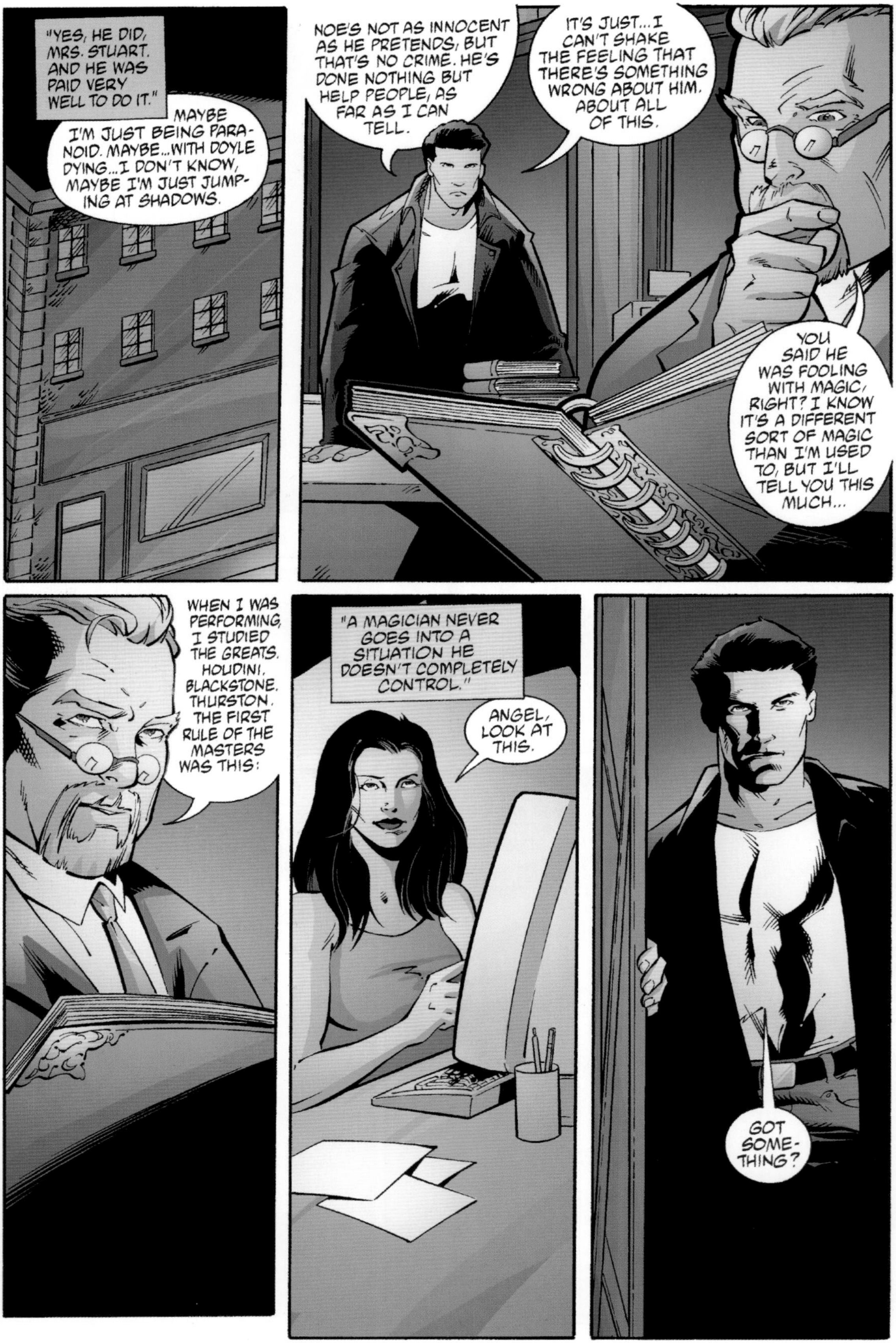
"YES, HE DID, MRS. STUART. AND HE WAS PAID VERY WELL TO DO IT."
MAYBE I'M JUST BEING PARANOID. MAYBE...WITH DOYLE DYING...I DON'T KNOW, MAYBE I'M JUST JUMPING AT SHADOWS.
NOE'S NOT AS INNOCENT AS HE PRETENDS, BUT THAT'S NO CRIME. HE'S DONE NOTHING BUT HELP PEOPLE, AS FAR AS I CAN TELL.
IT'S JUST...I CAN'T SHAKE THE FEELING THAT THERE'S SOMETHING WRONG ABOUT HIM. ABOUT ALL OF THIS.
YOU SAID HE WAS FOOLING WITH MAGIC, RIGHT? I KNOW IT'S A DIFFERENT SORT OF MAGIC THAN I'M USED TO, BUT I'LL TELL YOU THIS MUCH...
WHEN I WAS PERFORMING, I STUDIED THE GREATS. HOUDINI. BLACKSTONE. THURSTON. THE FIRST RULE OF THE MASTERS WAS THIS:
"A MAGICIAN NEVER GOES INTO A SITUATION HE DOESN'T COMPLETELY CONTROL."
ANGEL, LOOK AT THIS.
GOT SOMETHING?

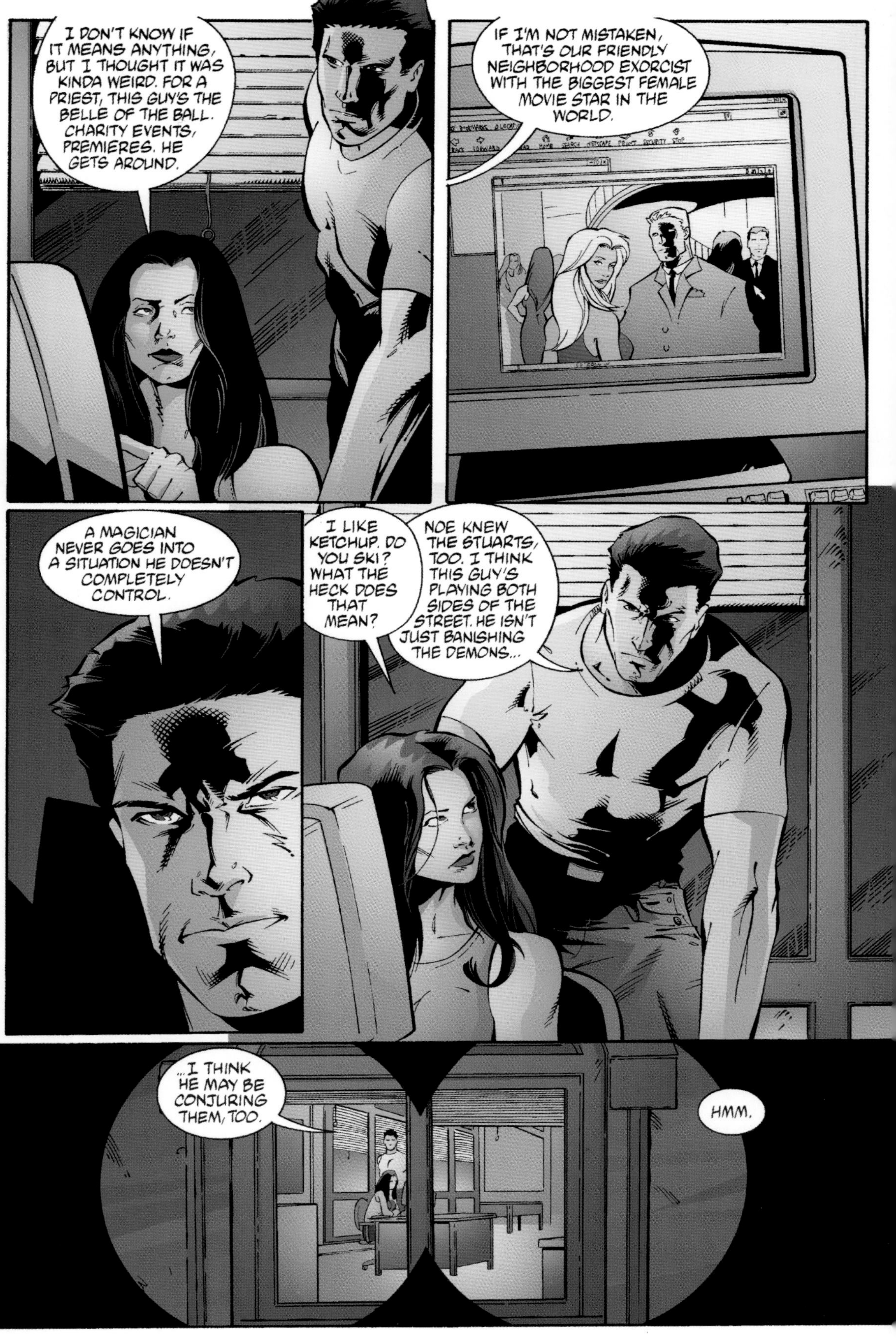
I DON'T KNOW IF IT MEANS ANYTHING, BUT I THOUGHT IT WAS KINDA WEIRD. FOR A PRIEST, THIS GUY'S THE BELLE OF THE BALL. CHARITY EVENTS, PREMIERES. HE GETS AROUND.
IF I'M NOT MISTAKEN, THAT'S OUR FRIENDLY NEIGHBORHOOD EXORCIST WITH THE BIGGEST FEMALE MOVIE STAR IN THE WORLD.
A MAGICIAN NEVER GOES INTO A SITUATION HE DOESN'T COMPLETELY CONTROL.
I LIKE KETCHUP. DO YOU SKI? WHAT THE HECK DOES THAT MEAN?
NOE KNEW THE STUARTS, TOO. I THINK THIS GUY'S PLAYING BOTH SIDES OF THE STREET. HE ISN'T JUST BANISHING THE DEMONS...
...I THINK HE MAY BE CONJURING THEM, TOO.
HMM.

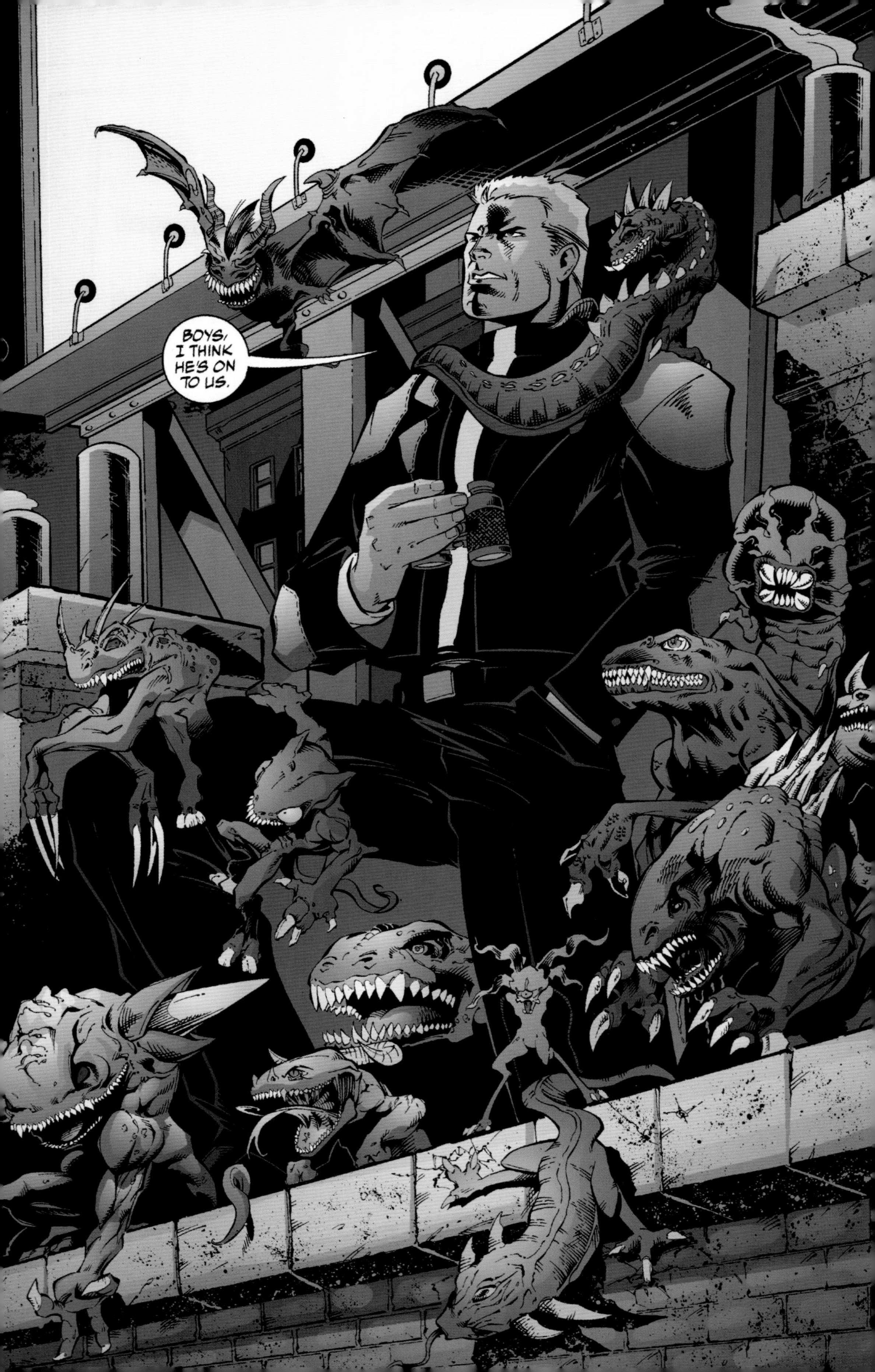
BOYS, I THINK HE'S ON TO US.

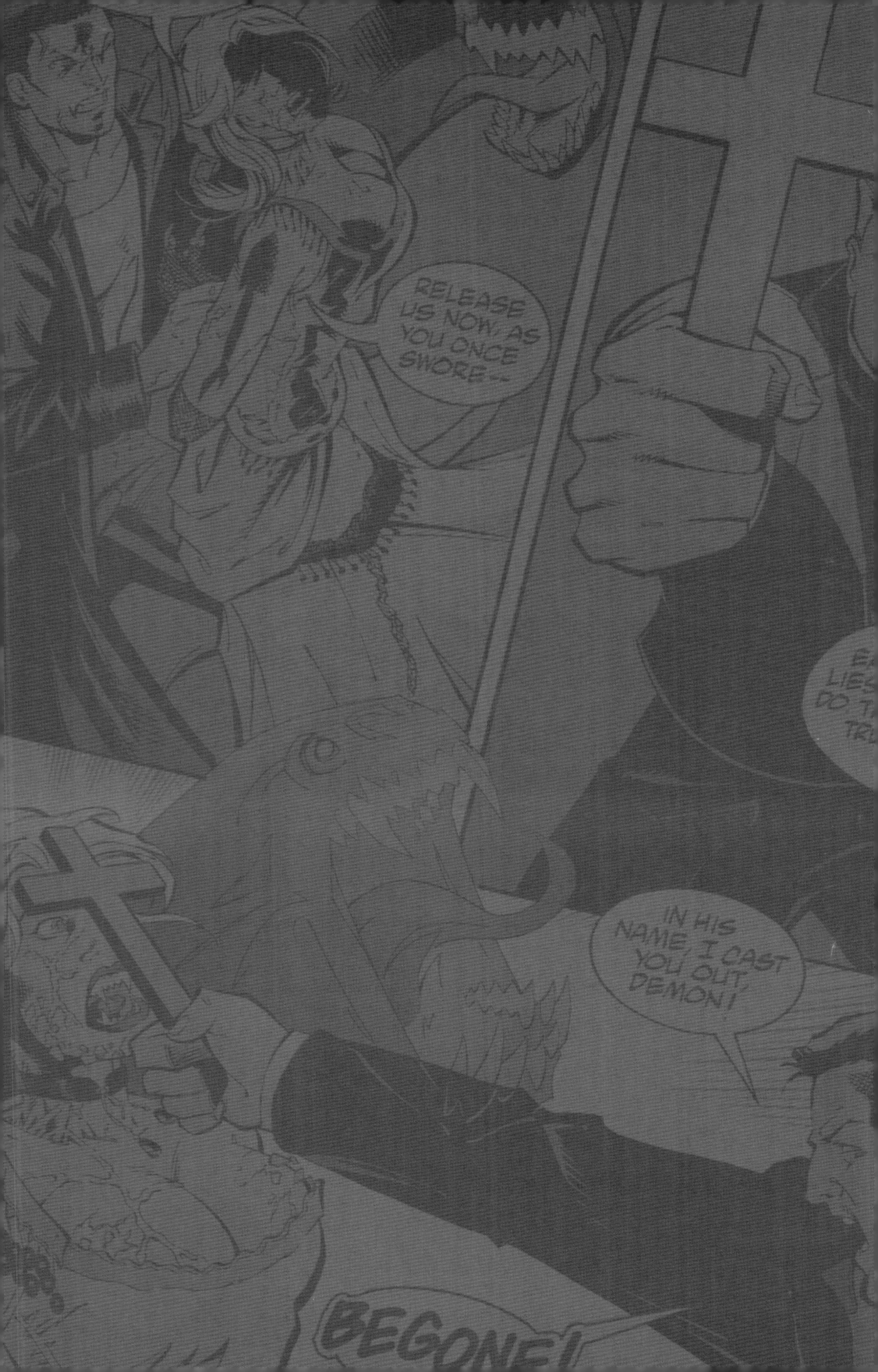
RELEASE US NOW, AS YOU ONCE SWORE--
IN HIS NAME, I CAST YOU OUT, DEMON!
BEGONE!

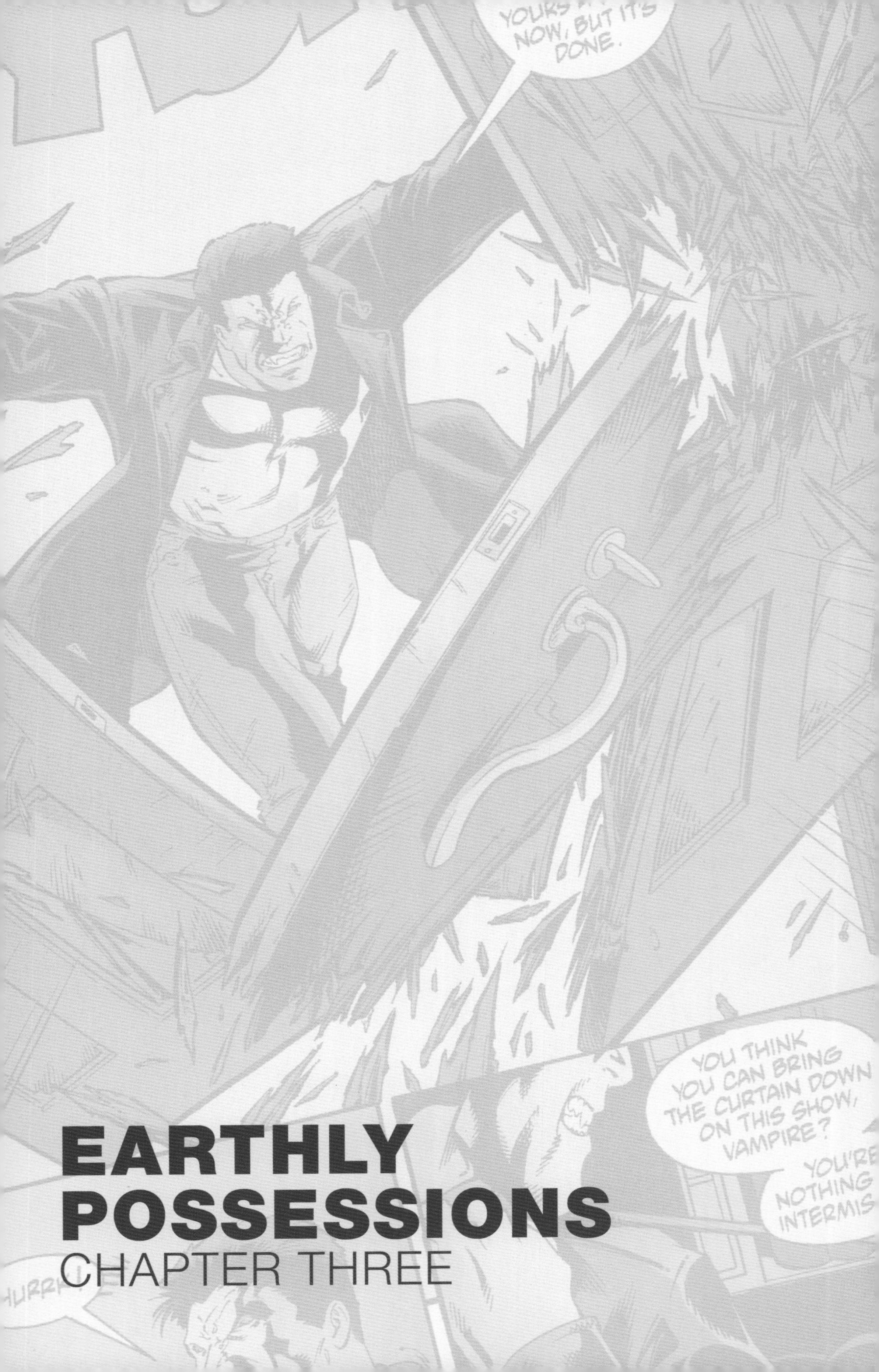
NOW, BUT IT'S DONE.
YOU THINK YOU CAN BRING THE CURTAIN DOWN ON THIS SHOW, VAMPIRE?
YOU'RE NOTHING INTERMIS

EARTHLY POSSESSIONS
CHAPTER THREE

THE ROMAN CATHOLIC ARCHDIOCESE OF LOS ANGELES.

"YOU UNDERSTAND, OF COURSE, THAT THE INFORMATION YOU SEEK IS CONFIDENTIAL. I'M NOT AT LIBERTY EVEN TO HAVE THIS CONVERSATION."

I DO. THE QUESTION IS, DO *YOU* UNDERSTAND THAT YOUR SILENCE IS PROBABLY ENDANGERING LIVES... NOT TO MENTION SOULS?

WHAT *EXACTLY* DO YOU WANT TO KNOW? I HAVE NO IDEA WHERE HE'S LIVING NOW, IF THAT'S WHAT YOU'RE AFTER.

ALL RIGHT, THEN, TELL ME THIS...

NOE WAS EXCOMMUNICATED BECAUSE HE WASN'T JUST DOING EXORCISMS-- HE WAS TOYING WITH MAGIC. I NEED TO KNOW WHAT KIND. WHAT IS HE CAPABLE OF?

OFFICIALLY, THE CATHOLIC CHURCH DOES NOT RECOGNIZE THE EXISTENCE OF MAGIC.

AND UNOFFICIALLY?

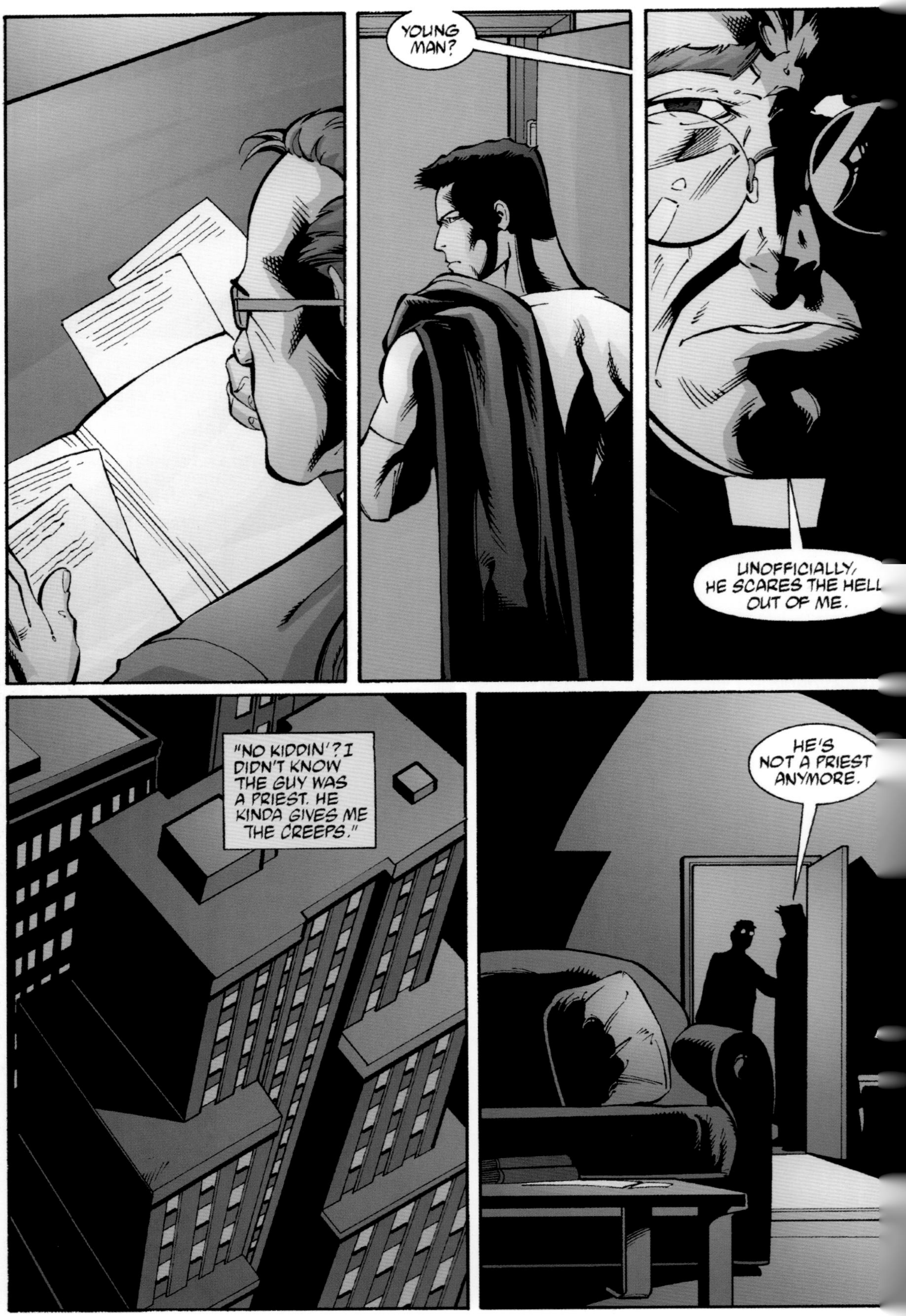
YOUNG MAN?
UNOFFICIALLY, HE SCARES THE HELL OUT OF ME.
"NO KIDDIN'? I DIDN'T KNOW THE GUY WAS A PRIEST. HE KINDA GIVES ME THE CREEPS."
HE'S NOT A PRIEST ANYMORE.

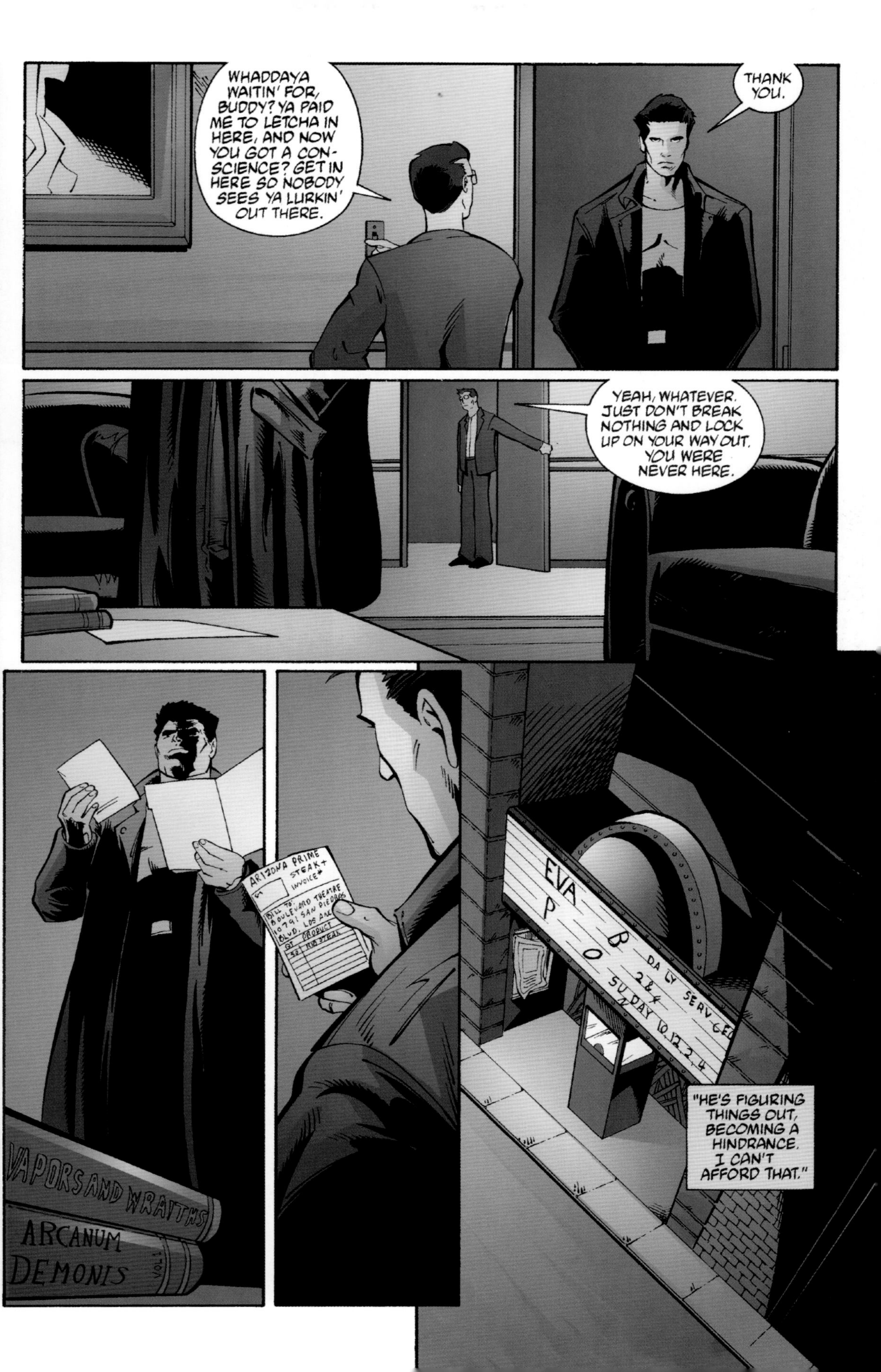
WHADDAYA WAITIN' FOR, BUDDY? YA PAID ME TO LETCHA IN HERE, AND NOW YOU GOT A CON-SCIENCE? GET IN HERE SO NOBODY SEES YA LURKIN' OUT THERE.
THANK YOU.
YEAH, WHATEVER. JUST DON'T BREAK NOTHING AND LOCK UP ON YOUR WAY OUT. YOU WERE NEVER HERE.
ARIZONA PRIME STEAK
BOULEVARD THEATRE
"HE'S FIGURING THINGS OUT, BECOMING A HINDRANCE. I CAN'T AFFORD THAT."
VAPORS AND WRAITHS
ARCANUM DEMONIS

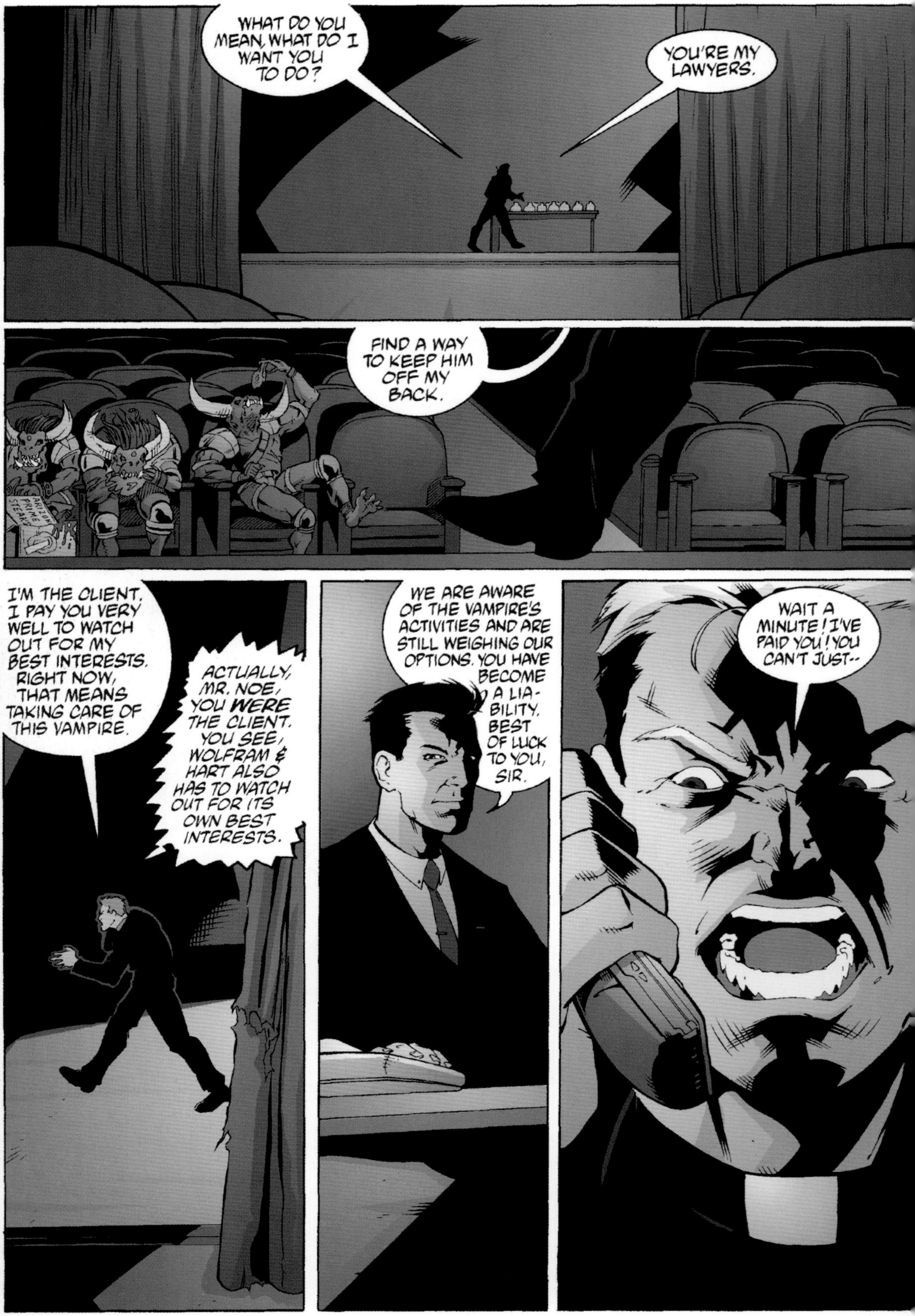
WHAT DO YOU MEAN, WHAT DO I WANT YOU TO DO?
YOU'RE MY LAWYERS.
FIND A WAY TO KEEP HIM OFF MY BACK.
ARIZONA PRIME STEAKS
I'M THE CLIENT. I PAY YOU VERY WELL TO WATCH OUT FOR MY BEST INTERESTS. RIGHT NOW, THAT MEANS TAKING CARE OF THIS VAMPIRE.
ACTUALLY, MR. NOE, YOU *WERE* THE CLIENT. YOU SEE, WOLFRAM & HART ALSO HAS TO WATCH OUT FOR ITS OWN BEST INTERESTS.
WE ARE AWARE OF THE VAMPIRE'S ACTIVITIES AND ARE STILL WEIGHING OUR OPTIONS. YOU HAVE BECOME A LIABILITY. BEST OF LUCK TO YOU, SIR.
WAIT A MINUTE! I'VE PAID YOU! YOU CAN'T JUST--

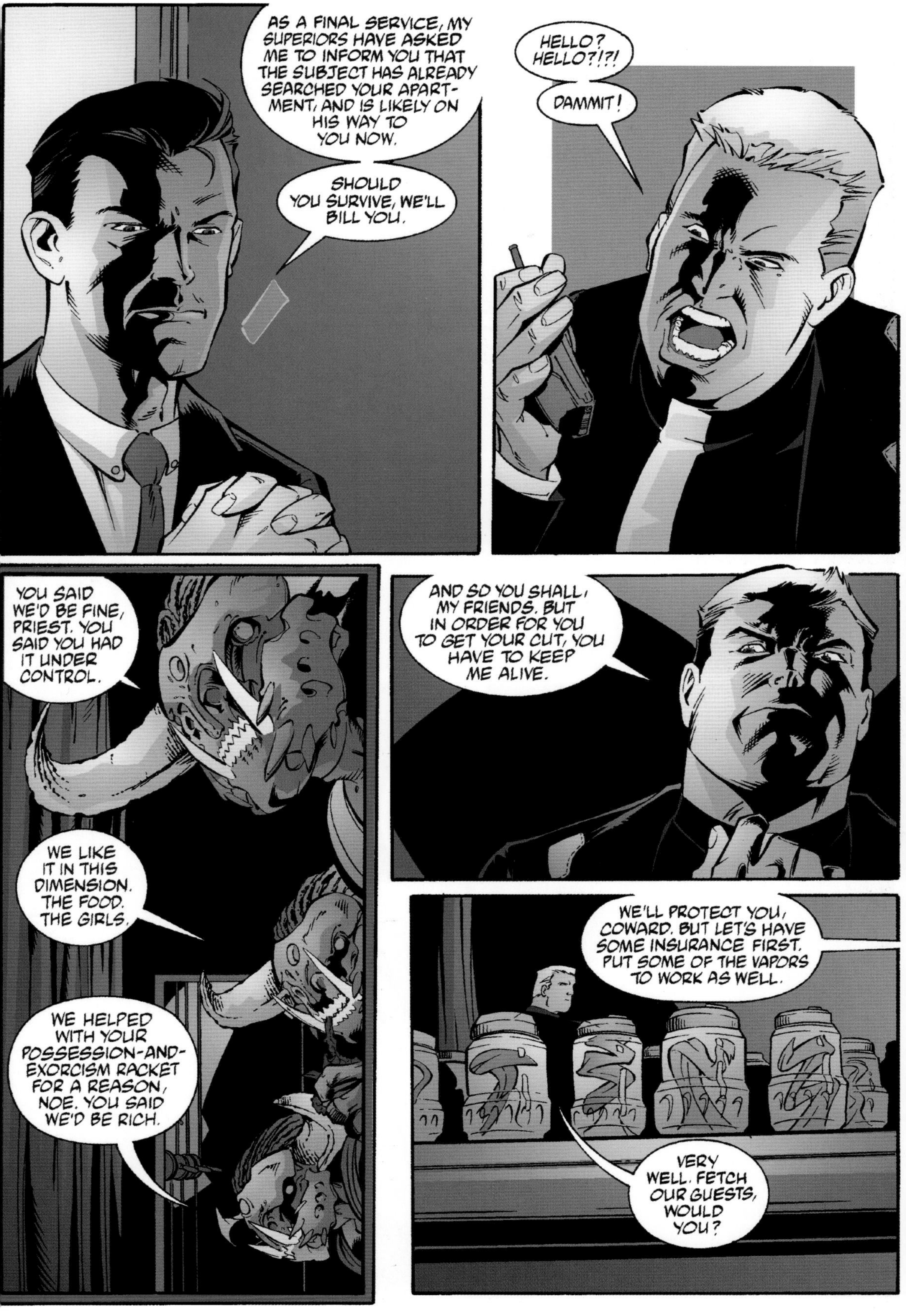
AS A FINAL SERVICE, MY SUPERIORS HAVE ASKED ME TO INFORM YOU THAT THE SUBJECT HAS ALREADY SEARCHED YOUR APARTMENT, AND IS LIKELY ON HIS WAY TO YOU NOW.
SHOULD YOU SURVIVE, WE'LL BILL YOU.
HELLO? HELLO?!?!
DAMMIT!
YOU SAID WE'D BE FINE, PRIEST. YOU SAID YOU HAD IT UNDER CONTROL.
WE LIKE IT IN THIS DIMENSION. THE FOOD. THE GIRLS.
WE HELPED WITH YOUR POSSESSION-AND-EXORCISM RACKET FOR A REASON, NOE. YOU SAID WE'D BE RICH.
AND SO YOU SHALL, MY FRIENDS. BUT IN ORDER FOR YOU TO GET YOUR CUT, YOU HAVE TO KEEP ME ALIVE.
WE'LL PROTECT YOU, COWARD. BUT LET'S HAVE SOME INSURANCE FIRST. PUT SOME OF THE VAPORS TO WORK AS WELL.
VERY WELL. FETCH OUR GUESTS, WOULD YOU?

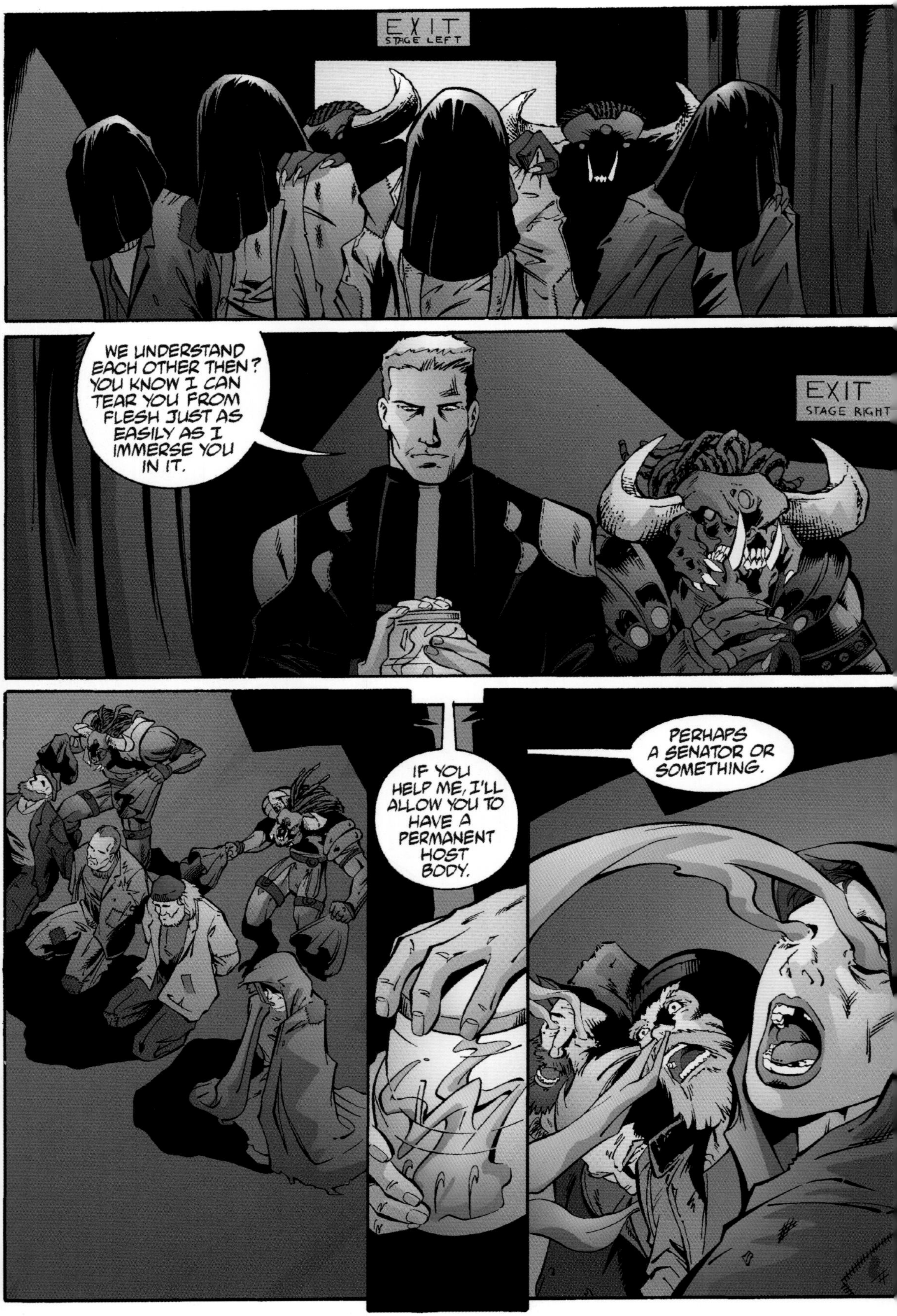
EXIT
STAGE LEFT
WE UNDERSTAND EACH OTHER THEN? YOU KNOW I CAN TEAR YOU FROM FLESH JUST AS EASILY AS I IMMERSE YOU IN IT.
EXIT
STAGE RIGHT
IF YOU HELP ME, I'LL ALLOW YOU TO HAVE A PERMANENT HOST BODY.
PERHAPS A SENATOR OR SOMETHING.

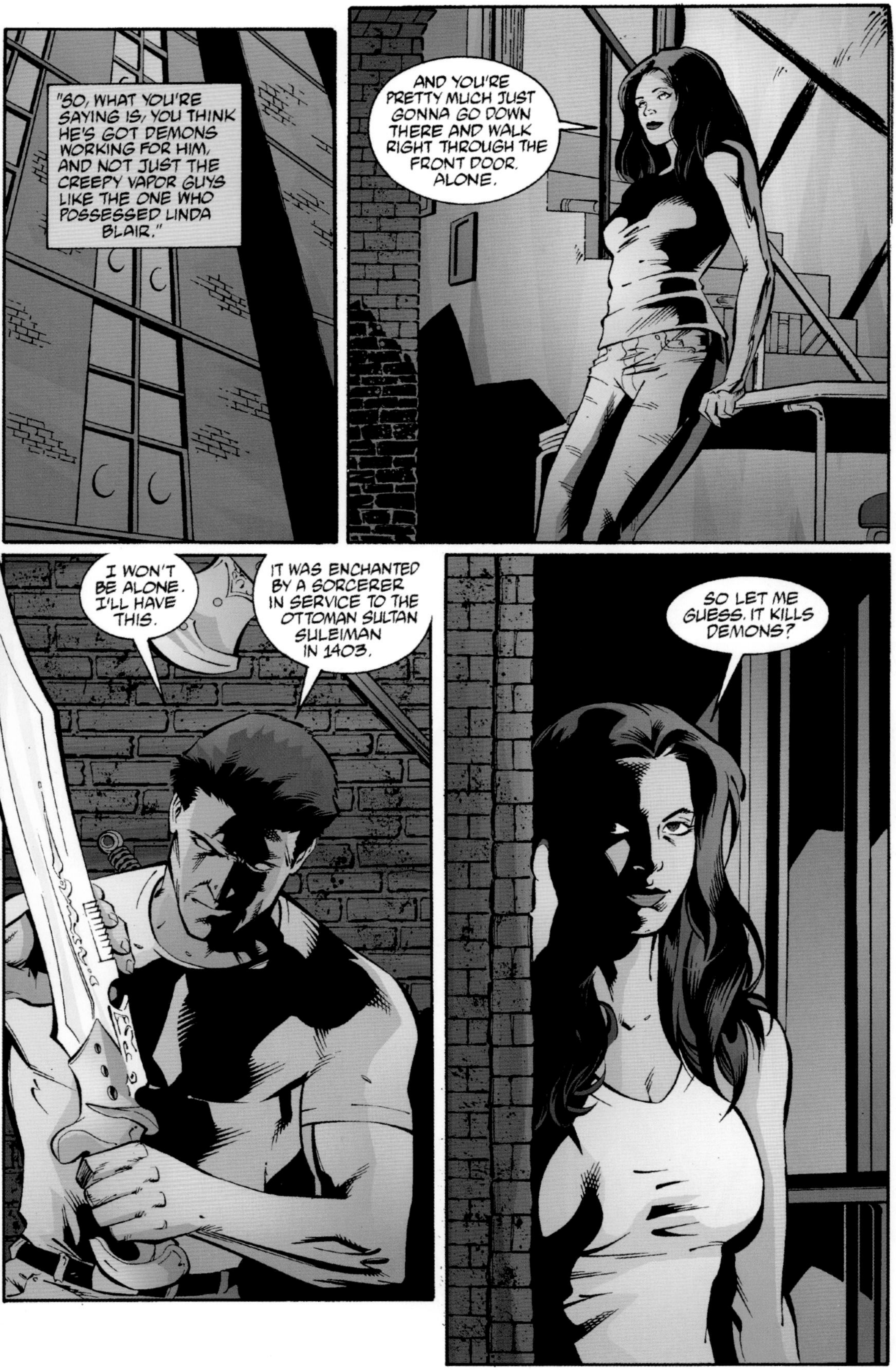
"SO, WHAT YOU'RE SAYING IS, YOU THINK HE'S GOT DEMONS WORKING FOR HIM, AND NOT JUST THE CREEPY VAPOR GUYS LIKE THE ONE WHO POSSESSED LINDA BLAIR."
AND YOU'RE PRETTY MUCH JUST GONNA GO DOWN THERE AND WALK RIGHT THROUGH THE FRONT DOOR. ALONE.
I WON'T BE ALONE. I'LL HAVE THIS.
IT WAS ENCHANTED BY A SORCERER IN SERVICE TO THE OTTOMAN SULTAN SULEIMAN IN 1403.
SO LET ME GUESS. IT KILLS DEMONS?

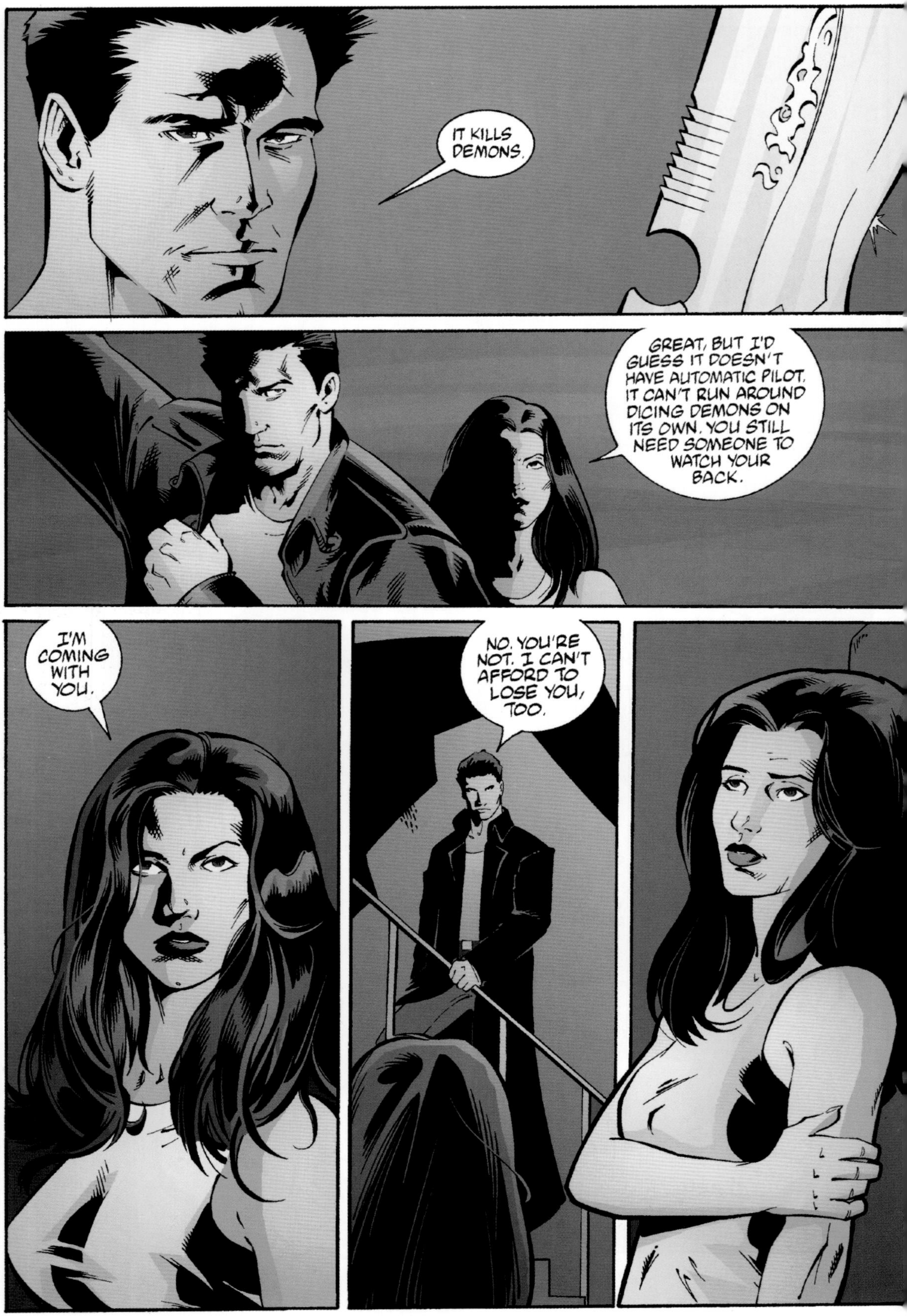
IT KILLS DEMONS.
GREAT, BUT I'D GUESS IT DOESN'T HAVE AUTOMATIC PILOT. IT CAN'T RUN AROUND DICING DEMONS ON ITS OWN. YOU STILL NEED SOMEONE TO WATCH YOUR BACK.
I'M COMING WITH YOU.
NO. YOU'RE NOT. I CAN'T AFFORD TO LOSE YOU, TOO.

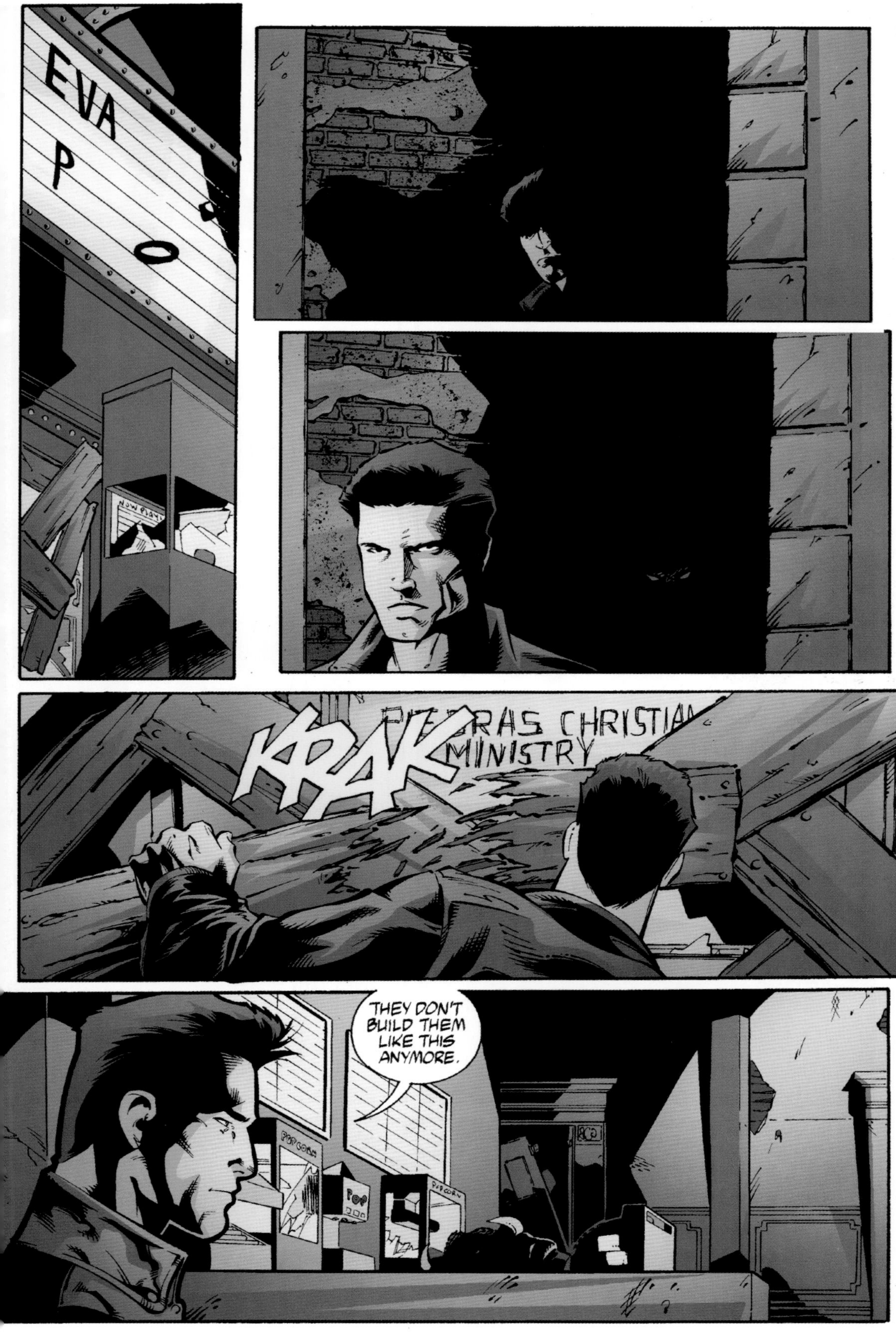
EVA
P
O
PIEDRAS CHRISTIAN MINISTRY
KRAK
THEY DON'T BUILD THEM LIKE THIS ANYMORE.

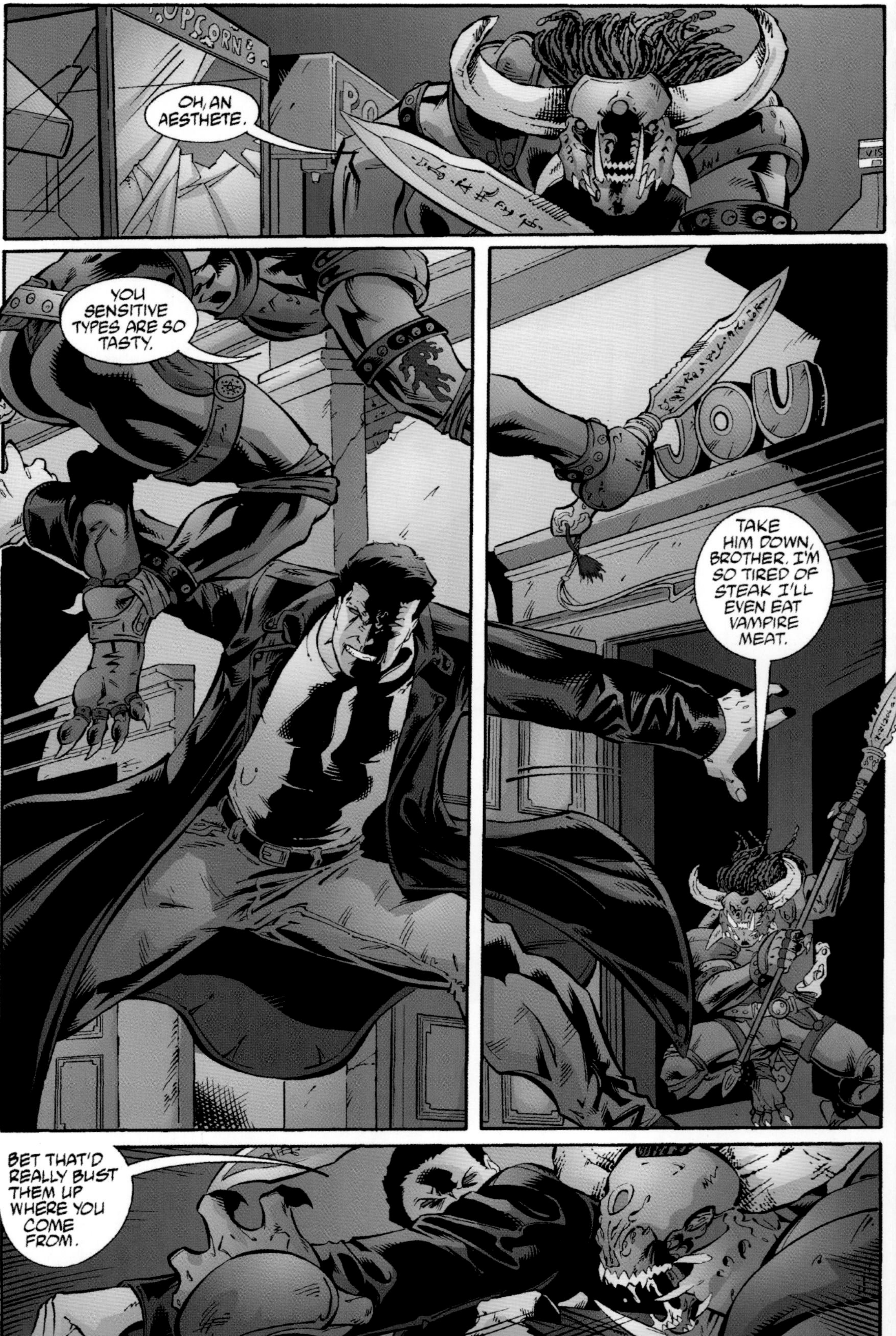
OH, AN AESTHETE.
YOU SENSITIVE TYPES ARE SO TASTY.
TAKE HIM DOWN, BROTHER. I'M SO TIRED OF STEAK I'LL EVEN EAT VAMPIRE MEAT.
BET THAT'D REALLY BUST THEM UP WHERE YOU COME FROM.

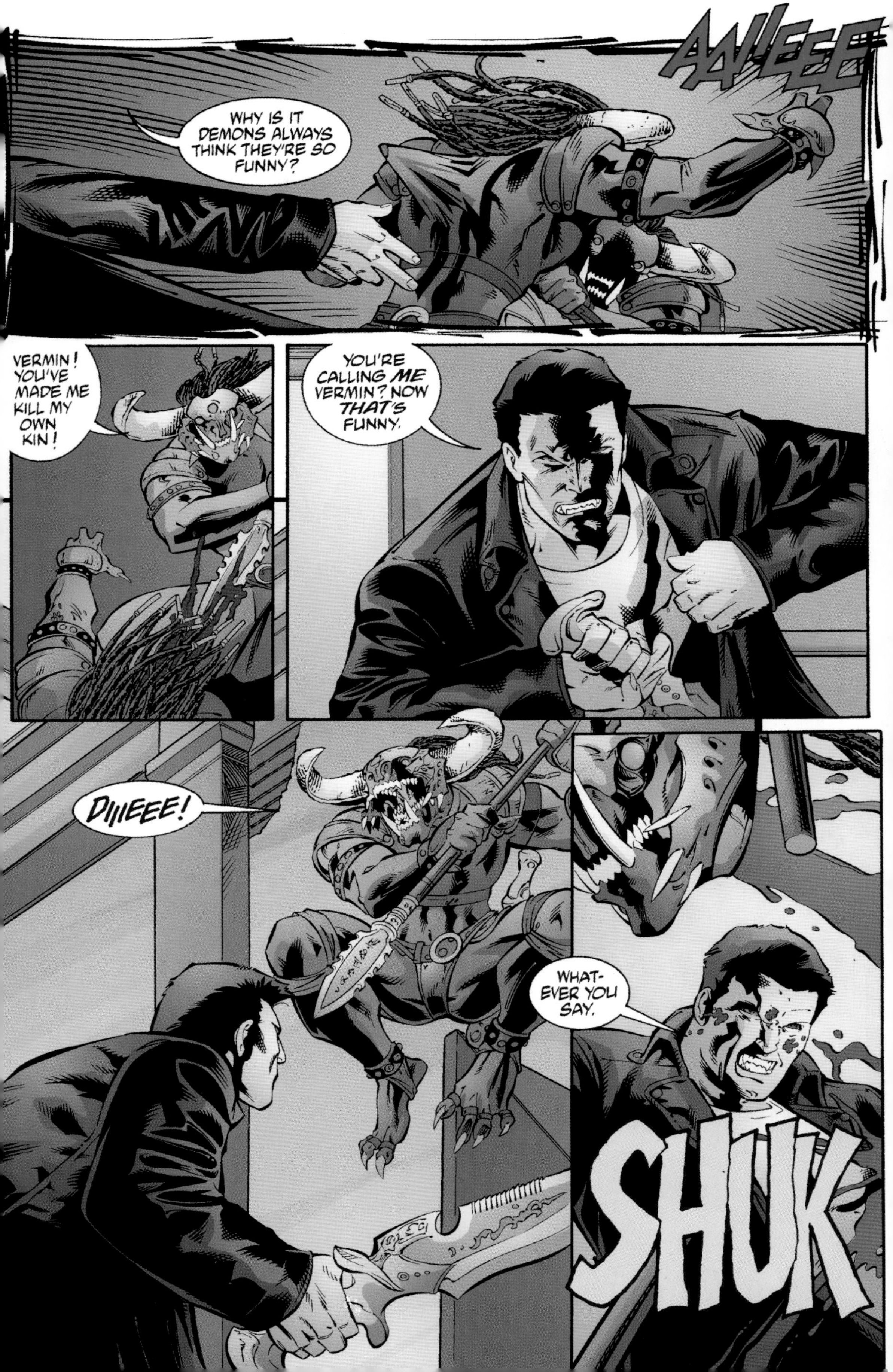
AAIIEEE
WHY IS IT DEMONS ALWAYS THINK THEY'RE SO FUNNY?
VERMIN! YOU'VE MADE ME KILL MY OWN KIN!
YOU'RE CALLING ME VERMIN? NOW THAT'S FUNNY.
DIIIEEE!
WHAT-EVER YOU SAY.
SHUK

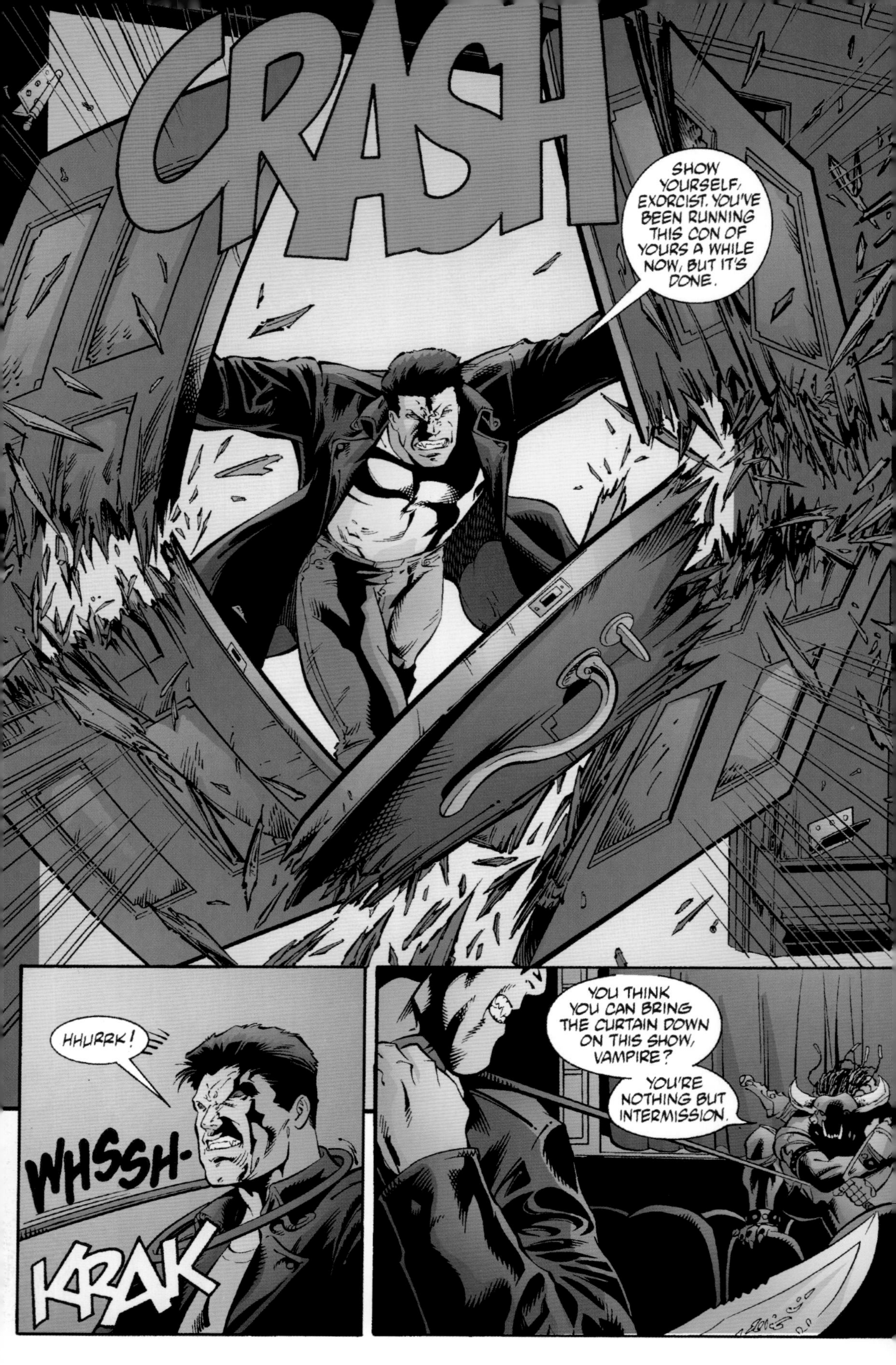
CRASH
SHOW YOURSELF, EXORCIST. YOU'VE BEEN RUNNING THIS CON OF YOURS A WHILE NOW, BUT IT'S DONE.
HHURRK!
WHSSH-
KRAK
YOU THINK YOU CAN BRING THE CURTAIN DOWN ON THIS SHOW, VAMPIRE?
YOU'RE NOTHING BUT INTERMISSION.

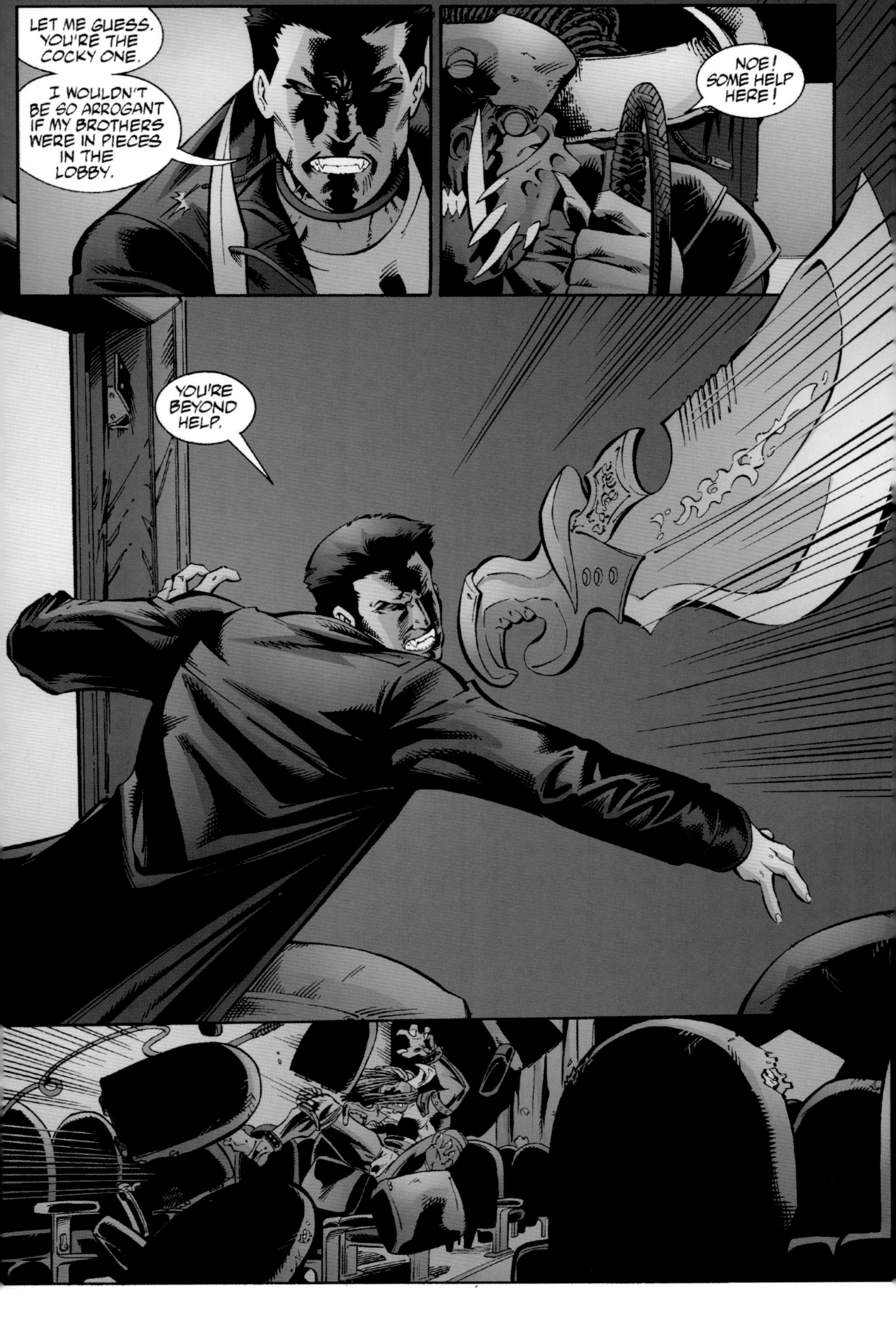
LET ME GUESS. YOU'RE THE COCKY ONE.
I WOULDN'T BE SO ARROGANT IF MY BROTHERS WERE IN PIECES IN THE LOBBY.
NOE! SOME HELP HERE!
YOU'RE BEYOND HELP.

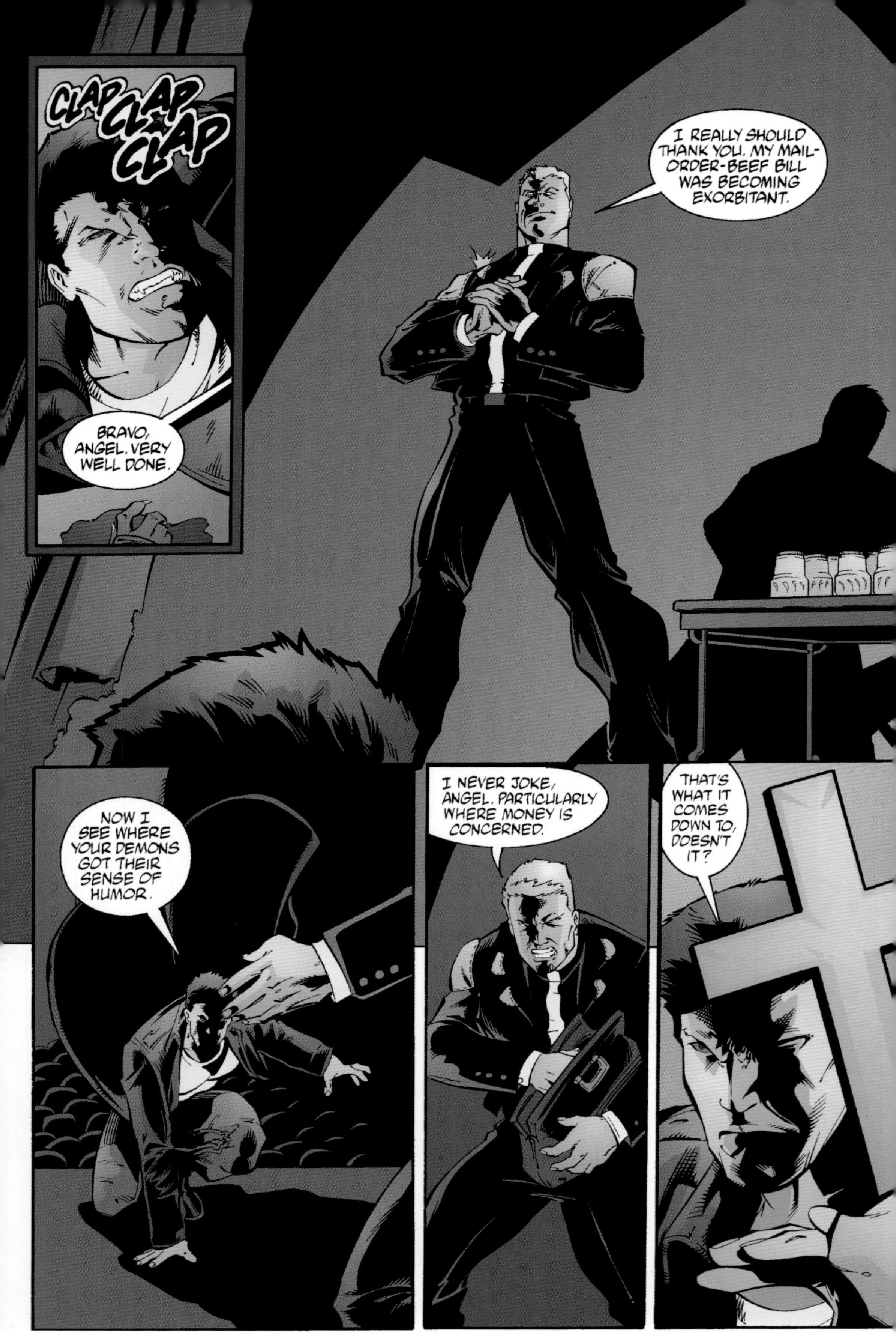

CLAP CLAP CLAP
BRAVO, ANGEL. VERY WELL DONE.
I REALLY SHOULD THANK YOU. MY MAIL-ORDER-BEEF BILL WAS BECOMING EXORBITANT.
NOW I SEE WHERE YOUR DEMONS GOT THEIR SENSE OF HUMOR.
I NEVER JOKE, ANGEL. PARTICULARLY WHERE MONEY IS CONCERNED.
THAT'S WHAT IT COMES DOWN TO, DOESN'T IT?

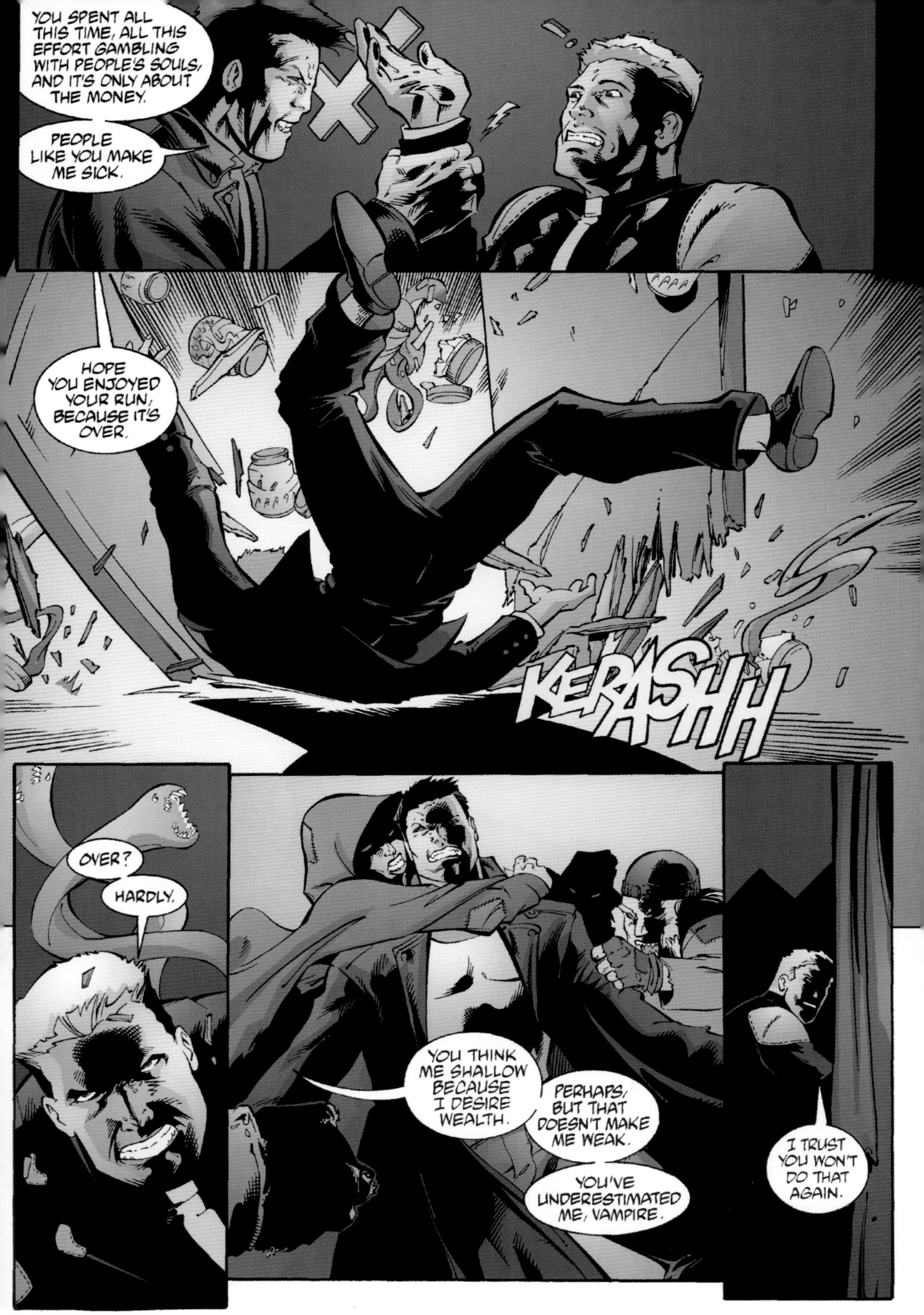

YOU SPENT ALL THIS TIME, ALL THIS EFFORT GAMBLING WITH PEOPLE'S SOULS, AND IT'S ONLY ABOUT THE MONEY.
PEOPLE LIKE YOU MAKE ME SICK.
HOPE YOU ENJOYED YOUR RUN, BECAUSE IT'S OVER.
KERASHH
OVER?
HARDLY.
YOU THINK ME SHALLOW BECAUSE I DESIRE WEALTH.
PERHAPS, BUT THAT DOESN'T MAKE ME WEAK.
YOU'VE UNDERESTIMATED ME, VAMPIRE.
I TRUST YOU WON'T DO THAT AGAIN.

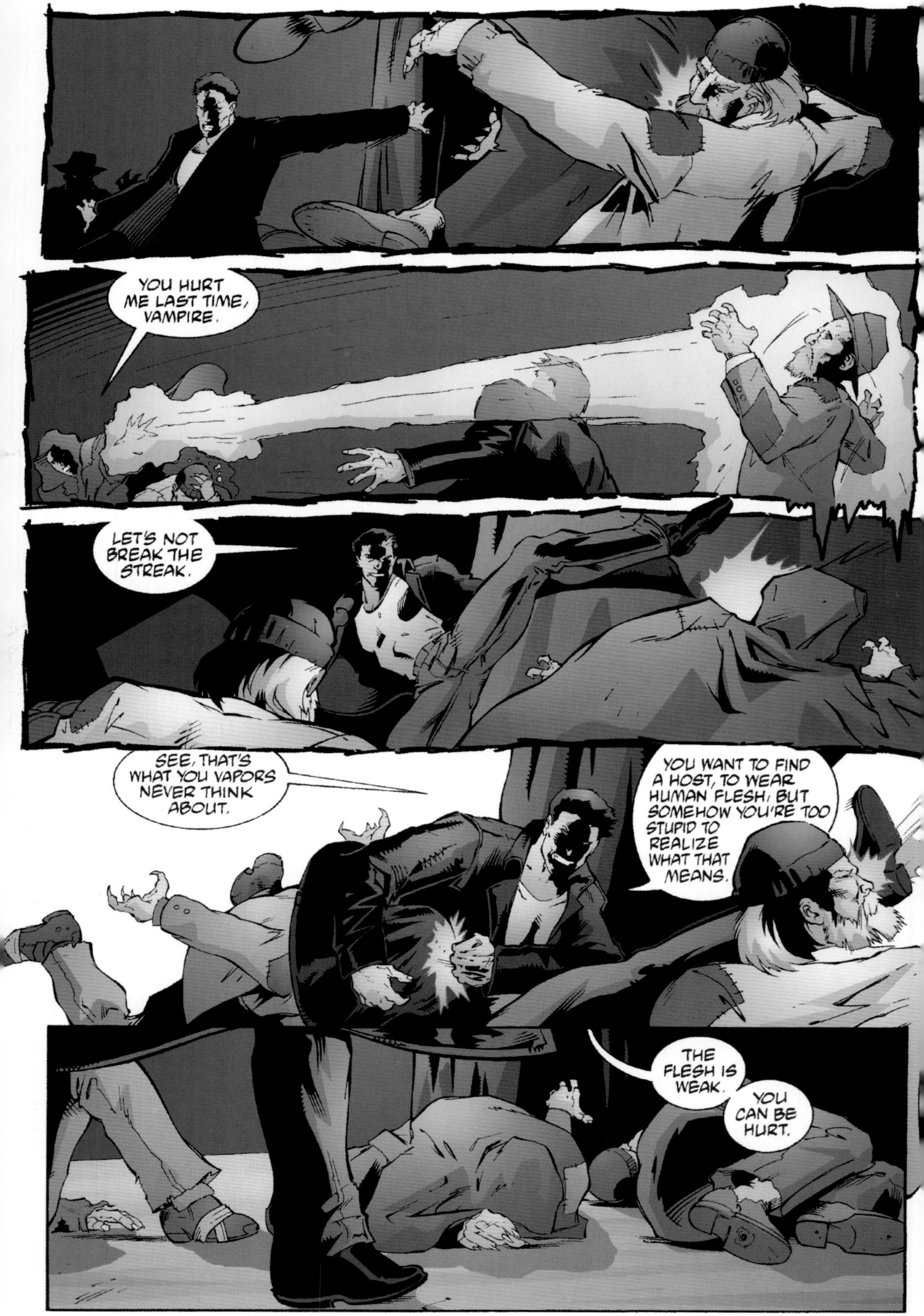
YOU HURT ME LAST TIME, VAMPIRE.
LET'S NOT BREAK THE STREAK.
SEE, THAT'S WHAT YOU VAPORS NEVER THINK ABOUT.
YOU WANT TO FIND A HOST, TO WEAR HUMAN FLESH, BUT SOMEHOW YOU'RE TOO STUPID TO REALIZE WHAT THAT MEANS.
THE FLESH IS WEAK.
YOU CAN BE HURT.

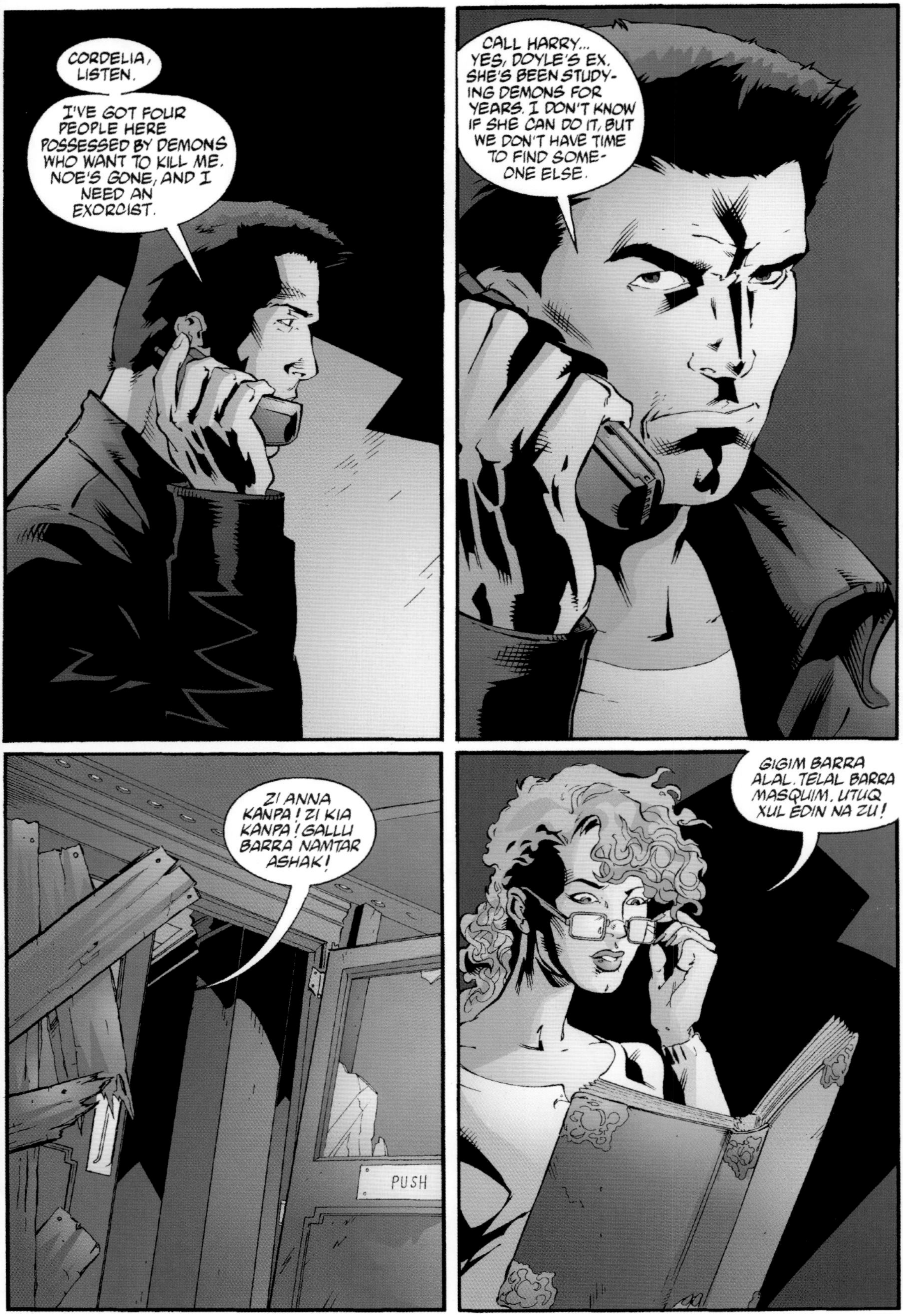
CORDELIA, LISTEN.
I'VE GOT FOUR PEOPLE HERE POSSESSED BY DEMONS WHO WANT TO KILL ME. NOE'S GONE, AND I NEED AN EXORCIST.
CALL HARRY... YES, DOYLE'S EX. SHE'S BEEN STUDYING DEMONS FOR YEARS. I DON'T KNOW IF SHE CAN DO IT, BUT WE DON'T HAVE TIME TO FIND SOMEONE ELSE.
ZI ANNA KANPA! ZI KIA KANPA! GALLU BARRA NAMTAR ASHAK!
PUSH
GIGIM BARRA ALAL. TELAL BARRA MASQUIM. UTUQ XUL EDIN NA ZU!

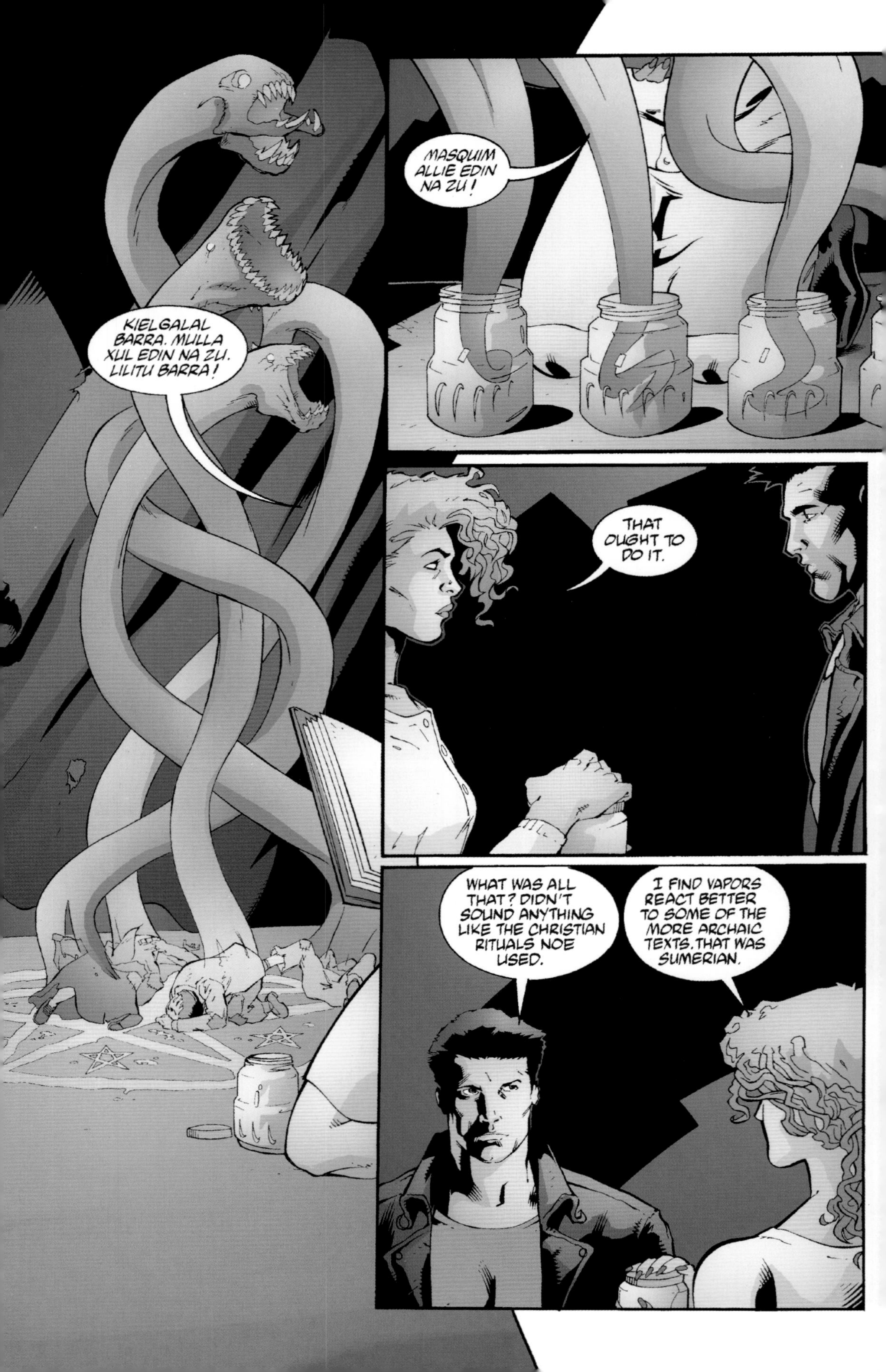
KIELGALAL BARRA. MULLA XUL EDIN NA ZU. LILITU BARRA!
MASQUIM ALLIE EDIN NA ZU!
THAT OUGHT TO DO IT.
WHAT WAS ALL THAT? DIDN'T SOUND ANYTHING LIKE THE CHRISTIAN RITUALS NOE USED.
I FIND VAPORS REACT BETTER TO SOME OF THE MORE ARCHAIC TEXTS. THAT WAS SUMERIAN.

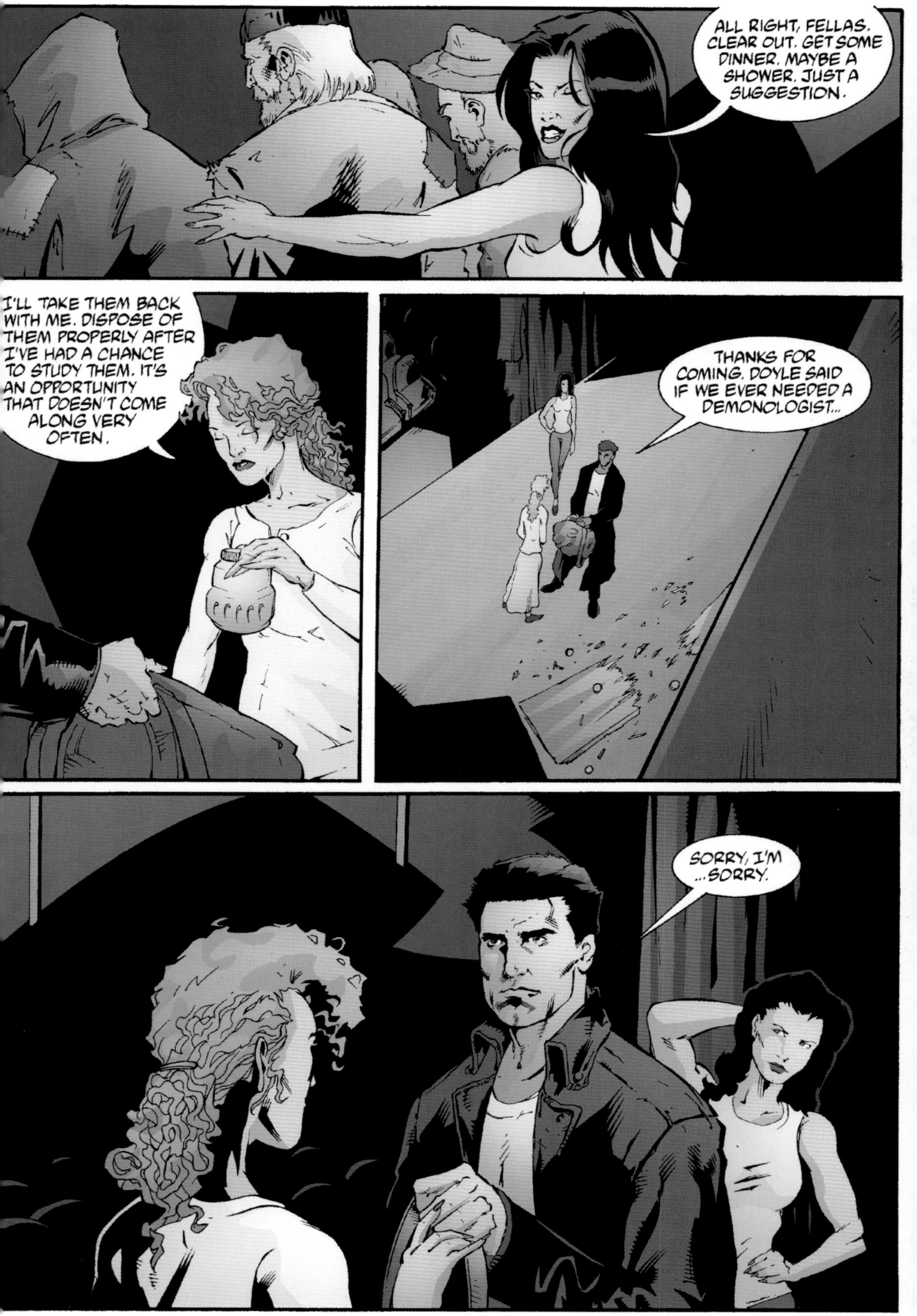
ALL RIGHT, FELLAS. CLEAR OUT. GET SOME DINNER. MAYBE A SHOWER. JUST A SUGGESTION.
I'LL TAKE THEM BACK WITH ME. DISPOSE OF THEM PROPERLY AFTER I'VE HAD A CHANCE TO STUDY THEM. IT'S AN OPPORTUNITY THAT DOESN'T COME ALONG VERY OFTEN.
THANKS FOR COMING. DOYLE SAID IF WE EVER NEEDED A DEMONOLOGIST...
SORRY, I'M ...SORRY.

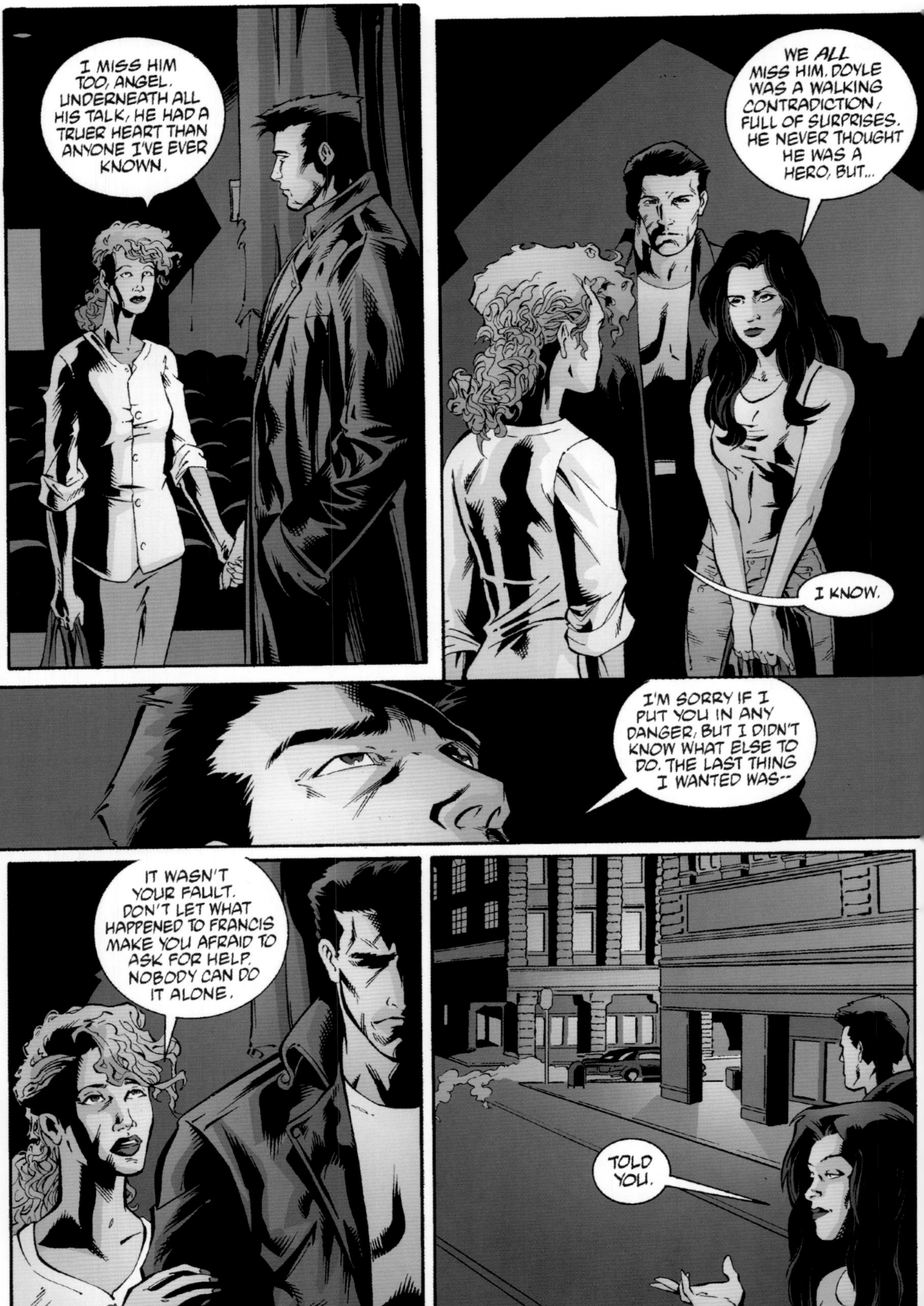
I MISS HIM TOO, ANGEL. UNDERNEATH ALL HIS TALK, HE HAD A TRUER HEART THAN ANYONE I'VE EVER KNOWN.
WE ALL MISS HIM. DOYLE WAS A WALKING CONTRADICTION, FULL OF SURPRISES. HE NEVER THOUGHT HE WAS A HERO, BUT...
I KNOW.
I'M SORRY IF I PUT YOU IN ANY DANGER, BUT I DIDN'T KNOW WHAT ELSE TO DO. THE LAST THING I WANTED WAS--
IT WASN'T YOUR FAULT. DON'T LET WHAT HAPPENED TO FRANCIS MAKE YOU AFRAID TO ASK FOR HELP. NOBODY CAN DO IT ALONE.
TOLD YOU.

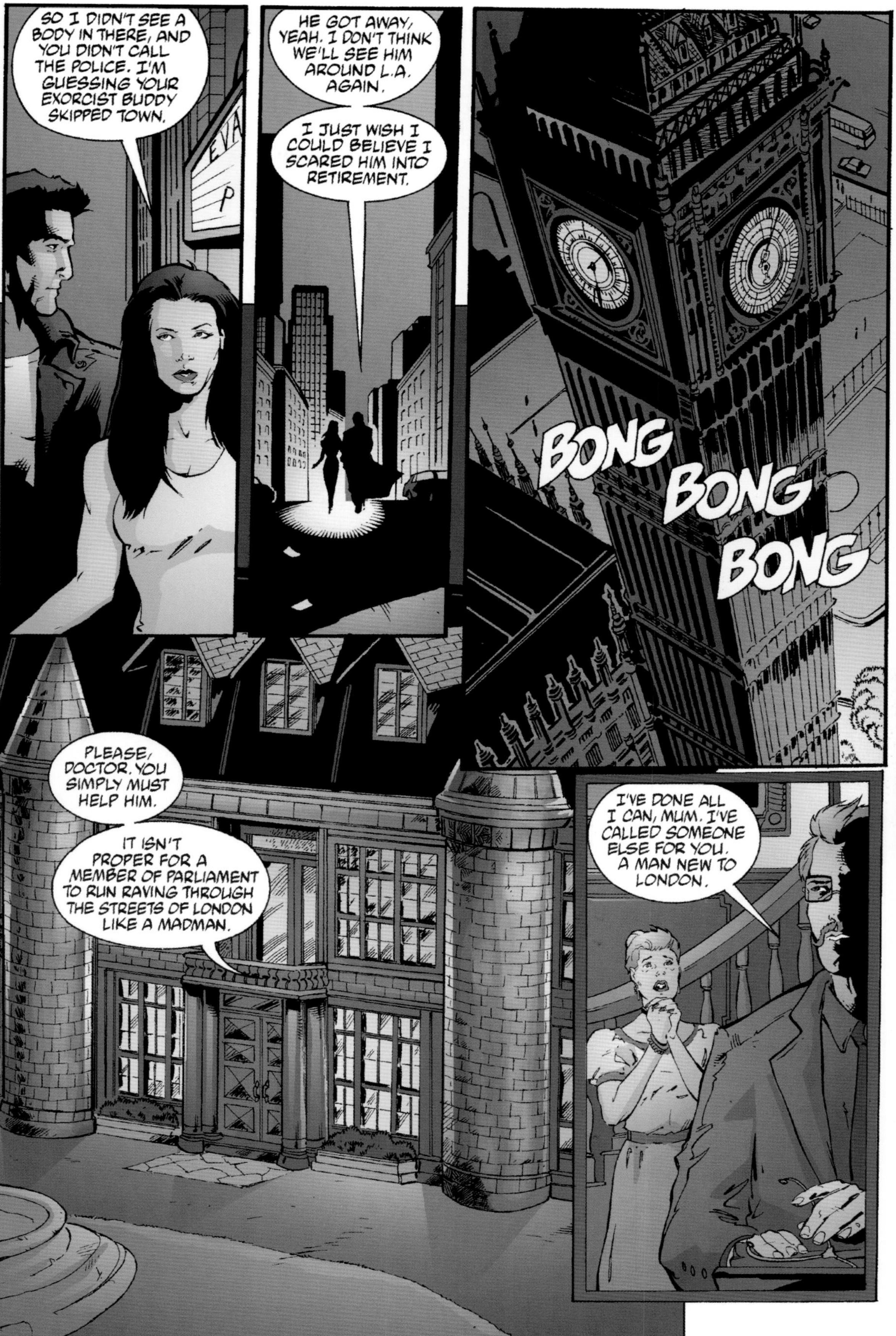
SO I DIDN'T SEE A BODY IN THERE, AND YOU DIDN'T CALL THE POLICE. I'M GUESSING YOUR EXORCIST BUDDY SKIPPED TOWN.
HE GOT AWAY, YEAH. I DON'T THINK WE'LL SEE HIM AROUND L.A. AGAIN.
I JUST WISH I COULD BELIEVE I SCARED HIM INTO RETIREMENT.
BONG
BONG
BONG
PLEASE, DOCTOR. YOU SIMPLY MUST HELP HIM.
IT ISN'T PROPER FOR A MEMBER OF PARLIAMENT TO RUN RAVING THROUGH THE STREETS OF LONDON LIKE A MADMAN.
I'VE DONE ALL I CAN, MUM. I'VE CALLED SOMEONE ELSE FOR YOU. A MAN NEW TO LONDON.

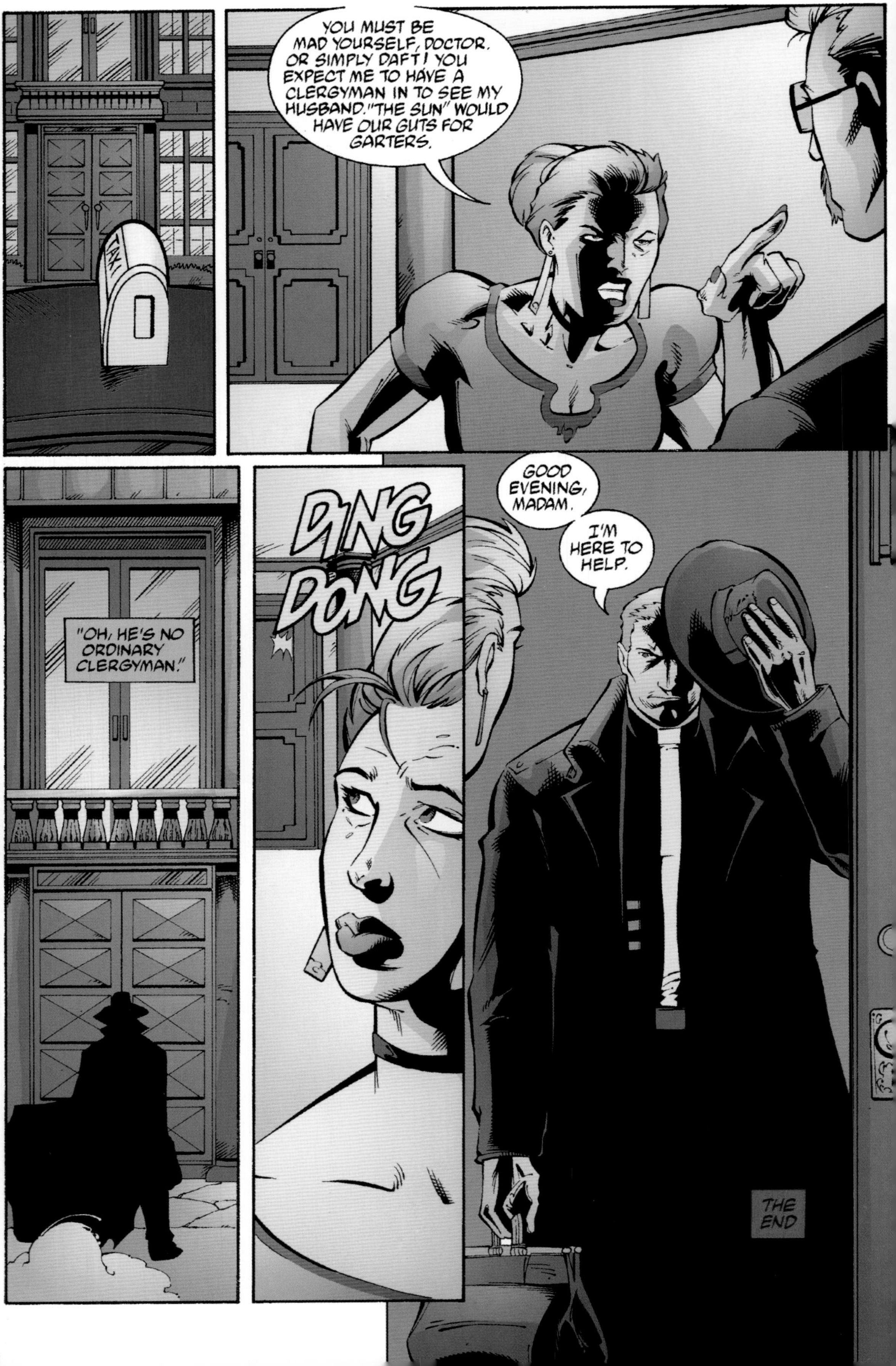
TAXI
YOU MUST BE MAD YOURSELF, DOCTOR. OR SIMPLY DAFT! YOU EXPECT ME TO HAVE A CLERGYMAN IN TO SEE MY HUSBAND."THE SUN" WOULD HAVE OUR GUTS FOR GARTERS.
"OH, HE'S NO ORDINARY CLERGYMAN."
DING DONG
GOOD EVENING, MADAM.
I'M HERE TO HELP.
THE END

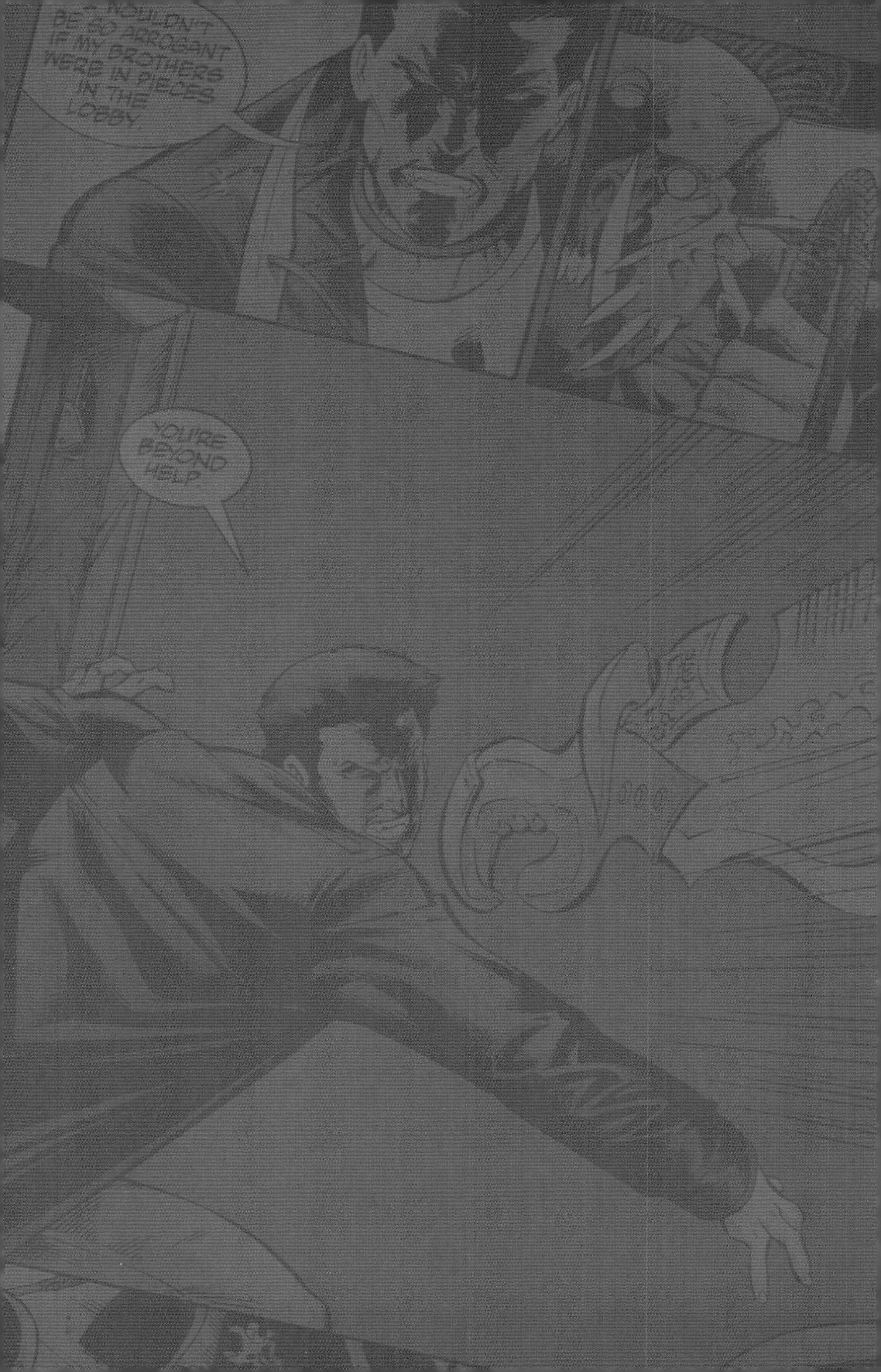

...WOULDN'T BE SO ARROGANT IF MY BROTHERS WERE IN PIECES IN THE LOBBY.
YOU'RE BEYOND HELP.

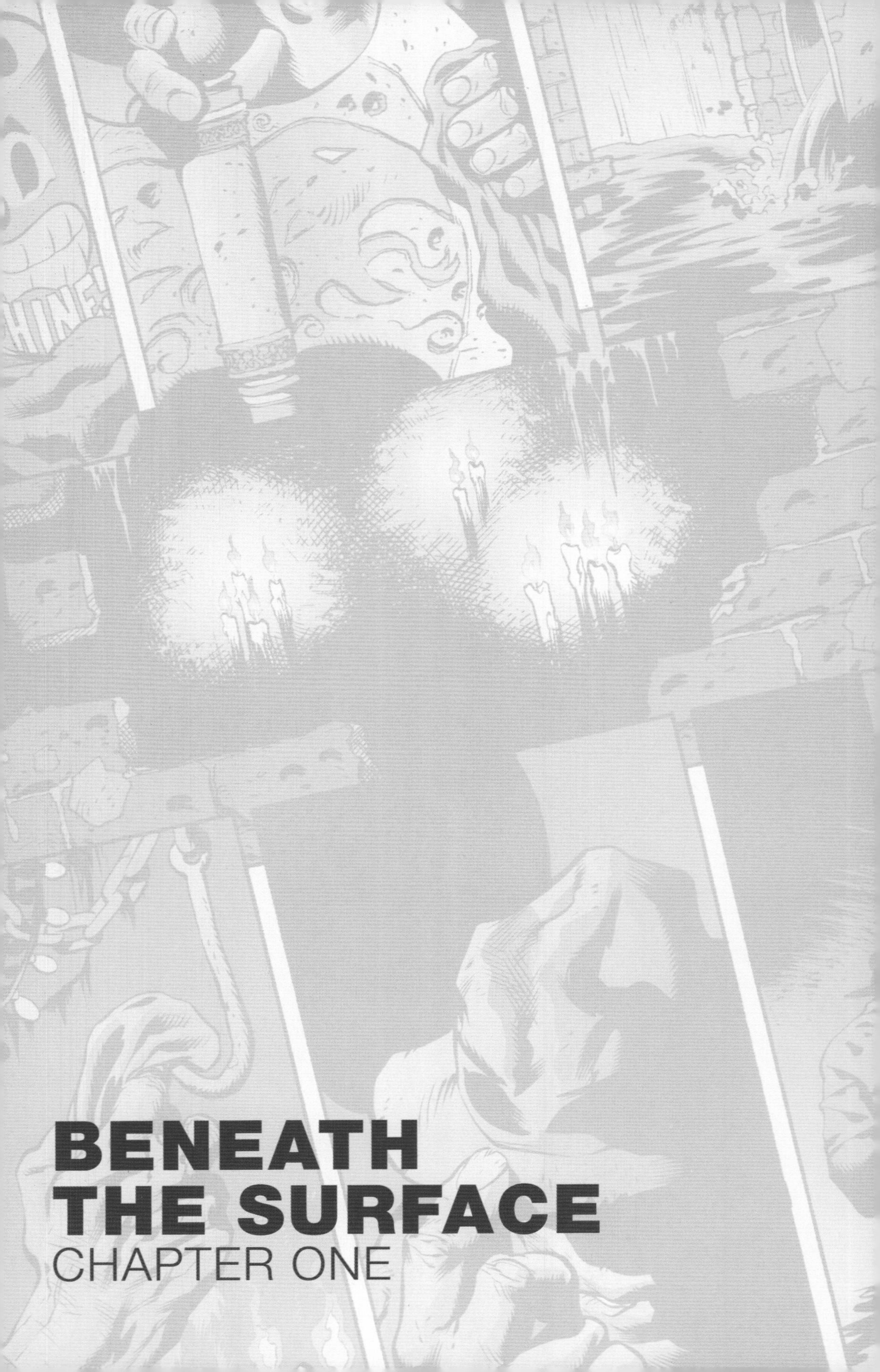

BENEATH THE SURFACE
CHAPTER ONE

DAWN OVER THE CITY OF ANGELS.

ALREADY, THE NEW DAY BEGINS, THE POPULATION STIRRING TO INDUSTRIOUS LIFE...

...EVEN AS THE CREATURES OF THE NIGHT...

...WITHDRAW INTO DEEPER SHADOWS...

THAT'S RIGHT, ANGEL. RUN OFF AND HIDE FROM THE SUN. BUT DON'T GET TOO COMFORTABLE. WON'T BE TOO LONG 'TIL THEY DRAG YOU OUT INTO THE LIGHT OF DAY, AND I'LL BE THERE TO SEE IT.

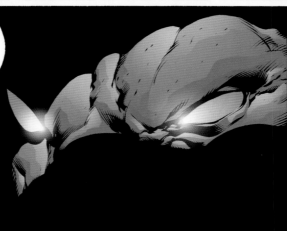

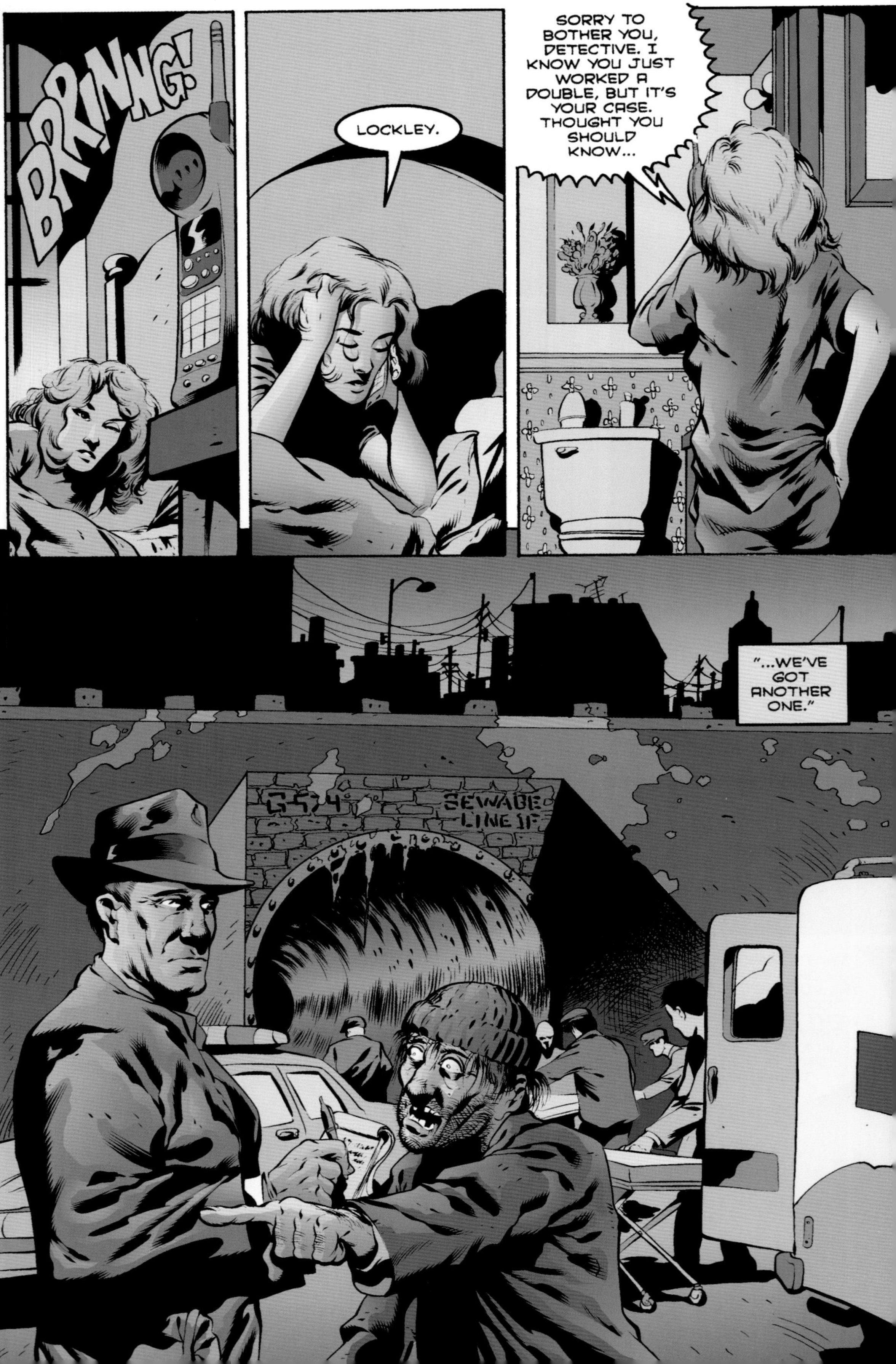
BRRINNG!
LOCKLEY.
SORRY TO BOTHER YOU, DETECTIVE. I KNOW YOU JUST WORKED A DOUBLE, BUT IT'S YOUR CASE. THOUGHT YOU SHOULD KNOW...
"...WE'VE GOT ANOTHER ONE."
SEWAGE LINE 1F

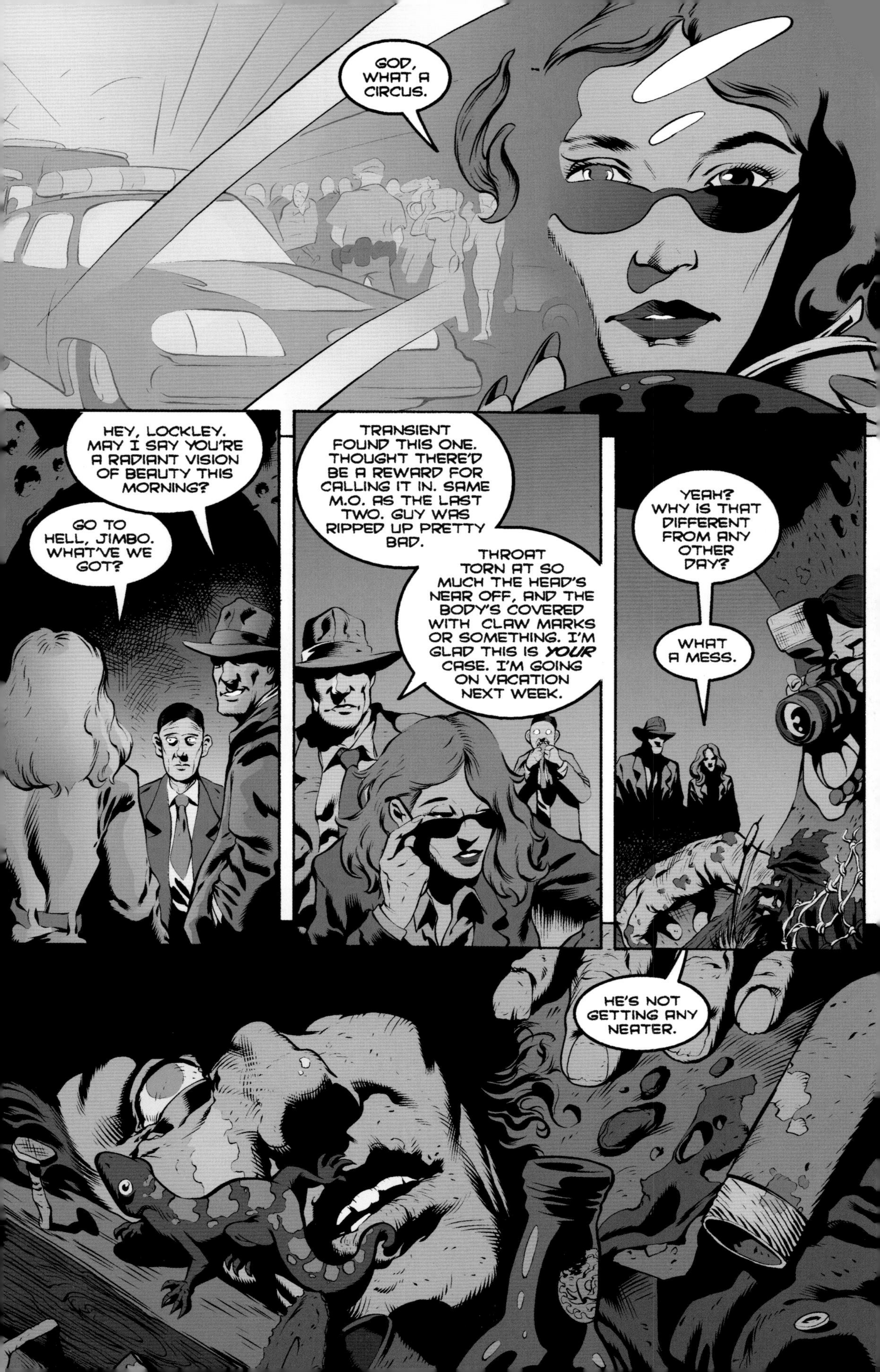
GOD, WHAT A CIRCUS.
HEY, LOCKLEY. MAY I SAY YOU'RE A RADIANT VISION OF BEAUTY THIS MORNING?
GO TO HELL, JIMBO. WHAT'VE WE GOT?
TRANSIENT FOUND THIS ONE. THOUGHT THERE'D BE A REWARD FOR CALLING IT IN. SAME M.O. AS THE LAST TWO. GUY WAS RIPPED UP PRETTY BAD.
THROAT TORN AT SO MUCH THE HEAD'S NEAR OFF, AND THE BODY'S COVERED WITH CLAW MARKS OR SOMETHING. I'M GLAD THIS IS *YOUR* CASE. I'M GOING ON VACATION NEXT WEEK.
YEAH? WHY IS THAT DIFFERENT FROM ANY OTHER DAY?
WHAT A MESS.
HE'S NOT GETTING ANY NEATER.

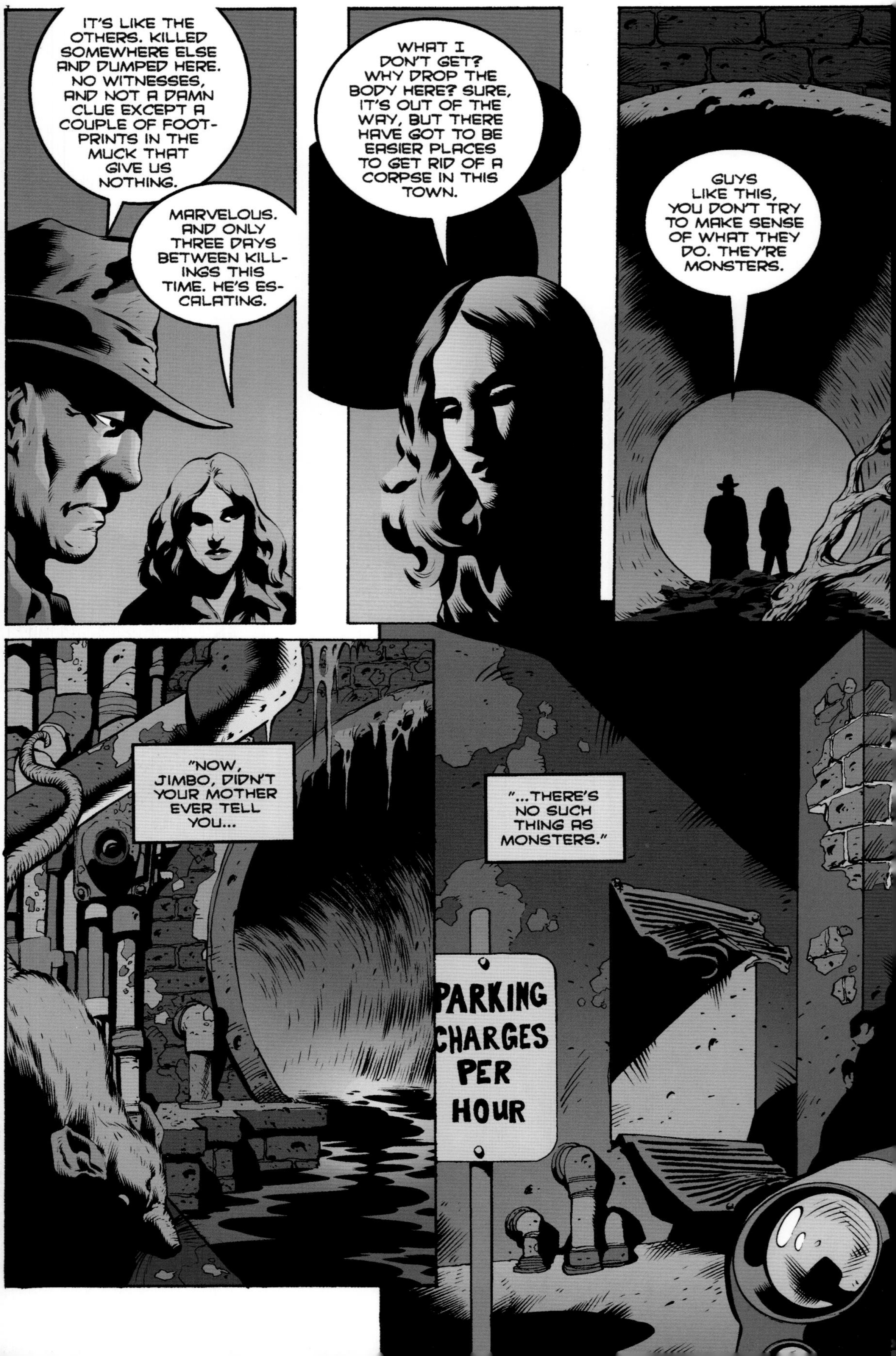
IT'S LIKE THE OTHERS. KILLED SOMEWHERE ELSE AND DUMPED HERE. NO WITNESSES, AND NOT A DAMN CLUE EXCEPT A COUPLE OF FOOT-PRINTS IN THE MUCK THAT GIVE US NOTHING.
MARVELOUS. AND ONLY THREE DAYS BETWEEN KILL-INGS THIS TIME. HE'S ES-CALATING.
WHAT I DON'T GET? WHY DROP THE BODY HERE? SURE, IT'S OUT OF THE WAY, BUT THERE HAVE GOT TO BE EASIER PLACES TO GET RID OF A CORPSE IN THIS TOWN.
GUYS LIKE THIS, YOU DON'T TRY TO MAKE SENSE OF WHAT THEY DO. THEY'RE MONSTERS.
"NOW, JIMBO, DIDN'T YOUR MOTHER EVER TELL YOU...
"...THERE'S NO SUCH THING AS MONSTERS."
PARKING CHARGES PER HOUR

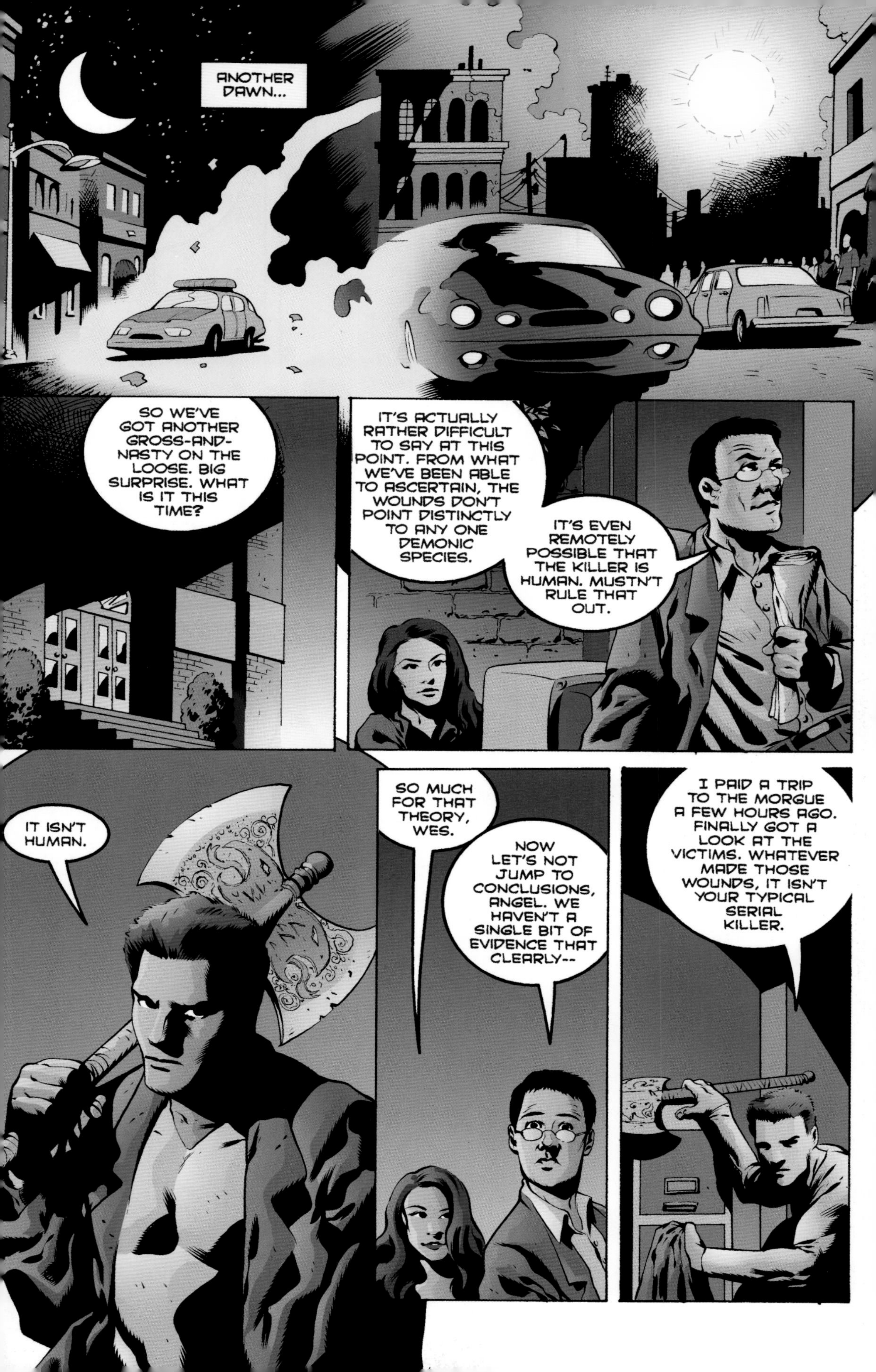
ANOTHER DAWN...
SO WE'VE GOT ANOTHER GROSS-AND-NASTY ON THE LOOSE. BIG SURPRISE. WHAT IS IT THIS TIME?
IT'S ACTUALLY RATHER DIFFICULT TO SAY AT THIS POINT. FROM WHAT WE'VE BEEN ABLE TO ASCERTAIN, THE WOUNDS DON'T POINT DISTINCTLY TO ANY ONE DEMONIC SPECIES.
IT'S EVEN REMOTELY POSSIBLE THAT THE KILLER IS HUMAN. MUSTN'T RULE THAT OUT.
IT ISN'T HUMAN.
SO MUCH FOR THAT THEORY, WES.
NOW LET'S NOT JUMP TO CONCLUSIONS, ANGEL. WE HAVEN'T A SINGLE BIT OF EVIDENCE THAT CLEARLY--
I PAID A TRIP TO THE MORGUE A FEW HOURS AGO. FINALLY GOT A LOOK AT THE VICTIMS. WHATEVER MADE THOSE WOUNDS, IT ISN'T YOUR TYPICAL SERIAL KILLER.

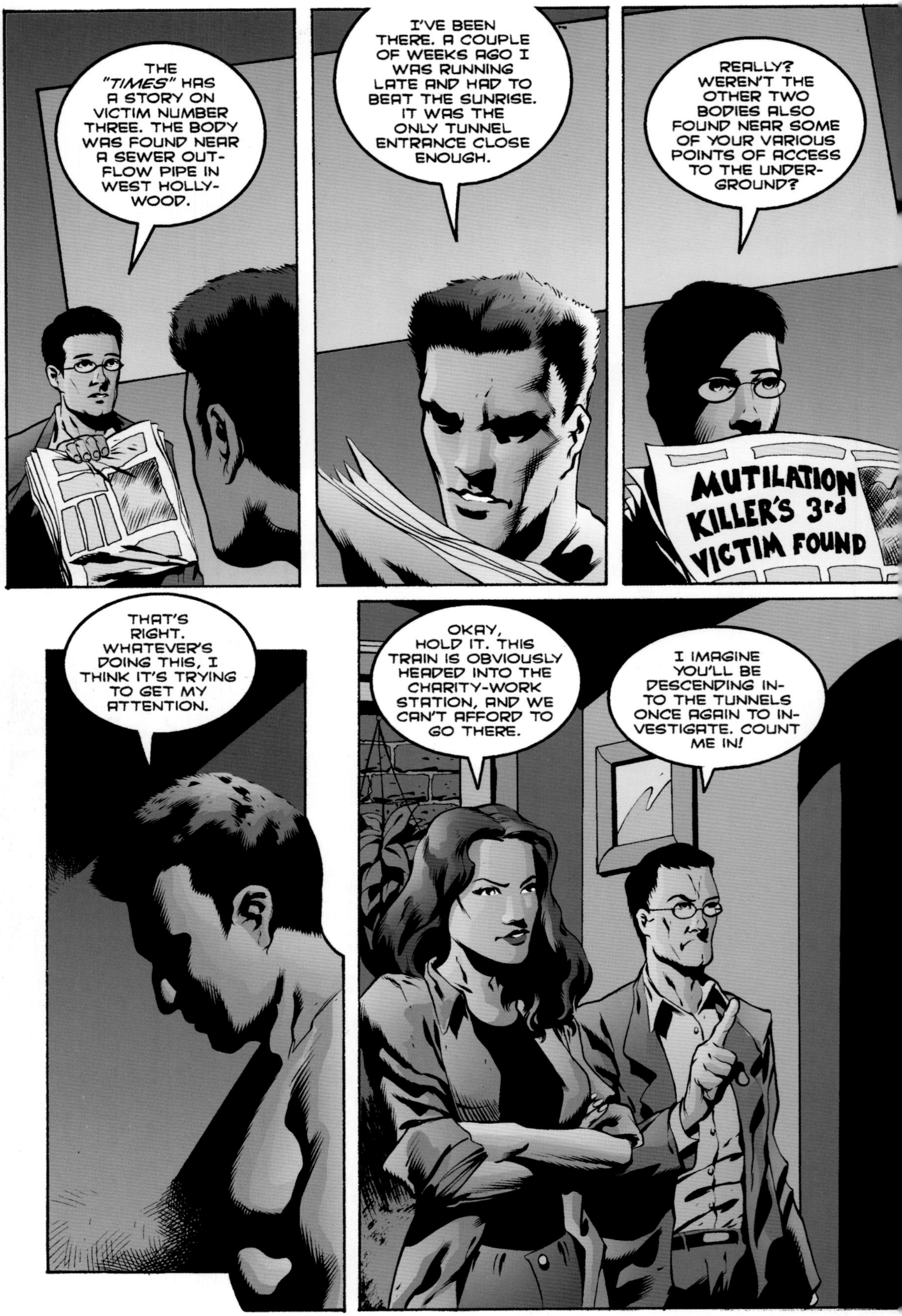
THE "TIMES" HAS A STORY ON VICTIM NUMBER THREE. THE BODY WAS FOUND NEAR A SEWER OUT-FLOW PIPE IN WEST HOLLY-WOOD.
I'VE BEEN THERE. A COUPLE OF WEEKS AGO I WAS RUNNING LATE AND HAD TO BEAT THE SUNRISE. IT WAS THE ONLY TUNNEL ENTRANCE CLOSE ENOUGH.
REALLY? WEREN'T THE OTHER TWO BODIES ALSO FOUND NEAR SOME OF YOUR VARIOUS POINTS OF ACCESS TO THE UNDER-GROUND?
MUTILATION KILLER'S 3rd VICTIM FOUND
THAT'S RIGHT. WHATEVER'S DOING THIS, I THINK IT'S TRYING TO GET MY ATTENTION.
OKAY, HOLD IT. THIS TRAIN IS OBVIOUSLY HEADED INTO THE CHARITY-WORK STATION, AND WE CAN'T AFFORD TO GO THERE.
I IMAGINE YOU'LL BE DESCENDING IN-TO THE TUNNELS ONCE AGAIN TO IN-VESTIGATE. COUNT ME IN!

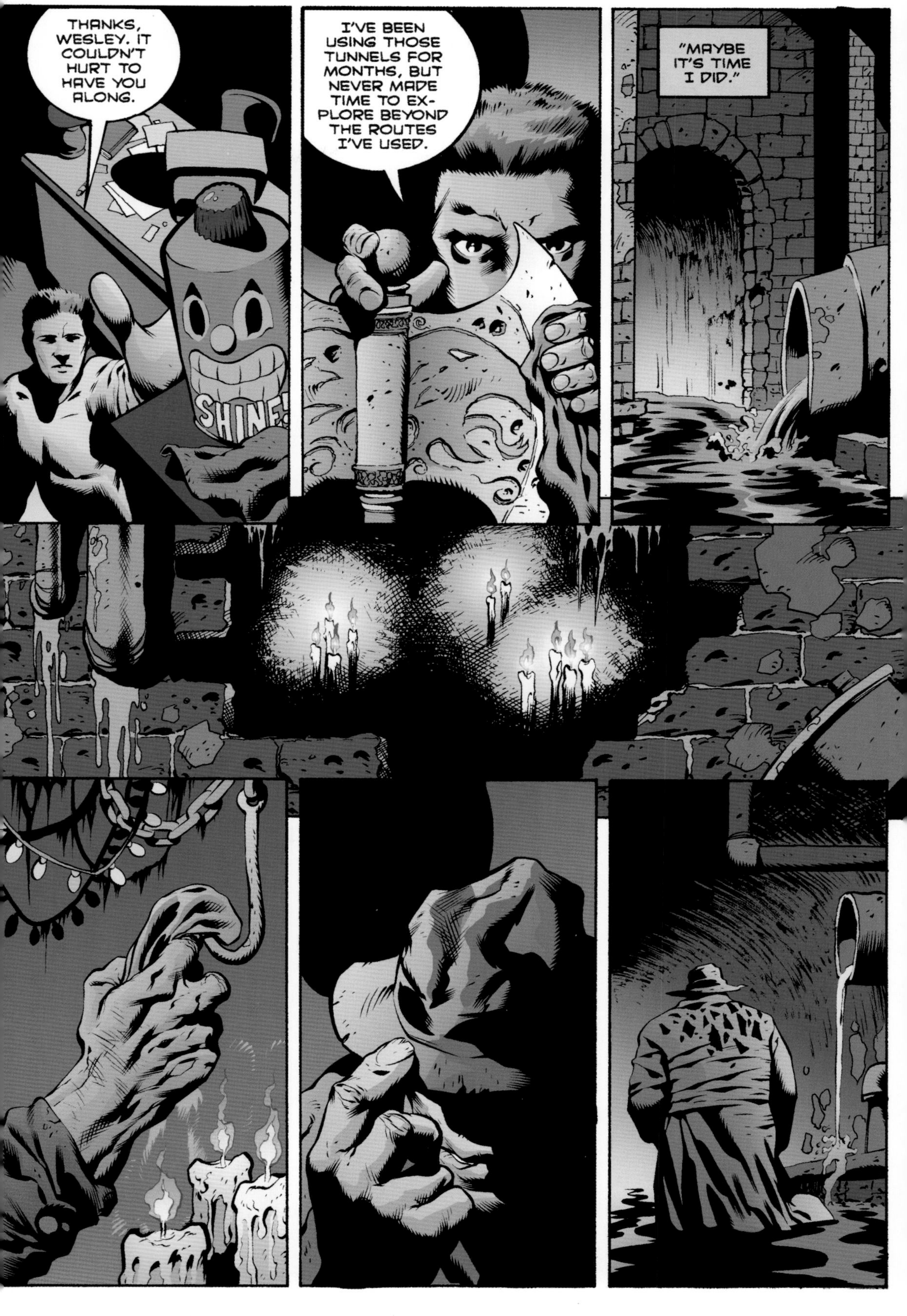
THANKS, WESLEY. IT COULDN'T HURT TO HAVE YOU ALONG.
SHINE!
I'VE BEEN USING THOSE TUNNELS FOR MONTHS, BUT NEVER MADE TIME TO EX-PLORE BEYOND THE ROUTES I'VE USED.
"MAYBE IT'S TIME I DID."

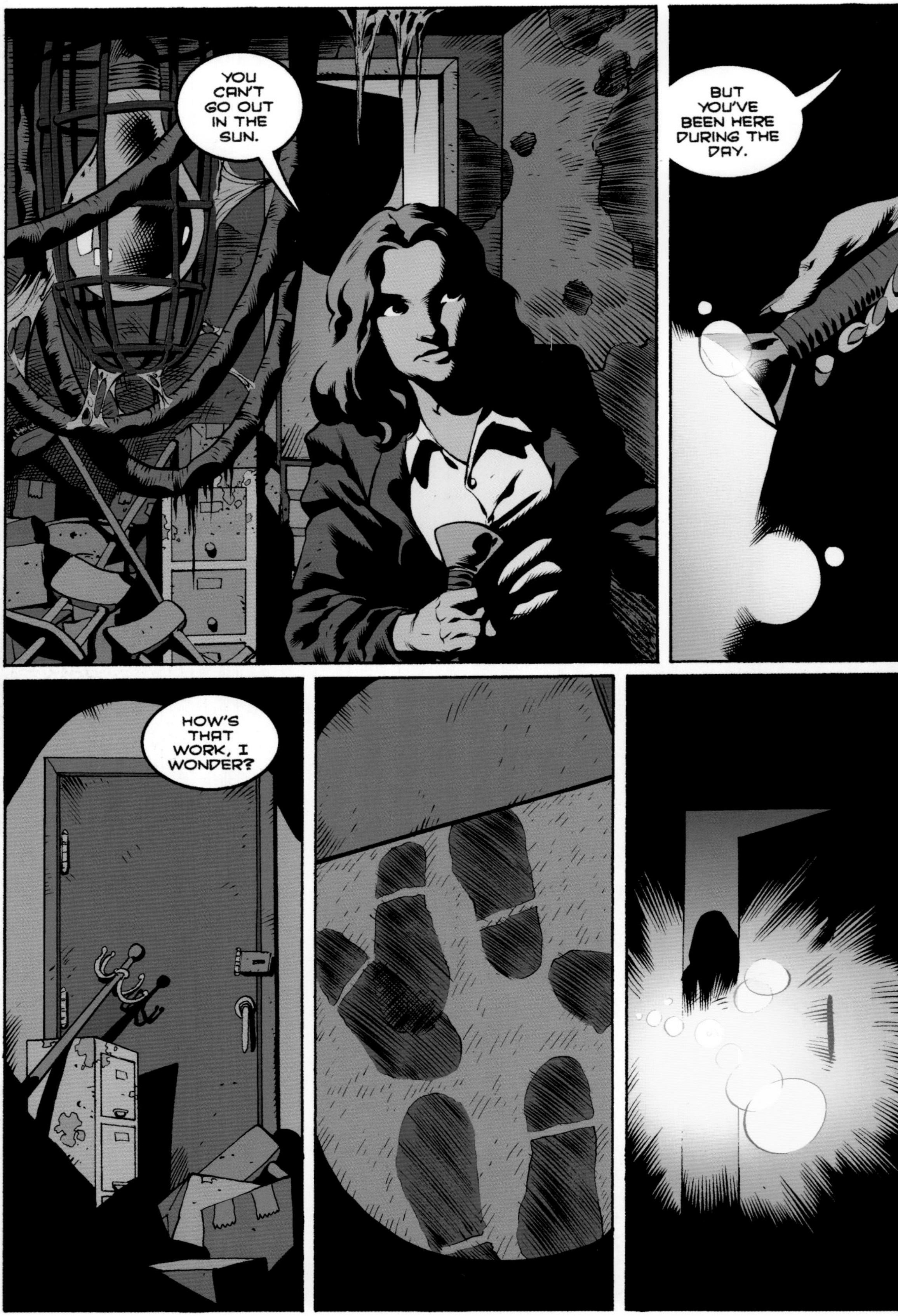
YOU CAN'T GO OUT IN THE SUN.
BUT YOU'VE BEEN HERE DURING THE DAY.
HOW'S THAT WORK, I WONDER?

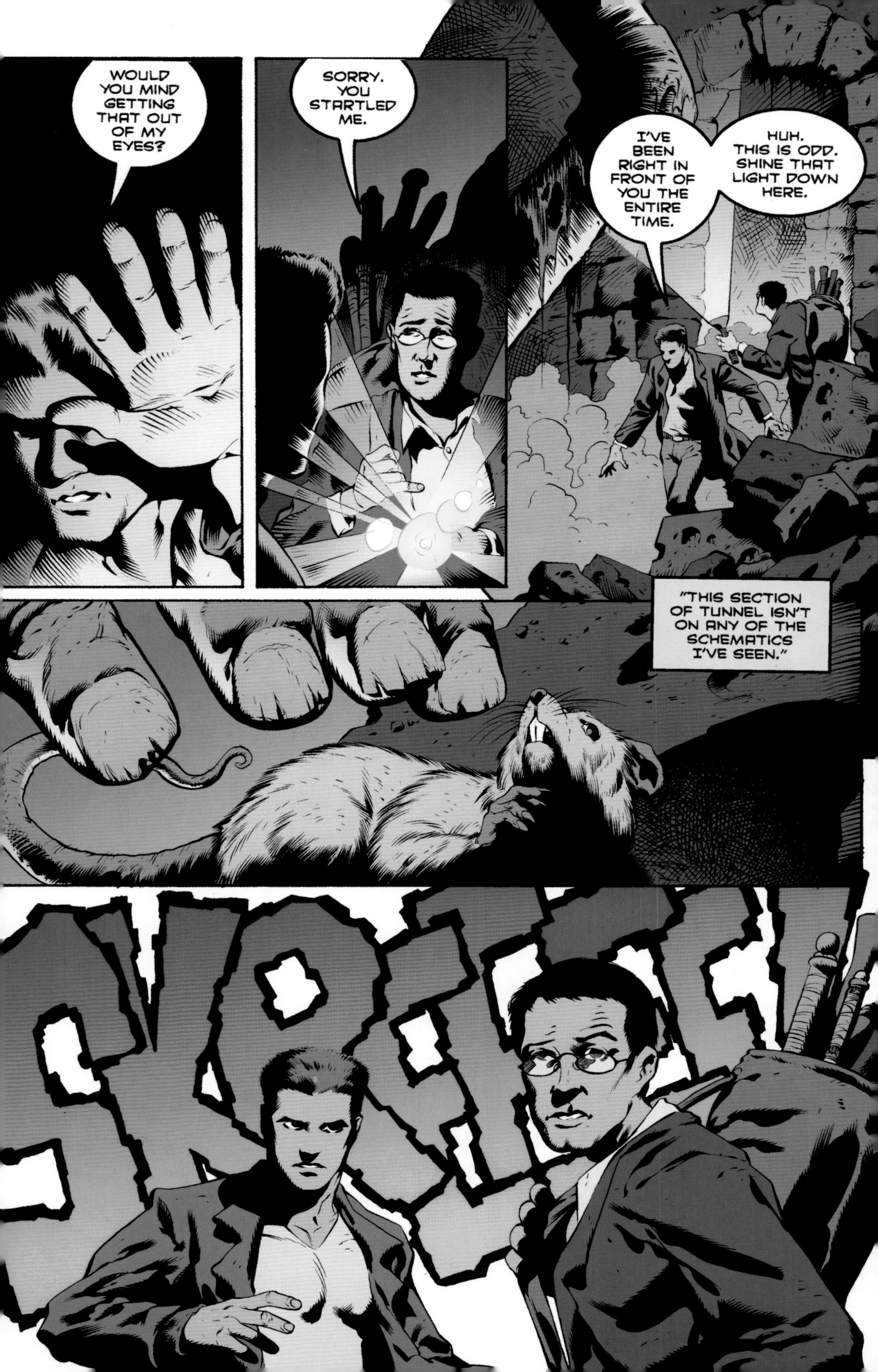
WOULD YOU MIND GETTING THAT OUT OF MY EYES?
SORRY. YOU STARTLED ME.
I'VE BEEN RIGHT IN FRONT OF YOU THE ENTIRE TIME.
HUH. THIS IS ODD. SHINE THAT LIGHT DOWN HERE.
"THIS SECTION OF TUNNEL ISN'T ON ANY OF THE SCHEMATICS I'VE SEEN."

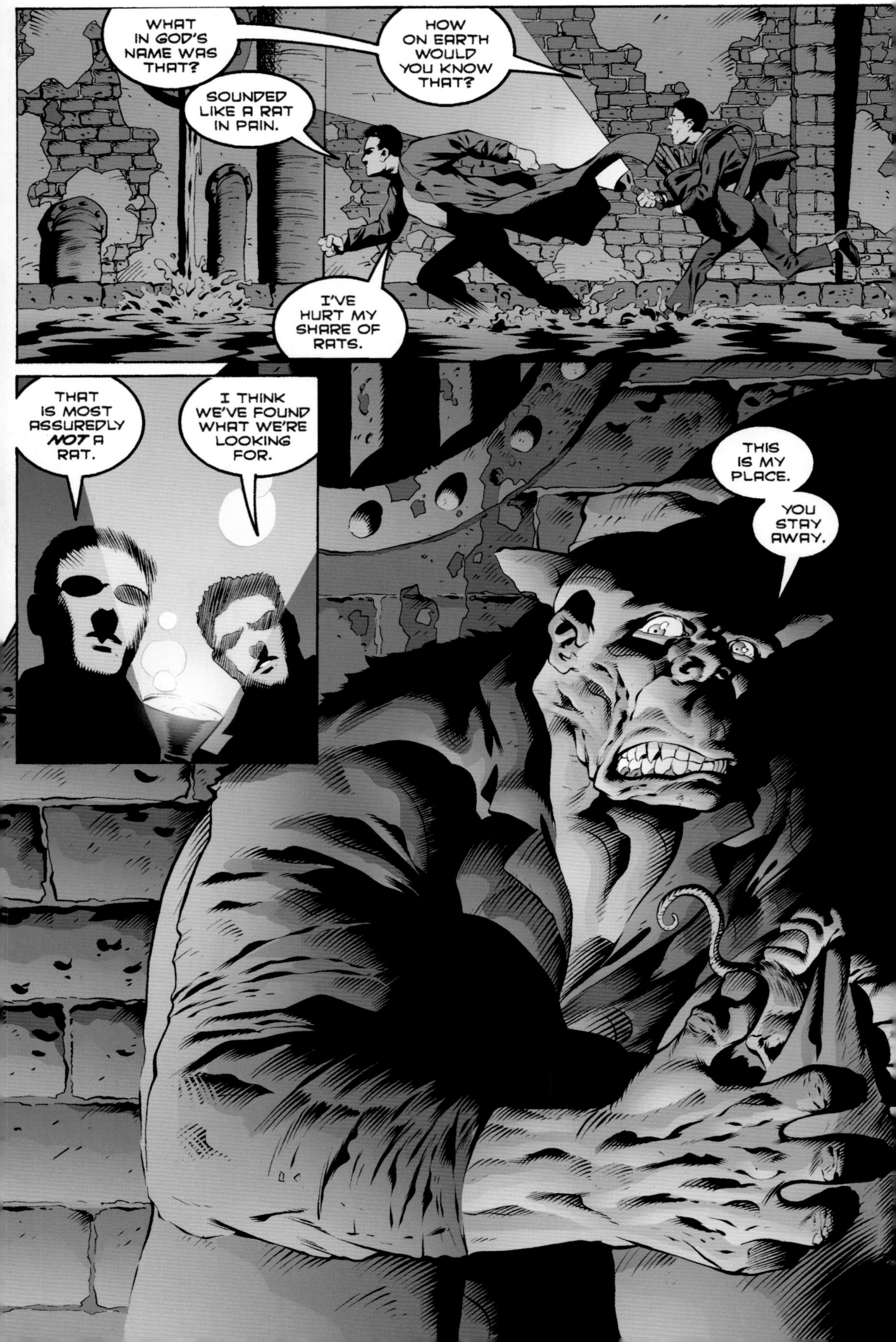
WHAT IN GOD'S NAME WAS THAT?
SOUNDED LIKE A RAT IN PAIN.
HOW ON EARTH WOULD YOU KNOW THAT?
I'VE HURT MY SHARE OF RATS.
THAT IS MOST ASSUREDLY NOT A RAT.
I THINK WE'VE FOUND WHAT WE'RE LOOKING FOR.
THIS IS MY PLACE.
YOU STAY AWAY.

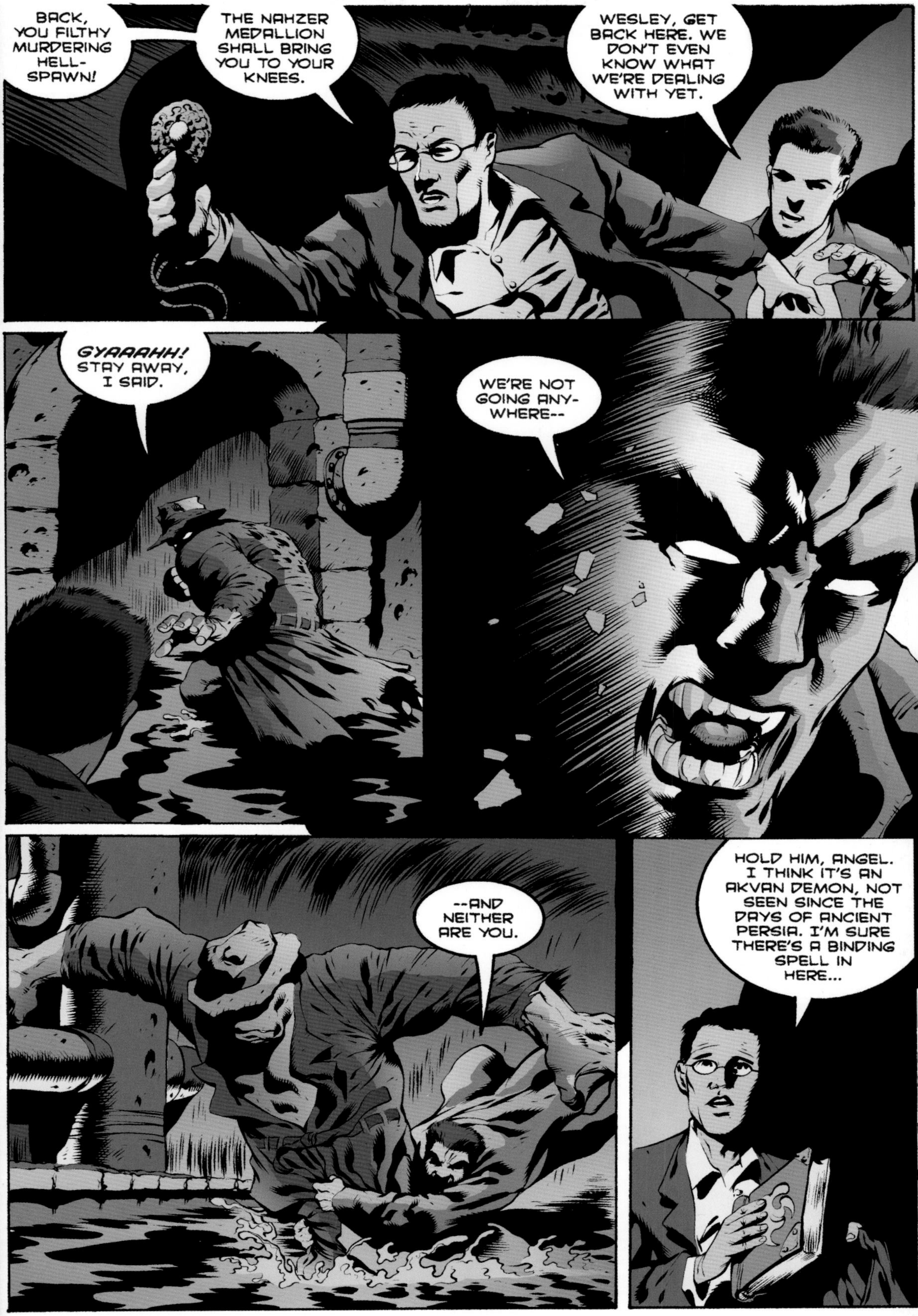
BACK, YOU FILTHY MURDERING HELL-SPAWN!
THE NAHZER MEDALLION SHALL BRING YOU TO YOUR KNEES.
WESLEY, GET BACK HERE. WE DON'T EVEN KNOW WHAT WE'RE DEALING WITH YET.
GYAAAHH! STAY AWAY, I SAID.
WE'RE NOT GOING ANY-WHERE--
--AND NEITHER ARE YOU.
HOLD HIM, ANGEL. I THINK IT'S AN AKVAN DEMON, NOT SEEN SINCE THE DAYS OF ANCIENT PERSIA. I'M SURE THERE'S A BINDING SPELL IN HERE...

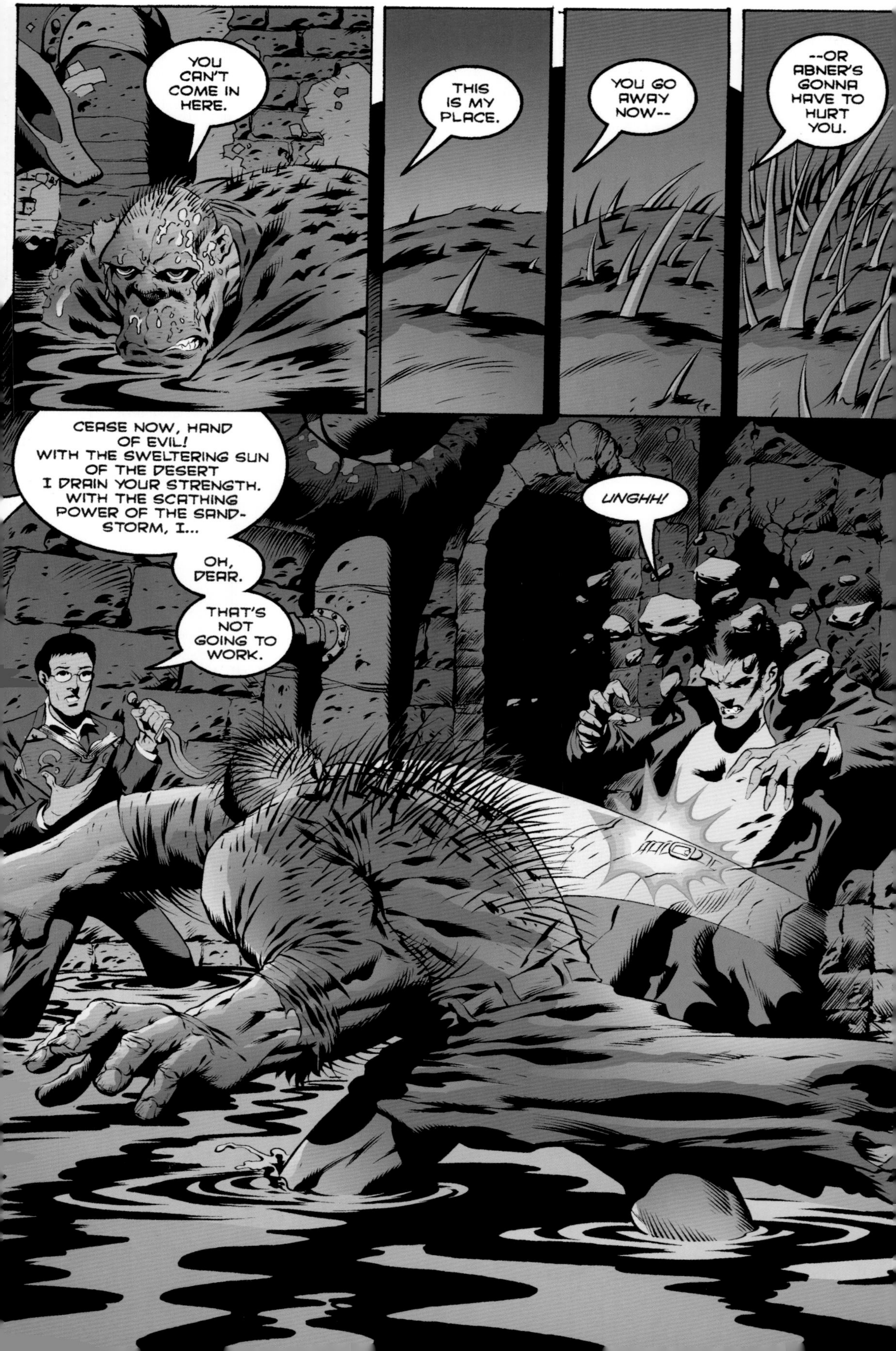
YOU CAN'T COME IN HERE.
THIS IS MY PLACE.
YOU GO AWAY NOW--
--OR ABNER'S GONNA HAVE TO HURT YOU.
CEASE NOW, HAND OF EVIL! WITH THE SWELTERING SUN OF THE DESERT I DRAIN YOUR STRENGTH. WITH THE SCATHING POWER OF THE SAND-STORM, I...
OH, DEAR.
THAT'S NOT GOING TO WORK.
UNGHH!

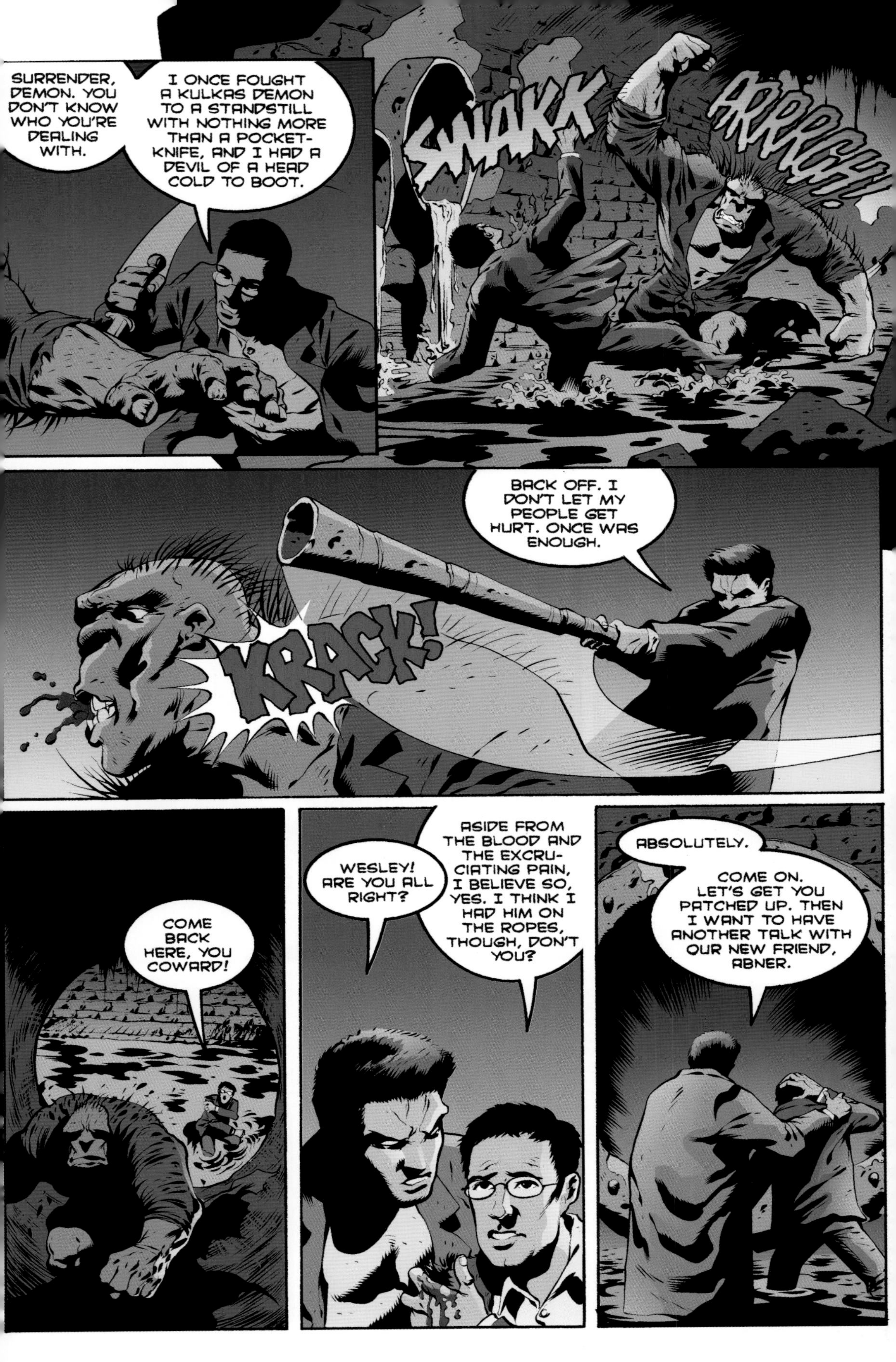
SURRENDER, DEMON. YOU DON'T KNOW WHO YOU'RE DEALING WITH.
I ONCE FOUGHT A KULKAS DEMON TO A STANDSTILL WITH NOTHING MORE THAN A POCKET-KNIFE, AND I HAD A DEVIL OF A HEAD COLD TO BOOT.
SWAKK
ARRRGH!
BACK OFF. I DON'T LET MY PEOPLE GET HURT. ONCE WAS ENOUGH.
KRACK!
COME BACK HERE, YOU COWARD!
WESLEY! ARE YOU ALL RIGHT?
ASIDE FROM THE BLOOD AND THE EXCRUCIATING PAIN, I BELIEVE SO, YES. I THINK I HAD HIM ON THE ROPES, THOUGH, DON'T YOU?
ABSOLUTELY.
COME ON. LET'S GET YOU PATCHED UP. THEN I WANT TO HAVE ANOTHER TALK WITH OUR NEW FRIEND, ABNER.

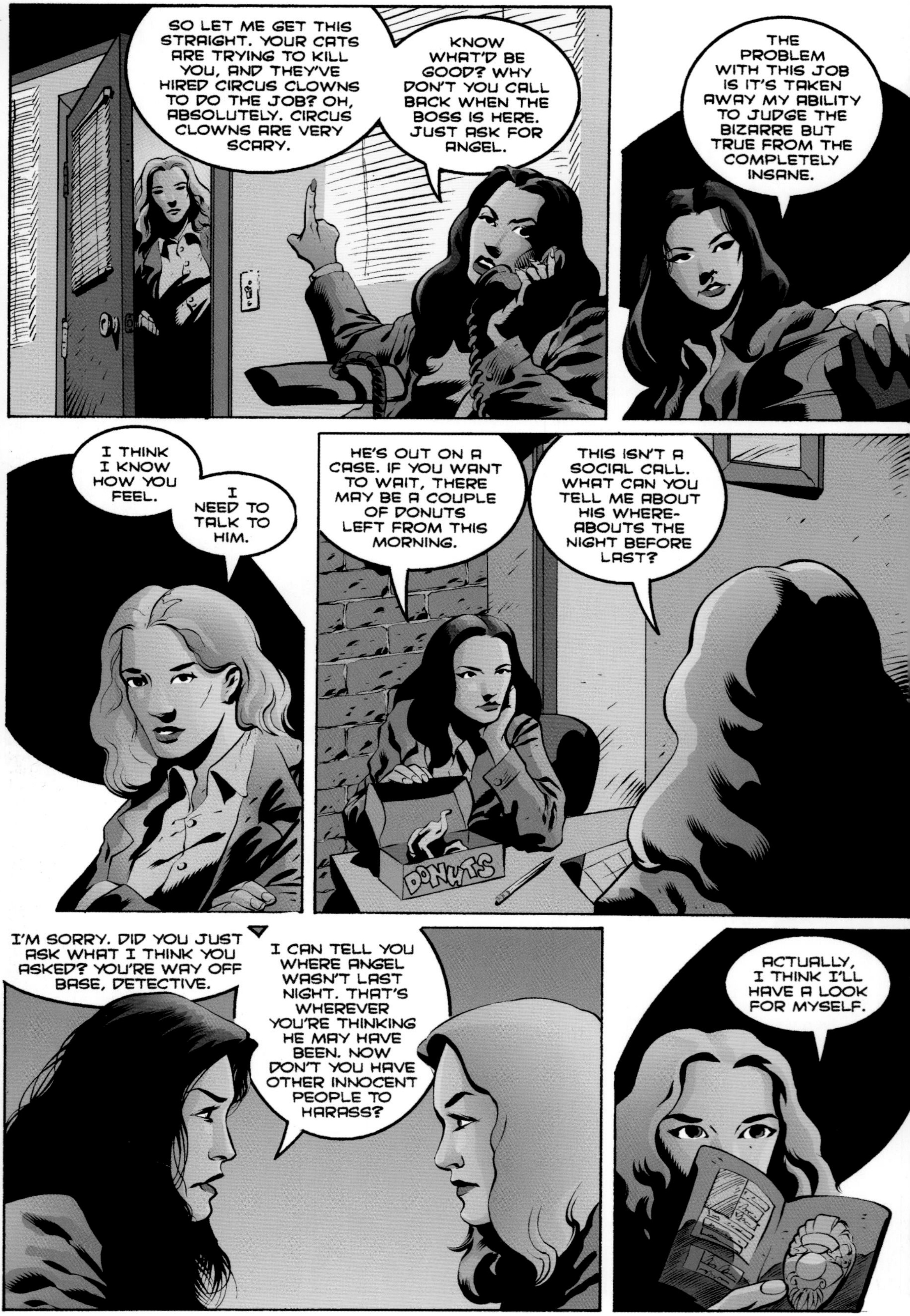
SO LET ME GET THIS STRAIGHT. YOUR CATS ARE TRYING TO KILL YOU, AND THEY'VE HIRED CIRCUS CLOWNS TO DO THE JOB? OH, ABSOLUTELY. CIRCUS CLOWNS ARE VERY SCARY.
KNOW WHAT'D BE GOOD? WHY DON'T YOU CALL BACK WHEN THE BOSS IS HERE. JUST ASK FOR ANGEL.
THE PROBLEM WITH THIS JOB IS IT'S TAKEN AWAY MY ABILITY TO JUDGE THE BIZARRE BUT TRUE FROM THE COMPLETELY INSANE.
I THINK I KNOW HOW YOU FEEL.
I NEED TO TALK TO HIM.
HE'S OUT ON A CASE. IF YOU WANT TO WAIT, THERE MAY BE A COUPLE OF DONUTS LEFT FROM THIS MORNING.
DONUTS
THIS ISN'T A SOCIAL CALL. WHAT CAN YOU TELL ME ABOUT HIS WHERE-ABOUTS THE NIGHT BEFORE LAST?
I'M SORRY. DID YOU JUST ASK WHAT I THINK YOU ASKED? YOU'RE WAY OFF BASE, DETECTIVE.
I CAN TELL YOU WHERE ANGEL WASN'T LAST NIGHT. THAT'S WHEREVER YOU'RE THINKING HE MAY HAVE BEEN. NOW DON'T YOU HAVE OTHER INNOCENT PEOPLE TO HARASS?
ACTUALLY, I THINK I'LL HAVE A LOOK FOR MYSELF.

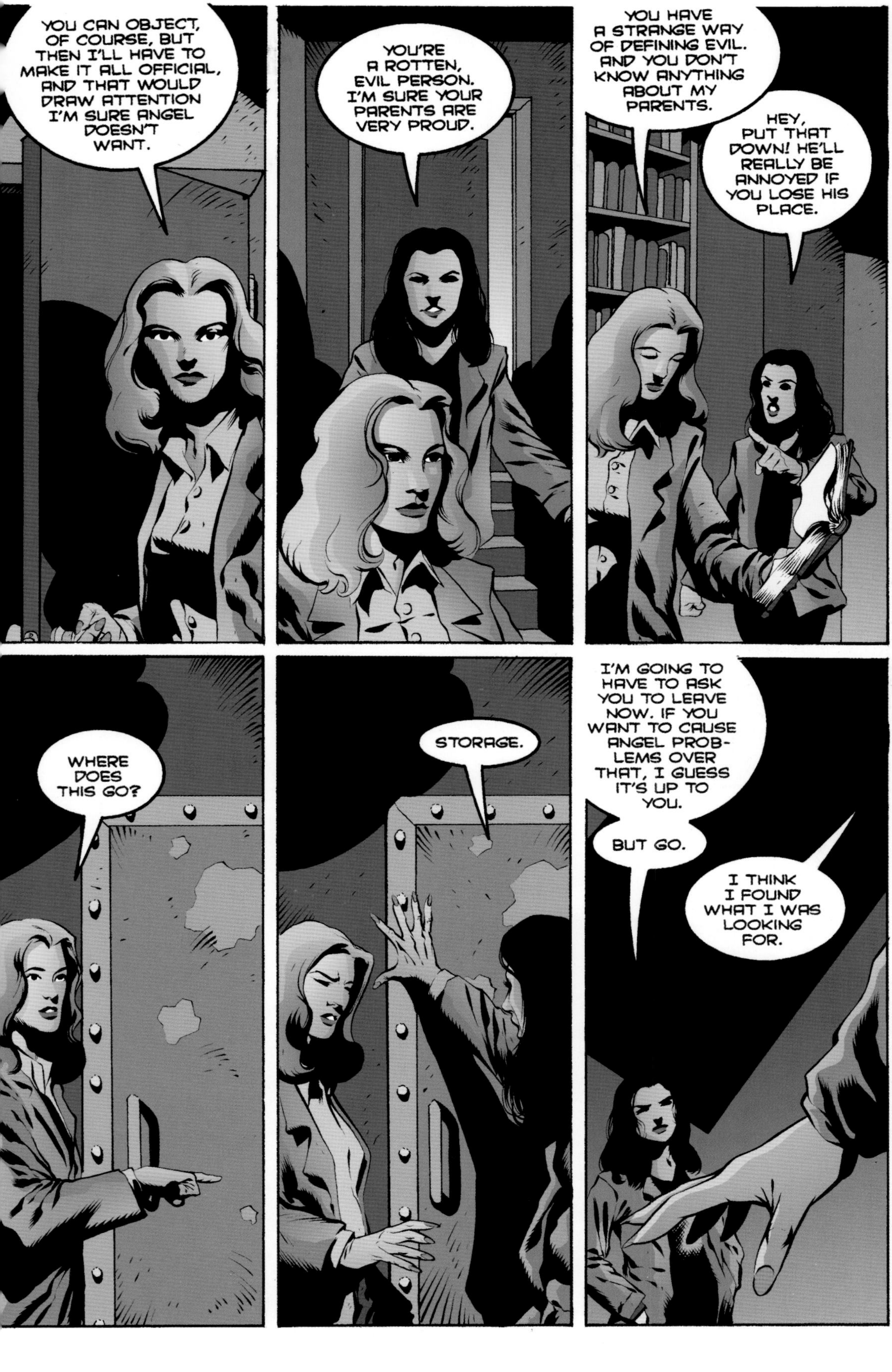
YOU CAN OBJECT, OF COURSE, BUT THEN I'LL HAVE TO MAKE IT ALL OFFICIAL, AND THAT WOULD DRAW ATTENTION I'M SURE ANGEL DOESN'T WANT.
YOU'RE A ROTTEN, EVIL PERSON. I'M SURE YOUR PARENTS ARE VERY PROUD.
YOU HAVE A STRANGE WAY OF DEFINING EVIL. AND YOU DON'T KNOW ANYTHING ABOUT MY PARENTS.
HEY, PUT THAT DOWN! HE'LL REALLY BE ANNOYED IF YOU LOSE HIS PLACE.
WHERE DOES THIS GO?
STORAGE.
I'M GOING TO HAVE TO ASK YOU TO LEAVE NOW. IF YOU WANT TO CAUSE ANGEL PROB-LEMS OVER THAT, I GUESS IT'S UP TO YOU.
BUT GO.
I THINK I FOUND WHAT I WAS LOOKING FOR.

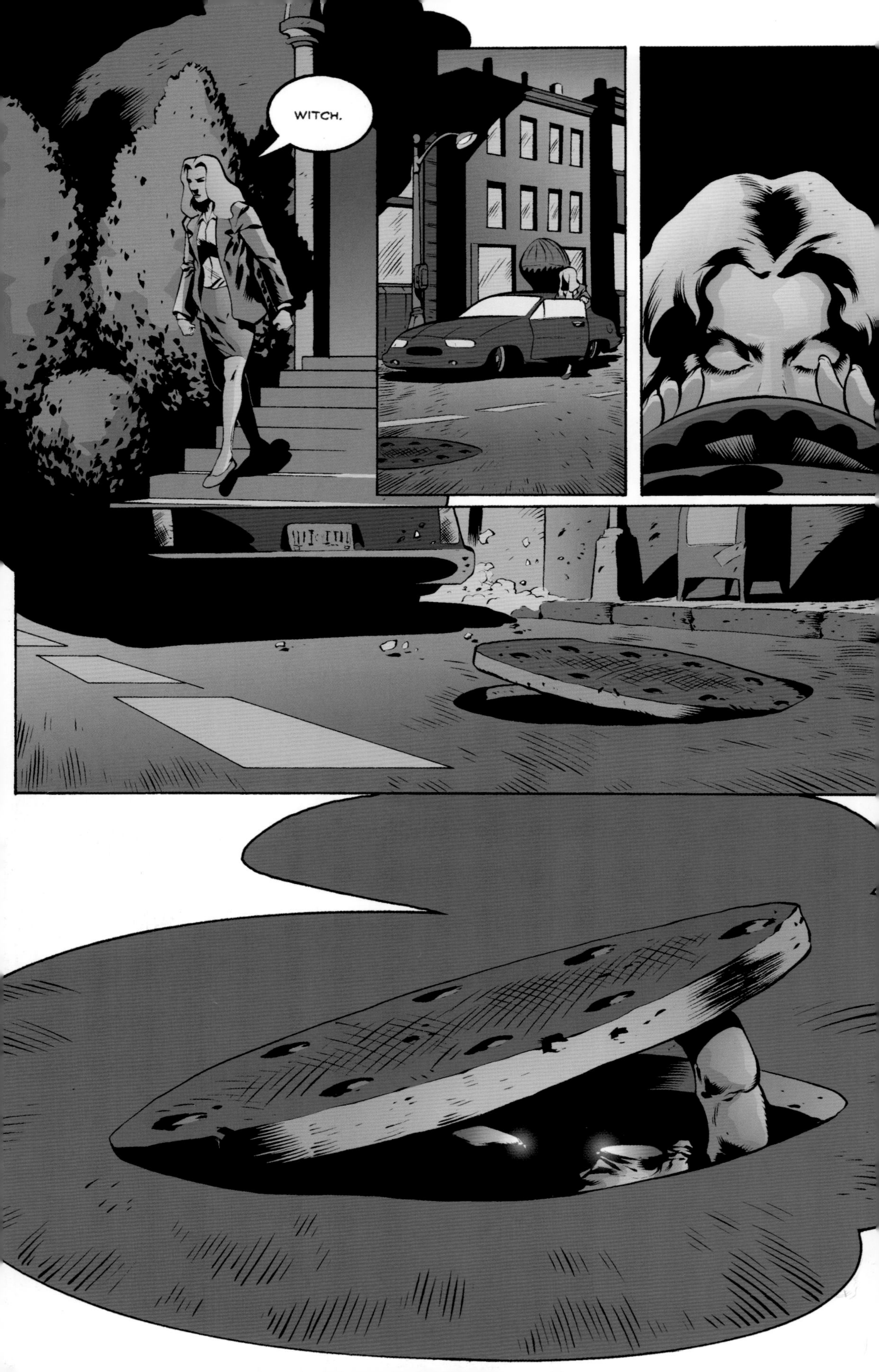
WITCH.

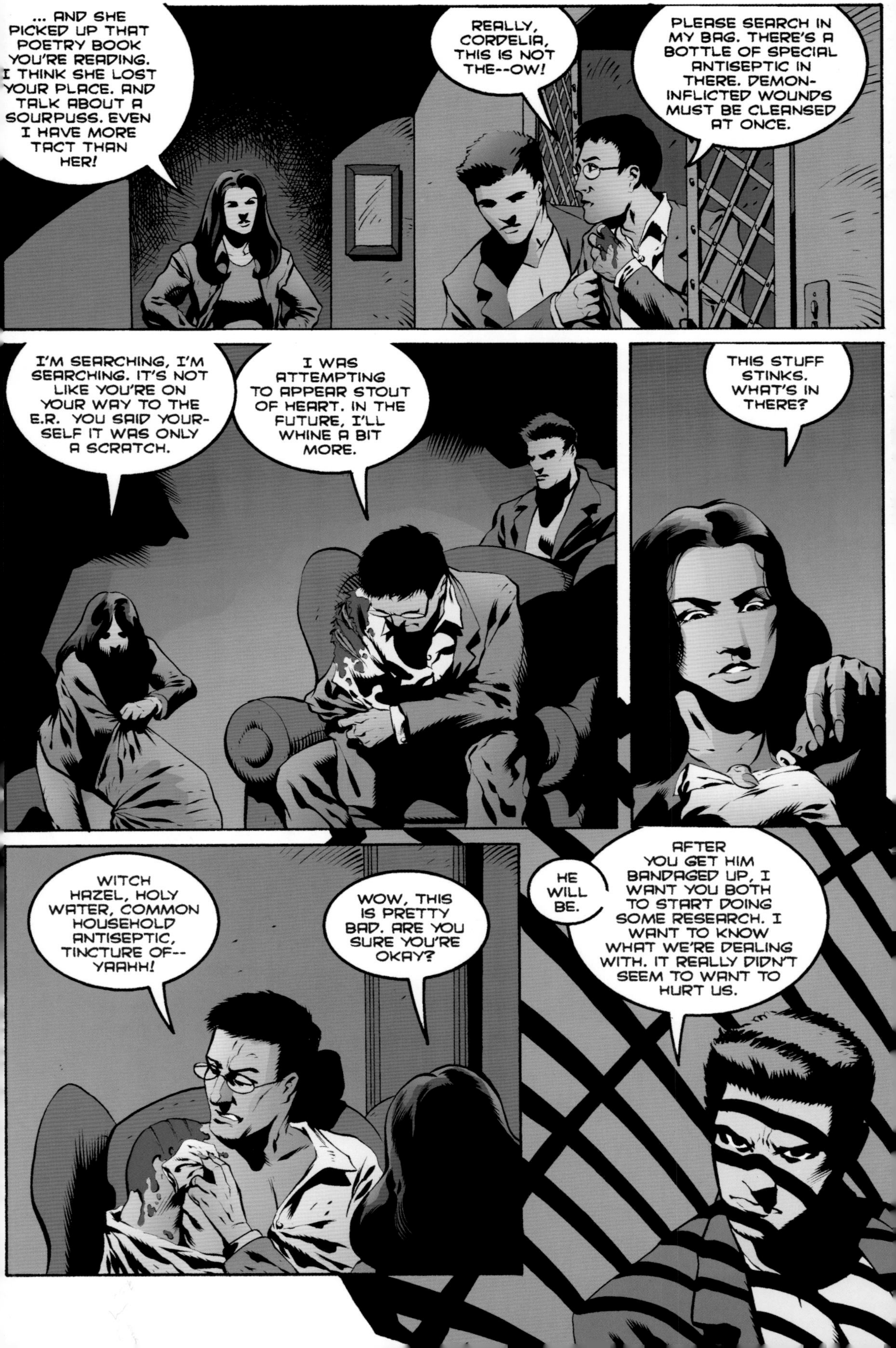
... AND SHE PICKED UP THAT POETRY BOOK YOU'RE READING. I THINK SHE LOST YOUR PLACE. AND TALK ABOUT A SOURPUSS. EVEN I HAVE MORE TACT THAN HER!
REALLY, CORDELIA, THIS IS NOT THE--OW!
PLEASE SEARCH IN MY BAG. THERE'S A BOTTLE OF SPECIAL ANTISEPTIC IN THERE. DEMON-INFLICTED WOUNDS MUST BE CLEANSED AT ONCE.
I'M SEARCHING, I'M SEARCHING. IT'S NOT LIKE YOU'RE ON YOUR WAY TO THE E.R. YOU SAID YOURSELF IT WAS ONLY A SCRATCH.
I WAS ATTEMPTING TO APPEAR STOUT OF HEART. IN THE FUTURE, I'LL WHINE A BIT MORE.
THIS STUFF STINKS. WHAT'S IN THERE?
WITCH HAZEL, HOLY WATER, COMMON HOUSEHOLD ANTISEPTIC, TINCTURE OF-- YAAHH!
WOW, THIS IS PRETTY BAD. ARE YOU SURE YOU'RE OKAY?
HE WILL BE.
AFTER YOU GET HIM BANDAGED UP, I WANT YOU BOTH TO START DOING SOME RESEARCH. I WANT TO KNOW WHAT WE'RE DEALING WITH. IT REALLY DIDN'T SEEM TO WANT TO HURT US.

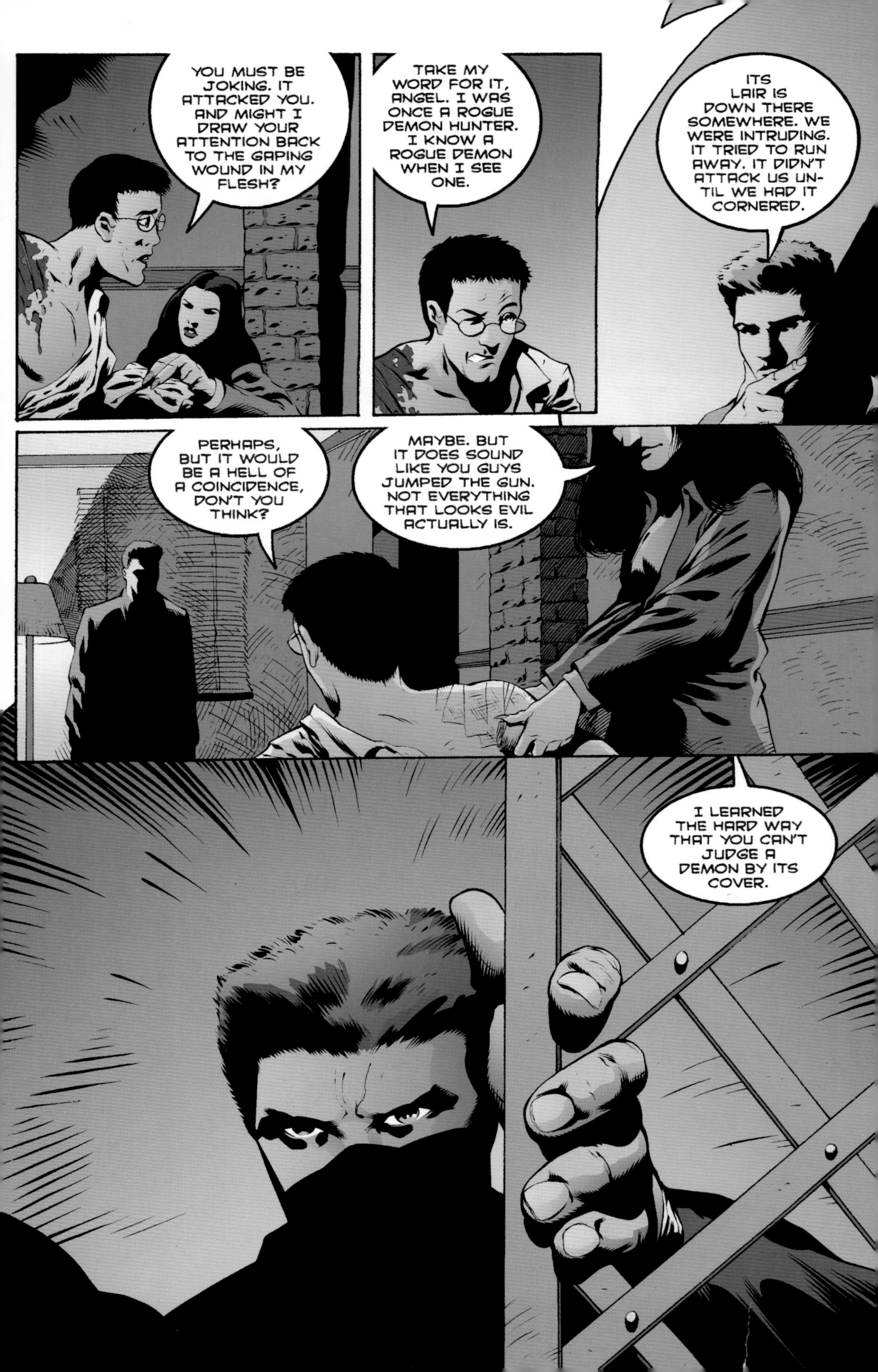
YOU MUST BE JOKING. IT ATTACKED YOU. AND MIGHT I DRAW YOUR ATTENTION BACK TO THE GAPING WOUND IN MY FLESH?
TAKE MY WORD FOR IT, ANGEL. I WAS ONCE A ROGUE DEMON HUNTER. I KNOW A ROGUE DEMON WHEN I SEE ONE.
ITS LAIR IS DOWN THERE SOMEWHERE. WE WERE INTRUDING. IT TRIED TO RUN AWAY. IT DIDN'T ATTACK US UN-TIL WE HAD IT CORNERED.
PERHAPS, BUT IT WOULD BE A HELL OF A COINCIDENCE, DON'T YOU THINK?
MAYBE. BUT IT DOES SOUND LIKE YOU GUYS JUMPED THE GUN. NOT EVERYTHING THAT LOOKS EVIL ACTUALLY IS.
I LEARNED THE HARD WAY THAT YOU CAN'T JUDGE A DEMON BY ITS COVER.

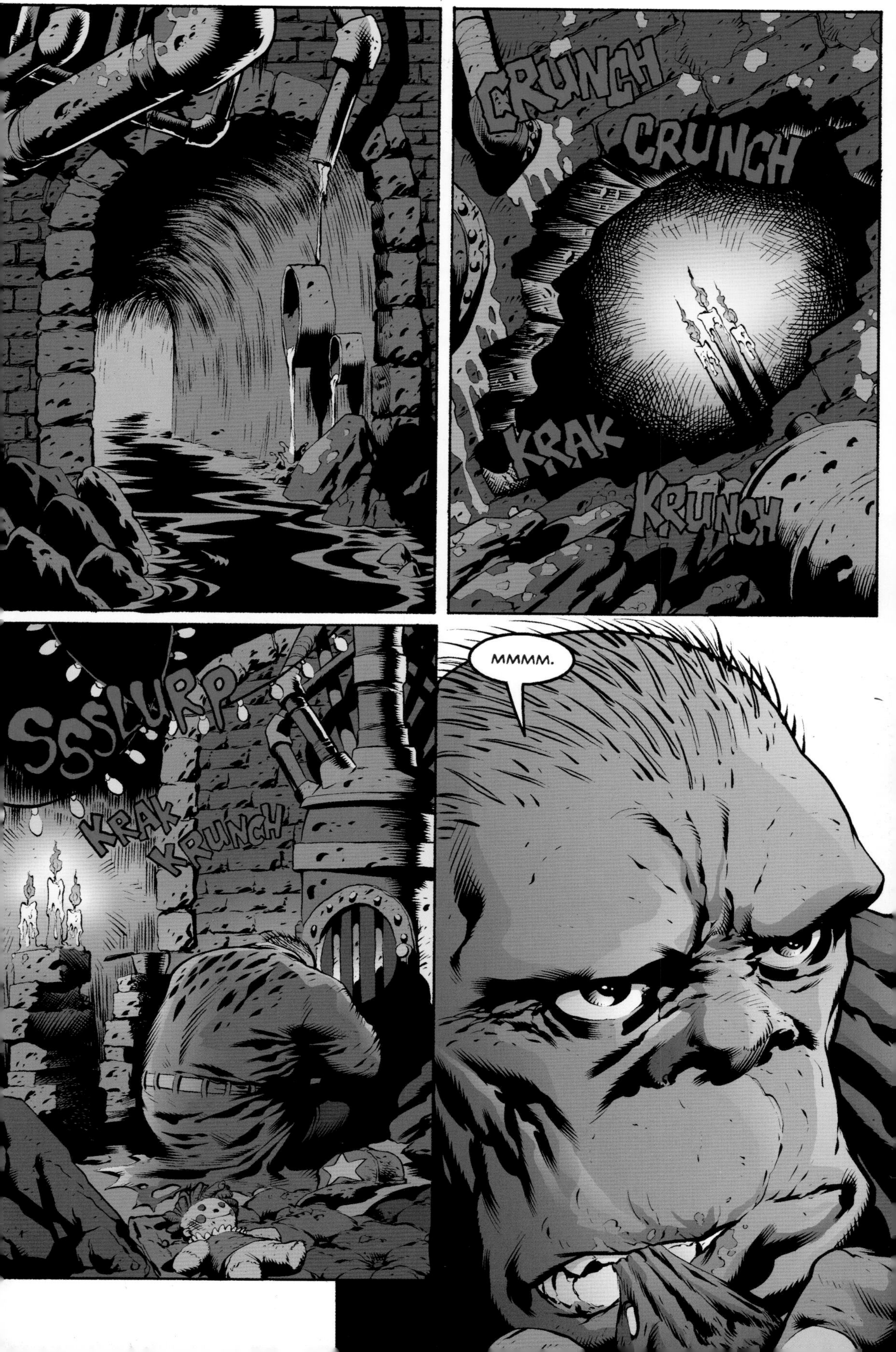
CRUNCH
CRUNCH
KRAK
KRUNCH
SSSLURP
KRAK
KRUNCH
MMMM.

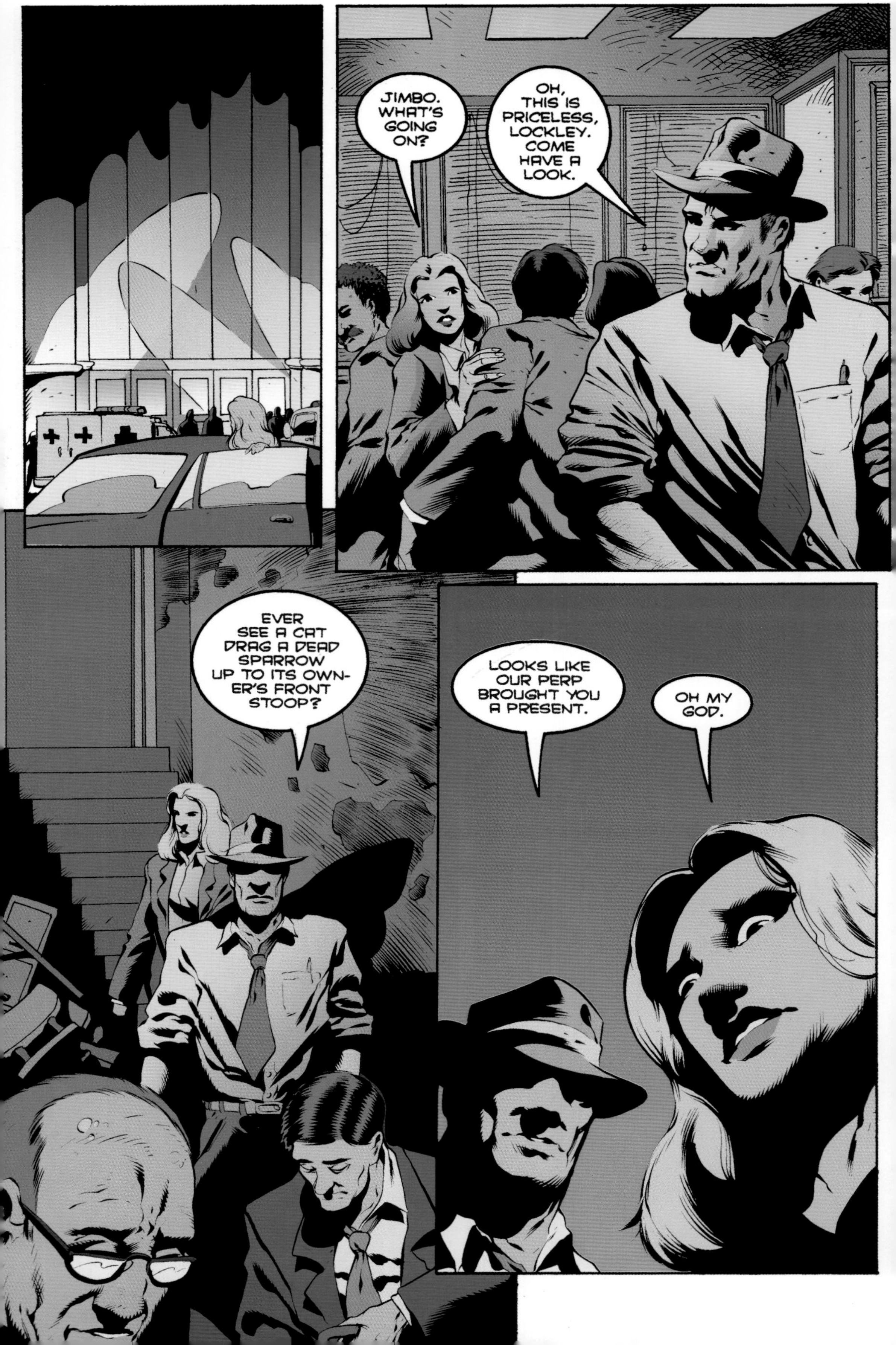
JIMBO. WHAT'S GOING ON?
OH, THIS IS PRICELESS, LOCKLEY. COME HAVE A LOOK.
EVER SEE A CAT DRAG A DEAD SPARROW UP TO ITS OWNER'S FRONT STOOP?
LOOKS LIKE OUR PERP BROUGHT YOU A PRESENT.
OH MY GOD.

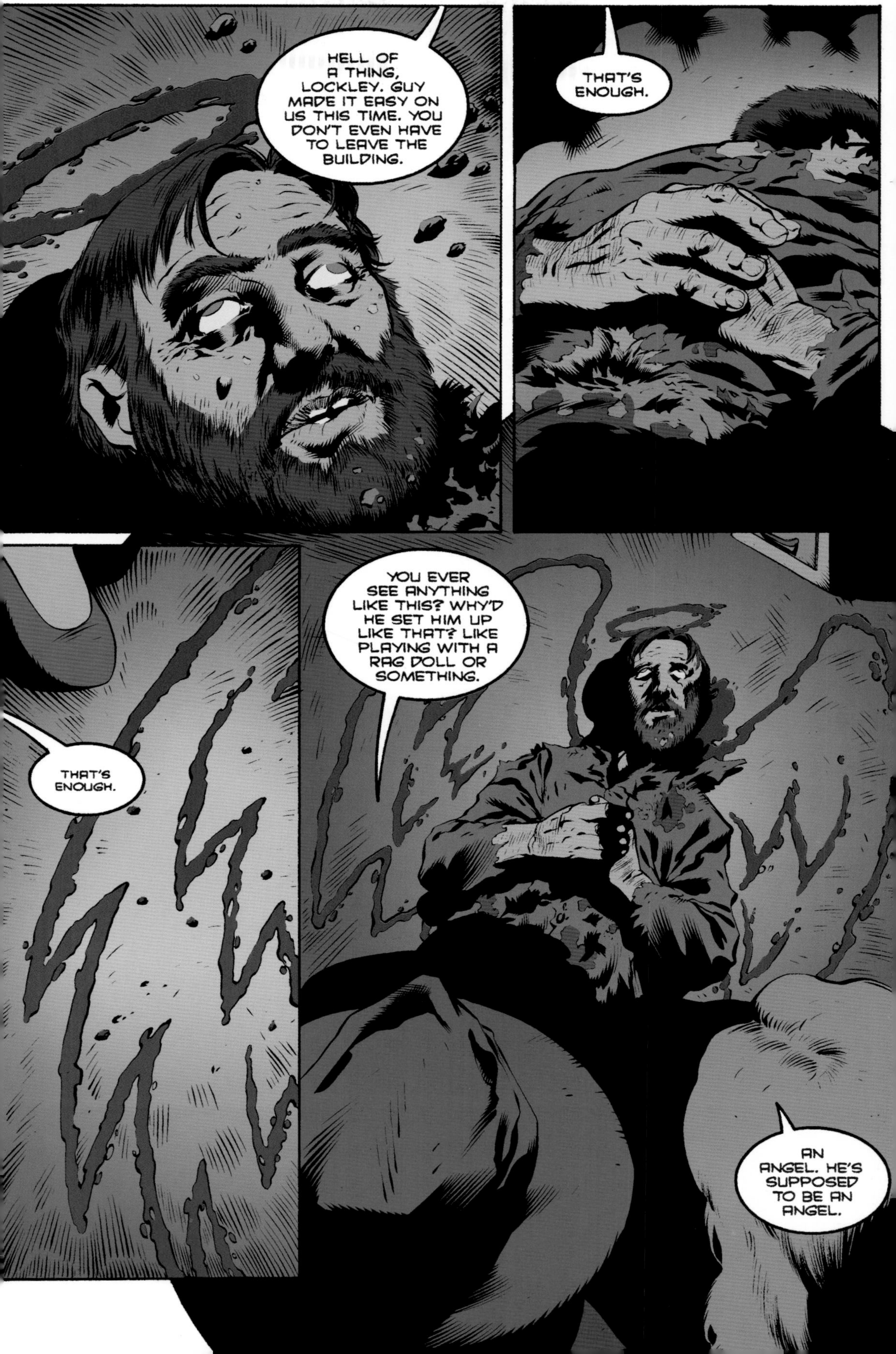
HELL OF A THING, LOCKLEY. GUY MADE IT EASY ON US THIS TIME. YOU DON'T EVEN HAVE TO LEAVE THE BUILDING.
THAT'S ENOUGH.
YOU EVER SEE ANYTHING LIKE THIS? WHY'D HE SET HIM UP LIKE THAT? LIKE PLAYING WITH A RAG DOLL OR SOMETHING.
THAT'S ENOUGH.
AN ANGEL. HE'S SUPPOSED TO BE AN ANGEL.

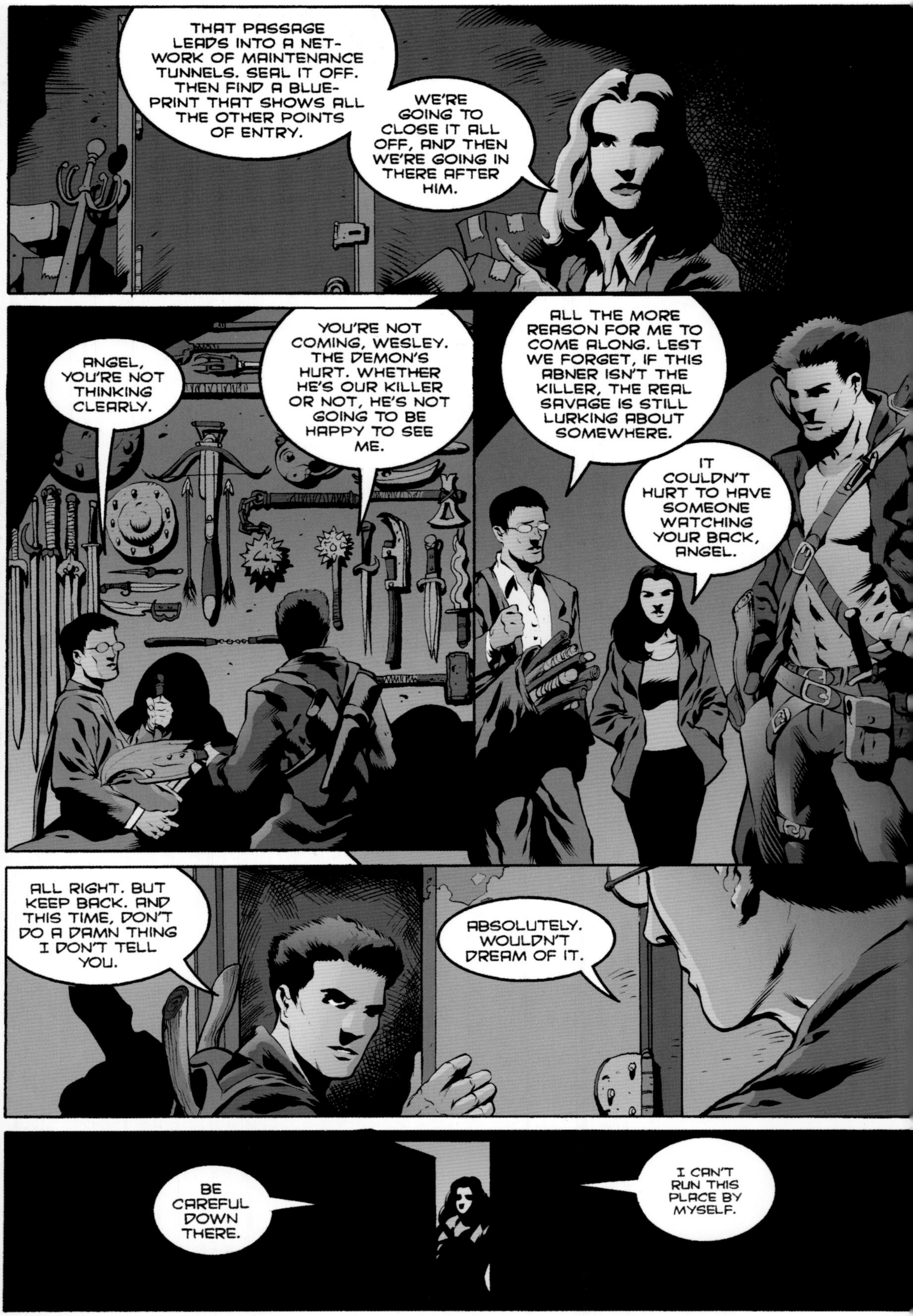
THAT PASSAGE LEADS INTO A NET-WORK OF MAINTENANCE TUNNELS. SEAL IT OFF. THEN FIND A BLUE-PRINT THAT SHOWS ALL THE OTHER POINTS OF ENTRY.
WE'RE GOING TO CLOSE IT ALL OFF, AND THEN WE'RE GOING IN THERE AFTER HIM.
ANGEL, YOU'RE NOT THINKING CLEARLY.
YOU'RE NOT COMING, WESLEY. THE DEMON'S HURT. WHETHER HE'S OUR KILLER OR NOT, HE'S NOT GOING TO BE HAPPY TO SEE ME.
ALL THE MORE REASON FOR ME TO COME ALONG. LEST WE FORGET, IF THIS ABNER ISN'T THE KILLER, THE REAL SAVAGE IS STILL LURKING ABOUT SOMEWHERE.
IT COULDN'T HURT TO HAVE SOMEONE WATCHING YOUR BACK, ANGEL.
ALL RIGHT. BUT KEEP BACK. AND THIS TIME, DON'T DO A DAMN THING I DON'T TELL YOU.
ABSOLUTELY. WOULDN'T DREAM OF IT.
BE CAREFUL DOWN THERE.
I CAN'T RUN THIS PLACE BY MYSELF.

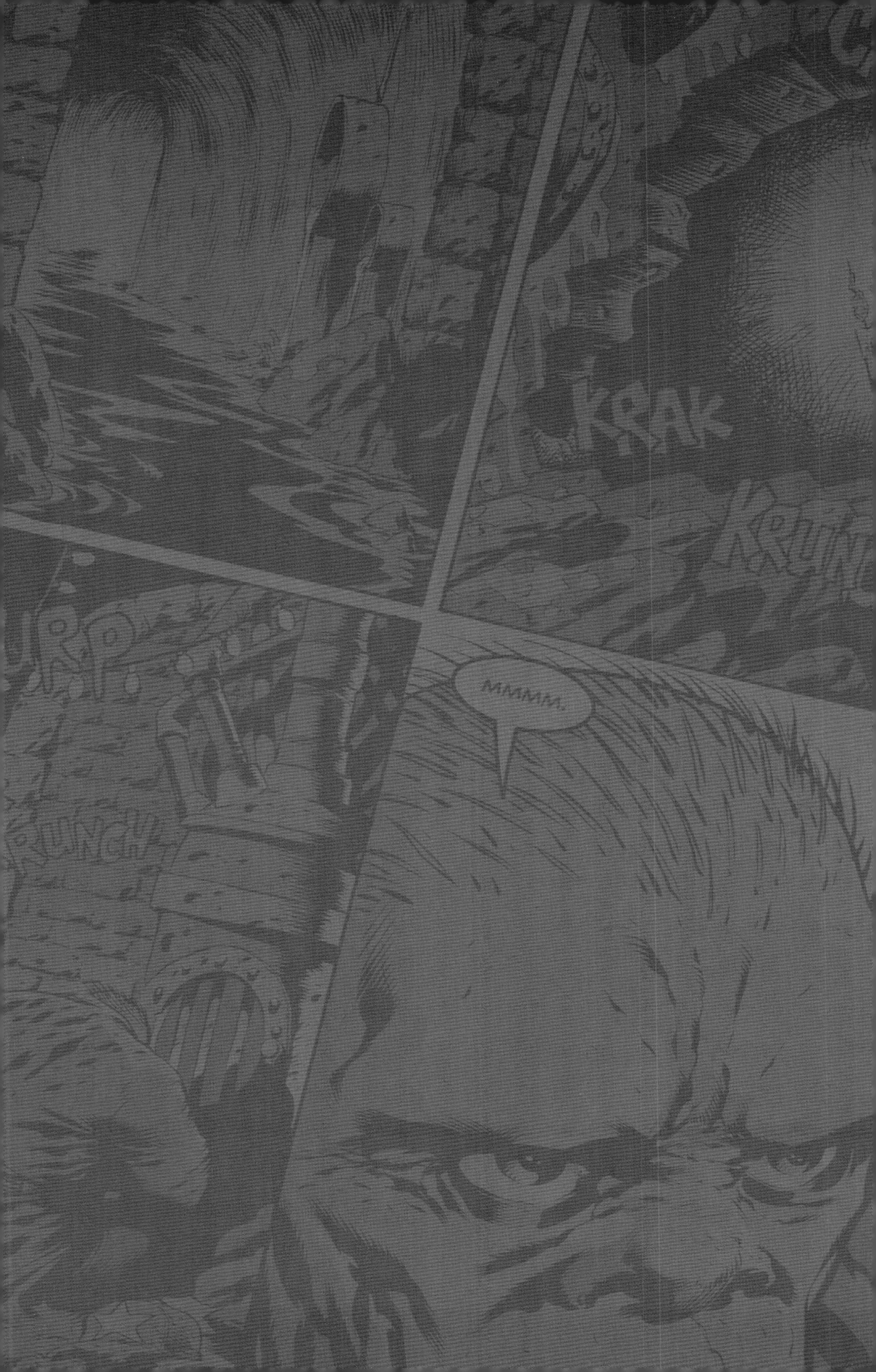
KRAK
MMMM.

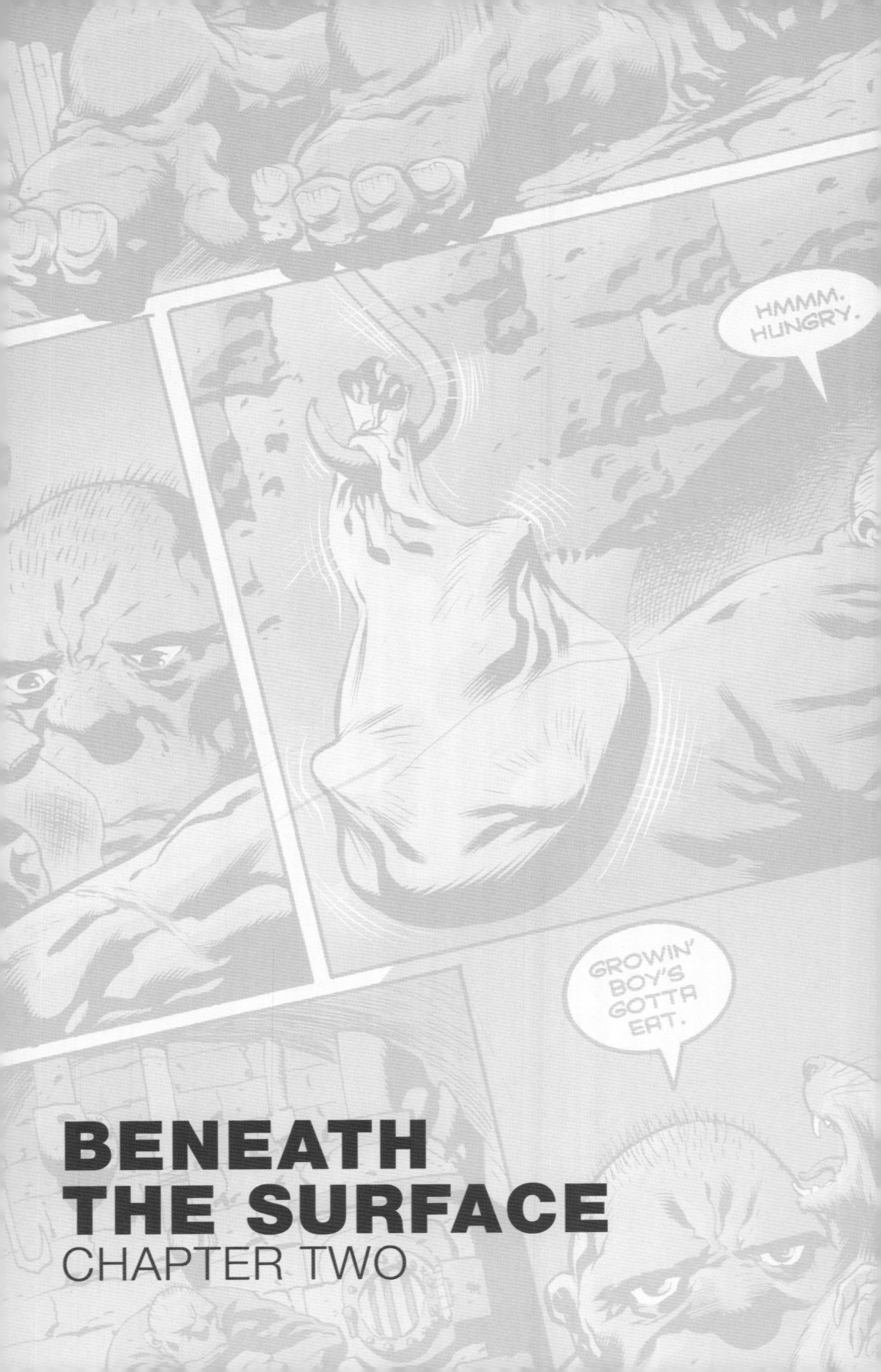
HMMM. HUNGRY.
GROWIN' BOY'S GOTTA EAT.

BENEATH THE SURFACE
CHAPTER TWO

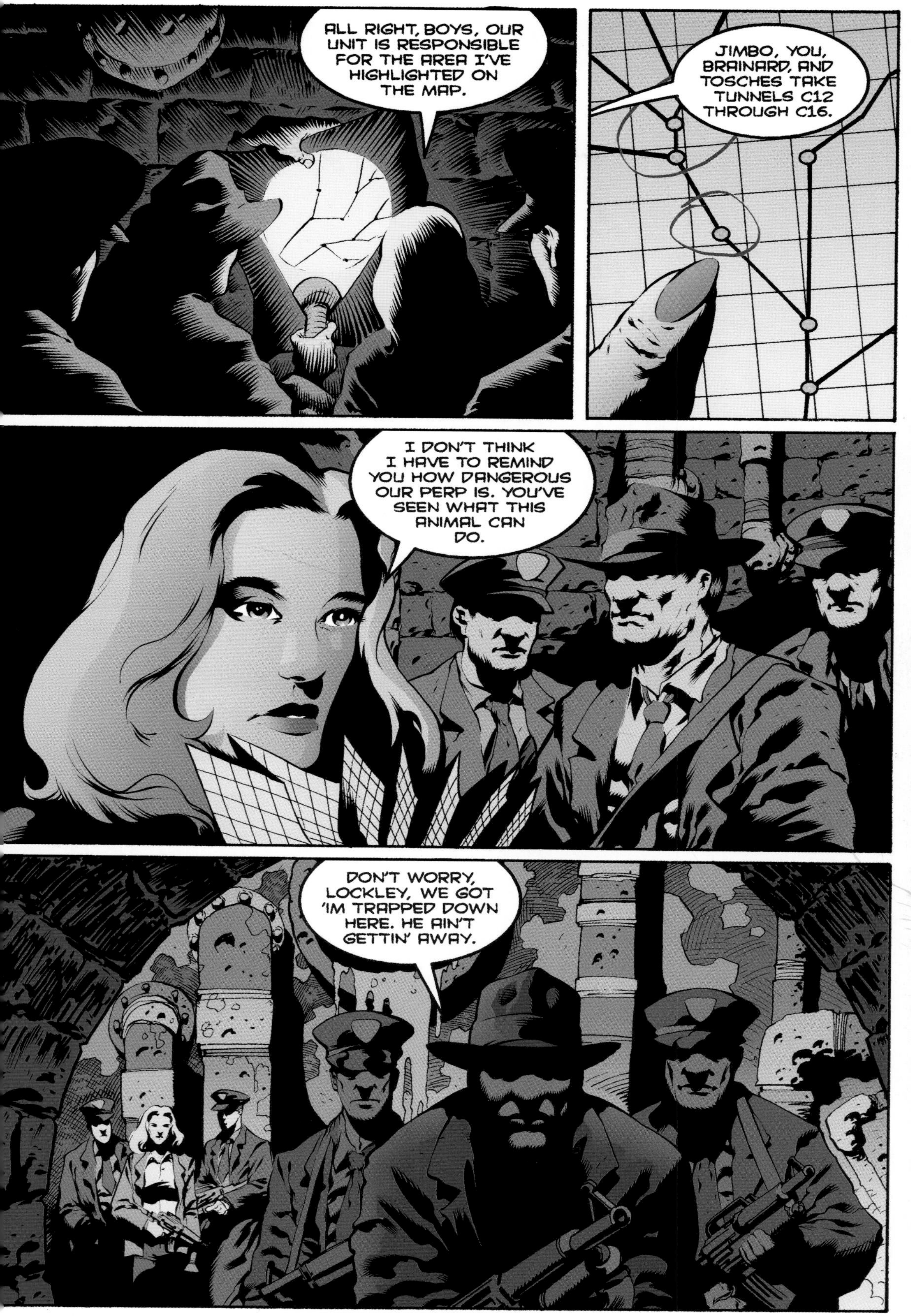
ALL RIGHT, BOYS, OUR UNIT IS RESPONSIBLE FOR THE AREA I'VE HIGHLIGHTED ON THE MAP.
JIMBO, YOU, BRAINARD, AND TOSCHES TAKE TUNNELS C12 THROUGH C16.
I DON'T THINK I HAVE TO REMIND YOU HOW DANGEROUS OUR PERP IS. YOU'VE SEEN WHAT THIS ANIMAL CAN DO.
DON'T WORRY, LOCKLEY, WE GOT 'IM TRAPPED DOWN HERE. HE AIN'T GETTIN' AWAY.

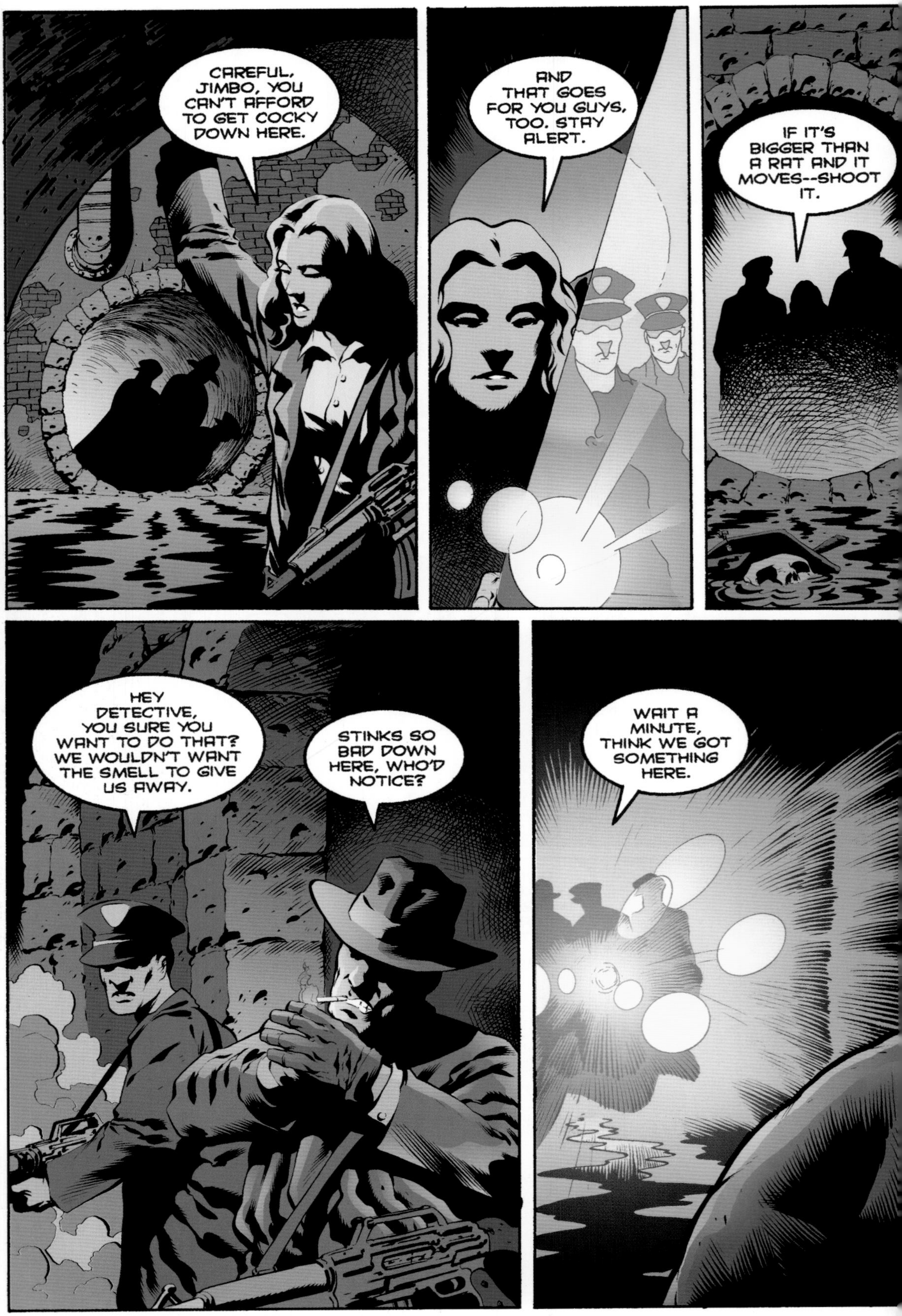
CAREFUL, JIMBO, YOU CAN'T AFFORD TO GET COCKY DOWN HERE.
AND THAT GOES FOR YOU GUYS, TOO. STAY ALERT.
IF IT'S BIGGER THAN A RAT AND IT MOVES--SHOOT IT.
HEY DETECTIVE, YOU SURE YOU WANT TO DO THAT? WE WOULDN'T WANT THE SMELL TO GIVE US AWAY.
STINKS SO BAD DOWN HERE, WHO'D NOTICE?
WAIT A MINUTE, THINK WE GOT SOMETHING HERE.

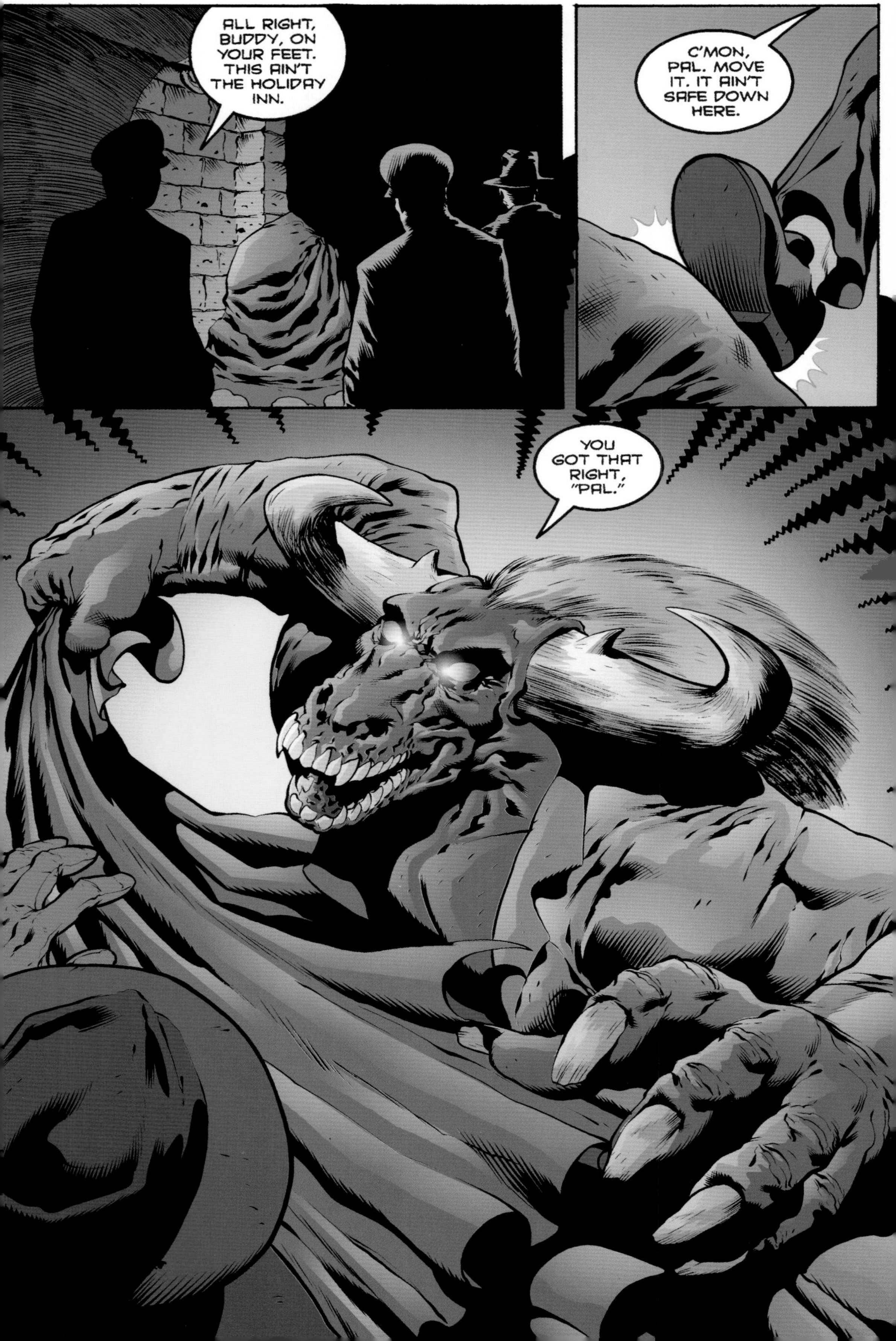
ALL RIGHT, BUDDY, ON YOUR FEET. THIS AIN'T THE HOLIDAY INN.
C'MON, PAL. MOVE IT. IT AIN'T SAFE DOWN HERE.
YOU GOT THAT RIGHT, "PAL."

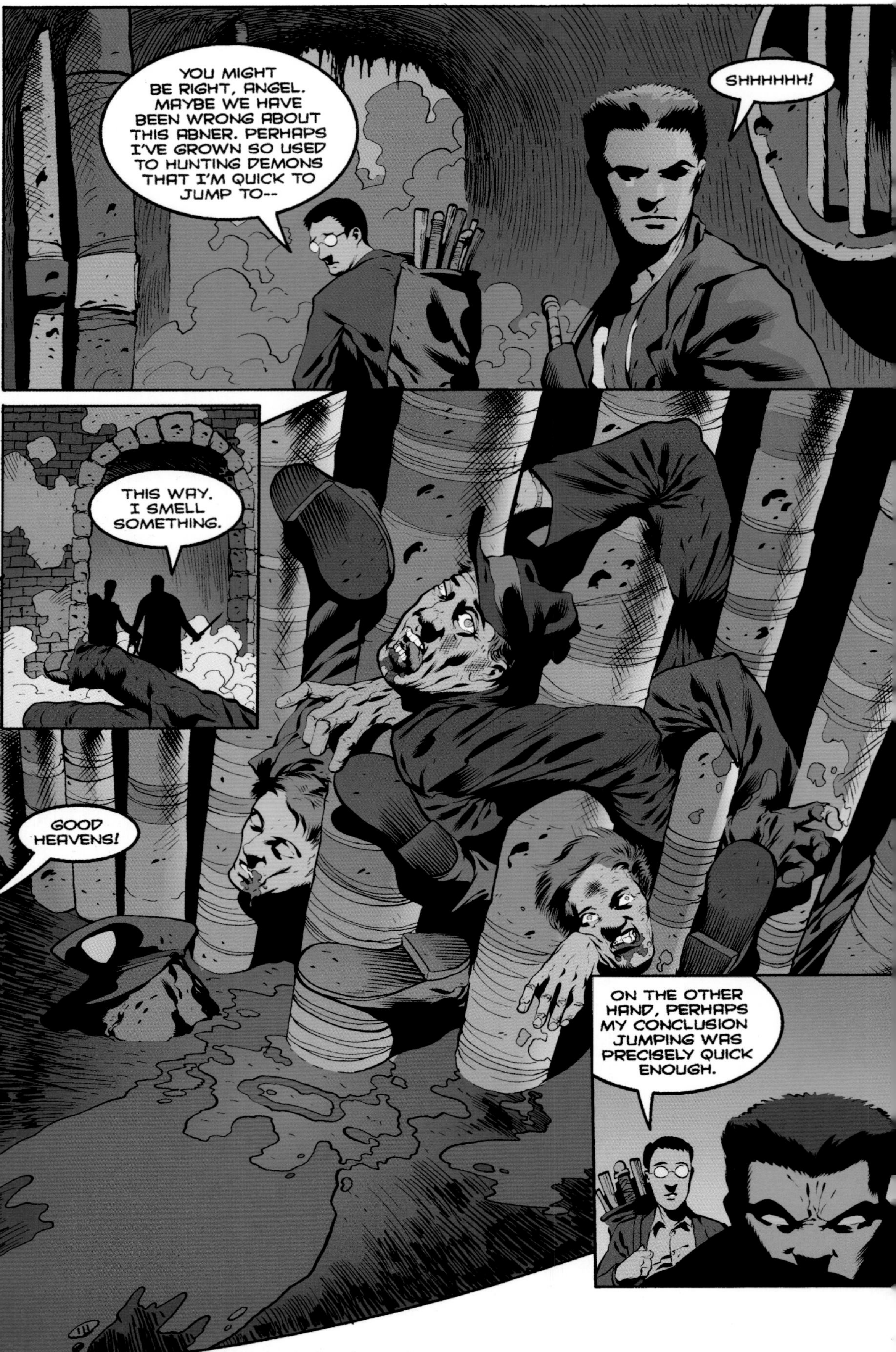
YOU MIGHT BE RIGHT, ANGEL. MAYBE WE HAVE BEEN WRONG ABOUT THIS ABNER. PERHAPS I'VE GROWN SO USED TO HUNTING DEMONS THAT I'M QUICK TO JUMP TO--
SHHHHHH!
THIS WAY. I SMELL SOMETHING.
GOOD HEAVENS!
ON THE OTHER HAND, PERHAPS MY CONCLUSION JUMPING WAS PRECISELY QUICK ENOUGH.

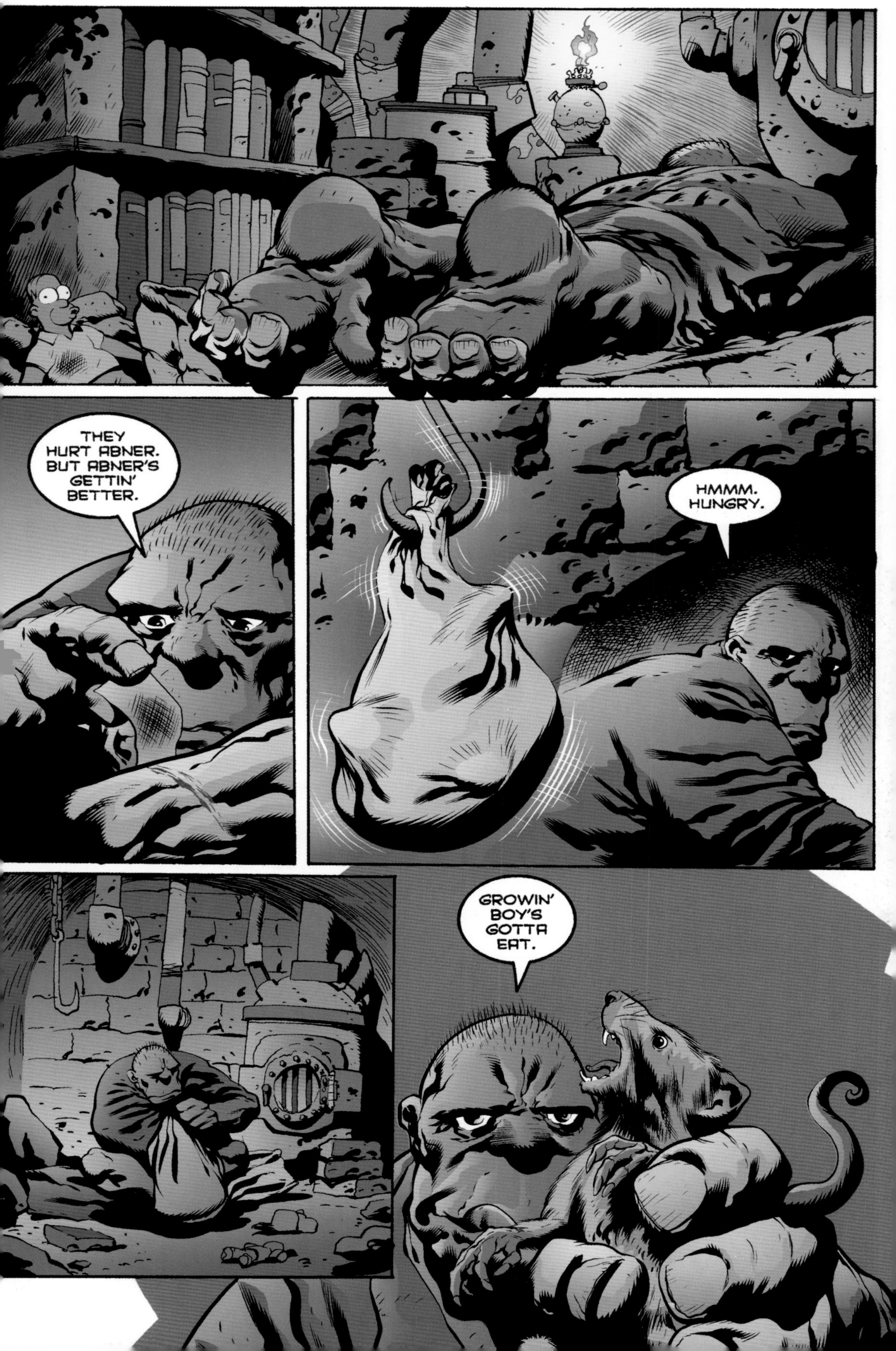
THEY HURT ABNER. BUT ABNER'S GETTIN' BETTER.
HMMM. HUNGRY.
GROWIN' BOY'S GOTTA EAT.

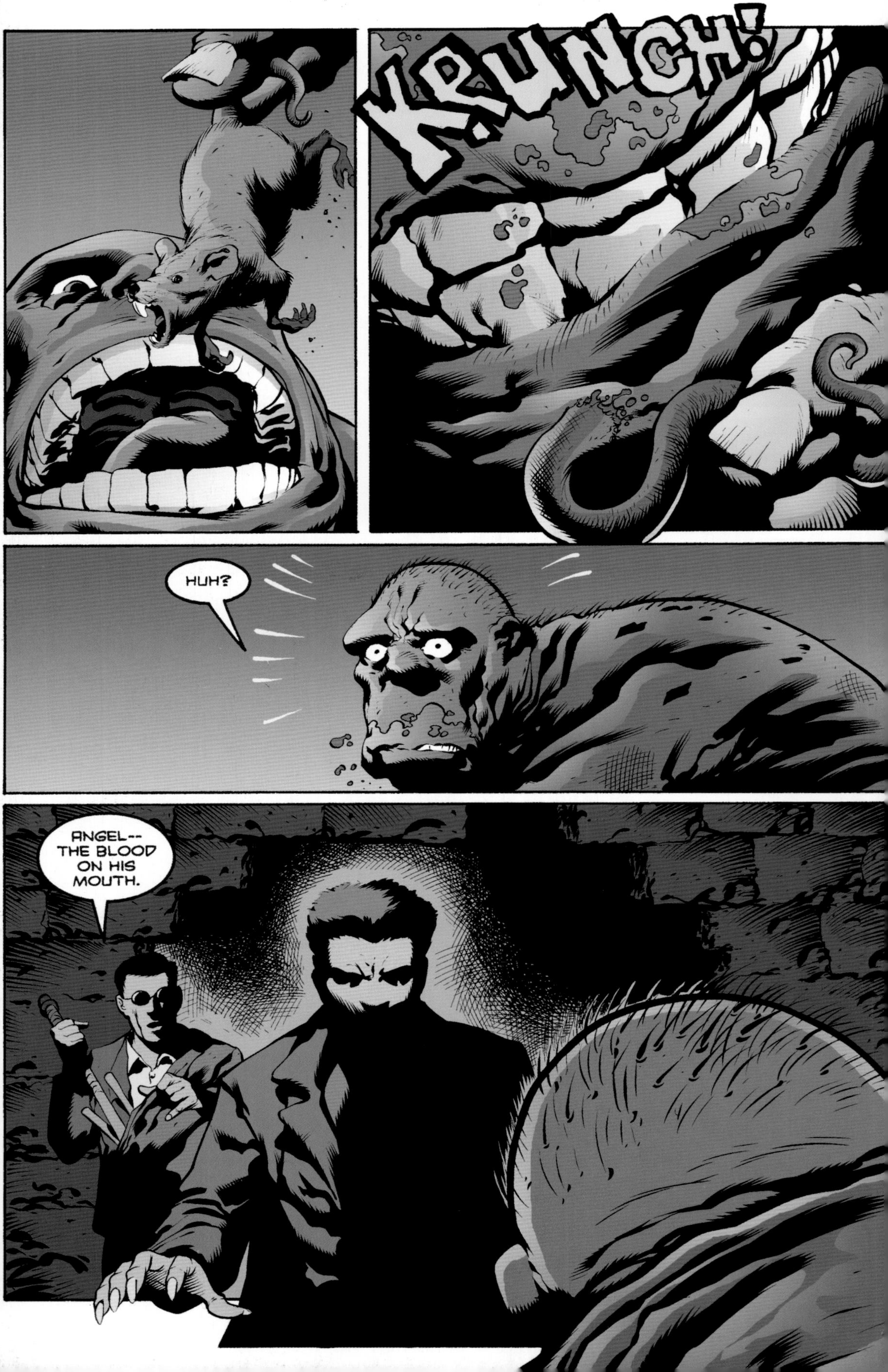
KRUNCH!
HUH?
ANGEL-- THE BLOOD ON HIS MOUTH.

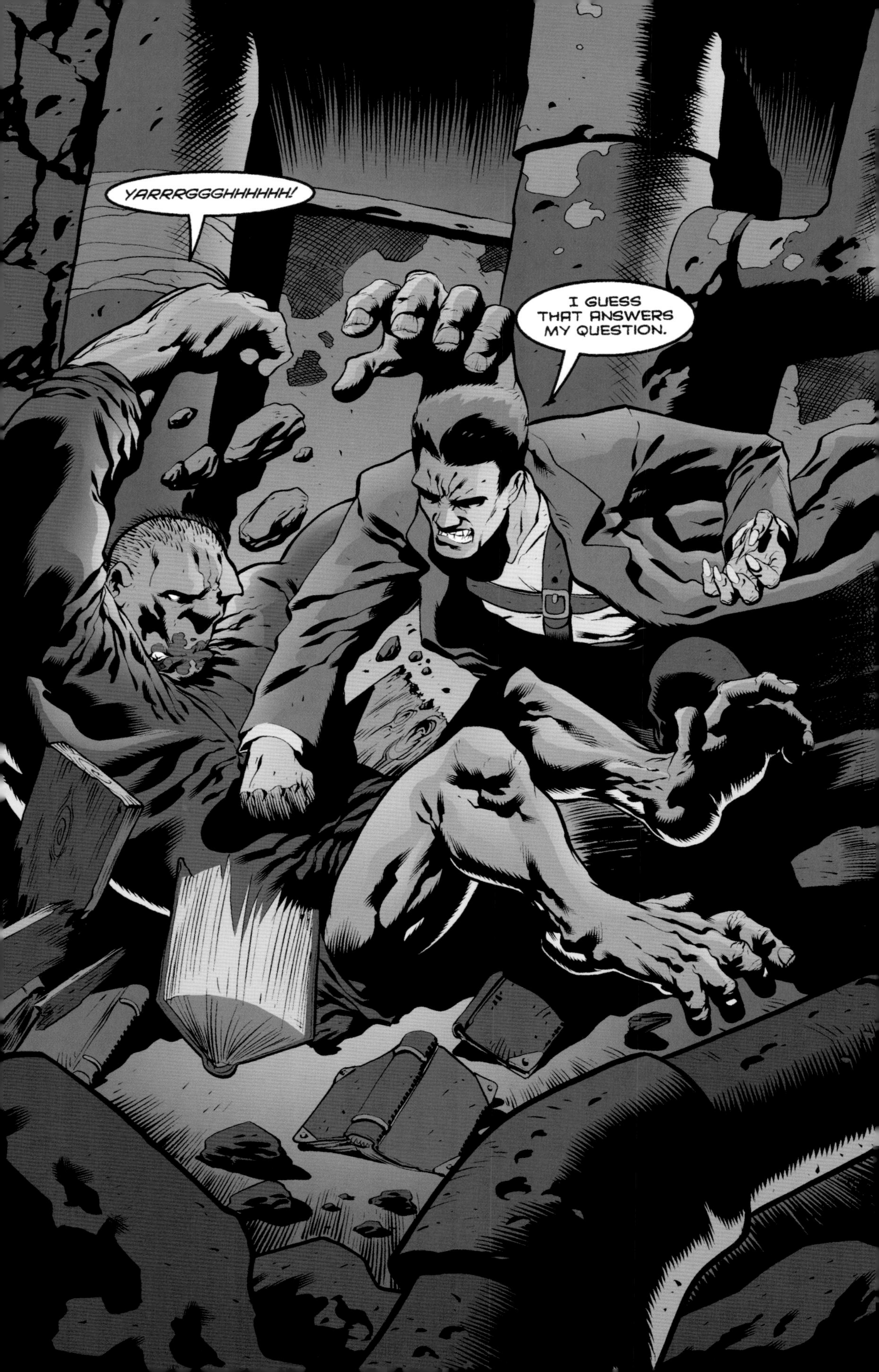
YARRRGGGHHHHHH!
I GUESS THAT ANSWERS MY QUESTION.

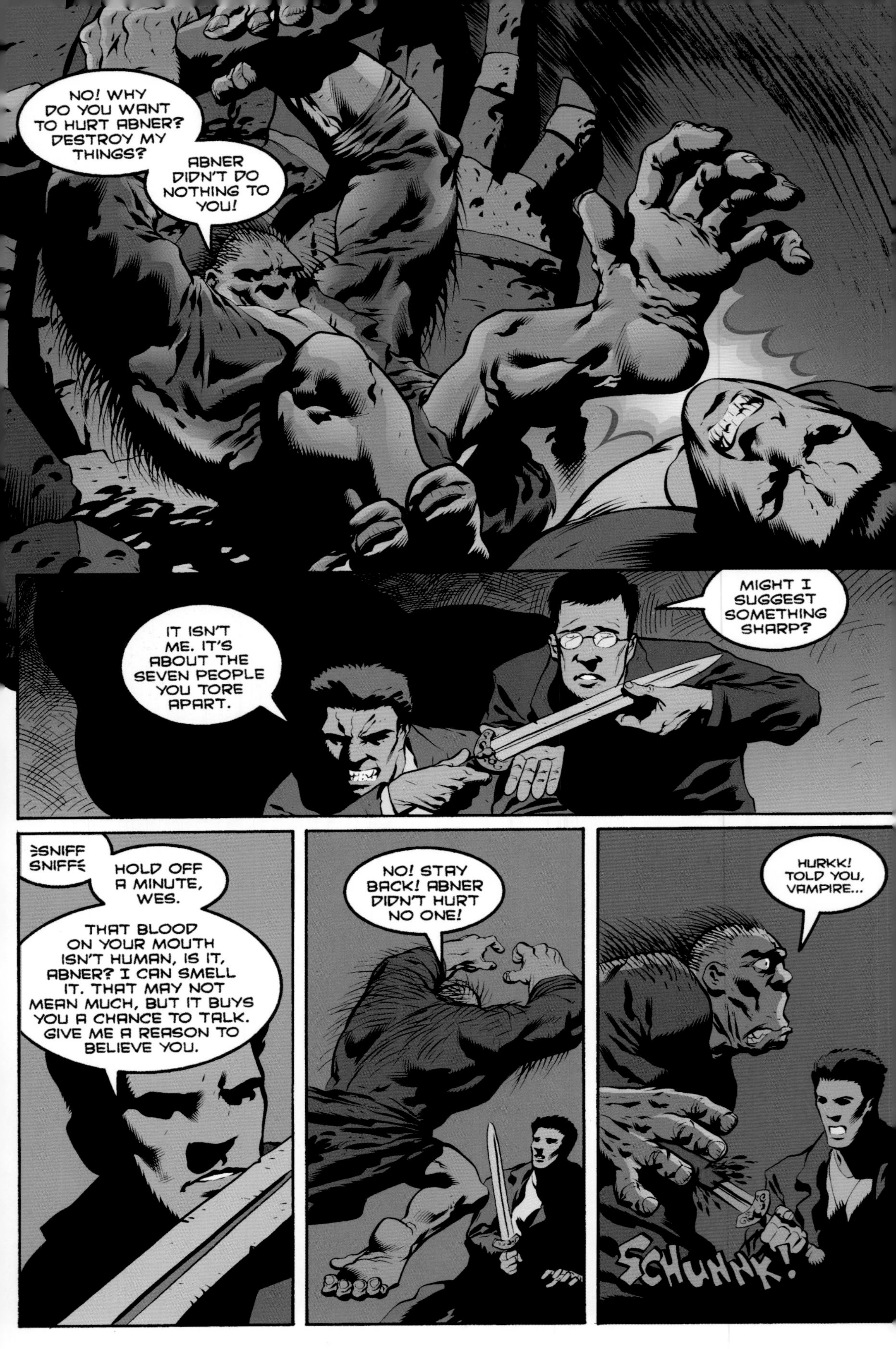
NO! WHY DO YOU WANT TO HURT ABNER? DESTROY MY THINGS?
ABNER DIDN'T DO NOTHING TO YOU!
IT ISN'T ME. IT'S ABOUT THE SEVEN PEOPLE YOU TORE APART.
MIGHT I SUGGEST SOMETHING SHARP?
SNIFF SNIFF
HOLD OFF A MINUTE, WES.
THAT BLOOD ON YOUR MOUTH ISN'T HUMAN, IS IT, ABNER? I CAN SMELL IT. THAT MAY NOT MEAN MUCH, BUT IT BUYS YOU A CHANCE TO TALK. GIVE ME A REASON TO BELIEVE YOU.
NO! STAY BACK! ABNER DIDN'T HURT NO ONE!
HURKK! TOLD YOU, VAMPIRE...
SCHUNNK!

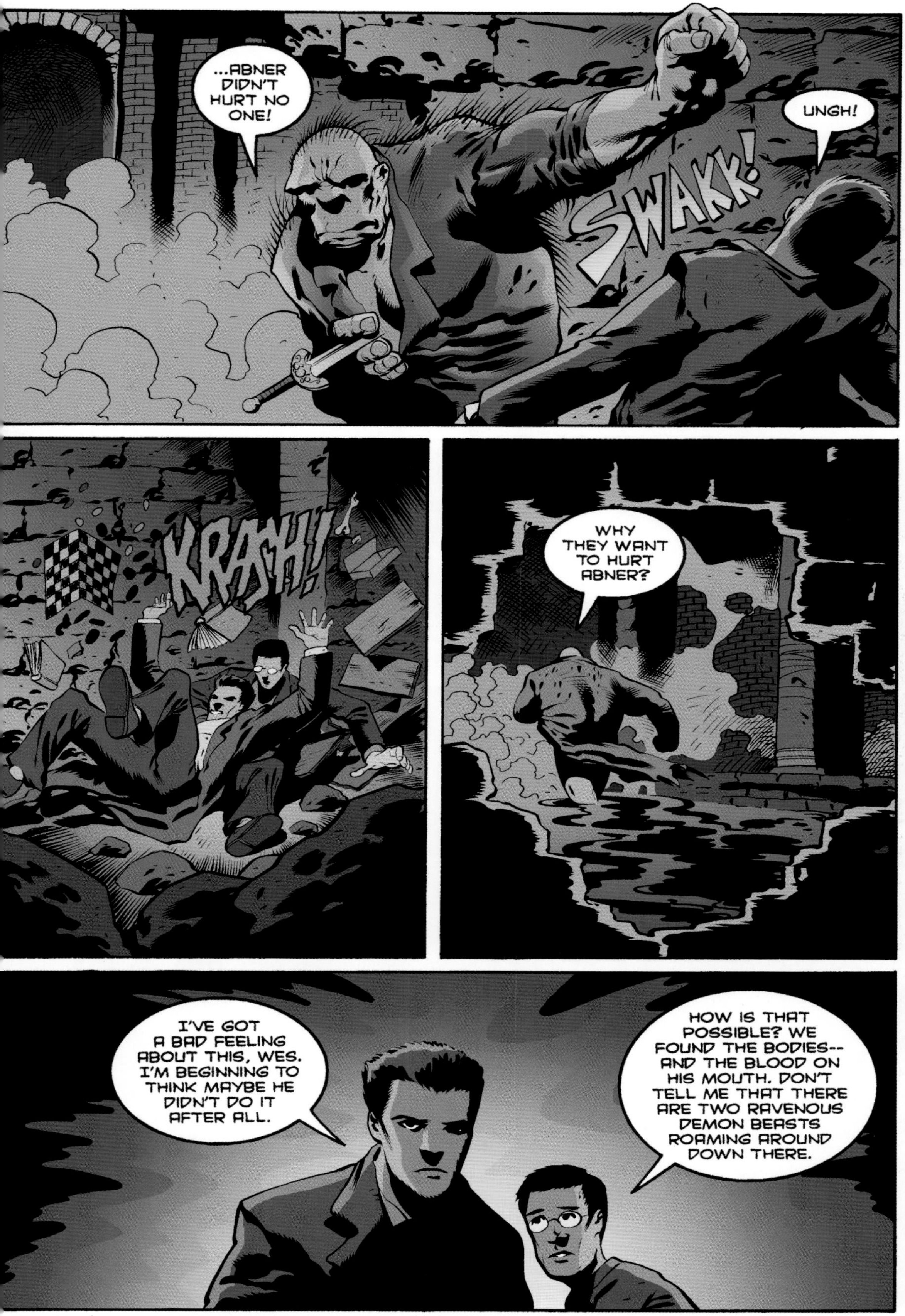
...ABNER DIDN'T HURT NO ONE!
UNGH!
SWAKK!
KRASH!
WHY THEY WANT TO HURT ABNER?
I'VE GOT A BAD FEELING ABOUT THIS, WES. I'M BEGINNING TO THINK MAYBE HE DIDN'T DO IT AFTER ALL.
HOW IS THAT POSSIBLE? WE FOUND THE BODIES-- AND THE BLOOD ON HIS MOUTH. DON'T TELL ME THAT THERE ARE TWO RAVENOUS DEMON BEASTS ROAMING AROUND DOWN THERE.

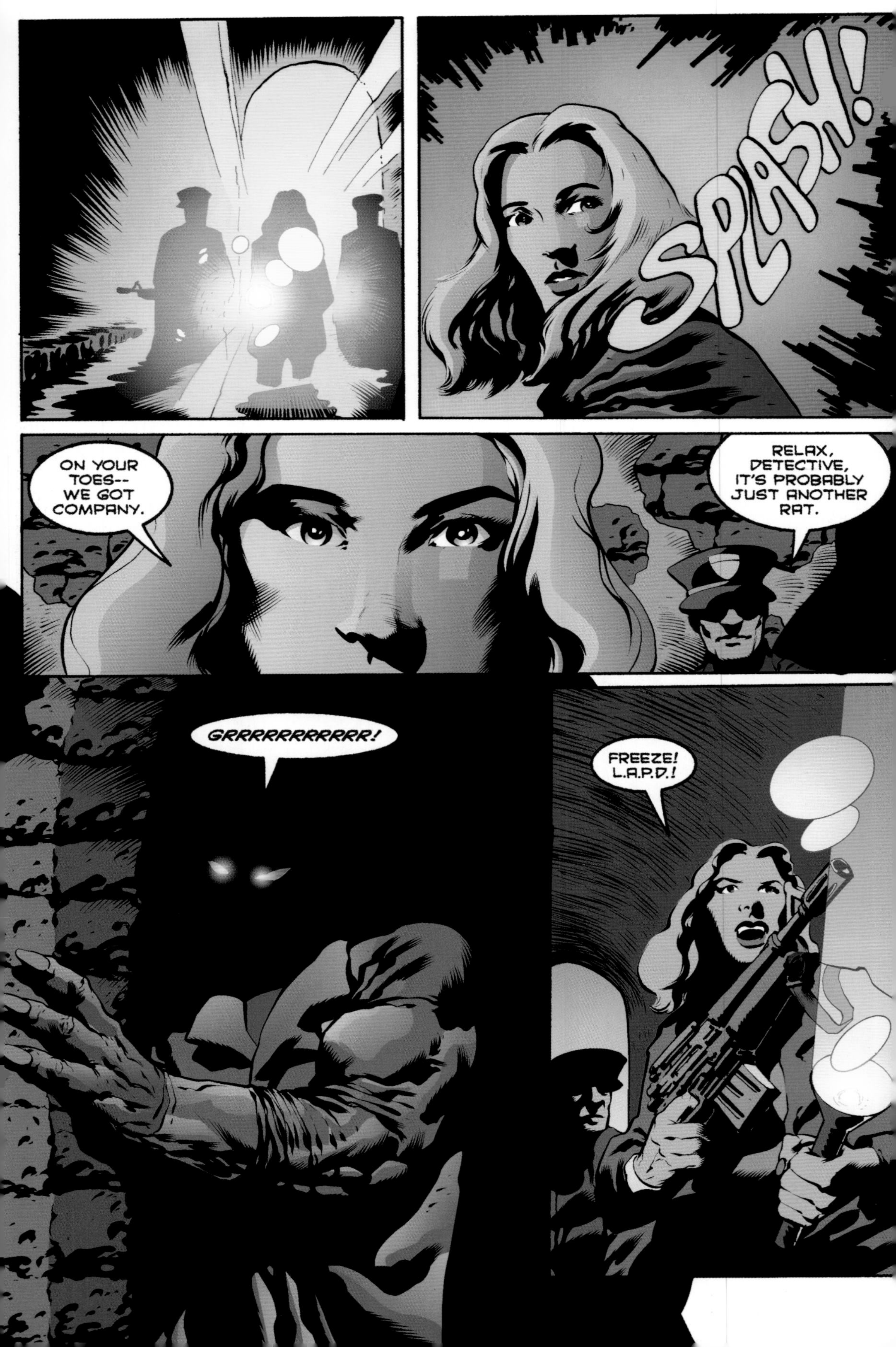
SPLASH!
ON YOUR TOES-- WE GOT COMPANY.
RELAX, DETECTIVE, IT'S PROBABLY JUST ANOTHER RAT.
GRRRRRRRRRRR!
FREEZE! L.A.P.D.!

STOP OR WE'LL OPEN FIRE!

JIMBO, COME IN-- IT'S LOCKLEY. WE'RE IN C9. THE PERP'S ON THE RUN.

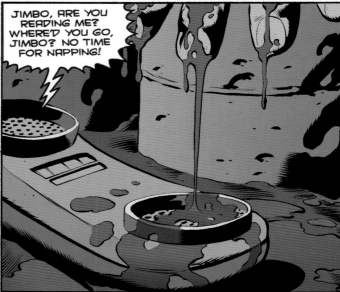

JIMBO, ARE YOU READING ME? WHERE'D YOU GO, JIMBO? NO TIME FOR NAPPING!

MUST BE INTERFERENCE FROM THE TUNNELS.

THAT MUST BE IT.

WHAT NOW, DETECTIVE?

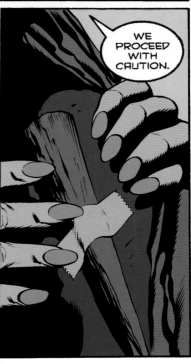

WE PROCEED WITH CAUTION.

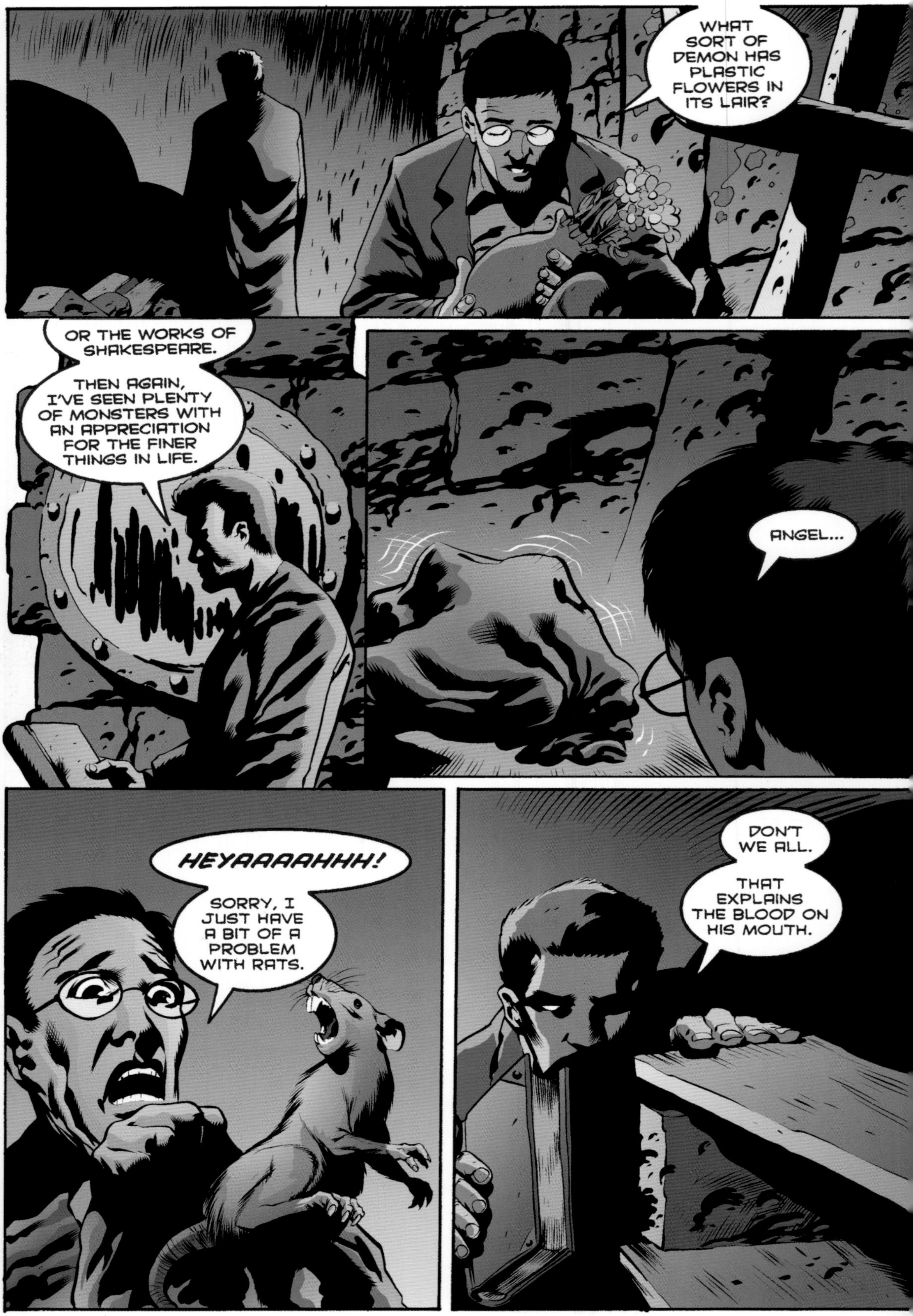
WHAT SORT OF DEMON HAS PLASTIC FLOWERS IN ITS LAIR?
OR THE WORKS OF SHAKESPEARE.
THEN AGAIN, I'VE SEEN PLENTY OF MONSTERS WITH AN APPRECIATION FOR THE FINER THINGS IN LIFE.
ANGEL...
HEYAAAAHHH!
SORRY, I JUST HAVE A BIT OF A PROBLEM WITH RATS.
DON'T WE ALL.
THAT EXPLAINS THE BLOOD ON HIS MOUTH.

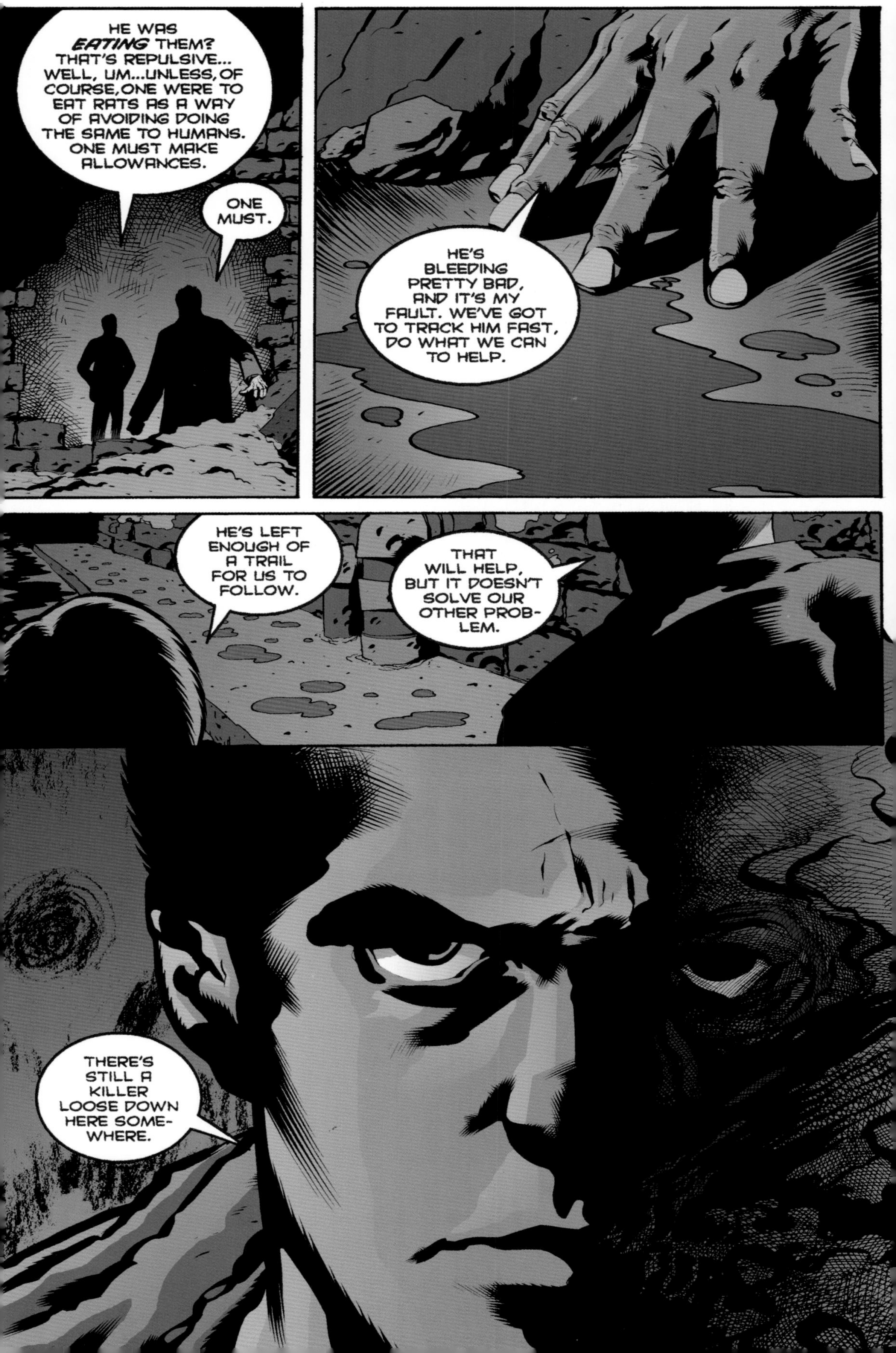
HE WAS *EATING* THEM? THAT'S REPULSIVE... WELL, UM...UNLESS, OF COURSE, ONE WERE TO EAT RATS AS A WAY OF AVOIDING DOING THE SAME TO HUMANS. ONE MUST MAKE ALLOWANCES.
ONE MUST.
HE'S BLEEDING PRETTY BAD, AND IT'S MY FAULT. WE'VE GOT TO TRACK HIM FAST, DO WHAT WE CAN TO HELP.
HE'S LEFT ENOUGH OF A TRAIL FOR US TO FOLLOW.
THAT WILL HELP, BUT IT DOESN'T SOLVE OUR OTHER PROB-LEM.
THERE'S STILL A KILLER LOOSE DOWN HERE SOME-WHERE.

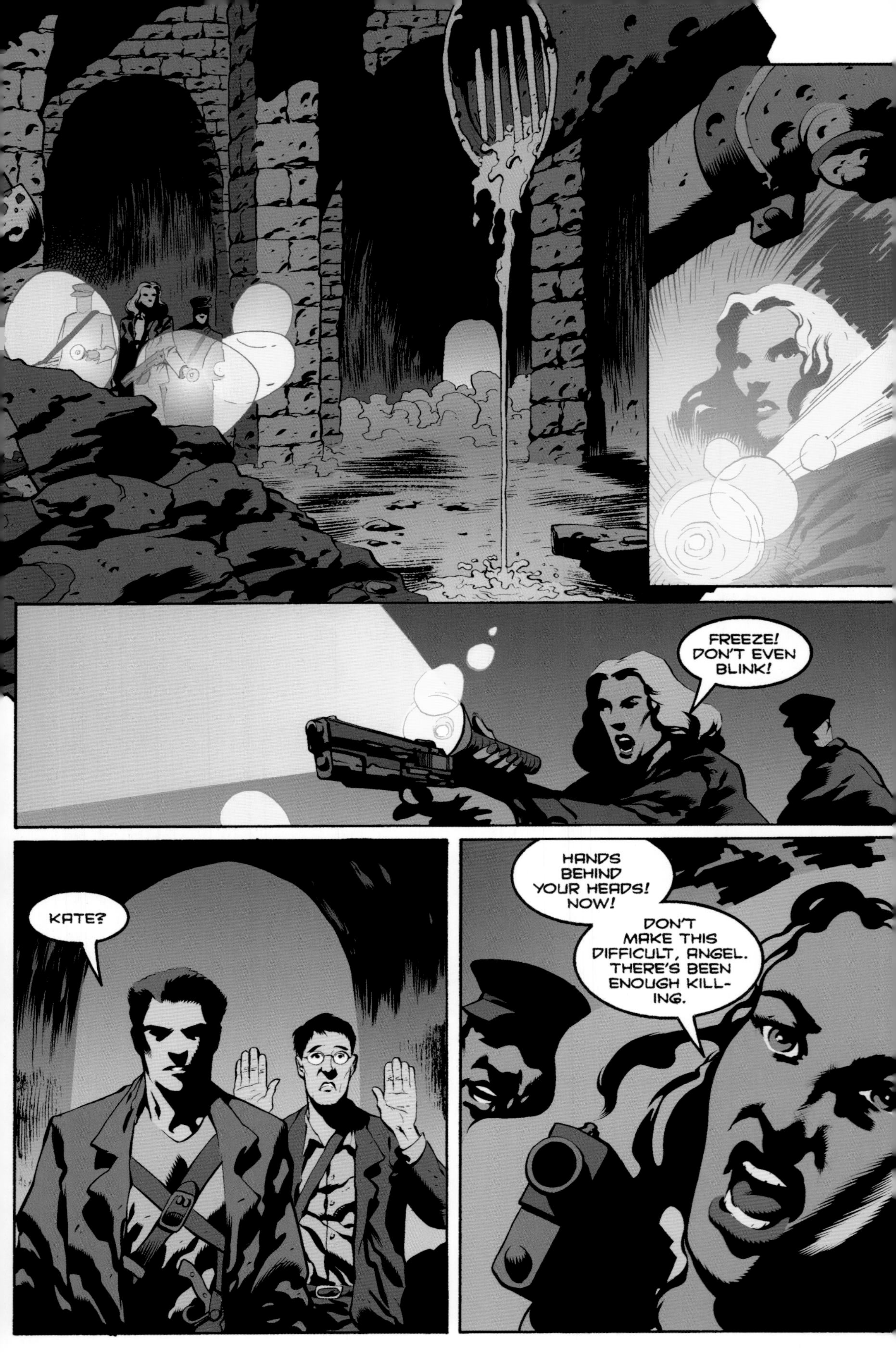
FREEZE! DON'T EVEN BLINK!
KATE?
HANDS BEHIND YOUR HEADS! NOW!
DON'T MAKE THIS DIFFICULT, ANGEL. THERE'S BEEN ENOUGH KILL-ING.

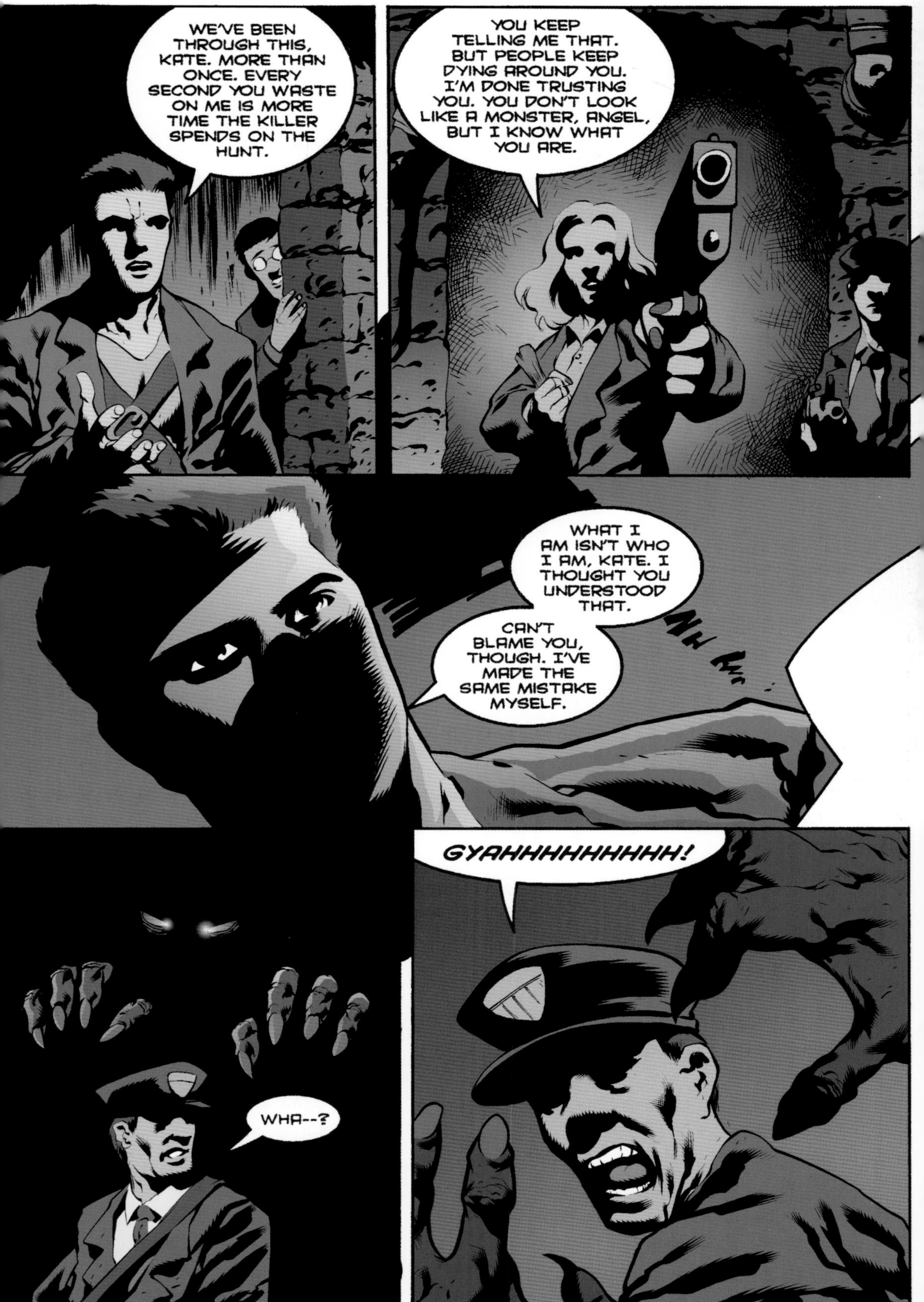
WE'VE BEEN THROUGH THIS, KATE. MORE THAN ONCE. EVERY SECOND YOU WASTE ON ME IS MORE TIME THE KILLER SPENDS ON THE HUNT.
YOU KEEP TELLING ME THAT. BUT PEOPLE KEEP DYING AROUND YOU. I'M DONE TRUSTING YOU. YOU DON'T LOOK LIKE A MONSTER, ANGEL, BUT I KNOW WHAT YOU ARE.
WHAT I AM ISN'T WHO I AM, KATE. I THOUGHT YOU UNDERSTOOD THAT.
CAN'T BLAME YOU, THOUGH. I'VE MADE THE SAME MISTAKE MYSELF.
WHA--?
GYAHHHHHHHHH!

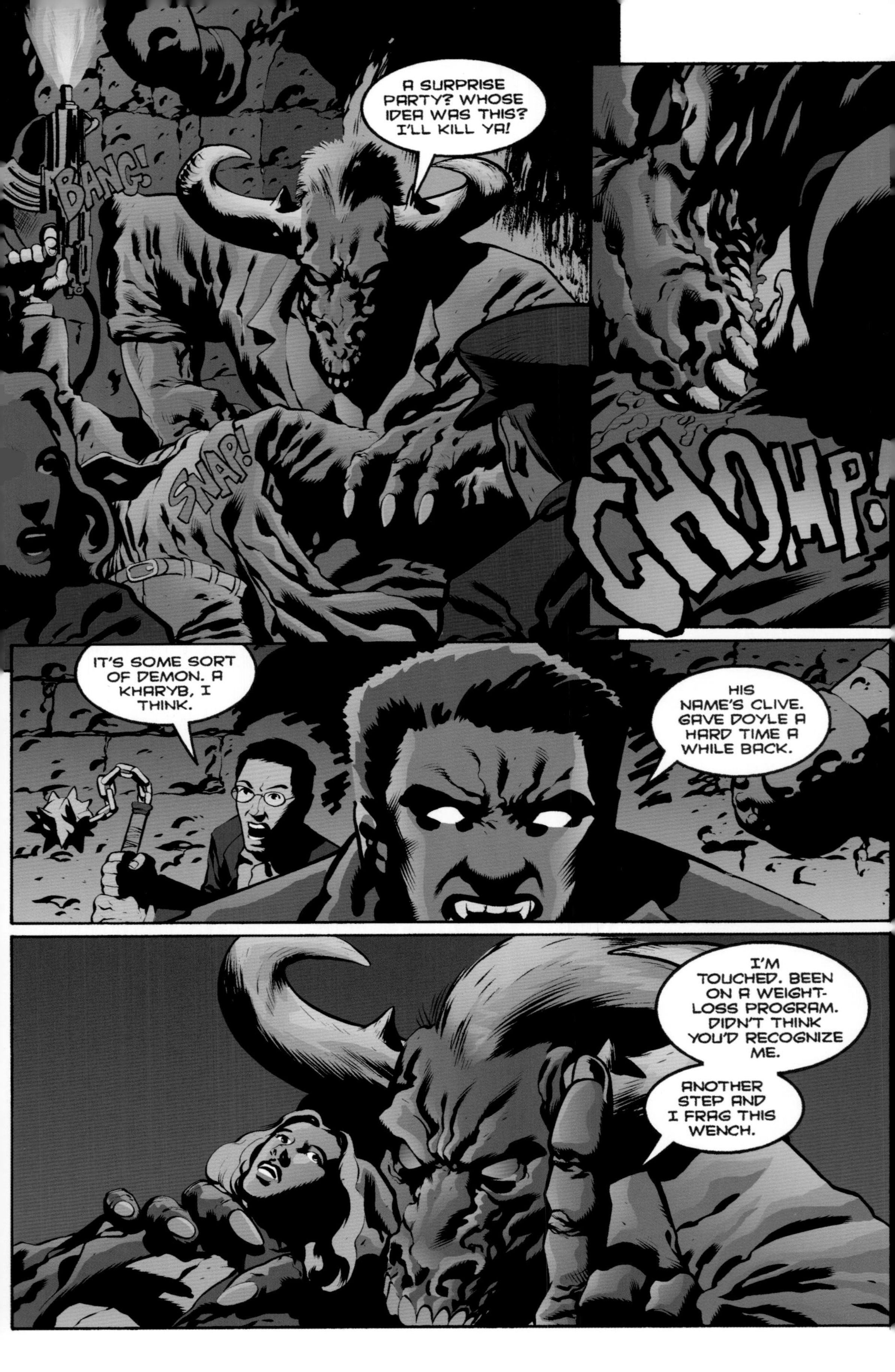
BANG!
A SURPRISE PARTY? WHOSE IDEA WAS THIS? I'LL KILL YA!
SNAP!
CHOMP!
IT'S SOME SORT OF DEMON. A KHARYB, I THINK.
HIS NAME'S CLIVE. GAVE DOYLE A HARD TIME A WHILE BACK.
I'M TOUCHED. BEEN ON A WEIGHT-LOSS PROGRAM. DIDN'T THINK YOU'D RECOGNIZE ME.
ANOTHER STEP AND I FRAG THIS WENCH.

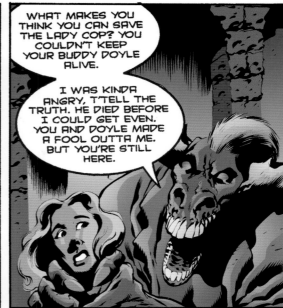

WESLEY. WAIT.

YOU'VE KILLED A LOT OF PEOPLE, CLIVE. I'M NOT LETTING YOU WALK AWAY FROM THAT.

WHAT MAKES YOU THINK YOU CAN SAVE THE LADY COP? YOU COULDN'T KEEP YOUR BUDDY DOYLE ALIVE.

I WAS KINDA ANGRY, T'TELL THE TRUTH. HE DIED BEFORE I COULD GET EVEN. YOU AND DOYLE MADE A FOOL OUTTA ME. BUT YOU'RE STILL HERE.

YOU'RE SAYING YOU KILLED THOSE PEOPLE, SET IT UP SO THE COPS WOULD THINK IT WAS ME, JUST BECAUSE I GAVE YOU A BEATING?

GUYS LIKE ME, WE LIVE AND DIE BY THE WORD ON THE STREET. NO WAY I COULD SURVIVE OUT THERE IF I LET YOU GET AWAY WITH WHAT YOU DID.

THIS WAY I GET TO TAKE YOU DOWN, GET MY STREET CRED BACK, AND THE POLICE BLAME YOU. KILLING ALL THE COPS? THAT'S JUST A BONUS.

SHLURP!

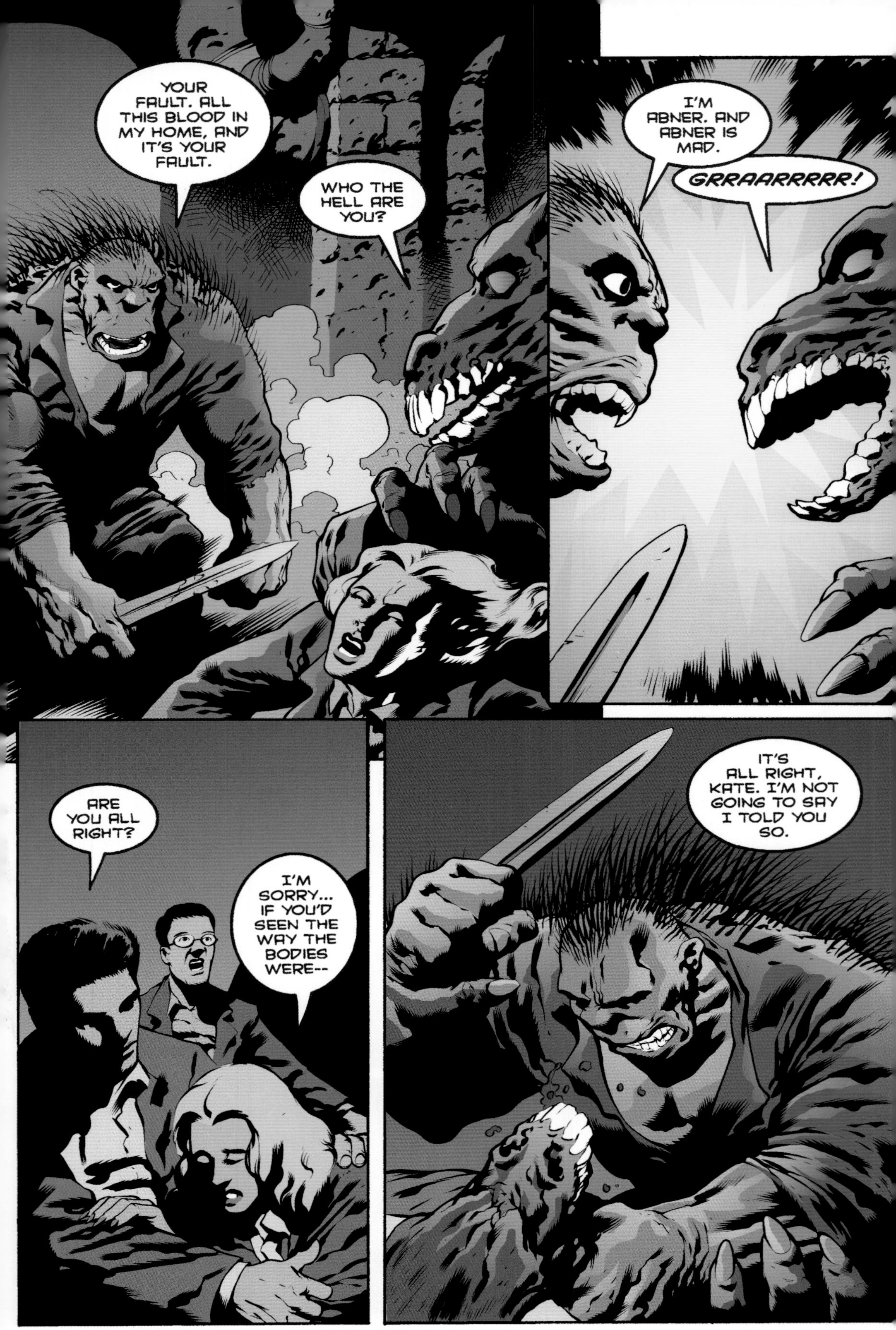
YOUR FAULT. ALL THIS BLOOD IN MY HOME, AND IT'S YOUR FAULT.
WHO THE HELL ARE YOU?
I'M ABNER. AND ABNER IS MAD.
GRRAAARRRRR!
ARE YOU ALL RIGHT?
I'M SORRY... IF YOU'D SEEN THE WAY THE BODIES WERE--
IT'S ALL RIGHT, KATE. I'M NOT GOING TO SAY I TOLD YOU SO.

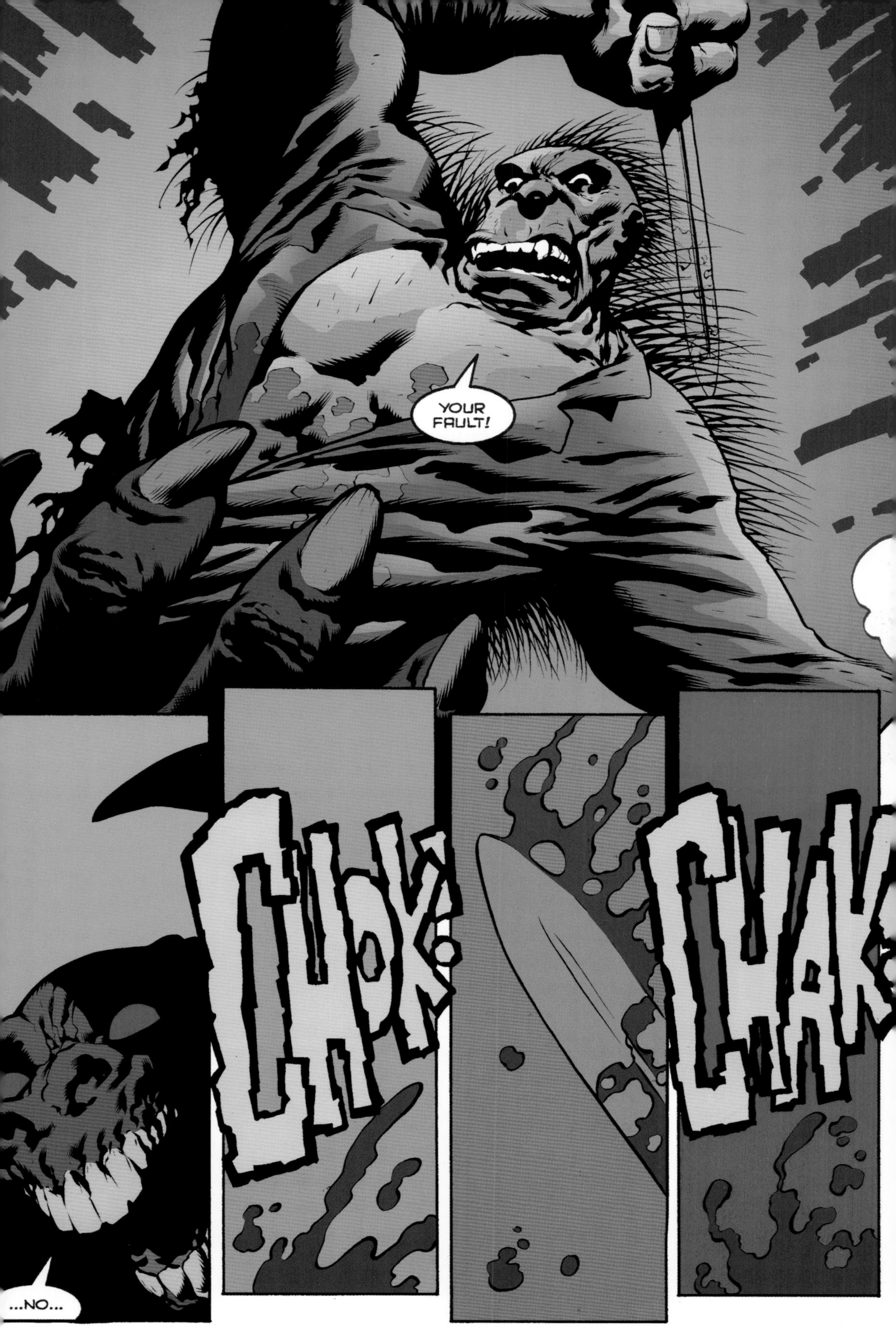
YOUR FAULT!
CHOK!
CHAK
...NO...

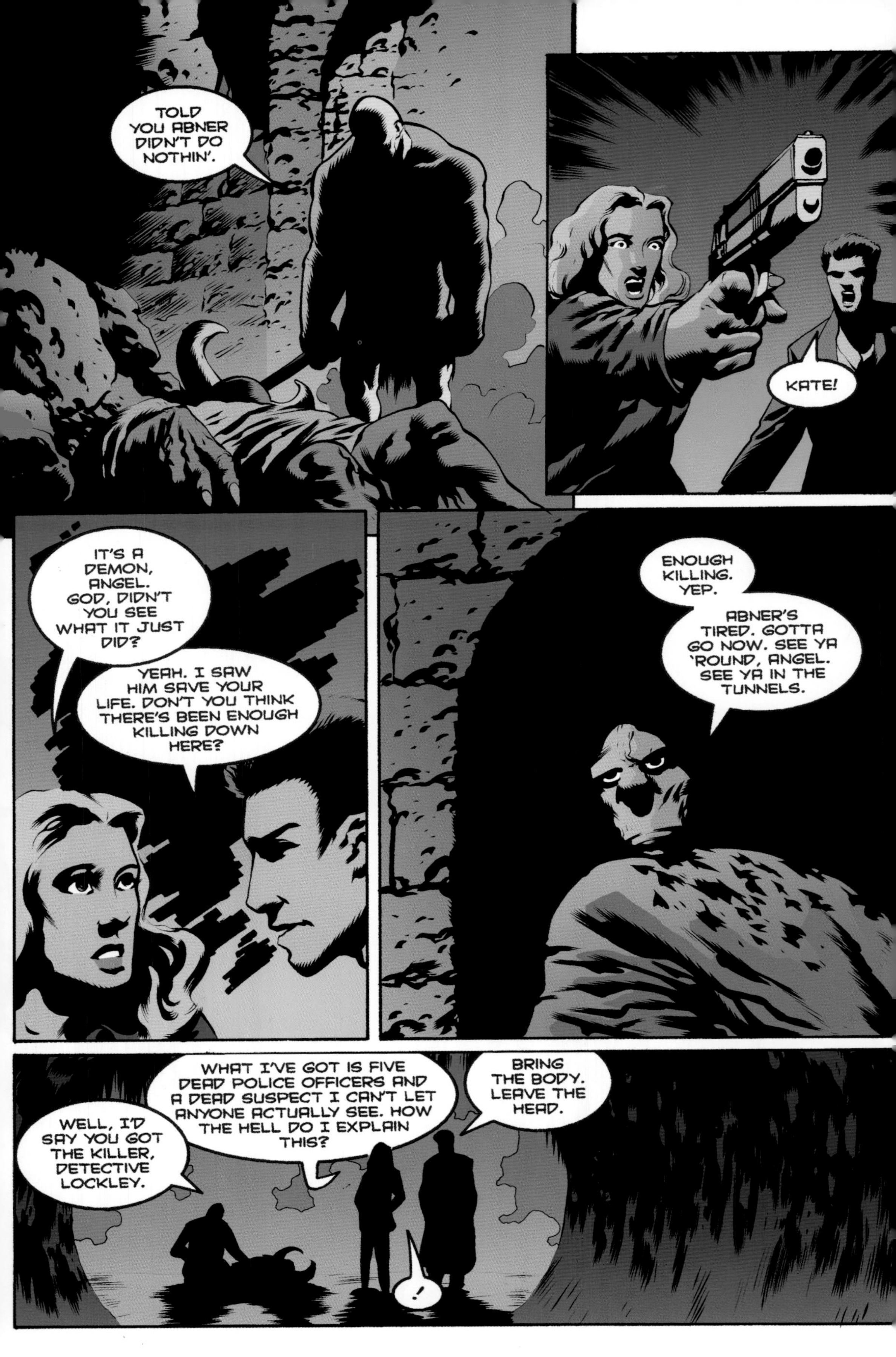
TOLD YOU ABNER DIDN'T DO NOTHIN'.
KATE!
IT'S A DEMON, ANGEL. GOD, DIDN'T YOU SEE WHAT IT JUST DID?
YEAH. I SAW HIM SAVE YOUR LIFE. DON'T YOU THINK THERE'S BEEN ENOUGH KILLING DOWN HERE?
ENOUGH KILLING. YEP.
ABNER'S TIRED. GOTTA GO NOW. SEE YA 'ROUND, ANGEL. SEE YA IN THE TUNNELS.
WELL, I'D SAY YOU GOT THE KILLER, DETECTIVE LOCKLEY.
WHAT I'VE GOT IS FIVE DEAD POLICE OFFICERS AND A DEAD SUSPECT I CAN'T LET ANYONE ACTUALLY SEE. HOW THE HELL DO I EXPLAIN THIS?
!
BRING THE BODY. LEAVE THE HEAD.

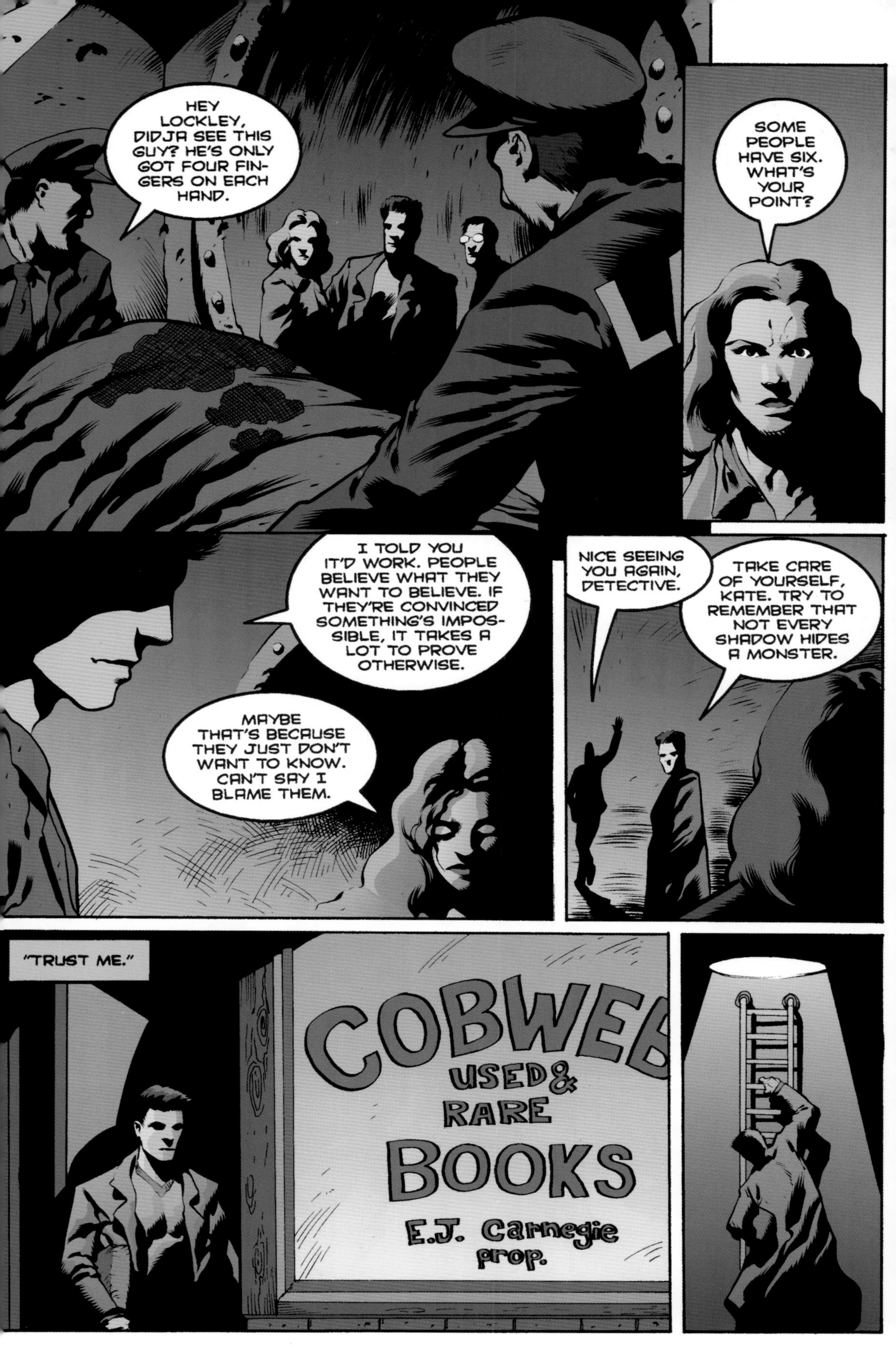
HEY LOCKLEY, DIDJA SEE THIS GUY? HE'S ONLY GOT FOUR FINGERS ON EACH HAND.
SOME PEOPLE HAVE SIX. WHAT'S YOUR POINT?
I TOLD YOU IT'D WORK. PEOPLE BELIEVE WHAT THEY WANT TO BELIEVE. IF THEY'RE CONVINCED SOMETHING'S IMPOSSIBLE, IT TAKES A LOT TO PROVE OTHERWISE.
MAYBE THAT'S BECAUSE THEY JUST DON'T WANT TO KNOW. CAN'T SAY I BLAME THEM.
NICE SEEING YOU AGAIN, DETECTIVE.
TAKE CARE OF YOURSELF, KATE. TRY TO REMEMBER THAT NOT EVERY SHADOW HIDES A MONSTER.
"TRUST ME."
COBWEB
USED & RARE BOOKS
E.J. Carnegie prop.

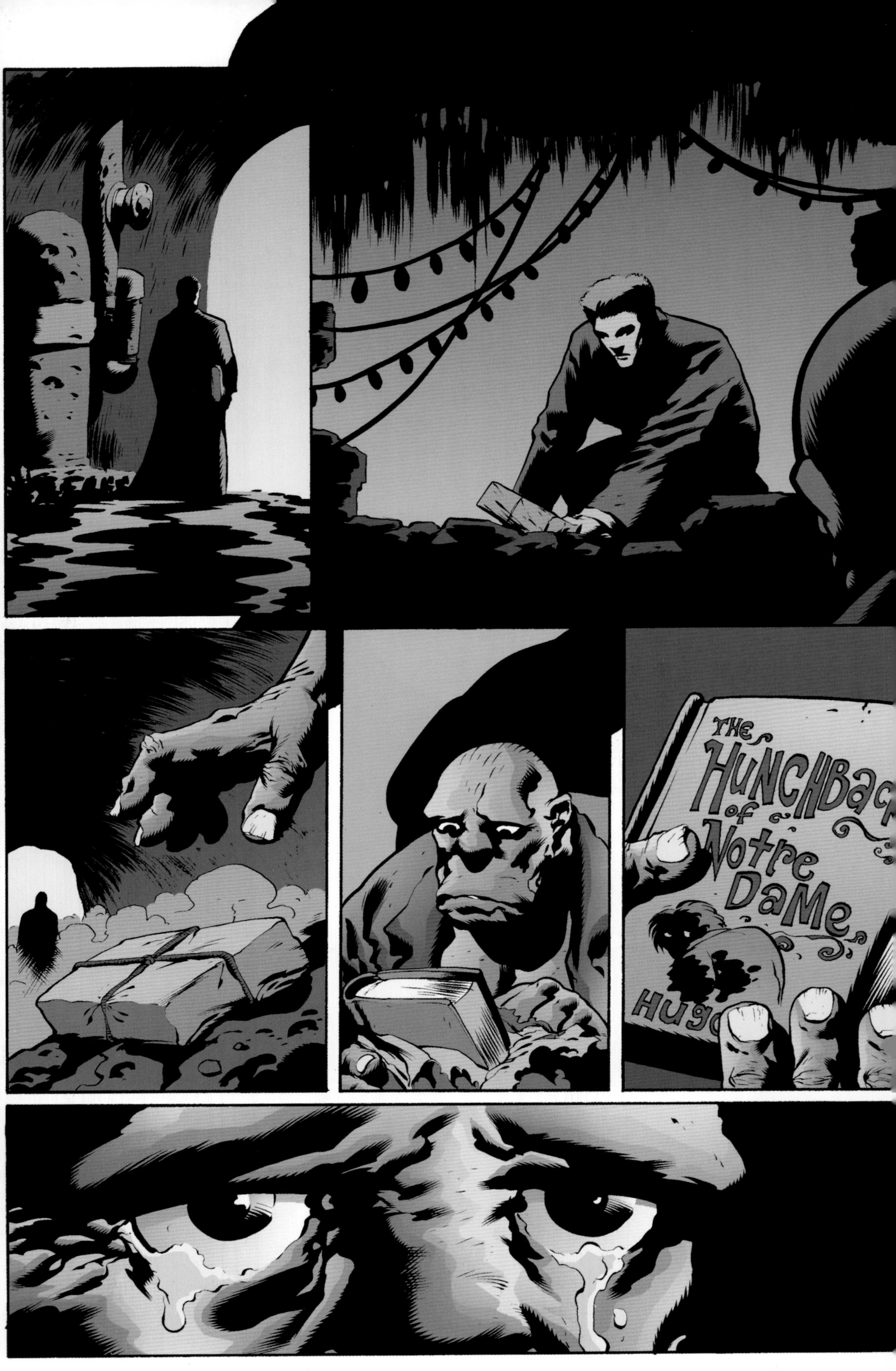
THE
HUNCHBAC
of
Notre
DaMe
HUGO

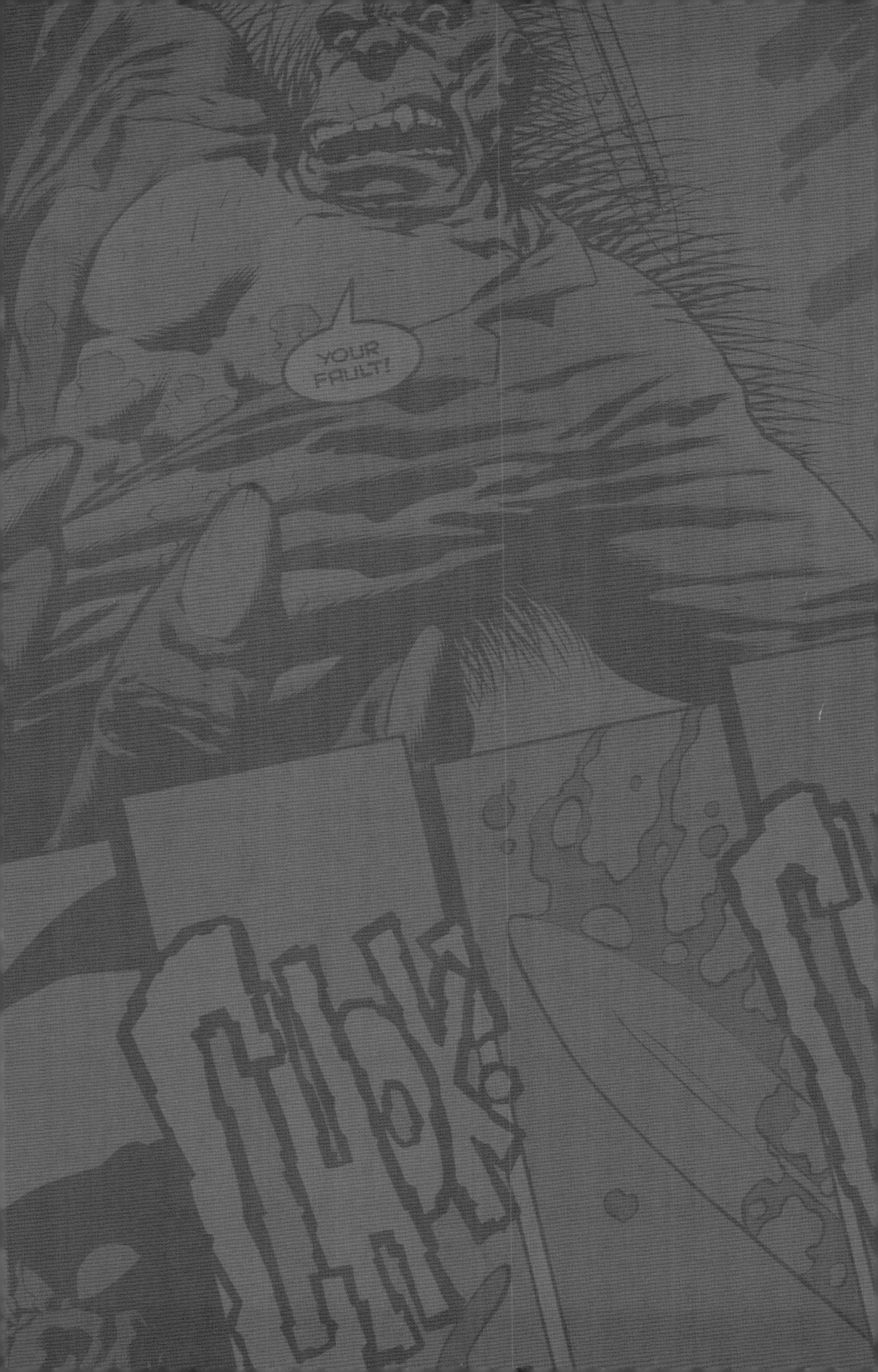
YOUR FAULT!

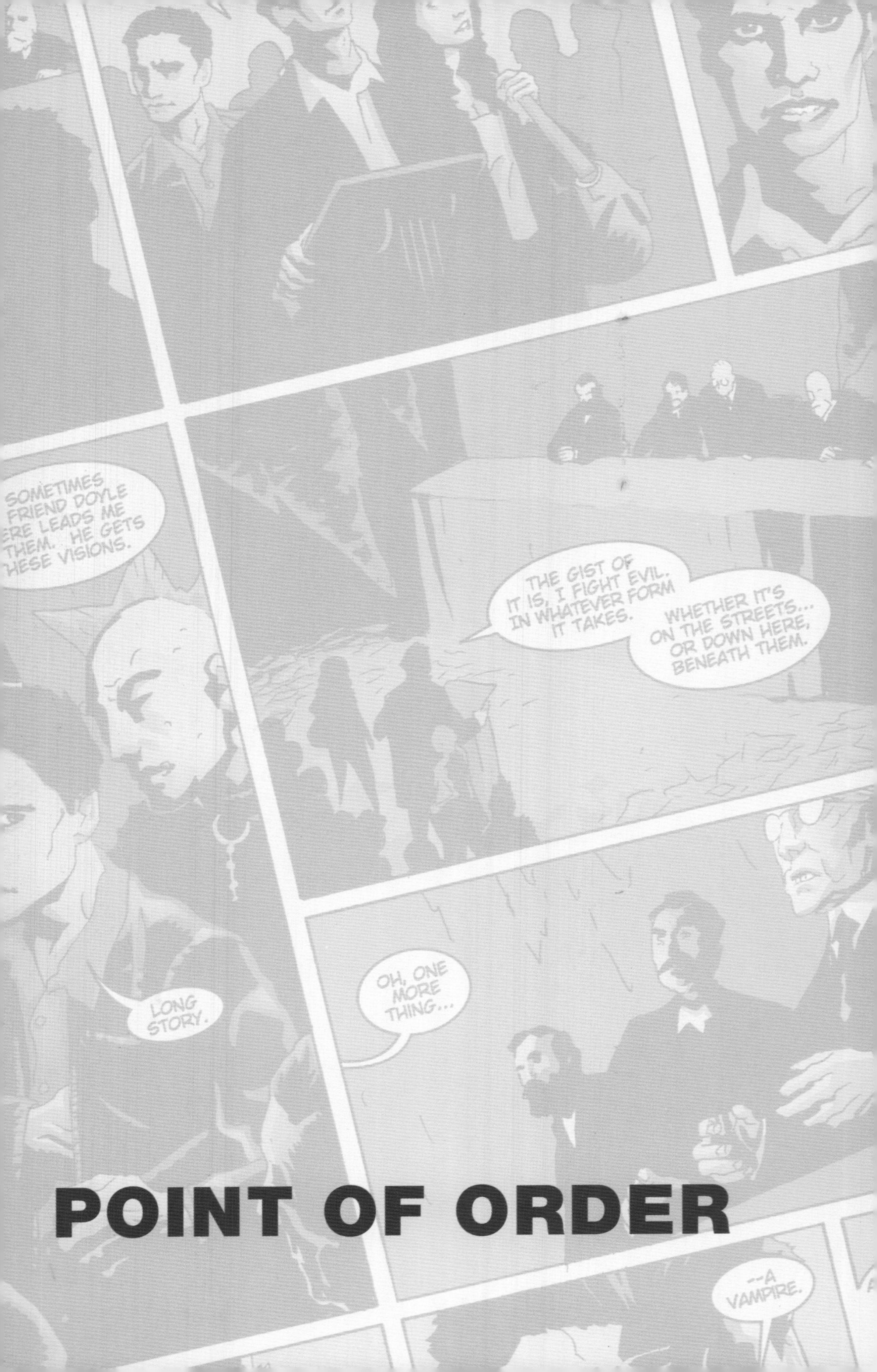

POINT OF ORDER

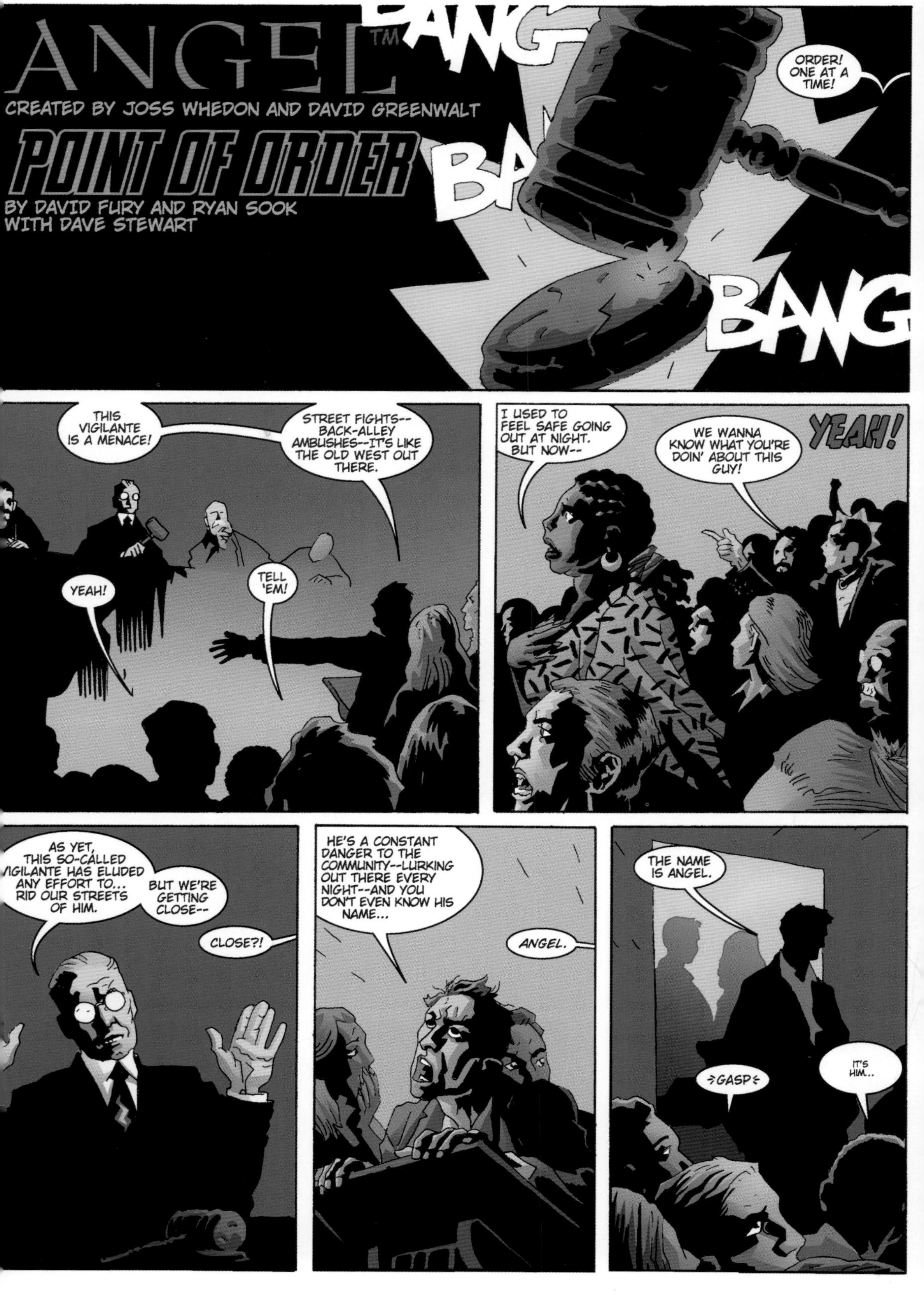
ANGEL™
CREATED BY JOSS WHEDON AND DAVID GREENWALT
POINT OF ORDER
BY DAVID FURY AND RYAN SOOK
WITH DAVE STEWART
BANG
BANG
BANG
ORDER! ONE AT A TIME!
THIS VIGILANTE IS A MENACE!
STREET FIGHTS--BACK-ALLEY AMBUSHES--IT'S LIKE THE OLD WEST OUT THERE.
YEAH!
TELL 'EM!
I USED TO FEEL SAFE GOING OUT AT NIGHT. BUT NOW--
WE WANNA KNOW WHAT YOU'RE DOIN' ABOUT THIS GUY!
YEAH!
AS YET, THIS SO-CALLED VIGILANTE HAS ELUDED ANY EFFORT TO... RID OUR STREETS OF HIM.
BUT WE'RE GETTING CLOSE--
CLOSE?!
HE'S A CONSTANT DANGER TO THE COMMUNITY--LURKING OUT THERE EVERY NIGHT--AND YOU DON'T EVEN KNOW HIS NAME...
ANGEL.
THE NAME IS ANGEL.
GASP
IT'S HIM...

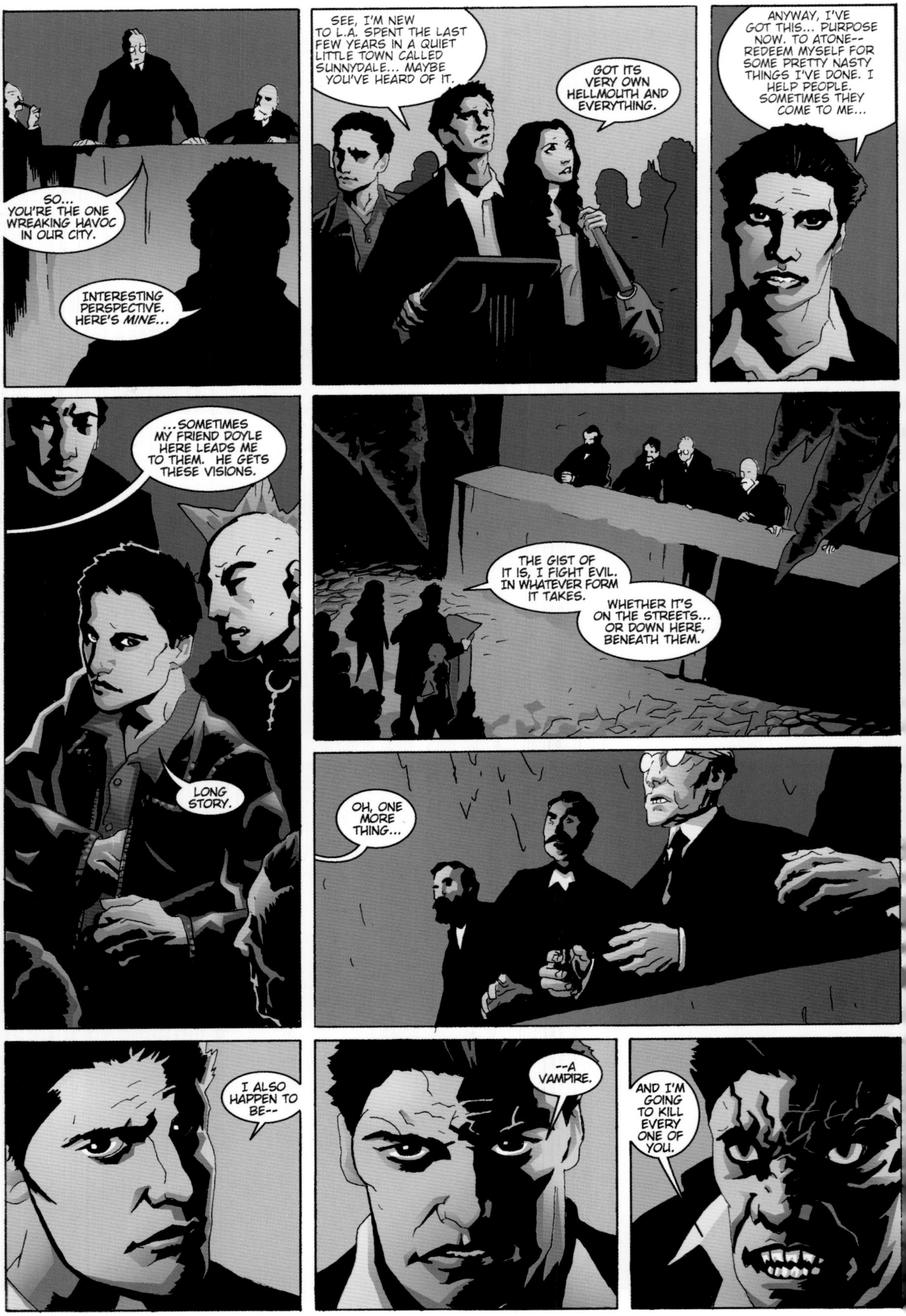
SO... YOU'RE THE ONE WREAKING HAVOC IN OUR CITY.
INTERESTING PERSPECTIVE. HERE'S MINE...
SEE, I'M NEW TO L.A. SPENT THE LAST FEW YEARS IN A QUIET LITTLE TOWN CALLED SUNNYDALE... MAYBE YOU'VE HEARD OF IT.
GOT ITS VERY OWN HELLMOUTH AND EVERYTHING.
ANYWAY, I'VE GOT THIS... PURPOSE NOW. TO ATONE-- REDEEM MYSELF FOR SOME PRETTY NASTY THINGS I'VE DONE. I HELP PEOPLE. SOMETIMES THEY COME TO ME...
...SOMETIMES MY FRIEND DOYLE HERE LEADS ME TO THEM. HE GETS THESE VISIONS.
LONG STORY.
THE GIST OF IT IS, I FIGHT EVIL. IN WHATEVER FORM IT TAKES.
WHETHER IT'S ON THE STREETS... OR DOWN HERE, BENEATH THEM.
OH, ONE MORE THING...
I ALSO HAPPEN TO BE--
--A VAMPIRE.
AND I'M GOING TO KILL EVERY ONE OF YOU.

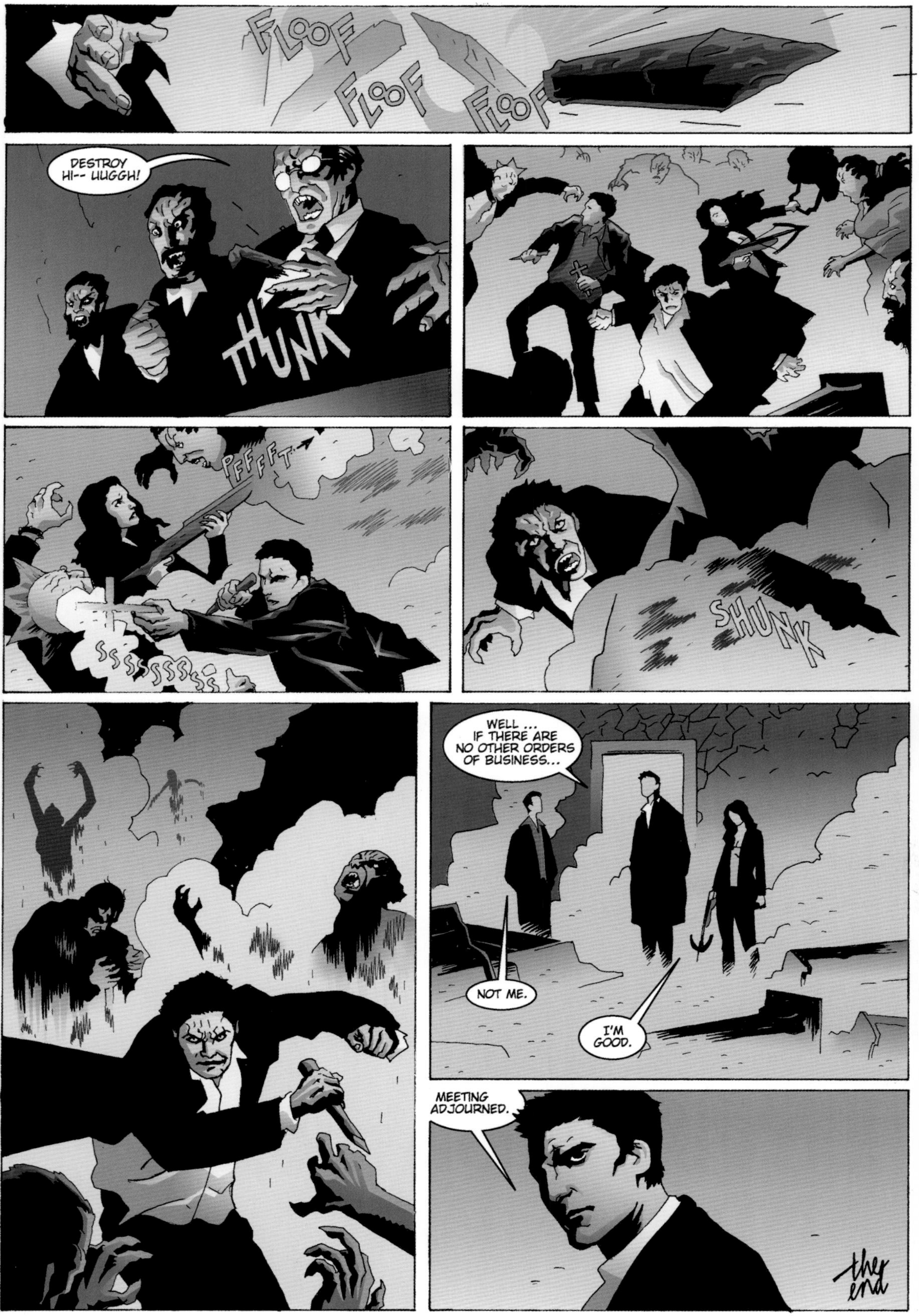
FLOOF
FLOOF
FLOOF
DESTROY HI-- UUGGH!
THUNK
PFFFFT
SSSSSSSSSS
SHUNK
WELL ... IF THERE ARE NO OTHER ORDERS OF BUSINESS...
NOT ME.
I'M GOOD.
MEETING ADJOURNED.
the end

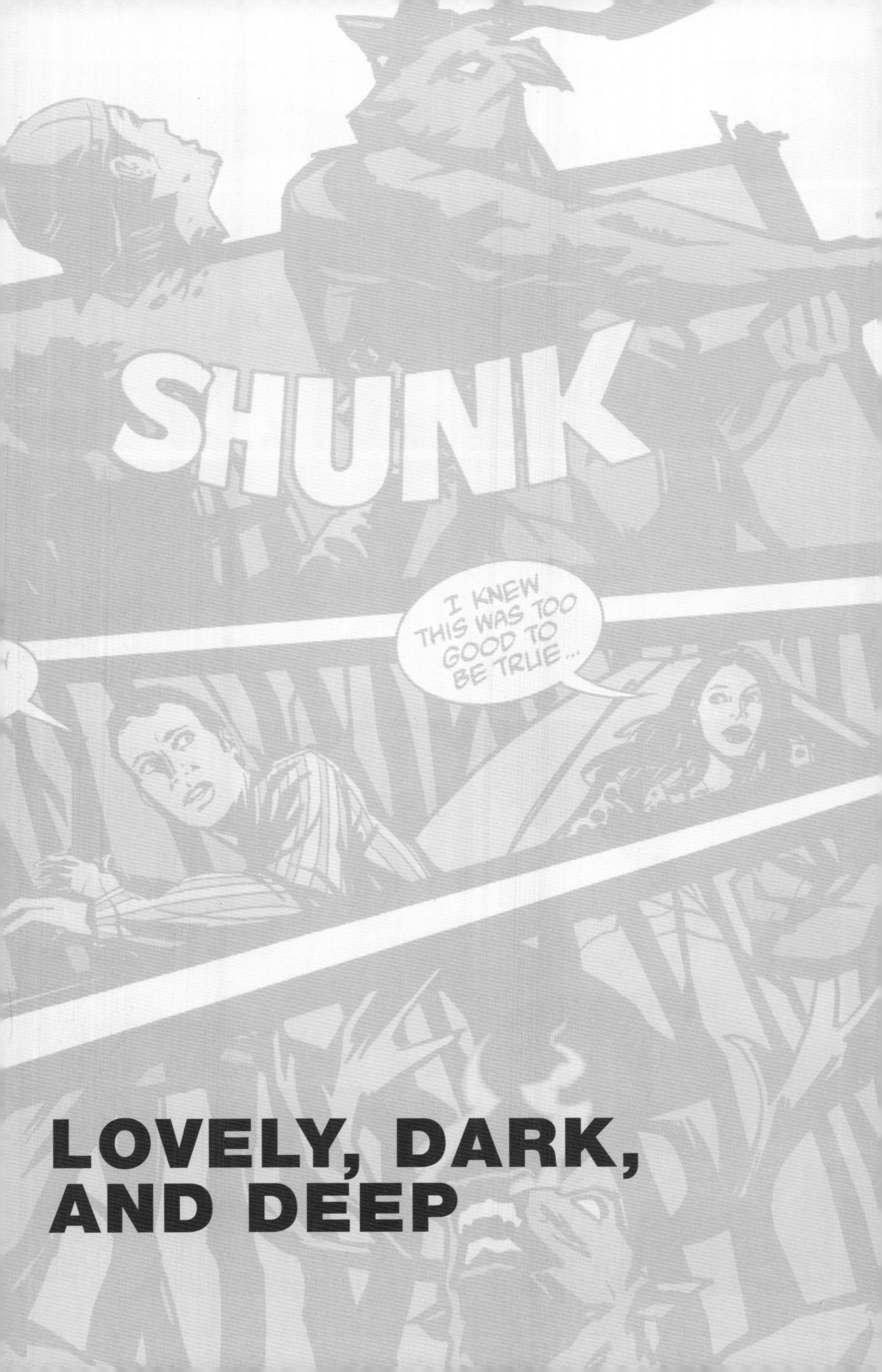
SHUNK
I KNEW THIS WAS TOO GOOD TO BE TRUE...

LOVELY, DARK, AND DEEP

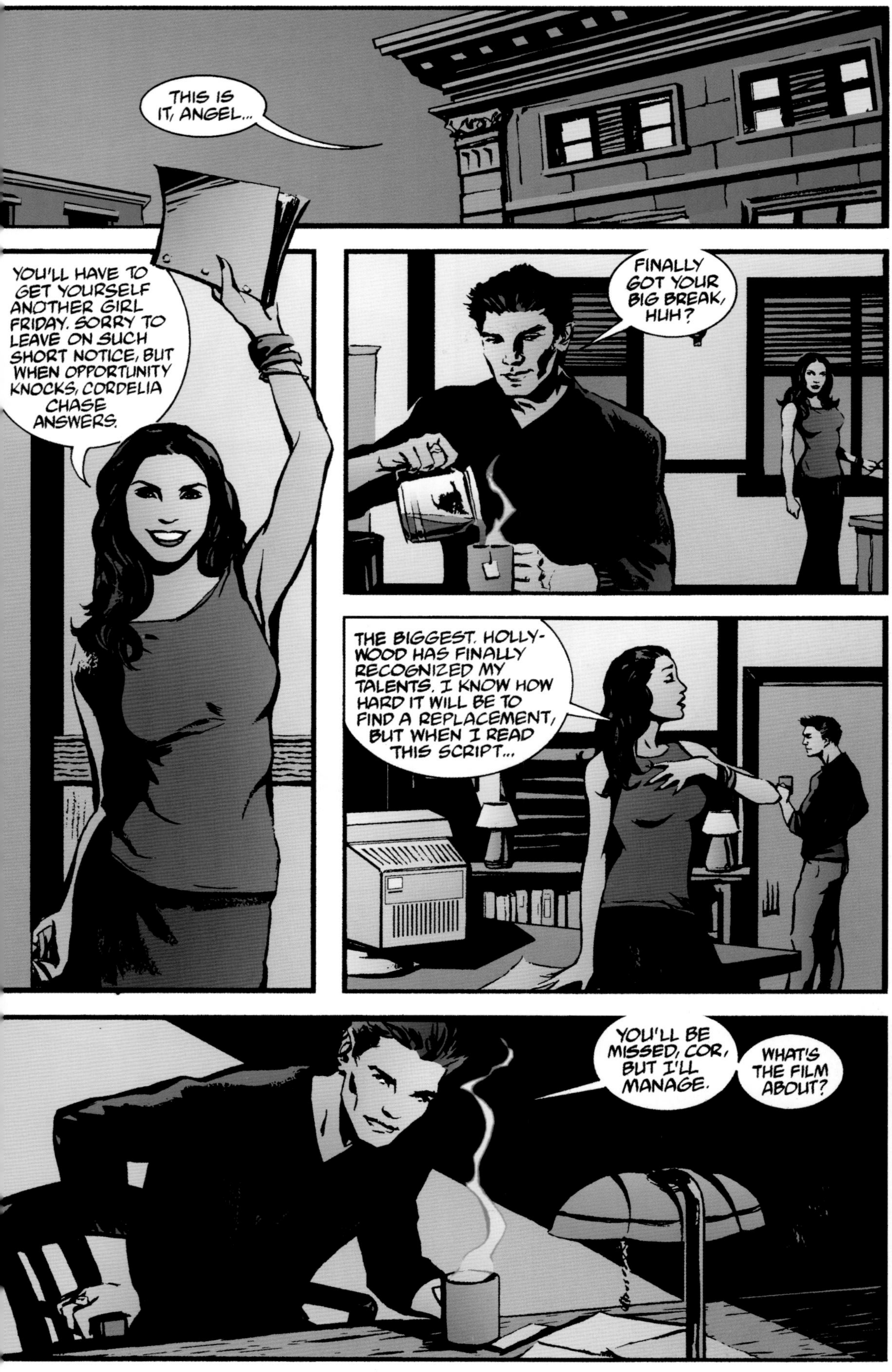
THIS IS IT, ANGEL...
YOU'LL HAVE TO GET YOURSELF ANOTHER GIRL FRIDAY. SORRY TO LEAVE ON SUCH SHORT NOTICE, BUT WHEN OPPORTUNITY KNOCKS, CORDELIA CHASE ANSWERS.
FINALLY GOT YOUR BIG BREAK, HUH?
THE BIGGEST. HOLLYWOOD HAS FINALLY RECOGNIZED MY TALENTS. I KNOW HOW HARD IT WILL BE TO FIND A REPLACEMENT, BUT WHEN I READ THIS SCRIPT...
YOU'LL BE MISSED, COR, BUT I'LL MANAGE.
WHAT'S THE FILM ABOUT?

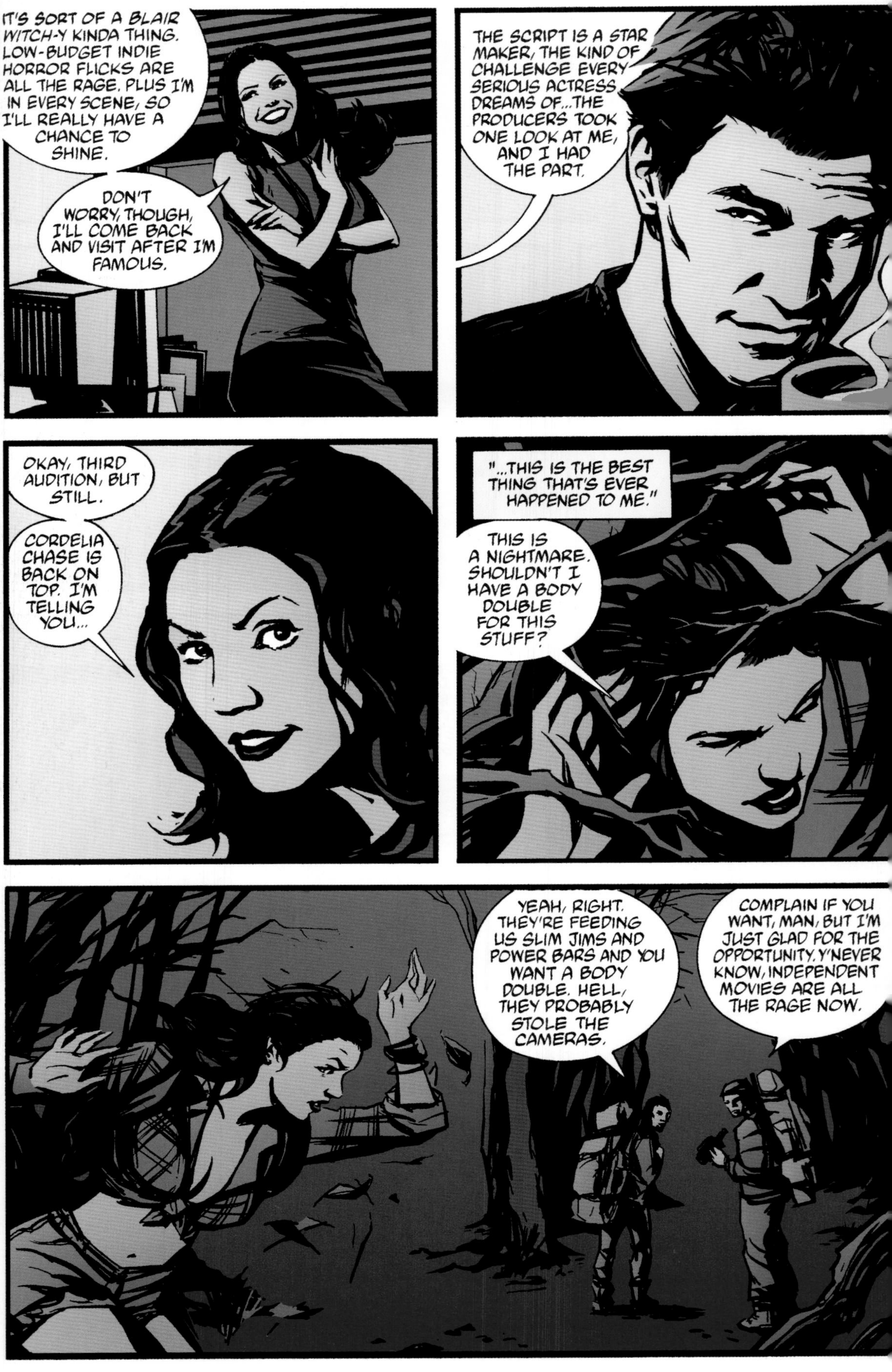
IT'S SORT OF A BLAIR WITCH-Y KINDA THING. LOW-BUDGET INDIE HORROR FLICKS ARE ALL THE RAGE. PLUS I'M IN EVERY SCENE, SO I'LL REALLY HAVE A CHANCE TO SHINE.
DON'T WORRY, THOUGH, I'LL COME BACK AND VISIT AFTER I'M FAMOUS.
THE SCRIPT IS A STAR MAKER, THE KIND OF CHALLENGE EVERY SERIOUS ACTRESS DREAMS OF... THE PRODUCERS TOOK ONE LOOK AT ME, AND I HAD THE PART.
OKAY, THIRD AUDITION, BUT STILL.
CORDELIA CHASE IS BACK ON TOP. I'M TELLING YOU...
"...THIS IS THE BEST THING THAT'S EVER HAPPENED TO ME."
THIS IS A NIGHTMARE. SHOULDN'T I HAVE A BODY DOUBLE FOR THIS STUFF?
YEAH, RIGHT. THEY'RE FEEDING US SLIM JIMS AND POWER BARS AND YOU WANT A BODY DOUBLE. HELL, THEY PROBABLY STOLE THE CAMERAS.
COMPLAIN IF YOU WANT, MAN, BUT I'M JUST GLAD FOR THE OPPORTUNITY. Y'NEVER KNOW, INDEPENDENT MOVIES ARE ALL THE RAGE NOW.

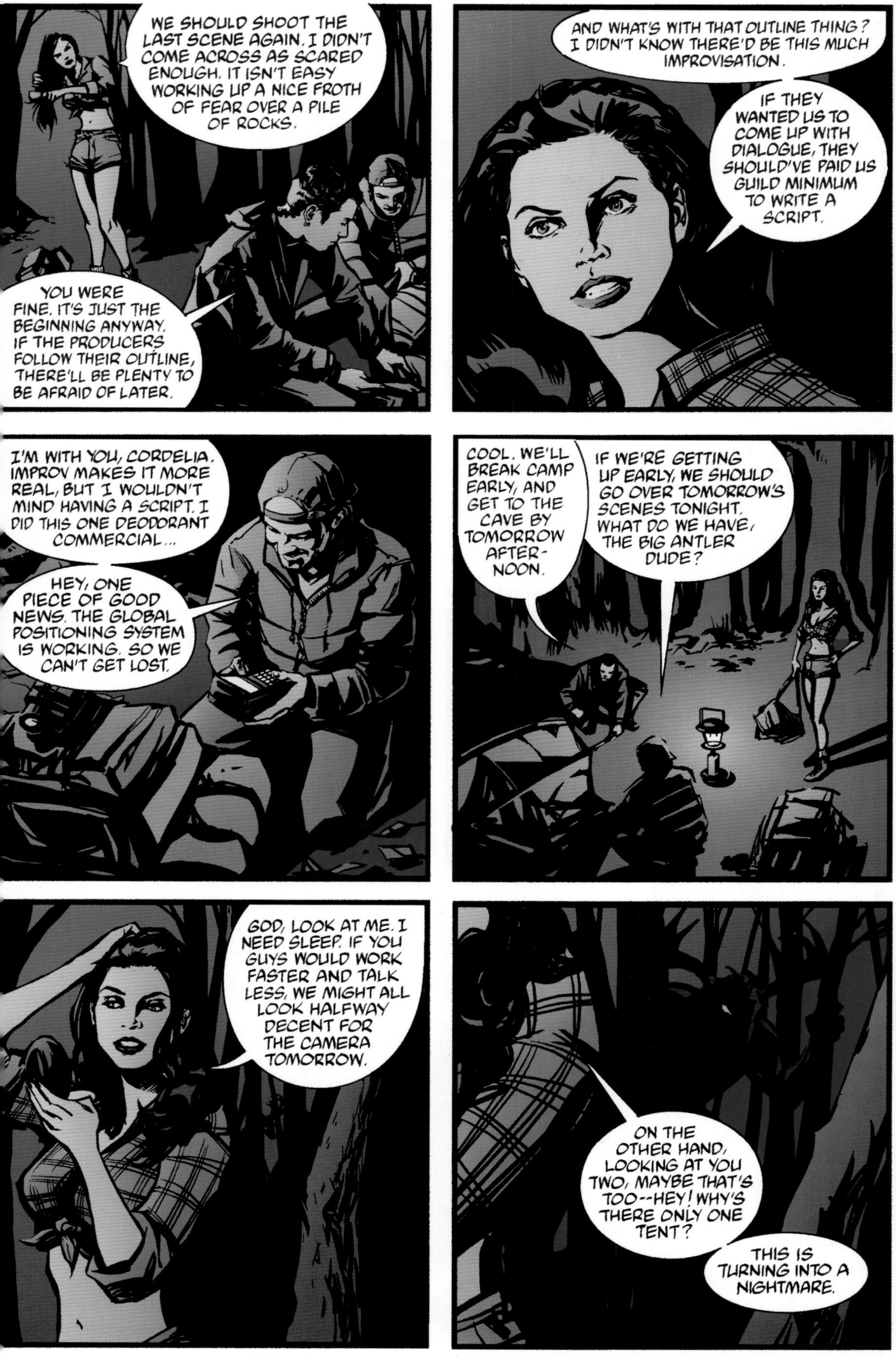
WE SHOULD SHOOT THE LAST SCENE AGAIN. I DIDN'T COME ACROSS AS SCARED ENOUGH. IT ISN'T EASY WORKING UP A NICE FROTH OF FEAR OVER A PILE OF ROCKS.
YOU WERE FINE. IT'S JUST THE BEGINNING ANYWAY. IF THE PRODUCERS FOLLOW THEIR OUTLINE, THERE'LL BE PLENTY TO BE AFRAID OF LATER.
AND WHAT'S WITH THAT OUTLINE THING? I DIDN'T KNOW THERE'D BE THIS MUCH IMPROVISATION.
IF THEY WANTED US TO COME UP WITH DIALOGUE, THEY SHOULD'VE PAID US GUILD MINIMUM TO WRITE A SCRIPT.
I'M WITH YOU, CORDELIA. IMPROV MAKES IT MORE REAL, BUT I WOULDN'T MIND HAVING A SCRIPT. I DID THIS ONE DEODORANT COMMERCIAL...
HEY, ONE PIECE OF GOOD NEWS. THE GLOBAL POSITIONING SYSTEM IS WORKING. SO WE CAN'T GET LOST.
COOL. WE'LL BREAK CAMP EARLY, AND GET TO THE CAVE BY TOMORROW AFTER-NOON.
IF WE'RE GETTING UP EARLY, WE SHOULD GO OVER TOMORROW'S SCENES TONIGHT. WHAT DO WE HAVE, THE BIG ANTLER DUDE?
GOD, LOOK AT ME. I NEED SLEEP. IF YOU GUYS WOULD WORK FASTER AND TALK LESS, WE MIGHT ALL LOOK HALFWAY DECENT FOR THE CAMERA TOMORROW.
ON THE OTHER HAND, LOOKING AT YOU TWO, MAYBE THAT'S TOO--HEY! WHY'S THERE ONLY ONE TENT?
THIS IS TURNING INTO A NIGHTMARE.

ANGEL INVESTIGATIONS.

HELLO? LISTEN, I GOTTA TALK FAST.

SOME BABE HANDED ME YOUR CARD IN A BAR A COUPLE MONTHS BACK. I MAY NEED YOUR HELP.

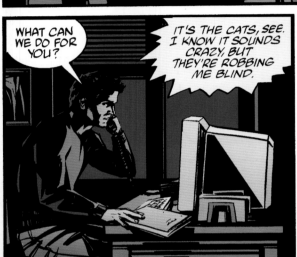

WHAT CAN WE DO FOR YOU?

IT'S THE CATS, SEE. I KNOW IT SOUNDS CRAZY, BUT THEY'RE ROBBING ME BLIND.

CAN'T LEAVE THE ROOM FOR A MINUTE. I COME BACK, AND THE FURNITURE'S MOVED.

The Helm of Haraxis

AND I THINK THEY PAWNED MY BOWLING BALL.

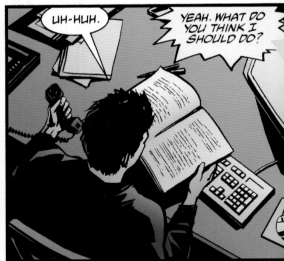

UH-HUH.

YEAH. WHAT DO YOU THINK I SHOULD DO?

RUN.

BRRINNGGG
BRRINNGGG

HELM PRODUCTIONS

KLIK

HELLO, YOU'VE REACHED THE OFFICES OF HELM PRODUCTIONS. NO ONE IS AVAILABLE TO TAKE YOUR CALL AT THE MOMENT, BUT IT IS IMPORTANT TO US...

PLEASE LEAVE A MESSAGE, AND SOMEONE WILL GET BACK TO YOU AS SOON AS POSSIBLE.

SOMETIMES I FEEL SO GUILTY ABOUT SCREENING OUR CALLS.

IT'S HOLLYWOOD. EVERYONE DOES IT.

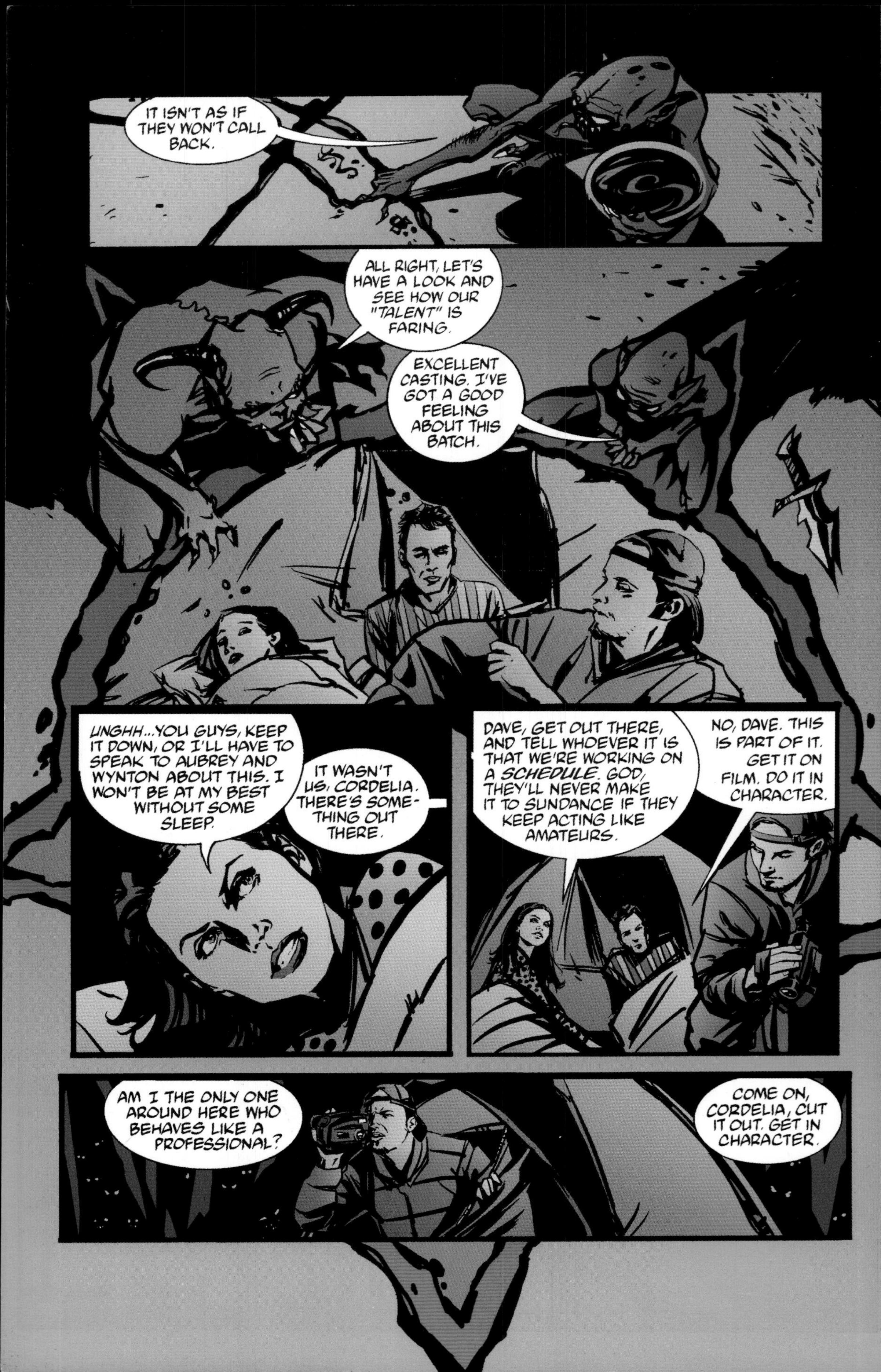
IT ISN'T AS IF THEY WON'T CALL BACK.
ALL RIGHT, LET'S HAVE A LOOK AND SEE HOW OUR "TALENT" IS FARING.
EXCELLENT CASTING. I'VE GOT A GOOD FEELING ABOUT THIS BATCH.
UNGHH...YOU GUYS, KEEP IT DOWN, OR I'LL HAVE TO SPEAK TO AUBREY AND WYNTON ABOUT THIS. I WON'T BE AT MY BEST WITHOUT SOME SLEEP.
IT WASN'T US, CORDELIA. THERE'S SOME-THING OUT THERE.
DAVE, GET OUT THERE, AND TELL WHOEVER IT IS THAT WE'RE WORKING ON A *SCHEDULE*. GOD, THEY'LL NEVER MAKE IT TO SUNDANCE IF THEY KEEP ACTING LIKE AMATEURS.
NO, DAVE. THIS IS PART OF IT. GET IT ON FILM. DO IT IN CHARACTER.
AM I THE ONLY ONE AROUND HERE WHO BEHAVES LIKE A PROFESSIONAL?
COME ON, CORDELIA, CUT IT OUT. GET IN CHARACTER.

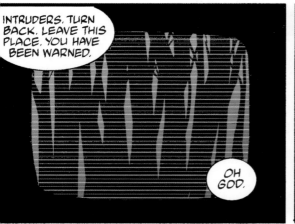

INTRUDERS, TURN BACK. LEAVE THIS PLACE. YOU HAVE BEEN WARNED.

OH GOD.

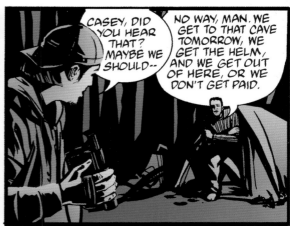

CASEY, DID YOU HEAR THAT? MAYBE WE SHOULD--

NO WAY, MAN. WE GET TO THAT CAVE TOMORROW, WE GET THE HELM, AND WE GET OUT OF HERE, OR WE DON'T GET PAID.

OOH, I HATE THIS PART!

DON'T BE SUCH A BABY, LIKE YOU HAVEN'T SEEN THIS HAPPEN BEFORE.

I DON'T HEAR ANY-THING.

IT CAME FROM OVER THERE, I SWEAR TO GOD. MAN, HOW LONG 'TILL SUN-UP?

DAVE, CALM DOWN. NOTHING'S GONNA HAPPEN. THERE'S NOTHING OUT THERE.

OH, MAN!

WOW, I DIDN'T THINK THEY HAD THE BUDGET FOR SOMETHING LIKE THAT.

WHAT THE HELL IS THAT?!

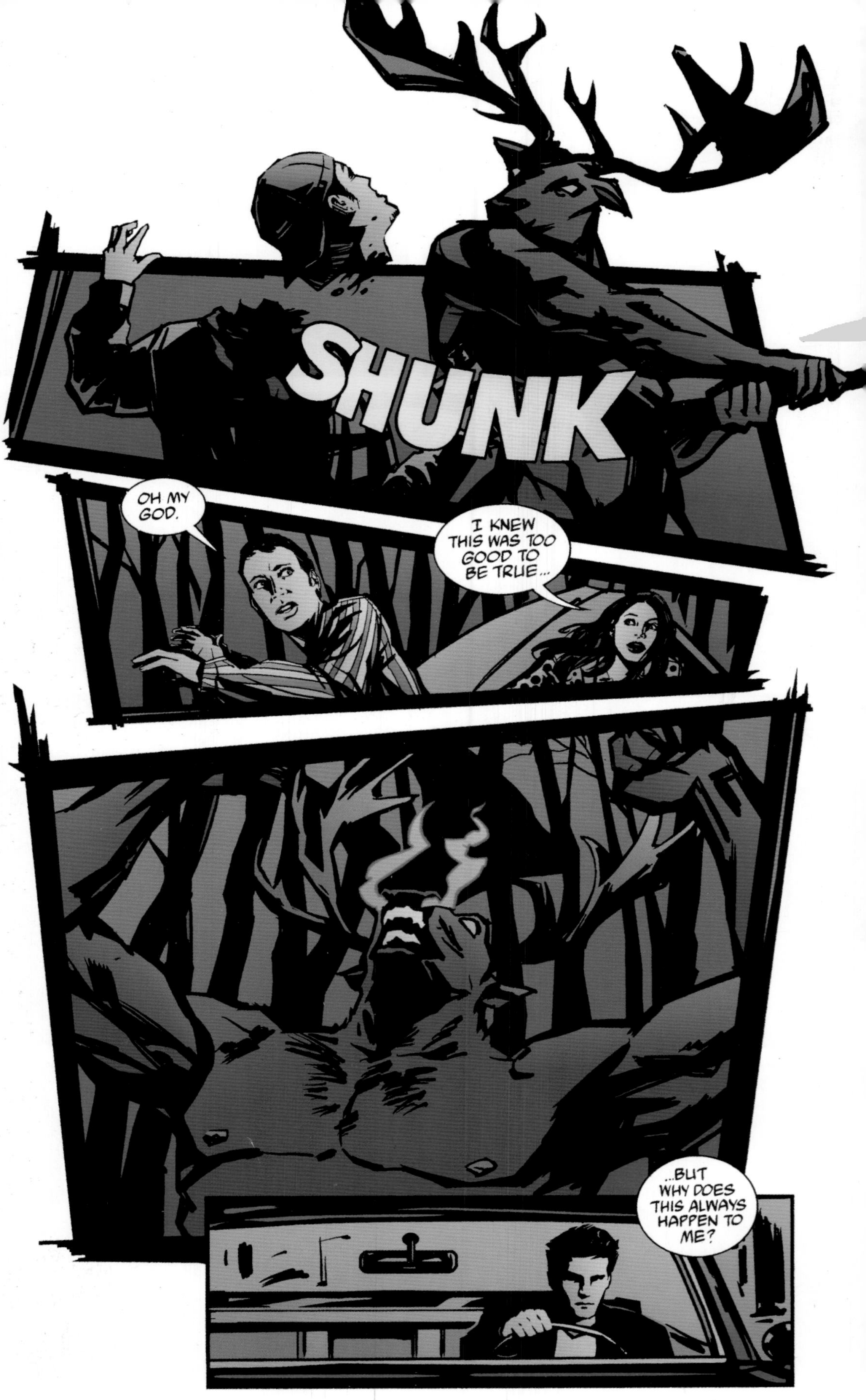
SHUNK
OH MY GOD.
I KNEW THIS WAS TOO GOOD TO BE TRUE...
...BUT WHY DOES THIS ALWAYS HAPPEN TO ME?

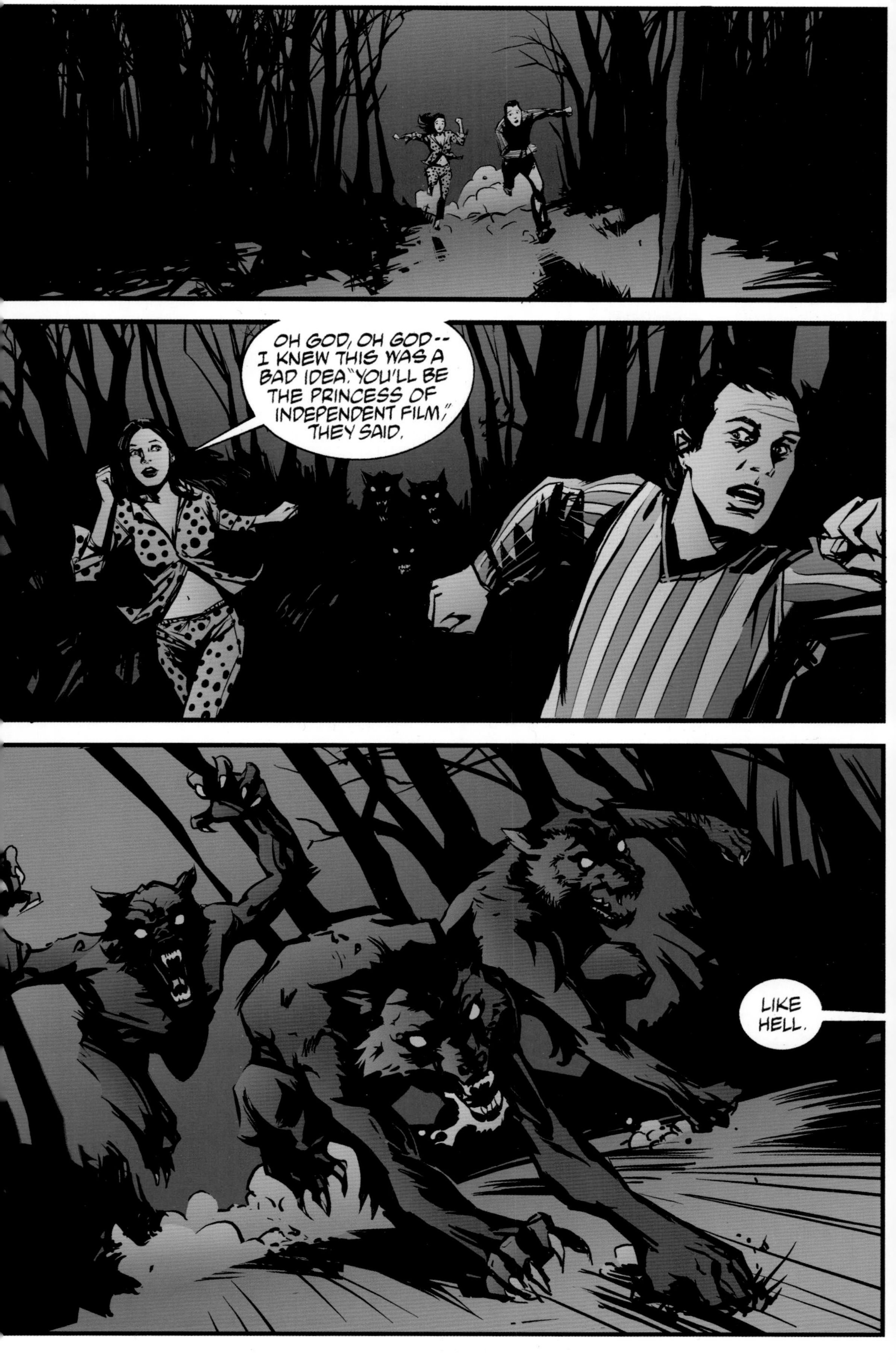
OH GOD, OH GOD-- I KNEW THIS WAS A BAD IDEA. "YOU'LL BE THE PRINCESS OF INDEPENDENT FILM," THEY SAID.
LIKE HELL.

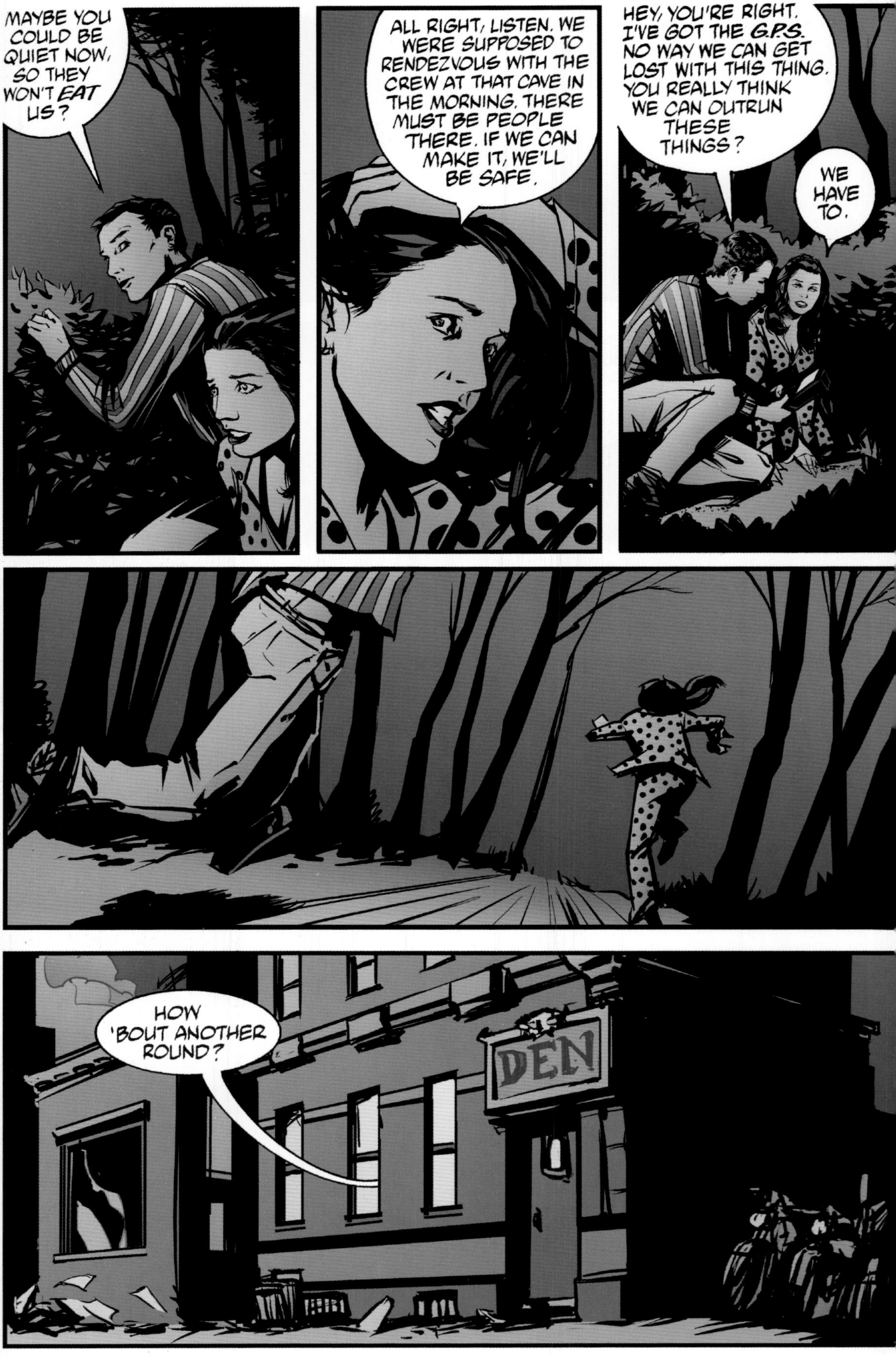
MAYBE YOU COULD BE QUIET NOW, SO THEY WON'T EAT US?
ALL RIGHT, LISTEN. WE WERE SUPPOSED TO RENDEZVOUS WITH THE CREW AT THAT CAVE IN THE MORNING. THERE MUST BE PEOPLE THERE. IF WE CAN MAKE IT, WE'LL BE SAFE.
HEY, YOU'RE RIGHT. I'VE GOT THE G.P.S. NO WAY WE CAN GET LOST WITH THIS THING. YOU REALLY THINK WE CAN OUTRUN THESE THINGS?
WE HAVE TO.
HOW 'BOUT ANOTHER ROUND?
DEN

THAT WAS THE LAST ONE, ZEKE. THE HELM OF HARAXIS. TALK.

NOT MUCH TO TELL, REALLY. LOTTA DEMONS DON'T BELIEVE IT EXISTS. IT WAS PART OF THE DEMON ARMOR HARAXIS MADE FOR HIMSELF BACK IN THE 9TH CENTURY.

LEGEND SAYS IT GAVE HIM POWER TO COMMAND OTHER DEMONS. LEASTWAYS 'TILL SOME WHITE HATS KILLED HIM, HID THE HELMET AWAY SOME-WHERES.

"SOMEWHERE AROUND HERE?"

"RUMORS HAVE IT THAT IT CAN BE FOUND SOMEWHERE IN A PATCH OF SEQUOIA NATIONAL PARK NICKNAMED THE WARNING WOOD.

"THE SPIRITS OF THE WOOD GUARD THE HELM TO KEEP IT FROM FALLING INTO THE WRONG HANDS. BUT NOW YOU KNOW WHAT YOU'RE LOOKING FOR, AND WHERE TO FIND IT.

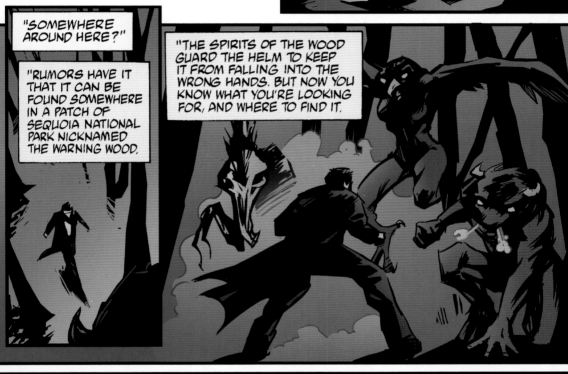

"THE HELM SHOULD BE EASY ENOUGH TO FIND FOR A BRIGHT BOY LIKE YOU.

"THOUGH WHY YOU WANNA GO ALL THAT WAY TO KILL YOURSELF I DON'T UNDERSTAND. YOU WANNA DIE, THERE'S PLENTY MORE FUN WAYS TO DO IT HERE IN L.A."

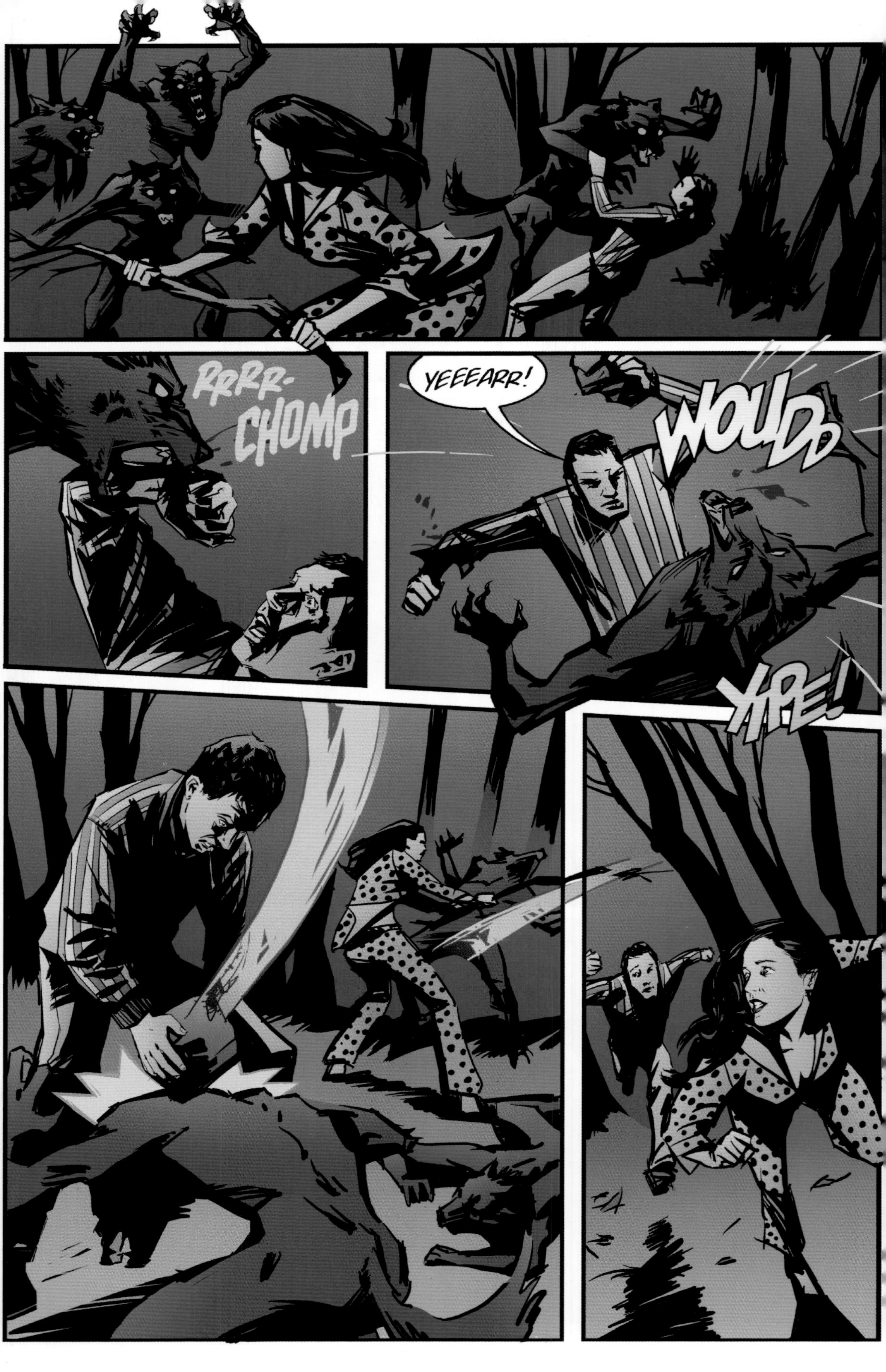
RRRR-
CHOMP
YEEEARR!
WOUD
YIPE!

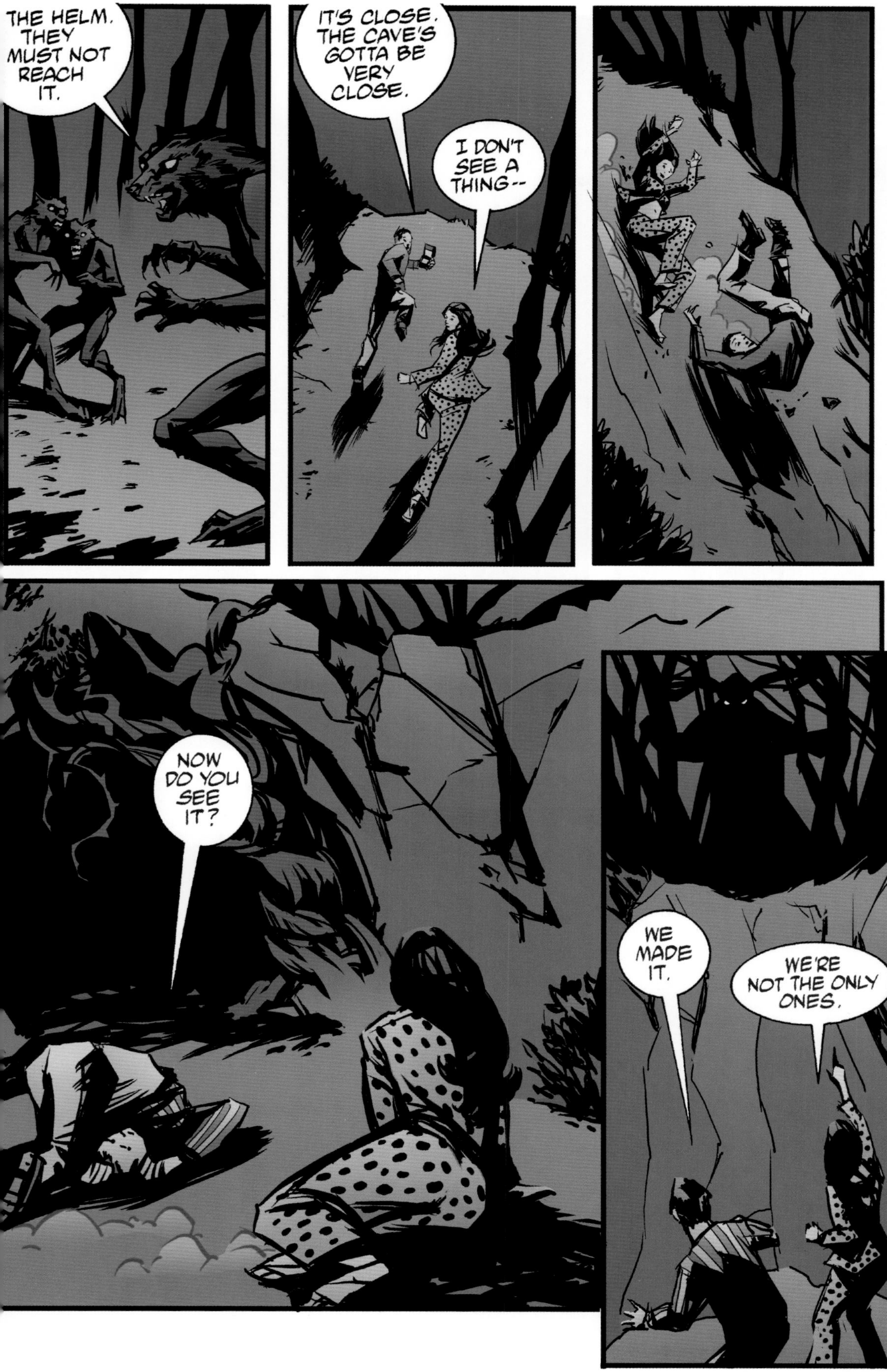
THE HELM. THEY MUST NOT REACH IT.
IT'S CLOSE. THE CAVE'S GOTTA BE VERY CLOSE.
I DON'T SEE A THING--
NOW DO YOU SEE IT?
WE MADE IT.
WE'RE NOT THE ONLY ONES.

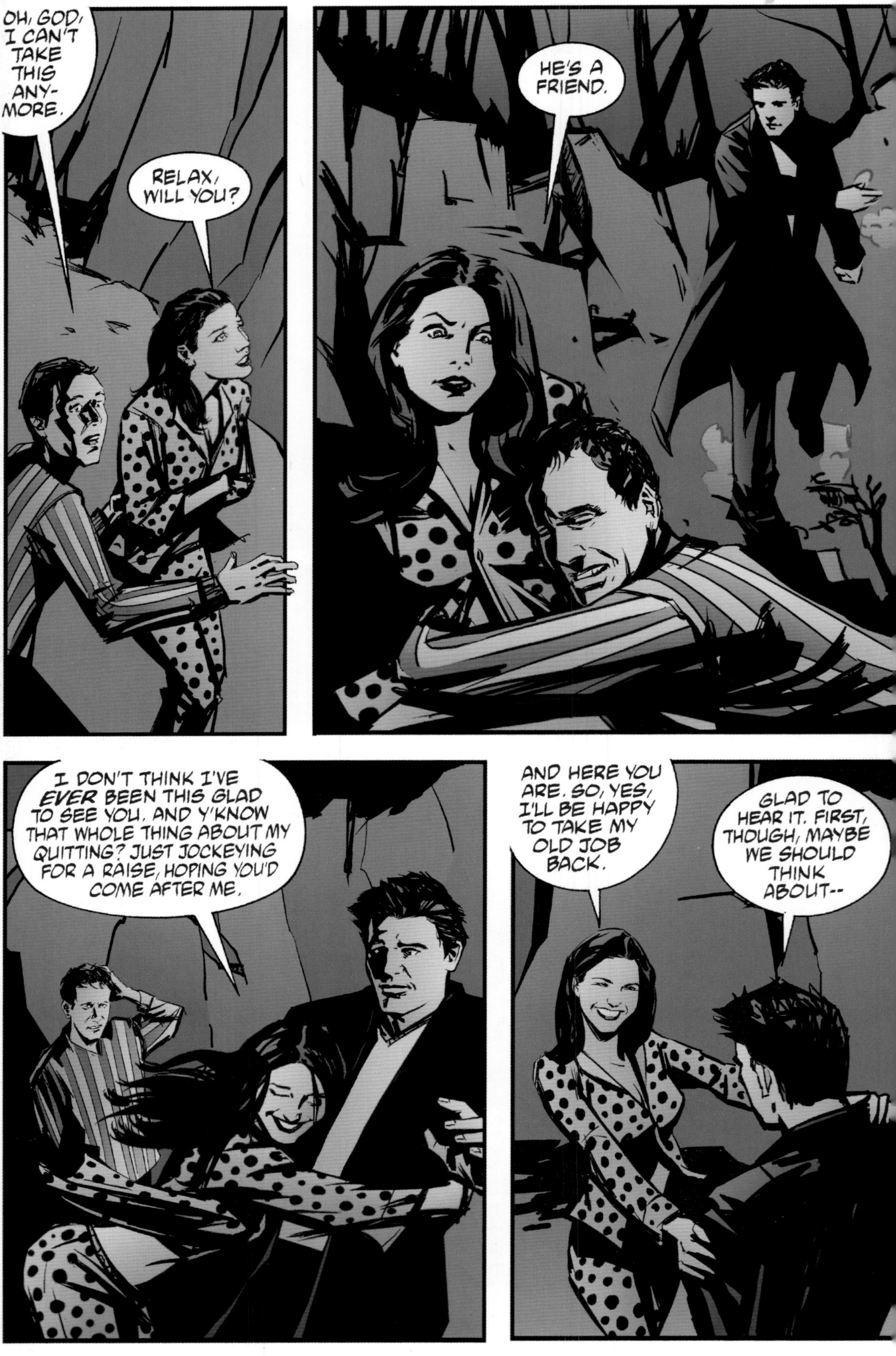
OH, GOD, I CAN'T TAKE THIS ANYMORE.
RELAX, WILL YOU?
HE'S A FRIEND.
I DON'T THINK I'VE EVER BEEN THIS GLAD TO SEE YOU. AND Y'KNOW THAT WHOLE THING ABOUT MY QUITTING? JUST JOCKEYING FOR A RAISE, HOPING YOU'D COME AFTER ME.
AND HERE YOU ARE. SO, YES, I'LL BE HAPPY TO TAKE MY OLD JOB BACK.
GLAD TO HEAR IT. FIRST, THOUGH, MAYBE WE SHOULD THINK ABOUT--

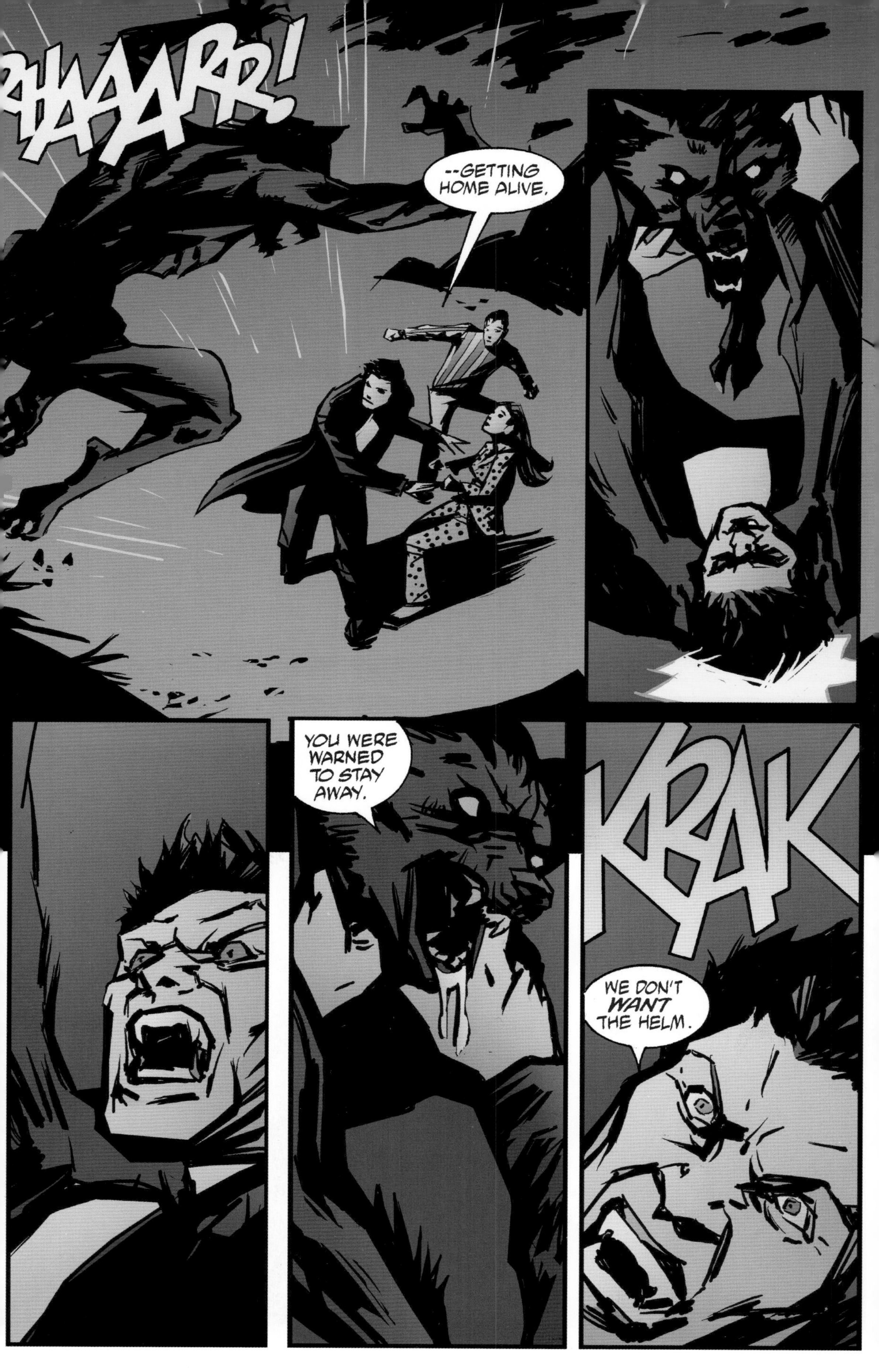
RHAAARR!
--GETTING HOME ALIVE.
YOU WERE WARNED TO STAY AWAY.
KRAK
WE DON'T WANT THE HELM.

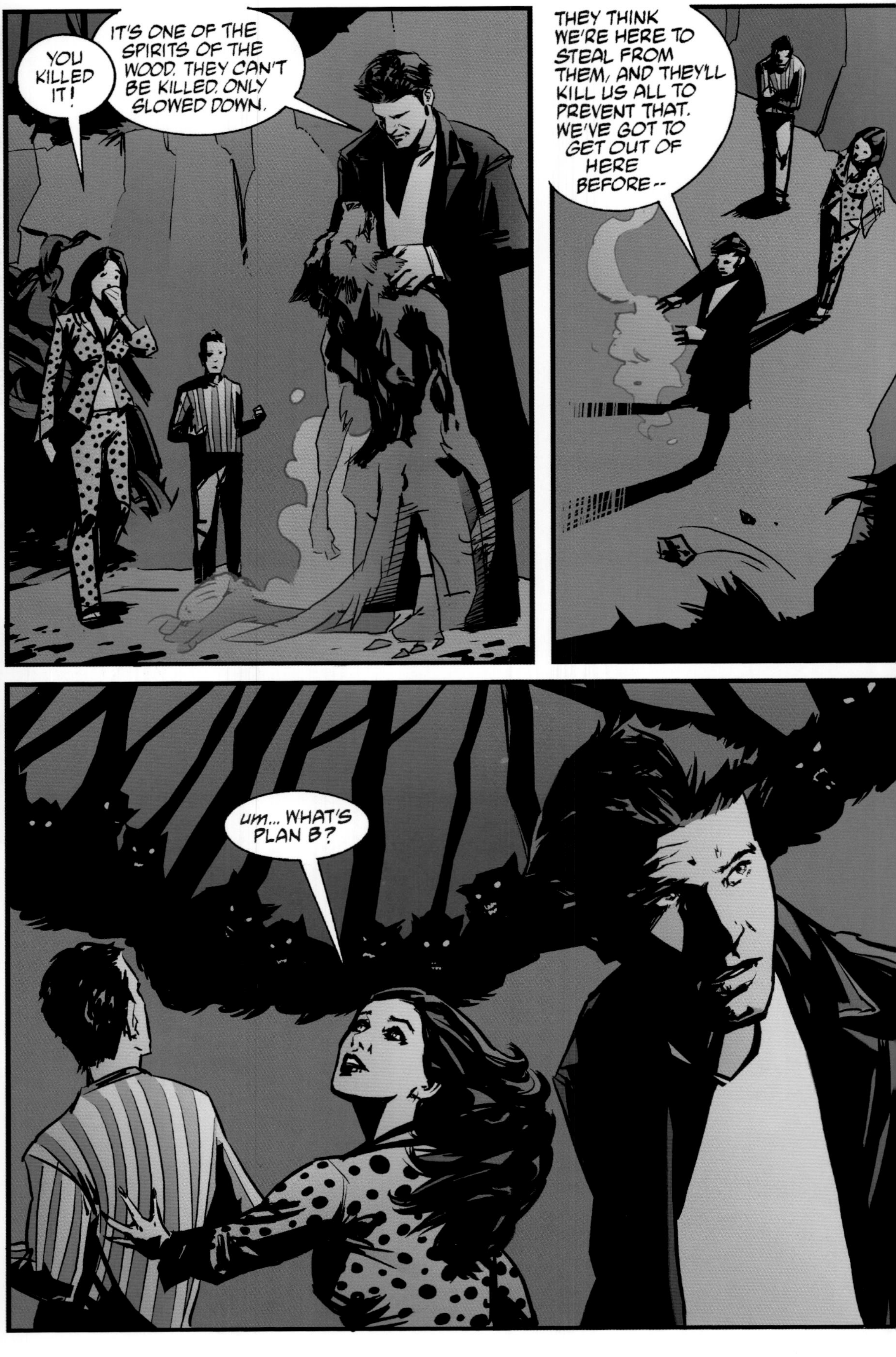
YOU KILLED IT!
IT'S ONE OF THE SPIRITS OF THE WOOD. THEY CAN'T BE KILLED, ONLY SLOWED DOWN.
THEY THINK WE'RE HERE TO STEAL FROM THEM, AND THEY'LL KILL US ALL TO PREVENT THAT. WE'VE GOT TO GET OUT OF HERE BEFORE--
um... WHAT'S PLAN B?

YOU READ THE TREATMENT. IT DIDN'T OCCUR TO YOU THAT THE PRODUCERS MIGHT BE DEMONS IN DISGUISE, HOPING YOU'D GET PAST THE FOREST SPIRITS?

HELLO? I'M AN ACTRESS. I WAS HIRED TO PLAY A PART. NOT *EVERY* HOLLYWOOD PRODUCER IS A DEMON.

CAN WE JUST GO NOW? I'LL DEAL WITH THIS CRUSHING BLOW TO MY CAREER LATER.

THEY THINK YOU'RE HERE TO STEAL THE HELM, THEY'RE NOT JUST GOING TO LET US LEAVE.

BUT WE DIDN'T. I MEAN...WE DID, BUT WE WERE JUST ACTING.

TRY TELLING *THEM* THAT.

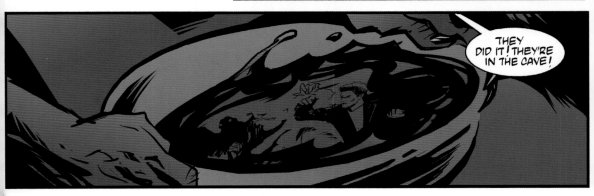

THEY DID IT! THEY'RE IN THE CAVE!

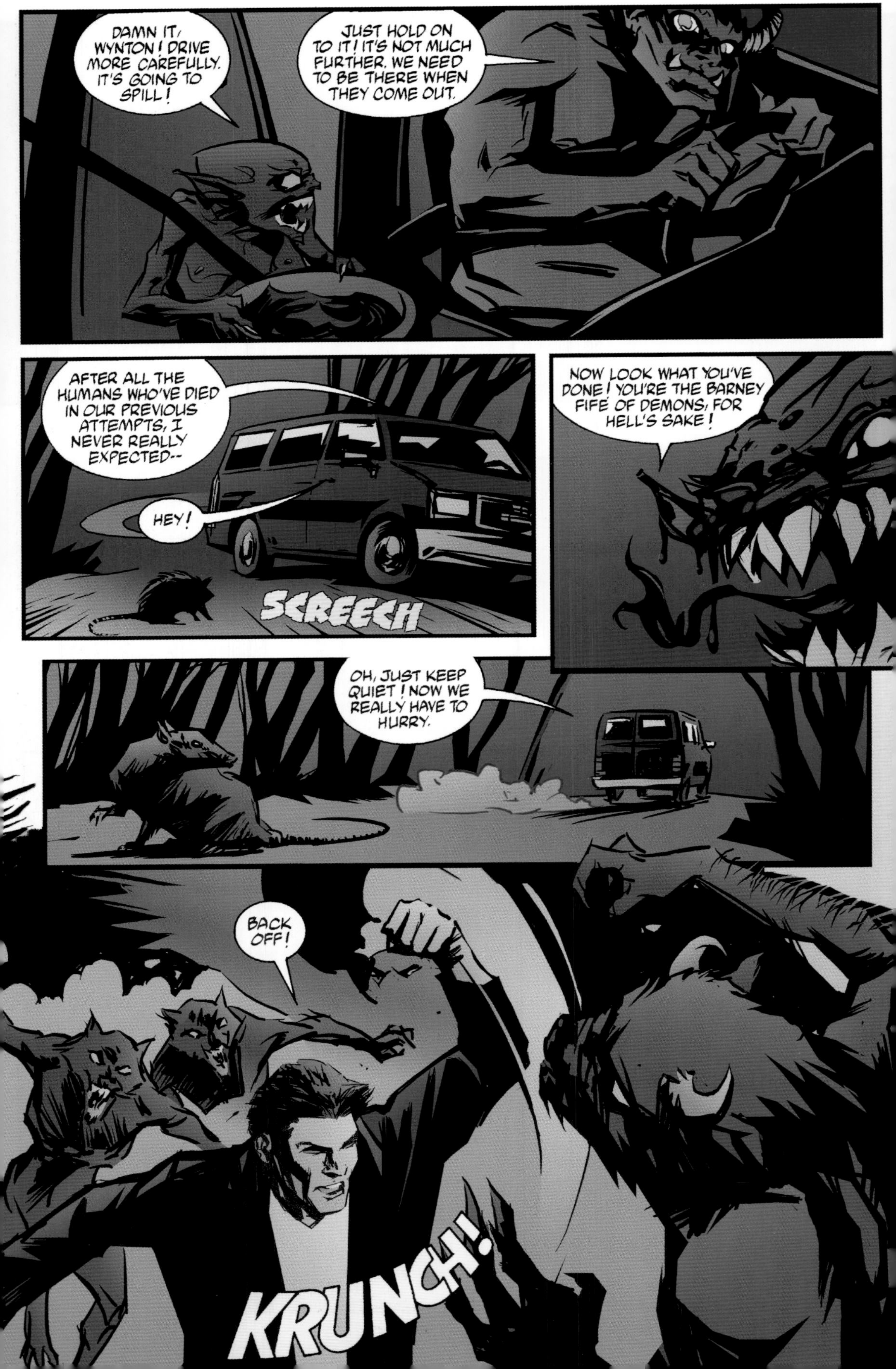
DAMN IT, WYNTON! DRIVE MORE CAREFULLY. IT'S GOING TO SPILL!
JUST HOLD ON TO IT! IT'S NOT MUCH FURTHER. WE NEED TO BE THERE WHEN THEY COME OUT.
AFTER ALL THE HUMANS WHO'VE DIED IN OUR PREVIOUS ATTEMPTS, I NEVER REALLY EXPECTED--
HEY!
SCREECH
NOW LOOK WHAT YOU'VE DONE! YOU'RE THE BARNEY FIFE OF DEMONS, FOR HELL'S SAKE!
OH, JUST KEEP QUIET! NOW WE REALLY HAVE TO HURRY.
BACK OFF!
KRUNCH!

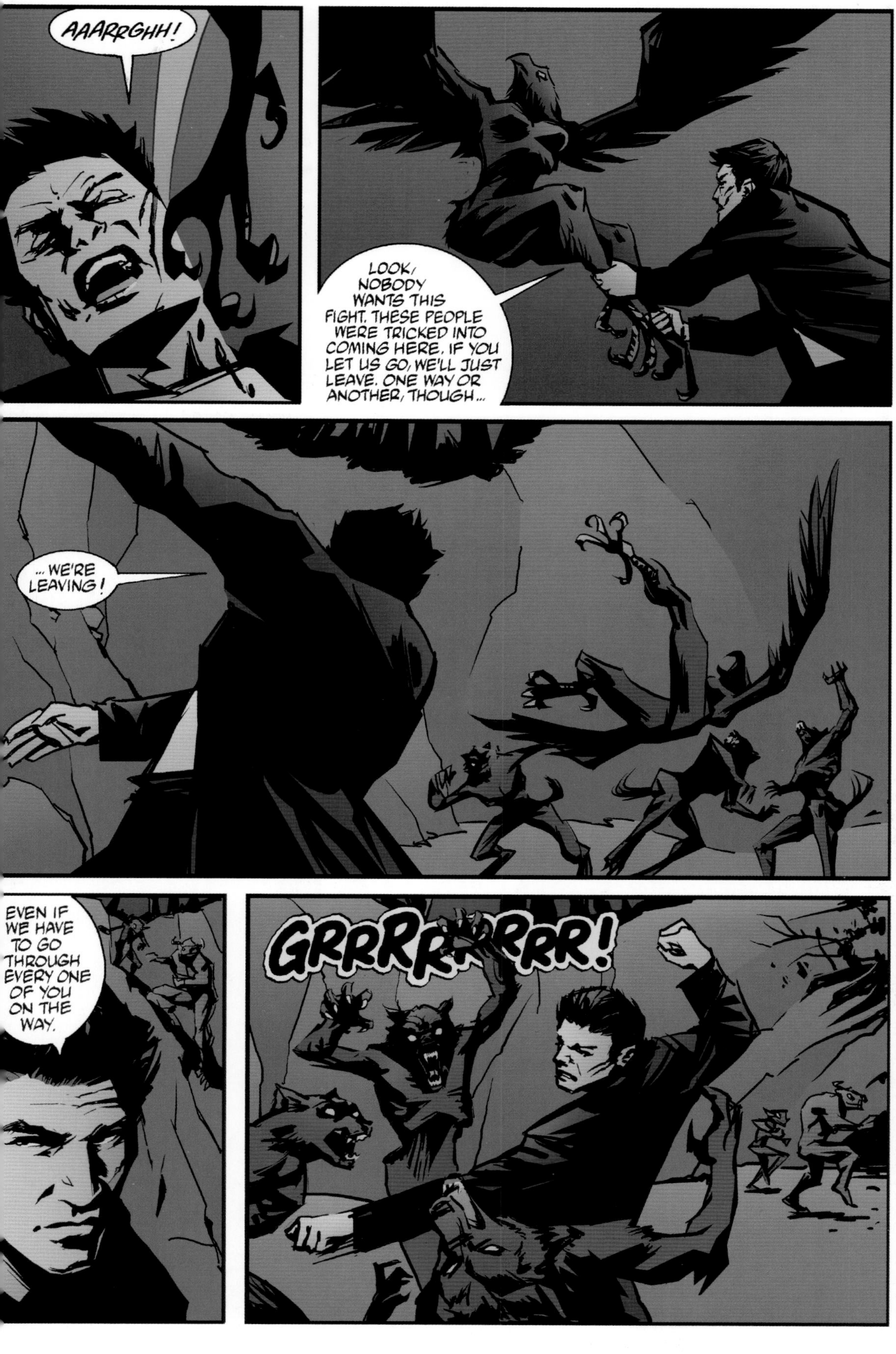
AAARRGHH!
LOOK, NOBODY WANTS THIS FIGHT. THESE PEOPLE WERE TRICKED INTO COMING HERE. IF YOU LET US GO, WE'LL JUST LEAVE. ONE WAY OR ANOTHER, THOUGH...
...WE'RE LEAVING!
EVEN IF WE HAVE TO GO THROUGH EVERY ONE OF YOU ON THE WAY.
GRRRRRRRRR!

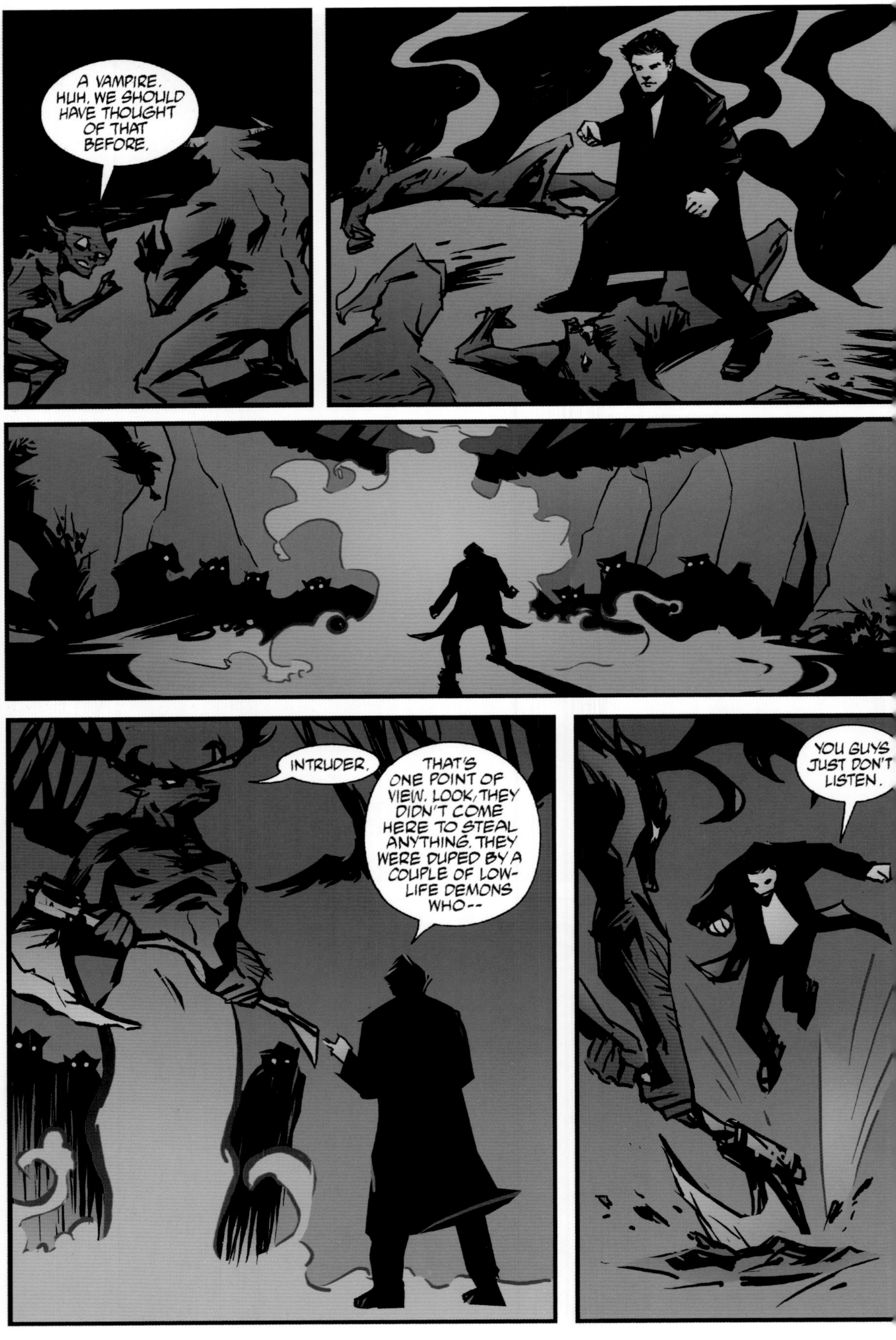
A VAMPIRE. HUH. WE SHOULD HAVE THOUGHT OF THAT BEFORE.
INTRUDER.
THAT'S ONE POINT OF VIEW. LOOK, THEY DIDN'T COME HERE TO STEAL ANYTHING. THEY WERE DUPED BY A COUPLE OF LOW-LIFE DEMONS WHO--
YOU GUYS JUST DON'T LISTEN.

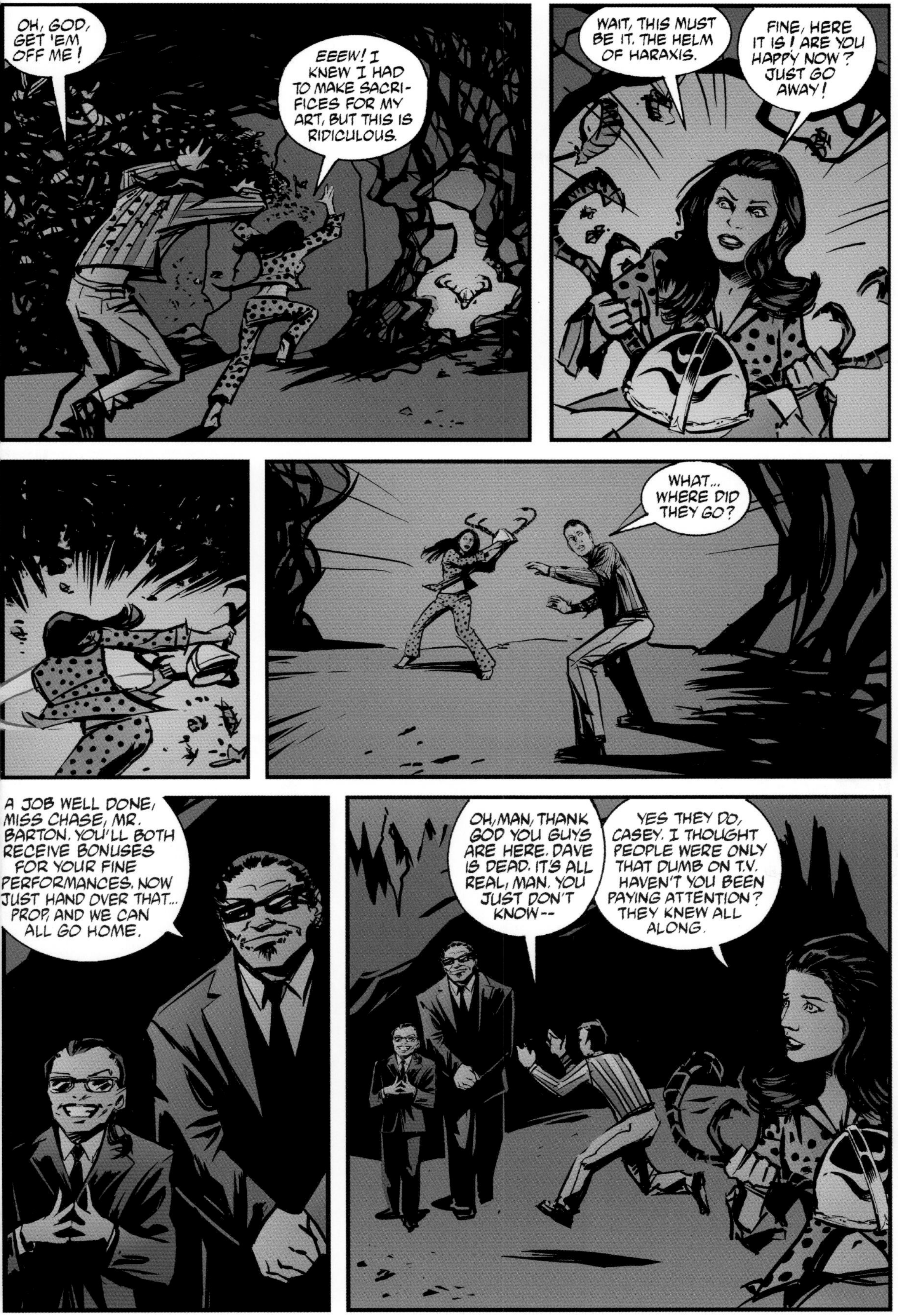
OH, GOD, GET 'EM OFF ME!
EEEW! I KNEW I HAD TO MAKE SACRI-FICES FOR MY ART, BUT THIS IS RIDICULOUS.
WAIT, THIS MUST BE IT. THE HELM OF HARAXIS.
FINE, HERE IT IS! ARE YOU HAPPY NOW? JUST GO AWAY!
WHAT... WHERE DID THEY GO?
A JOB WELL DONE, MISS CHASE, MR. BARTON. YOU'LL BOTH RECEIVE BONUSES FOR YOUR FINE PERFORMANCES. NOW JUST HAND OVER THAT... PROP, AND WE CAN ALL GO HOME.
OH, MAN, THANK GOD YOU GUYS ARE HERE. DAVE IS DEAD. IT'S ALL REAL, MAN. YOU JUST DON'T KNOW--
YES THEY DO, CASEY. I THOUGHT PEOPLE WERE ONLY THAT DUMB ON T.V. HAVEN'T YOU BEEN PAYING ATTENTION? THEY KNEW ALL ALONG.

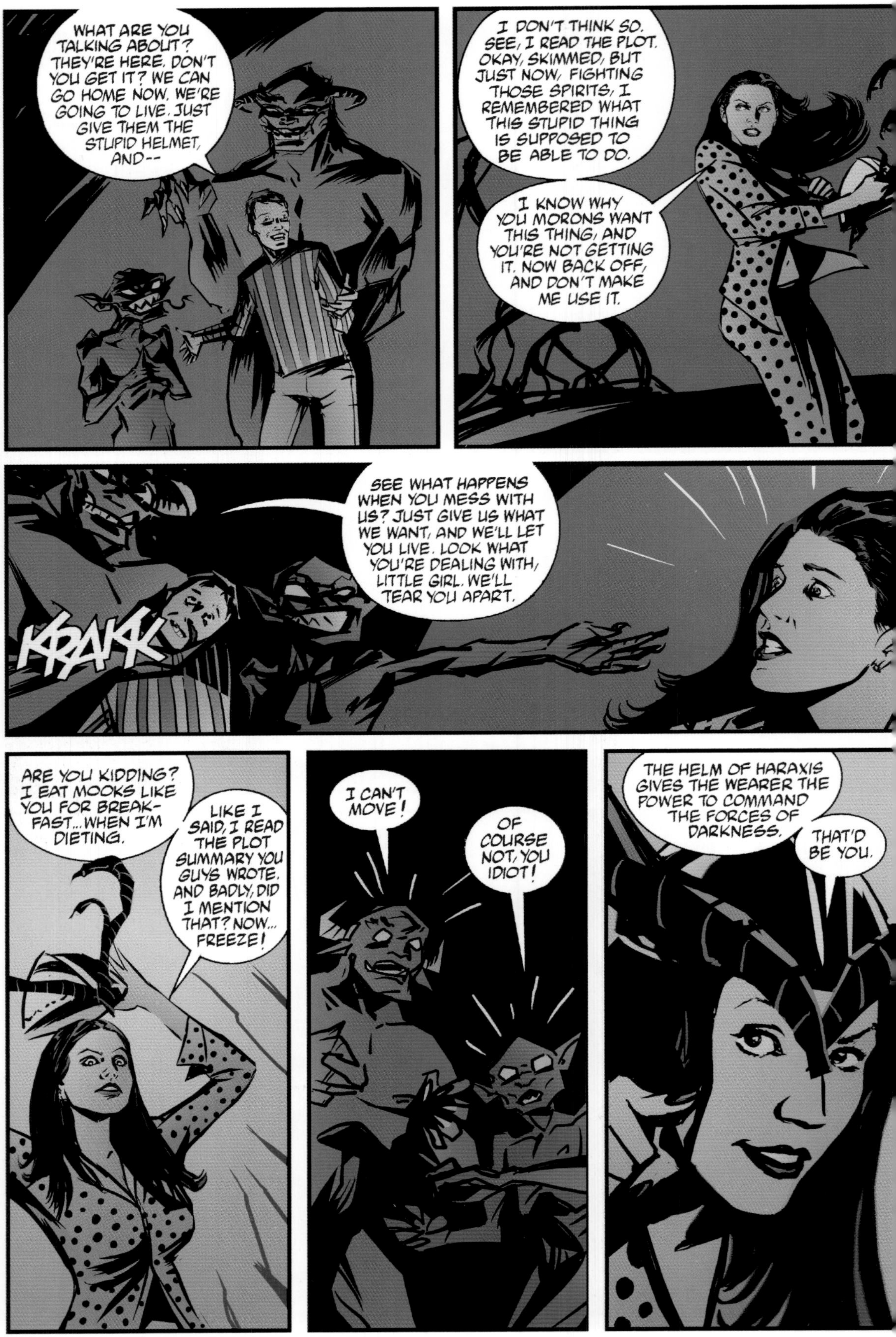
WHAT ARE YOU TALKING ABOUT? THEY'RE HERE. DON'T YOU GET IT? WE CAN GO HOME NOW. WE'RE GOING TO LIVE. JUST GIVE THEM THE STUPID HELMET, AND--
I DON'T THINK SO. SEE, I READ THE PLOT. OKAY, SKIMMED, BUT JUST NOW, FIGHTING THOSE SPIRITS, I REMEMBERED WHAT THIS STUPID THING IS SUPPOSED TO BE ABLE TO DO.
I KNOW WHY YOU MORONS WANT THIS THING, AND YOU'RE NOT GETTING IT. NOW BACK OFF, AND DON'T MAKE ME USE IT.
KRAKK
SEE WHAT HAPPENS WHEN YOU MESS WITH US? JUST GIVE US WHAT WE WANT, AND WE'LL LET YOU LIVE. LOOK WHAT YOU'RE DEALING WITH, LITTLE GIRL. WE'LL TEAR YOU APART.
ARE YOU KIDDING? I EAT MOOKS LIKE YOU FOR BREAK-FAST...WHEN I'M DIETING.
LIKE I SAID, I READ THE PLOT SUMMARY YOU GUYS WROTE. AND BADLY, DID I MENTION THAT? NOW... FREEZE!
I CAN'T MOVE!
OF COURSE NOT, YOU IDIOT!
THE HELM OF HARAXIS GIVES THE WEARER THE POWER TO COMMAND THE FORCES OF DARKNESS.
THAT'D BE YOU.

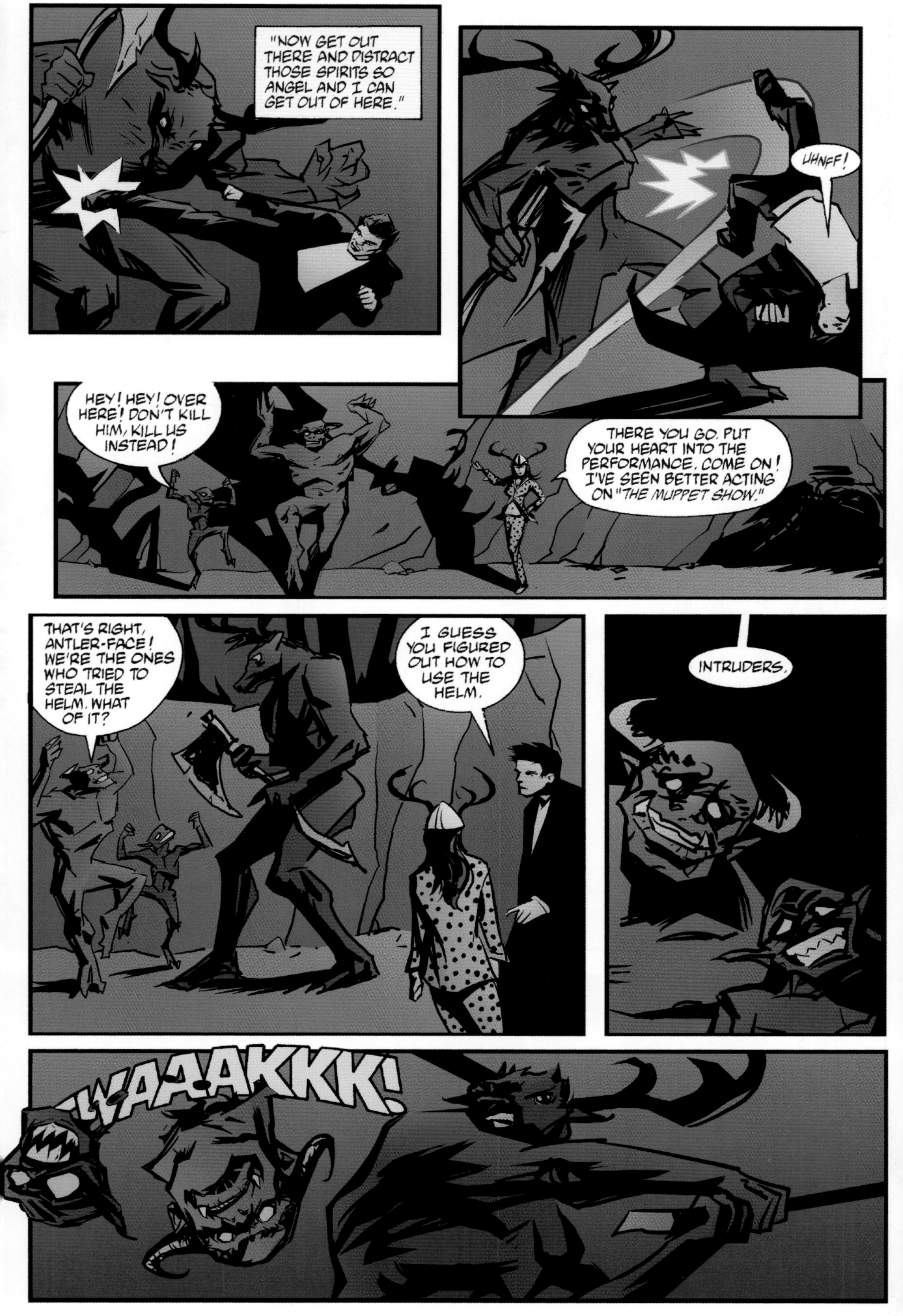
"NOW GET OUT THERE AND DISTRACT THOSE SPIRITS SO ANGEL AND I CAN GET OUT OF HERE."
UHNFF!
HEY! HEY! OVER HERE! DON'T KILL HIM, KILL US INSTEAD!
THERE YOU GO. PUT YOUR HEART INTO THE PERFORMANCE. COME ON! I'VE SEEN BETTER ACTING ON "THE MUPPET SHOW."
THAT'S RIGHT, ANTLER-FACE! WE'RE THE ONES WHO TRIED TO STEAL THE HELM. WHAT OF IT?
I GUESS YOU FIGURED OUT HOW TO USE THE HELM.
INTRUDERS.
WAAAKKK!

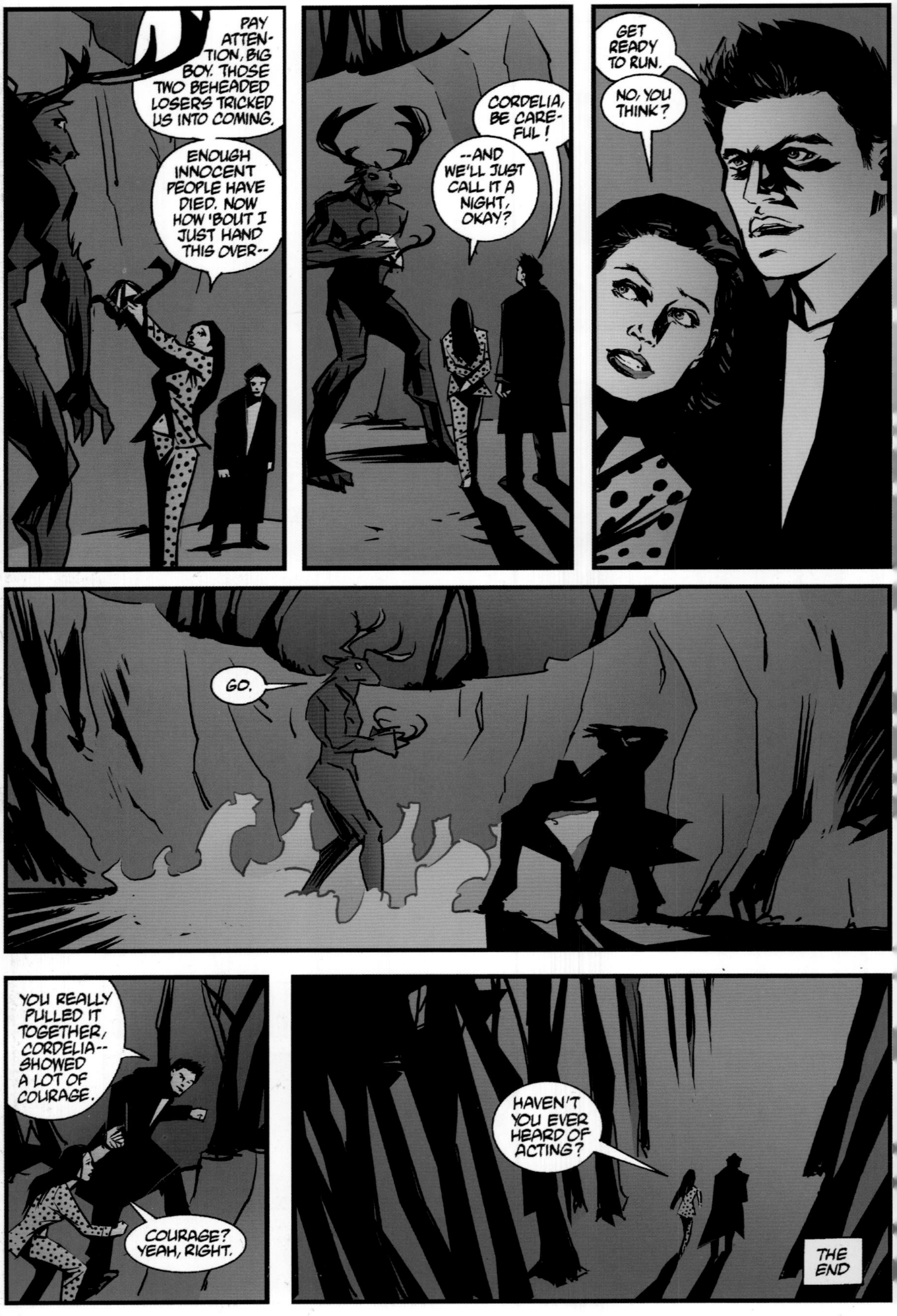
PAY ATTEN- TION, BIG BOY. THOSE TWO BEHEADED LOSERS TRICKED US INTO COMING.
ENOUGH INNOCENT PEOPLE HAVE DIED. NOW HOW 'BOUT I JUST HAND THIS OVER--
CORDELIA, BE CARE- FUL!
--AND WE'LL JUST CALL IT A NIGHT, OKAY?
GET READY TO RUN.
NO, YOU THINK?
GO.
YOU REALLY PULLED IT TOGETHER, CORDELIA-- SHOWED A LOT OF COURAGE.
COURAGE? YEAH, RIGHT.
HAVEN'T YOU EVER HEARD OF ACTING?
THE END